TORT:

CASES AND MATERIALS

URSULA CONNOLLY

B.Comm., LL.B. (Galway), LL.M. (KU Leuven)
Lecturer in Law, National University of Ireland, Galway

SHIVAUN QUINLIVAN

B.A., LL.B. (Galway), LL.M. (King's College, London),
B.L. (King's Inns, Dublin)
Lecturer in Law, National University of Ireland, Galway

THOMSON ROUND HALL
2006

Published in 2006 by
Thomson Round Hall Ltd
43 Fitzwilliam Place
Dublin 2
Ireland

Typeset by
Carrigboy Typesetting Services, County Cork

Printed by
ColourBooks, Dublin

10 Digit ISBN: 1-85800-443-8
13 Digit ISBN: 978-1-85800-443-3

A catalogue record for this book
is available from the British Library.

ACKNOWLEDGMENTS

The publishers have engaged best efforts to trace and contact the copyright holders of the materials contained in the various extracts in this book. We wish to thank the following for permission to print and edit material: The Incorporated Council of Law Reporting for Ireland for the *Irish Reports*; Thomson Round Hall for the *Irish Law Reports Monthly*, the *Irish Law Times* and the *Irish Law Times Reports*; The Courts Service for unreported judgments; the Incorporated Council of Law Reporting for England and Wales for the *Weekly Law Reports*, *Queen's Bench*, *Appeal Cases*, *Chancery Division*, and *House of Lords*. Material from the *Dominion Law Reports* is reproduced with the permission of Canada Law Book, A Division of The Cartwright Group Ltd. (1-800-263-3269, www.canadalawbook.ca). Material from the *All England Reports* is reproduced by permission of Reed Elsevier (UK) Limited trading as LexisNexis Butterworths. Material from the *Session Cases* is reproduced with permission of the Scottish Council of Law Reporting.

PREFACE

Few legal subjects depend as heavily on case law for their substantive content as does Tort Law. The area is almost entirely dictated by the pronouncements of judges in their capacity as decision-makers and this has not substantially altered over the years. Despite an increasing influence of statutory provisions in some areas (for an example, see Occupiers' Liability (Chapter 4)), a knowledge of the key cases is particularly relevant to even the most basic understanding of the law of Torts.

This cases and materials book has been written with the aim of making the consultation of key cases as unproblematic and rewarding as possible. Each chapter comes with an introduction to the topic in question, key extracts from relevant cases (both Irish and international), useful commentary to assist the reader's understanding of the major issues arising in the cases discussed, and questions to aid in further exploration. The impact of recent significant decisions such as *Glencar Explorations v County Council of Mayo* (duty of care), *Fletcher v Commissioners of Public Works* (occupational psychiatric injury) and *Delahunty v South Eastern Health Board & Others* (vicarious liability) are fully discussed. More historical cases have not been neglected, with extracts from *Rylands v Fletcher* and *Scott v Shepherd* (trespass) appearing in the relevant chapters.

Given the breadth of Tort Law, and the constraints of space, not all topics are discussed. However, care has been taken to ensure that all of the major Torts, with relevant cases and statutory provisions, have been included.

We would like to thank colleagues who offered advice, comments and support during the course of writing this book, in particular our colleagues at the Law Faculty at NUI, Galway, and Kathleen Moore-Walsh of the Waterford Institute of Technology. We are indebted to the staff of the Law Library, NUI, Galway, and in particular to Law Librarian Hugo Kelly, without whose endless patience and good humour in the face of endless requests for obscure cases with dubious citations, the completion of this book would have been far more difficult.

Finally, we would like to thank our publishers for their help, patience and guidance.

CONTENTS

TABLE OF CONTENTS

TABLE OF CASES

Note: Those page numbers marked in **bold** *are the case extracts contained in the book.*

IRELAND

ENGLAND

SCOTLAND

NORTHERN IRELAND

· EUROPEAN COURT OF JUSTICE

AUSTRALIA

NEW ZEALAND

SOUTH AFRICA

CANADA

USA

TABLE OF LEGISLATION

BUNREACHT NA hÉIREANN

IRISH STATUTES

IRISH STATUTORY INSTRUMENTS

EUROPEAN DIRECTIVES

EUROPEAN CONVENTION ON HUMAN RIGHTS

ENGLISH STATUTES

UNITED STATES OF AMERICA STATUTES

INTRODUCTION

This cases and materials book provides a comprehensive discussion of the key topics in Tort Law. It contains both extracts from key cases and additional materials to aid in the understanding of the judicial principles discussed. The following provides a general description of the layout of each chapter.

General commentary:
Each chapter gives a succinct overview of the tort in question and includes cases relevant to each aspect of the topic discussed. So, for instance, under Causation and Remoteness (Chapter 1), an overview of factual causes is given, followed by the relevant cases, before proceeding to an overview of legal causes, which is then, in turn, followed by the relevant cases, and so on. This approach has been taken to provide the maximum guidance to students in understanding the relevance of each case to the aspect of the tort in question.

Case extracts:
In the discussion of the cases, the authors have edited the cases somewhat. Each case comes with *Facts* and *Issues* as summarised by the authors in their own words. The *Facts* section includes the facts and case history. The *Issues* section describes the legal issues arising in the decision being considered. So for instance, if the case is a Supreme Court decision, the High Court findings will generally appear in the *Facts* section, while only the legal issues being dealt with in the Supreme Court decision will be stated in the *Issues* section.

The extract chosen from the court cases reflect, in the authors views, those extracts most relevant to understanding the legal principles applicable. In some decisions involving multiple judgments, only the leading opinion is given. In others, however, extracts from several opinions have been given. In all instances, the authors have attempted to strike a balance between including an extract which is too short, leading to a lack of clarity, to including one which is too long, leading to needless repetition.

Comments and Questions:
Most cases come with a section giving *Comments and Questions*. The *Comments* aspect seeks to highlight major issues in the case discussed or in the topic as a whole. The *Questions* are provided to provoke thought and analysis by the reader and to encourage further consideration of the case in question.

A line appears for the purposes of clarity between the end of the discussion of one case and the beginning of the discussion of the next case or aspect of the tort.

Statutory Provisions:

Where relevant, extracts from the applicable statutory provisions, or in some cases the statutory provision in its entirety, are included for ease of reference.

Feedback:

We are very interested in hearing how useful you, as a reader, have found this book. Any comments, suggestions or opinions are very welcome and can be made directly to the authors by email at the following address: tortcasebook@gmail.com.

CHAPTER 1

CAUSATION AND REMOTENESS

INTRODUCTION

To receive a remedy in tort the plaintiff must show that the defendant "caused" the injury or damage complained of (causation) and that the resulting injury is not one so far removed from the act of the defendant that s/he cannot be held liable for it (remoteness).

CAUSATION

Causation is an essential element of all torts for which damage is a necessary element (*i.e.* for torts which are not actionable *per se*). The cause of an injury is ascertained by determining, first, what the factual causes are, before going on to consider the legal cause of an injury.

In determining the legal cause the courts will ask whether a *novus actus interveniens* occurred. A *novus actus*, or new intervening act, is capable of breaking the chain of causation and relieving the initial defendant of liability.

Before we consider the identification of factual and legal cause, we must first discuss on whom the burden lies to prove causation.

PROVING CAUSATION

It is for the plaintiff to demonstrate, on the balance of probabilities, that the defendant caused the damage.

Hanrahan v Merck Sharp & Dohme (Ireland) Ltd.
Supreme Court [1988] I.L.R.M. 629

Facts: The plaintiffs sued the defendants, who operated a pharmaceutical company, for injury to livestock, plant life and personal health, which they alleged was caused by toxic emissions from the defendant's factory. The plaintiffs sued in nuisance, negligence and under the rule in *Rylands v Fletcher.* They lost their case in the High Court and appealed, *inter alia*, on the ground that, given the difficulty of proving causation in this case, the burden of proof ought to be reversed.

Issues: Should the burden of proving causation be reversed given the difficulty of proving that the defendants caused the injuries complained of. In particular, as the tort pleaded protected a constitutional right, did the constitutional guarantee allow for the burden of proof to be reversed?

The court found that the duty to prove causation always fell on the plaintiff.

Henchy J. (Finlay C.J. and Hederman J. concurring):

"The ordinary rule is that a person who alleges a particular tort must, in order to succeed, prove (save where there are admissions) all the necessary ingredients of that tort and it is not for the defendant to disprove anything. Such exceptions as have been allowed to that general rule seem to be confined to cases where a particular element of the tort lies, or is deemed to lie, pre-eminently within the defendants' knowledge, in which case the onus of proof as to that matter passes to the defendant. Thus, in the tort of negligence, where damage has been caused to the plaintiff in circumstances in which such damage would not usually be caused without negligence on the part of the defendant, the rule of *res ipsa loquitur* will allow the act relied on to be evidence of negligence in the absence of proof by the defendant that it occurred without want of due care on his part. The rationale behind the shifting of the onus of proof to the defendant in such cases would appear to lie in the fact that it would be palpably unfair to require a plaintiff to prove something which is beyond his reach and which is peculiarly within the range of the defendant's capacity of proof.

That is not the case here. What the plaintiffs have to prove in support of their claim in nuisance is that they suffered some or all of the mischief complained of and that it was caused by emissions from the defendants' factory. To hold that it is for the defendants to disprove either or both of those matters would be contrary to authority and not be demanded by the requirements of justice. There are of course difficulties facing the plaintiffs in regard to proof of those matters, particularly as to the question of causation, but mere difficulty of proof does not call for a shifting of the onus of proof. Many claims in tort fail because the plaintiff does not have access to full information as to the true nature of the defendant's conduct. The onus of disproof rests on the defendant only when the act or default complained of is such that it would be fundamentally unjust to require the plaintiff to prove a positive averment when the particular circumstances show that fairness and justice call for disproof by the defendant. The argument put forward in this case for putting a duty of disproof on the defendants would be more sustainable if the plaintiffs had to prove that the emissions complained of were caused by the defendants' negligence. Such is not the case. In my view, having regard to the replies given by the defendants to interrogatories and notices for particulars and to the full discovery of documents made by them, it is not open to the plaintiffs to complain that for want of knowledge on their part it would be unjust or unfair to require them to bear the ordinary onus of proof.

The plaintiffs have also invoked the Constitution in support of their argument as to the onus of proof. They contend that the tort relied on by them in support of their claim is but a reflection of the duty imposed on the State by Art.40.3 of the Constitution in regard to their personal rights and property rights. The relevant constitutional provisions are:

1° The State guarantees in its laws to respect, and, as far as practicable, by its laws to defend and vindicate the personal rights of the citizen.
2° The State shall, in particular, by its laws protect as best it may from unjust attack and, in the case of injustice done, vindicate the life, person, good name, and property rights of every citizen.

I agree that the tort of nuisance relied on in this case may be said to be an implementation of the State's duties under those provisions as to the personal rights and property rights of the plaintiffs as citizens. The particular duty pointed to by the plaintiffs is the duty to vindicate the personal right to bodily integrity and the property right to their land and livestock. They say that vindication of those rights under the constitutional guarantee is not properly effected by leaving them to their rights as plaintiffs in an action for nuisance and that the vindication they are guaranteed requires that once they show that they have been damnified in their person or property as alleged, it should be for the defendants to show that emissions from their factory were not the cause.

So far as I am aware, the constitutional provisions relied on have never been used in the courts to form the basis of any existing tort or to change the normal onus of proof. The implementation of those constitutional rights is primarily a matter for the State and the courts are entitled to intervene only when there has been a failure to implement or, where the implementation relied on is plainly inadequate, to effectuate the constitutional guarantee in question. In many torts—for example, negligence, defamation, trespass to person or property—a plaintiff may give evidence of what he claims to be a breach of a constitutional right, but he may fail in the action because of what is usually a matter of onus of proof or because of some other legal or technical defence. A person may of course, in the absence of a common law or statutory cause of action, sue directly for breach of a constitutional right (see *Meskell v CIE* [1973] I.R. 121), but when he founds his action on an existing tort he is normally confined to the limitations of that tort. It might be different if it could be shown that the tort in question is basically ineffective to protect his constitutional right; but that is not alleged here. What is said is that he may not succeed in having his constitutional rights vindicated if he is required to carry the normal onus of proof. However, the same may be said about many other causes of action. Lack of knowledge as to the true nature of the defendants' conduct or course of conduct may cause the plaintiff difficulty, but it does not change the onus of proof.

It is also to be noted that the guarantee to respect and defend personal rights given in Art.40.3.1° applies only *"as far as practicable"* and the guarantee to vindicate property rights given in Art.40.3.2° refers only to cases of *"injustice done"*. The guarantees, therefore, are not unqualified or absolute. I find it impossible to hold that Art.40.3.1° means that a plaintiff in an action for nuisance is to be relieved of the onus of proving the necessary ingredients of that tort. Neither, in my view, does Art.40.3.2° warrant such a dispensation, for the guarantee of vindication there given arises only *"in the case of injustice done"*, so it is for the plaintiff to prove that the injustice relied on was actually suffered by him and that it was caused by the defendant.

I would hold that the trial judge correctly rejected the submission of the plaintiffs that an onus of disproving the allegation as to causation should rest on the defendants."

Comments and Questions:
1. The case above demonstrates that, regardless of the difficulty in proving causation on the "balance of probabilities", this burden will always fall on the plaintiff. Compare this to the principle of *res ipsa loquitur* (see Chapter 2) which allows for the reversal of the burden of proof in negligence cases.

FACTUAL CAUSE

The first step in identifying the cause of an injury is the determination of the factual cause(s). This involves a factual or scientific examination of the defendant's actions to see if they can be linked to the plaintiff's injury. If no link can be made then no liability arises. The courts for this purpose have developed two principal tests: the "but for" test and the "material element and substantial factor test".

"But for" test

The "but for" test is useful in cases where there is only one defendant. Essentially it involves asking "but for the negligent action(s) of the defendant would the injury have arisen?" The application of this test can be seen in the following case.

Barnett v Chelsea and Kensington Hospital Management Committee
Queen's Bench Division [1969] 1 Q.B. 428

Facts: Barnett, a night watchman, and a number of his colleagues, attended at the defendant hospital complaining of stomach pains after drinking tea together. The nurse, after consulting with a doctor, sent them home on the doctor's instructions without having subjected them to an examination. Barnett went home and died five hours later from what transpired to have been arsenic poisoning. His wife sued, arguing that the defendant's negligence had caused her husband's death.

Issues: The legal issues to be decided were: whether the hospital was negligent and, if so, whether the negligence of the hospital in not examining the plaintiff's husband was the cause of his subsequent death.

In finding the hospital guilty of negligent conduct, the court (Nield J., Queen's Bench Division) held that the appropriate test in deciding causation was to ask whether the deceased would have died anyway, *i.e.* "but for the negligence of the defendant would the injury (in this case death) have arisen?" As the plaintiff on the facts would have died in any case, due to the late stage of his attendance at the hospital, the defendant was not found to have been the effective cause of his death and was not ultimately liable.

Nield J.:

"There are two main questions here: Has the plaintiff established, on the balance of probabilities, (1) that the medical casualty officer was negligent, and, if so, (2) that such negligence caused the death of the deceased? ...

[In finding that the defendants had been negligent in not seeing to the deceased he then went on to consider the second question.]

... It remains to consider whether it is shown that the deceased's death was caused by that negligence or whether, as the defendants have said, the deceased must have died in any event. In his concluding submission Mr. Pain submitted that the casualty officer should have examined the deceased and had he done so he would have caused tests to be made which would have indicated the treatment required and that, since the defendants were at fault in these respects, therefore the onus of proof passed to the defendants to show that the appropriate treatment would have failed, and authorities were cited to me. I find myself unable to accept that argument, and I am of the view that the onus of proof remains upon the plaintiff, and I have in mind (without quoting it) the decision cited by Mr. Wilmers in Bonnington Castings Ltd. v. Wardlaw [[1956] A.C. 613; [1956] 2 W.L.R. 707; [1956] 1 All E.R. 615, H.L.(Sc.)]. However, were it otherwise and the onus did pass to the defendants, then I would find that they have discharged it, as I would proceed to show.

There has been put before me a timetable which I think is of much importance. The deceased attended at the casualty department at five or 10 minutes past eight in the morning. If the casualty officer had got up and dressed and come to see the three men and examined them and decided to admit them, the deceased (and Dr. Lockett agreed with this) could not have been in bed in a ward before 11 a.m. I accept Dr. Goulding's evidence that an intravenous drip would not have been set up before 12 noon, and if potassium loss was suspected it could not have been discovered until 12.30 p.m. Dr. Lockett, dealing with this, said: 'If this man had not been treated until after 12 noon the chances of survival were not good.'

Without going in detail into the considerable volume of technical evidence which has been put before me, it seems to me to be the case that when death results from arsenical poisoning it is brought about by two conditions; on the one hand dehydration and on the other disturbance of the enzyme processes. If the principal condition is one of enzyme disturbance—as I am of the view it was here—then the only method of treatment which is likely to succeed is the use of the specific antidote which is commonly called B.A.L. Dr. Goulding said in the course of his evidence:

> 'The only way to deal with this is to use the specific B.A.L. I see no reasonable prospect of the deceased being given B.A.L. before the time at which he died'—and at a later point in his evidence—'I feel that even if fluid loss had been discovered death would have been caused by the enzyme disturbance. Death might have occurred later.'

I regard that evidence as very moderate, and it might be a true assessment of the situation to say that there was no chance of B.A.L. being administered before the death of the deceased.

For those reasons, I find that the plaintiff has failed to establish, on the balance of probabilities, that the defendants' negligence caused the death of the deceased."

Multiple causes of harm and the "material element" test

The "but for" test is useful where there is one significant cause of an injury, but can lead to an injustice where more than one cause exists or where it cannot be said on the balance of probabilities who caused the injury. In such a situation each defendant could argue that regardless of their negligent act the injury would have occurred anyway. For this reason the courts have also developed a further test which can be applied in cases of multiple causes of harm.

This test, favoured by Prosser & Keating, states that "[t]he defendant's conduct is a cause of the event if it was a material element and a substantial factor in bringing it about." The material element test can also find a defendant liable where conduct which is not tortious in itself, may be so when taken together with the conduct of others (*Lambton v Mellish* [1894] 3 Ch. 163). In cases of uncertain causes (where it is not clear who caused the injury or it may be impossible to show the level of contribution of each party) the courts have been willing (in England at least, see *Fairchild* below) to impose liability on all potential defendants, where policy considerations allow.

Fairchild v Glenhaven Funeral Services
House of Lords [2002] U.K.H.L. 22, [2002] 3 All E.R. 305,
[2002] I.C.R. 798, 67 B.M.L.R. 90

Facts: In three appeals to the House of Lords, claims were brought against employers by, or on behalf of, the estates of former employees. In each case the employee had been employed at different times and for differing periods by more than one employer and had inhaled asbestos dust due to the negligence of the employer. The employees had contracted mesothelioma. The question arose whether, in those circumstances, the employee was entitled to recover damages against either employer or both of them, even though, because of the current limits of scientific knowledge, he was unable to prove on the balance of probabilities which employer had caused his injury. The Court of Appeal answered that question in the negative, holding, on the basis of the conventional "but for" test of tortious liability, that the employee had failed to prove against either employer that his mesothelioma would not have occurred but for the breach of duty by that employer. The claims were therefore dismissed. The claimants appealed to the House of Lords.

Issues: Their Lordships were required to determine whether, in the special circumstances of such a case, a modified approach to proof of causation was required by principle, authority or policy.

The court held that, as each employer had breached a duty in exposing the employees to asbestos dust, each had materially contributed to their injury and would be held liable.

Lord Bingham (Nicholls, Hoffmann, Hutton and Rodger L.JJ. delivered concurring judgments):

"... The essential question underlying the appeals may be accurately expressed in this way. If (1) C was employed at different times and for differing periods by both A and B, and (2) A and B were both subject to a duty to take reasonable care or to take all practicable measures to prevent C inhaling asbestos dust because of the known risk that asbestos dust (if inhaled) might cause a mesothelioma, and (3) both A and B were in breach of that duty in relation to C during the periods of C's employment by each of them with the result that during both periods C inhaled excessive quantities of asbestos dust, and (4) C is found to be suffering from a mesothelioma, and (5) any cause of C's mesothelioma other than the inhalation of asbestos dust at work can be effectively discounted, but (6) C cannot (because of the current limits of human science) prove, on the balance of probabilities, that his mesothelioma was the result of his inhaling asbestos dust during his employment by A or during his employment by B or during his employment by A and B taken together, is C entitled to recover damages against either A or B or against both A and B? To this question (not formulated in these terms) the Court of Appeal (Brooke, Latham and Kay LJJ), in a reserved judgment of the court ([2001] EWCA Civ 1881, [2002] 1 WLR 1052), gave a negative answer. It did so because, applying the conventional 'but for' test of tortious liability, it could not be held that C had proved against A that his mesothelioma would probably not have occurred but for the breach of duty by A, nor against B that his mesothelioma would probably not have occurred but for the breach of duty by B, nor against A and B that his mesothelioma would probably not have occurred but for the breach of duty by both A and B together. So C failed against both A and B. The crucial issue on appeal is whether, in the special circumstances of such a case, principle, authority or policy requires or justifies a modified approach to proof of causation.

... In March v E & M H Stramare Pty Ltd (1991) 171 CLR 506 at 508, Mason CJ, sitting in the High Court of Australia, did not 'accept that the "but for" (causa sine qua non) test ever was or now should become the exclusive test of causation in negligence cases' and (at 516) he added:

> 'The "but for" test gives rise to a well-known difficulty in cases where there are two or more acts or events which would each be sufficient to bring about the plaintiff's injury. The application of the test "gives the result, contrary to common sense, that neither is a cause": Winfield and Jolowicz on Tort, 13th ed (1989), p. 134. In truth, the application of the test proves to be either inadequate or troublesome in various situations in which there are multiple acts or events leading to the plaintiff's injury: see, e.g., Chapman v. Hearse, Baker v Willoughby ([1969] 3 All ER 1528, [1970] AC 467); McGhee v. National Coal Board ([1972] 3 All ER 1008, [1973] 1 WLR 1); M'Kew (see M'Kew v Holland & Hannen & Cubitts (Scotland) Ltd 1970 SC (HL) 20) (to which I shall shortly refer in some detail). The cases demonstrate the lesson of experience, namely, that the test, applied as an exclusive criterion of causation, yields unacceptable results and that the results which it yields must be tempered by the making of value judgments and the infusion of policy considerations.'

In Snell v Farrell (1990) 72 DLR (4th) 289 at 294, Sopinka J, delivering the judgment of the Supreme Court of Canada, said:

> 'The traditional approach to causation has come under attack in a number of cases in which there is concern that due to the complexities of proof, the probable victim of tortious conduct will be deprived of relief. This concern is strongest in circumstances in which, on the basis of some percentage of statistical probability, the plaintiff is the likely victim of the combined tortious conduct of a number of defendants, but cannot prove causation against a specific defendant or defendants on the basis of particularized evidence in accordance with traditional principles. The challenge to the traditional approach has manifested itself in cases dealing with non-traumatic injuries such as man-made diseases resulting from the widespread diffusion of chemical products, including product liability

cases in which a product which can cause injury is widely manufactured and marketed by a large number of corporations.'

… The Supreme Court of Canada confronted this situation in Cook v Lewis [1951] SCR 830, in which Cartwright J, with whom a majority agreed, said (at 842):

> 'I do not think it necessary to decide whether all that was said in Summers v Tice should be accepted as stating the law of British Columbia, but I am of opinion, for the reasons given in that case, that if under the circumstances of the case at bar the jury, having decided that the plaintiff was shot by either Cook or Akenhead, found themselves unable to decide which of the two shot him because in their opinion both shot negligently in his direction, both defendants should have been found liable.'

… Conclusion

To the question posed in [2], above, I would answer that where conditions (1)–(6) are satisfied C is entitled to recover against both A and B. That conclusion is in my opinion consistent with principle, and also with authority (properly understood). Where those conditions are satisfied, it seems to me just and in accordance with common sense to treat the conduct of A and B in exposing C to a risk to which he should not have been exposed as making a material contribution to the contracting by C of a condition against which it was the duty of A and B to protect him. I consider that this conclusion is fortified by the wider jurisprudence reviewed above. Policy considerations weigh in favour of such a conclusion. It is a conclusion which follows even if either A or B is not before the court. It was not suggested in argument that C's entitlement against either A or B should be for any sum less than the full compensation to which C is entitled, although A and B could of course seek contribution against each other or any other employer liable in respect of the same damage in the ordinary way. No argument on apportionment was addressed to the House. I would in conclusion emphasise that my opinion is directed to cases in which each of the conditions specified in (1)–(6) of [2], above is satisfied and to no other case. It would be unrealistic to suppose that the principle here affirmed will not over time be the subject of incremental and analogical development. Cases seeking to develop the principle must be decided when and as they arise. For the present, I think it unwise to decide more than is necessary to resolve these three appeals which, for all the foregoing reasons, I concluded should be allowed."

Comments and Questions:

1. In cases such as that above, the question of the apportionment of liability becomes very complicated in view of the fact that it is not clear to what extent each party caused the resulting injury. In Ireland, s.11(3) of the Civil Liability Act 1961 provides a similar remedy and states that:

"Where two or more persons are at fault and one or more of them is or are responsible for damage while the other or others is or are free from causal responsibility, but it is not possible to establish which is the case, such two or more persons shall be deemed to be concurrent wrongdoers in respect of the damage."

2. In the above case all the employers were found to have been at fault. However, it appears that causation can also be proven where it is not possible to identify which party was at fault. Lord Bingham referred in this respect to the Canadian case of *Cook v Lewis* [1951] S.C.R. 830 where a man was shot by one of two men who fired simultaneously but it was impossible to identify which one was at fault. Each party was found to be a cause. A similar outcome occurred in the case of *Lambton v Mellish* [1894] 3 Ch. 163. These outcomes appear motivated primarily by policy considerations.

LEGAL CAUSE AND *NOVUS ACTUS INTERVENIENS*

A *novus actus interveniens*, or new intervening act, is capable of breaking the chain of causation and relieving the initial defendant of liability. The intervening act may be that of a third party, of the plaintiff himself, or it may be an independent cause, such as an act of God. While not all intervening acts will amount to a *novus actus*, the rules for distinguishing a *novus actus* from an otherwise innocent intervening act are less than clear. Some general principles have emerged, focusing on issues of the foreseeability and reasonableness of the intervening act, and to a lesser extent the criminal nature of it. In the case of *Crowley v Allied Irish Banks* [1987] I.R. 282, the court, in determining the issue of whether a *novus actus* existed, focused on the issue of the unforeseeability of the intervening act.

Crowley v Allied Irish Banks Limited, and O'Flynn
Supreme Court [1987] I.R. 282

Facts: The plaintiff, who was 16 years old at the time, was seriously injured when he fell from the roof of the building of the first named defendant (AIB) while playing a game of rugby with three other boys. The first named defendant (the manager of which was the plaintiff's father) was aware that the boys played on the roof. The plaintiff sued both the bank and the architects who designed the roof (third party) in negligence. In two separate actions taken in the High Court, the plaintiff succeeded as against the bank with 9 per cent contributory negligence awarded against the plaintiff. Liability against the bank and the architects was apportioned on a 70/30 per cent basis. The architects appealed, arguing that notwithstanding any negligence in failing to include a railing on the roof, the actions of the bank constituted a *novus actus interveniens* absolving them of liability.

Issues: The court had to consider whether the action of the bank in allowing the boys to play on the roof of the building constituted a *novus actus* so as to relieve the architects of liability. The court held that the unforeseeable nature of the bank's actions in allowing the boys onto the roof constituted a *novus actus* capable of breaking the chain of causation.

Finlay C.J. (Walsh, Henchy, Hederman and Barr JJ. concurring):

"… Firstly, it was contended, applying the principles laid down by this Court in the case of Conole v Redbank Oyster Co [1976] IR 191, that even if one assumed that the architects were negligent in failing to provide in their plans for protection of the lower roof, then the finding by the jury, that the defendant, its servants or agents was aware that boys, including the plaintiff, were liable to play on this roof before the date on which the accident happened, constituted their consequential negligence as a novus actus interveniens and therefore it was not open to the court to hold that there was any nexus between the negligence of the architects and the happening of this accident.

Secondly, it was contended in the alternative that a proper consideration of the degrees of fault as between the defendant and the third party and the plaintiff, even if the third party were properly to be held to be a concurrent wrongdoer with the defendant, was such that the fault of the third party was minimal and not such as would support any finding of contribution against them.

… With regard to these submissions I have come to the following conclusions. I am satisfied that having regard to the express finding made by the jury that the defendant, its servants or agents, was aware of the fact that boys, including the plaintiff, were liable to play on this unguarded roof and to the absence of evidence (which was not tendered at any part of the hearing) that they had attempted to prevent or prohibit the plaintiff and the other boys from playing on this roof, it was not open to the learned trial judge to hold that a sufficient nexus or connection existed between any negligence or default on the part of the third party and the happening of this accident so as to constitute the third party a concurrent wrongdoer with the defendant and therefore liable to make contribution or indemnity.

It was not suggested that any part of the design required by the defendant in the reconstruction of these bank premises involved an intended use of this lower roof otherwise than such use as might occasionally be required for the purpose of maintenance or repair. Accepting as this Court must, on appeal, the finding of the learned trial judge that it had been established that access to this lower, unguarded roof was easy, certainly for a fit boy of sixteen years of age, either by stepping over the wall adjoining the stone steps or by dropping down 4 or 5 feet from the parapet wall of the upper roof, there does not appear to me to have been any evidence which would indicate that the third party should reasonably have foreseen that boys would be permitted by the servants or agents of the defendant to play energetic games upon this unguarded roof which so obviously carried the ever-present danger of a fall from it. The legal position with regard to the potential liability of a third party in circumstances such as these is, in my view, correctly stated in the decision of this Court in Conole v Redbank Oyster Co [1976] IR 191 in the judgment of Henchy J where, dealing with the alleged liability to contribute of a firm named Fairway, who had, on the evidence constructed an unseaworthy boat, he said at p 196 as follows:—

> 'Assuming that Fairway were negligent in sending forth an unseaworthy boat, reliance on this negligence must, on the authorities, be confined to those whom Fairway ought reasonably to have foreseen as likely to be injured by it. Furthermore, the negligence must be such as to have caused a defect which was unknown to such persons. If the defect becomes patent to the person ultimately injured and he chooses to ignore it, or to an intermediate handler who ignores it and subjects the person ultimately injured to that known risk, the person who originally put forth the article is not liable to the person injured. In such circumstances the nexus of cause and effect, in terms of the law of tort, has been sundered as far as the injured person is concerned.'

There can be no doubt on all the evidence in this case that the servants or agents of the defendant, prior to the happening of this accident were completely and fully aware of the danger of permitting boys to play upon this unguarded roof and that, in the words of the extract which I have just read from the judgment of Henchy J, they ignored that danger and, by permitting the continuation of the playing by the boys upon the unguarded roof, subjected them to the risk which caused this accident. In these circumstances, I am satisfied that the third party is entitled to succeed on the first ground argued on its behalf in this appeal. Having reached that decision it is unnecessary for me to reach any conclusion and I express no view on issues raised in this case concerning in particular the provisions of ss 21, 22 and 29 of the Civil Liability Act, 1961, which may fall to be decided in some other case. I would accordingly allow this appeal, set aside the order made on the issue between the defendant and the third party and substitute therefore an order dismissing the claim of the defendant against the third party."

Comments and Questions:

1. In the *Crowley* case Finlay C.J. focused on the fact that the architects could not have foreseen that the bank would have allowed the boys to play on the roof as a sufficient reason for the chain of causation to be severed. He made reference to the judgment of Henchy J. in the case of *Conole* where the focus of Henchy J. was slightly different in that he referred both to the unforeseeability of the intervening act and also to the reckless disregard of the intervening actor to the risk.

2. Note that Henchy J., quoted above by Finlay C.J., also stated that the reckless actor could be the injured party themselves. Should this break the

chain of causation or should the carelessness of the injured party be seen as contributory negligence (see Chapter 14)?

In the following case of *Murray v Millar* (2002) 20 I.L.T. 252 the question of whether the intervening act was a *novus actus* capable of breaking the chain of causation was considered by McMahon J.

Murray v Millar and Brady
Circuit Court (2002) 20 I.L.T. 252

Facts: The third defendant, Mr Brady, struck a cow when driving along a main road on a winter evening. Unable to alert help and mistakenly believing the cow to be dead, Mr Brady went to a nearby house to alert the police. While Mr Brady was absent, the cow, still alive, dragged itself some way into the road where the plaintiff struck it. The plaintiff sued the owner of the cow and Mr Brady. The owner argued that the actions of Mr Brady in leaving the cow unattended amounted to a *novus actus interveniens* capable of relieving the farmer of liability.

Issue: The court was asked to consider whether the act of Mr Brady was a *novus actus*. McMahon J. held that it was not. To determine whether an act could constitute a *novus actus* capable of breaking the change of causation, McMahon J. held that a court had to consider a number of factors—the degree of foreseeability of the intervening act, whether the act was criminal or reckless, and the lapse of time between the initial act and that of the intervening act. On the basis of these considerations McMahon J. found that the act of Mr Brady leaving the cow was not a *novus actus* capable of breaking the chain of causation.

McMahon J.:

"… The Latin phrase usually used by lawyers to describe the situation when the intervening act relieves the original actor, *i.e., novus actus interveniens*, is of course an insufficient abbreviation to indicate the legal consequences when the principle comes into play. Lawyers frequently say, in a shorthand and misleading way, that the defendant is not liable because of a *novus actus interveniens*, as if any intervening act will have this disruptive effect. Nothing could be further from the truth. It is only some intervening acts that possess this disruptive quality. In so far as the three Latin words *novus actus interveniens* are intended to describe the circumstances when it will provide the original wrongdoer with a full defence, it should more meaningfully translate as an intervening act which is of such a kind that it attracts sole liability for the plaintiff's injury or is of such a kind that it becomes the sole legal cause of the plaintiff's injuries.

In these circumstances, we should first ask what is the general nature of the intervening act if it is to have this effect in these types of cases.

It can be said with some confidence that if the intervening act is predictable and inevitable, the original actor cannot shrug off responsibility since he practically programmed the intervention. [*See Scott v Shepherd* (1773) 2 Wm Bl 892.] In this case it can be truly said that the third party's act is not voluntary or independent. Similarly, if the original actor intended the intervention he will be responsible. [*O'Rourke v An Post et al., unreported decision of His Honour Judge McMahon, Circuit Court Dublin, July 19, 2000. The defendant, having conducted an inadequate investigation into thefts from its premises, reported its hasty conclusions to the Gardaí who then arrested the plaintiff. It subsequently transpired that the plaintiff was innocent. The argument put forward by the first defendant, that the intervention by the Gardaí constituted a novus actus interveniens, was dismissed. It was reasonable and foreseeable that the Gardaí, having been furnished with a report from the defendant's investigative department would rely on it. Indeed, it could be said that the Gardaí having a legal duty to act in the matter, were in fact primed to act.*] At the other end of the scale, however, it is equally clear that, if he could not reasonably foresee any intervening act, after his initial action, then he will not be responsible for the unpredictable intervention. [*Salmon and Houston on the Law of Torts, 21st ed. 521: "... if a consequence which actually results from the defendant's tort is an improbable or unforeseeable consequence, then the defendant is not liable". Ibid. See also Lamb v. Camden LBC* [1981] QB 625; *Muldoon v. Ireland and AG* [1988] ILRM 367; *Perl (Exporters) Ltd v. Camden LBC* [1983] 3 All ER 161.] In between these two extremes, the courts have been less sure-footed in defining when the intervening act will in effect hijack the causal element and erase the significance of the original wrong. The courts prefer to determine each case on its own facts. In examining the circumstances where the intervening act will have the effect of relieving the original perpetrator, two factors feature in the judges' approach: first, whether, and to what extent the intervening act was foreseeable by the original actor, and second, how does one characterise the attitude of the subsequent intervenor—was he careless, negligent, grossly negligent, reckless or, did he intend to do damage? [*McMahon and Binchy, Law of Torts, 3rd ed., 2000, pp. 69–70.*] If the intention of the intervenor can be properly characterised as being criminal or subjectively reckless, then it is likely (though not inevitable) that it would have the effect of breaking the chain that leads back to the initial wrongdoer. [*Conole v. Redbank Oyster* [1976] IR 191: *"A wholly unpredictable but non-tortious intervention may break the chain of causation in one case while in another even deliberate tortious conduct may not do so, though as a general proposition it is probably correct to say that the further along the scale from innocent mistake to wilful wrongdoing the third party's conduct moves the more likely it is to terminate the defendant's liability". Winfield and Jolowich on Tort, 15th ed., 1998, 226.*] Where the conduct of the intervenor does not invite such opprobrium, however, the courts

are not inclined to exonerate the first act, of all causative relevance. [*McMahon and Binchy, Law of Torts, 3rd ed., 2000, para. 2.28 et seq.: "To break the chain of causation it must be shown that there is something which I will call ultroneous, something unwarrantable, a new cause which disturbs the sequence of events, some thing which can be described as either unreasonable or extraneous or extrinsic" (The Oreposa [1943] p. 32, at 39, per Lord Wright).*]
A third factor should also be noted: the greater the delay there is between the original conduct and the intervening act the more likely is the latter to be considered as the sole operative cause. [*See Crowley v. AIB and O'Flynn* [1988] ILRM 225 *where the failure by the first defendant constituted a novus actus interveniens.*] If on the other hand, the intervening act is close in time to the original act the courts are more likely to say that the original conduct still possesses a causative relevance. The temporal proximity of the two acts to each other, therefore, is frequently relevant, although, in truth, it is only one of several factors which the courts will consider in coming to a conclusion. Working from these principles, which are extracted from the case law, it is necessary now to examine the nature of the third defendant's act to see if it possesses the necessary qualities to have the effect in the present case of rupturing the chain of causation back to the first and second defendants.

The case before the court is not particularly difficult to resolve since it is clear that the original wrongdoers could reasonably foresee the kind of intervention that occurred; moreover, the intervenor's act was not unreasonable in the circumstances. In fact, in the present case, the liability of the first and second defendants is so clear that it could be rationalised in terms of their duty of care (or the risk they created) in terms of remoteness or, as was argued here, in terms of causal principles. In a different and more difficult fact pattern, one might have to embark on a deeper analysis of the degree of foreseeability required, the nature and quality of the intervening act, and even then it might not be possible to avoid resort to policy considerations in coming to a just decision. But not here.

In the present case, the cause of the initial collision was the failure of the first and second defendants to keep the animal safely corralled. Undoubtedly, on the evidence before this court, these defendants will be liable to the third defendant for his injury suffered in the first collision. This liability to Mr Brady (the third defendant) was not in issue in these proceedings, however, and because of that no evidence was adduced in this case that the third defendant had in any way contributed to his own injury. The sole concern of this court is to determine if the conduct of Mr Brady relieved the other defendants of their liability to the plaintiff.

When Mr Brady hit the cow, he pulled into his own side of the road put on his dims and hazard lights and walked back to the point of impact. The animal was motionless and he wrongly concluded that it was dead. He appreciated the danger and he began to flag down the passing traffic. He had little success and the one car that did stop was not too helpful. He began to consider his options.

Having considered the matter further, he decided to go for help to a house which was no more than four hundred yards away. If he took the car he would only be gone for a few minutes. In the circumstances was this conduct negligent, grossly negligent or reckless? Was it of such a kind that it relieved the original wrongdoers? Further, in considering the matter it must be relevant to acknowledge that the predicament in which he found himself was caused by the very people who now want to place the liability on him.

The first and second defendants must have foreseen that if their cow escaped onto the road it was likely to cause an accident and that more than one vehicle might eventually become involved. In general, therefore, these defendants should be liable for all the reasonable foreseeable consequences of their initial negligence. Clearly, once a collision has taken place, a new sequence of events unfolds, involving the first driver (most likely), other motorists (probably) and rescuers (possibly). Provided the responses of such unwilling participants are not unreasonable gauged in the light of the emergency in which they find themselves, they will be rightly attributed to the original wrongdoers. Should the first and second defendants be relieved from liability by the act or omission of the third defendant in the present circumstances? In my opinion, the conduct of the third defendant does not in the present circumstances possess such defective qualities as to wrest responsibility entirely from the original perpetrators. As I have already said, the conduct of the third defendant given the emergency the other defendants created for him was certainly not criminal or subjectively reckless as the case law seems to demand if it is to amount to a *novus actus interveniens* which breaks the link back to the other defendants. [*"Where the third-party conduct was an attempt to cure the problem caused by the defendant's negligence, the courts will be very slow to describe it as unforeseeable or unreasonable, or to regard it as a novus actus interveniens"*. *Butterworths Common Law Series, The Law of Tort*, 654, para. 14.35. See also *Salmond and Heustons, supra,* at *524*.] That a car might collide with the straying cow in the dark was foreseeable, and that a further collision might occur when the first parties injured were seeking assistance, was also foreseeable. To allocate liability to the original actors it is not of course necessary that they should foresee exactly the sequence of events that would follow from their initial negligence. [*"The plaintiff need not prove that the defendant ought to have foreseen every step in the chain of events leading to the accident"* (citing *Wieland v. Cyril Lord Carpets Ltd* [1969] 3 All ER 1006, *1009*).] In my view the general sequence of events was reasonably foreseeable by a reasonably prudent person, and the conduct of the intervenor was not so unreasonable or of such a nature as to hijack the causative aspect of the second collision. [*If "a driver so negligently manages his vehicle as to cause it to obstruct the highway and constitute a danger to other road users, including those who are driving too fast or not keeping a proper lookout, but not those who deliberately or recklessly drive into the obstruction, then the first driver's negligence may be held to have contributed to the causation of the accident of* which the immediate cause was the negligent driving of the vehicle which because of the presence of the obstruction collides with it" (Rouse v. Squires [1973] QB 889 at 898, per Cairns LJ).] The first and second defendants must compensate the plaintiff for his loss. Moreover, from the facts of this case I have no hesitation in saying that the straying animal was the sole cause of the accident."

Comments and Questions:

1. A number of matters arose for consideration in the above case in determining if the intervening act had the necessary quality to relieve the initial wrongdoer of liability. It appears that no one factor is critical but all relevant factors must be considered in coming to a decision.

2. Recklessness was one of the considerations. McMahon J. highlighted that the nature of the recklessness had to be subjective (that the actor averted to the risk and acted in disregard of it). See further the case of *Connolly (def.) v South of Ireland Asphalt Co. Ltd. (third party)* [1977] I.R. 99 where the objective recklessness of Connolly was not sufficient to break the chain of causation between the damage caused and the South of Ireland Asphalt Co. Ltd.

REMOTENESS

The issue of remoteness arises in determining the cut-off point of liability for damage: in other words, what will the defendant be liable for? The early position was that a defendant would be liable for all injury that flowed from his/her negligent act, regardless of how foreseeable that injury was (*Re Polemis* [1921] 3 K.B. 560). The decision in *Polemis*, however, has since been overruled so that the current law is that a defendant will only be liable for that type of injury which can reasonably be foreseen. While the leading authority for this principle is that of *Wagon Mound (No.1)*, a similar finding was made in Ireland some 10 months earlier in the Irish case of *O'Mahony v Ford & Son* [1962] I.R. 146.

Overseas Tankship (UK) Ltd. v Morts Dock & Engineering Co. Ltd. Respondents (The Wagon Mound) [1961] A.C. 388

Facts: The appellants (Wagon Mound), moored at Sydney harbour, caused some oil to spill into the harbour. The oil caught fire due to welding operations carried on at the wharf, causing severe fire damage to the wharf. The respondents sued. It was contended by the appellants that it was not reasonably foreseeable that oil would catch fire when on water.

The Supreme Court of New South Wales dismissed an appeal by the appellants as to their liability. The appellants made a further appeal to the Judicial Committee of the Privy Council.

Issues: It fell to be determined by the court (Judicial Committee of the Privy Council) whether the appellants could be held liable for the damage which, while unforeseeable, was a direct consequence of their negligent act. The court held that the authority in *Polemis* was no longer good law. The correct legal principle to be applied was whether the injury caused was foreseeable. As there was no foreseeability in this case there was no liability. The appeal was upheld.

Viscount Simonds:

"... Enough has been said to show that the authority of Polemis has been severely shaken though lip-service has from time to time been paid to it. In their Lordships' opinion it should no longer be regarded as good law. It is not probable that many cases will for that reason have a different result, though it is hoped that the law will be thereby simplified, and that in some cases, at least, palpable injustice will be avoided. For it does not seem consonant with current ideas of justice or morality that for an act of negligence, however slight or venial, which results in some trivial foreseeable damage the actor should be liable for all consequences however unforeseeable and however grave, so long as they can be said to be 'direct.' It is a principle of civil liability, subject only to qualifications which have no present relevance, that a man must be considered to be responsible for the probable consequences of his act. To demand more of him is too harsh a rule, to demand less is to ignore that civilised order requires the observance of a minimum standard of behaviour.

This concept applied to the slowly developing law of negligence has led to a great variety of expressions which can, as it appears to their Lordships, be harmonised with little difficulty with the single exception of the so-called rule in Polemis. For, if it is asked why a man should be responsible for the natural or necessary or probable consequences of his act (or any other similar description of them) the answer is that it is not because they are natural or necessary or probable, but because, since they have this quality, it is judged by the standard of the reasonable man that he ought to have foreseen them. Thus it is that over and over again it has happened that in different judgments in the same case, and sometimes in a single judgment, liability for a consequence has been imposed on the ground that it was reasonably foreseeable or, alternatively, on the ground that it was natural or necessary or probable. The two grounds have been treated as coterminous, and so they largely are. But, where they are not, the question arises to which the wrong answer was given in Polemis. For, if some limitation must be imposed upon the consequences for which the negligent actor is to be held responsible—and all are agreed that some limitation there must be—why should that test (reasonable foreseeability) be rejected which, since he is judged by what the reasonable man ought to foresee, corresponds with the common conscience of mankind, and a test (the 'direct' consequence) be substituted which leads to no-where but the never-ending and insoluble problems of causation. 'The lawyer,' said Sir Frederick Pollock, 'cannot afford to adventure himself with philosophers in the logical and metaphysical controversies that beset the idea of cause.' Yet this is just what he has most unfortunately done and must continue to do if the rule in Polemis is to prevail ...

The validity of a rule or principle can sometimes be tested by observing it in operation. Let the rule in Polemis be tested in this way. In the case of the Liesbosch the appellants, whose vessel had been fouled by the respondents, claimed damages under various heads. The respondents were admittedly at fault; therefore, said the appellants, invoking the rule in Polemis, they were responsible for all damage whether reasonably foreseeable or not. Here was the opportunity to deny the rule or to place it secure upon its pedestal. But the House of Lords took neither course; on the contrary, it distinguished Polemis on the ground that in that case the injuries suffered were the 'immediate physical consequences' of the negligent act. It is not easy to understand why a distinction should be drawn between 'immediate physical' and other consequences, nor where the line is to be drawn. It was perhaps this difficulty which led Denning L.J. in Roe v. Minister of Health ([1933] A.C. 449; 49 T.L.R. 289, H.L.) to say that foreseeability is only disregarded when the negligence is the immediate or precipitating cause of the damage. This new word may well have been thought as good a word as another for revealing or disguising the fact that he sought loyally to enforce an unworkable rule.

In the same connection may be mentioned the conclusion to which the Full Court finally came in the present case. Applying the rule in Polemis and holding therefore that the unforeseeability of the damage by fire afforded no defence, they went on to consider the remaining question. Was it a 'direct' consequence? Upon this Manning J. said: 'Notwithstanding that, if regard is had separately to each individual occurrence in the chain of events that led to this fire, each occurrence was improbable and, in one sense, improbability was heaped upon improbability, I cannot escape from the conclusion that if the ordinary man in the street had been asked, as a matter of common sense, without any detailed analysis of the circumstances, to state the cause of the fire at Mort's Dock, he would unhesitatingly have assigned such cause to spillage of oil by the appellant's employees.'

Perhaps he would, and probably he would have added: 'I never should have thought it possible.' But with great respect to the Full Court this is surely irrelevant, or, if it is relevant, only serves to show that the Polemis rule works in a very strange way. After the event even a fool is wise. But it is not the hindsight of a fool; it is the foresight of the reasonable man which alone can determine responsibility. The Polemis rule by substituting 'direct' for 'reasonably foreseeable' consequence leads to a conclusion equally illogical and unjust.

At an early stage in this judgment their Lordships intimated that they would deal with the proposition which can best be stated by reference to the well-known dictum of Lord Sumner: 'This however goes to culpability not to compensation.' It is with the greatest respect to that very learned judge and to those who have echoed his words, that their Lordships find themselves bound to state their view that this proposition is fundamentally false.

It is, no doubt, proper when considering tortious liability for negligence to analyse its elements and to say that the plaintiff must prove a duty owed to him by the defendant, a breach of that duty by the defendant, and consequent damage. But there can be no liability until the damage has been done. It is not the act but the consequences on which tortious liability is founded. Just as (as it has been said) there is no such thing as negligence in the air, so there is no such thing as liability in the air. Suppose an action brought by A for damage caused by the carelessness (a neutral word) of B, for example, a fire caused by the careless spillage of oil. It may, of course, become relevant to know what duty B owed to A, but the only liability that is in question is the liability for damage by fire. It is vain to isolate the liability from its context and to say that B is or is not liable, and then to ask for what damage he is liable. For his liability is in respect of that damage and no other. If, as admittedly it is, B's liability (culpability) depends on the reasonable foreseeability of the consequent damage, how is that to be determined except by the foreseeability of the damage which in fact happened— the damage in suit? And, if that damage is unforeseeable so as to displace liability at large, how can the liability be restored so as to make compensation payable?

But, it is said, a different position arises if B's careless act has been shown to be negligent and has caused some foreseeable damage to A. Their Lordships have already observed that to hold B liable for consequences however unforeseeable of a careless act, if, but only if, he is at the same time liable for some other damage however trivial, appears to be neither logical nor just. This becomes more clear if it is supposed that similar unforeseeable damage is suffered by A and C but other foreseeable damage, for which B is liable, by A only. A system of law which would hold B liable to A but not to C for the similar damage suffered by each of them could not easily be defended. Fortunately, the attempt is not necessary. For the same fallacy is at the root of the proposition. It is irrelevant to the question whether B is liable for unforeseeable damage that he is liable for foreseeable damage, as irrelevant as would the fact that he had trespassed on Whiteacre be to the question whether he has trespassed on Blackacre. Again, suppose a claim by A for damage by fire by the careless act of B. Of what relevance is it to that claim that he has another claim arising out of the same careless act? It would surely not prejudice his claim if that other claim failed: it cannot assist it if it succeeds. Each of them rests on its own bottom, and will fail if it can be established that the damage could not reasonably be foreseen. We have come back to the plain common sense stated by Lord Russell of Killowen in Bourhill v. Young ([1943] A.C. 92). As Denning L.J. said in King v. Phillips ([1953] 1 Q.B. 429, 441): 'there can be no doubt since Bourhill v. Young that the test of liability for shock is foreseeability of injury by shock.' Their Lordships substitute the word 'fire' for 'shock' and endorse this statement of the law."

Comments and Questions:

1. The clear statement of the law is therefore that liability will only ensue for those injuries which are the "natural and probable" cause of a negligent act. Is this, however, altogether clear? How will the courts decide which injuries are foreseeable and which are not?

A similar finding to that in *Wagon Mound (No.1)* above was made in the Irish case of *O'Mahony v Ford* [1962] I.R. 146.

Edward O'Mahony v Henry Ford & Son Ltd.
Supreme Court [1962] I.R. 146

Facts: The plaintiff, who was employed by the defendants as a riveter and assembly operator, in the course of his work operated a riveting machine which he held against his chest when in use. He developed a small swelling of the left breast which was diagnosed as scirrhus carcinoma. He successfully brought proceedings in the High Court against the defendants for his injuries. The defendants appealed to the Supreme Court on the basis that the risk of cancer from the use of a riveter was not a foreseeable one and that they should not be held liable.

Issues: The court (Lavery, Ó Dálaigh JJ., Maguire C.J.) had to consider whether the principle in *Re Polemis* ought to be applied, in which case the defendants might be liable (causes of cancers being largely unknown at that time) or whether it ought to be rejected in favour of the principle that the defendant ought only to be liable for foreseeable injuries.

Lavery and Ó Dálaigh JJ. (Maguire C.J. dissenting) held that the defendants should only be liable for foreseeable injuries, rejecting the rule in *Polemis*. As cancer could not be seen to be a foreseeable injury from the use of a riveter, the defendants should not be held liable.

Lavery J. (Ó Dálaigh J. concurring):

"... I think the jury could find that the alleged system might cause some injury such as bruising of the chest, though the plaintiff did not suffer any such injury nor was there any evidence that any other worker did so.

There is not, in my opinion, any evidence that the defendants could have reasonably foreseen that the system of work would cause cancer. The evidence does support, assuming a particular view is taken, that the plaintiff's condition may have been in fact caused by his work. The particular form of the disease is very rare in men and doctors of great experience over many years gave evidence that a very small number of cases have come under their notice, in some of which the origin of the disease could not be determined. The evidence also establishes the well-known fact that the causation of cancer, notwithstanding all the research made, is still largely unknown.

This situation raises for consideration the much discussed case of In re Polemis and Furness, Withy & Co ((1921) 3 KB 560).

... The Polemis Case ((1921) 3 KB 560) has been followed in innumerable cases in England in the High Court and the Court of Appeal, but the issue has never been brought to the House of Lords [*see now Overseas Tankship (UK) Ltd*

v Morts Dock & Engineering Co Ltd (The Wagon Mound) (1961) AC 388–Ed].)
It has been the subject of discussion by judges, text-writers and essayists,
notably by Lord Wright (1951) 14 Modern LR 393); Lord Porter ((1934) 5
Cambridge LJ 176); Professor McNair (as he was at the time he wrote) ((1931)
4 Cambridge LJ 125); Dr Goodhart (68 LQR 514) and Professors H L Hart and
A M Honore (Causation in the Law, 1959). Some of these writers support the
decision, others challenge it.

The decision is not binding on this Court but it would be wrong not to give it
the most careful consideration so far as may be necessary on the facts of this
case.

I have read these essays carefully and it would be useless and is unnecessary
to discuss them at length in this judgment. I certainly could not hope to settle
the many difficulties and, unlike the essayists, I am not called on to attempt to
do so.

... In the Polemis Case ((1921) 3 KB 560) there was a finding by arbitrators
that the defendants were negligent. No attempt was made to challenge this
finding which, being one of fact, was accepted as binding, on the hearing of a
case stated by them.

... Though not considered, it was the position that in the Polemis Case
((1921) 3 KB 560) the foreseeable damage which might be caused by the fall of
the plank was not suffered and the damage actually caused, but not foreseeable,
was certainly not of the same 'exact kind.'

Whether an act or omission which might have caused but, in fact, did not
cause injury or damage which the reasonable man might be held to have
foreseen and had, therefore, a duty not to commit or to omit, is actionable
negligence because injury or damage of a different kind not foreseeable and
one, therefore, in respect of which there was no duty, has been suffered?

It is axiomatic that a failure to use the due care required by law, applying the
standard of care of the reasonable man, does not give a cause of action unless
injury or damage is caused. Is there a cause of action where there has been no
fault on the part of the defendant, considered as the reasonable man, because
damage which he could not foresee has been suffered? The risk of injury in this
case, which on the evidence might be held to have been foreseeable, was a
physical injury such as bruising of the chest—I shall use the term, 'physical
injury,' in this sense.

I distinguish between such an injury and the causation of the disease by
repeated vibration of the tools which was on the evidence not foreseeable and
therefore not a risk which the employers had a duty to guard against.

The only possible conclusion from this evidence, in my opinion, is that the
plaintiff did not suffer any physical injury and does not allege that he did. A
number of medical witnesses were examined. They differed in opinion on
several issues but none of them testified to having observed any physical
injury—in the sense in which I am using the phrase—or that the plaintiff told
them that he had at any time suffered any such injury.

The question is, therefore, definitely posed and must be faced.

There has been no verdict and, therefore, the questions of law must be considered on a hypothetical basis, assuming that a jury has found the facts on all issues proper to be submitted, in the way most favourable to the plaintiff.

1, The use of the tools as described by the plaintiff was known to the defendant company and was directed or permitted by them.

2, Such user was capable of causing physical injury to the plaintiff and therefore was in that respect an unsafe system.

3, No injury of this kind was suffered—it is not open to the jury to find otherwise.

4, The plaintiff is suffering from cancer of the breast.

5, This disease was caused by his work, done in the manner found in item 1.

6, This consequence could not have been foreseen by careful and prudent employers.

In my opinion, these findings, if made, would not entitle the plaintiff to judgment.

… A similar situation existed in the case of Carey v Cork Consumers' Gas Co (unreported; 5th March, 1958).

The plaintiff claimed damages against his employers because he contracted silicosis in the course of his work and by reason of the defendants' failure to provide a safe system to protect him.

Mr Justice Haugh at the trial withdrew the case from the jury, holding that while there was controversy as to whether the plaintiff had silicosis or some other ailment and as to whether if he had silicosis it was caused by his work, both of which questions might have been determined in the plaintiff's favour, the evidence could not support a finding that it could reasonably have been foreseen by the employers that the plaintiff in his work would be exposed to the risk. This Court sustained this ruling and the judgment for the defendants stood.

In my opinion, therefore, the trial Judge should have withdrawn the case from the jury and entered judgment for the defendants.

The appeal, in my opinion, should therefore be allowed and judgment should be entered for the defendants."

Comments and Questions:

1. Lavery J. held in the above case that for the defendant to be liable not only must there be injury but it must be of a "type" that was foreseeable. In the above case it was concluded that cancer is not a physical injury of a type foreseeable to the reasonable person and therefore no liability should have been applied. The determination of "type" appears to enjoy a wide latitude. In this sense it is sometimes argued (McMahon & Binchy) that it does not differ too greatly from the "direct consequences test". Some writers (see Fleming) argue that in fact the principle enjoys such flexibility that it appears that the courts simply use it to find as they wish in a particular case.

Outside of some general categorisations (physical, psychological, economic), how easy is it in your view to distinguish one "type" of injury from another?

"Egg-shell skull" rule

As stated above the injury must not only be foreseeable but must be of a type that is foreseeable. In some cases, however, while the type of injury suffered is a foreseeable one, the extent of damage may be much greater than expected due to some weakness on the part of the plaintiff. The defendant will still be held liable, reflecting the principle that has long existed in tort law that "the tortfeasor takes his victim as he finds him", a principle also referred to as the "egg-shell skull" rule.

This rule applied in the case of *Burke v John Paul & Co Ltd.* [1967] I.R. 277 below.

James Burke v John Paul and Company Limited
Supreme Court [1967] I.R. 277

Facts: The plaintiff, who worked as a steel-cutter for the defendant company, suffered severe muscle strain from using a blunt saw, supplied to him by his employers. Due to a predisposition of the plaintiff's, instead of simply suffering from muscle strain he developed a hernia from the exertion required to operate the saw. The High Court (McLoughlin J. and a jury) held that the injury suffered was too remote, in that the employer was not liable for the injury suffered as he could not have foreseen the weakness of the plaintiff which led to the more severe injury. The plaintiff appealed to the Supreme Court.

Issues: The Supreme Court (Ó Dálaigh C.J., Haugh and Budd JJ.) was required to consider whether the defendants ought to be liable for the plaintiff's hernia, despite the fact that it was a more extreme reaction to the strain suffered.

Budd J. (Ó Dálaigh C.J. and Haugh J. concurring):

"... Certain medical evidence was adduced at the hearing on behalf of the plaintiff with the object of proving that the hernia was caused by the man being required to work at the cutting of the steel bars with this allegedly blunt instrument. Dr McCarthy's evidence was to this effect. For a hernia to develop there is usually an area of congenital weakness on the surface of the abdomen. As a result of muscular exertion and the muscles being caught off-guard a piece of bowel may be pushed through that area, thus causing a hernia. He said that what would be noticed would be a pain in the groin and a swelling, and that what the plaintiff noticed would be consistent with a hernia. He also said, as I understand his evidence, that the exertion of pressure and the condition which the plaintiff noticed would be quite consistent with a hernia resulting from the pressure. Dr Lucey also said that a hernia comes from pressure on the abdominal muscles. The muscle tears or the pressure and force on the muscles causes the area to break. Her view was that the muscles become weaker having undergone pressure for some time. The gist of her further evidence was that hernia is caused by a strain too great for the muscles, and that the more pressure the workman is obliged to apply the more likely he is to produce a hernia.

... On the pleadings, the run of the case and the evidence given, the questions which the jury would have to answer in the affirmative to enable the plaintiff to succeed would be, first, were the defendants negligent in failing to provide the plaintiff with a proper appliance with which to do the work he was required to do, or in failing to maintain it in a proper condition; secondly, if the answer to the first question is in the affirmative, was the hernia caused by the negligent breach of duty; thirdly, if so, was the type of injury suffered one which an employer could and should reasonably have foreseen. The point to be decided is whether a reasonable jury could have answered these questions in the affirmative on the evidence adduced.

[Having accepted that the employers had been negligent in knowingly supplying the plaintiff with a blunt saw, and that the saw had caused the injury, Budd J. then went on to consider whether the injury suffered was too remote.]

There then remains the question of foreseeability. The test of foreseeability as adopted in Overseas Tankship (UK) Ltd v Morts Dock & Engineering Co Ltd (The Wagon Mound) ((1961) AC 388) has been accepted in this Court (and indeed was accepted in the argument in this case) and I proceed on the basis that, in determining liability for the consequences of a tortious act of negligence, the test is whether the damage is of such a kind as a reasonable man should have foreseen. What is said by the defendants is that there was no evidence given in this case to show that the type of injuries sustained might reasonably have been anticipated by the defendants. The argument, as it was developed, was that the medical evidence showed that before a person can develop a hernia there must be some congenital weakness—some predisposition to getting a hernia, and that, since this could not be discovered on any ordinary examination, it was impossible for the defendants to know of any predisposition of the plaintiff to develop a hernia, and that consequently they could not foresee that the use of extra exertion and pressure by the plaintiff in cutting the bars would result in a hernia developing. It was clearly implicit in the medical evidence that unwonted bodily exertion may cause straining or tearing of the muscles. It cannot, I think, be suggested that it is necessary to have the statement of a medical expert that an employer should know that if one of his employees is forced to use great exertion in the course of his work that may cause a straining, or even tearing, of muscles, as that is a matter of common knowledge; but the point taken is that it could not be reasonably anticipated that a hernia would result without knowledge that the plaintiff had a predisposition to hernia. The answer to this, I think, is what is generally referred to as 'the egg-shell skull rule' and I do not think that that rule has been impugned in any way by the Wagon Mound ((1961) AC 388) decision.

A somewhat similar point arose in the case of Smith v Leech Brain & Co Ltd ((1962) 2 QB 405). The case was a claim by the widow of a workman under the Fatal Accidents Acts, 1846 to 1908, and the Law Reform (Misc Provs) Act, 1934. The workman suffered an injury by reason of a piece of molten metal striking him on the lower lip and causing a burn. The burn was the promoting cause of cancer from which the workman died. The cancer developed in tissues which already had a premalignant condition. It was alleged that the employers were negligent in not providing adequate protection for the workman, the risk of his being burned being one which was readily foreseeable. Lord Parker CJ took the view that, but for the decision in the Wagon Mound ((1961) AC 388) case, it seemed perfectly clear to him that, assuming negligence was proved and the burn caused in whole or in part the cancer and death, the widow would be entitled to recover.

With regard to the effect of the Wagon Mound ((1961) AC 388) on the case he was dealing with, Lord Parker said at pp. 414 and 415 of the report—"For my part, I am quite satisfied that the Judicial Committee in the Wagon Mound ((1961) AC 388) case did not have what I may call, loosely, the thin skull cases in mind. It has always been the law of this country that a tortfeasor takes his victim as he finds him. It is unnecessary to do more than refer to the short passage in the decision of Kennedy J in Dulieu v White & Sons ((1901) 2 KB 669) "If a man is negligently run over or otherwise negligently injured in his body, it is no answer to the sufferer's claim for damages that he would have suffered less injury, or no injury at all, if he had not had an unusually thin skull or an unusually weak heart." To the same effect is a passage in the judgment of Scrutton LJ in The Arpad ((1934) p189, p202, p203). But quite apart from those two references, as is well known, the work of the courts for years and years has gone on on that basis. There is not a day that goes by where some trial judge does not adopt that principle, that the tortfeasor takes his victim as he finds him. If the Judicial Committee had any intention of making an inroad into that doctrine, I am quite satisfied that they would have said so. It is true that if the wording in the advice given by Lord Simonds in the Wagon Mound ((1961) AC 388) case is applied strictly to such a case as this, it could be said that they were dealing with this point. But, as I have said, it is to my mind quite impossible to conceive that they were and, indeed, it has been pointed out that they disclose the distinction between such a case as this and the one they were considering when they comment on Smith v London & South Western Railway Company (LR 6 CP 14). Lord Simonds in dealing with that case said: 'Three things may be noted about this case: the first, that for the sweeping proposition laid down no authority was cited; the second, that the point to which the court directed its mind was not unforeseeable damage of a different kind from that which was foreseen, but more extensive damage of the same kind.' In other words, Lord Simonds is clearly there drawing a distinction between the question whether a man could reasonably anticipate a type of injury, and the question whether a man could reasonably anticipate the extent of injury of the type which could be foreseen. The Judicial Committee were, I think, disagreeing with the decision in the Polemis ((1921) 3 KB 560) case that a man is no longer liable for the type of damage which he could not reasonably anticipate. The Judicial Committee were not, I think, saying that a man is only liable for the extent of damage which he could anticipate, always assuming the type of injury could have been anticipated. I think that view is really supported by the way in which cases of this sort have been dealt with in Scotland. Scotland has never, so far as I know, adopted the principle laid down in Polemis ((1921) 3 KB 560), and yet I am quite satisfied that they have throughout proceeded on the basis that the tortfeasor takes the victim as he finds him. In those circumstances, it seems to me that this is plainly a case which comes within the old principle. The test is not whether these employers could reasonably have foreseen that a burn would cause cancer and that he would die. The question is whether these employers could reasonably foresee the type of injury he suffered, namely, the burn. What, in the particular case, is the amount of damage which he suffers as a result of that burn, depends upon the characteristics and constitution of the victim."

With respect, I entirely adopt the reasoning of Lord Parker. Applying his reasoning to this case, the test is not whether the defendants could reasonably have foreseen that a straining or tearing of the muscles would cause a hernia in this particular man, but the question is rather whether they could have reasonably foreseen the type of injury that he did suffer, namely, the tearing or straining of the muscles which resulted in the hernia. A reasonable jury could, in my view, certainly find on all the facts and circumstances of the case that the defendants ought to have anticipated that a man in the plaintiff's position, being given a blunt instrument with which to cut steel bars, might, by reason of the unusual exertion he would be called upon to exercise, strain or injure his muscles; it is immaterial that the defendants could not anticipate the full extent of the damage. It follows that a reasonable jury could properly have answered the third question that I have posed in the affirmative, as well as the other two. The case, therefore, should not have been withdrawn from the jury and in the circumstances a new trial becomes necessary."

Comments and Questions:
1. A defendant must take his victim as he finds him. Is this requirement a further dilution of the principle that a defendant is only liable for the "type of injury" foreseeable or is it merely a question of degree?

2. The egg-shell skull rule is as equally applicable to financial weakness as it is to physical weakness. In this way a defendant may be liable for interest

payable on loans required due to the defendant's fault (see *Riordan's Travel Ltd. v Acres and Co. Ltd. (No.2)* [1979] I.L.R.M.).

3. Should the egg-shell skull principle apply equally to mental injury as well as physical injury? While the application of the principle to mental injury cases is generally accepted as the correct statement of the law, Keane C.J. threw some doubt on this proposition in *Glencar v Mayo County Council* [2002] 1 I.R. 84, [2002] 1 I.L.R.M. 481.

CHAPTER 2

NEGLIGENCE

INTRODUCTION

To succeed in a negligence action a plaintiff must satisfy a number of conditions. First, the plaintiff must show that the defendant owed him/her a duty of care. Secondly, the plaintiff must establish that the defendant fell below a reasonable standard of care (*i.e.* that the defendant was negligent). Generally speaking, it is for the plaintiff to prove that the defendant was negligent. The only exception to this is when the negligence of the defendant is clear, in which case negligence is presumed and it is for the defendant to rebut this presumption (the principle of *res ipsa loquitur*). Thirdly, the defendant must establish causation (see Chapter 1).

This chapter will discuss the guidelines developed by the courts to determine to whom a duty is owed, the standard and its breach (this element of the tort of negligence is also referred to as negligence), and the principle of *res ipsa loquitur*.

DUTY OF CARE

The initial view was that no general principle existed which could decide when a duty arose. Instead, claimants had to bring themselves within one of the established categories of claim and new categories could only be developed incrementally. Examples of established categories included recovery against an occupier for injury to entrants, recovery against the manufacturer of a dangerous product for injury caused by that product, and so on.

In England, the first significant case which sought to develop a general principle was that of *Donoghue v Stevenson* [1932] A.C. 562. In that case, Lord Atkin established the now famous "neighbour principle", which held that a duty was owed in cases where a relationship of proximity existed between the plaintiff and the defendant and the injury to the plaintiff was foreseeable.

Donoghue (or McAlister) v Stevenson
House of Lords [1932] All E.R. Rep 1, [1932] A.C. 562; 101 L.J.P.C. 119; 147 L.T. 281; 48 T.L.R. 494; 76 Sol Jo 396; 37 Com Cas 350

Facts: The appellant drank a bottle of ginger beer manufactured by the respondent, which a friend had ordered on her behalf from a retailer in a shop in Paisley, Scotland. The bottle was made of dark opaque glass. On pouring some of its contents into a glass of ice-cream, a snail which had been in the bottle floated out in a state of decomposition. The appellant alleged that as a result she had contracted a serious illness, and she sued the respondents as manufacturers of the product. The respondent, on the other hand, argued that, as there was no contract between them, there could be no claim. At that time the law stated that while manufacturers could be held liable for injury caused by a dangerous product, a bottle of ginger beer could not be classified as dangerous. The plaintiff sued but lost in the trial court, and an appeal was brought to the House of Lords.

Issues: The legal issue then to be decided was whether a duty of care was owed to her by the manufacturer and, if so, on what basis.

The House of Lords held, by a majority of three to two, that a duty of care was owed to her by the manufacturer (Lords Atkin, Macmillan and Thankerton, with Lords Buckmaster and Tomlin dissenting) on the basis of proximity and foreseeability.

Lord Atkin:

"The sole question for determination in this case is legal: Do the averments made by the pursuer in her pleading, if true, disclose a cause of action? ...

... In the present case we are not concerned with the breach of the duty; if a duty exists, that would be a question of fact which is sufficiently averred and for the present purposes must be assumed. We are solely concerned with the question whether as a matter of law in the circumstances alleged the defender owed any duty to the pursuer to take care.

It is remarkable how difficult it is to find in the English authorities statements of general application defining the relations between parties that give rise to the duty. The courts are concerned with the particular relations which come before them in actual litigation, and it is sufficient to say whether the duty exists in those circumstances. The result is that the courts have been engaged upon an elaborate classification of duties as they exist in respect of property, whether real or personal, with further divisions as to ownership, occupation or control, and distinctions based on the particular relations of the one side or the other, whether manufacturer, salesman or landlord, customer, tenant, stranger, and so on. In this way it can be ascertained at any time whether the law recognises a duty, but only where the case can be referred to some particular species which has been examined and classified. And yet the duty which is common to all the cases where liability is established must logically be based upon some element common to the cases where it is found to exist. To seek a complete logical definition of the general principle is probably to go beyond the function of the judge, for, the more general the definition, the more likely it is to omit essentials or introduce non-essentials. The attempt was made by LORD ESHER in

Heaven v Pender in a definition to which I will later refer. As framed it was demonstrably too wide, though it appears to me, if properly limited, to be capable of affording a valuable practical guide.

At present I content myself with pointing out that in English law there must be and is some general conception of relations giving rise to a duty of care, of which the particular cases found in the books are but instances. The liability for negligence, whether you style it such or treat it as in other systems as a species of 'culpa,' is no doubt based upon a general public sentiment of moral wrong-doing for which the offender must pay. But acts or omissions which any moral code would censure cannot in a practical world be treated so as to give a right to every person injured by them to demand relief. In this way rules of law arise which limit the range of complainants and the extent of their remedy. The rule that you are to love your neighbour becomes in law: You must not injure your neighbour, and the lawyers' question: Who is my neighbour? receives a restricted reply. You must take reasonable care to avoid acts or omissions which you can reasonably foresee would be likely to injure your neighbour. Who then, in law, is my neighbour? The answer seems to be persons who are so closely and directly affected by my act that I ought reasonably to have them in contemplation as being so affected when I am directing my mind to the acts or omissions which are called in question. This appears to me to be the doctrine of Heavens v Pender as laid down by LORD ESHER when it is limited by the notion of proximity introduced by LORD ESHER himself and AL SMITH, LJ, in Le Lievre and another v Gould. LORD ESHER, MR, says ([1893] 1 QB at p 497):

> 'That case established that, under certain circumstances, one man may owe a duty to another, even though there is no contract between them. If one man is near to another, or is near to the property of another, a duty lies upon him not to do that which may cause a personal injury to that other, or may injure his property.'

So AL SMITH, LJ, says ([1893] 1 QB at p 504):

> 'The decision of Heaven v Pender was founded upon the principle that a duty to take due care did arise when the person or property of one was in such proximity to the person or property of another that, if due care was not taken damage might be done by the one to the other.'

I think that this sufficiently states the truth if proximity be not confined to mere physical proximity, but be used, as I think it was intended, to extend to such close and direct relations that the act complained of directly affects a person whom the person alleged to be bound to take care would know would be directly affected by his careless act. That this is the sense in which nearness or 'proximity' was intended by LORD ESHER is obvious from his own illustration in Heaven v Pender (11 QBD at p 510) of the application of his doctrine to the sale of goods.

'This [*i.e.*, the rule he has just formulated] includes the case of goods, &c, supplied to be used immediately by a particular person or persons, or one of a class of persons, where it would be obvious to the person supplying, if he thought, that the goods would in all probability be used at once by such persons before a reasonable opportunity for discovering any defect which might exist, and where the thing supplied would be of such a nature that a neglect of ordinary care or skill as to its condition or the manner of supplying it would probably cause danger to the person or property of the person for whose use it was supplied, and who was about to use it. It would exclude a case in which the goods are supplied under circumstances in which it would be a chance by whom they would be used, or whether they would be used or not, or whether they would be used before there would probably be means of observing any defect, or where the goods would be of such a nature that a want of care or skill as to their condition or the manner of supplying them would not probably produce danger of injury to person or property.'

I draw particular attention to the fact that LORD ESHER emphasises the necessity of goods having to be 'used immediately' and 'used at once before a reasonable opportunity of inspection.' This is obviously to exclude the possibility of goods having their condition altered by lapse of time, and to call attention to the proximate relationship, which may be too remote where inspection even by the person using, certainly by an intermediate person, may reasonably be interposed. With this necessary qualification of proximate relationship, as explained in Le Lievre and another v Gould I think the judgment of LORD ESHER expresses the law of England. Without the qualification, I think that the majority of the court in Heaven v Pender was justified in thinking that the principle was expressed in too general terms. There will, no doubt, arise cases where it will be difficult to determine whether the contemplated relationship is so close that the duty arises. But in the class of case now before the court I cannot conceive any difficulty to arise. A manufacturer puts up an article of food in a container which he knows will be opened by the actual consumer. There can be no inspection by any purchaser and no reasonable preliminary inspection by the consumer. Negligently in the course of preparation he allows the contents to be mixed with poison. It is said that the law of England and Scotland is that the poisoned consumer has no remedy against the negligent manufacturer. If this were the result of the authorities, I should consider the result a grave defect in the law and so contrary to principle that I should hesitate long before following any decision to that effect which had not the authority of this House. I would point out that in the assumed state of the authorities not only would the consumer have no remedy against the manufacturer, he would have none against anyone else, for in the circumstances alleged there would be no evidence of negligence against anyone other than the manufacturer, and except in the case of a consumer who was also a purchaser no contract and no warranty of fitness, and in the case of the purchase of a specific article under its patent or trade name, which might well be the case in the purchase of some articles of food or drink, no warranty protecting even the purchaser-consumer. There are other instances than of articles of food and drink when goods are sold intended to be used immediately by the consumer, such as many forms of goods sold for cleaning purposes, when the same liability must exist. The doctrine supported by the decision below would not only deny a remedy to the consumer who was injured by consuming bottled beer or chocolates poisoned by the negligence of the manufacturer, but also to the user of what should be a harmless proprietary medicine, an ointment, a soap, a cleaning fluid or cleaning powder. I confine myself to articles of common household use, where everyone, including the manufacturer, knows that the articles will be used by persons other than the actual ultimate purchaser—namely, by members of his family and his servants, and, in some cases, his guests. I do not think so ill of our jurisprudence as to suppose that its principles are so remote from the ordinary needs of civilised society and the ordinary claims which it makes upon its members as to deny a legal remedy where there is so obviously a social wrong. ...

... It is always satisfaction to an English lawyer to be able to test his application of fundamental principles of the common law by the development of the same doctrines by the lawyers of the courts of the United States. In that country I find that the law appears to be well established in the sense which I have indicated. The mouse had emerged from the ginger-beer bottle in the United States before it appeared in Scotland, but there it brought a liability upon the manufacturer. I must not in this long judgment do more than refer to the illuminating judgment of CARDOZO, J, in MacPherson v Buick Motor Co (15) in the New York Court of Appeals, in which he states the principles of the law as I should desire to state them and reviews the authorities in States other than his own. Whether the principle which he affirms would apply to the particular facts of that case in this country would be a question for consideration if the case arose. It might be that the course of business, by giving opportunities of examination to the immediate purchaser or otherwise, prevented the relation between manufacturer and the user of the car from being so close as to create a duty. But the American decision would undoubtedly lead to a decision in favour of the pursuer in the present case.

If your Lordships accept the view that the appellant's pleading discloses a relevant cause of action, you will be affirming the proposition that by Scots and English law alike a manufacturer of products which he sells in such a form as to show that he intends them to reach the ultimate consumer in the form in which they left him, with no reasonable possibility of intermediate examination, and with the knowledge that the absence of reasonable care in the preparation or putting up of the products will result in injury to the consumer's life or property, owes a duty to the consumer to take that reasonable care.

It is a proposition that I venture to say no one in Scotland or England who was not a lawyer would for one moment doubt. It will be an advantage to make it clear that the law in this matter, as in most others, is in accordance with sound common sense. I think that this appeal should be allowed."

Lord Macmillan:

"On the one hand, there is the well-established principle that no one other than a party to a contract can complain of a breach of that contract. On the other hand, there is the equally well-established doctrine that negligence, apart from contract, gives a right of action to the party injured by that negligence—and here I use the term negligence, of course, in its technical legal sense, implying a duty owed and neglected. ...

... The law takes no cognizance of carelessness in the abstract. It concerns itself with carelessness only where there is a duty to take care and where failure in that duty has caused damage. In such circumstances carelessness assumes the legal quality of negligence and entails the consequences in law of negligence. What then are the circumstances which give rise to this duty to take care? In the daily contacts of social and business life human beings are thrown into or place themselves in an infinite variety of relationships with their fellows, and the law can refer only to the standards of the reasonable man in order to determine whether any particular relationship gives rise to a duty to take care as between those who stand in that relationship to each other. The grounds of action may be as various and manifold as human errancy, and the conception of legal responsibility may develop in adaptation to altering social conditions and standards. The criterion of judgment must adjust and adapt itself to the changing circumstances of life. The categories of negligence are never closed. The cardinal principle of liability is that the party complained of should owe to the party complaining a duty to take care and that the party complaining should be able to prove that he has suffered damage in consequence of a breach of that duty. Where there is room for diversity of view is in determining what circumstances will establish such a relationship between the parties as to give rise on the one side to a duty to take care and on the other side to a right to have care taken.

To descend from these generalities to the circumstances of the present case I do not think that any reasonable man or any twelve reasonable men would hesitate to hold that if the appellant establishes her allegations the respondent has exhibited carelessness in the conduct of his business. For a manufacturer of aerated water to store his empty bottles in a place where snails can get access to them and to fill his bottles without taking any adequate precautions by inspection or otherwise to ensure that they contain no deleterious foreign matter may reasonably be characterised as carelessness without applying too exacting a standard. But, as I have pointed out, it is not enough to prove the respondent to be careless in his process of manufacture. The question is: Does he owe a duty to take care, and to whom does he owe that duty? I have no hesitation in arming that a person who for gain engages in the business of manufacturing articles of food and drink intended for consumption by members of the public in the form in which he issues them is under a duty to take care in the manufacture of these articles. That duty, in my opinion, he owes to those whom he intends to consume his products. He manufactures his commodities for human consumption; he intends and contemplates that they shall be consumed.

By reason of that very fact he places himself in a relationship with all the potential consumers of his commodities, and that relationship, which he assumes and desires for his own ends, imposes upon him a duty to take care to avoid injuring them. He owes them a duty not to convert by his own carelessness an article which he issues to them as wholesome and innocent into an article which is dangerous to life and health.

It is sometimes said that liability can arise only where a reasonable man would have foreseen and could have avoided the consequences of his act or omission. In the present case the respondent, when he manufactured his ginger-beer, had directly in contemplation that it would be consumed by members of the public. Can it be said that he could not be expected as a reasonable man to foresee that if he conducted his process of manufacture carelessly he might injure those whom he expected and desired to consume his ginger-beer? The possibility of injury so arising seems to me in no sense so remote as to excuse him from foreseeing it. Suppose that a baker through carelessness allows a large quantity of arsenic to be mixed with a batch of his bread, with the result that those who subsequently eat it are poisoned, could he be heard to say that he owed no duty to the consumers of his bread to take care that it was free from poison, and that, as he did not know that any poison had got into it, his only liability was for breach of warranty under his contract of sale to those who actually bought the poisoned bread from him? Observe that I have said 'through carelessness' and thus excluded the case of a pure accident such as may happen where every care is taken. I cannot believe, and I do not believe, that neither in the law of England nor in the law of Scotland is there redress for such a case. The state of facts I have figured might well give rise to a criminal charge, and the civil consequences of such carelessness can scarcely be less wide than its criminal consequences. Yet the principle of the decision appealed from is that the manufacturer of food products intended by him for human consumption does not owe to the consumers whom he has in view any duty of care, not even the duty to take care that he does not poison them."

Comments and Questions:
1. Lord Atkin stated that a person owes a duty when he can foresee that he would injure his "neighbour" through negligent acts or omissions. However, the law generally deals with liability for negligent acts and negligent omissions differently. Only in certain cases will a duty of care exist for negligent omissions as we are generally not under any obligation to be "our brother's keeper".

2. Lord Atkin departed from the general consensus in attempting to identify general principles which could be used to determine whether a duty of care existed, but he himself did not fully support strict adherence to a general principle for fear of omitting certain "essentials" from the discussion. Do you think he was correct in his view?

The Atkin formula was affirmed by Lord Wilberforce in *Anns v Merton Urban District Council* [1978] A.C. 728, where Lord Wilberforce laid emphasis on proximity, foreseeability and the absence of any policy considerations that might exclude liability, as being the "test" to establish the existence of a duty of care.

Anns v London Borough of Merton
House of Lords [1978] A.C. 728, [1977] 2 All E.R. 492, [1977] 2 W.L.R. 1024, 75 L.G.R. 555, 141 J.P. 527, 5 Build L.R. 1, 4 I.L.R. 21, 243 E.G. 523, [1977] E.G.D. 604, (48 M.L.R. 88), (101 L.Q.R. 24)

Facts: The plaintiffs, occupiers of flats in a block of flats, sued the builders of the flats and the local authority (London Borough Council) when cracks began to appear in the building. The plaintiffs argued that the cracks were due to the flats being erected on inadequate foundations. Their claim against the local authority was that it was negligent in approving foundations laid contrary to building regulations. The case was argued largely on the basis of a procedural issue as to the statute of limitations, on which basis it proceeded from the trial court to the Court of Appeal and from there to the House of Lords, at which point the defendants also argued that no duty of care was owed to the plaintiffs.

Issues: The court (Wilberforce, Diplock, Simon of Glaisdale, Salmon and Russel of Killowen L.JJ.) was asked to consider whether a duty was owed to the plaintiffs by the local authority, a contention which the local authority denied.
    Their Lordships held that a duty of care was owed by the Council. This duty arose from the proximity of the parties, the foreseeability of injury and the absence of any policy considerations which might deny a duty.

Lord Wilberforce:

"Through the trilogy of cases in this House, Donoghue v Stevenson [[1932] AC 562, [1932] All ER Rep 1], Hedley Byrne & Co Ltd v Heller & Partners Ltd [[1963] 2 All ER 575, [1964] AC 465] and Home Office v Dorset Yacht Co Ltd [[1970] 2 All ER 294 at 297, 298, [1970] AC 1004], the position has now been reached that in order to establish that a duty of care arises in a particular situation, it is not necessary to bring the facts of that situation within those of previous situations in which a duty of care has been held to exist. Rather the question has to be approached in two stages. First one has to ask whether, as between the alleged wrongdoer and the person who has suffered damage there is a sufficient relationship of proximity or neighbourhood such that, in the reasonable contemplation of the former, carelessness on his part may be likely to cause damage to the latter, in which case a prima facie duty of care arises. Secondly, if the first question is answered affirmatively, it is necessary to consider whether there are any considerations which ought to negative, or to reduce or limit the scope of the duty or the class of person to whom it is owed or the damages to which a breach of it may give rise (see the Dorset Yacht case [[1970] 2 All ER 294 at 297, 298, [1970] AC 1004] at 1027 per Lord Reid). Examples of this are Hedley Byrne & Co Ltd v Heller & Partners Ltd [[1963] 2 All ER 575, [1964] AC 465] where the class of potential plaintiffs was reduced to those shown to have relied on the correctness of statements made, and Weller & Co v Foot and Mouth Disease Research Institute [[1965] 3 All ER 560, [1966] 1 QB 569] a (I cite these merely as illustrations, without discussion) case about 'economic loss' where, a duty having been held to exist, the nature of the recoverable damages was limited (see SCM (United Kingdom) Ltd v W J Whittall & Son Ltd [[1970] 3 All ER 245, [1971] 1 QB 337], Spartan Steel and Alloys Ltd v Martin & Co (Contractors) Ltd [[1972] 3 All ER 557, [1973] QB 27].)

… It must be in the reasonable contemplation not only of the builder but also of the local authority that failure to comply with the byelaws' requirement as to foundations may give rise to a hidden defect which in the future may cause damage to the building affecting the safety and health of owners and occupiers. And as the building is intended to last, the class of owners and occupiers likely to be affected cannot be limited to those who go in immediately after construction.

What then is the extent of the local authority's duty towards these persons? Although, as I have suggested, a situation of 'proximity' existed between the council and owners and occupiers of the houses, I do not think that a description of the council's duty can be based on the 'neighbourhood' principle alone or on merely any such factual relationship as 'control' as suggested by the Court of Appeal. So to base it would be to neglect an essential factor which is that the local authority is a public body, discharging functions under statute: its powers and duties are definable in terms of public not private law. The problem which this type of action creates, is to define the circumstances in which the law should impose, over and above, or perhaps alongside, these public law powers and duties, a duty in private law towards individuals such that they may sue for damages in a civil court. It is in this context that the distinction sought to be drawn between duties and mere powers has to be examined.

Most, indeed probably all, statutes relating to public authorities or public bodies, contain in them a large area of policy. The courts call this 'discretion', meaning that the decision is one for the authority or body to make, and not for the courts. … It is for the local authority, a public and elected body, to decide on the scale of resources which it can make available in order to carry out its functions … —how many inspectors, with what expert qualifications, it should recruit, how often inspections are to be made, what tests are to be carried out, must be for its decision. It is no accident that the Act is drafted in terms of functions and powers rather than in terms of positive duty. …

… to say that councils are under no duty to inspect, is not a sufficient statement of the position. They are under a duty to give proper consideration to the question whether they should inspect or not. Their immunity from attack, in the event of failure to inspect, in other words, though great is not absolute.

... Is there, then, authority against the existence of any such duty or any reason to restrict it? It is said that there is an absolute distinction in the law between statutory duty and statutory power—the former giving rise to possible liability, the latter not; or at least not doing so unless the exercise of the power involves some positive act creating some fresh or additional damage.

My Lords, I do not believe that any such absolute rule exists: or perhaps, more accurately, that such rules as exist in relation to powers and duties existing under particular statutes, provide sufficient definition of the rights of individuals affected by their exercise, or indeed their non-exercise, unless they take account of the possibility that, parallel with public law duties there may coexist those duties which persons, private or public, are under at common law to avoid causing damage to others in sufficient proximity to them.

To whom the duty is owed.
There is, in my opinion, no difficulty about this. A reasonable man in the position of the inspector must realise that if the foundations are covered in without adequate depth or strength as required by the byelaws, injury to safety or health may be suffered by owners or occupiers of the house. The duty is owed to them, not of course to a negligent building owner, the source of his own loss. I would leave open the case of users, who might themselves have a remedy against the occupier under the Occupiers Liability Act 1957. A right of action can only be conferred on an owner or occupier, who is such when the damage occurs (see below). This disposes of the possible objection that an endless, indeterminate class of potential plaintiffs may be called into existence."

Later decisions, including those of *Home Office v Dorset Yacht Club Co. Ltd.* [1970] 2 All E.R. 294 and *Caparo v Dickman* [1990] 2 A.C. 605, clearly rejected this dictum. These cases did two things. First, they placed emphasis on an additional criterion, namely, whether it was "just and reasonable" to impose a duty of care. Secondly, they rejected the development of a general principle which could automatically give rise to a duty of care. This they felt would be going too far and lead to an unfettered expansion of the law of negligence. Instead, proximity, foreseeability and the "just and reasonable" criteria would be necessary requirements for a duty to exist but would not be decisive. The courts would still make reference to established categories of claim in deciding whether a duty should apply.

Caparo Industries Plc v Dickman
House of Lords [1990] 2 A.C. 605, [1990] 1 All E.R. 568, [1990] 2 W.L.R. 358, [1990] B.C.L.C. 273

Facts: Caparo bought shares in a company called Fidelity Plc. They subsequently bought further shares on the basis of an auditor's report prepared by

Touche Ross, a firm of accountants, in the hope of launching a take-over bid for Fidelity Plc. The report prepared had shown that Fidelity Plc had made a profit when in fact it had made a substantial loss. Caparo sued the accountants for the loss suffered. On the trial of a preliminary issue of whether the auditors owed a duty of care to the respondents, the judge held that the auditors did not. The respondents appealed to the Court of Appeal, which allowed their appeal in part on the ground that the auditors owed the respondents a duty of care as shareholders but not as potential investors. The auditors appealed to the House of Lords and the respondents cross-appealed against the Court of Appeal's decision that they could not claim as potential investors.

Issues: The legal question to be decided was whether the accountants owed Caparo a duty of care, either in their capacity as shareholders or as potential investors.

The court (Bride, Roskill, Ackner, Oliver and Jauncey L.JJ.) held that no duty of care could be owed in this case. The Lords unanimously held that, in addition to the two-step Anns "test", a court would have to further consider whether it was "fair, just and reasonable to impose" a duty. However, the court rejected the view that these principles were the determining factor in establishing a duty of care. Instead the court stated that, while judges should be mindful of the general principles, they should only develop new categories of duty incrementally and by reference to established categories of claim.

Lord Bridge of Harwich (concurring judgments delivered by Lord Roskill, Lord Ackner, Lord Oliver of Aylmerton and Lord Jauncey of Tullichettle):

"The most comprehensive attempt to articulate a single general principle is reached in the well-known passage from the speech of Lord Wilberforce in Anns v Merton London Borough [1977] 2 All E.R. 492 at 498; [1978] A.C. 728 at 751–752: 'Through the trilogy of cases in this House, Donoghue v Stevenson [1932] AC 562, [1932] All ER Rep 1, Hedley Byrne & Co Ltd v Heller & Partners Ltd [1963] 2 All ER 575, [1964] AC 465, and Home Office v Dorset Yacht Co Ltd [1970] 2 All ER 294, [1970] AC 1004, the position has now been reached that in order to establish that a duty of care arises in a particular situation, it is not necessary to bring the facts of that situation within those of previous situations in which a duty of care has been held to exist. Rather the question has to be approached in two stages. First one has to ask whether, as between the alleged wrongdoer and the person who has suffered damage there is a sufficient relationship of proximity or neighbourhood such that, in the reasonable contemplation of the former, carelessness on his part may be likely to cause damage to the latter, in which case a prima facie duty of care arises. Secondly, if the first question is answered affirmatively, it is necessary to consider whether there are any considerations which ought to negative, or to reduce or limit the scope of the duty or the class of person to whom it is owed or the damages to which a breach of it may give rise (see the Dorset Yacht case [1970] 2 All ER 294 at 297–298, [1970] AC 1004 at 1027 per Lord Reid).'

But since Anns's case a series of decisions of the Privy Council and of your Lordships' House, notably in judgments and speeches delivered by Lord Keith, have emphasised the inability of any single general principle to provide a practical test which can be applied to every situation to determine whether a duty of care is owed and, if so, what is its scope: see Peabody Donation Fund v Sir Lindsay Parkinson & Co Ltd [1984] 3 All ER 529 at 533–534, [1985] AC 210 at 239–241, Yuen Kun-yeu v A-G of Hong Kong [1987] 2 All ER 705 at 709–712, [1988] AC 175 at 190–194, Rowling v Takaro Properties Ltd [1988] 1 All ER 163 at 172, [1988] AC 473 at 501 and Hill v Chief Constable of West Yorkshire [1988] 2 All ER 238 at 241, [1989] AC 53 at 60. What emerges is that, in addition to the foreseeability of damage, necessary ingredients in any situation giving rise to a duty of care are that there should exist between the party owing the duty and the party to whom it is owed a relationship characterised by the law as one of 'proximity' or 'neighbourhood' and that the situation should be one in which the court considers it fair, just and reasonable that the law should impose a duty of a given scope on the one party for the benefit of the other. But it is implicit in the passages referred to that the concepts of proximity and fairness embodied in these additional ingredients are not susceptible of any such precise definition as would be necessary to give them utility as practical tests, but amount in effect to little more than convenient labels to attach to the features of different specific situations which, on a detailed examination of all the circumstances, the law recognises pragmatically as giving rise to a duty of care of a given scope. Whilst recognising, of course, the importance of the underlying general principles common to the whole field of negligence, I think the law has now moved in the direction of attaching greater significance to the more traditional categorisation of distinct and recognisable situations as guides to the existence, the scope and the limits of the varied duties of care which the law imposes. We must now, I think, recognise the wisdom of the words of Brennan J in the High Court of Australia in Sutherland Shire Council v Heyman (1985) 60 ALR 1 at 43–44, where he said:

> 'It is preferable in my view, that the law should develop novel categories of negligence incrementally and by analogy with established categories, rather than by a massive extension of a prima facie duty of care restrained only by indefinable "considerations which ought to negative, or to reduce or limit the scope of the duty or the class of person to whom it is owed".'

One of the most important distinctions always to be observed lies in the law's essentially different approach to the different kinds of damage which one party may have suffered in consequence of the acts or omissions of another. It is one thing to owe a duty of care to avoid causing injury to the person or property of others. It is quite another to avoid causing others to suffer purely economic loss."

Comments and Questions:
1. Lord Bridge in his judgment introduced a new consideration to the "two-step" test outlined in *Anns* above, *i.e.* whether it was "fair, just and

reasonable" to impose a duty of care. Some commentators have argued that in effect this is no different to the policy considerations outlined by Lord Wilberforce in *Anns*. Would you agree? If not, how is it different?

Duty of care in Ireland

In Ireland the development occurred differently. The two-step test initiated in *Donoghue* and developed in *Anns* remained that accepted by our courts until the 2001 decision of *Glencar Exploration plc v Mayo County Council* [2002] 1 I.R. 84, [2002] 1 I.L.R.M. 481. This case heralded not so much a rejection by the Irish Supreme Court of the two-step test but more an adaptation of it in favour of the incrementalist approach currently applied in England. Prior to this decision the *Anns* test had been quoted with approval in a number of cases from *McNamara v ESB* [1975] I.R. 1 to *Ward v McMaster* [1988] I.R. 337.

Ward v McMaster, Louth County Council and Nicholas Hardy and Co. Limited
Supreme Court [1988] I.R. 337

Facts: The plaintiffs had purchased a house, built by the first defendant, with the aid of a local authority loan. In approving the loan, Louth County Council had had a valuation completed by the third defendant, an auctioneer, who had no building qualifications but nonetheless approved it as free from defects. The house subsequently developed significant structural defects which made it uninhabitable. The plaintiffs then sued the three defendants in negligence. The case was heard before Costello J., in the High Court, who found in favour of the plaintiffs against the first and second defendants but not the auctioneer. Louth County Council appealed the decision to the Supreme Court.

Issues: First, did Louth County Council owe the plaintiffs a duty of care and, if so, what was the correct test in determining whether a duty arose? Secondly, did the failure to carry out a structural survey constitute a policy decision which was not open to scrutiny by the courts?

The court held that a duty of care was owed to the Wards in light of the special relationship between them. McCarthy J. based his judgment on that of Lord Wilberforce in *Anns, i.e.* proximity, foreseeability and the absence of any policy considerations. He went on to note that any such considerations would have to be "compelling" in order to exclude liability.

Finlay C.J. and Griffin J. concurred with the judgments of Henchy and McCarthy JJ.; Walsh J. concurred with the decision of McCarthy J.

Henchy J.:

"... For my part I gratefully acknowledge the assistance given by counsel on both sides in presenting an extensive array of decided cases relevant to the liability of public authorities in circumstances similar to those in this case. I do not propose to analyse or assess the different and not always reconcilable approaches adopted in those cases, because I consider that the salient features of this case are sufficiently clear and distinctive to enable the point at issue to be decided on well-established principles.

The Council were plainly in breach of their public duty, imposed by the Regulations made under s.39 of the Act, to ensure by a proper valuation that the house was worth £24,000 and that it was a good security for a loan of £12,000 repayable over a period of 30 years. However, the breach of such a public duty would not in itself give a cause of action in negligence to the plaintiff: see *Siney v. Corporation of Dublin* [1980] IR 400. It is necessary for him to show that the relationship between him and the Council was one of proximity or neigh-bourhood which cast a duty on the Council to ensure that, regardless of anything left undone by the plaintiff, he would not end up as the mortgagor of a house which was not a good security for the amount of the loan. A paternalist or protective duty of that kind would not normally be imposed on a mortgagee in favour of a mortgagor, but the plaintiff was in a special position ..."

McCarthy J.:

The legal relationship
   "Costello J. held [1985] I.R. 29 at 52:

   'In the light of the facts to which I have referred it seems to me that there was a sufficient relationship of proximity or neighbourhood between the plaintiff and the Council such that in the reasonable contemplation of the Council carelessness on their part in the carrying out of the valuation of the bungalow the plaintiff was going to purchase might be likely to cause him damage. They should have been aware that it was unlikely that the plaintiff (in view of his knowledge that they were going to value the premises and his very limited means) would himself employ a professional person to examine it and so they should have known that if the valuation was carelessly done it might not disclose defects in the premises and as a result the plaintiff might suffer loss and damage. So it seems to me that a *prima facie* duty of care existed and there is nothing in the dealing between the parties which should restrict or limit that duty in any way. In particular no warning against reliance on the proposed valuation was given.'

Basing his view on s.39 of the Act of 1966, the learned trial judge held that there was a private law duty of care in favour of the first plaintiff, it being 'just and reasonable' that the court should so hold.

   Mr O'Flaherty S.C., on behalf of the second defendant, has rested his appeal upon three main propositions:—

(1) That since each party (the plaintiffs and the County Council) had to look to themselves to safeguard their situation, there was no duty of care cast upon the Council in respect of the first plaintiff. None such arose from their established proximity.

(2) Even if there was such a duty, that there was no risk of damage reasonably foreseeable to the County Council and, consequently, no breach of duty.

(3) That the omission held to be culpable arose from a decision of policy or discretion which was not open to question by the courts in an action such as this. It was, it is said, a policy decision within the discretion of the County Council not to have any inspection other than that which produced a valuer's certificate: to carry out such inspections in every instance through an engineer or like qualified person would greatly reduce the amount of money available in loans with consequent damage to the true purpose of the relevant part of the Housing Act.

It is convenient first to deal with the third proposition. The monetary argument does not bear critical examination. The County Council would not require to have an engineering inspection in any case in which the relevant house is newly built since procedures for grants involve inspections at the material times with regard to such things as foundations etc., whilst the house is being built. Likewise, houses of significant age would not require such inspections to deal with defects arising from subsidence; visual inspection by a relatively unqualified person would be quite adequate to disclose such defects. In any event, I see no bar to the County Council expressly excluding any representation to be inferred from the fact that it sanctions a particular loan.

Since preparing the draft of this judgment my attention has been drawn to the decision of the Court of Appeal in England in *Harris v. Wyre Forest D.C.* [1988] 1 All E.R. 691 where, in a somewhat analogous case, a local authority was relieved of liability in negligence because of such an exclusion clause.

Having regard to this conclusion, it is not necessary for me to express an opinion as to whether or not what so-called policy considerations are, in that context, free from review in the courts in an action of this kind. The argument traversed a wide field of authority all but four of which were cited to Costello J. *Curran v. Northern Ireland Co-Ownership Housing Association Ltd.* (1985) 8 N.I.L.R. Bulletin 22 was decided by Carswell J. in the Northern Ireland High Court after the High Court hearing in the instant appeal although before judgment was delivered. With the able assistance of counsel, we have travelled well charted legal seas seeking, for my part, to find a well marked haven, whether it be in Australia, Canada, Northern Ireland or England. Certainly, the judicial complements manning the several ports are not marked by unanimity. The Canadian Supreme Court divided three to two, the High Court of Australia similarly, and whilst the House of Lords in *Curran* [1987] A.C. 718 was unanimous it did not deal with a case like to the present one, the point in which it was dealt with in the Court of Appeal in Northern Ireland (1986) N.I.L.R.

Bulletin 1 was not the subject of an appeal itself. Much judicial eloquence and invention has been spent on examining and analysing the observations of Lord Atkin in *Donoghue v. Stevenson* [1932] A.C. 562. *Anns v. Merton London Borough* [1978] A.C. 728 was described by Lord Bridge in *Curran* as being the high-water mark of the application of *Donoghue* with particular reference to the words of Lord Wilberforce identifying two stages of establishing liability for breach of duty to take care. The elaborate analysis of Brennan J. in the High Court of Australia in *Sutherland Shire Council v. Heyman* (1985) 59 A.L.J.R. 564 led to the verbally attractive proposition of incremental growth in this branch of the law; such a proposition, however, suffers from a temporal defect—that rights should be determined by the accident of birth. Albeit that *Anns v. Merton London Borough* [1978] A.C. 728 is the high-water mark, I would not seek to dilute the words of Lord Wilberforce at pp. 751 and 752:

> '[T]he position has now been reached that in order to establish that a duty of care arises in a particular situation, it is not necessary to bring the facts of that situation within those of previous situations where a duty of care has been held to exist. Rather the question has to be approached in two stages. First one has to ask whether, as between the alleged wrongdoer and the person who has suffered damage there is a sufficient relationship of proximity or neighbourhood such that, in the reasonable contemplation of the former, carelessness on his part may be likely to cause damage to the latter—in which case a prima facie duty of care arises. Secondly, if the first question is answered affirmatively, it is necessary to consider whether there are any considerations which ought to negative, or to reduce or limit the scope of the duty or the class of person to whom it is owed or the damages to which a breach of it may give rise . . .'

... *Yuen Kun Yeu v. A.-G. of Hong Kong* [1987] 3 W.L.R. 776 was a decision of the Judicial Committee of the Privy Council in which the judgment of the Committee was delivered by Lord Keith of Kinkel. Having cited the familiar passage from Lord Wilberforce in *Anns* he pointed to the subsequent judicial resiling from the two-stage test in England and in Australia (by Brennan J. and Gibbs C.J. in *Sutherland*). Lord Keith disposed of the second stage of the *Anns* test, the public policy factor, by reference to *Rondel v. Worsley* [1969] 1 A.C. 191 dealing with the liability of a barrister for negligence in the conduct of proceedings in court, and *Hill v. Chief Constable of West Yorkshire* [1987] 2 W.L.R. 1126 the claim by the mother of the last victim of the 'Yorkshire Ripper' for damages on the grounds of the negligence of the police in failing to apprehend the murderer before the death of her daughter. Glidewell L.J. as an additional reason for dismissing the action at its preliminary stage, pointed to what might be termed the 'floodgates' or 'appalling vista' line of argument. Lord Wilberforce, in *McLoughlin v. O'Brian* [1983] 1 A.C. 410 had been unimpressed by the floodgates reasoning. Lord Keith concluded at p. 785 that:—

'In view of the direction in which the law has since been developing, their Lordships consider that for the future it should be recognised that the two-stage test in *Anns v. Merton London Borough Council* [1978] A.C. 728, 751–752, is not to be regarded as in all circumstances a suitable guide to the existence of a duty of care.'

Insofar as it is used to support the appellant's case, I find the reasoning lacking in force. Whilst Costello J. essentially rested his conclusion on the 'fair and reasonable' test, I prefer to express the duty as arising from the proximity of the parties, the foreseeability of the damage, and the absence of any compelling exemption based upon public policy. I do not, in any fashion, seek to exclude the latter consideration, although I confess that such a consideration must be a very powerful one if it is to be used to deny an injured party his right to redress at the expense of the person or body that injured him.

... I turn then to the two main propositions advanced in support of the appeal:—

1. The duty of care,
2. Reasonable foreseeability

1. *The duty of care*

The proximity of the parties is clear: they were intended mortgagors and mortgagee. This proximity had its origin in the Housing Act, 1966, and the consequent loan scheme. This Act imposed a statutory duty upon the County Council and it was in the carrying out of that statutory duty that the alleged negligence took place. It is a simple application of the principle in *Donoghue v. Stevenson* [1932] A.C. 562 confirmed in *Anns v. Merton London Borough* [1978] A.C. 728 and implicit in *Siney v. Corporation of Dublin* [1980] IR 400 that the relationship between the first plaintiff and the County Council created a duty to take reasonable care arising from the public duty of the County Council under the statute. The statute did not create a private duty but such arose from the relationship between the parties.

2. *Reasonable foreseeability*

In my view, it does not require much imagination for the officers of the Housing Authority to contemplate that a purchaser under the scheme will both lack the personal means of having an expert examination and may well think, as the first plaintiff thought, that the very circumstances of the housing authority investing its money in the house was a badge of quality.

These two considerations are both involved in the first leg of the *Anns* principle. I do not understand it to be argued that there are considerations which ought to negative or to reduce or limit the scope of duty or the class of person to whom it is owed or the damages to which a breach of it may give rise, within the second leg of the observations of Lord Wilberforce. It follows, in my view, without entering into the question of whether or not it is 'just and reasonable' to impose the duty, that the duty arose from the proximity of the parties, the injury caused was reasonably foreseeable, the breach was established, and the first plaintiff was entitled to succeed."

The decisions in *Glencar* and in *Fletcher v Commissioners of Public Works in Ireland* Supreme Court, unreported, February 21, 2003 (see Chapter 6) have demonstrated a retreat from the earlier position in Irish law as described above. In particular in the case of *Glencar* the Supreme Court considered that Irish courts ought also to consider, in addition to the considerations of proximity, foreseeability and policy, whether it was "just and reasonable" in the circumstances, to impose a duty of care.

Glencar Explorations Plc and Andaman Resources Plc v The County Council of Mayo
Supreme Court [2002] 1 I.R. 84, [2002] 1 I.L.R.M. 481

Facts: The two applicants in the case were two companies who in 1986 had been granted mining licences to carry out mining and prospecting in Mayo by the Minister for Natural Resources. In 1992 Mayo County Council included a ban on mining in its development plan, leading to a loss to the applicants of investments up to and following the ban. They took judicial review proceedings in the High Court, arguing that the decision of the Council in instituting a ban was *ultra vires* its power and also arguing for damages for negligence and breach of statutory duty. (In a later hearing they also added a number of other grounds.) Kelly J. in the High Court found that the actions of the Council were *ultra vires* its powers, and that it had acted negligently. He did not, however, accept that the Council owed the applicants a duty of care and therefore dismissed their action in negligence. The applicants appealed this decision to the Supreme Court.

Issues: On the issue of negligence the Supreme Court had to decide whether a duty of care was owed to the applicants and, if so, on what basis.

The Supreme Court (Keane C.J., Denham, Murray, McGuinness and Fennelly JJ.) held that Mayo County Council did not owe a duty of care to the applicants. While it was foreseeable that the applicants could suffer a loss from the Council's negligent act, no relationship of proximity existed such that it would be just and reasonable to impose a duty of care. Keane C.J. questioned whether the apparent adoption of the two-step test by McCarthy J. formed part of the *ratio* of that judgment. He felt that no injustice would be done if, in addition to the two-step test, the further consideration of whether it was just and reasonable to impose a duty of care was made.

Keane C.J.:

"… As to the finding of the High Court that the claim for damages for negligence was not maintainable because of the absence of any duty of care, they submitted that the existence of a duty of care had not been traversed in the points of defence furnished by the respondent. On the assumption that the respondent was entitled to argue that no duty of care existed, they submitted that this was not the law, having regard to the decision of the High Court and the Supreme Court in Ward v McMaster [1985] IR 29; [1988] IR 337. The duty of care arose by virtue of:—

(a) the foreseeability of damage to the applicants as a consequence of the respondent's action;
(b) the statutory framework under which the relationship between the parties existed;
(c) the relationship of proximity between the parties, there being no factors in the relationship between the parties that would negative a duty of care;
(d) the absence of any factors that would make it 'fair and reasonable' to relieve the respondent from any duty of care, applying the formulation adopted by Costello J at first instance in Ward v McMaster [1985] IR 29.

They further submitted that, if the criteria laid down by McCarthy J in Ward v McMaster [1988] IR 337 for determining whether a duty of care existed were to be adopted, the argument for holding that the respondent was under a duty of care was even more compelling.

[After dispensing with the issues of breach of statutory duty, legitimate expectation and breach of constitutional rights Keane C.J. then went on to consider the question of whether the Council was negligent.]

3) Negligence
… Although the trial judge found that the respondent had acted negligently in adopting the mining ban, I think that it is clear that, in so finding, he was not holding that they had been in breach of any duty of care they owed the applicants: a finding to that effect would have been inconsistent with the conclusions he later reached, after a consideration of the authorities, that the respondent had not been in breach of any duty of care it owed the applicants. He did, however, conclude that, in adopting the mining ban, it had done something which no reasonable local authority would have done.

[Keane C.J. then went on to give an analysis of the law on the development of a duty of care as it stood at that date from the starting point of *Donoghue v Stevenson* to the decision in *Caparo plc. v Dickman* before describing what he considered to be the position in Ireland.]

The law in Ireland must now be considered. The decisions in both Donoghue v Stevenson [1932] AC 562 and Hedley Byrne & Co Ltd. v Heller and Partners Ltd. [1964] AC 465 have been considered and adopted by our courts in a number of cases and unquestionably represent the law in this jurisdiction. It has also been said—see, for example, McMahon and Binchy on the Law of Torts (3rd ed.) chapter 6—that the two stage test adopted by Lord Wilberforce in Anns v Merton London Borough [1978] AC 728 is also the test which must be adopted in this jurisdiction, having regard to the decision of this court in Ward v McMaster [1988] IR 337.

The plaintiffs in that case, a married couple, had purchased a house from a builder. Shortly afterwards, they discovered that it contained serious structural defects which, if not repaired, would render it dangerous and a risk to health. The plaintiffs had bought the house with the assistance of a loan from the local authority under the relevant housing legislation. They had not had any independent examination of the house carried out by a surveyor before they bought it, but it had been examined on behalf of the local authority by an auctioneer. The plaintiffs sued both the builders/vendor and the local authority. Their claim against the latter was based on the contention that the local authority should have known that the plaintiffs, not being persons of means, would be unlikely to retain their own independent surveyor and would have relied on an appropriate inspection having been carried out on behalf of the authority. In fact, as already noted, the examination was carried out by an auctioneer who was not a qualified surveyor and whose report did not reveal the defects in the house.

In the High Court ([1985] IR 29), the plaintiffs' claim against both the builder and the local authority succeeded. Although the damage which resulted was, on one view, purely economic loss, Costello J in the High Court was satisfied that it was recoverable in the light of the decision in Junior Books Ltd. v Veitchi Co Ltd. [1983] 1 AC 520. Having considered the authorities in England, he stated at p. 49 the legal principles which were applicable in determining whether a duty of care arose in the circumstances of that case to be as follows:—

'(a) When deciding whether a local authority exercising statutory functions is under a common law duty of care the court must firstly ascertain whether a relationship of proximity existed between the parties such that in the reasonable contemplation of the authority carelessness on their part might cause loss. But all the circumstances of the case must in addition be considered, including the statutory provisions under which the authority is acting. Of particular significance in this connection is the purpose for which the statutory powers were conferred and whether or not the plaintiff is in the class of persons which the statute was designed to assist.

(b) It is material in all cases for the court in reaching its decision on the existence and scope of the alleged duty to consider whether it is just and reasonable that a common law duty of care as alleged should in all the circumstances exist.'

In the case of the local authority, he held that it was within the reasonable contemplation of the second defendant that carelessness on its part in carrying out the valuation of the house might be likely to cause damage to the purchaser. It was consistent with the local authority's public law powers that they should be accompanied by a common law duty of care in favour of the plaintiffs and he further held that, for similar reasons, it was 'just and reasonable' that the court should hold that a duty of care arose in that case.

The local authority appealed to this court which unanimously upheld the judgment of Costello J. However, although there was, as in this case, an extensive debate as to the nature and scope of the duty of care, Henchy J was satisfied that the facts of the case were such that it could be decided in accordance with what he described as 'well established principles'. In his view, the relationship between the first plaintiff and the local authority was such that the latter owed a duty to him to take due care in the valuation of the house since they should have known that, in the light of his lack of means, he would rely on their having carried out an appropriate valuation. There is, accordingly, nothing in his judgment to indicate that he was adopting the more expansive view of the extent of the duty of care, rightly or wrongly attributed to Lord Wilberforce in Anns v Merton London Borough [1978] AC 728, rather than the more restrictive approach subsequently adopted in the English authorities.

By contrast, in the only other judgment delivered in this court reported at [1988] IR 337, McCarthy J expressly endorsed the two stage test adopted by Lord Wilberforce and added at p. 349:—

> 'Whilst Costello J essentially rested his conclusion on the "fair and reasonable" test, I prefer to express the duty as arising from the proximity of the parties, the foreseeability of the damage, and the absence of any compelling exemption based upon public policy. I do not, in any fashion, seek to exclude the latter consideration, although I confess that such a consideration must be a very powerful one if it is to be used to deny an injured party his right to redress at the expense of the person or body that injured him.'

As to the passage already cited from the judgment of Brennan J in Sutherland Shire Council v Heyman (1985) 157 CLR. 424, the judge commented that:—

> 'This verbally attractive proposition of incremental growth suffers from a temporal defect—that rights should be determined by the accident of birth.'

Finlay CJ and Griffin J said that they were in agreement with the judgments of both Henchy J and McCarthy J. Walsh J confined his concurrence to the judgment of McCarthy J.

While the decision in Ward v McMaster [1988] IR 337 has been treated by some as an unqualified endorsement by this court of the two stage test adopted by Lord Wilberforce in Anns v Merton London Borough [1978] AC 728, it is by no means clear that this is so. As already noted, Henchy J was satisfied that the case could be decided by reference to 'well established principles' and made no reference in his judgment to the two stage test in Anns v Merton London Borough. Since Finlay CJ and Griffin J expressed their agreement with both the judgments of Henchy J and McCarthy J, it is not clear that the observations of the latter in relation to the two stage test in Anns necessarily formed part of the ratio of the decision. Given the far reaching implications of adopting in this jurisdiction a principle of liability in negligence from which there has been such powerful dissent in other common law jurisdictions, I would not be prepared to hold that further consideration of the underlying principles is foreclosed by the dicta of McCarthy J in Ward v McMaster.

In considering whether that approach, or the more cautious approach favoured in Caparo plc. v Dickman [1990] 2 AC 605 and Sutherland Shire Council v Heyman (1985) 157 CLR. 424 should be adopted, I think it is helpful to refer again to the philosophy reflected in Lord Atkin's approach in Donoghue v Stevenson [1932] AC 562. The bystander who sees a building on fire and knows that there are people inside no doubt foresees that if he waits for the fire brigade to arrive rather than attempting to rescue them himself they may die. But the law has never imposed liability in negligence on a person who fails to act as a more courageous citizen might in such circumstances. A strict moral code might censure his timidity: the law of negligence does not. It is precisely that distinction drawn by Lord Atkin between the requirements of morality and altruism on the one hand and the law of negligence on the other hand which is in grave danger of being eroded by the approach adopted in Anns v Merton London Borough [1978] AC 728, as it has subsequently been interpreted by some. There is, in my view, no reason why courts determining whether a duty of care arises should consider themselves obliged to hold that it does in every case where injury or damage to property was reasonably foreseeable and the notoriously difficult and elusive test of 'proximity' or 'neighbourhood' can be said to have been met, unless very powerful public policy considerations dictate otherwise. It seems to me that no injustice will be done if they are required to take the further step of considering whether, in all the circumstances, it is just and reasonable that the law should impose a duty of a given scope on the defendant for the benefit of the plaintiff, as held by Costello J at first instance in Ward v McMaster [1985] IR 29, by Brennan J in Sutherland Shire Council v Heyman (1985) 157 CLR. 424 and by the House of Lords in Caparo plc. v Dickman [1990] 2 AC 605. As Brennan J pointed out, there is a significant risk that any other approach will result in what he called a 'massive extension of a prima facie duty of care restrained only by undefinable considerations'.

I observe, in this context, that it has been suggested in England that the difference in approach between Anns v Merton London Borough [1978] AC 728 and Caparo plc. v Dickman [1990] 2 AC 605 may ultimately be of no great significance, since the considerations which, in a particular case, may negative the existence of a duty of care under the Anns formulation are consistent with an assessment as to whether it is just, fair and reasonable to impose such a duty in the particular circumstances: (see the comments of Lord Hoffman in Stovin v Wise [1996] AC 923 at p. 949).

In the present case, we are concerned with negligence alleged against a public authority in the performance of a statutory function. The circumstances in which a duty of care can be said to arise in the case of such authorities when exercising statutory functions has also given rise to an enormous volume of decided cases in the common law world, to many of which we were referred. There are, of course, many instances in which a public authority will be liable in negligence because the duty of care imposed by the law on them is no different from that arising in private law generally. Obvious examples are the duties owed by local and other public authorities arising out of their occupation of premises or their role as employers. In such cases, the plaintiff does not have to call in aid the fact that the defendants may have been exercising a statutory function: their duty of care as occupiers, employers, etc., is no greater, but also no less, than that of their counterparts in the private sector.

Difficulties have arisen, however, in determining whether, and to what extent, a statutory authority can be made amenable in damages for the negligent exercise of a power which they were entitled, but not obliged, to invoke. In Anns v Merton London Borough [1978] AC 728, it had been held that, although a local authority was not under a duty to inspect the foundations of buildings, it could be made liable where proper consideration had not been given to the question as to whether they should inspect or not. In Siney v Corporation of Dublin [1980] IR 400, this court held that, where a flat had been provided by a local authority pursuant to their duties under the relevant housing legislation, they were obliged to take reasonable care to ensure that it was fit for human habitation and that, accordingly, they were liable in damages because appropriate humidity tests had not been carried out in order to determine whether the flat would be sufficiently ventilated. In Ward v McMaster [1988] IR 337, as we have seen, the local authority were found liable in damages for having failed to carry out a valuation by a qualified surveyor in circumstances where it could not be suggested that they were under a statutory duty to provide themselves or anyone else with such a valuation, although they were undoubtedly authorised so to do. Again, in the judgments of Costello J at first instance ([1985] IR 29) and McCarthy J in this court [1988] IR 337, Anns v Merton London Borough [1978] AC 728 is cited with approval as authority for the proposition that a duty of care arises in such circumstances.

In Anns v Merton London Borough [1978] AC 728, it was suggested that the imposition of a duty of care in cases of this nature was justified where the nature of the statutory power was such that it was obviously the intention of the legislature that it would be exercised and that, accordingly, a negligent failure to exercise what were described as 'operational' powers or duties could give rise to liability. In subsequent cases in England, however, it has been said that the distinction between policy and operations may not be a particularly useful guide in determining whether a duty of care should be found to exist in any particular case. Similar considerations apply to the distinctions drawn in some of the authorities between discretionary and non-discretionary decisions.

For the purposes of this case, it is sufficient to say that the mere fact that the exercise of a power by a public authority may confer a benefit on a person of which he would otherwise be deprived does not of itself give rise to a duty of care at common law. The facts of a particular case, however, when analysed, may point to the reasonable foreseeability of damage arising from the non-exercise of the power and a degree of proximity between the plaintiff and the defendant which would render it just and reasonable to postulate the existence of a duty of care. That approach is consistent with the reluctance of the law to impose liability for negligence arising out of an omission to act rather than out of the commission of positive acts which may injure persons or damage property. In the present case, the decision by the respondent that it would not grant planning permission for any mining development within the area covered by the ban was, on the assumption that it was intra vires, the exercise by it of a statutory power which would result in the withholding of a benefit from the applicants which would foreseeably result in their suffering financial loss. But, although such a loss was undoubtedly reasonably foreseeable, when one bears in mind that the powers in question were exercisable by the respondent for the benefit of the community as a whole and not for the benefit of a defined category of persons to which the applicant belonged (as in Siney v Corporation of Dublin [1980] IR 400 and Ward v McMaster [1985] IR 29; [1988] IR 337), I am satisfied that there was no relationship of 'proximity' between the applicants and the respondent which would render it just and reasonable to impose liability on the respondent.

In considering whether such a relationship of 'proximity' existed and whether it would be just and reasonable to impose a duty of care on the respondent, I think one also has to bear in mind that this was not a case in which it could reasonably be said that the applicants, in incurring the expense of their prospecting activities, could be said to have been relying on the non-negligent exercise by the respondent of its statutory powers. Their position is in contrast to that of the plaintiffs in both Siney v Corporation of Dublin [1980] IR 400 and Ward v McMaster [1985] IR 29; [1988] IR 337 where, in each case, they belonged to a category of persons for whose benefit a particular statutory framework had been created and who might reasonably be said to have relied on the local authority in each case taking reasonable care in the exercise of the statutory powers vested in them. The applicants in the present case could rely on no more than a general expectation that the respondent would act in accordance with the law which is not, in my view, sufficient to give rise to the existence of a duty of care."

Comments and Questions:
1.   Keane C.J. clearly questioned whether the decision of McCarthy J. formed part of the *ratio* in the Ward case. Was he correct in your view?

2. Will the consideration of whether it is "just and reasonable" to impose a duty lead to a more restrictive approach by the courts to the duty of care question?

STANDARD OF CARE

An action in negligence requires not only that the plaintiff owes the defendant a duty of care but also that the defendant falls below the standard of the "reasonably careful man". It requires the court to take into account not only the nature and capacity of the litigants in question, but also the circumstances of the case itself.

The reasonable man has at times been referred to as the man of ordinary prudence, the man on the Clapham omnibus, or the man on the Bondi tram. Every person is expected to possess the knowledge of the reasonable person, but the law also recognises that differences in mental and physical capacity will affect the standard of care not only expected but owed.

The standard was outlined in the case of *Kirby v Burke* [1944] I.R. 207 (see Chapter 5) and in the case of *McComiskey v McDermott* [1974] I.R. 75 below (also discussed in Chapter 14).

McComiskey v McDermott
Supreme Court [1974] I.R. 75

Facts: The plaintiff and the defendant were travelling at night in the defendant's motor car. They were taking part as a team in a motor rally. The defendant was the driver and the plaintiff the navigator when, having driven around a corner on a muddy laneway, the defendant was faced with an obstruction. Believing he could not stop before reaching the obstruction, he drove his car into a ditch where it overturned and the plaintiff was injured. The plaintiff unsuccessfully claimed damages in the High Court for the negligence of the defendant.

Issues: On appeal to the Supreme Court it fell to be considered, *inter alia*, whether the jury in the High Court was correct to find that the defendant was not negligent. The court (Griffin and Henchy JJ., Walsh J. dissenting) held that the standard of care required was one of "reasonable care" and they saw no reason to disturb the jury's finding that the defendant had driven as a reasonable rally driver would. Walsh J., dissenting, held that the standard was that of the reasonable driver and not the reasonable rally driver and that this issue should be retried.

Walsh J. (dissenting):

"In the main, the submissions made on behalf of the defendant in the course of this appeal were to the effect that since a negligence action is an action for breach of duty, the duty is to be measured in the light of the circumstances governing the situation in which the act complained of happened. Reduced to simpler terms, the defendant has submitted that the only duty the defendant owed to the plaintiff was to act in accordance with the standards of the ordinary, reasonable and prudent rally driver. In my view this submission is an over-simplification. The most important and the governing circumstance of this episode was that it occurred on the public highway at a time when the highway was open to use and was being used by other members of the public. If this particular competition had taken place in a private place or on the highway at a time when it was closed to ordinary use by members of the public, the circumstances would be different even for such members of the public as attended as spectators. There have been a number of cases dealing with episodes leading to injury to either participants or spectators at horse shows, motor races, motor-cycle races or competitions held in places which were not open to ordinary public traffic. One of these cases (Wilks v Cheltenham Cycle Club ((1971) 1 WLR 668)) was cited and relied upon in the present case. In my view, there is no parallel between the circumstances of that case and the present one. Nettleship v Weston ((1971) 2 QB 691) is closer to the present case; in that case the act of a learner driver caused injury to a passenger instructor, who was seated beside the learner, while the car was being driven on the public highway and it was held by the English Court of Appeal that the duty owed by the learner driver to the passenger instructor was the same objective standard as was owed by every driver on the public highway to other persons using the highway. The fact that the driver in question was so inexperienced or so unskilled as not to have the ability or skill of the ordinary reasonable and prudent driver was irrelevant.

In my view, in the present case the governing circumstance is that the motor car was being driven on the public highway at a time when the highway was being used as such. The duty which the defendant owed to all persons using that highway, including the passenger in his own car, was the same. To hold otherwise would lead to rather absurd results. For example, if during the course of the rally the defendant had picked up a passenger who knew that he was in a participating motor car (but who was not himself in any sense a participant) and if the car had been involved in an accident, due to the negligent driving of the defendant, which injured not merely the navigator but also the casual passenger and a pedestrian who happened to be walking along the road at the same time, it could not be seriously contemplated that the liability of the driver of the motor car to each of the injured parties would be governed by different standards of duty. Apart from facts which would warrant the application of the statutory defence given by s34, subs1, of the Act of 1961, the conduct of the plaintiff during the course of the exercise or the fact that he participated in this competitive venture with the driver may be relevant in terms of contributory negligence but they are not relevant in determining the standard of care which is to be observed by the defendant. It was the duty of the defendant to use proper care not to cause injury to persons using the highway, including his own passengers, and that involved not merely avoiding excessive speed but also keeping a proper look out. This duty was owed to the plaintiff as he was a person who might reasonably expect to be injured by the omission to take such care. If a pedestrian had been hit by the defendant's motor car and the facts of the case warranted a finding of negligence against the defendant, then the plaintiff would have been equally entitled to a verdict on this issue against the defendant."

Henchy J.:

"... The law of negligence lays down that the standard of care is that which is to be expected from a reasonably careful man in the circumstances. Because the particular circumstances dictate the degree of care required, decisions in other cases are frequently of little guidance. In the present case we have been referred to cases such as Insurance Commissioner v Joyce ((1948) 77 CLR 39) and Nettleship v Weston ((1971) 2 QB 691) which raise the vexed question as to the standard or degree of care required to be shown by a driver towards a passenger who knows that the driver lacks the capacity to drive with reasonable care. In my view, such cases are not to the point in the present case where the passenger, far from committing himself to the care of a driver whom he knew to be incompetent, allied himself to the driver as navigator in the hope that by the assiduous application of their respective skills they would win a prize in the competition.

I consider that the duty of care owed by the defendant to the plaintiff was to drive as carefully as a reasonably careful, competitive rally-driver would be expected to drive in the prevailing circumstances. The jury were fully and carefully instructed by the trial judge to apply that standard to the facts as they found them. The jury were entitled to find that the accident happened because on a wet, dark night on a muddy, narrow road in the Wicklow hills, in the course of a motor rally, the defendant drove around a bend in the road only to find an unexpected motor car 45 yards ahead on a pronounced downhill slope, blocking the road and that, not being able to brake effectively because of the muddy downhill surface, he had to drive his car against a bank at the side of the road thus causing it to overturn.

The question whether the defendant was negligent on that version of the circumstances of the accident was pre-eminently one for the jury, and their answer in the negative cannot be disturbed unless it could be said to be unreasonable. I am unable to say that is was. For those reasons, I would uphold the jury's verdict of no negligence and dismiss this appeal."

Griffin J.:

"... The duty of care owed by the defendant to the plaintiff was a duty, having regard to all the circumstances, to take the care reasonably to be expected from a prudent and careful rally driver. The circumstances in this case included the fact that the plaintiff and the defendant were members of a team competing for prizes in a rally, that an average speed of 35 mph over difficult terrain and rough muddy roads had to be maintained and that, although the actual driving was being done by the defendant, the navigator's duty included directions to the driver to drive faster or slower as the case may be. In addition, it appears from the evidence that a speed test would have taken place on the next section. If, for example, the accident had occurred in the course of the speed test, when presumably the defendant and the plaintiff would be going all out to win, it appears to me that the plaintiff would be in no better position than an injured spectator in such cases as Wilks v Cheltenham Cycle Club ((1971) 1 WLR 668).

In my opinion, the trial judge correctly directed the jury on the matters to be considered by them in considering the question of the defendant's negligence at pp 84–87 of the transcript of evidence; no objection was taken to the judge's direction on this issue. The jury is the appropriate tribunal to consider the facts and, as they have found that the defendant was not negligent in all the circumstances of this particular case, in my opinion their verdict should not be disturbed."

Comments and Questions:
1. While the duty is one of reasonable care, the dissenting judgment of Walsh J. above highlights the difficulty of this concept. Should the standard required of McComiskey above have been that of the reasonable driver, or the reasonable rally driver as contended by the majority?

"In the circumstances"

In considering the circumstances that must be taken into account in determining whether the defendant behaved reasonably, the courts have focused on the following elements:

1) probability of the accident;
2) gravity of the threatened injury;
3) cost of eliminating the risk;
4) social utility of the defendant's conduct.

None of these considerations is definitive in itself but is balanced against the others in the determination of negligent behaviour.

In the case of *Whooley v Dublin Corporation* [1961] I.R. 60 below, the court considered the importance of the purpose served by a fire hydrant in determining whether in the circumstances a standard of reasonable care had been breached.

Whooley v Dublin Corporation
High Court [1961] I.R. 60

Facts: The plaintiff, walking along a footpath at night, fell when her foot lodged in an uncovered box containing a fire hydrant. The lid of the box had been removed by a "mischievous person". She sued the defendants, who were responsible for the maintenance of the fire hydrant box. The Circuit Court (Conroy J.) held for the plaintiff on the basis of the dangerous nature of the fire hydrant box. The defendants appealed to the High Court.

Issues: It fell to be determined by the court (McLoughlin J.) whether the defendants had fallen below the standard of reasonable care in the circumstances. In particular, taken into account was the high social utility of having an accessible fire hydrant and the difficulty of installing a fire hydrant that would be safe from interference while still serving its function.

McLoughlin J.:

"... It is not contended that the Corporation are not under a duty to maintain these hydrants on the footway and that they must be readily accessible for use by the Corporation fire brigade in case of fire, but reliance is placed by the plaintiff on the evidence of an engineer called on her behalf who stated that the type of hydrant and box in this case was thirty to forty years old, that the lid could be removed by a child inserting a stick or some instrument into a slot provided along one side of the lid for that purpose, and that a more modern type has a heavier, though smaller, lid without a slot but with a hole in the centre for the insertion of a simple type of key. He did not, however, suggest that this more modern type of lid was designed to make, or would make, interference by mischievous persons more difficult.

There was evidence also by a lady that some days previous to the accident water was spurting from a hydrant without a lid in Oxford Road which, I am inclined to believe, was this same hydrant.

For the defendant Corporation there was evidence that for paving purposes the hydrants in Oxford Road, including this particular one, were in use during that period, 21st October to 4th November, after which they were inspected and were left in proper and safe condition. There was also evidence of a turncock who was notified of the accident on the same night, shortly after its happening, and inspected this hydrant box and found nothing wrong with it. How the lid came to be replaced is not known.

Having carefully considered all the circumstances and the authorities quoted to me by counsel I cannot find that the Corporation through its officials maintained this hydrant box in a negligent way so as to cause the plaintiff's injuries. There is, in my view, no reason for holding that this type of hydrant box is of the kind that is likely to be interfered with by young irresponsible children to the knowledge of the Corporation's officials or that any such knowledge should be imputed to them. It is my opinion that this hydrant was interfered with by some mischievous person and that no other type of hydrant which could be devised, consistent with its necessary purpose, would be safe from such malicious interference.

Accordingly, this action must be dismissed and the order of the Circuit Judge reversed."

The effect of capacity and foreknowledge of incapacity on the standard of care expected was examined in the case of *O'Brien v Parker* [1997] 2 I.L.R.M. 170.

O'Brien v Parker
High Court [1997] 2 I.L.R.M. 170

Facts: The plaintiff was injured when the defendant's car collided with his car. The defendant, who had not suffered from epilepsy in the past, had had an epileptic fit. He gave evidence that moments before the crash he became aware of a strange smell and of lights becoming more vivid but had otherwise no foreknowledge that anything was wrong. In the Circuit Court the case against him was dismissed. The plaintiff appealed to the High Court.

Issues: The court (Lavan J.) had to consider whether the defendant had behaved reasonably in the circumstances. Critical to the decision was the degree to which the defendant had foreknowledge that he might be unwell. On the basis of the facts Lavan J. held that he had not behaved as a reasonable person would, as he had ignored the warning signals.

Lavan J.:

"The Defendant in his evidence said he had certain experiences at home. He said that he was able to get into his car and drove in the direction of where the accident occurred. He had some sense of smell and felt unwell as he approached the junction opposite Crumlin Children's Hospital and as he turned down the road passing Rafters Road, Crumlin. He says that he has no further recollection of the hundred or so yards he would have travelled until the collision took place. The next memory he says he has is of getting out of his car and being surrounded by people, an ambulance and the Gardaí. On cross-examination he stated that his vision had been affected and that he felt it was more like a dream. He said that he was conscious of the presence of other cars on the roadway.

Doctor Murphy, in concluding his evidence and commenting on the history as given, regarded the Plaintiff as suffering from a complex partial seizure. This would allow for some consciousness on an objective basis. This would allow a person suffering from this condition to make a decision. There was a degree of awareness and there was a major attack on his accepting the Defendant's case history. Finally, I heard from Garda Thomas Burke who investigated the accident and gave evidence as to the Plaintiff's condition following the collision and confirmed that the Defendant was unable to recollect questions that had been put to him moments before and did not seem to understand what was going on and was unaware of his surroundings. This witness accepted that the Defendant was unable to understand what was going on.

… In the case of Roberts v Ramsbottom Neill J stated (at p 832):—

> 'I am satisfied that in a civil action a similar approach should be adopted. The driver will be able to escape liability if his actions at the relevant time were wholly beyond his control. The most obvious case is sudden unconsciousness. But if he retained some control, albeit imperfect control, and his driving, judged objectively, was below the required standard, he remains liable. His position is the same as a driver who is old or infirm.'

Mr Mark de Blacam for the Plaintiff contends that even were I to conclude that at the actual time of the accident the Defendant was an automaton, there was negligence on his part because the evidence disclosed that he was, at various times, conscious and thus recollects symptoms which, had he exercised reasonable care, would have led him to stop driving. These symptoms included a ringing in his ears, an awareness of a pungent smell, an awareness of intense light and an alteration in his consciousness which he described in evidence as a 'difficulty in focusing'. Mr de Blacam further submits that the Defendant was conscious when he experienced these symptoms otherwise he would not be able to recollect them and that in these circumstances a driver who continues to drive having experienced this combination of unusual symptoms is guilty of negligence. He also relies on Roberts v Ramsbottom (Supra).

He went on to distinguish the case of Waugh v James K Allan Limited, (1964) 2 Lloyds Rep 1. There the defendant suffered from a coronary thrombosis while driving a lorry and died immediately after the accident. The evidence disclosed that he had been prone to gastric attacks and that 15 minutes before the accident he was taken ill while loading the lorry. However, it was also established that he had sufficiently recovered from this attack so as to have no ground for doubting that he was fit to drive.

In this case there is no evidence of such a recovery on the part of the Defendant. This situation in the Waugh case was described by Lord Reid in the following terms:—

> 'We get little help from the evidence on the question whether it is safe for a man to drive soon after a gastric attack of sickness and nausea. It does not appear that an early recurrence of these symptoms is likely. Nor does it appear that such an attack generally leaves any substantial disability after the sickness has passed off. Fitness to drive involves not merely ability to control the vehicle in ordinary traffic but also ability to react quickly in an emergency. I could well understand that if such an attack is followed by severe headache or mental lassitude, the man ought not to drive until this, too, has passed off.

But there is nothing to suggest that Gemmel (the lorry driver) was suffering or was likely to have been suffering from any such disability when he drove (before the accident).'

Finally, Mr de Blacam submitted that the crux of the matter is that the test in negligence is an objective one. The Court is not required to consider whether the Defendant did all he could in the circumstances nor, of course, is perfection required of him. The Defendant must however meet the standard of a reasonably careful driver. It is not sufficient for a person to do his best if his best is not up to the standard of the reasonable person. Conversely, the standard of perfection is not required, since even 'the most excessively careful man will sometimes have an accident'. The question is a normative one: the Judge should ask, not in a question 'how would you have acted?' or 'how would the average man have acted?' but rather 'how ought the Defendant, as a reasonable person have acted?'

As to the fact that the defence is more usually associated with the criminal law, I see no reason why it should not be a defence in the civil law.

Viewing the English case law, there would appear to be a consistent pattern of maintaining strict limits to the defence in the criminal law. For instance, in Bratty v Attorney General for Northern Ireland (1963) AC 386, at page 409, Lord Denning confined the defence to acts done while unconscious and to spasms, reflex actions and convulsions. In Broome v Perkins (1987) Crim LR at 271, the defendant was found guilty despite suffering from hypoglycaemia as it was found that he exercised control from time to time and only a total destruction of voluntary control is consistent with automatism. I also note that in Hill v Baxter (Supra), Lord Goddard CJ in the context of a driving offence essentially said the defence could arise in circumstances where the Accused 'could not really be said to be driving at all' such as a stroke or an epileptic fit. Pearson J also following this approach concludes that in order to get as far as he did the Defendant must have been exercising some skill and this implies some element of control thus inconsistent with the defence of automatism. From an assessment of the various authorities opened to this Court it seems clear that strict limits are emphasised before the defence can succeed. I am satisfied that the test to be applied is that the defence of automatism requires that there must be a total destruction of voluntary control on the Defendant's part. Impaired, reduced or partial control is not sufficient to maintain the defence.

Applying this test to the evidence some of which I have heard and some of which was presented on an agreed basis, I am satisfied that the Defendant has not established this defence on the balance of probabilities. Notwithstanding experiencing some difficulties at home he was able to make a decision to drive. He drove some distance. He was conscious of experiencing some symptoms as he passed the hospital and as he drove down the Old Crumlin Road seconds before the accident occurred. In these circumstances, I hold that there was not a total destruction of voluntary control on the Defendant's part. Impaired, reduced or partial control of which I have heard in evidence is not, in my view, sufficient to enable the Defendant to succeed in this case. In the circumstances, I will vacate the Order of the Circuit Court. There will be judgment in favour of the Plaintiff in the sum agreed together with an Order for costs same to be taxed in default of agreement."

Comments and Questions:

1. To what extent did the foreknowledge of the defendant of something being wrong affect the outcome of this case? Compare this decision with that of *Kelly v Gilmore*, unreported, Supreme Court, July 28, 1970, where a driver who lost consciousness and struck the plaintiff was found not to be negligent as he was narrowly held not to have any foreknowledge of his loss of consciousness.

2. Given that the defendant had not suffered an epileptic fit before as an adult and that he professed to not knowing what was happening to him at the time, do you think the decision of Lavan J. above was unduly harsh? Was the decision affected in your view by the potential gravity of any consequent harm?

In the following case of *Callaghan v Killarney Race Company Ltd* [1958] I.R. 366 the issues of cost and social utility were considered in determining whether the standard of care had been breached by the defendant racecourse.

Callaghan v Killarney Race Company Limited
Supreme Court [1958] I.R. 366

Facts: The plaintiff, attending at a race meeting, was standing at the railings viewing a race, when a horse, instead of taking the jump, jumped over the railing and into the group of onlooking spectators. The plaintiff was injured and sued the defendant racetrack owners in negligence. In the High Court, the trial judge withdrew the case from the jury on the basis that there was no evidence of negligence on the part of the defendants. The plaintiff appealed.

Issues: The Supreme Court (Maguire C.J., Lavery, Kingsmill Moore, O'Daly and Maguire JJ.) had to consider whether the defendants had breached the standard of reasonable care. In finding that they had not, particular emphasis was placed on the high social utility provided by the racecourse, balanced against the prohibitively high cost of eliminating the risk.

Maguire C.J. (Lavery J. concurring):

"The law in regard to injuries to spectators who pay to see an entertainment to which obvious risks are incidental has been considered in a number of cases. This Court considered it in the case of Coleman v Kelly and Others (85 ILTR 48). The leading English case is Hall v Brooklands Auto Racing Club ((1933)

1 KB 205)—'What then is the term to be implied on payment to see a spectacle, the nature of which is known to all people of ordinary intelligence who go to see it?' He answers this by citing a passage from Lord Wensleydale's judgment in Parnaby v Lancaster Canal Co (11 A&E 223, at p230)- 'This is not an absolute warranty of safety, but a promise to use reasonable care to ensure safety. What is reasonable care would depend on the perils which might be reasonably expected to occur, and the extent to which the ordinary spectator might be expected to appreciate and take the risk of such perils. Illustrations are the risk of being hit by a cricket ball at Lord's ... where any ordinary spectator ... takes the risk of a ball being hit with considerable force amongst the spectators...'

Further illustrations he gives are spectators who stand along the line at a football or hockey match. Lord Justice Greer's judgment is to the same effect. He adds the illustration of a man taking a ticket to see the Derby who would know quite well that there would be no provision to prevent a horse which got out of hand from getting amongst the spectators and would take the risk of such a possible but improbable accident happening to himself.

Applying these principles the Court set aside a verdict which the plaintiff had obtained and entered judgment for the defendants. As already stated, the principle laid down in the Brooklands Case ((1933) 1 KB 205) has been accepted by this Court in Coleman v Kelly and Others (85 ILTR 48). This latter was a case of an accident at a show ground. The Court distinguished it from the Brooklands Case ((1933) 1 KB 205) 'It was not the duty of the defendants to provide against improbable or unlikely happenings such as the dashing of a horse through the railings in amongst spectators.' That is what happened here. In my opinion, the plaintiff took the risk of a horse swerving off the course as this horse did and injuring him. That a horse might do so was an obvious possibility. If precautions were to be taken to prevent this happening there would need to be a substantial fence all the way round the track which would have to be so high that nobody standing behind it could see the horses. Mr McMahon of course does not suggest anything quite so absurd. It would prevent the spectators seeing what they paid to see. He does suggest a guard rail similar to that at the finishing-post. The double rail at that point is not for the purpose of protecting the spectators but for the purpose of preventing excited or over-eager spectators from invading the course. It is, in effect, to protect the horses and their riders from spectators and not vice versa.

In my opinion, the learned Judge was correct in withdrawing the case from the jury."

Kingsmill Moore J.:

"In judging what a reasonable and prudent man would think necessary more than one element has to be considered. The rarity of the occurrence must be balanced against the gravity of the injury which is likely to ensue if the occurrence comes about, and some consideration must be paid to the practicability of the precautions suggested. If there was an obligation to double fence the whole perimeter, or to surround it with an unbreakable fence, the expense might well put an end to many of the smaller race-courses, or involve a higher price for admission. Having regard to the unlikelihood of the occurrence and the difficulty and expense of taking adequate steps to make such an occurrence impossible, and the practice prevailing at other similar race-courses, I do not consider that a jury could properly find that the defendant Company were guilty of a lack of reasonable care.

It must be remembered that there was no obligation on the plaintiff to post himself so near the rails, and if he chose to do so it seems to me that the defendant Company can rely on the further limitation of liability which Scrutton L.J. and Greer L.J. laid down in *Hall* v. *Brooklands Auto Racing Club* [[1933] 1 K.B. 205] and which was approved by the English Court of Appeal in *Murray and Another* v. *Harringay Arena Ltd.* [[1951] 2 K.B. 529], namely, that a person paying for his licence to see a cricket match or a race or other sport takes upon himself the risk of unlikely and improbable accidents provided that there has not been on the part of the occupier a failure to take the usual precautions. A person placed near to the playing-ground takes the risk of being hit by a cricket ball or a hockey ball, or, as in *Murray's Case* [[1956] 1 W.L.R. 177], by an ice hockey puck. Lord Justice Greer in *Hall's Case* [1909 S.C. 807] at p. 224 says that 'a man taking a ticket to see the Derby would know quite well that there would be no provision to prevent a horse which got out of hand from getting amongst the spectators, and would quite understand that he was himself bearing the risk of any such possible but improbable accident happening to himself'; and, in *Coleman* v. *Kelly and Others* [[1951] A.C. 367], Maguire C.J. at p. 51 said:— 'It was not the duty of the defendants to provide against improbable or unlikely happenings such as the dashing of a horse through the railings in amongst spectators.'

Accordingly, I consider that this appeal must be dismissed."

O'Daly J. delivered a concurring judgment.
Lavery and Maguire JJ. concurred.

RES IPSA LOQUITUR

Generally speaking the burden of proving negligence falls on the plaintiff and it is not for the defendant to disprove anything. There is, however, an exception to this general rule, in the principle of *res ipsa loquitur* ("the thing speaks for itself").

One of the earliest cases to outline the principle was that of *Scott v London & St Katherine Docks Co.* (1865) 3 H & C 722. In that case it was held that *res ipsa loquitur* will apply if in the ordinary course of events the accident could not have happened without negligence on the part of the defendant. In addition, the "thing" which causes the damage must be under the management or control of the defendant. The effect of *res ipsa loquitur* is not to render the defendant automatically liable. The legal effect is that the burden of proof is reversed and it falls on the defendant to show that s/he was not negligent. The defendant does not have to show how the injury came about and in some cases it will in fact be impossible to do so.

A number of cases where the principle arises involve animals straying onto the highway, as in the case of *O'Shea v Tilman Anhold and Horse Holiday Farm Ltd.*, unreported, Supreme Court, October 23, 1996.

O'Shea v Tilman Anhold and Horse Holiday Farm Ltd.
Unreported, Supreme Court, October 23, 1996

Facts: The plaintiff was injured when a horse jumped onto the roof of his car causing him to crash. He sued the defendants in negligence. In the High Court, Costello J. found in favour of the plaintiff. The defendants appealed.

Issues: In this case it fell to the court to consider whether the defendants were liable. The court (Hamilton C.J., O'Flaherty, Keane JJ.) held that applying the principle of *res ipsa loquitur* was appropriate. However, this did not mean that the defendant was automatically liable and it did not require the defendants to prove what had happened. It simply required them to show that they had taken reasonable care. On the facts the Supreme Court accepted that the defendants had satisfied this burden and allowed the appeal.

O'Flaherty J. (Hamilton C.J. concurring):

"At the outset, Mr Nugent SC, for the appellants, submitted that even if there was negligence on the part of the defendants (which, of course, he disputed) there should, nonetheless, have been a finding of contributory negligence against the plaintiff. I disagree. Here was a man driving his motor car along a busy highway, on a dark night, on dimmed headlights, and out of the blue a horse crashes onto the roof of his car. Mr Fergus O'Hagan SC, for the plaintiff, has said that this horse resembled Pegasus, the winged horse of Greek mythology, in performing such a feat and, he asks: how was the plaintiff expected to cope with that? There is certainly substance in this submission. So, in my judgment, there was no negligence on the plaintiff's part. But, from the plaintiff's perspective, he still has to prove negligence on the defendants' part. Was there such negligence?

The first-named defendant, Tilman Anhold, gave evidence that he had purchased the lands adjacent to the highway from which the horse strayed in or about 1984. He runs a holiday company. This is the second-named defendant company. The horses are the only assets of the company. There were four horses in the field at the time. Mr Anhold fed the horses on the evening of the accident at about 4.30 pm. The horses were in a concrete portion between two gates when they were fed. The gate leading into the field was open. He left the horses on the concrete portion. He walked out through the roadside gate and closed it. The gate was spring-loaded. He had to lift up the gate and only then could the bolt be moved freely. He was sure that he had closed the gate. Mr Anhold said that he was involved with horses for the past twenty five years. Previously he had a horse removed from his lands.

Dr Joe Hart, an agricultural consultant, gave evidence that he was satisfied that the fencing was adequate for ordinary commercial horse purposes. He said that the horse would not itself have got out. It would not jump over the wall onto the road. On the public road, the horse would have been in a panic and would behave differently. He believed that someone must have let it out onto the road. In a similar vein, Mr Ray Gallagher, an equestrian expert, testified that the only way that the horse would get out was for somebody to have opened the gate. While he agreed that a horse could jump from three to seven feet, he said he would be surprised if a horse would do so without being urged or forced.

Section 2(1) of the Animals Act, 1985, provides:—

> So much of the rules of the common law relating to liability for negligence as excludes or restricts the duty which a person might owe to others to take such care as is reasonable to see that damage is not caused by an animal straying on to a public road is hereby abolished.

The 'rules of the common law' are well summarised for our present purposes in the decision of the House of Lords in Searle v Wallbank [1947] AC 341. For example, Lord du Parcq, in the course of his speech in that case said, at p 361:—

> 'Counsel disclaimed any suggestion that the respondent was bound to maintain a fence, and he recognised that for centuries both the law and the general sense of the community have sanctioned the depasturing of cattle on unfenced land. He contended, however, that one who keeps his cattle on land adjoining the highway behind an apparently secure fence must see to it that it is in fact secure, for otherwise (he said) a deceptive feeling of safety will be induced in the passing cyclist or motorist. My Lords, I should have thought that, on principle, where there is no duty to maintain a fence at all, it cannot be a breach of duty to maintain one which is imperfect. But, however that may be, the argument takes little account of rural conditions. A stray horse, even if it has come from the nearest field and not from one a mile or more away, may have escaped, not through a gap in the fence, but through a gate left open by a trespasser. Moreover, the suggested duty could only be to take reasonable care to maintain a reasonably secure fence, and it must be a very high fence which a horse cannot jump; indeed, we have it on the authority of Byles J that, in or about the year 1858, it was proved that a bull had leaped

over an iron fence six feet high (Bessant v Great Western Ry Co [(1860) 8CB NS 368,372]). The truth is that, at least on country roads and in market towns, users of the highway, including cyclists and motorists, must be prepared to meet from time to time a stray horse or cow, just as they must expect to encounter a herd of cattle in the care of a drover. An underlying principle of the law of the highway is that all those lawfully using the highway, or land adjacent to it, must show mutual respect and forbearance. The motorist must put up with the farmer's cattle: the farmer must endure the motorist.'

The position as recounted in Searle v Wallbank also represented the law in Ireland: see McMahon and Binchy, The Irish Law of Torts (2nd ed) pp 518–521 and the cases cited therein. But then the legislature stepped in to change the law. This was a recognition, no doubt, that public roads had got much busier with the increase in motor traffic and so, from everyone's point of view, it was best to impose a duty on landowners to provide proper fencing adjacent to the highway to prevent animals from straying thereon except where 'the land is situated in an area where fencing is not customary' (see s 2(2) of the Animals Act, 1985). The trial judge was faced with the question: in the circumstances, were the owners of the horse liable to the plaintiff? He concluded:—

'The situation was that either the fencing on the laneway or field was inadequate or someone had opened the gate, let out one horse and closed the gate again. On balance the first possibility was much more likely than the second. The problem of fencing is a difficult one and the defendant was unable to discharge the onus of proof on it. The plaintiff has shown a breach of duty. There was no contributory negligence on the part of the plaintiff.'

There is no doubt that having regard to the statutory provision an onus rested on the defendants to show that they had taken reasonable care; nonetheless, that is the extent of the burden that rested on them. They disproved any negligence on their part through the evidence of their expert witnesses that the fencing was adequate, which testimony was not contradicted by the plaintiff's engineer. They were not required to take the further step of proving how the animal came to be on the highway: whether through the act of a trespasser or however. The most that is required of a defendant in this situation where the onus of proof rests on him is to disprove any negligence on his part: cf Lindsay Mid-Western Health Board [1993] 2 IR 147. It is not as if this was a case of strict or absolute liability. The learned trial judge approached the matter on the basis that one possibility was more likely than another; however, that was not the proper frame in which to resolve the problem that was presented to him. The trial judge's essential task was to decide whether reasonable care had been taken by the owners of the horse in the circumstances of the case, as required by the Act. The judge, in effect, went close to imposing strict liability on the defendants. This is to go too far. Legislation enacted in the future may provide for strict liability dispensing with the necessity to prove negligence, but that is not now the law.

In any event, as between the two possibilities, I would regard the possibility that someone opened the gate and let the horse out as less unlikely than that the horse cleared the fencing.

In the circumstances, I would allow the appeal."

Keane J.:

"… In the present case, it was accepted that the horse which collided with the Plaintiff's motor car was the property of the second named Defendants and had escaped, in some fashion, from the first named Defendant's land on to the highway. Although counsel for the Defendants was reluctant to concede the point, it seems clear that at that stage, as the trial judge ruled, the onus shifted to the Defendants to prove, on the balance of probabilities, that they had taken such care as was reasonable to see that damage was not caused by horses escaping from the land on to the public road. This would seem to be a case in which the res ipsa loquitur principle clearly applies.

In Scott v London and St Katherine Docks Company (1865), 3 H & C 596 Erle CJ said:

> 'There must be reasonable evidence of negligence. But where the thing is shown to be under the management of the Defendant or his servants, and the accident is such as in the ordinary circumstances does not happen if those who have the management use proper care, it affords reasonable evidence, in the absence of explanation by the Defendants, that the accident arose from want of care.'

(I have used that classic formulation rather than the recent restatement of the doctrine by this court in Hanrahan v Merck Sharpe & Dohme (Ireland) Limited, [1988] ILRM 629 which has been criticised and may need to be reconsidered at some stage. [See, for example, McMahon & Binchy on the Irish Law of Torts [2nd Edition], at pp 142 to 144.])

In the present case, the Defendants were the persons who brought the horse into the field adjoining the highway and provided such fences and gates as were there. Matters were, accordingly, essentially under their control and the first element of res ipsa loquitur is present. As to the next requirement—that the accident was such as in ordinary circumstances does not happen if those who have the management use proper care—it is self evident that a horse will not normally escape from lands on to the public road if adequate fencing is provided and any gates are kept in a closed position. At the close of the Plaintiff's case, there was, accordingly, reasonable evidence, in the absence of explanation by the Defendants, that the accident arose from their want of care. I am, accordingly, satisfied that the trial judge was correct in refusing to accede to the application for a non-suit made on behalf of the Defendants.

As we have seen, however, an explanation was offered by the Defendants. The evidence both of the first named Defendant and the experts called on his behalf was that all the standard precautions in the way of fencing and gates had been taken by the first named Defendant to ensure that horses did not stray from the land on to the road. In addition, the first named Defendant gave evidence, which the trial judge appears to have accepted, that, having fed the horses in the feeding area, he then left the gate into the field open and closed the gate leading from the feeding area into the public road. The explanation offered by him as to how the accident happened was that someone had opened the gate and allowed the horse to get on to the road.

The trial judge considered it more likely that the fencing was 'inadequate' and, accordingly, he found that the Defendants had been negligent.

There is, with respect, a lacuna in this reasoning. Even if the trial judge was satisfied as a matter of probability that the horse had managed in some fashion to surmount the obstacle presented by the fencing, it would not necessarily follow that this was due to any want of reasonable care on the part of the Defendants. If it were the case that the Defendants had taken all the precautions which a reasonable person in their position ought to have taken to prevent the horse escaping, then the fact that the horse succeeded in getting on to the road was not the result of any negligence on their part.

As to whether the Defendants had taken all the steps which a reasonable person in their position would have taken, the evidence before the trial judge was all to the same effect. Two experts, whose qualifications were not challenged, gave evidence that the fencing was adequate for its purpose and that they would be surprised if any of the horses in the field either attempted to jump over it or succeeded in jumping over it on to the road. They never resiled from that evidence and there was no evidence to suggest that they were wrong in that view. On the contrary, the experienced accident engineer who gave evidence on behalf of the Plaintiff notably refrained from expressing any view as to the adequacy of the fencing.

… I would also allow the appeal."

CHAPTER 3

SPECIAL INCIDENCES

This chapter will deal with two areas in which the recovery of damages in negligence is at issue: namely those of recovery for pure economic loss and recovery for psychiatric injury (nervous shock).

ECONOMIC LOSS

Introduction

Traditionally the courts have had no difficulty in allowing recovery for economic loss sustained due to some personal injury or property damage. However, where the economic loss suffered has arisen independently of any property damage or personal injury (pure economic loss), courts have been consistently more reluctant to allow recovery.

As regards pure economic loss, it can be caused either by negligent misstatements (negligent advice or information) or by a negligent act and the law has dealt differently with both. In both Ireland and England recovery is allowed for pure economic loss arising from negligent misstatements (on the basis of the *Hedley Byrne* principle). The right to recover for pure economic loss arising from negligent acts is more uncertain.

Recovery for negligent misstatements

Recovery under the *Hedley Byrne* principles now allows recovery for negligent misstatements where the following criteria are fulfilled: there is clear reliance by the plaintiff on the statement made; reliance is foreseeable and reasonable; and a special relationship exists between the parties (proximity). Prior to this decision recovery had only been allowed where either a fiduciary or contractual relationship existed between the parties.

Hedley Byrne & Co. Ltd. v Heller & Partners Ltd.
House of Lords [1964] A.C. 465

Facts: In this case Hedley Byrne & Co., advertising agents, asked their bankers to look into the financial stability of a company they were dealing with. Their bankers (National Provincial Bank) sought information from the company's bankers (Heller & Partners). Heller & Partners mistakenly gave favourable reports about the company, on the basis of which Hedley Bryne carried out some advertising work on credit. The company for whom the work was done went into liquidation. Hedley Byrne then sued Heller & Partners for the advice negligently given. The advice had been given on the understanding that it was "without responsibility" on the part of Heller & Partners. The case was decided in favour of Heller & Partners in both the trial court and the Court of Appeal on the basis that no duty of care existed. Hedley Byrne appealed to the House of Lords.

Issues: Two issues arose for consideration. First, whether Heller & Partners could be liable for the pure economic loss suffered by Hedley Byrne arising from the negligent advice given and, secondly, whether the disclaimer could absolve them from responsibility.

The House of Lords (Reid, Morris, Hodson, Devlin and Pearce L.JJ.) held that the law would now impose a duty of care where one party, possessed of a special skill, gave advice to another who relied on that advice, and that reliance was foreseeable. However, the disclaimer in this case was upheld, absolving the defendants of liability.

Lord Reid:

"... So it seems to me that there is good sense behind our present law that in general an innocent but negligent misrepresentation gives no cause of action. There must be something more than the mere misstatement. I therefore turn to the authorities to see what more is required ...

... A reasonable man, knowing that he was being trusted or that his skill and judgment were being relied on, would, I think, have three courses open to him. He could keep silent or decline to give the information or advice sought: or he could give an answer with a clear qualification that he accepted no responsibility for it or that it was given without that reflection or inquiry which a careful answer would require: or he could simply answer without any such qualification. If he chooses to adopt the last course he must, I think, be held to have accepted some responsibility for his answer being given carefully, or to have accepted a relationship with the inquirer which requires him to exercise such care as the circumstances require."

Lord Morris:

"My Lords, I consider that it follows and that it should now be regarded as settled that if someone possessed of a special skill undertakes, quite irrespective of contract, to apply that skill for the assistance of another person who relies upon such skill, a duty of care will arise. The fact that the service is to be given by means of or by the instrumentality of words can make no difference. Furthermore, if in a sphere in which a person is so placed that others could reasonably rely upon his judgment or his skill or upon his ability to make careful inquiry, a person takes it upon himself to give information or advice to, or allows his information or advice to be passed on to, another person who, as he knows or should know, will place reliance upon it, then a duty of care will arise.

I do not propose to examine the facts of particular situations or the facts of recently decided cases in the light of this analysis but I proceed to apply it to the facts of the case now under review. As I have stated, I approach the case on the footing that the bank knew that what they said would in fact be passed on to some unnamed person who was a customer of the National Provincial Bank. The fact that it was said that 'they,' that is, the National Provincial Bank, 'wanted to know' does not prevent this conclusion. In these circumstances, I think some duty towards the unnamed person, whoever it was, was owed by the bank. There was a duty of honesty. The great question, however, is whether there was a duty of care. The bank need not have answered the inquiry from the National Provincial Bank. It appears, however, that it is a matter of banking convenience or courtesy and presumably of mutual business advantage that inquiries as between banks will be answered. The fact that it is most unlikely that the bank would have answered a direct inquiry from Hedleys does not affect the question as to what the bank must have known as to the use that would be made of any answer that they gave but it cannot be left out of account in considering what it was that the bank undertook to do. It does not seem to me that they undertook before answering an inquiry to expend time or trouble 'in searching records, studying documents, weighing and comparing the favourable and unfavourable features and producing a well-balanced and well-worded report.' (I quote the words of Pearson L.J. [[1962] 1 Q.B. 396, 414]). Nor does it seem to me that the inquiring bank (nor therefore their customer) would expect such a process. This was, I think, what was denoted by Lord Haldane in his speech in Robinson v. National Bank of Scotland Ltd. [1916 S.C.(H.L.) 154] when he spoke of a 'mere inquiry' being made by one banker of another. In Parsons v. Barclay & Co. Ltd. [(1910) 103 L.T. 196] Cozens-Hardy M.R. expressed the view that it was no part of a banker's duty, when asked for a reference, to make inquiries outside as to the solvency or otherwise of the person asked about or to do more than answer the question put to him honestly from what he knew from the books and accounts before him. There was in the present case no contemplation of receiving anything like a formal and detailed report such as might be given by some concern charged with the duty (probably for reward) of making all proper and relevant inquiries concerning the nature, scope and extent of a company's activities and of obtaining and marshalling all available evidence as to its credit, efficiency, standing and business reputation. There is much to be said, therefore, for the view that if a banker gives a reference in the form of a brief expression of opinion in regard to creditworthiness he does not accept, and there is not expected from him, any higher duty than that of giving an honest answer. I need not, however, seek to deal further with this aspect of the matter, which perhaps cannot be covered by any statement of general application, because, in my judgment, the bank in the present case, by the words which they employed, effectively disclaimed any assumption of a duty of care. They stated that they only responded to the inquiry on the basis that their reply was without responsibility. If the inquirers chose to receive and act upon the reply they cannot disregard the definite terms upon which it was given. They cannot accept a reply given with a stipulation and then reject the stipulation. Furthermore, within accepted principles (as illustrated in Rutter v. Palmer [[1922] 2 K.B. 87]) the words employed were apt to exclude any liability for negligence.

I would therefore dismiss the appeal."

Lord Hodson:

"... I do not think it is possible to catalogue the special features which must be found to exist before the duty of care will arise in a given case, but since preparing this opinion I have had the opportunity of reading the speech which my noble and learned friend, Lord Morris of Borth-y-Gest, has prepared. I agree with him that if in a sphere where a person is so placed that others could reasonably rely upon his judgment or his skill or upon his ability to make careful inquiry such person takes it upon himself to give information or advice to, or allows his information or advice to be passed on to, another person who, as he knows, or should know, will place reliance upon it, then a duty of care will arise ..."

Lord Devlin:

"A plaintiff cannot, therefore, recover for financial loss caused by a careless statement unless he can show that the maker of the statement was under a special duty to him to be careful. Mr. Foster submits that this special duty must be brought under one of three categories. It must be contractual; or it must be fiduciary; or it must arise from the relationship of proximity and the financial loss must flow from physical damage done to the person or the property of the plaintiff. The law is now settled, Mr. Foster submits, and these three categories are exhaustive. It was so decided in Candler v. Crane, Christmas & Co. [[1951] 2. K.B. 164] and that decision, Mr. Foster submits, is right in principle and in accordance with earlier authorities.

Mr. Gardiner, for the appellants, agrees that outside contractual and fiduciary duty there must be a relationship of proximity—that is Donoghue v. Stevenson [[1932] A.C. 562]—but he disputes that recovery is then limited to loss flowing from physical damage. He has not been able to cite a single case in which a defendant has been held liable for a careless statement leading, otherwise than through the channel of physical damage, to financial loss. But he submits that in principle such loss ought to be recoverable and that there is no authority which prevents your Lordships from acting upon that principle. Unless Mr. Gardiner can persuade your Lordships of this, his case fails at the outset. This, therefore, is the first and the most fundamental of the issues which the House is asked to decide.

Mr. Foster's second reason is that, if it is open to your Lordships to declare that there are or can be special or proximate relationships outside the categories he has named, your Lordships cannot formulate one to fit the case of a banker who gives a reference to a third party who is not his customer; and he contends that your Lordships have already decided that point in Robinson v. National Bank of Scotland Ltd. [1916 S.C.(H.L.) 154]. His third reason is that if there can be found in cases such as this a special relationship between bankers and third parties, on the facts of the present case the appellants fall outside it; and here he relies particularly on the fact that the reference was marked Strictly confidential and given on the express understanding that we incur no responsibility whatever in furnishing it.

... Originally it was thought that the tort of negligence must be confined entirely to deeds and could not extend to words. That was supposed to have been decided by Derry v. Peek [14 App.Cas. 337]. I cannot imagine that anyone would now dispute that if this were the law, the law would be gravely defective. The practical proof of this is that the supposed deficiency was in relation to the facts in Derry v. Peek [[1936] A.C. 85] immediately made good by Act of Parliament. Today it is unthinkable that the law could permit directors to be as careless as they liked in the statements they made in a prospectus.

... In my opinion, the appellants in their argument tried to press Donoghue v. Stevenson [[1932] A.C. 562] too hard. They asked whether the principle of proximity should not apply as well to words as to deeds. I think it should, but as it is only a general conception it does not get them very far. Then they take the specific proposition laid down by Donoghue v. Stevenson [[1932] A.C. 562] and try to apply it literally to a certificate or a banker's reference. That will not do, for a general conception cannot be applied to pieces of paper in the same way as to articles of commerce or to writers in the same way as to manufacturers. An inquiry into the possibilities of intermediate examination of a certificate will not be fruitful. The real value of Donoghue v. Stevenson [[1932] A.C. 562] to the argument in this case is that it shows how the law can be developed to solve particular problems. Is the relationship between the parties in this case such that it can be brought within a category giving rise to a special duty? As always in English law, the first step in such an inquiry is to see how far the authorities have gone, for new categories in the law do not spring into existence overnight ...

... The respondents in this case cannot deny that they were performing a service. Their sheet anchor is that they were performing it gratuitously and therefore no liability for its performance can arise. My Lords, in my opinion this is not the law. A promise given without consideration to perform a service cannot be enforced as a contract by the promisee; but if the service is in fact performed and done negligently, the promisee can recover in an action in tort ...

My Lords, it is true that this principle of law has not yet been clearly applied to a case where the service which the defendant undertakes to perform is or includes the obtaining and imparting of information. But I cannot see why it should not be: and if it had not been thought erroneously that Derry v. Peek [14 App.Cas. 337] negatived any liability for negligent statements, I think that by now it probably would have been. It cannot matter whether the information consists of fact or of opinion or is a mixture of both, nor whether it was obtained as a result of special inquiries or comes direct from facts already in the defendant's possession or from his general store of professional knowledge. One cannot, as I have already endeavoured to show, distinguish in this respect between a duty to inquire and a duty to state.

... I am satisfied, for the reasons I have given, that a person for whose use a banker's reference is furnished is not, simply because no consideration has passed, prevented from contending that the banker is responsible to him for what he has said.

[As regards the disclaimer LORD DEVLIN stated as follows:]

"A man cannot be said voluntarily to be undertaking a responsibility if at the very moment when he is said to be accepting it he declares that in fact he is not. The problem of reconciling words of exemption with the existence of a duty arises only when a party is claiming exemption from a responsibility which he has already undertaken or which he is contracting to undertake. For this reason alone, I would dismiss the appeal."

Lord Pearce:

"... The law of negligence has been deliberately limited in its range by the courts' insistence that there can be no actionable negligence in vacuo without the existence of some duty to the plaintiff. For it would be impracticable to grant relief to everybody who suffers damage through the carelessness of another.

The reason for some divergence between the law of negligence in word and that of negligence in act is clear. Negligence in word creates problems different from those of negligence in act. Words are more volatile than deeds. They travel fast and far afield. They are used without being expended and take effect in combination with innumerable facts and other words. Yet they are dangerous and can cause vast financial damage. How far they are relied on unchecked (by analogy with there being no probability of intermediate inspection—see Grant v. Australian Knitting Mills Ltd. [[1936] A.C. 85]) must in many cases be a matter of doubt and difficulty. If the mere hearing or reading of words were held to create proximity, there might be no limit to the persons to whom the speaker or writer could be liable. Damage by negligent acts to persons or property on the other hand is more visible and obvious; its limits are more easily defined, and it is with this damage that the earlier cases were more concerned. It was not until 1789 that Pasley v. Freeman [(1789) 3 Term Rep. 51] recognised and laid down a duty of honesty in words to the world at large—thus creating a remedy designed to protect the economic as opposed to the physical interests of the community. Any attempts to extend this remedy by imposing a duty of care as well as a duty of honesty in representations by word were curbed by Derry v. Peek [14 App.Cas. 337].

... How wide the sphere of the duty of care in negligence is to be laid depends ultimately upon the courts' assessment of the demands of society for protection from the carelessness of others. Economic protection has lagged behind protection in physical matters where there is injury to person and property. It may be that the size and the width of the range of possible claims has acted as a deterrent to extension of economic protection ...

... In this sphere the law was developed in the United States in Glanzer v. Shepherd, [233 N.Y. 236] where a public weigher employed by a vendor was held liable to a purchaser for giving him a certificate which negligently overstated the amount of the goods supplied to him. The defendant was thus engaged on a task in which, as he knew, vendor and purchaser alike depended on his skill and care and the fact that it was the vendor who paid him was merely an accident of commerce. This case was followed and developed in later cases.

... Was there such a special relationship in the present case as to impose on the defendants a duty of care to the plaintiffs as the undisclosed principals for whom the National Provincial Bank was making the inquiry? The answer to that question depends on the circumstances of the transaction. If, for instance, they disclosed a casual social approach to the inquiry, no such special relationship or duty of care would be assumed (see Fish v. Kelly [17 C.B.N.S. 194]). To import such a duty the representation must normally, I think, concern a business or professional transaction whose nature makes clear the gravity of the inquiry and the importance and influence attached to the answer. It is conceded that Salmon J. rightly found a duty of care in Woods v. Martins Bank Ltd. [[1959] 1 Q.B. 55] but the facts in that case were wholly different from those in the present case. A most important circumstance is the form of the inquiry and of the answer. Both were here plainly stated to be without liability. Mr. Gardiner argues that those words are not sufficiently precise to exclude liability for negligence. Nothing, however, except negligence could, in the facts of this case, create a liability (apart from fraud, to which they cannot have been intended to refer and against which the words would be no protection, since they would be part of the fraud). I do not, therefore, accept that even if the parties were already in contractual or other special relationship the words would give no immunity to a negligent answer. But in any event they clearly prevent a special relationship from arising. They are part of the material from which one deduces whether a duty of care and a liability for negligence was assumed. If both parties say expressly (in a case where neither is deliberately taking advantage of the other) that there shall be no liability, I do not find it possible to say that a liability was assumed.

I would therefore dismiss the appeal."

Comments and Questions:

1. In the above case liability would have been imposed, in the absence of a disclaimer, because of the proximity between the parties and the reasonable reliance on the advice given. The court stated that sufficient proximity would exist where there was a "special relationship" between the parties. They also stated that for reliance to be reasonable the advice had to be given in circumstances which were more than "casual", something closer to a business relationship (see Lord Pearce). Are these two considerations merely two ways of examining the same question, or are there differences in your view?

2. In the above case, liability would almost certainly have been imposed were it not for the existence of a disclaimer denying responsibility. Do you feel that courts will uphold such disclaimers in all circumstances?

3. In many pure economic loss cases arising out of negligent misstatements, a duty may exist in both contract and tort. It is important to remember that if such a situation arises a case can be taken in both (see *Finlay v Murtagh* [1979] I.R. 249 discussed in *Wall v Hegarty* below).

4. For a similar Irish case where in the absence of a disclaimer liability was imposed see *Tulsk v Ulster Bank Ltd.,* unreported, High Court, May 13, 1983.

Hedley Byrne applied in Ireland

In Ireland the decision in *Hedley Byrne* has been followed in a line of cases. It is clear from the decision in *Hedley Byrne* (in particular that of Lord Devlin) that a duty cannot be owed to the whole world. A duty is owed only to those with whom the defendant is in a "special relationship", *i.e.* those with whom the defendant has a high degree of proximity and for whom it is reasonable to rely on the advice given.

In the case of *Securities Trust Ltd. v Hugh Moore & Alexander Ltd.* [1964] I.R. 417 the question arose as to whether sufficient proximity existed between the parties so as to bring the case within the *Hedley Byrne* criteria.

Securities Trust Limited v Hugh Moore & Alexander Limited
High Court [1964] I.R. 417

Facts: A Mr Anderson held shares in the defendant company as a trustee for the plaintiff company. He requested a copy of the memorandum and articles of association of the defendant company from the defendant company in his own name. On the basis of information contained in the articles of association, he purchased further shares on behalf of the plaintiff company. The information in the articles of association was found to be erroneous resulting in a significant loss to the plaintiff company. The plaintiff company sued the defendant company for negligent misrepresentation.

Issues: The court (Davitt P.) was required to consider whether the case came within the *Hedley Byrne* criteria. He held that it did not, as there was an insufficient relationship of proximity between the plaintiff and the defendants to give rise to a duty of care.

Davitt P.:

"… The law to be applied in this case is not in controversy. It would appear that the proposition that innocent (ie nonfraudulent) misrepresentation cannot give rise to an action for damages is somewhat too broadly stated, and is based upon a misconception of what was decided by the House of Lords in Derry v Peek (14 App Cas 337). Such action may be based on negligent misrepresentation which is not fraudulent. This was pointed out in Nocton v Lord Ashburton ((1914) AC 932)—'Although liability for negligence in word has in material respects been developed in our law differently from liability for negligence in act, it is none the less true that a man may come under a special duty to exercise care in giving information or advice. I should accordingly be sorry to be thought to lend countenance to the idea that recent decisions have been intended to stereotype the cases in which people can be held to have assumed such a special duty. Whether such a duty has been assumed must depend on the relationship of the parties, and it is at least certain that there are a good many cases in which that relationship may be properly treated as giving rise to a special duty of care in statement.' It was apparently considered in some quarters that such a special duty could arise only from a contractual or fiduciary relationship. In Robinson v National Bank of Ireland (1916 SC (HL) 150)—'The whole of the doctrine as to fiduciary relationships, as to the duty of care arising from implied as well as express contracts, as to the duty of care arising from other special relationships which the Courts may find to exist in particular cases, still remains, and I should be very sorry if any word fell from me which would suggest that the Courts are in any way hampered in recognising that the duty of care may be established when such cases really occur.'

The proposition that circumstances may create a relationship between two parties in which, if one seeks information from the other and is given it, that other is under a duty to take reasonable care to ensure that the information given is correct, has been accepted and applied in the case of Hedley Byrne & Co Ltd v Heller and Partners Ltd ((1963) 3 WLR 101), recently decided by the House of Lords. Counsel for the defendant Company did not seek to dispute the proposition. He submitted, however, that the circumstances of this case created no such special relationship.

... At the time that Mr Anderson made his request to the secretary of the defendant Company for a copy of their Memorandum and Articles of Association he was a shareholder. The plaintiff Company had not then been registered as owner of any shares. He was a member of the defendant Company; his Company was not. The position was that he was entitled to receive a copy of the Memorandum and Articles; his Company was not. He was entitled to receive it personally qua member; he was not entitled to receive it qua agent of the plaintiff Company. In these circumstances I must, I think, conclude that the copy was requested and supplied, in accordance with the provisions of s18, subs1, of the Act, by the defendant Company to Mr Anderson personally and not as agent for the plaintiff Company. It seems to me that there was no relationship between the parties in this case other than such as would exist between the defendant Company and any person (other than Mr Anderson) who might chance to read the copy supplied to him; or, indeed, between that Company and any member of the community at large, individual or corporate, who chanced to become aware of the last sentence in Article 155 of the defective reprint of the Memorandum and Articles. It can hardly be seriously contended that the defendant Company owed a duty to the world at large to take care to avoid mistakes and printers' errors in the reprint of their Articles. In my opinion, counsel is correct in his submission that in this case the defendant Company owed no duty to the plaintiff Company to take care to ensure that the copy of the Articles supplied to Mr Anderson was a correct copy. For these reasons there must, in my opinion, be judgment for the defendant Company."

Comments and Questions:
1. Similarly, in the more recent case of *Bank of Ireland v Smith* [1966] I.R. 646 it was held that an auctioneer, acting for a vendor, did not owe a duty to buyers to ensure that statements made by him/her in relation to the property were correct. In this case the plaintiff, who relied to his detriment on an advertisement placed by the auctioneer, was not entitled to recover for his loss.

Proximity was found to have been established between a solicitor and all potential beneficiaries of a will in the case of *Wall v Hegarty* [1980] I.L.R.M. 24.

Wall v Hegarty and Callnan
High Court [1980] I.L.R.M. 124

Facts: The defendants, a firm of solicitors, had failed to properly attest a will, rendering it inoperative. As a result the plaintiff did not receive a legacy of £15,000 to which he was entitled under the will. He sued the defendants for the ensuing pure economic loss.

Issues: Barrington J. in the High Court had to consider whether a duty of care could be owed to a legatee under a will for pure economic loss. He held that a duty of care did exist (citing *Donoghue v Stevenson* [1932] A.C.) and that pure economic loss in this case was recoverable under the principles in *Hedley Byrne*.

Barrington J.:

"There is no doubt that [the defendants] owe a duty to a testator to show reasonable care and to exercise professional skills appropriate to a solicitor in ensuring that the testator's wishes are carried out. But if a legacy fails, the testator and his estate may suffer little or no damage. The legatee may suffer substantial damage but may have no right of action against the solicitor. The testator's estate may have a right of action against the solicitor in contract or in tort, but may be entitled only to nominal damages.

The plaintiff, in his statement of claim, pleads that a solicitor retained by a testator to prepare a will owes a duty to an executor and beneficiary named in the will to ensure that the testator's benevolent intentions in respect of the executor and beneficiary are not frustrated through lack of reasonable care on the part of the solicitor ...

... Traditionally, English law did not regard a solicitor as owing any such duty to a legatee in a testator's will and, so far as I am aware, the law of Ireland was no different in this respect.

[Barrington J. then went on to describe how the law had since then changed, particularly in light of the dicta of Lord Atkin in *Donoghue v Stevenson* [1932] A.C. 562.]

The second important legal development which has taken place ... is that it is now finally established, so far, at any rate, as the law of Ireland is concerned, that a solicitor owes two kinds of duties to his client. First, is his duty in contract to carry out the terms of his retainer. Second is a duty in tort to show reasonable professional skill in attending to his client's affairs. It is clear that this duty in tort arises simply because he is purporting to act as a solicitor for his client and is independent of whether he is providing his professional services voluntarily or for reward. (See the judgment of the Supreme Court in *Finlay v Murtagh*

[1979] IR 249 and the judgment of Oliver J., in *Midland Bank Trust Co. Ltd v Hetts, Stubbs & Kemp* [1979] Ch 384).

The Supreme Court in *Finlay v Murtagh* was merely dealing with a net point of law as to whether a solicitor owed a duty to a client in tort as well as in contract, but it is quite clear that the court, in holding that he did, derived the duty from the proximity principle outlined by Lord Atkin in *Donoghue v Stevenson*. For instance, the following passage appears at page 2 of the judgment of Kenny J:

> 'The professional person, however, owes the client a general duty and not one arising from contract from the '*proximity*' principle (*Donoghue v Stevenson, Hedley Byrne & Co. v Heller & Partners Ltd*), to exercise reasonable care and skill in the performance of the work entrusted to him. This duty arises from the obligation which springs from the situation that he knew or ought to have known that his failure to exercise care and skill would probably cause loss and damage. This failure to have or to exercise reasonable skill and care is tortious or delictual in origin.'

Indeed, Henchy J, in a passage at page ten of his judgment, appears to anticipate the situation which has arisen in the present case. He says:

> 'The solicitor's liability in tort under the general duty of care extends not only to a client for reward, but to any person for whom he undertakes to act professionally without reward, and also to those (such as beneficiaries under a will, persons entitled under an intestacy, or those entitled to benefits in circumstances such as a claim in respect of a fatal injury) with whom he has made no arrangement to act, but who, as he knows or ought to know, will be relying on his professional care and skill. For the same default there should be the same cause of action. If others are entitled to sue in tort for the solicitor's want of care, so also should the client.'

Since the decision of the Supreme Court in *Finlay v Murtagh*, the specific question which arises in the present case arose for consideration in the English High Court in the case of *Ross v Caunters* [1980] Ch. 297.

In that case, the testator instructed solicitors to draw up his will to include gifts of chattels and a share of his residuary estate to the plaintiff, who was his sister-in-law. The solicitors drew up the will naming the plaintiff as legatee. The testator requested the solicitors to send the draft will to him at the plaintiff's home where he was staying, to be signed and attested. The solicitors sent the will to the testator with a covering letter giving instructions on executing it, but failed to warn him that under *s. 15 of the Wills Act, 1837*, attestation of the will by the beneficiary's spouse would invalidate the gift to the beneficiary. The plaintiff's husband attested the will which was then returned to the solicitors who failed to notice that he had attested it. In fact, prior to the execution of the will, the testator had, in correspondence, raised with his solicitor, the question *'Am I right in thinking that beneficiaries may not be witnesses?'* The solicitors unfortunately did not answer this question which clearly provided them with an opportunity to warn the testator that the spouse of a beneficiary should not be a witness either.

The testator died two years after the execution of the will. Some time later, the solicitors wrote to the plaintiff informing her that the gifts to her under the will were void because her husband had attested it. The plaintiff brought an action against the solicitors claiming damages for negligence for the loss of the gifts under the will. Sir Robert Megarry VC, after an exhaustive analysis of the authorities, held that she was entitled to succeed.

... If a solicitor owes any duty to a named legatee, then it is quite clear that the solicitor in the present case has failed to show the appropriate care and skill. It is unnecessary to labour the point. The case has been frankly met. No effort has been made to defend what was done, except to say that the defendants owed no duty to the plaintiff.

To turn now to the question of the plaintiff's loss. Mr Matthews has suggested that the plaintiff had no more than a *'spes.'* His loss, it is suggested, is too remote to be taken into consideration by the law. I cannot accept this. The testator died without revoking his purported will. Had, therefore, the will been validly drawn, the plaintiff would have received his bequest of £15,000."

Comments and Questions:
1. The *Wall v Hegarty* case above was resolved applying the principles of *Donoghue v Stevenson* and *Hedley Byrne.* How are these principles different to those which apply in professional negligence cases (see Chapter 8)?

In addition to the requirement of close proximity, in order to recover under the *Hedley Byrne* principle a plaintiff must establish that it was foreseeable that s/he would rely on the statement negligently made and that such reliance was reasonable. An Irish case in which reliance was found to be reasonable was that of *McAnarney v Hanrahan* [1993] 3 I.R. 492.

McAnarney and McAnarney v Hanrahan
High Court [1993] 3 I.R. 492

Facts: The defendants, a firm of auctioneers, told the plaintiffs that a property they wished to purchase had attracted an offer of £54,000 at auction and, additionally, that the freehold for the premises could be purchased when the time came for £3,000. Both statements were untrue. The plaintiffs, acting on the advice given, purchased the property and, when they attempted to purchase the freehold, learnt that the owners wanted £40,000 and not £3,000. On learning this the plaintiffs sued the defendants for the advice negligently given.

Issues: The court was required to consider whether a "special relationship" existed between the parties, so as to establish a duty of care to protect the plaintiffs from the economic loss suffered.

Costello J. held that due to the circumstances in which the advice was given, a "special relationship" had been created. Applying the *Hedley Byrne* principles he held that there was a sufficient relationship to give rise to a duty of care, and the circumstances were such that it was reasonable for the plaintiffs to have relied on the advice given.

Costello J.:

"The plaintiffs do not maintain a claim for damages for deceit—their claim is for damages for negligence. It is claimed that Mr Hanrahan owed a duty of care to them and that this duty was breached and in support they rely on the principle established in Hedley Byrne and Co Ltd v Heller & Partners Ltd [1964] AC 465. It is important to bear in mind that this is not a case in which a party to a contract (or his agent) has made a negligent misstatement to another—it is a case of an auctioneer acting for a vendor making a statement to a proposed purchaser. The question for determination is whether in the particular circumstances the auctioneer owed a duty of care to the purchasers. As pointed out in Hedley Byrne & Co Ltd v Heller & Partners Ltd [1964] AC 465 by Lord Morris (at pages 502–503):—

> 'If, in a sphere in which a person is so placed that others could reasonably rely upon his judgment or his skill or upon his ability to make careful enquiry, a person takes it upon himself to give information or advice to, or allows his information or advice to be passed on to, another person who, as he knows or should know, would place reliance upon it, then a duty of care will arise.'

Here Mr Hanrahan took upon himself responsibility for giving his opinion about the purchase of the freehold. He should have known that the plaintiffs would place reliance on what he told them, particularly as he expressly stated that negotiations had already taken place with the landlords. In my opinion a special relationship thus arose between Mr Hanrahan and the plaintiffs which imposed on him the duty of care in giving the information. He breached that duty in that before making the statement he took no care to see what price the landlords would require for their interest. This case is different to that of the Bank of Ireland v Smith [1966] IR 646 in which Kenny J held that no duty of care towards prospective purchasers was imposed on an auctioneer when placing an advertisement which contained misleading information. In this case the particular circumstances of the negotiations and the express assumption of responsibility to which I have referred created a special relationship which was absent in the circumstances which Kenny J was considering.

It follows, therefore, that if the plaintiffs can establish loss arising from the negligent misstatement that damages are recoverable against Mr Hanrahan personally and against his employers, the second defendant, which is vicariously liable for his negligence."

Comments and Questions:
1. Contrast this decision with that of *Bank of Ireland v Smith* [1996] I.R. 646.
   How are these cases different?

Pure economic loss and negligent acts

The principles applicable to recovery for negligent acts in the realm of pure economic loss are not as certain as the position described above with respect to negligent misstatements. The earlier position reflected that which existed prior to the *Hedley Byrne* principles, *i.e.* that such recovery was not permissible outside of contract, in the absence of any physical damage or personal injury. In the English courts a relaxing of that strict view took place in the case of *Junior Books v Veitchi* [1983] 520 (H.L.). However, they have since held that the *Junior Books* case should be confined to its facts and was not a proposition for the general principle that recovery for pure economic loss arising from negligent acts was permissible. It is therefore, likely that recovery for pure economic loss in the English courts arising from negligent acts will be tightly controlled.

The Irish position

Ireland's earliest decisions, as in England, were clearly hostile to a right to recover for pure economic loss. In *Irish Paper Sacks Ltd v John Sisk & Son (Dublin) Ltd.,* High Court, May 18, 1972, for instance, the fact that the only loss sustained was economic barred recovery. In this case O'Keefe P. stated that "… a plaintiff suing for damages suffered as a result of an act or omission of the defendant cannot recover if the act or omission did not directly injure the plaintiff's person or property, but merely caused consequential loss."

More recently, however, the courts have held that recovery hinges on the issues of proximity and foreseeability and that the nature of the loss (physical or economic) is irrelevant (see for instance McCarthy J., in *Ward v McMaster* [1989] I.L.R.M. 400, Chap.2). Another case, often cited as supporting recovery for pure economic loss, is that of *McShane Wholesale Fruit & Vegetables Ltd. v Johnston Haulage Co. Ltd.* [1997] 1 I.L.R.M. 86.

McShane Wholesale Fruit and Vegetables Ltd. v Johnston Haulage Co. Ltd. and Carbrook Chemicals Ltd.
High Court [1997] 1 I.L.R.M. 86

Facts: The plaintiff and the defendants occupied adjoining business premises. In February 1991 a fire occurred on the defendants' premises which resulted in the loss of electrical power to the plaintiff's premises. The plaintiff claimed economic loss to its business and that the fire was due to the negligence of the defendants. The defendants contended that the loss was not reasonably foreseeable and that the damage was too remote. The parties agreed to have a preliminary issue determined, namely, whether damages are recoverable for economic loss consequent on a negligent act.

Issues: The court was asked to determine whether pure economic loss was recoverable in the Irish courts.

Flood J., relying on the judgment of McCarthy J. in *Ward v McMaster*, held that the type of damage suffered was irrelevant in determining whether a duty of care was owed. The question was to be decided on the basis of the principles of proximity, foreseeability and the absence of considerations of public policy that might deny recovery.

Flood J.:

"The defendants and each of them filed defences which may be generally described as being traverses of the allegations of fact, a plea that the loss or damage was not reasonably foreseeable and was too remote and a plea by way of estoppel on the premises that the said fire was an accidental fire and that in consequence no cause of action arose therefrom and there is an estoppel from maintaining the claim pursuant to *s. 1(1)(a) of the Accidental Fires Act 1943.*

On the matter being opened in this Court, I was advised that the plaintiff and defendants had agreed that I should try a preliminary issue as to whether economic loss consequent on a negligent act is recoverable as damages, within this jurisdiction.

In Ireland since the Supreme Court decision in *Ward v. McMaster* [1988] IR 337; [1989] ILRM 400, the test for actionable negligence is:

(a) A sufficient relationship of proximity between the alleged wrongdoer and the person who has suffered damage.
(b) Such relationship that in the reasonable contemplation of the former carelessness on his part may be likely to cause damage to the latter—in which case a *prima facie* duty of care arises.
(c) Subject always to any compelling exemption based on public policy.

McCarthy J stated the position as follows at pp. 349/409:

> ... I prefer to express the duty as arising from the proximity of the parties, the foreseeability of the damage and the absence of any compelling exemption based on public policy. I do not in any fashion seek to exclude the latter consideration although I confess that such a consideration must be a very powerful one if it is to be used to deny any injured party his right to redress at the expense of the person or body that injured him.

The quality of the damage does not arise. It can be damage to property, to the person, financial or economic—see *Sweeney v. Duggan* [1991] 2 IR 274. The question as to whether the damage (of whatever type) is recoverable is dependent on proximity and foreseeability subject to the caveat of compelling exemption on public policy.

In short, the proximity of the parties giving rise to the duty of care must be such, as a matter of probability to be causal of the damage. If it is not, the damage is too remote and the action will fail. It will fail not because the damage is of a particular type but because the relationship between the wrongdoer and the person who suffers the damage does not have the essential of sufficient relationship of proximity or neighbourhood.

It therefore follows that the fact that the damage is economic is not in itself a bar to recovery where the other elements above stated are present.

Whether the damage in this instance is or is not too remote is a question of fact to be determined on evidence."

Comments and Questions:

1. It is arguable whether Ireland has had a successful case involving pure economic loss outside of the area of negligent misstatement, in which case any comment on such recovery by the Irish courts is merely *obiter*. For instance, in both *Ward v McMaster* [1988] I.R. 377 and *McShane* some physical damage occurred. In the latter case it appeared that the fire had spread to the plaintiff's premises, although the plaintiff only appears to have sued for economic loss arising from the loss of electricity.

2. The most recent significant case to comment on the issue is that of *Glencar Explorations v County Council of Mayo* [2002] 1 I.R. 84 where Keane C.J. stated that, notwithstanding the judgment in *Ward*, it was still unclear whether recovery for pure economic loss was allowed in this jurisdiction outside of the area of negligent misstatement at p.143. The Chief Justice also questioned whether the *Junior Books* decision ought to be followed in Ireland. This statement casts significant doubt over whether any general right to recovery for pure economic loss exists in this country.

PSYCHIATRIC DAMAGE (NERVOUS SHOCK)

Introduction

The term "nervous shock" refers to an injury of the mind that may or may not be accompanied by a physical injury or a threat of such injury. Nervous shock is not to be confused with grief, or depression associated with a personal injury; it refers rather to a negligently inflicted disruption of a person's mental well-being. Denham J. in *Kelly v Hennessy* [1995] 3 I.R. 253 states:

"'Nervous shock' is a legal term used to connote a mental as opposed to physical injury to a person. It has been accepted in Irish law that such an injury can be the subject of damages. The term was used over a hundred years ago and accepted: see *Byrne v Great Southern and Western Railway Company of Ireland*, [1884] 26 LR (Ir) 428 *and Bell v Great Northern Railway Company of Ireland*, (1896) 26 LR (Ir) 428.

'Nervous shock' is a mental injury, being a recognisable and distinct psychiatric illness: *Hinz v Berry* [1970] 2 QB 40, 42. It is a term to be contrasted to mental distress, fear, grief or sadness."

History

Historically, common law jurisdictions have been slow to allow recovery for "nervous shock". In *Victoria Railway v Coultas,* 13 App. Cas. 222 (1888) the Privy Council stated:

"Damages arising from mere sudden terror unaccompanied by any actual physical injury but occasioning a nervous or mental shock cannot under such circumstances, their Lordships think, be considered a consequence which, in the ordinary course of things, would flow from the negligence ..."

The Irish courts have allowed nervous shock cases since the 1800s: see *Byrne v Great Southern and Western Railway Company of Ireland* [1884] 26 L.R. (Ir.) 428 and *Bell v Great Northern Railway Company of Ireland* (1896) 26 L.R. (Ir.) 428.

Bell v The Great Northern Railway Co. of Ireland
Exchequer Division (1896) 26 L.R. (Ir.) 428

Facts: The plaintiff was a passenger in the defendant's train, when the train was unhooked and reversed at high speed down a hill. This caused some panic among the passengers. At a curve the train stopped suddenly and the plaintiff, who was then standing up, was thrown down. She suffered severe shock and her mental health was severely affected. Three medical witnesses held that she was suffering from "fright and nervous shock" and one of the witnesses claimed that her condition may result in paralysis.

Issues: This is an appeal case, appealing the decision of Mr Justice Andrews and, more specifically, his directions to the jury as to the elements of the case they were entitled to take into consideration. Palles C.B. had to determine whether to follow the earlier Irish decision of *Byrne v Great Southern and Western Railway Company of Ireland* [1884] 26 L.R. Ir. 428, or the Privy Council decision in *Victoria Railway v Coultas,* 13 App. Cas. 222 (1888). Recovery for nervous shock was permitted by Palles C.B.

Palles C.B. (Murphy and Andrews JJ. concurring):

"In summing up, my brother Andrews told the jury that, if great fright was, in their opinion, the reasonable and natural consequence of the circumstances in which the defendants by their negligence had placed the female plaintiff, and that she was actually put in great fright by those circumstances; and if the injury to her health was, in their opinion, the reasonable and natural consequence of such great fright, and was actually occasioned thereby, damages for such injury would not be too remote. The defendant's counsel objected to this direction, and required the judge to tell the jury that if the injury was the result of, or arose from, mere fright, and was not accompanied by any physical injury, even though there might be a nervous or mental shock occasioned by the fright, such damages would be too remote.

This objection presupposes that the plaintiff sustained, by reason of the defendants' negligence, 'injury' of the class left to the consideration of the jury by summing-up, i.e. injury to health, which is bodily or physical injury; and the proposition presented is that damages for such injury are not recoverable, if two circumstances occur: (1) if the only connection between the negligence and this bodily injury is that the former caused fright, which caused nervous or mental shock, which shock caused the bodily injury complained of; and (2) that this so-called bodily injury did not accompany the fright, which I suppose means that the injury, although in fact occasioned by the fright, assumed the character of bodily injury subsequently to, and not at, the time of the negligence or fright. To sustain this contention, it must be true whether the shock which it assumed to have caused was either mental or nervous; and as the introduction of the word 'mental' may cause obscurity, by involving matter of a wholly different nature, unnecessary to be taken into consideration here, I eliminate it from the question. If there be a distinction between mental shock and nervous shock, and if the proposition be not true in the case of nervous shock, then the objection cannot be sustained.

If, then, such bodily injury as we have here, may be a natural consequence of fright the chain of reasoning is complete. But the medical evidence here is such that the jury might from it reasonably arrive at the conclusion that the injury, similar to that which actually resulted to the plaintiff from the fright, might reasonably have resulted to any person who had been placed in a similar position. It has not been suggested that there was anything special in the nervous organization of the plaintiff which might render the effect of the negligence or fright upon her different in character from that which it would have produced in any other individual. I do not myself think that proof that the plaintiff was an unusual nervous disposition would have been material to the question; for persons, whether nervous or strong-minded, are entitled to be carried by railway companies without unreasonable risk of danger; and my only reason for referring to the circumstance is to show that, in this particular case, the jury might have arrived at the conclusion that the injury which did, in fact, ensue was a natural and reasonable consequence of the negligence which actually caused it.

Again, it is admitted that, as the negligence caused fright, if the fright contemporaneously caused physical injury, the damage would not be too remote. The distinction insisted upon is one of time only. The proposition is that, although, if an act of negligence produces such an effect upon particular structures of the body as at the moment to afford palpable evidence of physical injury, the relation of proximate cause and effect exists between such negligence and the injury, yet such relation cannot in law exist in the case of a similar act producing upon the same structures an effect which, at a subsequent time—say a week, a fortnight, or a month—must result, without any intervening cause, in the same physical injury. As well it might be said that a death caused by poison is not to be attributed to the person who administered it because the moral effect is not produced contemporaneously with its administration. This train of reasoning might be pursued much further; but in consequence of the decision to which I shall hereafter refer, I deem it unnecessary to do so.

In support of their contention, the defendants relied upon the *Victoria Railway Commissioners v. Coultas* 13 App Cas 222. That was a remarkable case. The statement of claim alleged that through the negligence of the servants of the defendants, in charge of a railway gate at a level crossing, the plaintiffs, while driving over it, were placed in imminent peril of being killed by a train, and by reason thereof the plaintiff, Mary received a shock, and suffered personal injuries. It appeared that the female plaintiff, whilst returning with her husband and brother in the evening, from Melbourne to Hawthorn, in a buggy, had to cross the defendants' line of railway at a level crossing. When they came to it the gates were closed; the gatekeeper opened the gates nearest to the plaintiffs, and then went across the line to those on the opposite side. The plaintiffs followed him, and were partly on to the up-line (the further one), when the train was seen approaching on it. The gatekeeper directed them to go back, but James Coultas, who was driving, shouted to him to open the opposite gate, and went on. He succeeded in getting the buggy across the line, so that the train, which was going at rapid speed, did not touch it, although it passed close at the back of it. As the train approached, the plaintiff Mary, fainted. The medical evidence showed that she received a severe nervous shock from the fright, and that the illness from which she afterwards suffered (and which is stated in Mr Beven's book on *Negligence* to have included a miscarriage) was the consequence of the fright. One of the plaintiffs' witnesses said she was suffering from profound impression on the nervous system—nervous shock; and that the shock from which she suffered would be a natural consequence of the fright. Another said he was unable to detect any physical damage; he put her symptoms down to nervous shock.

It is to be observed that from this evidence the jury might have inferred that physical injury was sustained by the female plaintiff at the time of the occurrence in question. Although one witness spoke of nervous shock, as contradistinguished from physical damage, the question would still have been open for the jury whether the nervous shock was not—as in the generality of, if not indeed in all, cases it necessarily must be—physical injury. The jury found for the plaintiffs. Upon an appeal, the Privy Council without deciding that impact was necessary to sustain the action not only set aside the verdict, but entered judgment for the defendants. In delivering judgment, Sir R Couch says, 'Her fright was caused by seeing the train approaching, and thinking they were going to be killed. Damages arising from mere sudden terror, unaccompanied by any actual physical injury but occasioning a nervous or mental shock, cannot, under such circumstances (their Lordships think), be considered a consequence which, in the ordinary course of things, would flow from the negligence of the gatekeeper.'

Amongst the reasons stated in the judgment in support of this conclusion are: 1, that a contrary doctrine would involve damage on account of mental injury being given in every case where the accident caused by the negligence had given the person a severe nervous shock; 2, that no decision of an English court had been produced in which, upon such facts, damages were recovered; 3, that a decision of the Supreme Court of New York (*Vandebury v. Truax* 4 Denio Sup Ct NY Rep 464), which was relied upon was distinguishable, as being a case of palpable injury.

Of these reasons, the first seems to involve that injuries, other than mental, cannot result from nervous shock, and the third implies that injuries resulting from such a shock cannot be 'palpable'. I am unable (I say it with deference) to follow the reasoning; and further, it seems to me that even were the proposition of law upon which the judgment is based sustainable, the Privy Council were not warranted in assuming as a fact, against the verdict of the jury, and without any special finding with regard to it, that the fright was, in that particular case, unaccompanied by any actual physical injury. Further the judgment assumes, as a matter of law, that nervous shock is something which affects merely the mental functions, and is not in itself a peculiar physical state of the body. This error pervades the entire judgment. Mr Beven states, in his recent work on *Negligence* (p 67), and I entirely concur with him, that 'the starting-point of the reasoning there is that nervous shock and mental shock are identical; and that they are opposed to actual physical injury.'

Possibly, were there no decision the other way, I should from courtesy, defer my opinion to that of the Privy Council, and leave it to the plaintiff to question our decision on appeal. The very point, however, had been, four years before the decision of the Privy Council in the *Victoria Railway Commissioners v. Coultas* 13 App Cas 222, decided in this country, first in the Common Pleas Division, then presided over by the present Lord Morris, and afterwards in the Court of Appeal, in a judgment delivered by the late Sir Edward Sullivan; and it is a sad commentary upon our system of reporting that a decision so important and so novel has never found its way into our law reports. The case I refer to is *Byrne v. Great Southern and Western Railway Co,* unreported. It was tried before me on the 5th and 6th of December 1882; and a motion to enter a verdict for the defendants was heard in 1883 by the Common Pleas Division; and by the Court of Appeal in February 1884. It was an action by the Superintendent of the

Telegraph Office at the Limerick Junction station of the defendants' railway. His office consisted of a small building at the end of one of the defendants' sidings, between which and the railway points having been negligently left open, a train entered this siding, broke down the permanent buffer, and the wall of the telegraph office. The plaintiff's case was that by hearing the noise, and seeing the wall falling, he sustained a nervous shock, which resulted in certain injuries to his health. On cross-examination he said, 'A hair on my head was not touched; I swear I received no physical injury; I got a great fright and shock; I do not mean a physical shock; it was the crash and falling in of the office, and it was all falling in.' A verdict having been found for the plaintiff with £325 damages, a motion to set it aside, and enter a verdict for the defendants, on the ground that there was no evidence of injury sufficient to sustain the action, was refused by the Common Pleas Division; and this refusal was reaffirmed by the Court of Appeal.

This case goes much further than is necessary to sustain the direction here, as in it there was nothing in the nature of impact. As between it, by which we are bound, and the decision of the Privy Council, by which we are not, I must prefer the former. I desire, however, to add that I entirely concur in the decision in *Byrne v. Great Southern and Western Railway Co* and that I should have been prepared to have arrived at the same conclusion, even without its high authority. Its importance in the present case is that it renders unnecessary for me to yield my own opinion to the decision in *Victoria Railway Commissioners v. Coultas* 13 App Cas 222.

In conclusion, then, I am of the opinion that, as the relation between fright and injury to the nerve and brain structures of the body is a matter which depends entirely upon scientific and medical testimony, it is impossible for any court to lay down, as a matter of law, that if negligence causes fright, and such fright, in its turn, so affects such structures as to cause injury to health, such injury cannot be a 'consequence which, in the ordinary course of things would flow from the negligence, unless such injury accompany such negligence in point of time.'"

Comments and Questions:
1. Does Palles C.B. introduce any limits to establishing a case for negligently-inflicted nervous shock?

English position

The concern in jurisdictions such as England has been that it is difficult to determine the extent and impact of negligently-induced nervous shock, and that by allowing such claims the courts would be subject to bogus claims: the floodgates argument. Advances in medical knowledge recognised that people could suffer from nervous shock that was not accompanied by physical injury.

The legal issue related to the duty of care in negligence, and how to determine how far the duty should extend. Using straight foreseeability as the test to determine the duty could potentially spread the issue of liability very wide. The dilemma facing the courts was whether to decide that nervous shock is not foreseeable, or to introduce factors that must be present before nervous shock can be argued. The English courts have looked at a number of ways to limit the scope of liability—namely the introduction of primary and secondary victims, and the introduction of policy factors. The question of how to limit the scope of nervous shock came to the fore in *McLoughlin v O'Brian* [1983] 1 A.C. 410.

McLoughlin v O'Brian
Court of Appeal [1983] 1 A.C. 410, [1982] 2 All E.R. 298

Facts: The plaintiff's husband and four children were involved in an accident. The car they were driving was in collision with a lorry driven by the first defendant and owned by the second defendants. This lorry had just collided with an articulated lorry driven by the third defendant and owned by the fourth defendant. At the time of the accident the plaintiff was two miles away; she was informed of the accident by a neighbour and was taken to the hospital to see her family. The plaintiff's youngest daughter was killed and the others were seriously injured. She suffered severe shock and depression and this resulted in psychiatric injury.

This case was instigated against all four defendants for damages for shock-induced injuries. The defendants admitted liability for the death of the plaintiff's daughter and the injuries suffered by the plaintiff's family, but denied that the shock injury was due to their negligence. The claim was initially dismissed. The plaintiff's appeal was also dismissed—it was held that, although it was reasonably foreseeable that injury by shock would be caused to a wife and mother in the position of the plaintiff, it was settled law that the duty of care that was owed by the driver of a vehicle was limited to persons or owners of property at or near the scene of an accident and directly affected by his negligence; that considerations of policy limited the duty of care in that way and did not require it to be extended. This case was appealed to the House of Lords.

Issues: The House of Lords found for the plaintiff, but their Lordships did differ on how such cases should be determined. Below are extracts from two of the judgments in the case, Lord Bridge and Lord Wilberforce, as they represent most accurately the distinctions in reasoning. That distinction relates to whether there is a necessity to introduce policy factors to limit the scope of nervous shock.

Lord Wilberforce:

"Foreseeability, which involves a hypothetical person, looking with hindsight at an event which has occurred, is a formula adopted by English law, not merely for defining, but also for limiting, the persons to whom duty may be owed, and the consequences for which an actor may be held responsible. It is not merely an issue of fact to be left to be found as such. When it is said to result in a duty of care being owed to a person or a class, the statement that there is a 'duty of care' denotes a conclusion into the forming of which considerations of policy have entered. That foreseeability does not of itself, and automatically, lead to a duty of care is, I think, clear. I gave some examples *in Anns v. Merton London Borough Council* [1978] A.C. 728, 752, *Anns* itself being one. I may add what Lord Reid said *in McKew v. Holland & Hannen & Cubitts (Scotland) Ltd.* [1969] 3 All E.R. 1621, 1623:

 'A defender is not liable for a consequence of a kind which is not foreseeable. But it does not follow that he is liable for every consequence which a reasonable man could foresee.'

We must then consider the policy arguments ...

The policy arguments against a wider extension can be stated under four heads.

First, it may be said that such extension may lead to a proliferation of claims, and possibly fraudulent claims, to the establishment of an industry of lawyers and psychiatrists who will formulate a claim for nervous shock damages, including what in America is called the customary miscarriage, for all, or many, road accidents and industrial accidents.

Secondly, it may be claimed that an extension of liability would be unfair to defendants, as imposing damages out of proportion to the negligent conduct complained of. In so far as such defendants are insured, a large additional burden will be placed on insurers, and ultimately upon the class of persons insured—road users or employers.

Thirdly, to extend liability beyond the most direct and plain cases would greatly increase evidentiary difficulties and tend to lengthen litigation.

Fourthly, it may be said—and the Court of Appeal agreed with this—that an extension of the scope of liability ought only to be made by the legislature, after careful research. This is the course which has been taken in New South Wales and the Australian Capital Territory ...

[T]here remains, in my opinion, just because 'shock' in its nature is capable of affecting so wide a range of people, a real need for the law to place some limitation upon the extent of admissible claims. It is necessary to consider three elements inherent in any claim: the class of persons whose claims should be recognised; the proximity of such persons to the accident; and the means by which the shock is caused. As regards the class of persons, the possible range is between the closest of family ties—of parent and child, or husband and wife—

and the ordinary bystander. Existing law recognises the claims of the first: it denies that of the second, either on the basis that such persons must be assumed to be possessed of fortitude sufficient to enable them to endure the calamities of modern life, or that defendants cannot be expected to compensate the world at large. In my opinion, these positions are justifiable, and since the present case falls within the first class, it is strictly unnecessary to say more. I think, however, that it should follow that other cases involving less close relationships must be very carefully scrutinised. I cannot say that they should never be admitted. The closer the tie (not merely in relationship, but in care) the greater the claim for consideration. The claim, in any case, has to be judged in the light of the other factors, such as proximity to the scene in time and place, and the nature of the accident.

As regards proximity to the accident, it is obvious that this must be close in both time and space. It is, after all, the fact and consequence of the defendant's negligence that must be proved to have caused the 'nervous shock.' Experience has shown that to insist on direct and immediate sight or hearing would be impractical and unjust and that under what may be called the 'aftermath' doctrine one who, from close proximity, comes very soon upon the scene should not be excluded. In my opinion, the result in *Benson v. Lee* [1972] V.R. 879 was correct and indeed inescapable. It was based, soundly, upon 'direct perception of some of the events which go to make up the accident as an entire event, and this includes … the immediate aftermath …' (p. 880.) …

Finally, and by way of reinforcement of 'aftermath' cases, I would accept, by analogy with 'rescue' situations, that a person of whom it could be said that one could expect nothing else than that he or she would come immediately to the scene—normally a parent or a spouse—could be regarded as being within the scope of foresight and duty. Where there is not immediate presence, account must be taken of the possibility of alterations in the circumstances, for which the defendant should not be responsible.

Subject only to these qualifications, I think that a strict test of proximity by sight or hearing should be applied by the courts.

Lastly, as regards communication, there is no case in which the law has compensated shock brought about by communication by a third party. In *Hambrook v. Stokes Brothers* [1925] 1 K.B. 141, indeed, it was said that liability would not arise in such a case and this is surely right. It was so decided in *Abramzik v. Brenner* (1967) 65 D.L.R. (2d) 651. The shock must come through sight or hearing of the event or of its immediate aftermath. Whether some equivalent of sight or hearing, e.g. through simultaneous television, would suffice may have to be considered."

Lord Bridge:

"So, the first hurdle which a plaintiff claiming damages of the kind in question must surmount is to establish that he is suffering, not merely grief, distress or any other normal emotion, but a positive psychiatric illness. That is here not in issue. A plaintiff must then establish the necessary chain of causation in fact between his psychiatric illness and the death or injury of one or more third parties negligently caused by the defendant. Here again, this is not in dispute in the instant case. But when causation in fact is in issue, it must no doubt be determined by the judge on the basis of the evidence of psychiatrists. Then, here comes the all-important question. Given the fact of the plaintiff's psychiatric illness caused by the defendant's negligence in killing or physically injuring another, was the chain of causation from the one event to the other, considered ex post facto in the light of all that has happened, 'reasonably foreseeable' by the 'reasonable man'? A moment's thought will show that the answer to that question depends on what knowledge is to be attributed to the hypothetical reasonable man of the operation of cause and effect in psychiatric medicine ... Free of authority, and applying the ordinary criterion of reasonable foreseeability to the facts, with an eye 'enlightened by progressive awareness of mental illness' (the language of Stephenson L.J. [1981] Q.B. 599, 612), any judge must, I would think, share the view of all three members of the Court of Appeal, with which I understand all your Lordships agree, that, in the words of Griffiths L.J., at p. 617, it was

> 'readily foreseeable that a significant number of mothers exposed to such an experience might break down under the shock of the event and suffer illness.'

The question, then, for your Lordships' decision is whether the law, as a matter of policy, draws a line which exempts from liability a defendant whose negligent act or omission was actually and foreseeably the cause of the plaintiff's psychiatric illness and, if so, where that line is to be drawn. In thus formulating the question, I do not, of course, use the word 'negligent' as prejudging the question whether the defendant owes the plaintiff a duty, but I do use the word 'foreseeably' as connoting the normally accepted criterion of such a duty ...

My Lords, looking back I think it is possible to discern that there only ever were two clear lines of limitation of a defendant's liability for 'nervous shock' for which any rational justification could be advanced in the light both of the state of the law of negligence and the state of medical science as judicially understood at the time when those limitations were propounded. In 1888 it was, no doubt, perfectly sensible to say: 'Damages arising from mere sudden terror unaccompanied by any actual physical injury, but occasioning a nervous or mental shock, cannot ... be considered a consequence which, in the ordinary course of things, would flow from ... negligence' (Victorian Railway Commissioners v. Coultas, 13 App.Cas. 222, 225). Here the test, whether of duty or of remoteness, can be recognised as a relatively distant ancestor of the modern criterion of reasonable foreseeability. Again, in 1901 it was, I would suppose, equally sensible to limit a defendant's liability for 'nervous shock' which could 'reasonably or actually be expected' to be such as was suffered by a plaintiff who was himself physically endangered by the defendant's negligence (Dulieu v. White & Sons

[1901] 2 K.B. 669, 675). But once that line of limitation has been crossed, as it was by the majority in Hambrook v. Stokes Brothers [1925] 1 K.B. 141, there can be no logical reason whatever for limiting the defendant's duty to persons in physical proximity to the place where the accident, caused by the defendant's negligence, occurred. Much of the confusion in the authorities since Bourhill v. Young [1943] A.C. 92, including, if I may say so, the judgments of the courts below in the instant case, has arisen, as it seems to me, from the deference still accorded, notwithstanding the acceptance of the Hambrook principle, to dicta of their Lordships in Bourhill v. Young which only make sense if understood as based on the limited principle of liability propounded by Kennedy J. in Dulieu v. White & Sons [1901] 2 K.B. 669, and adopted in the dissenting judgment of Sargant L.J. in Hambrook v. Stokes Brothers ...

In approaching the question whether the law should, as a matter of policy, define the criterion of liability in negligence for causing psychiatric illness by reference to some test other than that of reasonable foreseeability it is well to remember that we are concerned only with the question of liability of a defendant who is, ex hypothesi, guilty of fault in causing the death, injury or danger which has in turn triggered the psychiatric illness. A policy which is to be relied on to narrow the scope of the negligent tortfeasor's duty must be justified by cogent and readily intelligible considerations, and must be capable of defining the appropriate limits of liability by reference to factors which are not purely arbitrary. A number of policy considerations which have been suggested as satisfying these requirements appear to me, with respect, to be wholly insufficient. I can see no grounds whatever for suggesting that to make the defendant liable for reasonably foreseeable psychiatric illness caused by his negligence would be to impose a crushing burden on him out of proportion to his moral responsibility. However liberally the criterion of reasonable foreseeability is interpreted, both the number of successful claims in this field and the quantum of damages they will attract are likely to be moderate. I cannot accept as relevant the well-known phenomenon that litigation may delay recovery from a psychiatric illness. If this were a valid policy consideration, it would lead to the conclusion that psychiatric illness should be excluded altogether from the heads of damage which the law will recognise. It cannot justify limiting the cases in which damages will be awarded for psychiatric illness by reference to the circumstances of its causation. To attempt to draw a line at the furthest point which any of the decided cases happen to have reached, and to say that it is for the legislature, not the courts, to extend the limits of liability any further, would be, to my mind, an unwarranted abdication of the court's function of developing and adapting principles of the common law to changing conditions, in a particular corner of the common law which exemplifies, par excellence, the important and indeed necessary part which that function has to play. In the end I believe that the policy question depends on weighing against each other two conflicting considerations. On the one hand, if the criterion of liability is to be reasonable foreseeability simpliciter, this must, precisely because questions of causation in psychiatric medicine give rise to difficulty and uncertainty, introduce an element of uncertainty into the law and open the way to a number of arguable claims which a more precisely fixed criterion of liability would exclude. I accept that the element of uncertainty is an important factor. I believe that the 'floodgates' argument, however, is, as it always has been, greatly exaggerated. On the other hand, it seems to me inescapable that any attempt to define the limit of liability by requiring, in addition to reasonable foreseeability, that the plaintiff claiming damages for psychiatric illness should have witnessed the relevant accident, should have been present at or near the place where it happened, should have come upon its aftermath and thus have had some direct perception of it, as opposed to merely learning of it after the event, should be related in some particular degree to the accident victim—to draw a line by reference to any of these criteria must impose a largely arbitrary limit of liability. I accept, of course, the importance of the factors indicated in the guidelines suggested by Tobriner J. in Dillon v. Legg, 29 A.L.R. 3d 1316 as bearing upon the degree of foreseeability of the plaintiff's psychiatric illness ...

My Lords, I have no doubt that this is an area of the law of negligence where we should resist the temptation to try yet once more to freeze the law in a rigid posture which would deny justice to some who, in the application of the classic principles of negligence derived from *Donoghue v. Stevenson* [1932] A.C. 562, ought to succeed, in the interests of certainty, where the very subject matter is uncertain and continuously developing, or in the interests of saving defendants and their insurers from the burden of having sometimes to resist doubtful claims."

Comments and Questions:

1. Lord Wilberforce states the necessity of policy arguments to limit the scope of liability in nervous shock cases: what are the policy arguments he sets out?

2. What are the necessary elements in establishing a case in nervous shock applying the principles used by Lord Bridge?

3. Compare and contrast the approaches taken by Lord Wilberforce and Lord Bridge.

In the immediate aftermath of this case the decision of Lord Bridge held sway in a number of cases: see *Attia v British Gas* [1988] Q.B. 304 and *Ravenscroft v Rederiaktiebølaget Transatlantic* [1991] 3 All E.R. 73. Ultimately, the policy factors espoused by Lord Wilberforce were adopted in the decision of *Alcock v Chief Constable of South Yorkshire* [1991] 3 W.L.R. 1055.

Alcock v Chief Constable of the South Yorkshire Police
House of Lords [1992] 1 A.C. 310, [1991] 4 All E.R. 907,
[1991] 3 W.L.R. 1057, 8 B.M.L.R. 37

Facts: This case arose out of the Hillsborough disaster. Prior to the commencement of a football match between Liverpool and Nottingham Forest at the
Hillsborough stadium, the police negligently allowed a large number of spectators
to have access to an already full stadium. A crush ensued, resulting in the death
of some 95 spectators and more than 400 injuries. The match, and the resulting
disaster, was shown live on television. However, in accordance with television
broadcasting guidelines, none of the television broadcasts depicted suffering or
dying of recognisable individuals. The claimants to this action all suffered forms
of nervous shock, and represented different groups that could be affected. Some
were present in the stadium, some watched events unfold on the television,
others listened to it on the radio. These plaintiffs also varied in relationships to
the dead and injured, including brothers, sisters, mothers, fathers, grandparents,
brothers-in-law and fiancés.

The Chief Constable admitted liability in negligence in respect of those who
were killed and injured in the disaster, but denied that he owed any duty of care
to the plaintiffs. The question was whether they were entitled in law to recover
damages for nervous shock. The judge found in favour of 10 of the plaintiffs
and against six of them. The defendant appealed in respect of nine of the 10
successful plaintiffs and the six unsuccessful plaintiffs cross-appealed. The
Court of Appeal allowed the appeals and dismissed the cross appeals, holding
that none of the plaintiffs were entitled to recover damages for nervous shock.
Ten of the plaintiffs appealed this decision to the House of Lords.

Issues: The essential issue in this case was whether nervous shock was foreseeable
or not. In *McLoughlin v O'Brian* Lord Bridge had opted for straight foreseeability,
whereas Lord Wilberforce wanted the introduction of policy factors: proximity of
time, space and relationship before allowing recovery for nervous shock. The
House of Lords held that a person who sustained nervous shock as a result of
apprehending physical injury to another person could only recover damages from
the person whose negligent act caused the physical injury if they satisfied both the
test of reasonable foreseeability and the test of proximity. The plaintiff needed to
establish a relationship to the primary victim that was sufficiently close, proximity
to the accident in both time and space, and to show that the plaintiff suffered
nervous shock as a result. As a result none of the appellants succeeded in
establishing nervous shock, and the appeals were dismissed.

Lord Ackner:

"In *Hay (or Bourhill) v Young* [1942] 2 All ER 396 at 402, [1943] AC 92 at 103
Lord Macmillan said:

'In the case of mental shock ... there are elements of greater subtlety than in the case of an ordinary physical injury and these elements may give rise to debate as to the precise scope of the legal liability.'

It is now generally accepted that an analysis of the reported cases of nervous shock establishes that it is a type of claim in a category of its own. Shock is no longer a variant of physical injury but a separate kind of damage. Whatever may be the pattern of the future development of the law in relation to this cause of action, the following propositions illustrate that the application simpliciter of the reasonable foreseeability test is, today, far from being operative.

(1) Even though the risk of psychiatric illness is reasonably foreseeable, the law gives no damages if the psychiatric injury was not induced by shock. Psychiatric illnesses caused in other ways, such as from the experience of having to cope with the deprivation consequent upon the death of a loved one, attracts no damages. Brennan J in *Jaensch's* case (1984) 54 ALR 417 at 429 gave as examples: the spouse who has been worn down by caring for a tortiously injured husband or wife and who suffers psychiatric illness as a result, but who, nevertheless, goes without compensation; a parent made distraught by the wayward conduct of a brain-damaged child and who suffers psychiatric illness as a result also has no claim against the tortfeasor liable to the child.

(2) Even where the nervous shock and the subsequent psychiatric illness caused by it could both have been reasonably foreseen, it has been generally accepted that damages for merely being informed of, or reading, or hearing about the accident are not recoverable. In *Bourhill v Young* [1942] 2 All ER 396 at 402, [1943] AC 92 at 103 Lord Macmillan only recognised the action lying where the injury by shock was sustained 'through the medium of the eye or the ear without direct contact'. Certainly Brennan J in his judgment in *Jaensch's* case 54 ALR 417 at 430 recognised that 'A psychiatric illness induced by mere knowledge of a distressing fact is not compensable; perception by the plaintiff of the distressing phenomenon is essential'. That seems also to have been the view of Bankes LJ in *Hambrook v Stokes Bros* [1925] 1 KB 141 at 152, [1924] All ER Rep 110 at 117...

(3) Mere mental suffering, although reasonably foreseeable, if unaccompanied by physical injury, is not a basis for a claim for damages. To fill this gap in the law a very limited category of relatives are given a statutory right by the Administration of Justice Act 1982, s 3, inserting a new s 1A into the Fatal Accidents Act 1976 to bring an action claiming damages for bereavement.

(4) As yet there is no authority establishing that there is liability on the part of the injured person, his or her estate, for mere psychiatric injury which was sustained by another by reason of shock, as a result of a self-inflicted death, injury or peril of the negligent person, in circumstances where the risk of such psychiatric injury was reasonably foreseeable. On the basis that there

must be a limit at some reasonable point to the extent of the duty of care owed to third parties which rests upon everyone in all his actions. Lord Robertson, the Lord Ordinary, in his judgment in Bourhill's case 1941 SC 395 at 399, did not view with favour the suggestion that a negligent window-cleaner who loses his grip and falls from a height, impaling himself on spiked railings, would be liable for the shock-induced psychiatric illness occasioned to a pregnant woman looking out of the window of a house situated on the opposite side of the street.

(5) 'Shock', in the context of this cause of action, involves the sudden appreciation by sight or sound of a horrifying event, which violently agitates the mind. It has yet to include psychiatric illness caused by the accumulation over a period of time of more gradual assaults on the nervous system.

I do not find it surprising that in this particular area of the tort of negligence, the reasonable foreseeability test is not given a free rein. As Lord Reid said in *McKew v Holland & Hannen & Cubitts (Scotland) Ltd* [1969] 3 All ER 1621 at 1623:

'A defender is not liable for the consequence of a kind which is not foreseeable. But it does not follow that he is liable for every consequence which a reasonable man could foresee.'

Deane J pertinently observed in *Jaensch's* case (1984) 54 ALR 417 at 443:

'Reasonable foreseeability on its own indicates no more than that such a duty of care will exist if, and to the extent that, it is not precluded or modified by some applicable overriding requirement or limitation. It is to do little more than to state a truism to say that the essential function of such requirements or limitations is to confine the existence of a duty to take reasonable care to avoid reasonable foreseeable injury to the circumstances or classes of case in which it is the policy of the law to admit it. Such overriding requirements or limitations shape the frontiers of the common law of negligence.'

Although it is a vital step towards the establishment of liability, the satisfaction of the test of reasonable foreseeability does not, in my judgment, ipso facto satisfy Lord Atkin's well-known neighbourhood principle enunciated in *M'Alister (or Donoghue) v Stevenson* [1932] AC 562 at 580, [1932] All ER Rep 1 at 11. For him to have been reasonably in contemplation by a defendant he must be:

'... so closely and directly affected by my act that I ought reasonably to have them in contemplation as being so affected when I am directing my mind to the acts or omissions which are called in question.'

The requirement contained in the words 'so closely and directly affected ... that' constitutes a control upon the test of reasonable foreseeability of injury. Lord Atkin was at pains to stress that the formulation of a duty of care, merely in the general terms of reasonable foreseeability, would be too wide unless it were 'limited by the notion of proximity' which was embodied in the restriction of the duty of care to one's neighbour' (see [1932] AC 562 at 580–582, [1932] All ER Rep 1 at 11–12).

The three elements
Because 'shock' in its nature is capable of affecting such a wide range of persons, Lord Wilberforce in *McLoughlin v O'Brian* [1982] 2 All ER 298 at 304, [1983] 1 AC 410 at 422 concluded that there was a real need for the law to place some limitation upon the extent of admissible claims and in this context he considered that there were three elements inherent in any claim. It is common ground that such elements do exist and are required to be considered in connection with all these claims. The fundamental difference in approach is that on behalf of the plaintiffs it is contended that the consideration of these three elements is merely part of the process of deciding whether, as a matter of fact, the reasonable foreseeability test has been satisfied. On behalf of the chief constable it is contended that these elements operate as a control or limitation on the mere application of the reasonable foreseeability test. They introduce the requirement of 'proximity' as conditioning the duty of care.

The three elements are: (1) the class of persons whose claims should be recognised; (2) the proximity of such persons to the accident—in time and space; (3) the means by which the shock has been caused.

I will deal with those three elements seriatim.

The class of persons whose claim should be recognised
When dealing with the possible range of the class of persons who might sue, Lord Wilberforce contrasted the closest of family ties—parent and child and husband and wife—with that of the ordinary bystander. He said that while existing law recognises the claims of the first, it denied that of the second, either on the basis that such persons must be assumed to be possessed with fortitude sufficient to enable them to endure the calamities of modern life, or that defendants cannot be expected to compensate the world at large. He considered that these positions were justified, that other cases involving less close relationships must be very carefully considered, adding ([1982] 2 All ER 298 at 304, [1983] 1 AC 410 at 422):

> 'The closer the tie (not merely in relationship, but in care) the greater the claim for consideration. The claim, in any case, has to be judged in the light of the other facts, such as proximity to the scene in time and place, and the nature of the accident.'

I respectfully share the difficulty expressed by Atkin LJ in *Hambrook v Stokes Bros* [1925] 1 KB 141 at 158–159, [1924] All ER Rep 110 at 117—how do you explain why the duty is confined to the case of parent or guardian and child and does not extend to other relations of life also involving intimate associations;

and why does it not eventually extend to bystanders? As regards the latter category, while it may be very difficult to envisage a case of a stranger, who is not actively and foreseeably involved in a disaster or its aftermath, other than in the role of rescuer, suffering shock-induced psychiatric injury by the mere observation of apprehended or actual injury of a third person in circumstances that could be considered reasonably foreseeable, I see no reason in principle why he should not, if in the circumstances, a reasonably strong-nerved person would have been so shocked. In the course of argument your Lordships were given, by way of an example, that of a petrol tanker careering out of control into a school in session and bursting into flames. I would not be prepared to rule out a potential claim by a passer-by so shocked by the scene as to suffer psychiatric illness.

As regards claims to those in the close family relationships referred to by Lord Wilberforce, the justification for admitting such claims is the presumption, which I would accept as being rebuttable, that the love and affection normally associated with persons in those relationships is such that a defendant ought reasonably to contemplate that they may be so closely and directly affected by his conduct as to suffer shock resulting in psychiatric illness. While as a generalisation more remote relatives and, a fortiori, friends, can reasonably be expected not to suffer illness from the shock, there can well be relatives and friends whose relationship is so close and intimate that their love and affection for the victim is comparable to that of the normal parent, spouse or child of the victim and should for the purpose of this cause of action be so treated ...

The proximity of the plaintiff to the accident
It is accepted that the proximity to the accident must be close both in time and space. Direct and immediate sight or hearing of the accident is not required. It is reasonably foreseeable that injury by shock can be caused to a plaintiff, not only through the sight or hearing of the event, but of its immediate aftermath.
Only two of the plaintiffs before us were at the ground. However, it is clear from McLoughlin's case that there may be liability where subsequent identification can be regarded as part of the 'immediate aftermath' of the accident. Mr Alcock identified his brother-in-law in a bad condition in the mortuary at about midnight, that is some eight hours after the accident. This was the earliest of the identification cases. Even if this identification could be described as part of the 'aftermath', it could not in my judgment be described as part of the immediate aftermath. McLoughlin's case was described by Lord Wilberforce as being upon the margin of what the process of logical progression from case to case would allow. Mrs McLoughlin had arrived at the hospital within an hour or so after the accident. Accordingly, in the post-accident identification cases before your Lordships there was not sufficient proximity in time and space to the accident.

The means by which the shock is caused
Lord Wilberforce concluded that the shock must come through sight or hearing of the event or its immediate aftermath but specifically left for later

consideration whether some equivalent of sight or hearing, e.g. through simultaneous television, would suffice (see [1982] 2 All ER 298 at 305, [1983] 1 AC 410 at 423). Of course it is common ground that it was clearly foreseeable by the chief constable that the scenes at Hillsborough would be broadcast live and that amongst those who would be watching would be parents and spouses and other relatives and friends of those in the pens behind the goal at the Leppings lane end. However he would also know of the code of ethics which the television authorities televising this event could be expected to follow, namely that they would not show pictures of suffering by recognisable individuals. Had they done so, Mr Hytner accepted that this would have been a 'novus actus' breaking the chain of causation between the chief constable's alleged breach of duty and the psychiatric illness. As the chief constable was reasonably entitled to expect to be the case, there were no such pictures. Although the television pictures certainly gave rise to feelings of the deepest anxiety and distress, in the circumstances of this case the simultaneous television broadcasts of what occurred cannot be equated with the 'sight or hearing of the event or its immediate aftermath'. Accordingly shocks sustained by reason of these broadcasts cannot found a claim. I agree, however, with Nolan LJ that simultaneous broadcasts of a disaster cannot in all cases be ruled out as providing the equivalent of the actual sight or hearing of the event or its immediate aftermath. Nolan LJ gave an example of a situation where it was reasonable to anticipate that the television cameras, whilst filming and transmitting pictures of a special event of children travelling in a balloon, in which there was media interest, particularly amongst the parents, showed the balloon suddenly bursting into flames (see [1991] 3 All ER 88 at 122). Many other such situations could be imagined where the impact of the simultaneous television pictures would be as great, if not greater, than the actual sight of the accident.

Conclusion

Only one of the plaintiffs who succeeded before Hidden J, namely Brian Harrison, was at the ground. His relatives who died were his two brothers. The quality of brotherly love is well known to differ widely from Cain and Abel to David and Jonathan. I assume that Mr Harrison's relationship with his brothers was not an abnormal one. His claim was not presented upon the basis that there was such a close and intimate relationship between them as gave rise to that very special bond of affection which would make his shock-induced psychiatric illness reasonably foreseeable by the chief constable. Accordingly, the learned judge did not carry out the requisite close scrutiny of their relationship. Thus there was no evidence to establish the necessary proximity which would make his claim reasonably foreseeable and, subject to the other factors, to which I have referred, a valid one. The other plaintiff who was present at the ground, Robert Alcock, lost a brother-in-law. He was not, in my judgment, reasonably foreseeable as a potential sufferer from shock-induced psychiatric illness, in default of very special facts and none was established. Accordingly their claims must fail, as must those of the other plaintiffs who only learnt of the disaster by watching simultaneous television. I, too, would therefore dismiss these appeals."

Comments and Questions:
1. The House of Lords in this action adopted the policy limitations first suggested by Lord Wilberforce. This serves to limit the potential actions in cases claiming nervous shock. This case represents the position currently adopted by the English courts to nervous shock; it is important to note that there is a divergence between Irish and English law on this area of law.

Irish position

Irish courts have historically been more open to allowing recovery for nervous shock. This position commenced with the cases of *Byrne v Southern and Western Railway Co.,* Court of Appeal, February 1884, and *Bell v Great Northern Railway Co,* 26 I.R. (Ir) 428 (above). In both of these cases the plaintiffs themselves were in physical danger; the more modern cases have focused on the position of plaintiffs who have come to the accident in its immediate aftermath, including *Mullally v Bus Éireann* [1992] I.L.R.M. 522, *Kelly v Hennessy* [1995] 3 I.R. 253, *Curran v Cadbury (Ireland) Ltd.* (2000) I.L.T. 140, and *Cuddy v May,* unreported, High Court, November 2003.

Mullally v Bus Éireann
High Court [1992] I.L.R.M. 522

Facts: The plaintiff's husband and three of their sons left Limerick to attend a soccer match; they travelled by means of a CIÉ bus. During the course of the day the plaintiff received news that there had been a serious bus accident that involved her family. The bus had overturned, resulting in three deaths and injuries to 49 passengers. The plaintiff went to the Regional Hospital in Limerick where two of her sons were being treated; the injuries were so serious that she did not recognise one of her sons. While at the hospital she witnessed some terrifying and appalling scenes. She then went to Barrington's Hospital where her other son and husband were in care and she was told that her husband was dying. In time two of her sons and her husband recovered and were able to come home. Her youngest son, Paul, was critically ill; he underwent several operations over the following months and suffered terribly. Some eight months after the accident he died.

Issues: This case represents the Irish courts' first attempt since *Bell v Great Northern Railway Company of Ireland* (1896) 26 L.R. (Ir.) 428 to address the issue of nervous shock. The question before the court was whether the negligence of the defendants which resulted in the accident and the illness of the plaintiff was reasonably foreseeable by a reasonable man. Should the courts adopt the ordinary criteria of reasonable foreseeability, or should they impose policy restrictions in the manner of our neighbouring jurisdiction? Denham J. was guided by Lord Bridge from the *McLoughlin v O'Brian* decision and held that nervous shock was reasonably foreseeable and that the issue was to establish the chain of causation from the crash to the illness of the plaintiff. The plaintiff succeeded in recovering for nervous shock.

Denham J.:

"Post traumatic stress disorder has five criteria and they are as follows:

1. Exposure to a recognisable stress or trauma outside the range of usual human experience, which would evoke significant symptoms of distress in almost anyone ...
2. Re-experiencing of the trauma through intrusive memories, nightmares or flashbacks or intensification of symptoms through exposure to situations resembling or symbolising the event ...
3. Avoidance of stimuli related to the trauma or numbing of general responsiveness indicated by avoidance of thoughts or feelings, or of situations associated with the trauma, amnesia for important aspects of the trauma, diminished interest in activities, feelings of estrangement from others, constricted effect, sense of foreshortened future ...
4. Increased arousal indicated by sleep disturbance, anger outbursts, difficulty concentrating, hyper vigilance, exaggerated startle response, psychological reactivity to situations resembling or symbolising the trauma ...
5. Duration of disturbance at least one month ...

It is established factually in this case that the plaintiff suffers from a psychiatric illness as a result of an accident caused by the defendants and its aftermath. It is not her grief which caused her illness, it was the accident and its aftermath. But the question of law from this Court is whether the chain of causation from the crash caused by the defendants to the illness of the plaintiff is reasonably foreseeable by the reasonable man. Applying the ordinary criteria of reasonable foreseeability to the facts, and in view of our ever advancing awareness of medical knowledge of mental illness, I consider it is readily foreseeable that a mother exposed to the experience herein, would break down and suffer illness, as did the plaintiff. I consider that the law does not create any bar to this conclusion. The law as to grief and anguish and mental distress is set out in the *Civil Liability Act 1961* but it is a different matter and has been met. Grief did not cause this illness. I consider that there is no policy in Irish law opposed to a finding of nervous shock, an old term covering post traumatic stress disorder.

Indeed the Irish courts were one of the first to find that such an illness existed and was compensatable: See *Byrne v Great Southern and Western Railway Company of Ireland (1884)* cited at 26 LR Ir 428 and *Bell v Great Northern Railway Company of Ireland* (1896) 26 LR (Ir) 428. Both are referred to in *Irish Law of Torts*, McMahon and Binchy, 2nd ed., p. 306–307. In the latter case Palles CB said:

> 'As the relation between fright and injury to the nerve and brain structures of the body is a matter which depends entirely upon scientific and medical testimony, it is impossible for any court to lay down, as a matter of law, that if negligence causes fright, and such fright, in its turn, so affects such structures as to cause injury to health, such injury cannot be *"a consequence which, in the ordinary course of things would flow from the negligence"* unless such injury *"accompany such negligence in point of time".'*

Murphy J also stated that it appeared to him:

> 'immaterial whether the injuries may be called nervous shock, brain disturbance, mental shock or injury. The only questions to be considered, in my opinion, are: was the health or capacity of the plaintiff for the discharge of her duties and enjoyment of life affected by what occurred to her whilst in the carriage? Next, was this caused by the negligence of the defendants?'

Thus the law is that a person who suffers nervous shock which results in psychiatric illness may succeed against the person who caused the nervous shock. The question then is whether the causation, nexus, exists between the defendant's negligence and the plaintiff's illness as the plaintiff was not at the scene of the accident.

It appears to me that the causal link is there; that the illness was reasonably foreseeable. The facts of this case clearly establish, an horrific situation for the plaintiff from the time of learning of the accident, through her journey to the hospital, to the appalling sights at the hospital, the terrifying sights of her sons Paul and Francis, and the fact of her apparently dying husband. All these events were caused by the accident caused by the defendants. It would be unjust, and contrary to the fundamental doctrine of negligence, not to find that there is a legal nexus between the actions of the defendants causing the accident, and the resultant aftermath of the accident in the scenes in the hospitals in the early hours of 27 April 1987 and the injuries of the plaintiff's three sons and husband. There was no other cause of the scenes in the hospital or the injuries to the children and the husband other than the defendant's negligence. The shock of the plaintiff was foreseeable. The duty of care of the defendants extends as to injuries which are reasonably foreseeable. Thus the defendants had a duty of care to the plaintiff. I consider that there is no bar in law, or under the Constitution, to this determination. If it causes commercial concern then that is a matter for another place, where a policy can be established in the law. It appears to me to come under the fundamental principles of the law of negligence to hold the defendants liable for reasonably foreseeable psychiatric illness caused by his negligence.

I have been referred to *McLoughlin v O'Brian* [1982] 2 All ER 298. I have been assisted by this case. While today's case would appear to fall within the parameters set by Lord Wilberforce, I am guided more by Lord Bridge."

Comments and Questions:

1. Denham J. clarifies that she is guided by the position Lord Bridge takes in *McLoughlin v O'Brian* [1982] 2 All E.R. 298. In applying this rule she sets out that the crucial question is whether "causation, nexus, exists between the defendant's negligence and the plaintiff's illness as the plaintiff was not at the scene of the accident." Based on Denham J.'s position here she clearly sets out the chain of events that are necessary to establish liability in an action of nervous shock. The illness must be foreseeable, and the result of defendant's negligence.

2. Denham J. legally recognises the condition of post-traumatic stress disorder and sets out the criteria necessary to establish same. What are those criteria?

The Supreme Court next dealt with the issue of nervous shock in the case of *Kelly v Hennessy* [1995] 2 All E.R. 298.

Kelly v Hennessy
Supreme Court [1995] 3 I.R. 253; [1996] 1 I.L.R.M. 321

Facts: The defendant was involved in a collision with the plaintiff's husband and two daughters who suffered severe personal injuries, loss and damage for which they have recovered damages against the defendant. The plaintiff to this action was not within sight or sound of the accident, but claimed that she suffered injury as a result of the defendant's negligence. The accident occurred when the plaintiff's husband and two daughters left home to travel to the airport to collect the plaintiff's niece. During that evening the niece telephoned the plaintiff and told her that her husband and two children were seriously injured in an accident. On hearing the news, the plaintiff began to vomit; and on arriving at the hospital she saw each of her family members, all of whom were in an appalling condition. She described one member of her family as looking like mince-meat. Her family remained in hospital for some time. The plaintiff's husband and daughter were brain-damaged and the plaintiff cared for both of them. The second daughter made a full recovery from her injuries. The plaintiff herself suffered from post-traumatic stress disorder, and continued to suffer serious depression. The High Court judge found for the plaintiff, and allowed her to recover damages against the defendant for nervous shock. The defendants appealed to the Supreme Court.

Issues: In this decision, Hamilton C.J. set out five principles that need to be complied with to establish nervous shock. He reiterated that there were no public policy criteria to limit a claim once the five principles were complied with. The court held that the plaintiff was entitled to recover for nervous shock.

Hamilton C.J. (Egan J. concurring):

"In the course of his judgment in *McLoughlin v O'Brien* [1982] 2 All E.R. 298 (hereinafter referred to as *McLoughlin's* case) Lord Wilberforce stated:—

> 'While damages cannot, at common law, be awarded for grief and sorrow, a claim for damages for nervous shock caused by negligence can be made without the necessity of showing direct impact or fear of immediate personal injuries for oneself.'

The cases seem to establish that in order to succeed in an action for damages for nervous shock a Plaintiff must establish the following:—

1. The Plaintiff must establish that he or she actually suffered 'nervous shock'. This term has been used to describe 'any recognisable psychiatric illness' and a plaintiff must prove that he or she suffered a recognisable psychiatric illness if he or she is to recover damages for 'nervous shock'…
2. A plaintiff must establish that his or her recognisable psychiatric illness was 'shock-induced'.

This principle was enunciated in the Australian case of *Jaensch v Coffey* [1984] 155 CLR 549, by Brennan J as follows:—

> 'A plaintiff may recover only if the psychiatric illness is the result of physical injury inflicted on him by the Defendant or if it is induced by shock. Psychiatric illness caused in other ways attracts no damages, though it is reasonably foreseeable that psychiatric illness might be a consequence of the defendant's carelessness.'…

3. A plaintiff must prove that the nervous shock was caused by a defendant's act or omission …
4. The nervous shock sustained by a Plaintiff must be by reason of actual or apprehended physical injury to the Plaintiff or a person other than the Plaintiff.

This view was clearly expressed by Deane J in *Jaensch v Coffey* 155 CLR 540 as being the present state of the law when he said that a duty of care (and hence liability for nervous shock) will not exist unless 'the reasonably foreseeable psychiatric injury was sustained as a result of the death, injury or peril of someone other than the person whose carelessness caused the injury' …

5. If a Plaintiff wishes to recover damages for negligently inflicted nervous
   shock he must show that the defendant owed him or her a duty of care not
   to cause him a reasonably foreseeable injury in the form of nervous shock.
   ...

It was stated by Brennan J now Chief Justice of Australia, in the case of *Jaensch
v Coffey*, 155 CLR 540 already referred to, that:—

> 'It is not necessary that the precise events leading to the administration of the
> shock should be foreseeable. It is sufficient that shock and a psychiatric
> illness induced by it are reasonably foreseeable'

and

> 'It is not necessary for a plaintiff to prove that a reasonable man in the
> defendant's position could foresee that any particular psychiatric illness might
> be caused by his conduct: it suffices that he could have foreseen that his
> conduct might cause some recognised psychiatric illness by shock.' ...

[T]he question relevant to this appeal is whether the Respondent came within
the scope of the Appellant's duty of care and the fact that she does so is not in
issue ...

There is no doubt but that nervous shock and a psychiatric illness induced by
it are reasonably foreseeable consequences of the Appellant's negligence in this
case.

Nor is there any doubt but that the Respondent came within the Appellant's
duty of care.

The acts of negligence on the part of the Appellant which occasioned the
injuries to her husband and two daughters occurred out of sight and earshot of
the Respondent.

However, the law permits of the recovery of damages for nervous shock and
psychiatric illness induced thereby where a plaintiff comes on the immediate
aftermath of the accident.

The relationship between the Plaintiff and the person injured must be close.
As stated by Gibbs CJ in *Jaensch v Coffey* 155 CLR 540:—

> 'where the relationship between the person killed or physically injured and
> the person who suffers shock is close and intimate ... it is readily defensible
> on grounds of policy to allow recovery'.

Lord Wilberforce in the course of his judgment in *McLoughlin v O'Brien* [1982]
2 All ER stated at page 304:—

> 'The closer the tie (nor merely in relationship but in care) the greater the claim
> for consideration' ...

Both the House of Lords and the High Court of Australia held that it was
sufficient that the psychiatric illness which the plaintiffs suffered were as a

result of what the plaintiffs saw or heard in the aftermath of the accident at the scene or even at the hospital where the injured relatives were taken as a result of the accidents.

As Brennan J stated:—

'liability cannot rationally depend on a race between a spouse and an ambulance.'

The Respondent's ties with her husband and daughters could not be closer and the effect of the learned trial judge's judgment in this case is that the nervous shock and psychiatric illness suffered by the Respondent was caused to her by what she learned in the phone call from her niece in the immediate aftermath of the accident and what she heard and saw at the hospital immediately thereafter.

...

There is no public policy that the Respondent's claim, if substantiated should be excluded."

Denham J.:

"PROXIMITY
This case turns on the issue of proximity. There are several aspects of proximity. These may include: (a) proximity of relationship between persons; (b) proximity in a spatial context; and (c) proximity in a temporal sense.

(a) PROXIMITY OF RELATIONSHIPS
The proximity of relationship between the primary victim and the secondary victim is a critical factor. In this case there is a close relationship between the persons injured in the accident and the Appellant. This concept was not an issue before the Court.

(b) SPATIAL PROXIMITY
It is evident that the Appellant was not at the scene of the accident. However, she was told of the event on the telephone shortly thereafter, and she went immediately to the hospital. She viewed her loved ones who were in a very serious condition. She perceived the aftermath of the road traffic accident in the hospital. These facts are not in contention.

(c) TEMPORAL PROXIMITY ie, PROXIMITY IN TIME
It is on the issue of proximity in time that this case turns. The Appellant's case is that the post-traumatic stress disorder arose later in time than the accident, that it arose as a result of the events in the weeks and months after the accident. The learned Trial Judge stated:—

'I am, therefore, satisfied that the [Respondent] suffered immediate nervous shock resulting in vomiting on receiving the telephone call concerning her family's accident. This condition was, in my view, gravely aggravated by the scenes she immediately thereafter witnessed in Jervis Street hospital.

I am satisfied that the post-traumatic stress disorder which Doctor Corry has given evidence of continued up to 1992, at the earliest.

... I ... find that this [Respondent] is entitled to recover as against the [Appellant] for nervous shock.'

It was conceded by Counsel for the Appellant that the Respondent suffered from a post-traumatic stress disorder some time after the accident. It was appropriate for Mr Haugh to so concede, in view of the facts found by the learned Trial Judge on the evidence and the jurisprudence of this Court: see *Hay v O'Grady* [1992] IR 210 at page 217. This case falls to be determined on the very precise issue as to the temporal proximity of the post-traumatic stress disorder, ie when did the post-traumatic stress disorder occur: did it arise after the accident or some weeks or months later? This is a question of fact. Several matters are relevant to this issue.

First, to take the commonsense approach. The illness in question arises as a result of a shock, of exposure to a trauma far outside the usual range of experience. There is no doubt that the accident exposed the Respondent to such a trauma.

Secondly, the learned Trial Judge has found a continuum of nervous stress, post-traumatic stress disorder, and depression from the accident. That continuum is based on credible evidence before the Court.

Thirdly, the finding of the learned Trial Judge is as to an immediate 'nervous shock' and then he refers to post-traumatic stress disorder. The shock is the trigger for the following events. There is evidence from Dr Corry that the psychiatric illness developed in the initial few days when the patients were in hospital ...

There was the above and other evidence upon which the High Court could (and did) conclude that the post-traumatic stress disorder occurred at a time proximate to the accident. These are facts found on credible evidence. It is clear from the text and context of the judgment that the learned Trial Judge used the term 'immediate nervous shock' to indicate the immediate reaction to the accident, the shock, which, together with the aftermath, triggered the on-set of the post-traumatic stress disorder.

LAW
The law on the issue is to be found in common law. It is useful to consider cases in other jurisdictions. In *McLoughlin v O'Brien*, [1983] AC 410, the plaintiff's husband and three children were involved in a road accident ...

Lord Bridge of Harwich stated:—

'The question, then, for your Lordships' decision is whether the law, as a matter of policy, draws a line which exempts from liability a defendant whose negligent act or omission was actually and foreseeably the cause of the plaintiff's psychiatric illness and, if so, where that line is to be drawn. In thus formulating the question, I do not, of course, use the word "negligent" as prejudging the question whether the defendant owes the plaintiff a duty, but I do use the word 'foreseeably' as connoting the normally accepted criterion of such a duty.'

After analysing the authorities he stated:—

"In approaching the question whether the law should, as a matter of policy, define the criterion of liability in negligence for causing psychiatric illness by reference to some test other than that of reasonable foreseeability it is well to remember that we are concerned only with the question of liability of a defendant who is, ex hypothesi, guilty of fault in causing the death, injury or danger which has in turn triggered the psychiatric illness. A policy which is to be relied on to narrow the scope of the negligent tortfeasor's duty must be justified by cogent and readily intelligible considerations, and must be capable of defining the appropriate limits of liability by reference to factors which are not purely arbitrary ... On the one hand, if the criterion of liability is to be reasonable foreseeability simpliciter, this must, precisely because questions of causation in psychiatric medicine give rise to difficulty and uncertainty, introduce an element of uncertainty into the law and open the way to a number of arguable claims which a more precisely fixed criterion of liability would exclude. I accept that the element of uncertainty is an important factor. I believe that the "floodgates" argument, however, is, as it always has been, greatly exaggerated . . .'

'My Lords, I have no doubt that this is an area of the law of negligence where we should resist the temptation to try yet once more to freeze the law in a rigid posture which would deny justice to some who, in the application of the classic principles of negligence derived from *Donoghue v Stevenson* [1932] AC 562 [1932] All ER Rep 1, ought to succeed, in the interests of certainty, where the very subject matter is uncertain and continuously developing, or in the interests of saving defendants and their insurers from the burden of having sometimes to resist doubtful claims.'

Lord Wilberforce took a more restricted view and held that the application of the reasonable foreseeability test for nervous shock cases should be limited in terms of proximity. The proximity has three elements: the proximity of the tie or relationship between the plaintiff and the injured person; the proximity of the plaintiff to the accident in time and space; and the proximity of the communication of the accident to the plaintiff, either through sight or hearing of the event or its immediate aftermath.

In Australia, in *Jaensch v Coffey*, 155 CLR 540, a wife, who was not at the scene of the road traffic accident was brought to hospital where she saw her husband who was 'pretty-bad'. Next morning he was in intensive care, she was told he had taken a change for the worse, and she was required to come to hospital as quickly as possible. Her husband survived but she suffered nervous shock as a result of what she had seen and been told. The driver of the car was held to owe a duty of care to her and that he had been in breach of that duty. Gibbs CJ stated:—

> 'In the present case there was a very close relationship, both legal and actual, between the respondent and her husband. She was notified of the accident, and went to the hospital, as soon as practicable on the evening when it occurred. She personally perceived the aftermath of the accident, although not at the scene but at the hospital.
>
> ... She was, in my opinion, a "neighbour" of the appellant within Lord Atkin's principle; it was foreseeable that a person in her position would suffer nervous shock, and there is no reason of policy why her claim should not succeed.'

A number of other members of the High Court of Australia held views similar to those of Bridge LJ in *McLoughlin v O'Brien.*

In this jurisdiction in *Mullally v Bus Eireann,* 1992 ILRM 722, it was found as a fact that the plaintiff, the wife and mother of primary victims, who was not at the scene of a serious bus accident but viewed its aftermath in hospitals, suffered the psychiatric illness of post-traumatic stress disorder which was triggered by the news of the accident and her experiences in its aftermath, the illness manifesting itself two days after the accident, was entitled to damages.

I have considered the above cases, and the 'neighbour' principle *in Donoghue v Stevenson*, [1932] AC 562. It is not necessary in this case to choose between either the general or the more restricted approach in common law. I have used the cases to isolate factors which are relevant in law and applied these factors to the facts of this case.

The relationship of the Respondent to the victims who were participants in the accident could not be closer, the victims were her daughter and husband who with her formed a close loving family. The Respondent was drawn into the trauma by a telephone call. She went to the hospital as soon as practicable. She saw the seriously injured victims in the immediate aftermath of the accident when they were in so serious a state of injury as to be disturbing to the normal person. She was told of the serious nature of the injuries of her husband, but especially the serious injuries of her daughter Shirley Anne.

I am satisfied that a person with a close proximate relationship to an injured person, such as the Respondent, who, while not a participant in an accident, hears of it very soon after and who visits the injured person as soon as practicable, and who is exposed to serious injuries of the primary victims in such a way as to cause a psychiatric illness, then she becomes a secondary victim to the accident. In reaching these determinations it is necessary to review the accident and immediate aftermath in an ex post facto way to test the situation."

Comments and Questions:

1. In this decision has Denham J. adopted a different position from the position she adopted in *Mullally v Bus Éireann*?

2. What does Denham J. mean when she refers to the principle of primary and secondary victims?

3. Hamilton C.J. speaks for the majority of the court; his five principles therefore set out the criteria necessary to establish the right to recover for negligently inflicted nervous shock. How do these criteria differ from straight foreseeability?

This area of law is still under development and the decision of *Curran v Cadbury (Ireland) Ltd.* reconfirms the above decisions. This case also seeks to clarify the area of law by means of an overview of the area.

Curran v Cadbury (Ireland) Ltd.
Circuit Court [2000] 2 I.L.R.M. 343; (2000) I.L.T. 140

Facts: The plaintiff worked at the defendant's factory for about 17 years. The plaintiff and another operative worked near a moving belt which carried chocolate bars to the plaintiff's work station. She was the more senior of the two operatives. On the day of the incident the machine feeding out the bars of chocolate was stopped without notification to the plaintiff, contrary to normal practice. On restarting the machine she became aware that there was a fitter inside the machine. The fitter was shouting and screaming; she could not see him but she could hear him, and she thought that he was being seriously injured. She suffered a nervous shock as a result of the incident.

Issues: In this action McMahon J. expressed unease at the distinction made between primary and secondary victims. He also stated that he was unconvinced about the arguments against recovery, and contended that the Irish courts should continue not to impose control mechanisms on recovery for nervous shock. The court held that the plaintiff was entitled to recover.

McMahon J.:

"[The facts of the case] show that the plaintiff was at the very centre of this frightening episode. She was in the eye of the storm. In the terminology that is gaining currency in other jurisdictions, she was 'a primary victim.' She was not 'a secondary victim,' that is a person who was not involved in the accident itself, but was removed from the direct action or came on the immediate aftermath of the accident. The plaintiff had a central role in this frightening drama.

Primary and Secondary Victims:

There has been a tendency in recent years, especially in English cases, to divide victims in these type of cases into two categories: primary victims and secondary victims (See Lord Oliver in *Alcock v Chief Constable of South Yorkshire Police* [1992] 1 AC 310 and Lord Lloyd in *Page v Smith* 1 AC 155). Such categorisation is not without difficulties and has been criticised (See Law Commission Report (England), Liability for Psychiatric Illness (1998) Law Coin No 249, at para 5.50, which followed the Law Commission's Consultation Paper No 137 (1995), where the suggestion is that the distinction should be abandoned as it is unhelpful). For my own part, I am not convinced that the separation of victims into these two categories does anything to assist the development of legal principles that should guide the courts in this complex area of the law. Hamilton CJ (with whom Egan J agreed) did not refer to the distinction in *Kelly v Hennessy* [1995] 3 IR 253 the leading Irish case on the matter, and while Denham J, in the same case used the term 'secondary victims' to describe the aftermath relatives who were plaintiffs in that case, her primary focus was naturally on the plaintiffs before her rather than on persons who were more directly involved in the accident. She did, however, give a clear definition as to what she meant by the terms when she said of the victim before her:

> 'The plaintiff was not a primary victim; that is to say she was not a participant in the accident. Her case is that she is a secondary victim; that is to say one who did not participate in the accident, but was injured as a consequence of the event' (at p 269).

It is clear from this that Mrs Curran, in the present case, was a 'primary victim' in Denham J's definition. For those who favour this categorisation, the advantage of being classified as a 'primary victim' is that the policy restrictions that might be justified in limiting the persons to whom a duty of care is owed, would apply only to 'secondary victims', as there is little 'flood-gate fears' in relation to primary victims ...

The Basic Principles:

The Supreme Court, in *Kelly v Hennessy* supra, in addressing the problem of compensating aftermath victims for negligently inflicted 'nervous shock' approached the problem from basic principles. Hamilton CJ, with whom Egan J agreed, was happy to start his analysis with the neighbour concept in *Donoghue v Stevenson* [1932] AC 562. He then listed 5 conditions which had to be complied with before recovery would be allowed. Denham J, likewise started from the basic concepts of neighbourhood and proximity, and she considered the question whether liability should be determined on reasonable foreseeability simpliciter (as suggested by Lord Bridge of Harwich in the English case of *McLoughlin v O'Brian* 1 AC 1410, an approach which she favoured in the earlier High Court decision of Mullally v Bus Eireann ILRM 722) or whether the reasonable foreseeability test for nervous shock cases should be restricted by proximity factors ie on policy grounds (as suggested by Lord Wilberforce in *McLoughlin v O'Brian* supra). In the end she concluded:

> 'It is not necessary in this case to choose between either the general or more restricted approach in common law. I have used the cases to isolate factors which are relevant in law and applied these factors in the facts of this case' (at p 274).

Bearing the Supreme Court's approach in mind, as indeed I must, it is appropriate therefore that I too should approach the present case from basic common law principles ...

The plaintiff was the defendant's employee; she was at the scene and she unwittingly caused the crisis. In the words of Denham J in *Mullally*, she was a participant in the accident.

Whether one applies the proximity test (of Wilberforce J *in Anns v Merton London Borough Council* AC 728 and adopted in this country in *Ward v McMaster* IR 337 and many cases since (see for recent example *HMW (nee F) v Ireland AG and Govt of Ireland*, unreported High Court, Costello J, 11 April 1997)), or the close and direct criterion (of Lord Atkin in *Donoghue v Stevenson*, supra) the plaintiff clearly qualifies as being within the range of persons to whom a duty of care is owed. The questions that rightly exercise the courts in *Mullally v Bus Eireann* supra, and *Kelly v Hennessy* supra, need not concern us in the present set of circumstances. The control mechanisms which Courts feel necessary to introduce in the case of bystanders and aftermath victims are not required here ...

The question that concerns us here, therefore, relates not so much to the duty aspect of the problem, but more to the nature of the harm which the plaintiff suffered and whether this kind of harm, psychiatric illness, could be reasonably foreseen as a consequence that would follow from the defendant's lack of care in the circumstances. ...

[From the facts of the case] which are supported by the evidence, I have little difficulty in concluding that the defendant was clearly in breach of its obligation to take reasonable care for the plaintiff in these circumstances.

Kind of Harm: Psychiatric Illness
The remaining issue is whether the Courts are willing to compensate the plaintiff for the kind of harm she suffered which was not physical injury as traditionally defined, but psychiatric injury previously described by lawyers as 'nervous shock'. A couple of preliminary points can be made.

First, Irish authorities clearly establish that the duty to compensate for nervous shock in negligence cases extends only to recognised psychiatric illnesses. In the present case, the medical evidence of both doctors was that the plaintiff suffered from a mild to moderate post traumatic stress disorder and this has been accepted in this jurisdiction as a recognisable psychiatric illness (*see Mullally v Bus Eireann,* supra) ...

Second, such harm is recognised as compensable in negligence only if it is brought about by a shock or sudden event. Compensation in this jurisdiction is not available for general grief or sorrow (*Hosford v John Murphy and Sons Ltd* ILRM 300) or for a condition which is brought about over a period of time, for example, the wear and tear which caring parents might suffer if they have to look after a son or daughter severely injured in an accident (*Kelly v Hennessy*, supra). Again, there was agreement in this case that the plaintiff's condition was brought about by the crisis which followed when she switched on the machine ...

Reasonably Foreseeable Psychiatric Illness.

Although the Courts have long since indicated their willingness to recognise nervous shock or psychiatric illness as harm which is compensateable in our jurisdiction (*see Bell v Great Northern Railway Company of Ireland* (1890) 26 LR (Ir) 428; *Byrne v Great Southern and Western Railway Company of Ireland* Irish Court of Appeal, February 1884, cited in Bell; *Mullally v Bus Eireann* supra; *Kelly v Hennessy* supra), it must of course be harm which is reasonably foreseeable by the defendant. If the plaintiff is within the range of persons who is likely to be affected by the defendant's actions or omissions, and to whom a duty is owed, and it is reasonably foreseeable that failure to take care on the part of the defendant will result in psychiatric illness, then the defendant will be liable for such psychiatric illness if it is negligently inflicted. Moreover, liability will be imposed in such circumstances even if no physical injury results from the lack of care. (See *Bell*, supra; *Byrne* supra; and *Kelly v Hennessy* supra). In determining whether such psychiatric illness is reasonably foreseeable or not it will be relevant to take into account, inter alia that there was fear for one's own physical safety (*Bell*, supra; *Byrne*, supra) the safety of one's family (*Hambrook v Stokes Bros* [1925] 1 KB 141), or the safety of one's fellow employees (*Dooley v Cammell Laird & Co Ltd* [1951] 1 Lloyd's Rep 271), or even fear for the safety of one's home (*Attia v British Gas plc* QB 304).

In the present case it is clear from the evidence and from the facts already outlined, that it was reasonably foreseeable, if the plaintiff switched on the machine while the fitter was inside the housing, that the fitter would in all probability be physically injured and that the plaintiff would get a great fright which could easily result in a serious assault on her nervous system and result in psychiatric illness. It must surely be conceded that when the machine was switched on with the fitter inside 'all hell would break loose', to use the Plaintiff's own phrase in evidence. The noise, the screams, the malfunctioning of the machine, the shout of alarm from others, all assaulting the plaintiff through her own senses, would frighten the most courageous. Add to this the guilt factor, irrationally assumed by the plaintiff as a result of her causative role, and one has a combination that would frighten the bravest soul. The psychiatric illness (PTSD) that these events triggered was acknowledged by the doctors who gave evidence.

It is clear therefore, that the defendant owed the plaintiff a duty of care in the circumstances; that there was a breach of its common law duty to take care; that the defendant attracted liability vicariously through the negligence of its employees; and, finally, that the plaintiff suffered a compensatable injury which was reasonably foreseeable in the circumstances.

Policy
Liability must follow unless there are policy reasons which would operate against the plaintiff (*Ward v McMaster*, supra). Hamilton CJ in *Kelly v Hennessy* supra, said, in allowing an aftermath claim that: "(there) is no public policy that the plaintiff's claim, if substantiated should be excluded" (p 262) echoing Gibbs CJ *in Jaensch v Coffey* (1984) 155 CLR 549, at p 556. He quoted Lord Russell of Killowen in *McLoughlin v O'Brian,* supra, who rejected the floodgates argument in that case. In *Mullally*, Denham J also took the view that there was no public policy which prevented the plaintiff from recovering, in a similar case, nor was there any legal or Constitutional ban to such recovery. If there is no policy argument against recovery in those cases, it would seem that, a fortiori, there should be none in the present case where the plaintiff was a participant in the accident ..."

In 2003 the Irish courts were given the opportunity to address the issue of nervous shock in the case of *Cuddy v May.*

Cuddy v May
Unreported, High Court, November 28, 2003

Facts: There was a car accident involving a car which contained nine occupants; five people were killed in the tragedy. The injured and dead were brought to Portlaoise General Hospital where the plaintiff was a porter. The plaintiff assisted in bringing in the injured and dead into the hospital—the first ambulance carried his cousin, who died a few days later; the second ambulance carried another cousin, who subsequently died; and his brother was also among the dead. His sister suffered extremely serious and life-threatening injuries. He also recognised the other injured and dead as they were either family or lifelong family friends. He was advised to leave Casualty, but the Garda required his assistance in identifying all involved in the accident; this included going to the mortuary to identify the deceased, where he found his brother. The plaintiff was severely traumatised, as were others present on the occasion. One member of the Gardaí was required to take a year's leave of absence from work.

Issues: The issues before the court were first, whether the injury sustained by the plaintiff was foreseeable. The second issue before the court related to the category of persons entitled to maintain an action as aftermath or secondary victims. Were brothers or more distant relatives included within that category? The plaintiff to this action was entitled to recover.

Kearns J.:

"The law in this area has been addressed in a number of Irish cases in recent years, including *Mullally v Bus Eireann and another* [1992] ILRM 722, *Kelly v Hennessy* [1995] 3 IR 253, *Curran v Cadbury (Ireland) Ltd* [2000] 2 ILRM 343, and most recently by the Supreme Court *in Fletcher v Commissioners of Public Works in Ireland* [2003] 1 IR 465, [2003] 2 ILRM 94 ...

The circumstances in which damages for nervous shock are recoverable were set out as follows by Hamilton, CJ in *Kelly v Hennessy* [1995] 3 IR 253, at pp 258–9:

'1. The plaintiff must establish that he or she actually suffered "nervous shock". This term has been used to describe "any recognisable psychiatric illness" and a plaintiff must prove that he or she suffered a recognisable psychiatric illness if he or she is to recover damages for "nervous shock".

2. A plaintiff must establish that his or her recognisable psychiatric illness was "shock induced".

3. A plaintiff must prove that the nervous shock was caused by a defendant's act or omission.

4. The nervous shock sustained by a plaintiff must be by reason of actual or apprehended physical injury to the plaintiff or a person other than the plaintiff.

5. If a plaintiff wishes to recover damages for negligently inflicted nervous shock he must show that the defendant owed him or her a duty of care not to cause him a reasonably foreseeable injury in the form of nervous shock.'

In the instant case, the Defendants accept that conditions 1–4 have all been fulfilled and the submissions in defence were entirely directed to the fifth consideration listed by Hamilton J.

Firstly, a submission was made that it was not reasonably foreseeable to a negligent defendant that a brother of one person killed and another injured in the same accident would happen to be present at the nearby hospital when the victims were admitted.

This point, it seems to me, can be quickly dealt with. There can, in my view, be no possible basis for excluding the Plaintiff on any such grounds. This is not a case where the Plaintiff claims qua employee or rescuer. His evidence to this court satisfies me that during the two-and-a-half years during which he worked in Casualty, he was frequently exposed, without suffering nervous shock, to the experience of dealing with road traffic accident victims. His employment circumstances per se have nothing to do with the onset of nervous shock. His injury was brought about partly because of his temporal and spatial proximity to the horrific sights, but was triggered or caused because of his relationship and intimate knowledge of those killed and injured in the collision. Had he not been present on the night in question in his capacity as a porter, he would almost certainly have come to the hospital in any event, as his parents did, on hearing the news that his brother and sister had been involved in this terrible accident and would, as a matter of probability have been exposed to most, if not all, of what he did actually see and experience.

The Defendants' central point, however, is that policy considerations should persuade the court not to allow a recovery of damages at the level of relationship which existed between the parties in the instant case, it not being a case of husband and wife or parent and child. Heavy reliance was place on the 'control mechanisms' emphasised by Lord Wilberforce in *McLoughlin v O'Brian* [1983] 1 AC 410 …

[Kearns J. then went on to consider the implications of *Fletcher v Commissioners of Public Works* [2003] 1 IR 465; [2003] 2 ILRM 94 on the question of policy considerations, and quoted from the following judgment of Geoghegan J. in that case.] In his judgment in the same case Geoghegan J also acknowledged the importance of policy considerations where attempts are made to define the limits either of what might be regarded as reasonably foreseeable or other questions in relation to the existence of a duty of care in stating (at p 144):

> 'It is against that background of the case law which I have reviewed that this court must decide as a matter of policy and of reasonableness whether claims for damages for psychiatric injury only and resulting from fear of asbestos related diseases of a degree which is objectively irrational are recoverable. Traditionally, courts do not always use the actual word "policy". They may attempt to draw artificial limits to what can be regarded as being reasonably foreseeable or they may in considering proximity or other questions in relation to the existence of a duty of care, invoke the concept of reasonableness so that a duty of care will not in fact be imposed if the court considers it unreasonable to do so. The third control mechanism which the court may impose is in relation to particular heads of damage or finally, they may expressly deny a claim on grounds of public policy.'

Geoghegan J was thus able to formulate a set of principles applicable to cases of this nature (albeit that *Fletcher* [2003] 1 IR 465, [2003] 2 ILRM 94, was more concerned with irrational fear of asbestos-related disease), to describe as his first principle the following (at p 145):

> 'Reasonable foreseeability is not the only determining factor in establishing a duty of care. "Proximity" which is given an elastic definition in the decided cases, the reasonableness of the imposition of a duty of care and questions of public policy can be additional determining factors.'

'Proximity' was dealt with in the judgment of Denham J in *Kelly v Hennessy* [1995] 3 IR 253 (at p 270). The learned judge said that there were several elements in the requirement of proximity being (a) proximity of relationship between persons; (b) proximity in a spatial context (ie the person must perceive the aftermath of the accident); and (c) proximity in a temporal sense (ie that 'shock' must be the cause of the illness).

It is on the issue of proximity of relationships that this case turns. The Defendants do not argue that the Plaintiff in the instant case has failed to meet any requirement of either spatial or temporal proximity to the accident.

In *Kelly v Hennessy*, the plaintiff's husband and one of her daughters suffered permanent brain damage in a serious car crash caused by the negligence of the defendant. There was no dispute in that case but that the plaintiff came within the scope of those to whom the defendant owed a duty of care. In his judgment, Hamilton CJ did not purport to fix any boundary by way of Rubicon whereby husbands and wives, parents and children would qualify and all other relationships, familial or otherwise, would not. Indeed the defendants did not even argue the relationship issue in that case. The judgment of Denham J, however, addressed the question of the scope of who might qualify when she stated (at p 274):

> 'I am satisfied that a person with a close proximate relationship to an injured person, such as the plaintiff who, while not a participant in the accident, hears of it very soon after and who visits the injured person as soon as practicable, and who is exposed to serious injuries of the primary victims in such a way as to cause a psychiatric illness, then she becomes a secondary victim to the accident.' ...

It certainly cannot be said in the instant case that the Plaintiff has failed to discharge the onus of proving that a 'close proximate relationship' existed between him and his deceased brother and also his seriously injured sister, both on the basis of close family relationship and indeed also on the basis of close ties of affection. I am, however, taking Denham J to mean 'family relationship' only by her observations in *Kelly v Hennessy* [1995] 3 IR 253. In the absence of any debate on the issue, which in any event did not require to be decided in that case, it would be quite wrong in my opinion to interpret what was said by Denham J in any way which would extend the boundaries beyond those of very close family relationships, amongst which that of brothers and sisters may clearly be one.

This court would certainly support the proposition that policy considerations would dictate that the ambit of recoverability and the category of relationships entitled to successfully claim damages for nervous shock should be tightly restricted. However, to recognise such a principle is not in any way to resolve the problems that arise in deciding who may recover in these cases. These problems were addressed extensively in the judgment of Geoghegan J in *Fletcher v Commissioner of Public Works* [2003] 1 IR 465, [2003] 2 ILRM 94. Having referred to how the House of Lords in *Alcock v Chief Constable of South Yorkshire Police* [1992] 1 AC 310, [1991] 4 All ER 907, held that the class of persons to whom a duty of care was owed on the basis of proximity was not limited by reference to particular relationships such as husband and wife or parent and child but was based also on ties of love and affection, the closeness of which would need to be proved in each case, Geoghegan J stated as follows (at p 131):

> 'The idea that as between siblings the plaintiff would have to prove special love and affection for the brother or sister in question with that perhaps being hotly opposed in cross-examination is certainly not a desirable vista, if it could be avoided in other ways.'

One of the ways is, of course, to exclude certain categories of relationships, invoking policy grounds to do so. But which relationships are included and which are excluded when such policy grounds are invoked? Where does the policy interest lie? For example, if siblings qualify, do stepbrothers and stepsisters also qualify? Do engaged or same-sex couples in a long and loving relationship qualify? Does a close and lifelong friendship offer any prospect that a court might qualify the severely traumatised survivor where a lifelong friend and companion dies through the negligence of another? At the opposite extreme, should policy considerations, which must include some recognition of the burden on insurers called upon to meet the cost of multiple claims, exclude secondary victims altogether? Ultimately, of course, this burden falls on the policy-holders and, by extension, the public. Should not the possibility of exaggerated, or even fraudulent claims, in this area not weigh heavily with judges whose sympathies may all too easily be won over by horrifying accounts of such accidents and their aftermath?

The difficulty of resolving these issues is self evident even where the other elements of the proximity test are met and the considerations last mentioned above would, it must be said, most commend themselves to this court. However, it seems to me that I must accept what has been decided in other cases and that in the instant case I therefore should apply a 'close proximate relationship' test which, by implication at least, seems to qualify the close family relationship between the Plaintiff and his brother and sister. At least such an interpretation has the benefit of being consistent with the legislative policy evident in Pt IV of the Civil Liability Act 1961 when it identified those entitled to recover damages for mental distress in fatal accident cases as being 'any member of the family of the deceased'. While the causes of action are different, the principle determining who may recover seems to me to be the same, even if the scope for far larger awards arises in cases of nervous shock.

For my own part, it seems to me that a policy based limit on the category of those entitled to recover is, in the absence of legislation, a less dangerous route to follow than one based on foreseeability. Under a foreseeability test, absent qualifications for policy reasons, there could be very significant numbers of persons who could advance claims for compensation for nervous shock having fulfilled the temporal and spatial requirements of the proximity text, particularly when and where a multiple tragedy takes place. It may make sense on policy grounds to exclude from the ambit of compensation a police officer who arrives qua 'rescuer' on the scene of an horrific accident. On any test of foreseeability, however, it is entirely understandable that a considerable range of persons may well suffer nervous shock as a result of exposure to a particular experience. To my way of thinking it is an entirely artificial exercise to assume degrees of 'resoluteness' or 'fortitude' on the part of secondary victims as a reason for excluding them from a qualifying category of claimant.

A clear policy which defines and limits the categories of persons to whom a duty is owed, with whatever drawbacks that approach may involve, seems to me to offer greater certainty in this difficult area. While the Civil Liability Act 1961 was eventually amended in 1996 to provide for larger compensation in fatal accident cases for mental distress, and while in the 'nervous shock' context it may not accord with my own views, I am not aware of any serious criticism over the years of the limited range of persons identified in the Civil Liability Act as potential or appropriate claimants."

Comments and Questions:
1. Has Kearns J. in this action attempted to re-open the debate, in the Irish context, on the introduction of policy criteria as espoused by Lord Wilberforce in *McLoughlin v O'Brian*?

CHAPTER 4

OCCUPIERS' LIABILITY

INTRODUCTION

The area of occupiers' liability deals with the tort of negligence as it applies to injuries to entrants onto land. Historically, the protection offered to entrants onto property who incurred an injury did not benefit to the same extent as other areas of negligence by the principles of *Donoghue v Stevenson*. This was due in part to the fact that the rights of property-owners was well developed at the time that *Donoghue v Stevenson* was decided through the seminal decision of *Indermaur v Dames* (1888) L.R. 1 C.P. 274. This decision, coupled with the *laissez-faire* approach which applied to property issues in the late 19th century, meant that the rights of entrants onto land were directly related to their benefit to the land-owner. As such, classifications of entrants were used, ranging from that of contractual invitees to trespassers, each with their own corresponding levels of protection. This remained the position for many years in Ireland before negligence principles began to be applied in the area, most notably through judgments such as that of *McNamara v ESB* [1975] I.R. 1. However, these decisions, although clarifying the duty owed to trespassers, did lead to some confusion as to the duty owed to other categories of claimants and raised the duty owed to trespassers to that of "reasonable care". Through lobbying by interest groups such as farmers, horrified by the extent of the duty owed to trespassers, the whole area of occupiers' liability has now been overhauled by the Occupiers' Liability Act 1995 (the Act). This Act now largely replaces the common law on occupiers' liability. The Act, however, only deals with injury arising from dangers due to the state of the premises and not due to activities carried out on it. This means that if the injury arises from activities on the premises, the Act will not apply. Although not clearly stated in the Act, the non-statutory negligence principles will apply in these cases. This is dealt with further below.

The Act is reproduced, for reference, at the end of this chapter.

SCOPE OF THE ACT

The Act imposes liability on the occupiers of premises for injury arising from dangers on that premises. "Premises" is defined as including land, water and any fixed or moveable structures thereon and also includes vessels, vehicles, trains, aircraft and other means of transport (s.1).

The definition of occupier in the Act reflects that which existed in the common law, *i.e.* the person who controls a premises. If there are a number of people who control the premises, the extent of the duty of each occupier depends on their respective degrees of control (s.1). Occupiers are liable under the Act for dangers existing on premises. "Danger", however, is defined narrowly to cover only the state of the premises and not activities carried out on it. Unfortunately, it is not always clear where the line between "activity" and "state" can be drawn.

Hackett v Calla Associates Ltd.
High Court [2004] I.E.H.C. 336 (transcript)

Facts: The plaintiff alleged that in an incident outside a nightclub known as Marley's Night Club, jointly run by both Calla Associates and the second defendant, Mr O'Reilly, a security man working for the nightclub (a "bouncer") hit him with a blunt instrument causing near permanent blindness to his right eye. The defendants, for their part, denied that any baton or blunt instrument was used at all, but accepted that a group of bouncers came out of the premises into the carpark to break up a crowd which was causing trouble outside the nightclub.

Issues: Two issues arose for consideration. First, who were the occupiers for the purpose of the case? Secondly, did the incident come within the scope of the Occupiers' Liability Act 1995, and if not, what was the correct law to be applied?

Peart J., in his decision, held that both parties were occupiers for the purpose of the case, given that both exercised a degree of control over how the business was run. He further held that the 1995 Act did not apply to the case as the injury arose from an "activity" and not from the "state of the premises" and that the non-statutory principles of the common law should be applied instead. Applying the *Glencar* criteria he ultimately held that a duty of care was owed to the plaintiff but attached 50 per cent to the plaintiff in light of his contributory negligence.

Peart J.:

"[In relation to who was the occupier Peart J. said the following:]
    In my view there is such a mingling of functions between both Calla and Mr O'Reilly, according to the evidence, and such a relationship created by the Agreement, that it can reasonably and properly be said that both the Defendants are occupiers of the premises and that each owe a duty to the visiting public, including the Plaintiff. Since the agreement actually refers to Mr O'Reilly as an occupier for the purposes of insurance, he cannot now say that he is not an occupier, particularly as he is the holder of the licence by virtue of the transfer of the licence to him by virtue of this agreement. Equally, Calla has accepted that as a matter of fact the bouncers were their employees. I am satisfied therefore that the liability to the Plaintiff is one which is joint and several. The

Plaintiff ought to be entitled to recover from either Defendant, and the paying Defendant will be entitled on the basis of joint and several liability to recover appropriately from the non-paying Defendant.

[Peart J. then went on to consider whether the incident fell within the scope of the Act.]

I should perhaps at the outset deal with the Plaintiff's plea in the statement of claim that the Defendants are in breach of statutory liability to him by virtue of failing to comply with s 3 of the Occupiers' Liability Act 1995. Section 3, sub-s (1) of that Act provides that an occupier of premises owes a duty of care towards a visitor, except in so far as the occupier extends, restricts, modifies or excludes that duty in accordance with s 5. Section 3(2) provides that this duty is to take such care as is reasonable in all the circumstances to ensure that a visitor to the premises 'does not suffer injury or damage by reason of any danger existing thereon'. It is important to note that the word 'danger' is defined in s 1 as meaning 'in relation to any premises, means a danger due to the state of the premises'. It must follow from this that the Plaintiff's claim is not one coming within the duty of care imposed by s 3 as the allegations of negligence are not related in any way to the state of the premises but rather the behaviour of the bouncers on the night in question. It is necessary to consider this claim by reference to the more usual non-statutory criteria in relation to the possible breach of the common law duty of care owed to the Plaintiff by the owners/occupier of the premises, diluted possibly by the contribution which the Plaintiff's own behaviour made to what befell him at the hands of their employees, servants or agents.

[In considering whether the non-statutory duty had been breached Peart J. applied the *Glencar* criteria, *i.e.* was there proximity, foreseeability of injury, policy considerations and was the imposition of a duty of care just and reasonable in the circumstances?]

... In this case there is no doubt in my mind that since the Plaintiff gained admission and his presence there was at least permitted throughout the evening, the necessary relationship of proximity exists for the purpose of establishing the duty of care. The fact that he had been barred previously and ought not to have gained entry is irrelevant since he was known to be there and was observed throughout the evening. A decision was apparently taken that he would not be removed.

It is trite law that these security staff members are not entitled to use more force than is reasonably necessary in any particular circumstances which might present during the evening. Each case will have to be considered on its own facts, since the variety of situations giving rise to intervention by security staff in this type of premises is infinite. But the requirement to use only reasonable force never disappears. It is beyond doubt that it is reasonably foreseeable that an excessive use of force by staff of this nature has the potential to cause injury to others. The next hurdle to be overcome under the test for liability as pronounced by Keane CJ in Glencar Exploration Ltd v Mayo County Council [2002] 1 IR 84, [2002] 1 ILRM 481 is to exclude any public policy consideration which ought to exclude liability arising. In my view there could be no public policy consideration which should result in no duty of care being owed by employers of security staff to members of the public in the circumstances of facts such as have occurred in this case. In fact the opposite would be the case, since a situation would then exist in which security could go about their tasks with complete impunity regarding the level of force they might use, and in effect a situation would exist where it was permissible for the owners of licensed premises and other such premises to hire their own private army in order to enforce their version of law and order. That could never be acceptable. The final hurdle to be overcome by a plaintiff under the Glencar principles is that the court must be satisfied that it would be fair, just and reasonable that the law should impose a duty of care on the Defendants for the benefit of the Plaintiff in this case. That consideration is for the purpose of this case quite closely linked to the public policy consideration, and there is also some blurring between consideration of that concept of fairness and reasonableness and the concept of any contributory negligence on the part of the Plaintiff. One could consider the concept of fairness, justice and reasonableness also from the point of view of the 'ex turpi causa' principle. In other words, the actions of the Plaintiff as proven in this case are so egregious that he ought not to be allowed to recover damages for an injury sustained which results from that behaviour.

The latter methodology must in my view be reserved for the very worst type of behaviour in order to serve the punitive purpose of denying an injured plaintiff any remedy for otherwise culpable behaviour on the part of a defendant. I believe that in the present case it is fair, just and reasonable that the Defendants remain under the duty of care towards the Plaintiff and other patrons even in the unpleasant and potentially dangerous circumstances which arose outside the premises on this night. The whole purpose of the job of being security staff member is to deal with situations which arise in premises of this kind and which cannot be reasonably dealt with by what I might conveniently describe as 'ordinary staff'. It is part of the normal working life of such security men to encounter patrons in various states of intoxication, and who even when not intoxicated, are nevertheless aggressive and sometimes violent. Such staff ought to be, and in most cases, are trained to deal efficiently with such situations. It is perfectly fair, just and reasonable that such persons should carry out their duties in a way which is consistent with a reasonable use of force and restraint, and I can see no reason why any special dispensation should be extended to them in the manner in which they carry out their tasks.

I am satisfied therefore that a duty of care was and ought to be owed by the Defendants and their servants and agents towards the Plaintiff, and that this duty extended to avoiding causing injury to the Plaintiff through an unreasonable or unnecessary use of force or violence in dealing with the situation which existed outside the premises in the car park ...

... However, the Plaintiff has to share in the responsibility for what happened to him that night. His involvement, as found by me, amounts to contributory negligence. The question as always is to what degree. One is more accustomed to assessing contributory negligence in the context of a car accident or an accident at work. In such cases it would be unusual to make a large deduction on account of contributory negligence, because in most cases the element of contributory negligence arises due to perhaps not wearing a seat-belt, exceeding a speed limit, failing to observe an on-coming car and so forth ... In my view, even though the Defendants are liable to him for an unreasonable use of force, and even though the court feels great sympathy for the fact that the Plaintiff has now only the use of one eye, he has himself to blame to a significant extent, and to an extent far in excess of the more normal type of case to which I have referred. In my view it is right to attribute to the Plaintiff a finding of contributory negligence to the extent of 50%."

Comments and Questions:
1. The case clearly places the activities of individuals in the category of "activity" and not "state" so that the non-statutory negligence provisions would apply. Is the distinction so clear when we consider other physical causes of injury, however, such as a recently dug hole, some bricks left lying temporarily at the entrance of a building and so on?

2. In a number of cases, slippages on wet surfaces have been considered in light of the Act without any debate as to whether the temporarily wet floor constituted the "state" of the premises (see *Collins v McDermot*, unreported, High Court, December 18, 2003 and *Power v Governor of Cork Prison* [2005] I.E.H.C. 253). On the other hand, in *McGovern v Dunnes Stores* a clothes hanger left lying on the ground was held not to be sufficiently permanent to constitute the "state" of the premises and hence fell outside of the Act. Does the law require further clarification in your view?

3. In the above case the entrant was quite clearly in any event, a visitor, and the applicable principles (statutory or non-statutory) are the same (reasonable care). The situation is made more difficult when we consider the cases where the plaintiff is a trespasser. Should the elevated duty outlined in *McNamara v ESB* apply or the lower earlier duty applicable in the common law and now in the Act?

4. Peart J. distinguished the consideration of public policy from that of whether the imposition of a duty of care was "fair, just and reasonable". In applying the public policy consideration he considered whether the nature of the

relationship (occupier and entrant) ought to warrant such an exclusion, holding that it did not. While applying the "fair, just and reasonable" criteria, Peart J. considered the plaintiff's own contribution to the incident and his character. As regards the latter, does this, in your view, represent an unwelcome blurring of the lines between the defences and duty of care principles? (See Chapter 13 on Defences for further guidance).

CATEGORIES OF ENTRANT

The Act now refers to three categories of entrants: visitors, trespassers and recreational users.

Visitors

Visitors are defined in s.1 as entrants who enter onto a premises with the express or implied right of the occupier, or those who are there as of right, or under contract and who are not recreational users. It also includes those who entered as visitors but no longer have permission to be there and are making reasonable efforts to leave. Once a person exceeds their permission to be on the premises they become trespassers.

The duty owed to visitors is to take reasonable care in all the circumstances to ensure that they do not suffer injury or damage by reason of any danger existing on the property (s.3). Note must also be taken of the duty of any other person in the company of the entrant to supervise the entrant, and the care which the entrant is expected to take for his or her own safety (s.3(2)).

In the *Sheehy v Devil's Glen Tours Equestrian Centre* case the court had to consider whether a duty of reasonable care had been breached.

Angela Sheehy v The Devil's Glen Tours Equestrian Centre Limited
Unreported, High Court, December 10, 2001

Facts: The plaintiff, while entering the reception area of the defendant's premises, tripped and fell over the door saddle of the door.

Issues: Lavan J. had to consider what category of entrant the plaintiff was, whether the duty to her had been breached and whether the plaintiff was liable in contributory negligence. Lavan J ultimately found in favour of the plaintiff, and against a finding of contributory negligence.

Lavan J.:

"The Occupiers' Liability Act, 1995 came into force on the 17th July, 1995. This Act created three categories of entrant:

(1) Recreational user;

Pursuant to section 1(1) recreational user means an entrant who with or without the occupier's permission or at the occupier's implied invitation is present on premises without a charge (other than a reasonable charge in respect of the cost of providing vehicle parking facilities) being imposed for the purpose of engaging in a recreational activity.

(2) A trespasser;

(3) A visitor;

Pursuant to section 1(1) 'visitor' means;

(a) an entrant other than a recreational user who is present on premises at the invitation or with the permission of the occupier or any other entrant specified in paragraph (a) (b) or (c) of the definition of recreational user,

(b) an entrant other that a recreational user who is present on premises by virtue of an express or employed term in a contract, and

(c) an entrant as of right;

(d) While he or she is so present as the case may be for the purpose for which he or she is invited or permitted to be there, for the purpose of the performance of the contract or for the purpose of the exercise of the right, and includes any such entrant who is present on premises has become unlawful after entry thereon and who is taking reasonable steps to leave.

In the case the Plaintiff along with her husband and two daughters were present on the Defendant's premises to avail of the horse riding facilities provided on a commercial basis by the Defendant. It is submitted that in those circumstances the Plaintiff was clearly on the premises at the invitation or 'with the permission' of the Defendant and was at all material times a visitor within the meaning of the Act of 1995 aforesaid.

The Defendant's duties in respect of dangers existing on their premises are therefore governed by the above Act of 1995.

Duty owed to a visitor:

Section 3 of the above Act specifies the duty owed to a visitor;

(1) an occupier of premises owes a duty of care ('the common duty of care') towards a visitor thereto accepting so far as the occupier extends, restricts, modifies or excludes that duty in accordance with Section 5.

(2) in this section 'the common duty of care' means a duty to take such care as is reasonable in all the circumstances (having regard to the care which a visitor may reasonably be expected to take for his or her own safety and, if the visitor is on the premises in the company of another person, the extent

of the supervision and control the later person may reasonably be expected to exercise over the visitors activities) to ensure that a visitor to the premises does not suffer injury of damage by reason of any danger existing thereof.

It is submitted therefore that the Defendants' duty was to take reasonable care to ensure that the Plaintiff did not suffer injury or damage from any danger on their premises and further that there is no suggestion that the Defendant by express agreement or notice under Section 5 aforesaid is attempting to restrict, modify or exclude the duty towards the visitors.

The Defendants ... submit that the 'common duty of care' which is owed to 'visitors' is higher than the duty owed to trespassers and recreational users under the Act. That the common duty of care is defined in classic negligence terms so that the occupier is only liable if such is 'reasonable'. That there is no judicial guidance from the decided cases as to the meaning and effect of subsection 3 of the Act but it is submitted that what constitutes reasonableness in all the circumstances of a given case is a mixed question of law-in [sic] and fact.

The Defendants in their submission comment on the facts as outlined in the evidence and submitted that a 'weather bar' of the type complained of in these proceedings does not constitute a danger as it is an integral part of the saddle of an external door.

They further submit that the Plaintiff approached the door with an unobstructed view of same and that she accepts that she did not see the threshold at all and that she was not looking down but significantly, from their point of view, that she was watching her daughter and talking to her. In the result that she was not looking where she was going and that this was the proximate cause of the accident.

Essentially the Defendants submit that the threshold was not a hazard or danger to the visitor. That in so far as there is a conflict between the engineers this is academic as the Plaintiff accepts that she did not see the threshold at all and the Plaintiff's engineer accepts that one inch is sufficient to cause a trip of the kind that occurred. That I should take account of the fact that thousands of visitors have stepped over this saddle without injury or complaint.

Turning to the facts—I accept the Plaintiff's evidence and where there is a conflict on the engineering evidence I prefer that of Mr Watson who gave evidence on behalf of the Plaintiff.

In the result I therefore find as a fact that the danger here complained of was a danger and hazard due to the state of the premises.

In the result I hold the Defendants liable in negligence to the Plaintiffs.

Turning to the issue of contributory negligence in the particular circumstances of this case I am guided by the following view of the law. There is an essential difference between contributory negligence arising out of a breach of statutory duty and contributory negligence arising out of a breach of a common law duty of care. In the latter case 'An act of inadvertence if it is an act which a reasonably careful workman(person) would not do will constitute contributory negligence'.

See Higgins-v-Siac 101 ILTR at 168.

In that same case I also noticed the opinion of Ó Dálaigh CJ at page 171 to the following effect:

'There may be acts of momentary inadvertence which a jury will properly excuse as being the acts which a reasonably careful (person) will do'.

These principals have been implemented in practice by Barron J in Dunne -v- Honeywell Control Systems Limited and Virginia Milk Products Limited [1991] IRLM at 595; by Budd J in Kelly -v- McNamara (unreported, The High Court 5th June, 1996) and by myself in a number of cases including Connell -v- McGing (unreported, The High Court 8th December, 2000).

I also note that the Supreme Court have pointed out in a number of cases the view that a Plaintiff, whilst walking is not required to look down at the ground.

In the case before me I'm satisfied that the Plaintiff and her family were visiting what, on any view of the case, was an interesting equestrian centre all of which were new to the Plaintiff on her first visit thereto.

I have seriously considered whether the actions of the Plaintiff constituted an act of inadvertence which a reasonably careful person would not do and likewise have considered the matter from the point of view as to whether I should deem the Plaintiff's actions in talking to her family and walking through the door as such an act of momentary inadvertence which a jury (and in this case which I) would properly excuse as being an act which a reasonably careful person will do. Taking all these matters into account I have concluded that it would be unreasonable to find the Plaintiff guilty of contributory negligence in the particular circumstances as pleaded in this case.

In the circumstances I find the Defendant liable in negligence. I find the Plaintiff not guilty of contributory negligence.

The Parties very sensibly had agreed the medical reports at outset of this case. Upon my invitation they agreed the general damages and the special damages. In the circumstances there will be judgment in the sum of £41,200; being as to £40,000 agreed general damages and £1,200 for special damages. For the purpose of completeness I note that the Plaintiff suffered a very serious injury with continuing sequelae and continues to carry a very severe scar."

Comments and Questions:
1. Lavan J. notes that the occupier of the premises did not seek to modify his duty as allowed under s.5. Consider how the occupier might have employed s.5 to do so.

Recreational users

A recreational user is defined as a person who enters onto the premises of the occupier with or without the occupier's permission to engage in a recreational activity. It does not include those who have paid to enter (other than the payment of a reasonable parking charge), are members of the occupier's family who are ordinarily resident on the premises, a person who has received express permission to be present, or a social guest (s.1(1)).

A recreational activity is defined in s.1 as an activity carried out in the open air, or any scientific research or nature study conducted in the open air, or exploring caves or visiting sites and buildings of historical, architectural, traditional, artistic, archeological or scientific importance.

The duty owed to recreational users is divided into two parts: (1) a duty not to injure or damage the property of the entrant intentionally and the duty not to act in reckless disregard for them or their property (for reckless disregard please see below); and (2) a duty to take reasonable care required in the maintenance of structures which are provided *primarily* for the use of recreational users.

Heaves v Westmeath County Council
Circuit Court (2002) 20 I.L.T. 236

Facts: The plaintiff entered the defendant's grounds and paid a fee for himself and his two small children when he parked his car. Presently the two children strayed from his sight. In seeking out the children he proceeded to descend a set of rustic steps, which his children had already successfully negotiated, when he slipped on an uneven indentation, which was partly covered in moss and lichen. He had moved down the right-hand side of the steps (rather than the left-hand side which was partly covered with ivy and other growth) with his right arm outstretched. He sued the defendant as occupiers of the premises for the injuries he received when he fell. In evidence, it was established that a good cleaning system was in place and that on an annual basis the defendant employed an independent contractor who accompanied the defendant's gardener on a tour of the premises. This annual consultation between the defendant and the contractor had taken place in the month previous to the events at issue and recommended spraying, including treating the steps in question, had been carried out.

Issues: Two issues arose for consideration. First, was the fee paid an entrance fee (which would classify the plaintiff as a visitor) or was it a parking fee (in which case he would be classified as a recreational user)? What was the correct duty owed to the entrant and was this duty breached?

McMahon J. held that the fee was an entrance fee as it would have been paid regardless of whether the plaintiff had parked his car or not. As such he was a visitor and owed a reasonable duty of care. However, that duty in this case was not breached, taking into account in particular the steps taken by the defendant to ensure the safety of the grounds.

McMahon J.:

"The law relating to occupiers' liability is now contained in the Occupiers' Liability Act 1995. Under the 1995 Act, persons who come on to another person's premises are divided into three categories: visitors, trespassers and recreational users. Briefly speaking to the visitor, the occupier owes a duty of care ('the common duty of care') defined in the act as a duty 'to take such care as is reasonable in all the circumstances—to ensure that a visitor to premises does not suffer injury or damage by reason of any danger existing thereon'. This duty is comparable to the duty of care in the ordinary negligence action. Trespassers and recreational users, however, are not so generously treated under the legislation. To these entrants, the occupier must merely ensure that he does not intentionally injure them, or does not act with reckless disregard for their safety. Not surprisingly, the plaintiff argued that he was a lawful visitor to the premises and was entitled to the common duty of care that is, a duty on the part of the defendant to take reasonable care. Somewhat more surprisingly the defendant argued that the plaintiff was a recreational user and was accordingly only owed the lower standard of care. In the alternative, the defendant claimed that even if the plaintiff was a visitor, the defendant was not in breach of its statutory duty in the circumstances.

Visitor or recreational user?

To determine the initial question one must look to the definitions in the Act 'visitor' in the definition section means:

(a) an entrant, other than a recreational user, who is present on premises at the invitation, or with the permission, of the occupier or any other entrant specified in paragraph (a), (b) or (c), of the definition of 'recreational user'.

(b) an entrant, other than a recreational user, who was present on premises by virtue of an express or implied term in contract, and

(c) an entrant as of right,

while he or she is so present, as the case may be, for the purpose for which he or she is invited or permitted to be there for the purpose of the performance of the contract or for the purpose of the exercise of the right, and includes any such entrant whose presence has become unlawful after entry thereon and who is taking reasonable steps to leave (section 1).

'Recreational user', on the other hand, under the Act means an entrant who, with or without the occupier's permission or at the occupier's implied invitation, is present on premises without a charge (other than a reasonable charge in respect of the cost of providing vehicle parking facilities) being imposed for the purpose of engaging in a recreational activity, including an entrant admitted without charge to a national monument pursuant to section 16(1) of the National Monuments Act, 1930.

In so far as the term 'visitor' *includes an entrant who was present on premises by virtue of a contract, it would seem clear that the plaintiff in the present case should be classified as a visitor.* After all, he paid an entry fee in respect of himself and his children. At common law he would have been classified as a contractual invitee. At common law he would he entitled to reasonable care. The history of the legislation in question indicates that there was no intention to downgrade the legal status of such an entrant. The act was primarily introduced to reverse *McNamara v. ESB* [1975] IR 1 in respect of trespassers, and to create a new category for recreational users who were causing some concern to the agricultural community who feared that the common law might treat them too leniently by according to them the duty of reasonable care.

'Recreational users', on the other hand, was intended to cover people who entered premises with or without permission without a charge, to engage in a recreational activity conducted in the open air (including any sporting activity), or to engage in scientific research and nature study or to explore caves, visit sites and buildings of historical, architectural, traditional artistic and archaeological or scientific importance (s. 1(1) of the 1995 Act).

From a careful reading of these definitions it is clear that, by entering under a contract the plaintiff is squarely in the category of 'visitor', and by paying a charge he is outside the category of 'recreational user' (See McMahon and Binchy, 3rd ed., 2000, p. 322).

It was suggested by counsel for the defence that, since the money from the plaintiff was paid in the car-park, it constituted a charge in respect of parking the car only, and since it did not amount to an entry fee, it accordingly, brought the plaintiff out of the visitor category and into the category of recreational user. There can be little doubt, from the definition of recreational user, that a parking charge, if that is all it is, will not take the entrant out of that category. The weakness of this argument in the present case, however, was fully exposed when in answer to the question, whether the plaintiff and his children would have been charged if they arrived on foot, the defendant's counsel had to concede that they would have had to pay in such an event also. In these circumstances, it is clear that the fees were not paid for the privilege of parking the car. They were clearly entry fees. And this made the plaintiff and his children 'visitors' under the act.

That the plaintiff also wandered at his leisure enjoying the garden and the grounds, is not in doubt. But engaging in a recreational activity does not necessarily and invariably make him a recreational user. The act is clear in declaring that if an entrant comes to the premises under a contract and pays a charge he is a visitor, and only a visitor. In this legislative classification it is important to remember that there are three, and only three categories; these categories are exhaustive; there are no more categories. Furthermore, it is equally important to realise that an entrant cannot be in two categories at the same time. A careful study of the legislation compels one to this conclusion and in this, it in no way departs from the common law (see for detailed consideration McMahon and Binchy, *Irish Law of Torts*, 1st ed., 1980, pp. 230–262). To accept the defendant's argument, that because the plaintiff was enjoying the scenery he must, therefore, be a recreational user, would ignore these principles, would distort the statute and would lead to unwarranted and unreasonable conclusions. For these reasons, I have little hesitation in rejecting it.

The common duty of care

The standard of care owed to a visitor is the common duty of care, that is, a duty to take such care as is reasonable in all circumstances (having regard to the care which the visitor may reasonably be expected to take for his own safety and, if the visitor is on the premises in the company of another person, the extent of the supervision and control the latter person may reasonably be expected to exercise over the visitor's activities) to ensure that a visitor to the premises does not suffer injury or damage by reason of any dangerous existing thereon (s. 3(1) of the 1995 Act).

Could it be suggested in the present circumstances, that the defendant did not act reasonably in the measures it took to protect its visitor from the danger which the rough-hewn steps in these grounds, carrying some moss and lichen as they did, presented to the plaintiff? ...

... Having considered the matter fully, I have come to the conclusion that the plaintiff's action should be dismissed. I find that the precautions which the defendant had taken in all the circumstances were reasonable. They had personnel appointed to address such risks; the gardener who was the relevant person had a satisfactory cleaning system in place, and it had worked for several years without a problem. The evidence of the defendant's witnesses that this was carried out in a proper way was not undermined in cross-examination. Moreover, in those matters where the gardener lacked competence he recognised his own limitations and engaged an outside expert to advise him. He duly implemented the advice he received, and this was exactly what the plaintiff's Engineer said the defendant should do to avoid the negligence label. Furthermore, the absence of a warning notice was not fatal to the defendant's case for the reasons I have already stated. In any event, the plaintiff in his own evidence said that, before he commenced his descent, he approached the steps with his eyes open and fully aware of the nature of the steps that confronted him. He was in full possession of all the requisite knowledge that a warning notice, had there been one there, would have given him and, in the circumstances, one cannot conclude that the absence of such a notice in any way contributed to the plaintiff's injury. Finally, it must be noted that the plaintiff's two young children, aged five and three years at the time, had safely negotiated the same steps some moments previous to the plaintiff's fall and, if it was safe for them, it cannot have represented a serious risk to an adult who was fully aware of what lay before him.

For these reasons, therefore, I conclude that, although the plaintiff was a visitor within the statutory definition, there was no failure on the part of the defendant to discharge its statutory duty to take reasonable care in respect of dangers existing on the premises. Since there was no breach of duty by the defendant, the question of contributory negligence does not arise."

Comments and Questions:
1. Do you think the finding of McMahon J. would have been the same had the injured party been one of the children and not Mr Heaves?

RECKLESS DISREGARD

The duty owed to recreational users is not to intentionally injure them or act with reckless disregard. While the Act outlines nine factors to be taken into consideration when judging whether an occupier has acted with reckless disregard, the concept is far from clear. An attempt was made in the following case to clarify what it might mean.

Weir-Rodgers v SF Trust Ltd.
Supreme Court [2005] I.E.S.C. 2

Facts: The respondent was sitting down with some friends close to the edge of a cliff on land owned by the appellant. When she stood up, she lost her footing and fell down the edge of the cliff, and suffered injuries. The respondent brought proceedings on the basis of a breach of the duty, under s.4 of the Occupiers' Liability Act 1995. She relied, *inter alia*, on the absence of any warning notice about the cliff, the gradient of which she maintained was deceptive. It was accepted in the High Court that Ms Weir-Rodgers was a recreational user. The High Court judge, Butler J., having regard to the criteria in s.4(2), found the appellant to be liable, but assessed contributory negligence at 25 per cent. The appellant (a company established by a Franciscan order who owned the land) appealed.

Issues: The court had to consider whether the appellants (SF Trust Ltd) had acted with reckless disregard with respect to the respondent. The Supreme Court held that they had not, holding that the High Court had erred in applying a standard more akin to "reasonable care" as opposed to the standard of "reckless disregard" which the court appeared to accept was more "indulgent" to the defendant. However, the court failed to establish whether the test of "reckless disregard" was an objective or a subjective one.

Geoghegan J. (Murray C.J. and Denham J. concurring):

"The law
As I have already indicated the respondent in order to succeed in this action had to establish a breach of duty towards her under s.4 of the Occupiers' Liability Act 1995. Under that section the same duty is owed to recreational users within the meaning of the Act and to trespassers. For this reason and for shorthand convenience, I will be referring from now on to the duty owed to trespassers but this does not mean that I am expressing any view as to whether the respondent was a recreational user within the meaning of the Act or not. I will begin my treatment of the law by quoting paragraph 12.16 of McMahon and Binchy Law of Torts 3rd edition under the heading of 'Occupiers Liability to Trespassers'. The learned authors say the following:

'This branch of the law was drastically overhauled twenty five years ago in Ireland. After McNamara v. ESB was handed down by the Supreme Court in 1975, the duty owed to trespassers in Ireland was the duty to take reasonable care. The Occupiers' Liability Act, 1995, however, has reversed this and has restored the old pre-McNamara common law standard, that is, that the duty owed to trespassers is not to injure them intentionally and not to act with reckless disregard (for) their person or property. All the common law case law on this branch of the law, which had become largely redundant during the period 1975 to 1995, is once more very relevant in determining what recklessness means in this context. Furthermore, the judicial techniques which were developed to mitigate this harsh common law rule must all be revisited as they represent real options for a judiciary wishing to avoid a draconian rule in particular situations.'

With the greatest respect to the learned trial judge there is nothing to indicate that he addressed himself to this much higher threshold now enacted for a plaintiff trespasser. In fairness to him he undoubtedly referred to the expression 'reckless disregard' and he said that he had been told by Mr. Whelehan that the expression had not been discussed in the courts or determined in any written judgment. Unfortunately, he did not then go on to consider what it meant but rather moved to certain matters which under the section, a judge should have regard to. To understand this point, I think it necessary to cite in full the first two subsections of s.4.

'4(1) In respect of a danger existing on premises, an occupier owes towards a recreational user of the premises or a trespasser thereon ("the person") a duty—
  (a) not to injure the person or damage the property of the person intentionally, and
  (b) not to act with reckless disregard for the person or the property of the person,
  except in so far as the occupier extends the duty in accordance with section 5.
(2) In determining whether or not an occupier has so acted with reckless disregard, regard shall be had to all the circumstances of the case, including—
  (a) whether the occupier knew or had reasonable grounds for believing that a danger existed on the premises;
  (b) whether the occupier knew or had reasonable grounds for believing that the person and, in the case of damage, property of the person, was or was likely to be on the premises;
  (c) whether the occupier knew or had reasonable grounds for believing that the person or property of the person was in, or was likely to be in, the vicinity of the place where the danger existed;
  (d) whether the danger was one against which, in all the circumstances, the occupier might reasonably be expected to provide protection for the person and property of the person;

(e) the burden on the occupier of eliminating the danger or of protecting the person and property of the person from the danger, taking into account the difficulty, expense or impracticality, having regard to the danger of the premises and the degree of the danger, of so doing;

(f) the character of the premises including, in relation to premises of such a character as to be likely to be used for recreational activity, the desirability of maintaining the tradition of open access to premises of such a character for such an activity;

(g) the conduct of the person, and the care which he or she may reasonably be expected to take for his or her own safety, while on the premises, having regard to the extent of his or her knowledge thereof;

(h) the nature of any warning given by the occupier or another person of the danger; and

(i) whether or not the person was on the premises in the company of another person and, if so, the extent of the supervision and control the latter person might reasonably be expected to exercise over the other's activities.'

At paragraph 12.109 of the third edition of McMahon and Binchy the following is stated:

'It is clear from consideration of the several factors prescribed in the legislation that recklessness connotes objective default rather than necessarily requiring any subjective advertence on the part of the occupier to the risk of injury.'

I do not intend to express any view on the subjective/objective question. Such consideration should be left for a case where it properly arises. My concern in this regard arises from the fact that notwithstanding the recommendations contained in both the Consultation Paper and the ultimate report of the Law Reform Commission that the liability towards trespassers and recreational users should be one of 'gross negligence', the Oireachtas appears to have rejected this recommendation and adopted the phrase arising from the old case law namely 'reckless disregard'. It may well be, therefore, that the liability is something more than what might be described as 'gross negligence'. However, this is a case of a lady falling down the edge of a cliff. It is suggested that there was an inherent danger in the nature of the actual ground and portion of cliff where she fell. This, of course, is so but only in the sense that wherever there is a cliff edge it is to be reasonably expected that there may be parts of it more dangerous than others. At any rate, it would be reasonable to assume that the occupiers in this case would have had some awareness of the danger. For the purposes of this case and without deciding the issue, I am prepared to accept that the test of recklessness is an objective one as suggested by the authors of McMahon and Binchy. In the same paragraph of that work the authors make a very astute and prescient remark. They state the following:

'One can only speculate about the extent to which the courts are in practice going to set the standard at a lower level than the (equally objective) standard of reasonable care. The 1995 Act gives no guidance as to how much lower the level should be. The nine factors specified in section 4(2) contain no such yardstick; indeed, they might constitute a trap to an unwary judge who could easily seek to apply them without adverting to the fact that, although they are similar to criteria applicable for determining the issue of negligence, they have to be pitched at a level more indulgent to the defendant.'

It would seem to me that that is exactly what happened in this case and that the learned trial judge unconsciously fell into this trap.

As it happens, I take the view that even if the duty on the occupier in this case was the ordinary Donoghue v. Stevenson neighbourly duty of care the respondent would not be entitled to succeed. Interestingly in Donovan v. Landy's Limited [1963] I.R. 441 a case in which, as the Law Reform Commission noted, Kingsmill Moore J. reviewed all the Irish and English authorities, Lavery J. gave a judgment agreeing with the judgment of Kingsmill Moore J. but making the following apposite comment:

'I agree with his conclusions and in the main with the reasons which he has given. I am, however, in some doubt as to whether the distinction between negligence and reckless disregard is necessary to be drawn and I fear that such a distinction may well lead to difficulty in a trial before a jury in explaining a case of this kind. There are already so many distinctions which have been elaborately explained in innumerable judgments.'

More or less the same view was taken by Judge McMahon one of the authors of McMahon and Binchy in his submission to the Law Reform Commission between the time of the Consultation Paper and the ultimate report. He was strongly of the view that the duty should be an ordinary duty of reasonable care.

The Commission rejected his advice and again recommended a threshold of 'gross negligence'. The Oireachtas, however, did not adopt that expression in the legislation and instead went back to the old expression 'reckless disregard'. It may well be reasonable to argue therefore that the threshold is even higher than 'gross negligence'. I do not find it necessary to express any definitive view on any of this because as I have already indicated I believe that even if the duty was merely a duty of reasonable care and not the obviously higher duty not to act with reckless disregard for the personal property of the person the result in this case would be the same. It is perfectly obvious to all users of land higher than sea level but adjoining the sea that there may well be a dangerous cliff edge and in those circumstances the occupier of the lands cannot be held to be unreasonable in not putting up a warning notice. Still less has he reckless disregard for the safety of the person using the land. The whole area of reasonableness in an outdoor land situation has been quite recently considered by the House of Lords in Tomlinson v. Congleton Borough Council [2003] 3 All E.R. 1122. That case involved potential liability under the English Occupiers' Liability Act, 1957 and there were some views expressed in the speeches of the Law Lords relating also to the Occupiers' Liability Act, 1984 which was the Act dealing with duty to trespassers. While there is some overlap, the wording of the English Acts is sufficiently different to render it of limited assistance in interpreting the Irish legislation. But at least one aspect of that case is relevant to this case. The Law Lords in their speeches referred to the common sense expectations of persons engaged in outdoor activities such as, for instance, mountain climbing or walking or swimming in dangerous areas. The other side of that coin is that the occupier is entitled to assume that knowledge of such dangers and risks would exist and safety measures would be taken. For this purpose, I find it sufficient to refer only to some passages from the speech of Lord Hutton. At p. 1155 of the report he cited with approval a Scottish case Stevenson v. Corporation of Glasgow [1908] SC 1034 at 1039 where Lord M'Laren stated:

> '... in a town, as well as in the country, there are physical features which may be productive of injury to careless persons or to young children against which it is impossible to guard by protective measures. The situation of a town on the banks of a river is a familiar feature; and whether the stream be sluggish like the Clyde at Glasgow, or swift and variable like the Ness at Inverness, or the Tay at Perth, there is always danger to the individual who may be so unfortunate as to fall into the stream. But in none of these places has it been found necessary to fence the river to prevent children or careless persons from falling into the water. Now, as the common law is just the formal statement of the results and conclusions of the common sense of mankind, I come without difficulty to the conclusion that precautions which have been rejected by common sense as unnecessary and inconvenient are not required by the law.'

That passage would seem to be apposite to this case also and would seem to apply to any suggestion that a warning notice should have been put up. Lord Hutton also cites Corporation of the City of Glasgow v. Taylor [1922] 1 A.C. 44 where at 61 Lord Shaw of Dunfermline stated:

> 'Grounds thrown open by a municipality to the public may contain objects of natural beauty, say precipitous cliffs or the banks of streams, the dangers of the resort to which are plain.'

In support of these propositions, Lord Hutton cited yet another Scottish case Hastie v. Magistrates of Edinburgh [1907] SC 1102 where the Lord President (Lord Dunedin) at 1106 said that there are certain risks against which the law in accordance with the dictates of common sense, does not give protection—such risks are 'just one of the results of the world as we find it'.

I would heartily endorse the sentiments expressed in these passages. The person sitting down near a cliff must be prepared for oddities in the cliff's structure or in the structure of the ground adjacent to the cliff and he or she assumes the inherent risks associated therewith. There could, of course, be something quite exceptionally unusual and dangerous in the state of a particular piece of ground which would impose a duty on the occupier the effect of which would be that if he did not put up a warning notice he would be treated as having reckless disregard. But this is certainly not such a case. While obviously sympathetic to the respondent in her serious injuries, I am quite satisfied that there was no liability on the part of the appellant in this case and I would set aside the judgment of the High Court and dismiss the action. The issues on the notice to vary do not, therefore, arise in any view."

Comments and Questions:
1. Geoghegan J. refused to adjudge whether the test of reckless disregard was an objective or a subjective one, but he did appear to give more weight to the possibility as advocated by McMahon & Binchy that the test was an objective one. However, given that the first three propositions in s.4(2) relate to what the occupier knew or ought reasonably to know, does this not require a certain element of subjectiveness? In this way is the test not more correctly stated as a mix of objective and subjective considerations?

2. McMahon, in his submission to the Law Reform Commission, suggested that the standard be one of reasonable care. What difference does it make, in your view, that it is instead one of reckless disregard, given the balance of competing interests which takes place when one considers what is "reasonable" in a given situation?

Trespassers

A trespasser is defined simply as a person who is not a recreational user or a visitor (s.1(1)).

The duty owed is divided into two parts: a duty not to injure the entrant or damage their property intentionally and not to act with reckless disregard for them or their property (s.4(1)). If the entrant has a criminal intent, or commits a criminal act while on the premises, the duty is simply not to injure the entrant or damage his property intentionally, there is no duty not to act with reckless disregard. This applies except where the court determines otherwise "in the interests of justice". It is also subject to the "defence of property" principle.

Williams v TP Wallace Construction Ltd. and Crickley Roofing Ltd.
High Court [2002] 2 I.L.R.M. 62

Facts: The plaintiff was the general manager of the third party, a company which had distributed the guttering used by the defendants during a construction project. During a visit to the site to inspect the guttering he fell from a ladder and was injured. A dispute arose as to the circumstances in which he came to be on the ladder. The defendants argued that at the relevant time the plaintiff was on the site as a trespasser as he had arrived during a tea-break and he had been asked to come back at a later time. The plaintiff, however, contended that he was accompanied to the site of the guttering by a workman who was not taking his tea-break at that time.

Issues: The issue of fact to be decided was whether the plaintiff had received permission to investigate the guttering at the time the accident occurred. Once that was decided the legal issue to be decided was whether any duty to him had been breached.

Morris P. believed the evidence of the defendants to be the more credible. On that basis he held that the plaintiff was a trespasser and that the duty not to intentionally injury him or act with reckless disregard as to his safety had not been breached.

Morris P.:

"In my view it is clear that the duty owed to Mr Williams must be identified by reference to his status on site at the relevant time. It is submitted by Counsel on behalf of the Defendants that at the relevant time Mr Williams was on the building site as a trespasser, which is defined in the Occupiers Liabilities Act, 1995 as meaning 'an entrant other than a recreational user or visitor.' It is submitted that in these circumstances the only duty owed to the Plaintiff by the First Named Defendant was, as is provided in Section 4 of the Act:

> '(a) Not to injure the person or damage the property of the person intentionally and
> (b) Not to act with reckless disregard for the person or the property of the person.'

It is submitted that, as occurred in this case, to leave a ladder leaning against scaffolding but untied is not to act with reckless disregard for the person or his property.

On behalf of the Plaintiff it is submitted that he was on site as a visitor. The term 'visitor' is defined by the 1995 Act as

> 'An entrant, other than a recreational user, who is present on the premises at the invitation or with the permission of the occupier or any other entrant specified in paragraph (a), (b) or (c) of the definition of "recreational user."'

It is further submitted on the Plaintiff's behalf that as he was invited on to the site by the workman in the circumstances which are outlined above and since he was therefore a visitor, he was owed the duty of care referred to in paragraph (3) of the 1995 Act. That duty of care is the 'common law duty of care' which is defined as meaning an obligation to 'take such care as is reasonable in all the circumstances having regard to the care which the visitor may reasonably be expected to take for his or her own safety and if the visitor is on the premises in the company of another person the extent of the supervision and control the latter person may reasonably expected to exercise over the visitor's activities.' To ensure that the visitor to the premises does not suffer injury or damage by reason of any danger existing thereon.

I turn first to consider the status of Mr Williams on the site at the relevant time.

Even allowing for the fact that this incident occurred over three years ago I am struck by the lack of harmony between the accounts which were given by Mr Williams and the two other persons in his group as to the circumstances in which they came to be on the roof. I find it quite inconceivable that a workman on site would:

(a) be working during the tea break (even though I do accept that Mr Maher said that in the boom times that existed in 1998 it occasionally happened) but that he would

(b) identify the group as the persons who had come in connection with the faulty guttering and

(c) take it upon himself to escort them on to the flat roof for the purpose of Mr Williams climbing on the scaffolding to carry out his inspection.

I cannot believe that a workman would behave in such a busy body way. I do not believe that the party came to be on the roof in the manner described on behalf of the Plaintiff.

It is not alone the unlikely nature of this part of the story told by the Plaintiff's witnesses. There is also the contradiction and conflict between the stories told by Mr Cooke and Mr McConnell of what transpired later on. Having brought Mr Williams to hospital it is said that they went back to the building site as a 'courtesy visit' but were as a result of the visit able to glean information which would be of relevance and importance for Mr Williams in his litigation. To instance but one stark contrast between the two accounts. Mr Cooke says that when he returned with Mr McConnell he was able to make his observations from the road and that he did not go back on site. Mr McConnell on the other hand says that they went back up on the flat roof and made the observations of the ladder from there.

I approach the evidence of these three gentlemen on the basis that the Plaintiff is a long term business associate of Mr McConnell and was at the relevant time employed by the same company as Mr Cooke. I am unable to accept their evidence on their account of how they came to be on the roof as being at the invitation of the workman or anybody else. I have not been satisfied that the Plaintiff is entitled to be regarded at law as a visitor within the meaning of the Occupiers' Liability Act, 1995.

That being so the standard of care imposed upon the First Named Defendant was not to injure the Plaintiff intentionally and not to act with reckless disregard for his person. I am satisfied that no case has been made out that the First Named Defendant acted in such a reckless way and therefore the Plaintiff is not entitled to any relief under the Occupiers' Liability Act."

Comments and Questions:

1. The injury in this case was brought about as a result of a ladder which had been insufficiently secured. Does this in your view constitute a "state" of the premises as required by the Act?

The Occupiers' Liability Act 1995

AN ACT TO AMEND THE LAW RELATING TO THE LIABILITY OF OCCUPIERS OF PREMISES (INCLUDING LAND) IN RESPECT OF DANGERS EXISTING ON SUCH PREMISES FOR INJURY OR DAMAGE TO PERSONS OR PROPERTY WHILE ON SUCH PREMISES AND TO PROVIDE FOR CONNECTED MATTERS.

[17*th June*, 1995]

BE IT ENACTED BY THE OIREACHTAS AS FOLLOWS:
Interpretation.
1.—(1) In this Act, unless the context otherwise requires—

"damage" includes loss of property and injury to an animal;

"danger", in relation to any premises, means a danger due to the state of the premises;

"entrant", in relation to a danger existing on premises, means a person who enters on the premises and is not the sole occupier;

"injury" includes loss of life, any disease and any impairment of physical or mental condition;

"occupier", in relation to any premises, means a person exercising such control over the state of the premises that it is reasonable to impose upon that person a duty towards an entrant in respect of a particular danger thereon and, where there is more than one occupier of the same premises, the extent of the duty of each occupier towards an entrant depends on the degree of control each of them has over the state of the premises and the particular danger thereon and whether, as respects each of them, the entrant concerned is a visitor, recreational user or trespasser;

"premises" includes land, water and any fixed or moveable structures thereon and also includes vessels, vehicles, trains, aircraft and other means of transport;

"property", in relation to an entrant, includes the property of another in the possession or under the control of the entrant while the entrant is on the premises of the occupier;

"recreational activity" means any recreational activity conducted, whether alone or with others, in the open air (including any sporting activity), scientific research and nature study so conducted, exploring caves and visiting sites and buildings of historical, architectural, traditional, artistic, archaeological or scientific importance;

"recreational user" means an entrant who, with or without the occupier's permission or at the occupier's implied invitation, is present on premises without a charge (other than a reasonable charge in respect of the cost of providing vehicle parking facilities) being imposed for the purpose of engaging in a recreational activity, including an entrant admitted without charge to a national monument pursuant to section 16(1) of the National Monuments Act, 1930, but not including an entrant who is so present and is—

(*a*) a member of the occupier's family who is ordinarily resident on the premises,

(*b*) an entrant who is present at the express invitation of the occupier or such a member, or

(*c*) an entrant who is present with the permission of the occupier or such a member for social reasons connected with the occupier or such a member;

"trespasser" means an entrant other than a recreational user or visitor;

"visitor" means—

(*a*) an entrant, other than a recreational user, who is present on premises at the invitation, or with the permission, of the occupier or any other entrant specified in *paragraph (a), (b)* or *(c)* of the definition of "recreational user",

(*b*) an entrant, other than a recreational user, who is present on premises by virtue of an express or implied term in a contract, and

(*c*) an entrant as of right,

while he or she is so present, as the case may be, for the purpose for which he or she is invited or permitted to be there, for the purpose of the performance of the contract or for the purpose of the exercise of the right, and includes any such entrant whose presence on premises has become unlawful after entry thereon and who is taking reasonable steps to leave.

(2) In this Act—

(*a*) a reference to a section is to a section of this Act, unless it is indicated that reference to some other enactment is intended,

(*b*) a reference to a subsection is to the subsection of the provision in which the reference occurs, unless it is indicated that reference to some other provision is intended, and

(*c*) a reference to any enactment shall be construed as a reference to that enactment as amended, adapted or extended by or under any subsequent enactment including this Act.

Replacement of common law rules.
2.—(1) Subject to *section 8*, the duties, liabilities and rights provided for by this Act shall have effect in place of the duties, liabilities and rights which heretofore attached by the common law to occupiers of premises as such in respect of dangers existing on their premises to entrants thereon.

(2) This Act does not apply to a cause of action which accrued before the commencement of this Act.

Duty owed to visitors.
3.—(1) An occupier of premises owes a duty of care ("the common duty of care") towards a visitor thereto except in so far as the occupier extends, restricts, modifies or excludes that duty in accordance with *section 5*.

(2) In this section "the common duty of care" means a duty to take such care as is reasonable in all the circumstances (having regard to the care which a visitor may reasonably be expected to take for his or her own safety and, if the visitor is on the premises in the company of another person, the extent of the supervision and control the latter person may reasonably be expected to exercise over the visitor's activities) to ensure that a visitor to the premises does not suffer injury or damage by reason of any danger existing thereon.

Duty owed to recreational users or trespassers
4.—(1) In respect of a danger existing on premises, an occupier owes towards a recreational user of the premises or a trespasser thereon ("the person") a duty—
(*a*) not to injure the person or damage the property of the person intentionally, and
(*b*) not to act with reckless disregard for the person or the property of the person, except in so far as the occupier extends the duty in accordance with *section 5*.
    (2) In determining whether or not an occupier has so acted with reckless disregard, regard shall be had to all the circumstances of the case, including—
(*a*) whether the occupier knew or had reasonable grounds for believing that a danger existed on the premises;
(*b*) whether the occupier knew or had reasonable grounds for believing that the person and, in the case of damage, property of the person, was or was likely to be on the premises;
(*c*) whether the occupier knew or had reasonable grounds for believing that the person or property of the person was in, or was likely to be in, the vicinity of the place where the danger existed;
(*d*) whether the danger was one against which, in all the circumstances, the occupier might reasonably be expected to provide protection for the person and property of the person;
(*e*) the burden on the occupier of eliminating the danger or of protecting the person and property of the person from the danger, taking into account the difficulty, expense or impracticability, having regard to the character of the premises and the degree of the danger, of so doing;
(*f*) the character of the premises including, in relation to premises of such a character as to be likely to be used for recreational activity, the desirability of maintaining the tradition of open access to premises of such a character for such an activity;
(*g*) the conduct of the person, and the care which he or she may reasonably be expected to take for his or her own safety, while on the premises, having regard to the extent of his or her knowledge thereof;
(*h*) the nature of any warning given by the occupier or another person of the danger; and
(*i*) whether or not the person was on the premises in the company of another person and, if so, the extent of the supervision and control the latter person might reasonably be expected to exercise over the other's activities.

(3) (*a*) Where a person enters onto premises for the purpose of committing an offence or, while present thereon, commits an offence, the occupier shall not be liable for a breach of the duty imposed by *subsection (1)* (*b*) unless a court determines otherwise in the interests of justice.

   (*b*) In *paragraph (a)* "offence" includes an attempted offence.

(4) Notwithstanding *subsection (1)*, where a structure on premises is or has been provided for use primarily by recreational users, the occupier shall owe a duty towards such users in respect of such a structure to take reasonable care to maintain the structure in a safe condition:

Provided that, where a stile, gate, footbridge or other similar structure on premises is or has been provided not for use primarily by recreational users, the occupier's duty towards a recreational user thereof in respect of such structure shall not be extended by virtue of this subsection.

Modification of occupiers' duty to entrants.
5.—(1) An occupier may by express agreement or notice extend his or her duty towards entrants under *sections 3* and *4*.

   (2) (*a*) Subject to this section and to *section 8*, an occupier may by express agreement or notice restrict, modify or exclude his or her duty towards visitors under *section 3*.

     (*b*) Such a restriction, modification or exclusion shall not bind a visitor unless—

       (i) it is reasonable in all the circumstances, and

       (ii) in case the occupier purports by notice to so restrict, modify or exclude that duty, the occupier has taken reasonable steps to bring the notice to the attention of the visitor.

     (*c*) For the purposes of *paragraph (b) (ii)* an occupier shall be presumed, unless the contrary is shown, to have taken reasonable steps to bring a notice to the attention of a visitor if it is prominently displayed at the normal means of access to the premises.

   (3) In respect of a danger existing on premises, a restriction, modification or exclusion referred to in *subsection (2)* shall not be taken as allowing an occupier to injure a visitor or damage the property of a visitor intentionally or to act with reckless disregard for a visitor or the property of a visitor.

   (4) In determining for the purposes of *subsection (3)* whether or not an occupier has acted with reckless disregard, regard shall be had to all the circumstances of the case including, where appropriate, the matters specified in *subsection (2)* of *section 4*.

   (5) Where injury or damage is caused to a visitor or property of a visitor by a danger of which the visitor had been warned by the occupier or another person, the warning is not, without more, to be treated as absolving the occupier from liability unless, in all the circumstances, it was enough to enable the visitor, by having regard to the warning, to avoid the injury or damage so caused.

Duty of occupiers towards strangers to contracts.

6.—(1) The duty which an occupier of premises owes to an entrant under this Act shall not be capable of being modified or excluded by a contract to which the entrant is a stranger, whether the occupier is bound by the contract to permit the entrant to enter or use the premises or not.

(2) For the purposes of this section, an entrant shall be deemed to be a stranger to a contract if the entrant is not for the time being entitled to the benefit of the contract as a party to it or as the successor by assignment or otherwise of a party to it, and, accordingly, a party to the contract who has ceased to be so entitled shall be deemed to be a stranger to the contract.

(3) This section applies to contracts entered into before the commencement of this Act, as well as to those entered into after such commencement.

Liability of occupiers for negligence of independent contractors.

7.—An occupier of premises shall not be liable to an entrant for injury or damage caused to the entrant or property of the entrant by reason of a danger existing on the premises due to the negligence of an independent contractor employed by the occupier if the occupier has taken all reasonable care in the circumstances (including such steps as the occupier ought reasonably to have taken to satisfy himself or herself that the independent contractor was competent to do the work concerned) unless the occupier has or ought to have had knowledge of the fact that the work was not properly done.

Saver

8.—Nothing in this Act shall be construed as affecting any enactment or any rule of law relating to—

(*a*) self-defence, the defence of others or the defence of property,

(*b*) any liability imposed on an occupier as a member of a particular class of persons including the following classes of persons:

    (i) persons by virtue of a contract for the hire of, or for the carriage for reward of persons or property in, any vessel, vehicle, train, aircraft or other means of transport;

    (ii) persons by virtue of a contract of bailment; and

    (iii) employers in respect of their duties towards their employees, or

(*c*) any liability imposed on an occupier for a tort committed by another person in circumstances where the duty imposed on the occupier is of such a nature that its performance may not be delegated to another person.

Short title and commencement.

9.—(1) This Act may be cited as the Occupiers' Liability Act, 1995.

(2) This Act shall come into operation one month after the date of its passing.

CHAPTER 5

PRODUCTS LIABILITY

INTRODUCTION

The area of products liability concerns the right of a plaintiff to recover for damage arising from a defective product. Since the introduction of the Liability for Defective Products Act 1991 (the Act) there are now two avenues which a claimant can pursue in the Irish courts. One is to prove a case in tort under the negligence principles. The other is to pursue a claim under the 1991 Act. To sue in negligence a plaintiff must show that a duty of care existed, that that duty has been breached and that causation has been established. The benefit of pursuing a claim under the Act is that no breach of a duty of care needs to be proved as strict liability applies (strict liability refers to liability without fault or negligence). Causation must also be established under the Act. The Act, however, may not always be the most favourable route. For instance, the Act will only allow recovery for dangerous defects, which threaten safety. On the other hand, in a negligence action it appears to be the case that recovery for non-dangerous defects is permissible.

AN ACTION IN NEGLIGENCE

Historically, there was a reluctance to allow anyone other than a contractual customer to recover against those responsible for defective products. This position, however, was eventually altered by the seminal decision in *Donoghue v Stevenson* [1932] A.C. 562 (see Chapter 2) where the plaintiff was allowed to recover against the manufacturer of a defective product despite the absence of a contract between the parties. The first significant Irish case to allow recovery against a manufacturer was that of *Kirby v Burke and Holloway* [1944] I.R. 207. What is of particular interest in this case is that Gavan Duffy J. chose not to follow *Donoghue v Stevenson* [1932] A.C. 562 but rather based his decision on the writings of the famous American jurist, Oliver Wendell Holmes.

Kirby v Burke and Holloway
High Court [1944] I.R. 207

Facts: The plaintiff's wife bought a pot of jam in a grocer's shop and gave some of the jam to the plaintiff and their infant children who became ill as a consequence of eating it. The plaintiff brought an action in the Circuit Court claiming damages, suing the grocer for breach of warranty in that he had implicitly warranted that the jam was of merchantable quality and fit for human consumption, and also suing the jam manufacturer for negligence in manufacturing and issuing the jam for sale. The Circuit Court judge dismissed the action against the grocer, but awarded damages against the manufacturer. The manufacturer appealed to the High Court.

Issues: Could the manufacturer of a product be held liable to someone injured by his product in the absence of a contract between the parties?

Gavan Duffy J. held that the manufacturer was bound to conform to the standards of a reasonable man in protecting consumers against injury caused by his product (basing his decision on the writings of Oliver Wendell Holmes). As the manufacturer in this case had allowed his jam to become contaminated (unreasonable behaviour) he found the manufacturer liable. Liability was imposed by finding that the manufacturer had failed to conform to the standard of a reasonable man, without considering specifically the question of whether the manufacturer owed a duty of care.

Gavan Duffy J.:

"This appeal from the Circuit Court turns on a point of law of exceptional public importance, unquestionably fit for the decision of the final tribunal, but neither party has asked me to state a case for the Supreme Court and there is no other right of appeal.

… On 6th May, 1942, Mrs. Josephine Kirby, finding butter to be unobtainable, bought for her family from a grocer a pot of rhubarb and ginger jam; the pot was wrapped in cellophane of amber hue, and the jam had a cardboard cover and under the cover, immediately over the jam, a piece of waxed paper. This was the sort of jam known to the trade as 'slip' jam, from a slip of paper affixed to the pot, designating the fruit; the main attraction of slip jam seems to have been that it passed with an innocent public as home-made; and it bore no tell-tale label with the maker's name.

Mrs. Kirby brought the pot home, opened it forthwith and spread the jam on slices of bread for her husband's lunch; shortly afterwards she gave a similar luncheon to three of her young children, who had the like meal again for their supper. Mr. Gerald Kirby, the husband, suffered that afternoon and subsequently from an attack of gastro-enteritis, and that night the children had very severe attacks of the same malady with its unpleasant symptoms, which persisted; the eldest boy, Gabriel, aged 9 years, recovered very slowly. Mrs. Kirby herself had a toothache and took no jam, and she gave none to her baby daughter; neither she nor the baby fell ill.

I am satisfied that the members of the family who suffered did so as the direct result of eating that jam … I find that the pot of jam came from the defendant, Holloway, through two intermediate grocers, one of whom had kept it for some six months; and, though neither of these reluctant gentlemen was an impressive witness, I do not on the evidence see any reason to believe that there had been any tampering with the jam pot after it left the defendant's factory.

Professor Bayley Butler, with whose views generally Dr. John Magrath, the pathologist, agreed, ... reached the conclusion that some species of fly, carrying bacteria, must have made its way into the jam pot at the factory, probably while the jam was cooling or before its cardboard cap was affixed; that seemed to me a probable theory, unless it should be rebutted or countered by evidence for the defendant ... In my opinion, the initial burden of proof was discharged by the plaintiffs, and it remained for the defendant, with his own special knowledge of the conditions under which his jam was made, to displace that *prima facie* case, and to call any expert evidence which might undo it.

... I have now to consider whether the law sustains the claim of the plaintiffs to make the manufacturer liable for the unpleasant consequences to them of eating his jam. The defendant manufactures a common article of food, jam, made from fruit of the particular season; he then distributes it for sale by retail grocers to members of the public; he intends it to be sold as food for human consumption and bought as food for human consumption. Before sending it out he pots the jam and places waxed paper over it, closes the pot with a cover and packs it in a coloured cellophane wrapper, with the result that the jam, when sold over the counter, will be taken to be (as it is meant to be) in the condition in which it left the factory, and that the purchaser will have no reasonable opportunity to examine the contents for any visible defects; and a manufacturer must know, as a matter of ordinary experience, that a housewife, the probable purchaser, does not usually, on opening the pot at home, begin by scrutinising the contents for signs of corruption; why should she?

A particular pot of jam turns out to be unwholesome when bought, and injurious to the consumers, and the question at once arises on what principle is the alleged liability of the maker, who intended no injury and made no contract with the consumers, to be determined? The inquiry involves the ascertainment of the foundation, upon the authorities, of liability for tort at common law.

In 1869, an Irish Court, following English decisions, held on demurrer that, in the absence of fraudulent misrepresentation, the law could give no redress against the manufacturers to a man (the purchaser's servant) injured by the explosion of a boiler in a steam engine, upon an allegation that the boiler was unsafe by reason of negligence in its construction: *Corry* v. *Lucas* I. R. 3 C. L. 208. The confusion and conflict in later cases in England left the basis of liability in tort at common law so uncertain that at the time of the Treaty nobody could find in case law any sure guide to the actual legal position, and I have no Irish decision to guide me.

I am thus thrown back upon first principles in the endeavour to ascertain where the line is drawn at common law between conduct resulting in unintended hurt which entails liability for damage, and conduct resulting in unintended hurt which entails no liability.

In the quandary produced by the baffling inconsistencies among the pre-Treaty judicial pronouncements, I turn from the Courts to one of the outstanding juristic studies of the nineteenth century, 'The Common Law' by Oliver Wendell Holmes, afterwards Mr. Justice Holmes of the Supreme Court of the United

States. The work was published in London in 1887. The law which I apply to this case is taken from his penetrating Lectures III and IV on torts and the theory of torts.

That master of the common law shows that the foundation of liability at common law for tort is blameworthiness as determined by the existing average standards of the community; a man fails at his peril to conform to those standards. Therefore, while loss from accident generally lies where it falls, a defendant cannot plead accident if, treated as a man of ordinary intelligence and foresight, he ought to have foreseen the danger which caused injury to his plaintiff.

Applying that norm to the facts, I have to inquire whether a man in the position of the defendant, making jam for the public to eat, is bound, according to the standards of conduct prevailing among us, to take specific precautions against the danger, to the hurt of consumers, of infection to his jam from external causes before it finally leaves his factory; or, more exactly, though he may not have anticipated the precise injury that ensued to the plaintiffs from infection, was he bound, in conformity with those standards, to safeguard his jam from access by flies, as notoriously ubiquitous as they are notoriously dirty, during the interval between the moment when the jam is poured into a jam pot after boiling and the moment, three or four days later, when the jam pot is finally enveloped for sale and sent out? I answer this question, as I believe a jury of practical citizens would answer it, in the affirmative, because our public opinion undoubtedly requires of a jam manufacturer that he shall take care to keep flies out of his jam. Any novice would foresee that a fly might get in, given the chance, and I have already found as facts that the defendant failed to take adequate precautions and that the buyer was in no way at fault.

On the facts of the case now before me, there is no question of remoteness of damage. The test, as Holmes J. puts it is whether the result actually contemplated was near enough to the remoter result complained of to throw the peril of that result upon the actor. The plaintiffs are therefore entitled to succeed.

The much controverted 'Case of the Snail in the Bottle,' while leaving subsidiary questions open, has settled the principle of liability on a similar issue finally against the manufacturer in Great Britain. But the House of Lords established that memorable conclusion only twelve years ago in *Donoghue* v. *Stevenson* [1932] A.C. 562, by a majority of three Law Lords to two, 'a Celtic majority,' as an unconvinced critic ruefully observed, against an English minority. Where lawyers so learned disagreed, an Irish Judge could not assume, as I was invited to assume, as a matter of course, that the view which prevailed must of necessity be the true view of the common law in Ireland. One voice in the House of Lords would have turned the scale; and it is not arguable that blameworthiness according to the actual standards of our people depends upon the casting vote in a tribunal exercising no jurisdiction over them. Hence my recourse to the late Mr. Justice Holmes. His classic analysis supports the principle of Lord Atkin and the majority. And to that principle I humbly subscribe."

Comments and Questions:

1. Do you find it curious that, despite referring to the decision in *Donoghue v Stevenson* [1932] A.C. 562, Gavan Duffy J. did not specifically deal with the question of a duty of care separately but simply imposed one on the basis of the manufacturer's standard of care?

2. Why was Gavan Duffy J. reluctant, in your view, to follow the decision in *Donoghue v Stevenson* [1932] A.C. 562?

Development of negligence actions

To succeed in negligence a plaintiff has to establish a duty of care, a failure to attain the reasonable standard of care and causation.

In the case law that followed that of *Kirby* a duty was extended to all groups who came within the duty of care principles, including repairers (*Power v Bedford Motor Co.* [1959] I.R. 391), installers and assemblers (*Brown v Cotterill* (1938) 51 T.L.R. 21 (KBD)), suppliers (*Keegan v Owens* [1953] I.R. 267 (SC)) and retailers (*Duffy v Rooney and Dunnes Stores (Dundalk) Ltd.*, High Court, June 23, 1997. The following case law focuses on identifying whether a duty exists and ascertaining whether the defendant breached the standard of care owed.

Repairers

Power v The Bedford Motor Company Ltd. and Harris Brothers Ltd.
Supreme Court [1959] I.R. 391

Facts: The plaintiff's husband was injured and subsequently died after the car he was driving crashed into a wall. The car had been repaired at various times by both defendant garages when the car was in the ownership of another person. The car was then sold to the second named defendants, Harris Garages, who sold it to the deceased. The plaintiff successfully sued both garages in the High Court for negligence. The defendants appealed to the Supreme Court.

Issues: The Supreme Court had to consider whether the defendants owed a duty of care to the subsequent owners of a car they had serviced and if so if they had failed in this duty. It was held by the court (Maguire C.J., Lavery, O'Daly and Maguire JJ.; Kingsmill Moore J., dissenting) that a duty was owed by both defendants and that this duty had been breached.

Lavery J. (Maguire C.J., O'Daly and Maguire JJ. concurring):

"... The claim against both defendants is in negligence and is based on the principle stated in Donoghue v Stevenson ((1932) AC 562). That principle is now well established. It has been followed—and, as some think, been extended in later cases in Great Britain—and it has been followed and applied in this Court in several cases—notably in Robinson v Technico Ltd (unreported). The principle may be stated in the well-known passage from the speech of Lord Atkin. I quote (at p599)—'… manufacturer of products, which he sells in such a form as to show that he intends them to reach the ultimate consumer in the form in which they left him with no reasonable possibility of intermediate examination, and with the knowledge that the absence of reasonable care in the preparation or putting up of the products will result in an injury to the consumer's life or property, owes a duty to the consumer to take that reasonable care.'

Lord Atkin states the nature of the duty and defines the persons to whom it is owed in the following passage (at p580)—'You must take reasonable care to avoid acts or omissions which you can reasonably foresee would be likely to injure your neighbour. Who, then, in law is my neighbour? The answer seems to be—persons who are so closely and directly affected by my act that I ought reasonably to have them in contemplation as being so affected when I am directing my mind to the acts or omissions which are called in question.'

—'This appears to me to be the doctrine of Heaven v Pender (11 QBD 503, at p509).'

Lord Atkin's opinion commanded the support of the majority of the House— three against two— a division of opinion which demonstrates that the law was then difficult and unsettled. However, it must now be taken as settled.

It is clear in principle that the obligation is not confined to manufacturers of goods but extends to persons undertaking repairs to articles which will be dangerous to users who should be in contemplation if there is a want of reasonable care in the work. It must also apply to persons doing work on an article which they foresee would be used by others without examination.

This view has been taken in many cases in Great Britain, eg, Haseldine v C A Daw & Son, Ltd ((1941) 2 KB 343) (defective lift), Andrews v Hopkinson ((1957) 1 KB 229) (motor car), Herschtal v Stewart and Ardern, Ltd ((1940) 1 KB 155) (reconditioned motor car), Stennett v Hancock ((1939) 2 ALL ER 578) (motor lorry defectively repaired).

This Court was not referred to any such case in this country, but if my memory serves me the liability of a repairer to persons injured, for defective work, the other conditions being satisfied, has been maintained in actions in the High Court.

If this is the law, as in my opinion it is, the liability of Messrs Harris is established by the findings of the jury …

… In the case of Bedfords a further matter of great difficulty has to be considered.

The work done by them on the car was done on the 1st November, 1954, and the accident happened on the 14th May, 1955, an interval of six months and fourteen days. During that period the car had been driven by Dr Byrne and by employees of Harris and for the short period of sixteen days by the deceased.

No accident occurred until the fatal one. In reviewing the evidence, I have dealt with the suggested reasons for this freedom from accident notwithstanding the alleged dangerous set up of the steering. It is submitted that the damage is therefore not a direct result of these defendants' negligence and is too remote to found a claim by the plaintiff ...

... My first conclusion is that the deceased did belong to the class of persons whom Bedfords should have contemplated as being exposed to the danger if the work were done wrongly. That class of persons included any person who might drive or be a passenger in the car and perhaps others who might be injured if the car went out of control—though it is unnecessary to consider them.

My second conclusion is that this duty would continue to operate so long as the car remained in the same dangerous condition but limited to such period as within which it might be contemplated an examination of the car would be made.

My third conclusion is that Bedfords should have anticipated that the car would be used by various drivers without such an examination as would have discovered the incorrect fittings, and that there were no intervening 'contingencies' between the lack of care and the casualty.

I do not overlook that Harris's did make an examination—indeed, more than one and did not discover the defect, and that they, as the jury have found, were guilty of negligence—as I think rightly.

This has given me much thought but I have come to the conclusion that Bedfords cannot escape liability because an actual examination was made but done negligently. It is not a question of what happened, but of what should have been contemplated.

On these issues I therefore consider that both Harris and Bedfords are liable to the plaintiff."

Suppliers

Keegan v Owens, Ward & McMahon
Supreme Court [1953] I.R. 267

Facts: The plaintiff, an employee at a carnival, was injured by a protruding wire nail when attempting to stop a swing-boat. The swing-boat, supplied by the third-named defendant, did not have a mechanical lever by which to stop the boat. The carnival had been organised as a benefit to aid the Sisters of Saint Louis, in Kiltimagh (the first two named defendants being sisters of that order). In an action against the nuns and McMahon for damages for negligence and breach of duty, the trial judge, at the conclusion of the plaintiff's case, directed a verdict for the defendants on the ground that there was no evidence upon which the jury could find in favour of the plaintiff. The plaintiff appealed to the Supreme Court.

Issues: The court was asked to consider if the nuns were the plaintiff's employers at the time of the accident, in which case they would owe the plaintiff a duty to provide him with safe plant and equipment (see Chapter 6). On this issue they found that they were not and therefore did not owe him a duty of care. Similarly they found that they were not occupiers of the field in which the carnival took place and therefore owed no duty under this heading (see Chapter 4).

With respect to the potential liability of the suppliers of a product the court was asked to consider whether the supplier in this case, McMahon, owed the plaintiff a duty of care in respect of the swing-boats supplied. The court held for the plaintiff on this point, stating that the defendant supplied them for his own reward and ought to owe a duty of care.

Maguire C.J., Murnaghan and O'Byrne JJ. (judgment delivered by Maguire C.J.):

"It is now necessary to consider the plaintiff's claim as against the last-named defendant, Michael McMahon. It appears that this defendant was the owner of the mechanical contrivances, including swing-boats, used at the carnival, and that it was his business to hire out these contrivances for such a purpose. We have no express evidence of the contract under which the machines were supplied; but on the evidence that was adduced, and in the absence of any evidence from Mr. McMahon, we are of opinion that it would be open to the jury to hold that they were supplied by him for reward. He was himself present during the carnival and his employees took part in the management of the machines. It is, however, clear from the evidence that he did not supply sufficient employees of his own to manage all the machines and, in our view, it would be open to the jury to hold, on the evidence produced at the trial, that it was part of the arrangement that the persons running the carnival should supply other men to assist in the working of the machines. On the night in question the plaintiff was directed by Mr. Forde, the steward in charge on that night, to go and assist at the boats. He did so and was injured when attempting to stop one of the boats. We are of opinion that Mr. McMahon owed a duty to the plaintiff and that there was evidence from which a jury might properly hold that he failed in that duty. Accordingly, we are of opinion that the learned trial Judge's direction in favour of this defendant was improperly given and that, as against him, the case should have gone to the jury."

Establishing causation

In the case of *Duffy v Rooney and Dunnes Stores (Dundalk)* in addition to determining whether the retailer (Dunnes Stores) owed a duty of care, and fell below the standard owed, the question of causation in determining liability proved to be fatal to the claimant's case.

Duffy (A Minor) v Rooney and Dunnes Stores (Dundalk) Limited
High Court, 1992, No. 3439P (transcript)

Facts: The plaintiff, a young girl aged two years and 10 months, suffered serious burns when her coat caught fire by an unguarded open fire in her grandfather's house. She sued her grandfather as occupier of the house, and Dunnes Stores, from whom the coat had been purchased. The coat did not have a warning label advising of the dangers of fire. The plaintiff, however, was wearing trousers and a sweatshirt purchased from the same party which bore a warning label: "Keep Away From Fire".

Issues: Two issues arose for consideration. First, did the grandfather, as occupier of the house, owe a duty to the plaintiff and did he fall below the standard of care owed, causing injury to the plaintiff? On this issue the court found in favour of the plaintiff.

Secondly, did Dunnes Stores as retailers owe a duty of care to the plaintiff and did they fall below the standard of care owed causing injury to the plaintiff? On this issue, while they found that the second-named defendants had owed a duty of care and fallen below the standard owed in not attaching a warning label to the coat, they found Dunnes Stores not liable on the basis that a causative link between the absence of a warning label and the injury suffered was not established.

Laffoy J.:

"Before outlining the contentions of the Plaintiff and the first Defendant which form the basis of the allegation of negligence and breach of duty against the second Defendant, I think it is important to point out that it is not contended by any party that the coat worn by Amy on 9 February, 1992 differed from the other similar raincoats manufactured by LC (Tailorwear) Limited for the Group in any respect that rendered it defective. There was no suggestion by any party that Amy's coat was a 'rogue' coat. The complaints of defective and unsafe product relate, as it were, to the whole genus of which Amy's coat formed part. On 18 September, 1992, flammability tests were carried out on the remains of Amy's coat by Lambeg Industrial Research Association (LIRA). The results of the LIRA tests were relied on by the Plaintiff's expert witness, Dr Caroline Maguire, and the expert called by the first Defendant, Mr Joseph O'Neill. The accuracy of the results of the LIRA tests was accepted by the second Defendant and its experts, Mr Stephen Eckersley and Mr John Morris. Three tests were carried out by LIRA using the Test 3 method prescribed in BS 5438: 1976—on the outer fabric and the lining in combination, on the lining alone, and on the outer fabric alone. On each test the result was that the flammability of the test specimen indicated that it did not comply with the requirements of BS 5722: 1984. LIRA also carried out two minimum ignition time tests using the methodology of Test 1 prescribed by BS 5438: 1976—on the lining only, and on the outer fabric only. The results of these tests were that the minimum time of ignition in the case of the lining was three seconds and in the case of the outer fabric it was two seconds.

In 1991, the only Irish standard in force in relation to children's apparel was IS 148: 1988, which the National Standards Authority of Ireland (EOLAS) brought into force in 1988 and which set out the flammability and labelling requirements of fabrics and fabric assemblies used in children's nightwear. In IS 148: 1988, the expression 'children's nightwear' was defined as meaning any nightwear which is designed for wear and would normally be worn by a person over the age of three months and under the age of 13 years and as including children's night-dresses, children's dressing gowns and children's pyjamas. The expressions 'children's night-dresses', 'children's dressing gowns' and 'children's pyjamas' were also defined. It is undoubtedly the case, and indeed it was not contended otherwise, that Amy's coat did not come within any of those definitions so that IS 148: 1988 was not applicable to it. IS 148: 1988 stipulated that fabrics and fabric assemblies used in children's night-dresses and in children's dressing gowns must comply with the flammability requirements of clause 5 and the labelling requirements of clause 6, and those used in children's pyjamas and children's cotton terry-towelling bathrobes must comply with the labelling requirements of clause 6, although they were not required to comply with the flammability requirements of clause 5. It was acknowledged in IS 148: 1988 that the method of test and technical requirements of the standard were based on BS 5438: 1976 (Methods of test for Flammability of vertically oriented textile fabrics and fabric assemblies subjected to a small igniting flame) and BS 5722: 1984 (Flammability performance of fabrics and fabric assemblies used in sleepwear and dressing gowns). In general terms, accordingly, under IS 148: 1988, children's night-dresses and dressing gowns were required to comply with the performance criteria stipulated in BS 5722: 1984 when tested by the test method prescribed in Test 3 of BS 5438: 1976. Having regard to the results of the LIRA tests, the fabrics of which Amy's coat was made up could not have been used either individually or in combination in the manufacture of a child's night-dress or a dressing gown. Clause 6 of IS 148: 1988 required fabrics used in children's night-dresses and children's dressing gowns to bear, inter alia, a label with the words 'Low flammability to IS 148'. In the case of children's pyjamas and children's cotton terry-towelling bathrobes not in compliance with the flammability requirements of BS 5722: 1984, clause 6 of IS 148: 1988 required that they bear a warning label in red letters with the words 'Keep away from Fire'. Accordingly, if the fabrics used in Amy's coat had been used in the make-up of children's pyjamas, the pyjamas would have had to carry such a warning label.

The Plaintiff's contention that Amy's coat was inherently dangerous and unsafe was founded on the expert evidence of Dr Caroline Maguire. In Dr Maguire's opinion, as the fabric failed to comply with the requirements of BS

5722: 1984, which would have entitled it to be classified as of 'low flamma-bility', it was classifiable as being highly flammable. In her view, having regard to the composition of the fabrics and the design and the configuration of the garment, it was 'uniquely dangerous'. The fact that the outer fabric stood out from the body in a bell shape increased the risk of contact with a fire or a flame. The outer fabric was very flammable. The inner fabric or lining, which was closest to the body, was even more flammable. The fact that the wadding, which was a safer material, was attached to the lining created a scaffold effect so that the wadding's limited flame spread characteristic was obliterated. The air space between the outer fabric and the lining and the air space surrounding the fibres in the wadding facilitated combustion. Dr Maguire argued that in the case of children the distinction between nightwear and daywear, as reflected in IS 148: 1988, is illogical at the present time. The trend in recent years has been towards lightweight outer garments, and Amy's coat represented this vogue. Lighter fabrics are more easily combustible. In her view, the hazard identified thirty years ago as applying to nightwear must now be regarded as applying to all clothing for children. Dr Maguire did not contend that Amy's coat should not have been put into circulation. She recognised its popularity in the market place. However, in her opinion, the coat should not have been sold without a warning label and preferably should not have been sold without having been treated with a fire retardant in the case of coats' intended for use by low age groups, by which I understood her to mean young children …

The main thrust of the response of the second Defendant and of the evidence which supported it was that the coat Amy was wearing on 9 February, 1992 was neither dangerous nor unsafe. It did not infringe any standard or regulation in relation to children's wearing apparel in force either in the United Kingdom or in this jurisdiction. In terms of fabric composition, design and in every respect, including the absence of a warning label, it conformed with the universal practice in the manufacture of other raincoats for girls available in the market place at the time.

Mr Stephen Eckersley, the joint Managing Director of Fastech Testing Limited, the largest independent testing house specialising in textile testing in the United Kingdom, who was called by the second Defendant, testified that there was nothing unusual in the fabric composition, the design or the construction of the coat. He would classify the fabric as 'flammable', not as 'highly flammable'. It was common practice in 1991, and it still is the practice, to put this type of garment for a child on the market without testing for flammability. In his view, the fabric was perfectly safe to be put on the market. At the time, it was not the practice of retailers to put warning labels on this type of garment. More recently, one major retailer, Marks & Spencers, has introduced voluntary flammability testing for lightweight fabrics. The coat in issue here would have passed the Marks & Spencers test. In recent years, some retailers in the United Kingdom have commenced voluntarily putting warning labels on all children's clothing.

Mr John Morris, who serves on a number of British Standard, European (CEN) and International (ISO) Committees concerned with textile standards, including BSI TCI 63, which deals with all textile flammability testing, corroborated Mr Eckersley's evidence as to the then current practice in the United Kingdom in 1991. In his view, prevailing informed opinion was that it was not necessary to extend the nightwear standard, that is to say, the standard on which IS 148: 1988 is based, which applies to all nightwear in the United Kingdom whether for adults or children, to other end uses. In his opinion, the nightwear standard is not a suitable yardstick for testing the flammability of garments intended to be worn out of doors. He emphasised that night-dresses are of a different structure to outdoor wear, in that they are considerably longer and more flowing. They are typically of lighter fabrics which are generally knitted, not woven, now. Mr Morris could not recall any fabrics, apart from the occasional nightwear fabric, being treated with flame retardant in the early 1990s.

The evidence establishes that since approximately the end of 1992 to the present day, the Group puts warning labels on all children's garments.

It is not in issue that the second Defendant as the retailer of the coat owed a duty of care to Amy, the ultimate user of the coat. What is in issue is whether the second Defendant observed the standard of care in retailing that product which the law required of it. In considering what standard the law required of the second Defendant in the circumstances of this case, I find it useful to start with the following passage from a judgment dating from the middle of the last century quoted by the authors of McMahon and Binchy on Irish Law of Torts, 2nd Edition, at page 102, even if somewhat maligned by them:—

> 'Negligence is the omission to do something which a reasonable man, guided upon those considerations which ordinarily regulate the conduct of human affairs, would do or doing something which a prudent and reasonable man would not do.'

In applying the standard of the 'reasonable man' to different factual scenarios, varying factors and considerations emerge ...

... However, I am of the view that a reasonably prudent manufacturer or retailer, had he properly addressed the issue, would have, and the second Defendant ought to have, affixed a label to Amy's coat warning that it should be kept away from fire. The reasonable and prudent manufacturer or retailer properly addressing the issue would have taken the following factors into account, namely:—

(a) that the trend in recent times has been to utilise lighter weight and more flammable fabrics in making up garments intended for wear by children out of doors than thitherto was the case;

(b) that in design terms there are a lot of similarities between a coat such as Amy's coat and a night-dress or dressing gown particularly in terms of length and looseness and particularly having regard to the fact that frequently a garment such as a raincoat or a winter-coat a size bigger than is appropriate to the child's age is worn by the child, as happened in Amy's case;

(c) that very young children have to be dressed by a parent or other adult and that even a garment primarily designed for outdoor wear is normally put on the child in the house and may be worn around the house for some time before the child goes out;

(d) that open fires and gas heaters are a common feature of domestic life in Ireland;

(e) that young children are unpredictable and lack a sense of danger;

(f) the gravity of the consequences of fire accidents; and

(g) the relatively low cost of labelling garments.

Accordingly, in my view, the second Defendant was in breach of its duty of care to Amy in failing to affix a warning label to the coat.

CAUSATION

The absence of adequate supervision, which permitted Amy to come in close proximity to the fireplace, and the absence of a fireguard, which allowed Amy's coat to come in contact with the fire, caused her injuries in the sense that had she been prevented from coming into close proximity with the fireplace or, alternatively, had the fireguard been in place, it is highly improbable, if not absolutely out of the question, that her coat would have caught fire and that she would have sustained the injuries she sustained.

It was submitted on behalf of the second Defendant that there was no causal link between the fact that Amy was wearing the coat which was purchased from the second Defendant and her injuries. Irrespective of what she was wearing, it was urged, the accident would have occurred. This argument seems to me to be somewhat facile as a response of the case made against it by the first Defendant. However, having found that the second Defendant was in breach of its duty of care to Amy in not affixing a warning label to the coat, the issue I have to consider is whether there is a causal link between the absence of a warning label and Amy's injuries or, conversely, whether even if the coat had been labelled 'Keep away from the fire' the accident would have occurred. It seems to me that two questions require to be addressed on this issue.

The first is whether had the coat been labelled it would not have been purchased by Mrs Rooney and would not have been given as a gift to Amy or, alternatively, whether Mrs Duffy would not have dressed Amy in it because of the risk disclosed by the warning label. Mrs Rooney said that had there been a warning label on the coat she would have adverted to it and she would have been hesitant to buy something which would have been dangerous, particularly for her granddaughter. I have no doubt that Mrs Rooney honestly believes this but I think the belief is informed by more than a modicum of hindsight and, on the evidence as a whole, I am not satisfied that had the coat been labelled 'Keep away from fire' Mrs Rooney would have considered it inappropriate to buy for her granddaughter. Mrs Duffy also testified that had there been a warning label on the coat she would probably not have bought it. Later in her evidence, she said that she would be very conscious of a warning label now and when she goes out to buy clothes for Amy now it is the first thing she looks for. She very candidly testified that up to the time of the accident she would have concentrated on the age (ie the size of the garment) and maybe on the material. However the most telling fact which emerged was that on the fateful day Amy was wearing trousers and a sweatshirt to which warning labels were attached and the existence of the warning labels did not deter Mrs Duffy from purchasing the garments and dressing Amy in them. I am unable to infer from the evidence either that Mrs Rooney and Mrs Duffy may have been lulled into a false sense of safety by the absence of a warning label or that had the coat been labelled 'Keep away from fire' Amy would not have been wearing it at 3.00 pm on the 9 February, 1992.

The second question which arises is whether, if the coat had had a warning label affixed and Mrs Rooney and Mrs Duffy had taken on board the import of the warning label, affairs in the household on that day would have been conducted in such a way that Amy's coat would not have come in contact with the fire. The evidence establishes that Mr and Mrs Rooney and Mrs Duffy were fully aware of the risk an unguarded fire represents of itself when a young child is present. On this point also I am unable to infer that the circumstances would have been any different on the day if the coat had been labelled."

Questions and Comments:
1. The above case highlights the importance of proving causation in a negligence action. Even though the court found that Dunnes Stores had fallen below the standard of care owed to the plaintiff, the case ultimately failed as Dunnes Stores' negligent act (not attaching a warning label) did not legally cause the accident; it would, in the view of the court, have happened anyway (see further Chapter 1).

2. Note that the court, in taking into account whether Dunnes Stores had fallen below a standard of care, considered issues of foreseeability, social utility, gravity of threatened injury and the potential cost of eliminating the risk.

Recovery for non-dangerous defects

Once the courts overcame their initial reluctance to allow recovery in negligence for defective products, there was no difficulty in compensating for dangerous defects. However, there has been greater reluctance in extending this duty to allow recovery for non-dangerous defects, which by their nature result in economic loss only. The *Junior Books Ltd v Veitchi* [1983] A.C. 520 decision in Britain represented a temporary change in the attitude of the English Courts to such claims. This case, however, proved to be the exception rather than the rule and was quickly overruled by the English courts on their return to a more incremental development of incidents of duty (see Chapter 2). *Junior Books* was followed in Ireland in the case of *Ward v McMaster* [1985] I.R. 29 (see Chapter 2). This decision, while supportive of a right to recover for non-dangerous defects, is not however the last word on these types of claims in Irish courts. Disapproval for such an approach has been expressed by our Supreme Court in the recent decision of *Glencar Exploration plc v Mayo County Council* [2002] 1 I. R. 84. Keane C.J., in that case, stated that the question of whether "the decision of the House of Lords in *Junior Books Ltd v Veitchi Co. Ltd* should be followed in this jurisdiction" was yet to be decided, demonstrating a marked reluctance to apply the principles of negligence to loss arising from non-dangerous defects. See also Chapter 3 for further guidance in this area.

LIABILITY FOR DEFECTIVE PRODUCTS ACT 1991

The Liability for Defective Products Act 1991 was introduced to implement a European Directive on products liability, Directive 85/374/EC. Rather than replace the existing common law, the Products Liability Act merely provides another avenue whereby a party may seek a remedy. As is the position with Directives, an implementation period applied, in this case, three years. However, Ireland failed to implement the Directive in time, not introducing the Act until 1991. Given the principles of direct effect, it is unclear what the position is for products introduced between 1988 and 1991. In the case of *Duffy v Rooney and Dunnes Stores* above, for instance, the plaintiff sought to rely on the Act but was unsuccessful, given that the product in question (the coat) had been put into circulation after the Act came into effect, but had the Act been implemented in time, the plaintiff may well have been able to rely on it. It would have made little difference in that case however, given that the plaintiff lost her claim against Dunnes Stores on a causation issue, which also needs to be proven under the Act. While very few cases have been taken on the basis of the Act, in Ireland especially, a number of cases are being prepared and should appear before the courts in the coming years. So far they have simply appeared on procedural issues and not as a trial on the facts. Of particular interest for this jurisdiction, given developments in the United States, is a case being taken by a Ms Delahunty against the tobacco company Player & Wills for what she alleges is injury sustained from smoking their products (namely cigarettes—for a hearing on this case please see *Delahunty v Player & Wills (Ireland) Ltd and others* [2006] I.E.S.C. 21).

The Act is reproduced at the end of this section for reference, but a number of issues are worthy of particular note. The principal difference between a negligence action and the Act is that the Act imposes strict liability. Despite this it does have its shortcomings. The Act will only provide a remedy where products fail to provide the safety levels expected. Thus the Act clearly excludes recovery for any non-dangerous defects. The presentation of the product, the use to which it has been put and the time it was put into circulation are all factors to be considered when deciding the level of safety one could "reasonably expect" (see s.5). The principal sections of the Act are reproduced at the end of this chapter.

Issues of safety were considered in the UK case of *Richardson v LRC Products Ltd* (2000) 59 B.M.L.R. 185, where the Directive has been implemented by the adoption of the Consumer Protection Act 1987, a piece of legislation virtually identical to our own Act. In that case the plaintiff failed in arguing that a malfunctioning condom was defective under that Act, as Kennedy J., held that the condom had not fallen below the level of safety expected stating, "There are no claims made by the defendants that [a condom] will never fail and no one has ever supposed that any method of contraception intended to defeat nature will be 100% effective. This must particularly be so in the case of a condom, where the product is required, to a degree at least, to be 'user friendly'. So to the question 'Does a fracture prove a defect?' I answer 'No not by itself'."

The Act also provides a number of defences (see s.6). These have not yet been tested in an Irish court, but again, in the United Kingdom defences arose for consideration in the case of *A and others v National Blood Authority and another* [2001] 3 All E.R. 289. This case also dealt with the concept of what constituted a "defective product."

A and others v National Blood Authority and another
Queen's Bench Division [2001] 3 All E.R. 289, 60 B.M.L.R. 1

Facts: The plaintiffs in the case had been infected with Hepatitis C through blood transfusions. The plaintiffs sued the defendants, who had supplied the blood, arguing that the product (blood) was defective within the meaning of the Directive and the UK Consumer Protection Act 1987.

The defendants for their part argued that the blood was not defective, as consumers could not expect blood to be free from contamination. They further argued that they could rely on the defence available in Art.7(e), *i.e.* that the existence of the defect could not be known given the state of scientific and technical knowledge existing at that time (the "unavoidable risks" defence).

Issues: The court (Burton J.) had to consider whether the product was defective within the meaning of Art.6(1) (*i.e.* that it did not provide the safety which a person was entitled to expect, taking all circumstances into account, including the presentation of the product, the use to which it could reasonably be expected that the product would be put, and the time when the product was put into circulation). In addition the court had to consider whether the defence in Art.7(e) could be relied on.

The court held that while the medical profession was aware of the risk of contamination, the public was entitled to expect clean blood, therefore the blood had fallen below the level of safety expected and was "defective" within the meaning of Art.6.

The court also held that even though the state of scientific knowledge could not help the defendants to identify the exact batches of blood that were contaminated, it did enable them to know of the risk of contamination, therefore they could not rely on the defence of Art.7(e).

Burton J.:

"... THE DIRECTIVE

[13] The directive, resolved by the Council on 25 July 1985, had taken a long time in coming. In the first instance this was because discussion of it, which had begun in 1969/1970 in the light of the Thalidomide scandal, was held up largely due to the impending arrival of a number of new members of the Community, including the United Kingdom; but then because of the very lengthy processes of discussion and negotiation, and of intergovernmental and parliamentary discussion, which then took place. A number of matters appear to be common ground between the parties to these proceedings: (i) that its purpose was to increase consumer protection; (ii) that it introduced an obligation on producers which was irrespective of fault, by way of objective or strict liability, but not absolute liability; (iii) that its aim was to render compensation of the injured consumer easier, by removing the concept of negligence as an element of liability and thus of the proof of liability; and (iv) that it left an escape clause (in those Community jurisdictions, like the United Kingdom, where such provision was desired) for products otherwise found pursuant to the directive to be defective, if the producer could bring himself within what was, in the course of the 'travaux preparatoires', described as a 'development risks' defence.

... [16] The relevant articles are as follows:
'Article 1
The producer shall be liable for damage caused by a defect in his product:
Article 4
The injured person shall be required to prove the damage, the defect and the causal relationship between defect and damage:
Article 6
1. A product is defective when it does not provide the safety which a person is entitled to expect, taking all circumstances into account, including: (a) the presentation of the product; (b) the use to which it could reasonably be expected that the product would be put; (c) the time when the product was put into circulation.
2. A product shall not be considered defective for the sole reason that a better product is subsequently put into circulation.
Article 7
The producer shall not be liable as a result of this Directive if he proves: (a) that he did not put the product into circulation; or (b) that, having regard to the circumstances, it is probable that the defect which caused the damage did not

exist at the time when the product was put into circulation by him or that this defect came into being afterwards; or ... (d) that the defect is due to compliance of the product with mandatory regulations issued by the public authorities; or (e) that the state of scientific and technical knowledge at the time when he put the product into circulation was not such as to enable the existence of the defect to be discovered.

ARTICLE 6
The common ground
[31] I turn then to consideration of art 6. There is a foundation of common ground. (i) Article 6 defines 'defective', and hence a defect. A harmful characteristic in a product, which has led to injury or damage, may or may not be a defect as so defined, and thus within the meaning of the directive. It is common ground that the liability is 'defect-based' and not 'fault-based', ie that a producer's liability is irrespective of fault (Recitals 2, 6). (ii) The purpose of the directive is to achieve a higher and consistent level of consumer protection throughout the Community and render recovery of compensation easier, and uncomplicated by the need for proof of negligence. Both these propositions are expressed by Christopher Newdick in two published articles, first in the Law Quarterly Review 'The Future of Negligence in Product Liability' [1987] 103 LQR 288:

> '... liability for defective products is no longer to be dependent on fault, but rather on the mere fact of defectiveness. The broad reasons of policy for the change continue to be articulated by the injuries suffered by the thalidomide children. By the attention it devotes to consideration of the alleged fault of the defendant, the law of Negligence is unable to consider the interests of the person for whom the action has been brought.'

and also in 'The Development Risk Defence of the Consumer Protection Act 1987' [1988] CLJ 455 where, before going on to deal with art 7(e) as a possible exception, he states:

> 'The ... Directive ... introduces a new regime of strict product liability to the member states of the Community. Those injured by products may recover by showing that the product is "defective", i.e., that it "does not provide the safety which a person is entitled to expect . . ." The advantage of this approach for the individual is that liability turns on the existence of a defect alone. Unlike the law of Negligence, no question of foresight of the danger, or of the precautions taken to avoid it, arises for consideration. Strict product liability depends on the condition of the product, not the fault of its maker or supplier.'

(iii) The onus of proof is upon the claimants to prove the product to be defective. (iv) The question to be resolved is the safety or the degree or level of safety or safeness which persons generally are entitled to expect. The test is not that of an absolute level of safety, nor an absolute liability for any injury caused by the harmful characteristic. (v) In the assessment of that question the expectation is that of persons generally, or the public at large.

(vi) The safety is not what is actually expected by the public at large, but what they are entitled to expect. At one stage Mr Forrester QC contended that the process was to discover what the expectation was, and then see if it was legitimate; but, not least for the reasons set out in the next following sub-paragraph, he no longer actively pursued that contention. The common ground is that the question is what the legitimate expectation is of persons generally, ie what is legitimately to be expected, arrived at objectively. 'Legitimate expectation', rather than 'entitled expectation', appeared to all of us to be a more happy formulation (and is analogous to the formulation in other languages in which the directive is published); the use of that expression is not intended to import any administrative law concepts.

(vii) The court decides what the public is entitled to expect: Dr Harald Bartl in Produkthaftung nach neuem EG-Recht (1989) described the judge (as translated from the German) as 'an informed representative of the public at large'. Mr Brown did not like this, and preferred to suggest simply that the judge is determining what level of safety the public is entitled to expect, but I do not consider the two descriptions inconsistent. Such objectively assessed legitimate expectation may accord with actual expectation; but it may be more than the public actually expects, thus imposing a higher standard of safety, or it may be less than the public actually expects. Alternatively the public may have no actual expectation-eg in relation to a new product-the word coined in argument for such an imaginary product was a 'scrid'. (viii) There are some products, which have harmful characteristics in whole or in part, about which no complaint can be made. The examples that were used of products which have obviously dangerous characteristics by virtue of their very nature or intended use, were, on the one hand knives, guns and poisons and on the other hand alcohol, tobacco, perhaps foie gras …

(ix) Article 6(2) means that such test must be applied as at the date when the product is put into circulation, ie tested against the safety then to be expected. It is apparent that a product may be compared with other products said to be safer, but will not be condemned simply because another safer product is subsequently put into circulation. (x) There is also important factual common ground. It has, as set out in [8] above, been known, at least since the 1970s, by blood producers and the medical profession, primarily blood specialists, hepatologists and epidemiologists, that there was a problem of infection by Hep C (formerly NANBH) in transfused blood, and that a percentage of such blood-in the United Kingdom thought to be between 1% and 3% was infected with NANBH/Hep C. The claimants say that such knowledge by the medical profession and blood producers is on the one hand irrelevant to art 6, and to the public's expectation, and legitimate expectation, and on the other rules out the producers from the protection of art 7(e). The defendants say that such risks so known, which they allege to be impossible to avoid or prevent, affect the legitimate expectation of the public, such as to exclude art 6, and, because they were unavoidable, qualify them, if necessary, for art 7(e).

The differences between the parties

[32] Having set out what is common ground, I now summarise briefly the difference between the two parties, some of which is already apparent from my setting in context of the factual common ground. (i) As to art 6, the claimants assert that, with the need for proof of negligence eliminated, consideration of the conduct of the producer, or of a reasonable or legitimately expectable producer, is inadmissible or irrelevant. Therefore questions of avoidability cannot and do not arise: what the defendants could or should have done differently; whether there were any steps or precautions reasonably available; and whether it was impossible to take any steps by way of prevention or avoidance, or impracticable or economically unreasonable. Such are not 'circumstances' falling to be considered within art 6. In so far as the risk was known to blood producers and the medical profession, it was not known to the public at large (save for those few patients who might ask their doctor, or read the occasional article about blood in a newspaper) and no risk that any percentage of transfused blood would be infected was accepted by them.

(ii) The defendants assert that the risk was known to those who mattered, namely the medical profession, through whom blood was supplied. Avoiding the risk was impossible and unattainable, and it is not and cannot be legitimate to expect the unattainable. Avoidability or unavoidability is a circumstance to be taken into account within art 6. The public did not and/or was not entitled to expect 100% clean blood. The most they could legitimately expect was that all legitimately expectable (reasonably available) precautions-or in this case tests-had been taken or carried out. The claimants must therefore prove that they were legitimately entitled to expect more, and/or must disprove the unavoidability of the harmful characteristic. There would need to be an investigation as to whether it was impossible to avoid the risk and/or whether the producers had taken all legitimately expectable steps. In so far as there was thus an investigation analogous to, or involving similar facts to, an investigation into negligence, it was not an investigation of negligence by the individual producer and was necessary and, because it was not an investigation of fault, permissible. If, notwithstanding the known and unavoidable risk, the blood was nevertheless defective within art 6, then it is all the more necessary to construe art 7(e) so as to avail those who could not, in the then state of scientific and technical knowledge, identify the defect in a particular product so as to prevent its supply.

(iii) The claimants respond that art 7(e) does not apply to risks which are known before the supply of the product, whether or not the defect can be identified in the particular product; and there are a number of other issues between the parties in respect of art 7(e) to which I shall return later.

... CONCLUSIONS ON ARTICLE 6

[55] I do not consider it to be arguable that the consumer had an actual expectation that blood being supplied to him was not 100% clean, nor do I conclude that he had knowledge that it was, or was likely to be, infected with

Hepatitis C. It is not seriously argued by the defendants, notwithstanding some few newspaper cuttings which were referred to, that there was any public understanding or acceptance of the infection of transfused blood by Hepatitis C. Doctors and surgeons knew, but did not tell their patients unless asked, and were very rarely asked. It was certainly, in my judgment, not known and accepted by society that there was such a risk, which was thus not 'sozialadaquat' (socially acceptable), as Professor Taschner and Count von Westphalen would describe such risks: Taschner and Riesch Produkthaftungsgesetz und EG Produkt-haftungsrichtlinie (1990) at p 291 and von Westphalen Produkthaftungs-handbuch at 27. Thus blood was not, in my judgment, the kind of product referred to in the Flesch/Davenant question and answer in the European Parliament ie 'a product which by its very nature carries a risk and which has been presented as such (instructions for use, labelling, publicity, etc.)', 'risks which are … inherent in [a] product and generally known': nor as referred to by Professor Howells at para 1.17 as being risks which 'consumers can be taken to have chosen to expose themselves to in order to benefit from the product'.

[56] I do not consider that the legitimate expectation of the public at large is that legitimately expectable tests will have been carried out or precautions adopted. Their legitimate expectation is as to the safeness of the product (or not). The court will act as what Dr Bartl called the appointed representative of the public at large, but in my judgment it is impossible to inject into the consumer's legitimate expectation matters which would not by any stretch of the imagination be in his actual expectation. He will assume perhaps that there are tests, but his expectations will be as to the safeness of the blood. In my judgment it is as inappropriate to propose that the public should not 'expect the unattainable'—in the sense of tests or precautions which are impossible-at least unless it is informed as to what is unattainable or impossible, as it is to reformulate the expectation as one that the producer will not have been negligent or will have taken all reasonable steps.

[57] In this context I turn to consider what is intended to be included within 'all circumstances' in art 6. I am satisfied that this means all relevant circumstances. It is quite plain to me that (albeit that Professor Stapleton has been pessimistic about its success) the directive was intended to eliminate proof of fault or negligence. I am satisfied that this was not simply a legal consequence, but that it was also intended to make it easier for claimants to prove their case, such that not only would a consumer not have to prove that the producer did not take reasonable steps, or all reasonable steps, to comply with his duty of care, but also that the producer did not take all legitimately expectable steps either. In this regard I note para 16 of the Advocate General's opinion in European Commission v UK [1997] All ER (EC) 481 at 487 where, in setting out the background to the directive, he pointed out that:

> 'Albeit injured by a defective product, consumers were in fact and too often deprived of an effective remedy, since it proved very difficult procedurally to prove negligence on the part of the producer, that is to say, that he failed to take all appropriate steps to avoid the defect arising.'

[58] The Court of Justice in its judgment perhaps refers implicitly to this when it states (at 494 (para 24)): 'In order for a producer to incur liability for defective products under art 4 of the directive, the victim must prove the damage, the defect and the causal relationship between defect and damage, but not that the producer was at fault.' It seems to me clear that, even without the full panoply of allegations of negligence, the adoption of tests of avoidability or of legitimately expectable safety precautions must inevitably involve a substantial investigation. What safety precautions or tests were available or reasonably available? Were they tests that would have been excessively expensive? Tests which would have been more expensive than justified the extra safety achieved? Are economic or political circumstances or restrictions to be taken into account in legitimate expectability? Once it is asserted that it is legitimately expectable that a certain safety precaution should have been taken, then the producer must surely be able to explain why such was not possible or why he did not do it; in which case it will then be explored as to whether such tests would or could have been carried out, or were or would have been too expensive or impracticable to carry out. If risk and benefit should be considered, then it might be said that, the more beneficial the product, the lower the tolerable level of safety; but this could not be arrived at without consideration as to whether, beneficial or not, there would have nevertheless been a safer way of setting about production or design. As Mr Brown pointed out, even if an alleged impracticability is put forward by a producer, it would still be possible to go back further, and see why it was impracticable, and whether earlier or different research and expenditure could not have resolved the problem.

… [63] I conclude therefore that avoidability is not one of the circumstances to be taken into account within art 6. I am satisfied that it is not a relevant circumstance, because it is outwith the purpose of the directive, and indeed that, had it been intended that it would be included as a derogation from, or at any rate a palliation of, its purpose, then it would certainly have been mentioned; for it would have been an important circumstance, and I am clear that, irrespective of the absence of any word such as 'notamment' in the English-language version of the directive, it was intended that the most significant circumstances were those listed.

CONCLUSIONS ON ARTICLE 7(e)

[74] As to construction: (i) I note (without resolving the question) the force of the argument that the defect in art 7(b) falls to be construed as the defect in the particular product; but I do not consider that to be determinative of the construction of art 7(e), and indeed I am firmly of the view that such is not the case in art 7(e); (ii) the analysis of art 7(e), with the guidance of European Commission v UK, seems to me to be entirely clear. If there is a known risk, ie the existence of the defect is known or should have been known in the light of non-Manchurianly accessible information, then the producer continues to produce and supply at his own risk. It would, in my judgment, be inconsistent

with the purpose of the directive if a producer, in the case of a known risk, continues to supply products simply because, and despite the fact that, he is unable to identify in which if any of his products that defect will occur or recur, or, more relevantly in a case such as this, where the producer is obliged to supply, continues to supply without accepting the responsibility for any injuries resulting, by insurance or otherwise; and (iii) the existence of the defect is in my judgment clearly generic. Once the existence of the defect is known, then there is then the risk of that defect materialising in any particular product.

[75] The purpose of the directive, from which art 7(e) should obviously not derogate more than is necessary (see Recital 16) is to prevent injury, and facilitate compensation for injury. The defendants submit that this means that art 7(e) must be construed so as to give the opportunity to the producer to do all he can in order to avoid injury: thus concentrating on what can be done in relation to the particular product. The claimants submit that this will rather be achieved by imposing obligation in respect of a known risk irrespective of the chances of finding the defect in the particular product, and I agree.

[76] The purpose of art 7(e) was plainly not to discourage innovation, and to exclude development risks from the directive, and it succeeds in its objective, subject to the very considerable restrictions that are clarified by European Commission v UK: namely that the risk ceases to be a development risk and becomes a known risk not if and when the producer in question (or, as the CPA inappropriately sought to enact in s 4(1)(e) 'a producer of products of the same description as the product in question') had the requisite knowledge, but if and when such knowledge were accessible anywhere in the world outside Manchuria. Hence it protects the producer in respect of the unknown (inconnu). But the consequence of acceptance of the defendants' submissions would be that protection would also be given in respect of the known ...

The consequence

[82] In those circumstances the claimants recover against the defendants because their claim succeeds within art 4, the blood bags being concluded to be defective within art 6, and art 7(e) does not avail."

Comments and Questions:
1. In considering whether a product is defective within the meaning of the Directive one must look at the level of safety which can be expected taking into account issues such as the characteristics of the product, packaging and so on. In the above case the court held that a decision as to the level of safety expected is made based not on what the general public actually expects (actual expectation) but rather what they are entitled to expect (legitimate expectation). The decision as to legitimate expectation is one made by the courts (para.31 above).

2. The court also held that once the risk becomes a known risk, (as in the *Richardson* case) then the public is not entitled to expect that that product is entirely safe. Do you consider, given the level of publicity given to blood contamination, that the public is still "entitled" to expect clean blood?

LIABILITY FOR DEFECTIVE PRODUCTS ACT, 1991

Interpretation.

1.—(1) In this Act, except where the context otherwise requires—

"the Council Directive" means Council Directive No. 85/374/EEC of 25 July 1985(1) the text of which in the English language is set out for convenience of reference in the Schedule to this Act;

"damage" means—

(*a*) death or personal injury, or

(*b*) loss of, damage to, or destruction of, any item of property other than the defective product itself:

Provided that the item of property—

(i) is of a type ordinarily intended for private use or consumption, and

(ii) was used by the injured person mainly for his own private use or consumption;

"initial processing" means, in relation to primary agricultural products, any processing of an industrial nature of those products which could cause a defect therein;

"injured person" means a person who has suffered damage caused wholly or partly by a defect in a product or, if he has died, his personal representative (within the meaning of section 3 of the Succession Act, 1965 or dependants (within the meaning of section 47 (1) of the Civil Liability Act, 1961);

Member State" means a Member State of the European Communities;

"the Minister" means the Minister for Industry and Commerce;

"personal injury" includes any disease and any impairment of a person's physical or mental condition;

"primary agricultural products" means the products of the soil, of stock-farming and of fisheries and game, excluding such products and game which have undergone initial processing;

"producer" shall be construed in accordance with *section 2* of this Act;

"product" means all movables with the exception of primary agricultural products which have not undergone initial processing, and includes—

(*a*) movables even though incorporated into another product or into an immovable, whether by virtue of being a component part or raw material or otherwise,

(*b*) electricity where damage is caused as a result of a failure in the process of generation of electricity.

(2) A word or expression that is used in this Act and is also used in the Council Directive has, unless the contrary intention appears, the meaning in this Act that it has in the Council Directive.

(3) In construing a provision of this Act, a court shall give it a construction that will give effect to the Council Directive, and for this purpose a court shall have regard to the provisions of the Council Directive, including its preamble.

(4) In this Act a reference to any other enactment shall be construed as a reference to that enactment as amended by or under any other enactment, including this Act.

Liability for damage caused by defective products.

2.—(1) The producer shall be liable in damages in tort for damage caused wholly or partly by a defect in his product.

(2) In this Act, "producer" means—

(*a*) the manufacturer or producer of a finished product, or

(*b*) the manufacturer or producer of any raw material or the manufacturer or producer of a component part of a product, or

(*c*) in the case of the products of the soil, of stock-farming and of fisheries and game, which have undergone initial processing, the person who carried out such processing, or

(*d*) any person who, by putting his name, trade mark or other distinguishing feature on the product or using his name or any such mark or feature in relation to the product, has held himself out to be the producer of the product, or

(*e*) any person who has imported the product into a Member State from a place outside the European Communities in order, in the course of any business of his, to supply it to another, or

(*f*) any person who is liable as producer of the product pursuant to *subsection (3)* of this section.

(3) Without prejudice to *subsection (1)* of this section, where damage is caused wholly or partly by a defect in a product, any person who supplied the product (whether to the person who suffered the damage, to the producer of any product in which the product is comprised or to any other person) shall, where the producer of the product cannot by taking reasonable steps be identified, be liable, as the producer, for the damage if—

(*a*) the injured person requests the supplier to identify any person (whether still in existence or not) to whom *paragraph (a)*, *(b)*, *(c)*, *(d) or (e)* of *subsection (2)* of this section applies in relation to the product,

(*b*) that request is made within a reasonable time after the damage occurs and at a time when it is not reasonably practicable for the injured person to identify all those persons, and

(*c*) the supplier fails, within a reasonable time after receiving the request, either to comply with the request or to identify the person who supplied the product to him.

Limitation of damages.

3.—(1) Where, but for this section, damages not exceeding £350 in respect of loss of or damage to, or destruction of, any item of property other than the defective product itself would fall to be awarded by virtue of this Act, no damages shall be awarded, and where, but for this section, damages exceeding that amount would fall to be awarded, only that excess shall be awarded.

(2) The Minister may by order vary with effect from a date specified in the order, being a date subsequent to the making of the order, the amount specified in *subsection (1)* of this section but such variation shall not apply to proceedings pending in any court at that date.

(3) The Minister may by order amend or revoke an order made under this section.

Proof of damage and defect.

4.—The onus shall be on the injured person concerned to prove the damage, the defect and the causal relationship between the defect and damage.

Defective product.

5.—(1) For the purposes of this Act a product is defective if it fails to provide the safety which a person is entitled to expect, taking all circumstances into account, including—

(a) the presentation of the product,

(b) the use to which it could reasonably be expected that the product would be put, and

(c) the time when the product was put into circulation.

(2) A product shall not be considered defective for the sole reason that a better product is subsequently put into circulation.

Defences.

6.—A producer shall not be liable under this Act if he proves—

(a) that he did not put the product into circulation, or

(b) that, having regard to the circumstances, it is probable that the defect which caused the damage did not exist at the time when the product was put into circulation by him or that that defect came into being afterwards, or

(c) that the product was neither manufactured by him for sale or any form of distribution for an economic purpose nor manufactured or distributed by him in the course of his business, or

(d) that the defect concerned is due to compliance by the product with any requirement imposed by or under any enactment or any requirement of the law of the European Communities, or

(e) that the state of scientific and technical knowledge at the time when he put the product into circulation was not such as to enable the existence of the defect to be discovered, or

(f) in the case of the manufacturer of a component or the producer of a raw material, that the defect is attributable entirely to the design of the product in which the component has been fitted or the raw material has been incorporated or to the instructions given by the manufacturer of the product.

CHAPTER 6

EMPLOYERS' LIABILITY

INTRODUCTION

Employers' liability deals with the liability of employers for occupational injuries to employees arising from an employer's negligence. An employer owes employees a duty to act reasonably in protecting their health and safety while at work. Initially there was very little protection for employees within the workplace with respect to their health and safety. In addition, very strong defences existed for employers such as that of common employment and voluntary assumption of risk (see below). This has largely changed, partly as a result of legislation (see the Factories Acts, the General Applications Regulations 1993 and supplementary legislation), but also as a result of developments within the common law tort of negligence with respect to the duty of the employer to care for his employees' health and safety.

An action may also be brought by an employee under any piece of legislation which provides a remedy for injury. This is referred to as an action for breach of a statutory duty. Breach of statutory duty torts may arise under all torts where appropriate legislation exists, but are particularly common in the employment context.

A further means by which an employer may be sued is by invoking the principle of vicarious liability. This principle holds that an employer will be liable for the negligent action of an employee under his/her control even if the employer himself/herself has not acted negligently (see Chapter 7).

The duty owed by the employer is often discussed under four headings: the duty to provide a safe place of work; a safe system of work; safe plant and equipment; and competent fellow employees. There is a significant degree of overlap between these headings. The majority of cases deal with physical injury to employees, but a duty also exists to protect an employee against psychological injury. Before we consider the case law in this area we will first look at the standard of care owed by an employer to employees.

STANDARD OF CARE

The standard of care owed by the employer is not an absolute one but that of the "reasonable and prudent" employer.

Barclay v An Post
High Court [1998] 2 I.L.R.M. 385

Facts: Barclay, a postman who worked for An Post, injured his back in June 1993 while delivering some post to an estate with low-lying letter-boxes. He took some months off and on returning to work undertook some overtime in October 1993, also on an estate with low-lying letter-boxes, resulting in a second injury to his back. He sued his employer, An Post, for his injuries.

Issues: The court was required to consider whether the employer could be held liable for Barclay's work-related injury.

The court (McGuinness J.) ultimately held that the employer was not liable for the first injury suffered, given the steps taken by An Post in response to the dangers posed by low-lying letterboxes. However, the court found that An Post had fallen below the standard of "reasonable and prudent" employers in allowing Barclay to undertake the overtime concerned and found them liable for the second injury sustained.

McGuinness J.:

"… As far as the case law is concerned, the classic case in this jurisdiction on the standard of care owed by an employer to an employee in regard to safety is Bradley v CIE [1976] 1R 217. In that case the Plaintiff, a railwayman, was injured when he fell from a ladder attached to a signal post. Engineering evidence suggested that a protective cage would have prevented such a fall but there was no evidence that such cages were provided by other railway companies. There had been no similar accidents within the previous 10 years. The Supreme Court, as is stated in the head note, held that the suggested precaution had not been shown either to have been one which had been commonly taken by other railway operators or to have been one which a reasonably prudent employer would think was obviously necessary in the prevailing circumstances for the protection of its employees. At page 223 of the report Henchy J stated 'the law does not require an employer to ensure in all circumstances the safety of his workmen. He will have discharged his duty of care if he does what a reasonable and prudent employer would have done in the circumstances'. Henchy J went on to say 'even where a certain precaution is obviously wanted in the interest of the safety of the workmen, there may be countervailing factors which would justify the employer in not taking that precaution.'

However, as was submitted by Mr Trainor [counsel for the plaintiff], more recent cases have taken a somewhat less harsh line. In Kennedy v Hughes Dairies [1989] ILRM 117, where an employee suffered a cut from broken glass at a bottling plant, the Supreme Court held that there was sufficient evidence to enable a jury reasonably to conclude that there had been a foreseeable risk of injury to the Plaintiff in the area in which he was injured, because of the nature of his work. The learned McCarthy J (at page 123 of the report) stated 'the essential question in all actions of negligence is whether or not the party charged has failed to take reasonable care whether by act or omission.'

In Dunne v Honeywell [1991] ILRM 595, Barron J dealt with the situation where an employee is working on a third party's premises. At page 600 of the report he stated

> 'An employer has a duty to take reasonable care for the safety of his employees. Where an employee is working on premises other than that of his employer the duty of the employer to use reasonable care for his safety does not in any way diminish. Nevertheless what might be reasonable for an employer to do for the safety of his employee on his own premises may no longer be reasonable where the employee is working elsewhere.'

Dr White, in his book 'Civil Liability for Industrial Accidents' (Volume 1 page 434) summarises the situation of the worker on a third party's premises thus 'the employer owes the like duty of care with regard to the safety of the premises of third parties on which he requires his servants to work as he does in respect of his own premises, but what reasonable care requires in relation to the latter is not necessarily the same as what reasonable care requires in relation to the former'. Having referred to Dunne v Honeywell, he then goes on (at page 486) to deal with the situation where, as in the instant case the employer is aware of the hazard. He refers to the English case of Smyth v Austin Lifts Limited [1959] 1 All ER 81, where the Plaintiff employee had reported to the employer a faulty door mechanism on the third party's premises. When the employee was injured as a result of the hazard, the House of Lords held that the employer had indeed been negligent. Lord Denning said

> 'notwithstanding what was said in Taylor v Sims & Sims [1942] 2 All ER 375, it has since been held, I think rightly, that employers who send their workmen to work on the premises of others cannot renounce all responsibility for their safety. The employers still have an over-riding duty to take reasonable care not to expose their men to unnecessary risk. They must, for instance take reasonable care to devise a safe system of work (see General Contract Cleaning Contractors v Christmas [1952] 2 All ER 1110) and, if they know or ought to know of a danger on the premises to which they send their men, they ought to take reasonable care to safeguard them from it. What is reasonable care depends of course on the circumstances: see Wilson v Tyneside Window Cleaning Company [1958] 2 All ER 265.'

… Mr Mc Govern, for the Defendant, referred to Charlesworth on Negligence (9 Edition) at paragraph 6-18, where the learned author refers to the necessity of balancing the risk against the measures necessary to eliminate it, as follows:

> 'Very few activities can be done without some risk. Crossing the street in a town incurs a risk but the street must be crossed. Cleaning the windows of a high building is a risk and yet the windows must be cleaned. Going to sea is

a risky occupation but shipping must be carried on, regardlessly ... There are some cases where the risk can be reduced or eliminated only at great cost. But the question then arises, at what point can the matter of costs be taken into account when considering the degree of care to be taken?'

The learned author then considers a number of cases in which this question arose and concludes at paragraph 6–21

'In taking stock of the situation, including the difficulty or cost of remedial measures, it is necessary to take into account not only the risk but also the importance of the object to be attained by the activity which creates the risk. If the activity in question is of little or no national importance, it might be that costs should not be taken into account, but in other cases there must be, as in practice there is, a point beyond which further remedial measures are prohibitive by reason of cost.'

At paragraph 6–23 he concludes

'it is a question of degree in each case to be considered, together with the importance of the object to be achieved.'

An Post, Counsel submitted, had taken all possible and reasonable measures and could not be held liable for their failure to eliminate the risk.

It is necessary to consider the evidence in the light of the case law set out above. It is accepted by the Defendant that the positioning of letter boxes a few inches from the ground causes both extreme inconvenience and also a hazard to the health and safety of postmen; a moment's thought would convince one that this form of door design is totally contrary to common sense. An Post had received numerous complaints from the employees' trade union and from individual postmen; the matter had been raised in Dáil Eireann by Deputy James Tully as early as 1971. The hazard was therefore known to the Defendant and the risk was a foreseeable one. The Defendant from its own research and that of its consultants was aware that the practice in other jurisdictions was to regulate the size and position of letter boxes by statute or statutory regulation.

An Post and its predecessor the Department of Posts and Telegraphs did, however, make some response to the situation. By 1976 the Department had succeeded in having proper height and other specifications included in the Irish Standard. Over many years efforts were made to deal with the problem through building regulations or the planning code. It is true that until the late 1980s or early 1990s these efforts were somewhat lethargic and some blame for this attaches to the Defendant, but the main difficulty in my view lay with other bodies in whose hands the remedy lay—the Oireachtas and the Department of the Environment. Given the wide terms of Section 3 of the Building Control Act, 1990, I find it difficult to disagree with the contention of Counsel for the Plaintiff that the relevant regulations could have been made under that Act. However, the power to make such regulations lay outside the remit of the Defendant. Finally, in more recent times the Defendant has made sustained and genuine efforts to improve the situation in regard to letter boxes generally in both urban and rural areas. They have not succeeded in eliminating the hazard but that has not been due to any major negligence on their part. They have, in addition, provided a training course in manual handling to the Plaintiff and his fellow workers. The course may not have been ideal but it warned of the hazards of bending and twisting and I was impressed by the level of commitment and enthusiasm shown by Mr Bolger in his evidence. It is true that he did not provide a satisfactory answer to the problem of delivering letters to low letter boxes, but if one thing emerges from the evidence in this case it is that there is in fact no practical satisfactory answer to this problem other than to eliminate low letter boxes.

On balance, therefore, up to the time of the Plaintiffs injury in June, 1993 I conclude that the Defendant had taken reasonable care in the circumstances to deal with the undoubted hazard. The Defendant has, in general terms, continued to deal with the matter with reasonable care insofar as lies within its power. It can only be hoped that cases such as this may persuade the legislature to take the relevant action.

As far as this particular Plaintiff is concerned, however, that is not the end of the matter. He had suffered a severe injury to his back in June 1993; he had reported this matter to his supervisor; he had attended the company doctor; he had been forced to take time off work. His injury and his consequent vulnerability were by late August/early September 1993 well known to his employers. Yet on 21 October, 1993 he was sent out on overtime to deliver mail to the development at Mount Argus, where some 350 houses had low letter boxes. This overtime delivery to Mount Argus was not, on the evidence, a sudden emergency. It was a regular part of the system at the Fortfield Office because no arrangements had yet been made to set up a separate round for Mount Argus. The Plaintiff accepts that he took on this overtime duty voluntarily; he could have refused it. But he had been out of work for some time and he needed the extra money.

The question of voluntary assumption of risk is dealt with in convenient summary by McMahon and Binchy in their work The Irish Law of Torts (second edition) at 336 as follows:

> 'Formerly the defence of voluntary assumption of risk was fairly readily accepted in cases dealing with employer's liability. In recent years however, the defence "has virtually disappeared in such cases which turn on common law negligence" (O'Hanlon v Electricity Supply Board [1969] IR 75). The Courts, even before the statutory reform of 1961, had shown an increasing sympathy for the dilemma of an employee who was aware of a dangerous work practice for which his employer was responsible. If he said nothing, he might be held to have accepted the risk; if he protested, he might lose his livelihood. Today only a communicated waiver of a right of action will constitute a voluntary assumption of the risk; an uncommunicated determination will not suffice. The employee may, however, still be defeated by holding that, having regard to the risks inherent in a particular business, the employer was not in breach of his duty of care to the employee.'

In the particular circumstances of the Plaintiff in this case it seems to me that the Defendant's duty of care towards Mr Barclay included a duty to ensure that, at least in the short term after his illness, he did not take up duties which would put undue and extraordinary strain on his back. The delivery to 350 low letter boxes in Mount Argus was eminently such a duty...

In summary, I find that the Defendant did not properly discharge the employer's reasonable duty of care in the case of the Plaintiff's second injury and as such the Defendant is liable for that injury."

Comments and Questions:

1. Note that when considering what a reasonable employer would have done, issues which the court took into account above were: standards in the industry as a whole (as in *Bradley v CIÉ* [1976] 1.R. 217); the implications of cost; and whether the employee was on the employer's property when the injury occurred. A duty will still be owed when away from the employer's premises, but it is a factor which will affect what a reasonable employer could do to prevent the injury (see *Mulcare v Southern Health Board* [1988] I.L.R.M. 689 below).

2. McGuinness J. did not accept that the voluntary nature of the overtime was enough to relieve the defendants of liability, highlighting the restrictive nature of the defence of voluntary assumption of risk in recent times (see further Chapter 13).

3. Do you think it reasonable that the court placed a greater duty on An Post to prevent Barclay from undertaking the overtime than it did on Barclay to protect himself from further injury?

SAFE PLACE OF WORK

The employer is obliged to supply a safe place of work in the prevention of any accidents that could reasonably be foreseen by the employer. The question of an employer's liability for injuries incurred away from the workplace is more troublesome. While it will not be a bar to recovery that the employer did not control the premises, there is no doubt that it is something to which the court will have regard (as in *Barclay v An Post,* above).

Mulcare v Southern Health Board
High Court [1988] I.L.R.M. 689

Facts: For about seven years Ms Mulcare worked as a home-help for an elderly woman as an employee of the Southern Health Board. On one particular visit she twisted her ankle on an uneven part of the elderly woman's floor and successfully sued her employer in the Circuit Court for damages. Her employer appealed the decision to the High Court.

Issues: The issue to be addressed was whether the Southern Health Board had failed in its duty of reasonable care to Ms Mulcare in not having inspected the premises to ensure that it was safe for employment. The court held that while a duty might exist, "at most", to inspect the premises, there was no duty to bring it to a modern standard. The court also held that the house, in its view, was not unsafe and therefore found the defendants not liable.

Murphy J.:

"In 1985, she claims she fell in the hallway of Miss Pearse's house as a result of there being worn lino, or an otherwise uneven and rough surface. In these proceedings, the case as to fact and law proposed by the plaintiff is adequately summarised in Paragraph 6 of the plaintiff's reply to notice for particulars, date 14 July 1986, as follows:

> 'The defendants were negligent and in breach of duty in requiring the plaintiff to work in premises which were unsafe. It is clear that the defendant or their representatives should have surveyed the plaintiff's place of work to satisfy themselves that the premises on which she was required to work, did not include any unnecessary danger, or dangers, of which they should have been aware, or if such dangers were present on the premises, that they should warn the plaintiff. The floor of the room in which the plaintiff was required to work was uneven and unsafe, and had a very rough surface on it.'

The defence is that, firstly, the premises were not unsafe, secondly there was no obligation on the defendant to inspect, thirdly they were given no notice of the condition of the floor surface, and, fourthly, an inspection in any event would have been futile as they have no power in law, or no right or entitlement to remedy any defect in the floor. The plaintiff's reply to this is that if inspection had been carried out, and the premises found to be dangerous, the defendant would then have a duty to say to its employee, *'Don't work there'*, or alternatively, they should say to Miss Pearse that they cannot allow their employee to attend unless she carried out certain remedial works on the premises.

I have been referred to a useful decision in *Wilson v Tyneside Cleaning Company* [1958] 2 QB 110, in which it was held that employers of a window cleaner allowed him to work in a customer's premises. The employers were not held to be responsible. The case was decided on the question of the employee not being on the employer's premises. An employer continues to have responsibility for an employee, and in that case, it was held that the employer had fulfilled his duty. I was also referred to a very helpful extract and reference in the *Irish Law of Torts* by McMahon and Binchy (1981) and I will refer to page 315:

> 'The extent to which an employer must protect an employee from injury on premises not under the employer's control is somewhat less certain. While the fact that the premises are not under his control does not constitute an automatic ground for exemption from responsibility, clearly it is an important factor to which the court would have regard. There are obvious limits to the

> employer's duty in this regard: *"if a master sends a plumber to mend a leak in a respectable private house, no-one could hold him negligent for not visiting the house himself to see if the carpet in the hall creates a trap"*. Although some decisions have approached this issue under the fourth heading, of failure to provide a safe system of work, whatever approach is favoured, it seems that no hard and fast rule has been articulated on this question, and that the courts have generally been content to hide behind the rationale that it is no more than a *"question of fact".'*

I have no wish to hide behind the paragraph I have quoted, but it seems to me that what was involved in this case is a question of degree. A distinction must be drawn between an employee on his employer's property, and an employee on the property of others. There can be multiple variations, for example, a skilled craftsman who is sent out on a domestic emergency to a premises where no danger is likely, and where the premises would be safe. This must differ from the case of an apprentice who would be sent out to the demolition of a premises. It is a matter of degree and fact in every case. I think it unhelpful to consider the problem under the four general headings of workmen or competent staff, safe place of business, safe tools, safe premises, or safe system. I think that all that can be done is to simply state that the employer is bound to exercise reasonable care. The employer fixes the condition in which an employee works.

Let us for a moment assume that, at most, the obligation on the part of the defendant was to survey either initially or subsequently. That, at most, was a primary obligation. At worst, the condition of the premises in 1985 would have been slightly better than the condition which they were in when inspected by the plaintiff's engineer in 1986. What would that duty have been then? Are those conditions where the employer must say to an employee *'You cannot work there'*? Is one to say that a reasonable employer must say to the owner of the premises, *'My man will not go in there until certain works are done'*, be it in writing, or, in this case, remedying defects to a floor? At what stage is one to say the home help can only go to a moderately dilapidated premises?

I take the view that a Health Board is not bound by a duty, where an employee provides this type of service, to require the premises in which the employee is to provide those services, to be improved to modern standards.

Depressions will occur in a floor. While the floor may have been short of the ideal, I do not think it was unsafe. The plaintiff worked there for seven years, and never fell before the date of her accident. I cannot say that the premises were so unsafe that the defendant should have had Miss Pearse carry out improvements, or not provide the services. Consequently, I must accede to the defendant's request, and dismiss the plaintiff's claim."

Comments and Questions:

1. While considering that a duty to inspect a premises that an employee visits might exist, Murphy J. fell short of imposing an obligation in all cases to do so. Contrast this with the case of *McMahon v Irish Biscuits*, below, where

the court went further in requiring that an employer assure him/herself that all premises the plaintiff visits are safe. Do you think that an absolute duty to inspect ought to be imposed or should each case be decided on its own facts?

2. Murphy J., above, did not find on the facts that the house was unsafe. Had he, however, found the contrary, what do you think the court would have decided the Southern Health Board ought to have done to avoid liability?

When employees work away from the employer's premises, Murphy J. in *Mulcare* did not impose a duty to inspect—in the following case, however, the court was much more emphatic in its imposition of a duty on employers to satisfy themselves that all premises that an employee visits are safe and free from inherent dangers.

McMahon v Irish Biscuits Ltd. and Power Supermarkets T/A Quinnsworth
Unreported, High Court, January 28, 2002

Facts: The plaintiff, a sales representative, was injured while checking stock in a Quinnsworth supermarket on behalf of his employer, Irish Biscuits Ltd. The plaintiff, Mr McMahon, engaged in stock-taking every Monday for the purpose of placing orders for Quinnsworth with his employer. The only means of accessing all shelving was to climb onto the shelves in question, during which exercise Mr McMahon fell from the shelves. It was accepted in evidence that while his employers, Irish Biscuits, were aware of the circumstances in which Mr McMahon undertook the stock-taking, the management of Quinnsworth was not.

Issues: In relation to employers' liability, the issues to be decided were whether Irish Biscuits as his employers owed him a duty to inspect the premises that he visited as part of his employment and, having had knowledge of the dangers present, whether they were liable for the injury caused. The court (O'Donovan J.) held that Irish Biscuits owed a duty to ensure that the facilities their employees visited were free from danger. They had not only failed in that duty but also failed to take steps after having become aware of the dangers on the property of Quinnsworth, to eliminate that danger.

O'Donovan J.:

"... Insofar as Irish Biscuits Limited are concerned, it is settled law that, as the Plaintiff's employers, they owed him a duty, as was stated by the Supreme Court in the unreported case of Dalton v Frendo (judgment delivered on the 15 December 1977) 'to take reasonable care for the servants' safety in all circumstances of the case'. This does not mean that Irish Biscuits Limited are the insurers of the safety of the Plaintiff in the course of his employment with them but, in my view, it does mean that they were required to take all reasonable steps to ensure that he was not exposed to avoidable risk of injury in the course of his employment.

To that end, it is my view that they had a duty to acquaint themselves of the facilities which were provided by their customers to enable their (Irish Biscuits Ltd) sales staff to carry out duties, which were for their mutual benefit, and to satisfy themselves that those facilities and the system operated by their customers whereby their sales staff carried out their duties did not pose a threat to their well being. In my view, Irish Biscuits Ltd. fell down badly with regard to that duty. In this regard, it was clear from the evidence of Ms Derbhla O'Brien, the National Sales Manager for Irish Biscuits Ltd. at the material time, that she and, presumably, her employers did not consider it necessary to visit their various sales outlets to ensure that the facilities afforded to their sales staff were appropriate. Indeed, in the circumstance that Irish Biscuits Ltd. appear to have 1,000 outlets for their product, Ms O'Brien maintained that it was not practicable for them to inspect all those outlets. I do not agree. However difficult it might be, it is my opinion that the duty of care which Irish Biscuits Ltd. owed to its employees obliged them to ensure that the facilities afforded to their employees by their customers to enable their employees to carry out duties for the mutual benefit of themselves and their customers did not threaten the safety of their employees. This, it appears, Irish Biscuits Ltd. did not do; at least, insofar as the Plaintiff was concerned. However, the Plaintiff's immediate superior at the material time, Mr Michael McHugh, was aware of the risks which the Plaintiff was taking and, indeed, he gave evidence that he passed on the Plaintiff's complaints in that regard to his superior, a Mr Freehill so that the fact of the matter appears to be that while Irish Biscuits Ltd. do not, as a matter of practice, inspect all of the facilities afforded by their customers for their sales staff, insofar as the Plaintiff was concerned, senior management in Irish Biscuits Ltd. were aware of the risks to which the Plaintiff was exposed while checking stock in the Quinnsworth warehouse and, yet, they did nothing about it. In my view, their failure to do so amounted to negligence which significantly contributed to the Plaintiff's fall and the resultant injuries which he suffered. In this regard, I reject the submission by Counsel for Irish Biscuits Ltd that, in the absence of any relevant complaint, it is unreasonable to expect an employer to inspect premises of a third party in which members of the employer's staff are expected to carry out duties on behalf of the employer, or to make enquiries with regard to the system of work maintained for members of their staff on the premises of the third party for the purpose of satisfying themselves that their staff are not exposed to avoidable risks. If that were so, it seems to me that an employer would be entitled to abrogate the duty of care he owes to his employee in favour of a third party which I do not perceive to be the law in this country and neither do I think that the judgment of the Court in the case of Mulcare v Southern Health Board [1988] ILRM at page 689, to which I was referred, is authority for that proposition. Accordingly, it is my view that, not only were Irish Biscuits Ltd negligent for their failure to act upon the complaint made by Mr McMahon but I think that they were also negligent for failing to appraise themselves of the system of work involving their employee which was tolerated in the Quinnsworth warehouse.

Insofar as Powers Supermarkets are concerned, there is no doubt but that they were in control of the situation at the time of the Plaintiff's accident and I have no doubt but that members of their staff, including members at managerial level, were aware of the manner in which the Plaintiff was accustomed to checking stocks of biscuit and, being aware of that, they must also have been aware of the risk of injury to which the Plaintiff was exposed and, yet, they did nothing to avoid that risk. In my view, that also was a negligent omission which contributed to the Plaintiff's accident, and indeed, was the main contributing factor. In my view, as between Irish Biscuits Ltd. and Powers Supermarkets, insofar as blame worthiness is concerned, in the circumstance that Powers Supermarkets were in control of the situation at the material time and had the immediate opportunity of doing something which might have avoided the accident which befell the Plaintiff, I think that they are the more to blame. In this regard, I am very much influenced by the fact that the Plaintiffs visit to the Quinnsworth warehouse on a Monday morning was a scheduled visit of which Powers supermarket were well aware and a scheduled visit during which the Plaintiff would be under severe constraints with regard to the time within which he had to do whatever was necessary to ensure that they (Powers Supermarkets) got a fresh supply of biscuits on the following Wednesday, as the second-named Defendants were also well aware. Accordingly, they should have ensured that their premises were in a state of preparedness for the Plaintiff which they, obviously, were not.

In the light of the foregoing, I would apportion fault for the Plaintiff's accident as to 60% against Powers Supermarkets, 30% against Irish Biscuits Ltd, and, notwithstanding that the negligence of the Defendants would, in my view, also amount to breach of their statutory obligations under the relevant provisions of the Factories Acts and Regulations made thereunder, I find that the blameworthiness of the Plaintiff to which I have already referred amounts to contributory negligence to the extent of 10%."

Comments and Questions:
1. Do you think it was appropriate that contributory negligence of 10 per cent was apportioned to Mr McMahon?

2. The defendants in the above case stated in their defence that it was not practical for them to inspect all premises that their employees visited, but O'Donovan J. disagreed. Do you think he was correct and that a duty to inspect all premises would apply in every case?

3. In respect of the duty of employers to employees who work from home, the Department of Enterprise, Trade and Employment has drawn up a Code of Practice on E-Working as a guide to employers on best practice (available at http://www.entemp.ie/publications/trade/2000/ework.pdf).

SAFE SYSTEM OF WORK

While the courts accept that no system of work is entirely free from risk, an employer is required to provide a method of working which is safe as far as is reasonable. The fact that an employee is experienced and aware of the risks is not enough to absolve the employer of all liability but, as demonstrated by the *McSweeney v McCarthy* case, it is a factor the courts will take into account. In that case the court held that the appropriate test in deciding liability arising from an unsafe system of work is the degree of control each party had or could reasonably be regarded to have had. While an employer is always in primary control, an employee may also be found liable to the extent that they controlled or could be regarded to have controlled, how the work was done. However, for this principle to apply a system must first have been established.

McSweeney v McCarthy
Supreme Court, 1986/9039 P (transcript)

Facts: The plaintiff, an experienced painter, fell from an unsecured ladder when carrying out some painting work for the defendants at the factory of a client. His action was dismissed in the High Court, a decision he appealed to the Supreme Court.

Issues: The court had to consider whether, given the experience of the plaintiff, it was reasonable to impose liability on the employer for the unsafe system of work which left the ladder unsecured and therefore dangerous. The court held that, while the experience of the employee was not a complete defence, it was a factor to be considered when deciding what steps should reasonably have been taken. The test for liability could be decided on the basis of control; while ordinarily it is the employer who is in control, in some cases the employee also can be said to control how work is done.

The court held that a system did not exist in this case and that, as the injury was foreseeable, the defendants were liable. As the employee had also behaved unreasonably, liability was apportioned between both parties.

Murray J.:

"Safe System of Work
The first submission made on behalf of the Plaintiff in this appeal is to the effect that in leaving the Plaintiff to carry out the work according to his own devices the Defendants, by their servants or agents, failed to provide the Plaintiff with a reasonably safe system of work. The Defendants for their part contend that this was essentially a one man job and the Plaintiff had sufficient experience to carry it out himself. In particular, he was well aware of the danger

of climbing an unsecured ladder and also that he knew that the foreman would hold the ladder when he was climbing it, if asked to do so. In these circumstances, the work could have been carried out safely provided the Plaintiff himself exercised reasonable care. There was no want of care, it was submitted, on the part of the Defendants.

It is well established that an employer is under a common law duty to provide his employees with a reasonably safe system of work. I know of no principle which exempts an employer from this duty only because their employee(s) are experienced, or know or ought to have known, of the dangers inherent in the work. Certainly, there are many factors which come into play in assessing whether, in the circumstances of the particular case, the system of work was reasonably safe or not. Among these are the experience of the workman concerned, the level of danger involved, its complexity and so on. As regards a safe system of work Murnaghan J observed in Caulfield v Bell [1958] IR (326 at 333):

> 'The expression, "a safe system of work," ... has not, as far as I am aware, ever been precisely defined. The expression has to be considered in every case, to which it is appropriate, in relation to the particular circumstances of the job in hand. In the expression the word, "safe," means no more than "as safe as is reasonably possible in the circumstances." The degree of safety would depend on the particular job, and would vary between wide limits.'

Indeed, the expression 'a safe system of work' is not susceptible to a single all embracing definition. One may look at what it encompasses.

The word 'system' may in this context be said to comprehend a set of procedures according to which something is done; an organised scheme or method. (see New Oxford English Dictionary, Oxford University Press, 1998).

The organisation of procedures or methods according to which the work of an employee(s) should be carried out necessarily involves foresight and forethought on the part of the employer.

It is the employer who assigns the work; he sets the scene, so to speak. He is in control at this point. It follows that an employer must have addressed, in advance, the foreseeable risks inherent in the work which the employee is being required to carry out, so as to ensure that the method or procedures to be followed in carrying out the work are sufficient so as to reasonably protect him from those risks. The extent of the duty will evidently vary considerably according to the circumstances of the case. In cases where the work is complex and/or highly dangerous the duty may involve the establishment of an elaborate system which is strictly supervised and enforced. In other circumstances a mere warning or specific instruction may suffice.

In these proceedings it is common case that it was foreseeable that the Plaintiff at some point in the course of his duties would require the assistance of someone else to secure the ladder at its foot when he had to mount it. This is because the climbing of an unsecured ladder is inherently dangerous. It is also common case that, in the circumstances of this case, it would be placing too onerous a duty on the employer to contend that he should have provided the Plaintiff during his entire period of work with an assistant ready to hold the ladder, as the isolated need arose.

The reality of cases like the present is that both employer and employee had an opportunity to consider how the work should be carried out, whether it involved any dangers, and, if so, how they should be avoided. By denying liability because only the employee was present is in effect to seek to plead some sort of last opportunity rule. That, however, is not the basis of liability. Admittedly, the employee is more proximate to the events leading up to the circumstances in which the injury occurred. But this is not the test of liability. The test is dependent upon control of the work.

In the ordinary case, it is the employer who controls the work and liability on the part of the employer derives from his control. That does not mean that the employee cannot also be liable to the extent that he or she is in control or should be regarded as being in control.

If both have an opportunity to consider how the work should be done, what dangers might arise and how to avoid them, as between them, it is the employer who will normally exercise, or be required to exercise, primary control. That was the case here where the Defendant's foreman had the task of determining and assigning the work to be done.

In the present case when the Plaintiff arrived at a point, in the early afternoon, where he needed the assistance of a fellow worker to secure the ladder, the only person who could be considered reasonably to be available to secure the ladder for the Plaintiff, in the circumstances was the Defendant's foreman. The carrying out of the Plaintiff's work safely, therefore, required some co-ordination between him and the foreman who had assigned the work to him. Of this, the foreman was in control. As previously noted, the Plaintiff looked around the factory building 101 and did not find him there. As it happens, he was in the Defendant's compound at the time but there is nothing in the evidence or in the findings to indicate that the Plaintiff actually knew that he was there at the time, even if he certainly knew that the compound was a likely place to find him. Walking around the complex would have involved a search of 15 minutes, or if he had gone directly to the compound, 5 minutes walk there and five minutes walk back. At this point, the Plaintiff was confronted with a choice of searching further afield for the foreman or taking a chance that the ladder would hold. The latter option was what Counsel for the Defendants described in the course of the Appeal as 'a transient danger for a brief period'. This was the option he took.

This was not a case of an employee failing to observe a safe system of work. As the evidence clearly shows, there was no system of work. On the evidence of the foreman, Mr Murphy, already referred to, the Plaintiff was left entirely to his own devices and had to devise his own method of work.

Counsel for the Defendants submitted that the Plaintiff was an experienced painter, fully aware of the danger of climbing an unsecured ladder and knew that the foreman would hold the ladder if requested to do so. While the experience and competence of the workman is a relevant factor in considering whether, in the circumstances, a system of work has been made reasonably safe, his experience cannot be a reason for ignoring completely the duty to ensure that there is a safe system of work in place and leaving it up to the employee rather than the employer to devise such a system or whether there should be such a system.

In General Cleaning Contractors Ltd v Christmas [1952] 2 All ER 1110 Lord Oaksey sitting in the Court of Appeal in England and Wales observed at page 1114.

> 'In my opinion, it is the duty of an employer to give such general safety instructions as a reasonably careful employer who has considered the problem presented by the work would give to his workman. It is, I think, well known to employers, and there is evidence in this case that it was well known to the appellants, that their workpeople are very frequently, if not habitually, careless about the risks which their work may involve. It is, in my opinion, for that very reason that the common law demands that employers should take reasonable care to lay down a reasonably safe system of work. Employers are not exempted from this duty by the fact that their men are experienced and might, if they were in a position of an employer, be able to lay down a reasonably safe system of work themselves. Workmen are not in the position of employers. Their duties are not performed in the calm atmosphere of a boardroom with the advice of experts. They have to make their decisions on narrow windowsills and other places of danger, and in circumstances in which the dangers are obscured by repetition.'

This is a succinct summary of the common law duty of an employer in this context.

It is clear from the caselaw on employer's liability that workmen will be tempted to take risks on the spur of the moment in order to get on with the job, particularly when that risk is a momentary or transient one, such as was the case here. It is to protect him from such foreseeable risks from an inherent danger that a safe system of work is required.

Having taken the option which he did, the Plaintiff on his own admission, did so knowing that there was a risk of the ladder slipping, as it did, and also knowing that if he had sought out the foreman, Mr Murphy, he would have held the ladder while he climbed it. In this he was clearly negligent.

On the other hand, the Plaintiff was faced with the decision of delaying the work, while he searched out and located the foreman, or just getting on with it. Alternatively, as had been put to him, he could have got on, at least for the time being, with an easier part of the work by skipping the duct area, something for which, rightly or wrongly, he felt he could be criticised by the foreman. If the danger was foreseeable by the Plaintiff it was at least equally foreseeable by the Defendants and it is clear that they took no steps whatsoever to cater for this risk. The Defendants contend that only the Plaintiff had knowledge of the specific point in time when he would need assistance and the Defendants, that is the foreman, could only have responded when informed of the need for assistance. This, it seems to me, begs the question. It was at all times foreseeable that the Plaintiff working without assistance was likely to need such assistance to secure the ladder for access to one or more points at which he had to work and during one or more stages of his working day. The foreman, Mr Murphy, did not inspect the site to identify when or where this was likely to arise or how the Plaintiff should deal with this situation or how he might or should be contacted by the Plaintiff when assistance was needed.

A straightforward but specific instruction to postpone the work until the Plaintiff sought out and located the foreman, whatever delay was involved, would have been one means of addressing it. There may have been alternative procedures, but the Defendants, in any case, did nothing.

Each case must, of course, depend upon its own facts. This was a case where each was in a position to consider whether any problems might arise and to determine how the work should be carried out in safety. But there can also be cases where an employee may be solely liable for what occurs.

In Fennell v E Stone & Sons Ltd [1967] IR 204, the plaintiff was a general labourer engaged in carrying out renovation work to premises in Dublin. He was engaged in dismantling and moving scaffolding from one room to another. While doing so, he caused an electric lamp to fall on his head. There was nothing intrinsically dangerous about the layout of the rooms. What occurred was something which could have been avoided with a little care. It was held that the employers were not insurers and were not negligent because they had not in effect warned their employee to be careful in the course of what he was doing.

The case is a further illustration of the principle of control. It was the plaintiff himself who was actually in control of what he was doing. Neither was there an inherent danger in the work. His employer could not be responsible for every trivial aspect of his work which might cause him difficulty and which he was perfectly capable of avoiding.

In this case the circumstances are otherwise. Assigning a man on his own to use a ladder to work at a height poses immediately the question as to how he is to mount an unsecured ladder, whether it is for the purpose of tying it at the top or getting to his place of work. That was an inherent danger which was primarily, though not exclusively, under the control of the Defendants as the employer.

As O'Dalaigh J observed in Connor v Malachy Burke (Contractors) Limited (Unreported, Supreme Court, 31 March, 1955) the duty to provide a safe system of work 'arises because by reason of the nature of the work certain perils are to be anticipated'.

Since there was a foreseeable danger to a workman left on his own and to his own devices when using a ladder to climb such heights, the Defendants were under a duty to provide a reasonably safe system of work. They didn't do so and their failure to do so was a causative factor in the accident which gave rise to the Plaintiff's injuries.

[The court then went on to consider whether the employer was in breach of his statutory duties, which the court found he was].

... Having found that it had not been established that there was negligence on the part of the Defendants, the learned trial judge did not consider the question whether the Plaintiff was guilty of contributory negligence.

Again it is clear from the undisputed facts in this case that the Plaintiff himself was guilty of negligence and breach of statutory duty in failing to take reasonable care for his own safety.

The Plaintiff, who was an experienced painter and workman, fully appreciated the danger of ascending an unsecured ladder and the risk of injury attached thereto, but in spite of such knowledge, he knowingly took the risk of ascending a ladder which was not secured and when there was no person holding the ladder while he was ascending it.

In so doing, he, as an experienced workman was not taking reasonable care for his own safety.

... In apportioning degrees of fault, the Courts have traditionally adopted a more lenient view of the contributory negligence of a workman when there is a breach of statutory duty on the part of the employer.

In this case, however, the conduct of the Plaintiff amounted to more than mere 'inadvertence' referred to in the authorities. It consisted of a deliberate act in his part when he knew of the risk involved.

Having regard to the particular circumstances of this case I am satisfied that the negligence and breach of statutory duty of the Plaintiff contributed substantially to the injury which he sustained.

I would apportion degrees of fault under both headings as 40% to the Plaintiff and 60% to the Defendant and remit the matter back to the High Court for the assessment of damages."

Comment and Questions:
1. Was it correct of Murray J. to say that there was not a system of work at play in the above case? Might it also be true to say that the system (*i.e.* procedure) employed was to leave the decision-making to the employee?

2. See also *Barclay v An Post*, above, for an example of an unsafe work practice.

An employer is under a duty to take reasonable care to ensure that proper appliances are provided and maintained in a proper condition so as not to subject those employed to unnecessary risk. In considering what steps are reasonable the court will take into account standards in the industry as a whole (as in *Bradley v CIÉ*). Each case, however, must be decided on its own facts and on the basis of what is reasonable.

Bradley v Córas Iompair Éireann
Supreme Court [1976] I.R. 217

Facts: The plaintiff was employed by the defendants as a signalman on the railway. After having replaced a damaged signal light, and while descending by way of a ladder, he fell and was injured. In the High Court evidence was submitted that had a steel cage surrounded the ladder the accident could have been prevented. The defendants were found liable for failing to provide a safe place of work. The defendants appealed this finding to the Supreme Court.

Issues: The issue to be decided was whether the defendants had fallen below the standard of a reasonable and prudent employer in failing to have installed a safety cage around the ladder. The court held that this issue was to be decided taking into account the following: whether the cage in question was one commonly used in the industry; if not, whether it was something that was obviously wanting in the interests of health and safety; and finally, if it was so wanting, whether it was reasonable (taking into account issues such as risk and cost) to impose such a requirement on the defendants.

On the basis of an assessment of all of these considerations the court held that the defendants were not liable in not having installed the safety cages.

Henchy J. (Griffin and Kenny JJ. concurring):

"Having regard to the run of the case and the judge's charge to the jury, it is clear that the jury's finding that the defendants had not provided the plaintiff with a safe place of work was tantamount to an acceptance by them of the contention that the ladder should have been fitted with a safety cage. Therefore, the real question is whether the evidence justified such a finding ...

... Where a workman founds a claim for damages for negligence against his employer on an allegation that something was left undone that should have been done in the interests of his safety, the most commonly cited statement of the necessary degree of proof is that formulated by Lord Dunedin at p809 of the report of Morton v William Dixon Ltd (1909 SC 807)—

'… I think it is absolutely necessary that the proof of that fault of omission should be one of two kinds, either—to shew that the thing which he did not do was a thing which was commonly done by other persons in like circumstances, or—to shew that it was a thing which was so obviously wanted that it would be folly in anyone to neglect to provide it.'

This rule has been applied in numerous cases including the decision of the Supreme Court in Christie v Odeon (Ir) Ltd ((1956) 91 ILTR 25) usually with the gloss given to it by Lord Normand in Paris v Stepney Borough Council ((1951) AC 367, 382)—

'The rule is stated with all the Lord President's trenchant lucidity. It contains an emphatic warning against a facile finding that a precaution is necessary when there is no proof that it is one taken by other persons in like circumstances. But it does not detract from the test of the conduct and judgment of the reasonable and prudent man. If there is proof that a precaution is usually observed by other persons, a reasonable and prudent man will follow the usual practice in the like circumstances. Failing such proof the test is whether the precaution is one which the reasonable and prudent man would think so obvious that it was folly to omit it.'

See per Lord Tucker in Cavanagh v Ulster Weaving Co Ltd ((1960) AC 145, 162). In fact, it does no more than provide a mode of testing whether in the class of cases to which it refers the employer has taken reasonable care for the safety of his employee or, as it is sometimes put, whether he has subjected him to unnecessary risk.

In the present case, the first part of the test laid down by Lord Dunedin in Morton's Case (1909 SC 807) was answered by uncontroverted evidence that the safety cage suggested by the plaintiff's engineer was unknown in railway practice. The defendants' engineer (who was the only expert in railway engineering called in evidence) said that although he was familiar with the systems of railway signals in Ireland, the United Kingdom and some continental countries, he had never seen a signal-post ladder with such a cage. His evidence to the effect that such a cage was unheard-of passed without cross-examination or any other attempt to controvert it. That being so, it would have been impossible for counsel for the plaintiff to argue that the provision of a safety cage was 'a thing which was commonly done by other persons in like circumstances.'

Although the defendants were following general practice in not having fitted the ladder with a safety cage, was such a cage so obviously wanted for the protection of the plaintiff from injury by falling that the defendants could be said to have been imprudent or unreasonable in not providing it? In applying this test it is important to bear in mind what was pointed out by Lord Reid in General Cleaning Contractors v Christmas ((1953) AC 180, 192)—

'if he is right it means that all, or practically all, the numerous employers in the trade have been habitually neglecting their duty to their men.'

As far as the evidence in this case goes, it shows that no railway company in Ireland, the United Kingdom or Holland (and possibly other European countries) fits a safety cage to this kind of ladder. Was it open on the evidence for the jury to say, as in effect they did say, that they are all wanting in reasonable care for the safety of their workmen? The answer lies in whether, notwithstanding the general practice, the provision of a safety cage was an obvious safety precaution which could reasonably have been provided.

First, as to whether the defendants ought to have noticed that a safety cage was obviously wanted. There was no suggestion in the evidence that the experience from a century and a half of railway operations had thrown up any need for a safety cage on these ladders. A specific search of the records of the defendants for the ten years prior to this accident showed that, despite the fact that over 1000 of these uncaged ladders were being operated in the defendants' railway system, not one accident related to their use was reported. Looking outside railways, the plaintiff's engineer could produce from his experience only two instances of a ladder with a safety cage, one being in the Ford factory in Cork city and the other in an Aer Rianta installation in West Cork. But cross-examination elicited that in each of those two cases the ladder in question was used as a stairway for regular access to a higher level of a building. So, in fact, no instance was given of a safety cage on an external vertical or near-vertical fixed ladder of this kind, although such ladders are to be seen on quaysides, ships, silos, gasometers, building sites and other buildings and installations. It is impossible, therefore, to say that it was, or should have been, obvious to the defendants that a safety cage was wanted on this ladder. The combination of long-established operation, the widespread use elsewhere of similar ladders, and the unbroken experience of an absence of a likelihood that these ladders would cause accidents must be held to rule out the conclusion that a safety cage was obviously wanted. Of course, a ladder such as this carries a risk of injury to a person working on it, particularly if he is carrying an object such as a lamp in one hand, but no more than does any other fixed ladder of this kind on which a person is required to work. In all such cases it might be said, at the most, that a safety cage would be desirable, but certainly as far as this case is concerned, it could not be said that it was obviously wanted.

However, even if the evidence enabled the jury to say that a safety cage was obviously wanted, it would not necessarily follow that the plaintiff had established negligence by proving that the defendants had not fitted one. It would be further necessary in such a case as this for the plaintiff to show that the obviously wanted precaution is one that a reasonably careful employer would have taken. The law does not require an employer to ensure in all circumstances the safety of his workmen. He will have discharged his duty of care if he does what a reasonable and prudent employer would have done in the circumstances. Thus, even where a certain precaution is obviously wanted in the interests of the safety of the workman, there may be countervailing factors which would justify the employer in not taking that precaution. As Lord Reid said in Morris v West Hartlepool Steam Navigation Co Ltd ((1956) AC 552, 574)—

> '... It is the duty of an employer, in considering whether some precaution should be taken against a foreseeable risk, to weigh, on the one hand, the magnitude of the risk, the likelihood of an accident happening and the possible seriousness of the consequences if an accident does happen, and, on the other hand, the difficulty and expense and any other disadvantage of taking the precaution.'

The defendants were entitled to measure against the desirability of installing a safety cage on this ladder the fact that they would also have to install a safety cage on each of the thousand or more similar ladders scattered throughout their railroad system, thus incurring heavy installation and maintenance expenses, notwithstanding that such installations are not deemed necessary in neighbouring countries and notwithstanding the absence over a period of at least ten years of a single accident to suggest the necessity of taking such a precaution. Of even greater weight is the fact that, if they installed a safety cage on this particular ladder, they would reduce the clearance between the steel fixture thus created and each of the two adjoining railway lines from 4 foot 6 and a half inches to 3 foot 9 and a half inches—thus breaching the rule of a minimum clearance of 4 foot 6 inches which the defendants observe. That rule apparently derives from Board of Trade regulations which are not binding in this State.

Therefore, it would have been open to the plaintiff to show that the margin of clearance observed by the defendants is unnecessarily wide and that they could reduce it to 3 foot 9 and a half inches without undue risk. However, no evidence on the matter was given on behalf of the plaintiff. The only witness who dealt with it was the defendants' expert, and he left the witness box without a single question having been put to him in cross-examination to suggest that the observance of a 4 foot 6 inches clearance was unnecessary. Therefore, at the end of the case there was no evidence to support a finding that a 4 foot 6 and a half inches clearance could responsibly be reduced to a 3 foot 9 and a half inches clearance. It may be that a minimum clearance of 4 foot 6 inches is pitched unnecessarily high, but it would be unjustifiable to say so without evidence to that effect. It is implicit in the jury's verdict that they reached that conclusion. In doing so without evidence, they took a leap in the dark. For all they knew, a reduction of the clearance to 3 foot 9 and a half inches might have produced a hazard of injury to others that would outweigh the risk of injury to the plaintiff through not fitting the ladder with a safety cage.

For the foregoing reasons, I am of opinion that there was not evidence to support the jury's verdict, and that the application to have the case withdrawn from the jury should have been allowed. I would therefore allow the appeal and, in lieu of the order of the High Court, enter judgment for the defendants. I would allow the appeal without costs because counsel for the defendants, when applying to have the case withdrawn from the jury, did not direct the trial judge's attention to any of the authorities relied on in this Court or, indeed, to any authority."

Comments and Questions:
1. While the issues of cost and convenience were taken into account in the case above, in more recent years cost has been less of an influencing factor where safety concerns are high.

COMPETENT FELLOW EMPLOYEES

An employer is under a duty to use due care to select proper and competent staff. If the employer fails to take reasonable care in the selection of competent staff and an accident ensues as a result, then an employer will be liable.

However, in incidents where employees injure fellow employees, or members of the public, an employer is more likely to be sued on the basis of a vicarious liability action (where the employer is liable not because s/he was negligent but because s/he is in a position of "control" over the negligent employee).

Hough v Irish Base Metals Ltd.
Unreported, Supreme Court, December 8, 1967

Facts: The plaintiff suffered serious burns when a workmate placed a gas fire under his legs. The plaintiff sued in negligence. In the High Court McLoughlin J. (and a jury) found that the employers had failed to meet the standard of a reasonable and prudent employer in that supervision was inadequate and found the defendants liable on that basis. The employer appealed the finding to the Supreme Court.

Issues: The Supreme Court was asked to consider whether the defendant employers had fallen below the standard of care required. The court, on considering the recent occurrence of the larking which gave rise to the injury, and the levels of supervision provided, held that the employer had not fallen below the standard of a reasonable and prudent employer and allowed the appeal.

Ó Dálaigh J. (Walsh and Haugh JJ. concurring):

"The appellant sued the respondents for failure to provide a safe system of work; and the case made at the trial, which took place before Mr. McLoughlin J and jury, was that the system of work was unsafe because the employers had failed to exercise supervision over the repair shop. It was not said that there was evidence that the employers had actual knowledge of this dangerous larking, but it was submitted that the employers ought to have known of it and prevented it and could have known of it by a proper system of supervision.

Mr. Justice McLoughlin ruled that there was no evidence of a consistent practice which was known, or should be known, or could be known, to the employer and withdrew the case from the jury. He pointed out that Reilly's act was an act which was done for his own purposes and not for his employers' and therefore was not an act for which his employers could be vicariously liable.

Appellant's counsel accepted that there was no evidence that the employers had actual knowledge of the 'larking' complained of, but his submission here has been that the larking was so general that it ought to have been known to the employers if they had a proper system of supervision. And it is said that an employer who ought to know should be in no better position than an employer who does know.

Counsel for the respondents submitted that actual knowledge is necessary; then he asked a number of alternative submissions. He said there was evidence that the plaintiff was a person in authority, in charge not only of the fitters but also of general maintenance; in effect that the plaintiff was himself the supervisor and that as he was in default in not reporting the larking he cannot be heard to complain of his injuries. Further it was submitted that the plaintiff had given no evidence of absence of supervision; further still that the conduct complained of occurred momentarily and was a kind that would most probably be concealed in the presence of a supervisor.

The supervision which is in question here is supervision which is referable to the ordinary work of the repair shop. The evidence affords no assistance as to what amount of supervision would be required in a repair shop and store of this type; and moreover the evidence was not directed to what, if any, supervision took place ... It is therefore not possible to accept the submission that there was evidence from which the jury could infer that the employers ought to have known of this dangerous larking ...

It must be noted that there is no evidence that either the plaintiff or any of his fellow-workers made any complaint to anyone in authority in respect of this larking. It seems rather to have been looked upon by all as a 'bit of fun' or 'devilment'. The whole thing would be over in an instant ... The nature of the larking was therefore such as to not make it easily detectable; and in any event it could not reasonably be said that an employer who did not detect it, had failed in his duty to provide a safe system of supervision as the larking in question was of such recent origin and was not of such frequency as must necessarily have been detected in any system of reasonable supervision."

STATUTORY OBLIGATIONS

Statutory obligations are particularly significant in the field of employers' liability as a range of Acts and Regulations impose civil liability on employers for breaches of health and safety standards. The piece of legislation most often used for this purpose is the General Application Regulations 1993 (S.I. No. 44

of 1993) as amended. These Regulations, divided into nine sets of Regulations, are far-reaching, covering issues of the place of work, plant and equipment, first aid, fellow employees, notification of accidents and so on. While the liability imposed is similar, in the sense that it is civil liability, a question has arisen as to the standard of care the Regulations impose. The Regulations themselves do not specify what the standard is, but case law has stated that for some of the Regulations at least, the standard is an absolute one.

Everitt v Thorsman Ireland Limited
High Court [2000] 1 I.R. 256

Facts: The plaintiff was injured when attempting to open a bin with a lever supplied for that purpose. The lever snapped, causing him to fall backwards. The plaintiff was employed by the first named defendants, but the lever was supplied by the second named defendants (Jumbo Bins Ltd.).

Issues: Had the employer breached his duty in negligence or under statute (legislation relied on included the Factories Act 1955 and the General Applications Regulations 1993)?

The court (Kearns J.) held that the employer had not been negligent as there was no way that the employer could reasonably have identified the defect in the lever. The Factories Act 1955 did not apply as the lever was not a piece of equipment covered by that Act. However, the General Applications Regulations were held to apply and it was held that as they imposed a "virtually absolute duty", the employer was liable under this heading.

Kearns J.:

"[Having discussed the issue of liability under negligence Kearns J. found that the first named defendants were not liable as they could not reasonably have discovered the defect in the lever. He then went on to consider the case under the Regulations.]

... The only breach of statutory duty upon which the Plaintiff relies (and in this regard no details of breach of statutory duty appear either in the original civil bill or amended statement of claim) is the suggestion that under Section 34 (1) (a) of the Factories Acts, 1955, the Defendants failed to provide 'lifting tackle' which was of good construction, sound material, adequate strength and free from patent defect. I do not believe the lever in question can be regarded as 'lifting tackle' and as the decision in Doherty -v- Bowaters Irish Wool Board Limited [1968] IR 277 related to a hook which was carrying a load which was suspended from a travelling crane, that case does not seem to me to be a binding authority in the present instance. What does, however, seem to me to cover the situation is regulation 19 of the Safety, Health and Welfare at Work (General

Application) Regulations, 1993 (SI No 44 of 1993) which imposes virtually an absolute duty on employers in respect of the safety of equipment provided for the use of their employees. Article 19 provides:—

'It shall be the duly of every employer, to ensure that—
(a) The necessary measures are taken so that "the work equipment is suitable for the work to be carried out or is properly adapted for that purpose and may be used by employees without risk to their safely and health."'

Article 20 requires employers to comply with the requirements of the fifth schedule which includes the following requirement at Requirement 7:—

'Where there is a risk of rupture or disintegration of parts of work equipment, likely to pose significant danger to the safely and health of employees, appropriate protection measures shall be taken.'

Accordingly, while there is no blameworthiness in any meaningful sense of the word on the part of the employers in this case, these regulations do exist for sound policy reasons at least, namely, to ensure that an employee who suffers an injury at work through no fault of his own by using defective equipment should not be left without remedy. As O'Flaherty J. pointed out an employer in such a situation may usually, though not always, be in a position to seek indemnity from the third party who supplied the work equipment. Accordingly, I find there has been breach of statutory duty on the part of the first named Defendant in this case ...

... For the reasons which are entirely obvious on the particular facts of this case, it seems to me to be a situation where the first named Defendants are entitled to indemnities/contributions from the second named Defendants to the extent of 100% and I so hold."

Comments and Questions:
1. Kearns J. above states that the absolute duty imposed by the Regulations exists for "sound policy reasons". Do you agree with this view?
2. See *McGrath v Trintech Technologies* below for an application of the Regulations to an action for psychological damage.

LIABILITY FOR PSYCHOLOGICAL INJURY

Employers are responsible for the protection of both the mental and physical health of employees. The courts appear to have identified a number of types of mental injury for which liability may be imposed, namely, nervous shock (please see Chapter 3), injury arising from "fear of disease" (through being exposed to dangers to their health), also known as "worried well" cases, and injury arising from occupational stress.

The principles applicable to the latter two cases are broadly similar, in that they involve a consideration of the general negligence principles. However, further judicial guidance on the application of these principles has proved necessary, demonstrating the difficulty of applying traditional negligence principles to psychological injury cases. For the principles applicable to nervous shock cases, please see Chapter 3, in particular the case of *Curran v Cadbury*.

"Fear of disease"

These cases involve those plaintiffs who through anxiety at the prospect of developing a physical illness, worry themselves into a psychological one. Case law in this area is limited. However, the approach of the courts thus far has been to deny recovery to claimants who do not have a pre-existing physical condition which would provide a "rational" basis for their fears (as occurred in the case of *Fletcher*) and to provide a remedy to those who do.

Stephen Fletcher v Commissioners of Public Works
Supreme Court [2003] 1 I.R. 465, [2003] 2 I.L.R.M. 94

Facts: The plaintiff had been employed with the defendants as a general operative and from 1985 to 1989 worked as such in Leinster House. During this time he was regularly exposed to asbestos dust, which his employers knew carried a risk of causing mesothelioma, a potentially lethal disease. The trial judge (O'Neill J.) found the defendants guilty of gross negligence and held that the illness suffered was a foreseeable injury given the risk of harm he had been exposed to. The defendants appealed to the Supreme Court stating that, while they had been negligent, they should not be found liable for the harm suffered.

Issues: The issue to be decided was whether the defendants ought to be held liable for the psychiatric condition which the plaintiff developed.
    The court (Keane C.J., Denham, Murray, Hardiman and Geoghegan JJ.) held that the test was not simply whether the employer fell below a reasonable standard of care but whether a duty of care should be imposed for a psychiatric illness arising from a fear of disease. In the determination of this issue factors to be considered were proximity, foreseeability, the reasonableness of imposing a duty of care and public policy (including whether any physical injury existed which might justify the fear of disease). On the basis of the foregoing they found that no duty existed to protect the employee against the harm suffered.

Keane C.J. (Geoghegan J. also delivered a concurring judgement; Denham, Murray and Hardiman JJ. concurred with both judgments):

"... The issue ... which this court has to resolve is whether the plaintiff was entitled to recover damages for the impairment of his 'mental condition' which, according to the evidence of the psychiatrist, has resulted from his exposure to the risk of contracting mesothelioma, a risk which, it is beyond argument, was created by the failure of the defendants to take the precautions which a reasonable employer would have taken to ensure that he was not exposed to any such risk.

That in turn depends, initially at least, on whether the consequences which have ensued for the plaintiff ought reasonably to have been foreseen by the defendants. It is unnecessary, in my view, to arrive at any conclusion as to whether this is so because, if the personal injury was not foreseeable, liability in negligence cannot arise or because, if it was not foreseeable, the damage was too remote. In either case, reasonable foreseeability is a precondition to liability. The question as to whether those consequences were reasonably foreseeable cannot, of course, be answered by assessing the state of knowledge of the defendants at the material time. The test is an objective one, i.e., as to whether a reasonable person would have foreseen that the consequences suffered by the plaintiff might be the result of the defendants' want of care. Moreover, as Lord Bridge of Harwich pointed out in McLoughlin v. O'Brian [1983] 1 A.C. 410 at p. 433, the court must assume in applying this test that the hypothetical reasonable person would be properly informed as to the real, painful and disabling nature of psychiatric illness and would not dismiss the possibility of the plaintiff becoming subject to a similar illness simply because it is less susceptible to precise medical diagnosis and treatment than at least some purely physical disorders.

Recovery of damages for psychiatric illness

However, the fact that it is reasonably foreseeable that particular acts or omissions will cause loss or injury to another person does not, of itself, give rise to liability in negligence. There must also be what judges have called, as the law has evolved, a relationship of 'proximity' between the plaintiff and the defendant which gave rise to the legal duty to take care that the foreseeable consequence was avoided. That, of itself, does not present any difficulty for the plaintiff; if this were a case in which the injuries sustained by him were purely physical, then, given that they were the foreseeable consequence of the actions or omissions of the defendants as his employers there would, of course, be not the slightest difficulty in concluding that the latter were liable in negligence.

Nor is the fact that the injury of which the plaintiff complains, is purely psychiatric sufficient of itself to relieve the defendants from the consequences of their actions and omissions in the present case. Since Bell v. Great Northern Railway Company of Ireland (1890) 26 L.R. (Ir.) 428 (following the earlier unreported decision of Byrne v. Great Southern and Western Railway Company of Ireland (1884) cited at 26 L.R. (Ir.) 428), it has been the law in Ireland that a plaintiff who sustains what has usually been described as 'nervous shock', even where unaccompanied by physical injury can recover damages, where the other ingredients of negligence are established. It was undoubtedly the law that damages were not recoverable for grief or sorrow alone; no degree of mental anguish arising from the wrongful acts or omissions of another was compensatable at common law. But nervous shock, even where there was no physical injury or even fear of such injury, was compensatable when caused by the negligence of a defendant.

[Keane C.J. then went on to consider the principles applicable in cases of recovery for nervous shock.]

... In the present case, there was no shock of that nature: no sudden perception of a frightening event or its immediate aftermath, disturbing the mind of the witness to such an extent that a recognisable psychiatric illness supervened. If the plaintiff is entitled to recover damages it must be because such damages can be recovered in respect of a psychiatric disorder brought about otherwise than by 'nervous shock', in this case, by a combination of anger and anxiety which was the result of the plaintiff having been informed of his exposure to the risk of contracting mesothelioma because of his employer's negligence.

This, as Geoghegan J. points out in his judgment, is uncharted territory for our courts. It has been argued in this case that there is no reason in principle why the law should differentiate between a psychiatric illness which is induced by nervous shock and one such as the plaintiff in the present case has suffered, where both are the foreseeable result of the wrongdoing of the defendants. That issue must be resolved by determining whether or not the extension of the law to permit the recovery of damages in cases such as the present should be excluded on policy grounds.

I would have no hesitation in rejecting the proposition that, in considering whether particular categories of negligence which have not hitherto been recognised by judicial decision should be so recognised, policy decisions should play no part. That doctrine, in its most extreme form, is to be found in the speech of Lord Scarman in McLoughlin v. O'Brian [1983] 1 A.C. 410. However, as the speech of Lord Edmund-Davies in the same case demonstrated, judges have for long invoked policy considerations in determining where the boundaries of legal liability for negligence should be fixed. Thus, in principle, it would have been possible to extend liability for negligence far beyond the traditional ambit of wrongs causing personal injuries or physical damage to property; the ground for not extending liability to all forms of economic loss (save where caused by negligent misstatement) is the undesirability of courts extending the range of possible liability in so uncontrolled and indeterminate a manner without any legislative intervention. Thus, if Irish courts were to adopt the same approach to the law of tort in cases of economic loss as the English courts have more recently adopted, it would be because of policy considerations which outweigh what otherwise would be seen as a principled development of the existing law. As the decision of this court in Glencar Exploration plc. v.

Mayo County Council (No. 2) [2002] 1 I.R. 84 made clear, the question as to whether economic loss is recoverable in cases other than those of negligent misstatement and within the categories laid down in Siney v. Corporation of Dublin [1980] I.R. 400 and Ward v. McMaster [1988] I.R. 337 still awaits authoritative resolution.

The policy issues

Before considering the policy arguments that arise in the present case, it is right to say that although, as I have already pointed out, the courts have for long approached cases of psychiatric disorder on the basis that illness of that nature can be as real, painful and disabling as physical injuries, that is not to say that there are not special considerations applicable to such cases which must be borne in mind when the broader policy arguments are being considered.

Thus, as I have already noted, the law, while recognising that damage, in the form of a recognisable psychiatric disorder, is compensatable, does not permit the recovery of damages for mental anguish or grief which results from a bereavement or injury to a member of one's family caused by another's wrong. It is clear, however, that grief or mental anguish of that nature can result in recognisable psychiatric illnesses such as a reactive depression, and, in the light of developments in psychiatric medicine in recent decades, it must surely be questionable whether the inflexible boundary drawn by the law between recognisable psychiatric conditions, which are compensatable and grief or mental anguish, which is not, is entirely logical. The fact that the latter category is not compensatable is because the courts have adopted a pragmatic approach and have left it to the legislature to determine when and to what extent, such undoubted suffering should be the subject of an award of damages (as under s.49 of the Civil Liability Act 1961).

Secondly, it is an inescapable fact that, because psychiatric illness is frequently less susceptible to precise diagnosis, the courts may have to adopt a more circumspect approach to such cases. Thirdly, the phenomenon, familiar to all judges and practitioners who have been concerned in personal injury cases, that the prospect of compensation at a subtle and subconscious level does nothing to assist a plaintiff's recovery from physical injury and may positively impede it, can arise even more acutely in cases of alleged psychiatric illness.

Again, as pointed out by Lord Steyn in his instructive discussion of the problem in White v. Chief Constable of South Yorkshire Police [1999] 2 A.C. 455, the abolition or relaxation of the special rules governing the recovery of damages for psychiatric harm would greatly increase the class of person who can recover damages in tort and may result in a burden of liability on defendants disproportionate to the wrongful conduct involved. He cites the example of motorcar accidents which may involve a momentary lapse of concentration.

However, the policy arguments in the present case against a finding of liability for psychiatric injury are not confined to those factors or the so-called 'floodgates' factors, i.e., the possibility of the courts being swamped with trivial and unmeritorious claims, imposing particular strains on the legal system and making severe demands on judges who have to segregate serious claims from the trivial or even fraudulent. That is not to say that such considerations may not be important, but, in my view, there are specific policy considerations which, in the case of what can be conveniently catagorised as 'fear of disease' cases, such as the present, argue even more powerfully against the imposition of liability.

There is first the undesirability of awarding damages to plaintiffs who have suffered no physical injury and whose psychiatric condition is solely due to an unfounded fear of contracting a particular disease. A person who prefers to rely on the ill-informed comments of friends or acquaintances or inaccurate and sensational media reports rather than the considered view of an experienced physician should not be awarded damages by the law of tort. As McNulty J. put it, delivering the judgment of the Appellate Court of Illinois in Majca v. Beekil (1997) 682 N.E.2d. 253:—

> 'Where hysterical fear of disease is sufficiently widespread, and popular knowledge concerning its etiology is limited, a plaintiff may foreseeably experience severe emotional distress without medically verifiable evidence of a substantially increased risk of contracting the disease. Most courts have held that recovery for fear of disease should not extend to such foreseeable fears, because, as commentators have noted, such broad recovery rewards ignorance about the disease and its causes.'

The second policy argument is closely related to that first consideration. It relates to the implications for the health care field of a more relaxed rule as to recovery for psychiatric illness which were summarised as follows by Baxter J. giving the opinion of the majority of the Californian Supreme Court in Potter v. Firestone Tyre and Rubber Company (1993) 25 Cal. Rptr. 2d 550:—

> 'Access to prescription drugs is likely to be impeded by allowing recovery of "fear of cancer" damages in negligence cases without the imposition of a heightened threshold. To wit, thousands of drugs having no known harmful effects are currently being prescribed and utilised. New data about potentially harmful effects may not develop for years. If and when negative data are discovered and made public, however, one can expect numerous law suits to be filed by patients who currently have no physical injury or illness but who nonetheless fear the risk of adverse effects from the drugs they used. Unless meaningful restrictions are placed on this potential plaintiff class, the threat of numerous large, adverse monetary awards, coupled with the added cost of insuring against such liability (assuming insurance would be available) could diminish the availability of new, beneficial drugs or increase their price beyond the reach of those who need them most.'

It was also pointed out that there would also be serious implications for medical negligence cases grounded on the fear of the plaintiff's having contracted a disease as the result of having been prescribed a particular drug.

At an earlier point in this judgment, I expressed the view that the law would be in an unjust and anomalous state if a plaintiff who was medically advised that he would probably suffer from mesothelioma as a result of his negligent exposure to asbestos could not recover damages for a recognisable psychiatric illness which was the result of his being so informed. I am also satisfied, however, that in cases where there is no more than a very remote risk that he will contract the disease, recovery should not be allowed for such a psychiatric illness. That is because the policy considerations, which I have summarised, point clearly to the necessity for imposing some limitation on the number of potential claims which might otherwise come into being.

Claims for emotional distress arising out of exposure to asbestos came before the United States Supreme Court in Consolidated Rail Corporation v. Gottshall (1994) 512 U.S. 532, and Metro-North Commuter Railroad Corporation v. Buckley (1997) 521 U.S. 424. In both cases, a majority of the court concluded that it was an essential precondition to the recovery of damages for emotional distress under the Federal Employers Liability Act that the plaintiff should have sustained a 'physical impact' and that the plaintiff's contact in each case with asbestos laden insulation dust did not constitute such a 'physical impact'. Again, the majority of the court rested their conclusions on policy considerations, Breyer J. observing in the latter case that:—

> '... the common law in this area does not examine the genuineness of emotional harm case by case. Rather, it has developed recovery permitting categories the contours of which more distantly reflect this, and other, abstract general policy concerns. The point of such categorisation is to deny courts the authority to undertake a case by case examination.'

A similar approach was adopted by the Supreme Court of Texas in Temple-Inland Forest Products Corporation v. Carter (1999) 993 S.W.R.2d. 88. Delivering the unanimous judgment of the court, Hecht J., having referred to Metro-North Commuter Railroad Corporation v. Buckley (1997) 521 U.S. 424, went on to say:—

> 'A person exposed to asbestos can certainly develop serious health problems, but he or she also may not. The difficulty in predicting whether exposure will cause any disease and if so, what disease and the long latency period characteristic of asbestos related diseases, makes it very difficult for judges and juries to evaluate which exposure claims are serious and which are not. This difficulty in turn makes liability unpredictable, with some claims resulting in significant recovery while virtually indistinguishable claims are denied altogether. Some claimants would inevitably be over-compensated, when, in the course of time, it happens that they never develop the disease they feared, and others would be under-compensated when it turns out that they developed a disease more serious even than they feared. Also, claims for exposure could proliferate because in our society, as the Supreme Court observed, 'contacts, even extensive contacts, with serious carcinogens are

common'. Indeed, most Americans are daily subjected to toxic substances in the air they breathe and the food they eat. Suits for mental anguish damages caused by exposure that has not resulted in disease would compete with suits for manifest diseases for the legal system's limited resources. If recovery were allowed in the absence of present disease, individuals might feel obliged to bring suit for such recovery prophylactically, against the possibility of future consequences from what is now an inchoate risk. This would exacerbate not only the multiplicity of suits but the unpredictability of results.'

Conclusions

I am, accordingly, satisfied that the law in this jurisdiction should not be extended by the courts so as to allow the recovery by plaintiffs of damages for psychiatric injury resulting from an irrational fear of contracting a disease because of their negligent exposure to health risks by their employers, where the risk is characterised by their medical advisors as very remote.

I would add two final observations. First, we are not in this case concerned with the question as to whether an employer should be held liable where it is reasonably foreseeable that an employee might suffer a nervous breakdown because of the stress and pressures of his workload, an issue resolved in favour of the plaintiff by the English High Court in Walker v. Northumberland County Council [1995] 1 All E.R. 737. Secondly, the claim of the plaintiff in the present case was grounded on breach of statutory duty in addition to common law negligence. It is clear, that in the absence of any specific statutory provision entitling the plaintiff to recover damages for psychiatric injury, the same principles as to liability must apply.

I would allow the appeal and substitute for the order of the High Court an order dismissing the plaintiff's claim."

Comments and Questions:
1. In the High Court, O'Neill J. accepted that injury arising from fear of developing a disease was one which was foreseeable to a person of "reasonable fortitude"; however, Keane C.J. described such a fear as being irrational and therefore not compensatable. Which view do you favour?

2. Consider the policy considerations proffered by Keane C.J. above in relation to expanding the law to allow recovery for fear of disease cases. Do you find them convincing?

3. Might the Supreme Court have been more rational in discussing the type of injury suffered as a remoteness issue and not as an issue to be considered in determining whether a duty of care existed?

Stress-related injury

McGrath v Trintech Technologies Limited
High Court [2004] I.E.H.C. 342

Facts: The plaintiff worked as a project manager with the defendant company from April 2000. In 2001 he was promoted to Director of Professional Services, his immediate supervisor being Mr Downes, the Vice-President of Professional Services. The plaintiff clearly had a series of medical problems, predominantly physical, which led to his seeing a bewildering array of medical personnel both in Ireland and the US and, when on assignment, in those locations also. He alleged that he had suffered stress-related psychiatric injury caused by his employer's failure to provide him with a safe working environment.

Issues: The court (Laffoy J.) had to consider whether the defendants could be liable for stress-induced psychiatric injury and, if so, which principles were applicable.

Laffoy J., noting that this was the first time an Irish court had had to consider the issue, held that an employer owed a duty to prevent stress-induced mental injury, liability for which was to be decided on the basis of negligence principles. In particular, and in the absence of Irish jurisprudence, the principles provided by the English decision of *Sutherland v Hatton* [2002] 2 All E.R. 1 were applicable. Applying these principles Laffoy J. held that the injury suffered by the plaintiff was not foreseeable and the defendants were therefore not liable.

Laffoy J.:

"... While the Supreme Court in recent years has considered claims for compensation for psychiatric or psychological damage alleged to have been negligently inflicted in various contexts, for example, in the so-called 'nervous shock' context (Kelly v Hennessy [1996] 1 ILRM 321) and in the so-called 'fear of disease' context (Fletcher v Commissioner for Public Works [2003] 1 IR 465, [2003] 2 ILRM 94), as yet it has not had to consider directly the circumstances in which occupational stress resulting in psychiatric injury will give rise to liability on the part of an employer. That issue has been considered recently by courts in the United Kingdom. In reviewing the authorities from the United Kingdom referred to by counsel in their submissions, it seems to me that the most useful starting point is the decision of the Court of Appeal in Hatton v Sutherland [2002] EWCA Civ 76, [2002] 2 All ER 1.

The Hatton judgment related to four conjoined appeals in each of which the defendant employer appealed against a finding of liability for an employee's psychiatric illness caused by stress at work. Two of the plaintiffs (Hatton and Barber) were teachers in public sector comprehensive schools. The third (Jones) was an administrative assistant at a local authority training centre and the fourth

(Bishop) was a raw material operative in a factory. In all of the cases except that of Jones the decision at first instance was reversed by the Court of Appeal. The judgment of the Court was delivered by Hale LJ. Having analysed the law on liability in negligence under the headings of duty, foreseeability, breach of duty, causation and apportionment and quantification, the Court listed sixteen 'practical propositions' in determining liability for stress induced psychiatric injury in an employment context. The propositions are as follows:

(1) There are no special control mechanisms applying to claims for psychiatric (or physical) illness or injury arising from the stress of doing the work the employee is required to do. What this means is that 'policy' considerations of the type referred to by Geoghegan J in his judgment in the Fletcher case (at p 518) do not arise. Distinctions which are made in determining liability for psychiatric harm in other circumstances, for example, distinguishing between 'primary' and 'secondary' victims, have no application in the case of psychiatric injury arising from stress in the workplace.

(2) The threshold question is whether this kind of harm to this particular employee was reasonably foreseeable. This has two components: (a) an injury to health (as distinct from occupational stress), which (b) is attributable to stress at work (as distinct from other factors). In the earlier analysis of the issue of foreseeability, it was stated (at p 13) that the question is not whether psychiatric injury is foreseeable in a person of 'ordinary fortitude'. The employer's duty is owed to each individual employee.

(3) Foreseeability depends upon what the employer knows, or ought reasonably to know, about the individual employee. Because of the nature of mental disorder, it is harder to foresee than physical injury, but it may be easier to foresee in a known individual than in the population at large. An employer is usually entitled to assume that the employee can withstand the normal pressures of the job unless he knows of some particular problem or vulnerability.

(4) The test is the same whatever the employment: there are no occupations which should be regarded as intrinsically dangerous to mental health.

(5) Factors likely to be relevant in answering the threshold question included the following:
  (a) The nature and extent of the work done by the employee. Is the workload much more than is normal for the particular job? Is the work particularly intellectually or emotionally demanding for this employee? Are the demands being made of this employee unreasonable when compared with the demands made of others in the same or comparable jobs? Or are there signs that others doing the job are suffering from harmful levels of stress? Is there an abnormal level of sickness or absenteeism in the same job or the same department?
  (b) Signs from the employee of impending harm to health. Has he a particular problem or vulnerability? Has he already suffered from illness attributable to stress at work? Have there recently been frequent

or prolonged absences which are uncharacteristic of him? Is there reason to think that these are attributable to stress at work, for example, because of complaints or warnings from him or others?

(6) The employer is generally entitled to take what he is told by his employee at face value, unless he has good reason to think to the contrary. He does not generally have to make searching enquiries of the employee or seek permission to make further enquiries of his medical advisers.

(7) To trigger a duty to take steps, the indications of impending harm to health arising from stress at work must be plain enough for any reasonable employer to realise that he should do something about it.

(8) The employer is only in breach of duty if he has failed to take the steps which are reasonable in the circumstances, bearing in mind the magnitude of the risk of harm occurring, the gravity of the harm which may occur, the costs and practicability of preventing it, and the justifications for running the risk.

(9) The size and scope of the employer's operation, its resources and the demands it faces are relevant in deciding what is reasonable; these include the interests of other employees and the need to treat them fairly, for example, in any redistribution of duties.

(10) An employer can only reasonably be expected to take steps which are likely to do some good and the court is likely to need expert evidence on this.

(11) An employer who offers a confidential advice service, with referral to appropriate counselling or treatment services, is unlikely to be found in breach of duty.

(12) If the only reasonable and effective step would have been to dismiss or demote the employee, the employer will not be in breach of duty in allowing a willing employee to continue in the job.

(13) In all cases, therefore, it is necessary to identify the steps which the employer both should and could have taken before finding him in breach of his duty of care.

(14) The plaintiff must show that the breach of duty has caused or materially contributed to the harm suffered. It is not enough to show that occupational stress has caused the harm. Earlier, in its analysis of the issue of causation, the Court (at p 16) illustrated the distinction inherent in this proposition. Where there are several different causes, as will often be the case with stress related illness of any kind, the plaintiff may have difficulty proving the employer's fault was one of them. This will be a particular problem if the main cause was a vulnerable personality which the employer knew nothing about.

(15) Where the harm suffered has more than one cause, the employer should only pay for that proportion of the harm suffered which is attributable to his wrongdoing, unless the harm is truly indivisible. It is for the defendant to raise the question of apportionment.

(16) The assessment of damages will take account of any pre-existing disorder or vulnerability and of the chance that the claimant would have succumbed to a stress-related disorder in any event. Earlier, in dealing with the issue of quantification, the Court (at p 18) stated that where the tortfeasor's breach of duty has exacerbated a pre-existing disorder or accelerated the effect of pre-existing vulnerability, the award of general damages for pain, suffering and loss of amenity will reflect only the exacerbation or acceleration. Further, the quantification of damages for financial losses may take some account of contingency for example, the chance that the plaintiff would have succumbed to a stress-related disorder in any event and this may be reflected in the multiplier to be applied in quantifying future loss of earnings.

The Court of Appeal then went on to apply the foregoing principles to the facts of the four cases under appeal. In only one appeal, Jones, was the decision at first instance upheld. Mrs. Jones had been employed as an administrative assistant in a local authority training centre from August 1992 until January 1995 when she went off sick with anxiety and depression. She never returned and was made redundant when the centre closed at the end of 1996. While there was no specific medical event which might have alerted her employers to the risk of the breakdown which occurred in January 1995, her employers did know that excessive demands were being placed upon her. They also knew that she was complaining of unreasonable behaviour by her immediate manager, in that she had been threatened with non-renewal of her temporary post if she persisted in her complaints of overwork. These factors were taken sufficiently seriously for extra help to be arranged, not once but twice, but it was not actually provided. She had made two written formal complaints, one in July and one in November 1994, that problems at work were causing harm to her health. It was not disputed that they did in fact cause her breakdown in January 1995. On the basis of the foregoing facts, the Court stated (at p 24) that the question was not whether her employers had in fact caused harm to her health before January 1995, but whether it was sufficiently foreseeable that they would do so for it to be a breach of duty for the employers to carry on placing unreasonable demands upon her and not to follow through their own decision that something should be done about it. The Court concluded, not without some hesitation, that the evidence at first instance was sufficient to entitle the judge to reach the conclusion that it was. It was pointed out that, unlike the other appeals before the Court, Jones was one where the employer knew that the employee was being badly treated by another employee and could have done something to prevent it.

One of the appellants before the Court of Appeal, Barber, appealed to the House of Lords against the decision of the Court of Appeal. The speeches of the Law Lords were delivered on 1 April 2004 and are reported as Barber v Somerset County Council [2004] 2 All ER 385, [2004] 1 WLR 1089. The decision of the Court of Appeal was reversed. However, there was broad acceptance of the propositions put forward by the Court of Appeal. In his speech, Lord Walker of Gestingthorpe described the exposition and commentary in, inter alia, the part of the judgment dealing with the law as a valuable contribution to the development of the law. He referred to the recognition by the Court of Appeal that the causes of mental illness will often be complex and depend upon the interaction between the patient's personality and a number of factors in a patient's life and that it is not easy to predict who will fall victim, how, why or when. He stated that this uncertainty has two important consequences. First, overworked people have different capacities for absorbing stress, and different breaking points. Secondly, senior employees—especially professionals—will usually have quite strong inhibitions against complaining about overwork and stress, even if it is becoming a threat to their health. Commenting on the portion of the judgment of the Court of Appeal (para [29] at p 15) from which the proposition set out at (6) above was abstracted, Lord Walker emphasised that the analysis was useful practical guidance and must be read as that and not as having anything like statutory force. He emphasised that every case will depend on its own facts and stated that the following statement of Swanwick J in Stokes v Guest, Kean and Nettlefold (Bolts & Nuts) Ltd [1968] 1 WLR 1776 at 1783 remains the best statement of general principle:

> '... the overall test is still the conduct of the reasonable and prudent employer, taking positive thought for the safety of his workers in the light of what he knows or ought to know; where there is a recognised and general practice which has been followed for a substantial period in similar circumstances without mishap, he is entitled to follow it, unless in the light of common sense or newer knowledge it is clearly bad; but where there is developing knowledge, he must keep reasonably abreast of it and not be too slow to apply it; and where he has in fact greater than average knowledge of the risks, he may be thereby obliged to take some more than the average or standard precautions. He must weigh up the risk in terms of the likelihood of injury occurring and the potential consequence if it does; he must balance against this the probable effectiveness of the precautions that can be taken to meet it and the expense and inconvenience they involve. If he is found to have fallen below the standard to be properly expected of a reasonable and prudent employer in these respects, he is negligent.'

In dissenting from the majority view, Lord Scott of Foscote expressed a preference for the statement of the law contained in para 29 of the judgment of the Court of Appeal over the statement of general principle quoted above, pointing out that Swanwick J did not have in mind the problems of psychiatric illness caused by stress. He contrasted an appreciation of the existence of physical dangers of the sort which arose in the Stokes case (the risk of the plaintiff contracting cancer of the scrotum from exposure at work over a long period to mineral oils which, on a daily basis, had saturated his clothing and come in contact with his skin), which is dependent on scientific and medical knowledge, with psychiatric illness caused by stress as in the case of the Barber appeal, where the employers could only know what Mr Barber told them.

... The effect of the decisions of the Court of Appeal and the House of Lords in the Hatton/Barber case [2002] EWCA Civ 76, [2002] 2 All ER 1, is to assimilate the principles governing an employer's liability at common law for physical injury and for psychiatric injury where an employee claims that the psychiatric injury has resulted from the stress and pressures of his or her working conditions and workload. In my view, there is no reason in law or in principle why a similar approach should not be adopted in this jurisdiction. I consider that the practical propositions summarised in the judgment of the Court of Appeal in the Hatton case are helpful in the application of legal principle in an area which is characterised by difficulty and complexity, subject, however, to the caveat of Lord Walker in the Barber case—that one must be mindful that every case will depend on its own facts.

Application of the law to the facts

As a first step in the process of applying the law to the facts of this case, I propose considering the expert and other evidence which is before the court in relation to the plaintiff's medical and psychiatric condition before, during and after his sojourn in Uruguay. I will then summarise:

– the allegations of breach of duty against the factual backdrop of the plaintiff's employment from early 2003 to the commencement of these proceedings, and
– the submissions on foreseeability.

I will then apply the Hatton [2002] EWCA Civ 76, [2002] 2 All ER 1 propositions to the facts. Finally, I will set out my conclusions on the claim for breach of statutory duty.

[Laffoy J. then went on to describe the facts leading to the plaintiff's allegations.]

Application of the Hatton propositions

My conclusions on the application of the Hatton propositions to the facts of this case are as follows:
(a) The defendant did not have any actual knowledge of the plaintiff's vulnerability to psychological injury or harm.
(b) It clearly emerged from the evidence that the 'corporate culture' in the defendant's companies is competitive and demanding of their employees. Mr Cleary described it as the American model where employees work hard and play hard against the background of 'economic ups and downs'. It was

not a place where one would admit weakness. The plaintiff came to the defendant with experience of working in the IT sector both in the United States and in Ireland. On the evidence I conclude that there was no reason why the defendant should not assume that the plaintiff could withstand the stresses and pressures of this type of work environment and of the workload which he was required to undertake. Prior to his posting to Uruguay he had worked for two and a half years for the defendant and had undertaken foreign assignments in locations as diverse as the United States, Mauritius, South Africa and Korea without any apparent stress-related or psychological problems or susceptibility to such problems.

(c) As to the actual nature and extent of the workload undertaken by the plaintiff in Uruguay, it was undoubtedly the case that it was, and it was clear from the CMS document that it was going to be, an inherently difficult task. However, the evidence indicates that senior management in the defendant considered that the plaintiff had the attributes to do the job and it is to be inferred that the plaintiff also believed that he had. No issue at all arose on the evidence as to the manner in which the plaintiff performed the task. In fact there was general consensus among the defendant's witnesses as to his dedication and competence and that he had positively contributed to the resolution of the industrial relations difficulties in Uruguay. While the job proved to be more demanding than might have been anticipated, the crises which arose were unpredictable. The evidence of the defendant's witnesses was that all of the personnel of the defendant involved in trying to manage the crises were under stress and pressure and they handled it. On an objective appraisal of the evidence, I am satisfied that the senior management in Dublin did not subject the plaintiff to any greater pressure than was assumed by any other member of the management team or to unreasonable demands.

(d) Insofar as there were signs of vulnerability on the part of the plaintiff and possible harm to his health, these were adequately addressed by the defendant. The defendant was aware of the plaintiff's physical problems and procured medical advice from Dr Hastings before the plaintiff took up the post. Dr Hastings took the initiative of speaking to the plaintiff's general practitioner with the plaintiff's consent. The plaintiff did not inform the defendant of his medical problems while in Uruguay and he was not absent on sick leave.

(e) On the evidence, in my view, there was no sign or warning which the defendant's personnel ought to have picked up that the plaintiff was prone to psychological injury attributable to work-related stress. Nothing emerged on the examination carried out by Dr Hastings or his conversation with Dr Al Bayari. The plaintiff had not apprised the defendant of his psychological history. He had made no complaints in relation to work-related stress before he went to Uruguay. He made no direct complaints while there or on his return. In my view, the conversation with Mr Downes in November was a casual conversation, which did not put Mr Downes on any further inquiry as to the plaintiff's psychological condition. Insofar as the defendant was put on inquiry in relation to the plaintiff's health problems, by procuring medical advice the defendant discharged its duty of care to the plaintiff. The circumstances during the posting which the plaintiff contends the defendant's personnel should have taken as signs—the episode during Mr Cleary's visit to Montevideo in March and the subsequent e-mail of 20 March 2003 to Mr Downes—in the light of what the plaintiff had told the defendant and what the defendant had found out through having the plaintiff examined by Dr Hastings, in my view, were not such as to put a reasonable and prudent employer on further inquiry.

(f) On the evidence, I am satisfied that there was no good reason why the defendant should not have taken the information it obtained from the plaintiff before and during his employment, either directly or through Dr Hastings, at face value. In their submissions counsel for the plaintiff emphasised that he was not aware that he was suffering from a stress-related injury while in Uruguay. That inexorably leads to the question how could the defendant reasonably be expected to know of the plaintiff's vulnerability or the fact that he had succumbed. In my view, it would be wholly unreasonable to impute to the defendant knowledge of a vulnerability or condition of which the plaintiff was unaware in circumstances in which the defendant had not been apprised of the plaintiff's psychological history and the existence of the vulnerability and the likelihood of psychological harm was not ascertained through Dr Hastings' examination and inquiries.

(g) In my view, there were no indications of impending harm to the plaintiff's physical or mental health before, during or after his posting to Uruguay which triggered a duty on the part of the defendant to take any step other than the step which the defendant had taken—obtaining the opinion of Dr Hastings.

That situation prevailed up to the notification to the plaintiff of the defendant's intention to terminate his employment on 26 August 2003. The law did not require either Mr Downes or Mr Cleary to question the certification of the plaintiff's condition by his own general practitioner, which was silent on the existence of psychological injury.

My general conclusion is that the plaintiff has not crossed the foreseeability threshold. The risk of psychological harm to the plaintiff was not reasonably foreseeable. The fundamental test is whether the defendant fell below the standard to be properly expected of a reasonable and prudent employer. In my view it did not. Having done what was reasonable in the circumstances, the defendant did not breach its duty of care and has no liability to the plaintiff either in contract or in tort.

In relation to the failures which the plaintiff specifically ascribed to the defendant, I make the following findings.

I am satisfied on the evidence that the crisis management which the strike necessitated was conducted on a number of fronts. The plaintiff undoubtedly had a subjective perception that he was not being properly supported. However, viewed objectively in the light of what the defendant knew about the plaintiff, what his role was, and what was expected of him, the manner of deployment by the defendant of its personnel and outside advisers as it did in the resolution of the strike cannot be seen as giving rise to a breach of the defendant's duty of care to the plaintiff. To put it another way, I do not think that it would have been clear to a reasonable employer that, if the plaintiff was not supported in his role by the constant physical presence in Montevideo of a member of the management team with human resources or industrial relations experience during the currency of the strike, he would be at risk of injury arising from stress. The plaintiff was in constant contact with management personnel in Dublin by telephone and email throughout the strike.

Further, even if the defendant's safety statement had addressed the issue of stress, and structures were in place for monitoring stress in the workplace and, even if the defendant had an employee assistance programme in place in its Irish operations, it is difficult to see, given the factual circumstances, what difference these measures would have made to the outcome. In particular, notwithstanding the plaintiff's testimony that he would have availed of an employee assistance programme had one been in place, having regard to the totality of the evidence, it seems improbable that he would have. To the extent that the plaintiff bases his case on the fallout from the strike and, in particular, the attitude of the personnel in Uruguay to him, the reality is that after the strike the plaintiff was only on site in Montevideo for a matter of weeks when Mr Doran was appointed to replace him. He had access, if he wished, to his general practitioner while on trips home at the beginning of April and the beginning of May.

Liability for breach of statutory duty

In their written submission counsel for the plaintiff implicitly recognised that there is a difficulty in establishing a causative link between the alleged breaches of statutory obligations of the defendant upon which they rely and the injury of which the plaintiff complains. While acknowledging that the onus of proof is on the plaintiff, it was submitted that the plaintiff had made out a prima facie case and that the onus shifted to the defendant to advance an alternative cause for the plaintiff's injuries. Alternatively, it was submitted that the fact that the defendant had failed to offer any tenable explanation as to how the plaintiff could have sustained the psychological injuries was a consideration which the court could have regard to in considering whether the plaintiff had discharged the onus which rests on him.

The issue is not whether the stress the plaintiff suffered was caused by work, but whether the stress-induced injury was a consequence of a breach by the defendant of its statutory duties. Where an employee is injured because of the malfunction of a faulty piece of equipment given to him by his employer, the causative link is obvious. The injury would not have been inflicted if the faulty piece of equipment had not been given to the employee. The question which arises here is whether it can be said, as a matter of probability, that if the defendant took all of the steps which the plaintiff contends it was statutorily obliged to take (dealing with workplace stress in the safety statement, having in place a system for monitoring stress and an employee assistance programme and providing further training for the plaintiff) the plaintiff would not have suffered psychological injury. In my view it cannot.

By way of general observation, if the submissions made on behalf of the plaintiff were correct, in my view, the law would impose a wholly unrealistic burden on employers."

Comments and Questions:
1. Consider the criteria outlined by Hale L.J. in the *Sutherland* case and adopted by Laffoy J. above. In your view do they represent a fair balance between the rights of employees and employers?

CHAPTER 7

VICARIOUS LIABILITY

INTRODUCTION

Vicarious liability refers to the liability of one person for the actions of another although that person is free from any personal blameworthiness or fault. Before a defendant can be found liable for the wrongs of another, the person for whom the defendant is said to be vicariously liable must have acted negligently and the defendant must be in a position of control over the negligent actor. The most common situation in which vicarious liability arises is in the case of employers, who can be found vicariously liable for the negligent acts of their employees. Car-owners can also be liable for wrongs committed by those travelling in their cars and partners in firms can be held liable for the wrongs of their co-partners. While these examples are useful to note, it is true that a person may be held liable for another in any situation where they can be seen to exercise control over that person's actions.

CONTROL

For vicarious liability to arise the defendant must be in a position of control over the negligent actor. This requirement was demonstrated in the case of *Moynihan v Moynihan* [1975] I.R. 192.

Moynihan v Moynihan
Supreme Court [1975] I.R. 192

Facts: The plaintiff, who was two years old at the time, was injured when visiting her paternal grandmother's house, when she accidentally pulled a teapot containing hot tea over herself causing serious scalding. The tea had been prepared by the defendant's daughter, Marie, and left unattended and within reach of the unsupervised plaintiff. She sued the defendant in the High Court for negligence and vicarious liability where Murnaghan J. withdrew the case from the jury on the basis that no reasonable grounds for liability existed. The case was appealed to the Supreme Court.

Issues: The court (O'Higgins C.J. and Walsh J.; Henchy J. dissenting) held that the defendant's daughter had been negligent and that the defendant, as the householder and as the person in control of the hospitality being provided by her in her own house, would be vicariously liable for damage resulting from the negligence of her daughter.

Walsh J. (O'Higgins C.J. concurring):

"... the first question to be considered is whether on the evidence a jury could hold that Marie was negligent. If the jury had found, as in my view they could have found, that Marie put a teapot with freshly-made tea in a position on a table which was within reach of a two-year-old child and then left the room, leaving the child alone in the room, it would be open to a jury to hold that Marie was negligent. It is not the law that, in the circumstances of the case, the mother of the plaintiff was the only person who had to watch out for the plaintiff's safety or who owed her a duty to take care.

The next question is whether the defendant is vicariously liable for the negligence of her daughter Marie, if she was negligent. If the person who left the teapot on the table, in the circumstances already outlined, had been a domestic servant or other employee of the defendant, there could be no doubt about the defendant's vicarious liability for the negligence, if established, of that person. The question to be decided is whether, in the circumstances of the case, the relationship between the defendant and her daughter Marie was sufficient to make the defendant vicariously liable for the negligence alleged against Marie.

If the defendant had put the teapot there herself, she could have been found guilty of negligence and the case would not depend on whether or not she was the occupier of the premises in question or whether the child was or was not an invitee: see *Purtill* v. *Athlone U.D.C.* [1968] I.R. 205. In my view the present case turns upon the position of the defendant as the person extending hospitality to the child.

The defendant invited to her house for dinner the plaintiff and her parents. As the evidence shows, the defendant was the owner and occupier of the house and was the head of the household. She had two daughters employed outside the household but who resided with her and assisted her in the domestic chores. One of the domestic duties on the day in question was the giving of this dinner; in the service of this meal the daughter Marie, apart from whatever other duties may have been assigned to her, was given or permitted the task of making the tea and putting the teapot upon the table. The negligence attributed to Marie was not the casual negligence of a fellow guest but may be regarded as the negligence of a person engaged in one of the duties of the household of her mother, the defendant, which duties were being carried out in the course of the hospitality being extended by the defendant. The nature and limits of this hospitality were completely under the control of the defendant, and to that extent it may be said that her daughter Marie in her actions on this occasion was standing in the shoes of the defendant and was carrying out for the defendant a task which would primarily have been that of the defendant, but which was in this case assigned to Marie. As the defendant was the person providing the hospitality, the delegation of some of that task to her daughter Marie may be regarded as a casual delegation. Marie's performance of it was a gratuitous service for her mother. It was within the control of the defendant to decide when the tea would be served and where it would be served and, indeed, if it was to be served at all. It was also within the control of the defendant to decide how it would be served.

This power of control was not in any way dependent upon the relationship of mother and daughter but upon the relationship of the head of a household with a person to whom some of the duties of the head of the household had been delegated by that head. The position would be no different, therefore, from that of a case where the head of a household had requested a neighbour to come in and assist in the giving of a dinner-party because she had not any, or not sufficient, hired domestic help. It would produce a strange situation if in such a case the 'inviter' should be vicariously liable for the hired domestic help who negligently poured hot sauce over the head of a guest but should not be equally liable for similar negligence on the part of the co-helper who was a neighbour and who had not been hired. In my view, in the latter case the person requested to assist in the service, but who was not hired for that purpose, is in the *de facto* service of the person who makes the request and for whom the duty is being performed.

Most, if not all, of the cases of gratuitous service in respect of which a vicarious liability has been imposed upon the person for whom the service is performed relate to motor cars, but these cases confirm the view that, even if the doctrine of vicarious liability depends upon the existence of service, the service does not have to be one in respect of which wages or salary is paid but may be a gratuitous service or may simply be a *de facto* service. For example, in the present case if the defendant had requested or permitted her daughter Marie to drive the plaintiff home in the defendant's motor car and the plaintiff had been injured through Marie's negligence, there would have been no doubt about the vicarious liability of the defendant. It may well be, as has been suggested by one noted writer, that the fact that this imposition of vicarious liability has apparently been confined to motor-car cases is because it was developed as a means of reaching the insurance company of the owner of the car. Whatever may be the reasons for the development of the doctrine in a particular area, the reasons cannot mask the basic principle of law involved.

In my view, on the evidence so far adduced in the present case, the necessary element of control was vested in the defendant and her daughter Marie was in the *de facto* service of the defendant for the purpose of the act in which Marie was alleged to be negligent. If further or other evidence should indicate that the household was a joint one and that the defendant and her two daughters were engaged in a joint enterprise and were offering joint hospitality, then different considerations might arise; but it is not at this stage necessary to express any view whether in such a case persons engaged in such a joint enterprise would be vicariously responsible for each other.

In my view, the learned trial judge was wrong in withdrawing the case from the jury on the ground that in law the defendant could not be held vicariously liable for the act of negligence alleged against her daughter Marie. I would allow the appeal and direct a new trial."

Henchy J.:

"... Much as one might wish that the law would allow this plaintiff to recover damages from some quarter for the consequences of the unfortunate accident that befell her, the inescapable fact is that there is a complete absence of authority for the proposition that liability should fall on the defendant (who was innocent of any causative fault) rather than on Marie whose conduct is alleged to have been primarily responsible for the accident. I see no justification for stretching the law so as to make it cover the present claim when, by doing so, the effect would be that liability in negligence would attach to persons for casual and gratuitous acts of others, as to the performance of which they would be personally blameless and against the risks of which they could not reasonably have been expected to be insured. To transfer or extend liability in those circumstances from the blameworthy person to a blameless person would involve the redress of one wrong by the creation of another. It would be unfair and oppressive to exact compensatory damages from a person for an act done on his behalf, especially in the case of an intrinsically harmless act, if it was done in a negligent manner which he could not reasonably have foreseen and if—unlike an employer, or a person with a primarily personal duty of care, or a motor-car owner, or the like—he could not reasonably have been expected to be insured against the risk of that negligence.

Since in my view it would not have been open to the jury to hold that the defendant was liable for Marie's negligence, it is not necessary to come to any firm conclusion as to how the jury might permissibly have dealt with the question of Marie's negligence, having regard to the dicta of Devlin J. in *Phipps v. Rochester Corporation* [1955] 1 Q.B. 450 as to the degree of care that is owed to a child of tender years who comes accompanied by a parent or other custodian. I am prepared to hold, for the purpose of this judgment, that it would have been open to the jury to find that Marie was negligent. However, even if the jury were to make such a finding, they could not have gone on (for the reasons I have given) to hold the defendant liable for that negligence. I would therefore dismiss this appeal."

Comments and Questions:
1. Does the decision of Walsh J. above (and O'Higgins C.J. concurring) mean that a person can be held vicariously liable for any act done on a person's behalf, as Henchy J. argued, or does the decision of Walsh J. require something closer to the employment relationship, in the form of being entrusted, whether or not for gain, to carry out the act complained of?

The *Duffy* case below, while factually similar, demonstrates the distinction between an act done while in the *de facto* service of the defendant and an act done independently of the defendant (in which case no vicarious liability will lie).

Duffy (a minor) v Rooney and Dunnes Stores (Dundalk) Limited
High Court, 1992 No. 3439P (transcript)

Facts: The plaintiff was injured when a coat which she was wearing caught fire. The fire at the time was unguarded and evidence was submitted that a guard which had been in front of the fire had been removed by the first defendant's daughter. The plaintiff sued, *inter alia*, on the basis that the first defendant as occupier of the house should be held vicariously liable for the act of removing the fireguard.

Issues: The issue to be addressed by the court was whether the first defendant was in such a position of "control" over his daughter that he ought to be liable for the negligent act of removing the fireguard.
The court (Laffoy J.) held that the defendant's daughter could not be said to be acting in the service of the defendant.

Laffoy J.:

"… The basis on which the Supreme Court held in Moynihan v Moynihan that the defendant in that case could be found to be vicariously liable is succinctly summarised in the following passage from the headnote:—

> '… the defendant, as the householder and as the person in control of the hospitality being provided by her in her own house, would be vicariously liable for damage resulting from the negligence of her daughter in performing a gratuitous service for the defendant in the course of the provision of such hospitality.'

It is clear from the judgment of Walsh J that in order to establish vicarious liability in the type of factual context which arose in Moynihan v Moynihan and which arises in the instant case, where the defendant householder was extending hospitality to a visiting child, two matters must be proven—that the necessary element of control was vested in the defendant and that the doer of the act which is alleged to be negligent was in the de facto service of the defendant for the purpose of the act. Even if Emma did remove the fireguard, in my view, the evidence does not establish that she was in de facto service of the first Defendant for the purpose of that act, in the sense that the daughter of the defendant in Moynihan v Moynihan was in the de facto service of that defendant doing the task of making the tea and putting the teapot on the table. Even if Emma did remove the fireguard, on the evidence, in doing so she acted totally independently of the first Defendant and not in any sense in pursuance of the performance of a gratuitous service for the first Defendant and, accordingly, the principle of vicarious liability is not applicable."

VICARIOUS LIABILITY OF EMPLOYERS

An employer can be held liable for the negligent act of employees, but only if the negligent act was carried out while the employee was acting within the "scope of employment". This is a very important concept but unfortunately not one which is particularly clear.

Before we go on to consider the principles developed by the courts in determining when an act comes within an employee's scope of employment, we must first clarify who the employee is for the purpose of vicarious liability and how the employer is identified.

Who are the employees?

Not all workers are employees. Some workers who perform functions or provide services for pay, are classed as independent contractors, which means that they effectively work for themselves (plumbers, hairdressers and so on are examples). A person is not generally speaking held vicariously liable for the act of an independent contractor but there are exceptions (essentially hinging on the element of control similar to the case of *Moynihan v Moynihan* above).

In determining who is an employee for the purpose of vicarious liability the courts have developed a number of tests, such as the control test (the greater the extent to which the worker is controlled the greater the likelihood that s/he is an employee), the integration test (the extent to which a worker is integrated), the contract test (which looks to the terms of the contract) and the entrepreneurial test (the extent to which the worker can be said to be in business on their own account). In practice no one test is applied but a decision is reached by a consideration of all tests and all the circumstances of the case.

The case of *Denny v Minister for Social Welfare*, which follows, while essentially an employment law case, is illustrative of the application of these tests in determining the employee question, and is equally useful for the purposes of vicarious liability in tort.

Henry Denny & Sons (Ireland) Limited v Minister for Social Welfare
Supreme Court [1998] 1 I.R. 34

Facts: The appellants employed a Ms Mahon as a shop demonstrator (offering samples of Denny products). They argued that she was employed under a "contract for services" (an independent contractor) and therefore they were not required to make any social insurance payments on her behalf. An officer, an appeals officer and the chief appeals office within the Department of Social

Welfare disagreed and required that the insurance payments be made. In the High Court Carroll J. upheld the view of the Department and the appellants appealed to the Supreme Court.

Issues: The court (Hamilton C.J., Keane and Murphy JJ.) was required to consider whether the worker was an independent contractor or an employee.

Applying the available tests, but in particular considering whether the worker was "in business on her own account", the court found that Ms Mahon was an employee of the appellants and not an independent contractor.

Keane J. (Hamilton C.J. and Murphy J. also delivering concurring judgments):

"Demonstrators who offer passing shoppers free samples of wine, cigarettes, sausages or whatever are a familiar feature of supermarkets today. The net issue in this case is as to whether they are properly regarded in law as engaged in their tasks under a 'contract of service' or a 'contract for services'.

The significance of the distinction is that if such a demonstrator is regarded as being employed under a contract of service, then he or she is an insurable person for the purposes of the Social Welfare Acts, 1993 to 1997.

... [Ms Mahon] was engaged on the terms of a written contract. The contract expired at the end of each year and a fresh contract was then entered into annually between her and the appellant.

The manner in which Ms Mahon's services were availed of by the appellant was as follows. The particular retail store which required one of the appellant's food products to be demonstrated got in touch with the local customer service manager of the appellant and asked for such a demonstration specifying the day or days upon which it was required. Three or four days before the date of the proposed demonstration, the manager would telephone a demonstrator on the panel to inquire whether or not the demonstrator was available to provide her services on the particular days at the specified shop. Generally speaking, neither the demonstrator nor the appellant knew prior to this time whether or not a demonstration was to be given at any particular shop or store during the immediately following weekend. If the demonstrator was available, it was agreed that the service should be provided. The demonstration was carried out without any supervision by the appellant.

Ms. Mahon submitted an invoice in respect of the services provided after each demonstration to the appellant. The invoices were not treated as valid unless they were signed by the manager of the particular store in which the demonstration was carried out. Her fees were discharged on a fortnightly basis on production of the completed invoices. She was paid approximately L28.32 per day for her services and was also paid travelling expenses at the rate of 27p per mile. She was not a member of any pension scheme of the appellant nor was she a member of a trade union.

New contracts were entered into by the appellant with Ms Mahon in respect of each of the years ending the 31st December, 1991, the 31st December, 1992, and the 31st December, 1993. While there were some differences, the contracts for each of the years in question were in broadly the same terms. That in force for the year ending the 31st December, 1993, contained a number of important provisions which must be set out in full.

The letter from Ms Bernie Campbell, the customer services manager, confirming the retention of Ms Mahon and enclosing the terms and conditions of her employment, began as follows:—

'This is to confirm that [the appellant] is willing to retain your services as a demonstrator/merchandiser commencing on the 1st January, 1993 and ending on the 31st December, 1993.

For the avoidance of all doubt, I am obliged to point out to you that you will not be an employee of [the appellant], you will be providing it with your services as an independent contractor as and when they are required during the term of the contract.

The contract shall be subject to the standard terms and conditions, a copy of which is attached thereto ...'

Attached to this letter were what were described as 'NOTES' which stated as follows:—

'(1) You will be responsible for your own tax affairs. [The appellant] will be making returns to the revenue of all payments made to you. These payments will be made gross.

(2) You will not be an employee of [the appellant], you will be an independent contractor. This has implications in the area of employment legislation and from the point of view of injury or health and damages sustained or caused while you are providing services under the general terms and conditions to [the appellant].'

[Keane J. then considered some of the other terms of the contract and the background to the Supreme Court appeal before considering the merits of the case.]

... The criteria which should be adopted in considering whether a particular employment, in the context of legislation such as the Act of 1981, is to be regarded as a contract 'for service' or a contract 'of services' have been the subject of a number of decisions in Ireland and England. In some of the cases, different terminology is used and the distinction is stated as being between a 'servant' and 'independent contractor'. However, there is a consensus to be found in the authorities that each case must be considered in the light of its particular facts and of the general principles which the courts have developed: see the observations of Barr J, in McAuliffe v Minister for Social Welfare [1995] 2 IR 238.

At one stage, the extent and degree of the control which was exercised by one party over the other in the performance of the work was regarded as decisive. However, as later authorities demonstrate, that test does not always provide satisfactory guidance. In Cassidy v Ministry of Health [1951] 2 K.B. 343, it was pointed out that, although the master of a ship is clearly employed under a contract of service, the owners are not entitled to tell him how he should navigate the vessel. Conversely, the fact that one party reserves the right to exercise full control over the method of doing the work may be consistent with the other party being an independent contractor: see Queensland Stations Property Ltd. v Federal Commissioner of Taxation [1945] 70 CLR. 539.

In the English decision of Market Investigations v Min. of Soc. Security [1969] 2 Q.B. 173, Cooke J, at p. 184 having referred to these authorities said:—

'The observations of Lord Wright, of Denning L.J. and of the judges of the Supreme Court suggest that the fundamental test to be applied is this: "Is the person who has engaged himself to perform these services performing them as a person in business on his own account". If the answer to that question is "yes", then the contract is a contract for services. If the answer is "no", then the contract is a contract of service. No exhaustive list has been compiled and perhaps no exhaustive list can be compiled of considerations which are relevant in determining that question, nor can strict rules be laid down as to the relative weight which the various considerations should carry in particular cases. The most that can be said is that control will no doubt always have to be considered, although it can no longer be regarded as the sole determining factor; and that factors which may be of importance are such matters as whether the man performing the services provides his own equipment, whether he hires his own helpers, what degree of financial risk he takes, what degree of responsibility for investment and management he has, and whether and how far he has an opportunity of profiting from sound management in the performance of his task.'

It should also be noted that the Supreme Court of the Irish Free State in Graham v Minister for Industry and Commerce [1933] IR 156, had also made it clear that the essential test was whether the person alleged to be a 'servant' was in fact working for himself or for another person.

It is, accordingly, clear that, while each case must be determined in the light of its particular facts and circumstances, in general a person will be regarded as providing his or her services under a contract of service and not as an independent contractor where he or she is performing those services for another person and not for himself or herself. The degree of control exercised over how the work is to be performed, although a factor to be taken into account, is not decisive. The inference that the person is engaged in business on his or her own account can be more readily drawn where he or she provides the necessary premises or equipment or some other form of investment, where he or she employs others to assist in the business and where the profit which he or she derives from the business is dependent on the efficiency with which it is conducted by him or her.

The question remains as to whether the appeals officer, in the light of the legal principles to which I have referred, was entitled to arrive at the conclusion he did on the facts as found by him. I have no doubt that he was. Obviously, having regard to the nature of the work for which she was employed, there was no continuous supervision of Ms Mahon by the appellant. That cannot be regarded as a decisive factor, any more than it was in the case of the market researcher, the nature of whose employment was in issue in the case decided by Cooke J. On the other side of the equation are the facts that Ms Mahon was provided by the appellant with the clothing and equipment necessary for the demonstration and made no contribution, financial or otherwise, of her own and that the remuneration she earned was solely dependent on her providing the demonstrations at the times and in the places nominated by the appellant. The amount of money she earned was determined exclusively by the extent to which her services were availed of by the appellant: she was not in a position by better management and employment of resources to ensure for herself a higher profit from her activities. She did not as a matter of routine engage other people to assist her in the work: where she was unable to do the work herself, she had to arrange for it to be done by someone else, but the person in question had to be approved by the appellant.

The written agreement was undoubtedly drafted with understandable care with a view to ensuring, so far as possible, that Ms Mahon was regarded in law as an independent contractor. However, as I have already pointed out, although this was a factor to which the appeals officer was bound to have regard, it was by no means decisive of the issue. When he took into account all the circumstances of her employment, he was perfectly entitled to arrive at the conclusion, as he did, that she was employed under a contract of service.

As to the submission that the appeals officer should have treated himself as bound by the unreported decision of the Circuit Court in Cronin, it is sufficient to say that, since it was a decision on different facts in another statutory context and no written judgment appears to have been available, the appeals officer was entitled to adopt the approach he did, ie of applying to the facts as found by him the legal principles laid down in decisions of the High Court and this Court. This he clearly did and, for the reasons I have already given, I am satisfied that the High Court Judge was entirely correct in holding that his conclusions could not be disturbed.

I would dismiss the appeal."

Comments and Questions:
1. The case demonstrates that no one test will be decisive in determining who an employee is and also serves as a warning to employers who may feel that they can be absolved of responsibility by virtue of a contractual term.

Who is the employer?

It is generally clear who the employer is in a given case, but confusion may arise. The employer for the purpose of vicarious liability is deemed to be the person who controlled the employee at the time the negligent act was carried out. Where an employee is hired out a question arises as to whether the temporary employer or the original employer is the true employer for the purposes of an action. The answer will generally be that the employee remains the employee of the first employer as the temporary employer will not have the desired degree of control. However, in some cases, particularly in the case of unskilled workers, control will be deemed to have passed to the second, albeit temporary, employer.

Lynch v Palgrave Murphy Limited
Supreme Court [1964] I.R. 150

Facts: The plaintiff was injured when the driver of a forklift negligently lowered the prongs of the forklift, crushing his fingers between the prongs and a bale of paper. The forklift and its driver were on loan from a third party named Crosbie. The plaintiff sued his own employer, Palgrave Murphy Limited, claiming that they were vicariously liable for the negligent acts of the forklift operator. The High Court (Teevan J.) held that the forklift driver was working as an agent of the defendants and that they were therefore liable for his negligent act. The defendants appealed this finding to the Supreme Court.

Issues: The court (Ó Dálaigh C.J., Lavery, Kingsmill Moore, Haugh and Walsh JJ.) had to consider whether the defendants were the employers of the negligent forklift driver for the purposes of vicarious liability.

Kingsmill Moore J.:

"This appeal raises once again the question as to when and in what circumstances a workman, whose services have been lent temporarily by his permanent employer to another employer, can be considered to have become the servant of the second employer so as to make the second employer liable vicariously for his negligence. Various terms have been used in the decided cases to describe the second employer, such as 'dominus pro tempore' and 'dominus pro hac vice.' I will use the terms, 'permanent master' and 'temporary master,' as being the simplest, though I realise that the use of the word 'master' begs the question to a certain degree.

It was accepted by counsel on both sides that it was a question of fact whether in all the circumstances the control and direction of the workman could be said to have passed so completely from the permanent master to the temporary master as to make the workman a servant of the temporary master to the extent that the temporary master became responsible for his negligence; and it was conceded by counsel for the defendants that in certain circumstances such a result could be brought about. But counsel for the defendants contended that the presumption always was that the workman remained in the service of the permanent master and that the onus of disproving this rested on anyone who wished to challenge it; moreover, he said that the onus was very heavy and that the burden could only be shifted in exceptional circumstances, none of which had been proved in the present case...

... A great number of cases, ranging over a century, were cited but it is unnecessary to review them in detail. Though the question whether the permanent master or the temporary master is responsible for the negligence of the workman is a conclusion of fact based on the establishment or non-establishment of various other facts, it seems to be established by authority that the mere power to assign the task to be done—and even to direct in a general way how the desired object is to be accomplished—does not, by itself, make the temporary master responsible for the workman's negligence, unless there is also the power to control the way in which the act involving negligence was done. In the present case Crosbie engaged, paid and could dismiss Byrne. He directed him each day where to go to work. He left the driving of the truck and the operation of the controls to the discretion of Byrne, but he, Crosbie, would have had the power, by himself or by an engineer if he had chosen to employ one, to direct Byrne in his method of handling the controls. The defendants could only indicate to Byrne the load to be taken, the place from which it was to be taken, the place where it was to be deposited and the arrangements made to facilitate the depositing. The lifting of the forks, the driving of the truck and the management of the forks to deposit the load were not under the control of the defendants. This being so, there was no fact which would warrant a jury in finding that Byrne had become a servant of the defendants so as to involve them in vicarious liability. Nor is the position altered by the fact that, in order to achieve the desired end of stacking the bales in tiers, Byrne had so to operate his forks as to co-operate with a servant or servants of the defendants ...

... *M'Cartan* v. *Belfast Harbour Commissioners* [1910] 2 I. R. 470; [1911] 2 I. R. 143 was a case where the facts closely resembled *Donovan* v. *Laing, Wharton, and Down Construction Syndicate* [1893] 1 Q. B. 629. The Commissioners hired out one of their cranes with its driver to the master of a ship which was discharging at their wharves. The craneman raised and lowered the buckets containing the cargo, and swung the jib, on the direction of a servant of the ship-master. Owing to the negligence of the craneman in lowering a bucket at a high speed, the plaintiff was injured and he sued the Commissioners. The jury found that the plaintiff was injured as a result of the negligence of the craneman who let the bucket get out of control; but in answer to the special question, 'Had the hirer authority to control Duffy otherwise than in respect of the time and place of movement of the crane, and the time of raising and lowering the buckets?' they replied, 'No.' On those findings the trial judge entered judgment for the plaintiff. Upon motion by the defendants, the King's Bench Division set aside the judgment for the plaintiff and entered a verdict and judgment for the defendants with costs. The judgment of the King's Bench Division was reversed by the Court of Appeal who were affirmed by the House of Lords. In the Court of Appeal Holmes L.J., who gave the judgment of the Court, said that the work of unloading the vessel was a joint operation, but in that part of it which consisted of the manipulation of the crane the ship-master had no control over the craneman. For this reason he held that he had not become the servant of the ship-master so as to make the ship-master liable for the craneman's negligence in conducting that operation.

In the House of Lords the decision again rested on the limited amount of control exercised by the ship owner. *Donovan's Case* [1893] 1 Q. B. 629 was distinguished because in that case all control over the craneman had passed to the wharfinger while in *M'Cartan's Case* [1910] 2 I. R. 470; [1911] 2 I. R. 143 the control was limited as found by the jury. Lord Dunedin cited with approval the words of Bowen L.J. in *Moore* v. *Palmer* 2 T. L. R. 781 (a case almost identical in the relevant facts):—"The great test was this, whether the servant was transferred or only the use and benefit of his work." *M'Cartan's Case* [1910] 2 I. R. 470; [1911] 2 I. R. 143, as a judgment of our Court of Appeal and of the House of Lords before 1922, would normally be regarded as a precedent which, even if not absolutely binding on us, should be followed in the absence of very special reasons, and if there is any discrepancy between *Donovan's Case* [1893] 1 Q. B. 629 and *M'Cartan's Case* [1910] 2 I. R. 470; [1911] 2 I. R. 143 then the latter should be followed.

Mersey Docks and Harbour Board v. *Coggins and Griffith (Liverpool), Ltd.* [1947] A. C. 14 in its facts again echoes *M'Cartan's Case* [1910] 2 I. R. 470; [1911] 2 I. R. 143. The plaintiff, McFarlane, was employed by forwarding agents who had engaged the respondent company as stevedores to load cargo on a ship. While so employed the plaintiff was injured by the negligence of a craneman in the management of his crane. The crane and its driver had been hired by the appellant Board to the respondent company. Lord Simon, at p. 10 of the report, compendiously states the facts which seemed to him relevant, and his conclusion:—'The appellant board had engaged Newall, and it paid his wages: it alone had power to dismiss him. On the other hand, the respondent company had the immediate direction and control of the operations to be executed by the crane driver with his crane, e.g., to pick up and move a piece of cargo from shed to ship. The respondent company, however, had no power to direct how the crane driver should work the crane. The manipulation of the controls was a matter for the driver himself. In the present case the accident happened because of the negligent way in which the crane driver worked his crane, and since the respondent company had no control over how he worked it, as distinguished from telling him what he was to do with the crane, it seems to me to follow that Newall's general employers must be liable for the negligence and not the hirers of the apparatus … It is not disputed that the burden of proof rests on the general or permanent employer—in this case the appellant board— to shift the *prima facie* responsibility for the negligence of servants engaged and paid by such employer so that this burden in a particular case may come to rest on the hirer who for the time being has the advantage of the service rendered.

And, in my opinion, this burden is a heavy one and can only be discharged in quite exceptional circumstances.'

Lord Simon refers to the test laid down by Bowen L.J. in *Donovan's Case* [1893] 1 Q. B. 629 when the latter said:—'... by the employer is meant the person who has a right at the moment to control the doing of the act,' and Lord Simon accepts such test only if the words are construed as meaning 'to control the way in which the act involving negligence was done.' At page 12 of the report he presents the test as being 'where the authority lies to direct, or to delegate to, the workman, the manner in which the vehicle is driven,' and he goes on to say:—'It is this authority which determines who is the workman's "superior." In the ordinary case, the general employers exercise this authority by delegating to their workmen discretion in method of driving, and so the Court of Appeal correctly points out ... that in this case the driver Newall, "in the doing of the negligent act, was exercising his own discretion as driver—a discretion which had been vested in him by his regular employers when he was sent out with the vehicle—and he made a mistake with which the hirers had nothing to do."'

Lord Macmillan, Lord Porter, Lord Simonds and Lord Uthwatt, in slightly varying language, agreed with Lord Simon. Thus Lord Macmillan states, at p. 13:—'The stevedores were entitled to tell him where to go, what parcels to lift and where to take them, that is to say, they could direct him as to what they wanted him to do; but they had no authority to tell him how to handle the crane in doing his work,' and at p. 14:—'Here the driver became the servant of the stevedores only to the extent and effect of his taking directions from them as to the utilization of the crane in assisting their work, not as to how he should drive it.' Lord Porter says that a change of employer must always be proved in some way and not presumed: and that the test is to ask who is entitled to tell the employee the way in which he is to do the work on which he is engaged. He says, at p. 17:—'But it is not enough that the task to be performed should be under his control, he must also control the method of performing it. It is true that in most cases no orders as to how a job should be done are given or required: the man is left to do his own work in his own way. But the ultimate question is not what specific orders, or whether any specific orders, were given but who is entitled to give the orders as to how the work should be done. Where a man driving a mechanical device, such as a crane, is sent to perform a task, it is easier to infer that the general employer continues to control the method of performance since it is his crane and the driver remains responsible to him for its safe keeping.'

Finally, I would quote Lord Uthwatt, who says, at p. 21:—'The principles established by the authorities are clear enough. The workman may remain the employee of his general employer, but at the same time the result of the arrangements may be that there is vested in the hirer a power of control over the workman's activities sufficient to attach to the hirer responsibility for the workman's acts and defaults and to exempt the general employer from that responsibility. The burden of proving the existence of that power of control in the hirer rests on the general employer. The circumstance that it is the hirer who alone is entitled to direct the particular work from time to time to be done by the workman in the course of the hiring is clearly not sufficient for that purpose. The hirer's powers in this regard are directed merely to control of the job and the part the workman is to play in it, not to control of the workman, and the workman in carrying out the behests of the hirer as to what is to be done is not doing more than implementing the general employer's bargain with the hirer and his own obligations as a servant of his general employer. To establish the power of control requisite to fasten responsibility on him, the hirer must in some reasonable sense have authority to control the manner in which the workman does his work, the reason being that it is the manner in which a particular operation (assumed for this purpose to be in itself a proper operation) is carried out that determines its lawful or wrongful character. Unless there be that authority the workman is not serving the hirer, but merely serving the interests of the hirer, and service under the hirer in the sense I have stated is essential.'

Donovan's Case [1893] 1 Q. B. 629 was considered by Lord Simon, Lord Macmillan, Lord Porter and Lord Simonds and was explained by the special finding of fact that 'entire and absolute control' over the workman had passed to the wharfingers—though some of their lordships question whether such a finding could be justified.

The *Mersey Docks Case* [1947] A. C. 1 is not binding on us but must command the full weight of so distinguished a Court. I am in agreement with the opinions expressed in that case and, applying the tests laid down, I can find no evidence in the present case to suggest that the defendants had been granted or had assumed any power to control the driver in his actual operation of the machinery of the fork lift. In my opinion the case should have been withdrawn from the jury. The appeal must be allowed and judgment entered for the defendants."

Comments and Questions:

1. It appears from the above decision that the presumption shall be that the permanent employer is the employer unless strong arguments exist which prove the contrary. Ultimately the question is one of control, and the greater the degree of skill of the employee the more likely that the employee remains within the control of the permanent employer.

Within the scope of employment

An employer will only be held liable for the acts of a negligent employee where that employee is acting within the "scope of employment". Generally speaking, when an employee is doing what they have been employed to do, even where they are doing it badly, they will still be held to be acting within the "scope of employment". However, if the employee's actions are clearly unconnected with the work that they were hired to do, then the employer will not be held liable (as in *Delahunty v South Eastern Health Board* below).

(Note also that the concept of "scope of employment" or "course of employment" may be defined differently for other branches of the law, such as the liability of employers under equality legislation. The discussion in this chapter concerns vicarious liability in tort only.)

In the case of *Reilly v Ryan*, which follows, the court noted with approval Salmond on Torts (10th ed.), p.89 and (18th ed.), p.437 which states that:

> "A master is not responsible for a wrongful act done by his servant unless it is done in the course of his employment. It is deemed to be so done if it is either (a) a wrongful act authorised by the master, or (b) a wrongful and unauthorised mode of doing some act authorised by the master."

Reilly v Ryan
High Court [1991] 2 I.R. 247

Facts: The plaintiff sued the defendant for injuries suffered while he was on the defendant's licensed premises. The incident occurred when an intruder, wearing a balaclava and wielding a knife, sought to steal money from the premises. The manager of the bar grabbed the plaintiff and, while using him as a human shield, the plaintiff was stabbed in the arm. The plaintiff sued the defendant, *inter alia,* on the basis that he was vicariously liable for the acts of his servant. The Circuit Court judge dismissed the action, following which the plaintiff appealed to the High Court.

Issues: The court (Blayney J.) had to consider whether the defendant was vicariously liable for the acts of the bar manager, and in particular whether the bar manager had been acting in the "course of his employment" when the incident happened.

Blayney J. held that the bar manager had exceeded his authority when he used the customer as a human shield and was therefore acting outside of the course of his employment.

Blayney J.:

"… The defendant stated in evidence that Mr. Heffernan's instructions were to look after the customers' needs and their safety. He said that if he had been in the bar when the intruder came in he would have given him the £40 in the interests of the safety of his customers. He said he had given these instructions to Mr. Heffernan about 14 years before and had renewed them from time to time. The customers always came first. He said he did not authorise Mr. Heffernan to do what he had done on the occasion in question. He said Mr. Heffernan did not get an opportunity to give the intruder the £40 he had asked for.

On these facts it was submitted by Mr. Seligman on behalf of the plaintiff that the plaintiff's injuries had been caused by Mr. Heffernan's using him as a shield against the intruder; that in acting as he had Mr. Heffernan had been acting in the course of his employment and accordingly the defendant was liable. Reliance was placed on the following passages from Winfield on Tort (13th Ed.) at pp. 568, 570 and 574:—

> 'A wrong falls within the scope of employment if it is expressly or impliedly authorised by the master or is an unauthorised manner of doing something which is authorised, or is necessarily incidental to something which the servant is employed to do. Course of employment has supplanted scope of authority, but it contains no criteria to decide when or why an act is within or outside the scope of employment and no single test is appropriate to cover all cases. It is often an extremely difficult question to decide whether conduct is or is not within the course of employment as thus defined, and it would seem that the question is ultimately one of fact to be decided in the light of general principles.
>
> Another application of the same principle is an act done in protection of the master's property. The servant has an implied authority to make reasonable efforts to protect and preserve it in an emergency which endangers it. For wrongful, because mistaken, acts done within the scope of that authority the master is liable, and it is a question of degree whether there has been an excess of the authority so great as to put the act outside the scope of authority.
>
> Similarly, if the servant has committed an assault upon the plaintiff, that will be in the course of his employment if his intention was to further his master's business, but if the assault was a mere act of personal vengeance, it will not.'

Mr. Seligman submitted that Mr. Heffernan had been acting within the course of his employment in that what he had done was for the purpose of protecting his master's property.

For the defendant Mr. Burke submitted that Mr. Heffernan had not been trying to protect his master's property but simply to protect himself. What he had done was solely actuated by self interest and, accordingly, was not within the course of his employment.

I accept as correct the statements of the law set out in Winfield. It is similar to the statement of law in Salmond on Torts (10th Ed.) p. 89 and (18th Ed.) p. 437 which was approved by the Court of Appeal in England in *Poland v. John Parr and Sons* [1927] 1 K.B. 236 at p. 240:—

> 'A master is not responsible for a wrongful act done by his servant unless it is done in the course of his employment. It is deemed to be so done if it is either (a) a wrongful act authorised by the master, or (b) a wrongful and unauthorised mode of doing some act authorised by the master.'

[Blayney J. then went on to outline the facts of the case.]

On these facts, can it be said that Mr. Heffernan was acting in the course of his employment by reacting as he did, that is, by assaulting the plaintiff and using him as a shield, thus causing him to be stabbed? Clearly what he did was not expressly authorised by the defendant, but was it a wrongful and unauthorised mode of doing something that he was, if not expressly, at least impliedly authorised to do?

In *Poland v. John Parr and Sons* [1927] 1 K.B. 236, a carter in the employment of the defendants, while on his way home in the middle of the day, was following close behind a wagon laden with sugar in bags and being driven by one of his employers. He saw the plaintiff, a boy, walking beside the wagon with his hand upon one of the bags. Honestly and reasonably thinking that the plaintiff was stealing sugar from the bag, he gave him a blow with his hand on the back of the neck. The plaintiff fell and the wheel of the wagon injured his foot. It was held that in the circumstances the carter had implied authority to make reasonable efforts to protect and preserve the defendants' property; that the violence exerted was not so excessive as to take his act outside the scope of the authority, and that the defendants were liable.

Atkin L.J. said in his judgment at page 245:—

> '... there is a class of acts which in an emergency a servant, though not bound, is authorised to do. And then the question is not whether the act of the servant was for the master's benefit but whether it is an act of this class. I agree that, where the servant does more than the emergency requires, the excess may be so great as to take the act out of the class. For example, if Hall had fired a shot at the boy, the act might have been in the interest of his employers, but that is not the test. The question is whether the act is one of the class of acts which the servant is authorised to do in an emergency. In the present case the man Hall was doing an act of this class—namely, protecting his masters' property, which was or which he reasonably and honestly thought was being pillaged. His mode of doing it was not, in my opinion, such as to take it out of the class. He was therefore doing an authorised act for which the respondents are responsible.'

Scrutton L.J. said in his judgment at page 243:—

> 'To make an employer liable for the act of a person alleged to be his servant the act must be one of a class of acts which the person was authorised or employed to do. If the act is one of that class the employer is liable, though the act is done negligently or, in some cases, even if it is done with excessive violence. But the excess may be so great as to take the act out of the class of acts which the person is authorised or employed to do. Whether it is so or not is a question of degree.'

In the light of these statements of the law, it seems to me that a second question has to be asked also. If Mr. Heffernan had authority to do what he did on the basis that it was a wrongful and unauthorised mode of doing something which he was impliedly authorised to do, did he exceed what was required by the emergency, and was the excess such as to take his action outside the class of acts impliedly authorised?

Whether Mr. Heffernan's conduct is construed as directed to protecting the defendant's property or defending himself, it seems to me that it should be held to have been impliedly authorised by the defendant. *Poland v. John Parr and Sons* [1927] 1 K.B. 236 is clear authority for the proposition that a servant has implied authority to protect his master's property and I consider that where an employee, who is in charge of his master's premises in the course of his employment, is attacked by an intruder intent upon stealing his master's property, it would be unreasonable to hold that he did not also have implied authority to defend himself. To hold otherwise would involve deciding that he was acting in two separate capacities in warding off the attack—acting as the defendant's servant in protecting the latter's property but acting in his personal capacity in defending himself, and to make such a distinction would in my opinion be unreal. So I consider that the answer to the first question is that Mr. Heffernan did have implied authority to defend himself as well as to protect the defendant's property. The subsidiary question is more difficult. As the facts are very different from anything to be found in the decided cases, it has to be decided in the light of general principles, and the conclusion I have come to is that Mr. Heffernan did exceed what was required by the emergency. There were two options open to him, to accede to the intruder's demand, and give him the £40, or to resist. He chose the latter. But the means he employed went well beyond what was reasonable. One could have imagined him picking up some makeshift implement in order to resist the intruder (such as the snooker cue with which he did arm himself after the plaintiff had been stabbed) and if in the course of using it he had, by accident, injured one of the customers, the latter would have a good cause of action against the defendant. What Mr. Heffernan did was very different. He chose to interpose a human barrier between himself and the intruder. This involved a physical assault on the plaintiff and putting him in a position of great danger. It was a wholly unreasonable and excessive means of dealing with the emergency.

Was it so excessive as to take it out of the class of acts which were impliedly authorised? In my opinion it was. What he did has to be looked at in the context of his duties as the defendant's manager. His principal duty was to serve the defendant's customers. This involved also, as the defendant said in evidence, looking after their comfort and safety. But instead of looking after the plaintiff's safety, as was his duty, Mr. Heffernan was the cause of his being injured. His reaction was accordingly excessive in the sense that what he did went wholly outside what he was employed to do, being in fact the precise opposite of what his duty was at the time. Instead of trying to protect the plaintiff, he assaulted him and was the cause of his being injured. In my opinion it could not be said that such behaviour was impliedly authorised by the defendant. For these reasons I agree with the decision of the learned Circuit Court Judge and must dismiss the appeal."

It seems that a more modern view is to consider whether the negligent act is "connected" to the work of the employee when determining whether the act is within the "course of employment". Where the negligent act is not "connected" to the work the employee was hired to carry out, the employer is unlikely to be held liable. In the case of *Delahunty* below the court cited with approval the Canadian case of *Bazley v Curry* (1999) 174 D.L.R. (4th) 45 when considering the issue of "connectedness".

Delahunty v South Eastern Health Board, St Joseph's Industrial School and Minister for Education and Sport
High Court [2003] 4 I.R. 361

Facts: The plaintiff was sexually assaulted by a housemaster while visiting a friend who was a resident at the second defendant's premises in May 1976. The plaintiff sued the second and third defendants, *inter alia,* on the basis that they were vicariously liable for the acts of the housemaster.

Issues: The court (O'Higgins J.) was required to determine, *inter alia*, whether the second and third defendants were vicariously liable for the acts of the housemaster, and in particular whether the housemaster was acting within the "scope of his employment" when the abuse took place.

O'Higgins J. held that the second defendant was not vicariously liable in negligence for the acts of its employee as there was not a sufficient connection between the functions the housemaster was employed to carry out and the assault on the plaintiff for it to be regarded as within the scope of his employment. The plaintiff in this case was a visitor to the institution in respect of whom the housemaster had no particular duties.

As regards the third named defendants, the housemaster was not considered to be an employee of the Minister and therefore the Minister was not vicariously liable for any wrongs the housemaster carried out.

O'Higgins J.:

"... Vicarious liability of the second defendant

The application of the doctrine of vicarious liability to the facts of a particular case can often be a matter of great difficulty. The difficulty arises in determining whether a particular act has been committed in the scope of employment so as to render the employer vicariously liable for the torts. The classic formulation of the test is contained in Salmond & Heuston's Law of Torts (21st ed., 1996) at p. 443:—

> '... if it is either (1) a wrongful act authorised by the master, or (2) a wrongful and unauthorised mode of doing some act authorised by the master ... it is clear that the master is responsible for acts actually authorised by him: for liability would exist in this case, even if the relation between the parties was merely one of agency, and not one of service at all. But a master, as opposed

to the employer of an independent contractor, is liable even for acts which he has not authorised, provided they are so connected with acts which he has authorised that they might rightly be regarded as modes—although improper modes—of doing them.'

The difficulty was referred to by McCarthy J. in McIntyre v. Lewis [1991] 1 I.R. 121 at p. 137, where he said:—

'In the course of the argument, counsel for the State was asked as to where the scope of employment or duty ends—at what particular time and in what circumstances. No satisfactory answer was obtained to this question because there is no satisfactory answer. The matter is summarised in the second edition of McMahon & Binchy, Irish Law of Torts, at p. 756 where it is suggested that the test is by looking to see if the acts complained of are so closely connected with the employment of the primary wrongdoer as to make the employer vicariously liable.'

The attention of the court was drawn by counsel for the second defendant, to two important Canadian decisions on the topic of vicarious liability, namely Bazley v. Curry (1999) 174 D.L.R. (4th) 45 and Jacobi v. Griffiths (1999) 174 D.L.R (4th) 71. In Bazley v. Curry an employer was found vicariously liable for an employee's tortious conduct in sexually abusing a child. In helping to distinguish between an unauthorised mode of performing an authorised act which attracts liability and an entirely independent act which does not, it was held that where a precedent was inconclusive the courts should turn to policy for guidelines. Two fundamental policy concerns were the provision of a just remedy for the harm and the deterrence of future harm. It was held that the fundamental question is whether the wrongful act was sufficiently related to conduct authorised by the employer as to justify the imposition of a vicarious liability. In determining the sufficiency of the connection between the employment and the act the court could have regard to:—

(a) the opportunities the enterprise afforded to the employee to abuse his power;
(b) the extent to which the wrongful act may have furthered the employer's aims and hence be more likely to be committed by the employee;
(c) the extent to which the wrongful act was related to friction, or confrontation or intimacy inherent in the employer's enterprise;
(d) the extent of power conferred on the employee in relation to the victim;
(e) the vulnerability of potential victims through wrongful exercise of the employee's power.

In that case the offending employee's functions were to do everything that a parent would do for a child, including general supervision and intimate duties such as bathing and putting the children to bed. The wrongful act in that case was held to be sufficiently related or closely connected to the conduct authorised by the employers to justify the imposition of vicarious liability.

In Jacobi v. Griffiths (1999)174 D.L.R. (4th) 71, the Supreme Court of Canada, held that the process for determining when a non-authorised act is so connected to the employer's enterprise that liability should be imposed involved two steps:—

1. firstly a court should determine whether there are precedents which unambiguously determine on which side of the line between vicarious liability and no liability the case falls.
2. if prior cases do not clearly suggest a solution the next step is to determine whether vicarious liability should be imposed in light of the broader policy rationales behind strict liability.

In the facts of the case, however, the court held that the strong connection test had not been satisfied. The offender was a programme director of a club whose job was to supervise volunteer staff and to organise after school recreational activities. Although it was part of his job to build up a positive rapport with children the relationship was not one of intimacy and in the circumstances the strong connection case was not satisfied.

In Lister v. Hesley Hall Ltd. [2001] UKHL 22; [2002] 1 A.C. 215 the leading United Kingdom authority, the plaintiffs were residents in a boarding house attached to a school owned and managed by the defendants. The warden of the boarding house, employed by the defendants, sexually abused the claimants. It was held in the words of the headnote:—

> '... having regard to the circumstances of the warden's employment, including the close contact with the pupils and the inherent risks that it involved, there was a sufficient connection between the work that he had been employed to do and the acts of abuse that he had committed for those acts to be regarded as having been committed within the scope of his employment and the defendants should be held vicariously liable for them.'

Lord Steyn said at para. 28 of the judgment, at p. 230:—

> 'Employing the traditional methodology of English law, I am satisfied that in the case of the appeals under consideration the evidence showed that the employers entrusted the care of the children in Axeholme House to the warden. The question is whether the warden's torts were so closely connected with his employment that it would be fair and just to hold the employers vicariously liable. On the facts of the case the answer is yes. After all, the sexual abuse was inextricably interwoven with the carrying out by the warden of his duties in Axeholme House. Matters of degree arise. But the present cases clearly fall on the side of vicarious liability.'

Lord Clyde at para. 50, at p. 237 stated:—

> 'In addition to the opportunity which access gave him, his position as warden and the close contact with the boys which that work involved created a

sufficient connection between the acts of abuse which he committed and the work which he had been employed to do. It appears that the respondents gave the warden a quite general authority in the supervision and running of the house as well as some particular responsibilities.'

Lord Millett, in holding the school liable, said at para. 83, at p. 250, that he would regard this decision '… in accordance, not only with ordinary principle deducible from the authorities but with the underlying rationale of vicarious liability'.

It is to be noted that both Canadian decisions referred to above disapproved of the decision in Trotman v. North Yorkshire C.C. [1999] L.G.R. 584 and Lister v. Hesley Hall overruled it. In Trotman v. North Yorkshire C.C. Butler-Sloss L.J. considered, at p. 591, that the sexual assaults in that case were 'far removed from an unauthorised mode of carrying out a teacher's duty on behalf of his employer'. She later stated at p. 591:—

'… in the field of serious sexual misconduct, I find it difficult to visualise circumstances in which an act of the teacher can be an unauthorised mode of carrying out an authorised act, although I would not wish to close the door on the possibility.'

In Bazley v. Curry (1999) 174 D.L.R. (4th) 45 at p. 58 para. 24, that reasoning was faulted in [*sic*] as depending:—

'on the level of generality with which the sexual act is described. Instead of describing the act in terms of the employee's duties of supervising and caring for vulnerable students during a study trip abroad, the Court of Appeal cast it in terms unrelated to those duties. Important legal decisions should not turn on such semantics.'

Lord Steyn agreed with that criticism in Lister v. Hesley Hall Ltd. [2002] 1 A.C. 215. In this jurisdiction, in The Health Board v. B.C. [1994] E.L.R. 27, some years before the decision in Trotman v. North Yorkshire C.C. [1999] L.G.R. 584, Costello J. spoke in strikingly similar terms at p. 33:—

'In the absence of express statutory provision the law in this country in relation to the liability of an employer for a tortious act (including statutory torts) of his employee is perfectly clear—an employer is vicariously liable where the act is committed by his employee within the scope of his employment.'

He went on to say, however at p. 34:—

'An employer may, of course, be vicariously liable when his employee is acting negligently, or even criminally … But I cannot envisage any employment in which they were engaged in respect of which a sexual assault could be regarded as so connected with it as to amount to an act within its scope.'

… The 'strong connection' argument does not avail the plaintiff in this case. No such connection can be established between the plaintiff in this case and the employment of the man who assaulted him. No such relationship as that existing in Bazley v. Curry (1999) 174 D.L.R. (4th) 45 or even in Jacobi v. Griffiths (1999) 174 D.L.R. (4th) 71 existed—the plaintiff was merely a visitor in the institution at the time of the assault. Moreover, the policy considerations mentioned in those cases as grounds to justify vicarious liability while possibly applicable in relation to residents of the second defendant, have no application in relation to a mere visitor. Even if the reasoning in Lister v. Hesley Hall Ltd. [2002] 1 A.C. 215 were to be preferred to the reasoning of Costello J. in The Health Board v. B.C. [1994] E.L.R. 27 this would not enable the plaintiff to establish vicarious liability. Counsel for the second defendant submitted that Lister v. Hesley Hall Ltd. was a departure in the law which had not been adopted in this country. That might perhaps be open to question on a fuller analysis of the judgment. However, whether it be a new departure of the law or the application of existing law matters not. There was not such a connection between the employment of Mr. Brady as a housemaster and the assault on the plaintiff as to fix liability on his employers. The plaintiff in this case was a visitor in respect of whom Mr. Brady had no particular duties, notwithstanding the fact that visitors were encouraged to visit the institution. This is in contrast to Lister v. Hesley Hall Ltd. where the abuser was a warden and the close contact with the pupils and inherent risks that it involved were important factors in the decision. In the circumstances of this case the vicarious liability of the second defendant to the plaintiff for the acts of Mr. Brady has not been established.

Vicarious liability of the third defendant
… The second defendant, although it employed Mr. Brady, is not vicariously liable for the assault on the plaintiff; a fortiori no vicarious liability attaches to the third defendant whose connection with Mr. Brady was quite remote. He was not the third defendant's employee and the third defendant had no function in the hiring or firing of Mr. Brady, nor was he responsible for the way in which he performed his duties."

Comments and Questions:
1. O'Higgins J. referred above to the case of the *Health Board v BC,* relied on by the defendants in their argument. In that case Costello J., although not ruling out the vicarious liability of employers for the criminal acts of employees, could not contemplate any situation where an act of sexual assault could be seen to be so "connected" to the functions of an employee as to come within the scope of their employment. Is this view necessarily inconsistent with the decision in *Lister*? If it is, which view is to be preferred in your opinion?

2. Would the "connected" test, as described above, lead to the same conclusion in the case of *Reilly v Ryan* as that Blayney J. arrived at?

<hr>

LIABILITY OF FIRM FOR PARTNER'S WRONGS

The liability of a firm for the torts of its partner is very similar to that of an employer for the torts of its employee. If the partner is said to be working within the course of his or her employment then liability will attach to the firm.

Vicarious liability under this heading is provided for by ss.5, 10 and 11 of the Partnership Act 1890.

Section 5 states that:

> "5. Every partner is an agent of the firm and his other partners for the purpose of the business of the partnership; and the acts of every partner who does any act for carrying on in the usual way business of the kind carried on by the firm of which he is a member bind the firm and his partners, unless the partner so acting has in fact no authority to act for the firm in the particular matter, and the person with whom he is dealing either knows that he has no authority, or does not know or believe him to be a partner."

Section 10 provides:

> "10. Where, by any wrongful act or omission of any partner acting in the ordinary course of the business of the firm, or with the authority of his co-partners, loss or injury is caused to any person not being a partner in the firm, or any penalty is incurred, the firm is liable therefore to the same extent as the partner so acting or omitting to act."

Section 11 states that:

> "In the following cases; namely—
> (a) Where one partner acting within the scope of his apparent authority receives the money or property of a third person and misapplies it; and
> (b) Where a firm in the course of its business receives money or property of a third person, and the money or property so received is misapplied by one or more of the partners while it is in the custody of the firm;
> the firm is liable to make good the loss."

<hr>

VICARIOUS LIABILITY OF THE OWNERS OF VEHICLES

Section 118 of the Road Traffic Act 1961 imposes vicarious liability on the owners of any "mechanically propelled vehicle" where injury arises. This liability, however, is limited to the extent that the vehicle must have been used with the consent of the owner and within the scope of the consent given.

Section 118 states:

"Where a person (in this section referred to as the user) uses a mechanically propelled vehicle, with the consent of the owner of the vehicle, the user shall, for the purposes of determining the liability or non-liability of the owner for injury caused by the negligent use of the vehicle by the user, and for the purposes of determining the liability or non-liability of any other person for injury to the vehicle or persons or property therein caused by negligence occurring while the vehicle is being used by the user, be deemed to use the vehicle as the servant of the owner, but only in so far as the user acts in accordance with the terms of such consent."

CHAPTER 8

PROFESSIONAL NEGLIGENCE

INTRODUCTION

Negligence is concerned with compensating people who suffer a loss as a result of the careless acts or omissions of others. To establish an action in negligence the defendant must owe a duty of care to the plaintiff; s/he must fail to conform to the required standard of care; there must be an actual loss or damage to the interests of the plaintiff and a sufficiently close causal connection between the conduct of the defendant and the resulting injury to the plaintiff. For professionals, the rules of negligence are nuanced to that particular profession. The rules are profession-dependent; and in this chapter reference will be made to both the medical and legal professions.

WHO IS A PROFESSIONAL?

There is no definition of what or who is a professional. Jackson & Powell (*Professional Negligence*, 4th ed., Sweet & Maxwell, 1997) suggest that professional negligence relates to specialised intellectual work. In *Hughes v JJ Power Ltd.*, unreported, High Court, May 11, 1988, the High Court adjudged that mechanics could be deemed to be professional, for the purposes of professional negligence. In contrast, the courts were not convinced that nurses should be assessed under the heading of medical negligence: *Kelly v St Laurence's Hospital* [1989] I.L.R.M. 437.

Kelly v St Laurence's Hospital
Supreme Court [1989] I.L.R.M. 437

Facts: Mr Kelly, the respondent, had epilepsy, and was admitted to hospital to determine whether certain attacks of the illness were a result of schizophrenia or a manifestation of his epileptic condition. Upon admission to hospital he was taken off all medication. Some nights after his admission, Mr Kelly left the ward, climbed onto a windowsill and fell 20 feet into the yard below sustaining severe personal injuries. Mr Kelly succeeded in his action in the High Court and the hospital appealed to the Supreme Court.

Issues: Mr Kelly succeeded in establishing negligence in the Supreme Court. The issue for the purposes of this extract is the discussion by the court of professional negligence, and particularly medical negligence. This case involved assessing the work of nursing staff, and what should be the practice for that profession. The court appears to suggest that nurses are not professionals in the sense that they attract assessment by the standards of medical negligence.

McCarthy J. (Finlay C.J., Henchy, Hederman and Walsh JJ. all suggested that this was not a real case of professional negligence):

"... In my view, this was not what is commonly called a medical malpractice case; it was a case concerning the standard of care and attention which the administration of a hospital might reasonably be expected to provide for a patient who had been admitted to the hospital and taken off all drug therapy; in particular, who had been admitted to the hospital for observation when not taking these drugs. Whilst the trial judge did refer to *O'Donovan*'s case (*O'Donovan v Cork County Council* [1967] IR 173) he made clear his own view as to the real issue in the case being that of the standard of care as I have sought to indicate. It is in that context that I approach a consideration of the several grounds of appeal advanced at the trial and detailed in the judgment of the Chief Justice, whose view that there was evidence of negligence to go to the jury I entirely share ..."

CONTRACT v TORT

Many professional relationships, such as doctor/patient and solicitor/client, give rise to relationships in contract. Does such a contractual relationship preclude a party taking an action in tort? This question was addressed in *Finlay v Murtagh* [1979] I.R. 249.

Finlay v Murtagh
Supreme Court [1979] I.R. 249

Facts: The plaintiff claimed damages from his solicitor, the defendant, in the tort of negligence. The plaintiff alleged that his solicitor was negligent in failing to institute an action on behalf of the plaintiff against a third party within the period permitted by the Statute of Limitations.

Issue: Whether there was a cause of action in tort, or whether the plaintiff was confined to taking the action in contract. The court found for the plaintiff, and held that it was permissible to take an action in tort.

Henchy J. (O'Higgins C.J. and Kenny J. concurring; Parke and Griffin JJ. also in agreement):

"… When a client complains that he has suffered loss because his solicitor has failed to show due care in the performance of his duty as solicitor, does the client's cause of action lie in contract or in the tort of negligence? Or has he a choice? That is the problem presented in this appeal …

… *Liston* v. *Munster and Leinster Bank*, [[1940] IR 77] was an action by the personal representative of a customer of the bank against the bank for damages for negligence, for conversion, and for money had and received. The issue being whether the entire cause of action arose out of a contract, in which case notice of trial by a judge without a jury would be appropriate, or whether it lay partly in tort, in which case the notice of trial that had been served specifying trial by a judge with a jury would have been correct. In holding that the claim was partly for breach of contract and partly for conversion, O'Byrne J. applied the following test which had been laid down by Greer LJ in *Jarvis* v. *Moy, Davies, Smith, Vandervell & Co.* [[1936] 1 KB 194] at p. 405 of the report:—

> 'The distinction in the modern view, for this purpose, between contract and tort may be put thus: where the breach of duty alleged arises out of a liability independently of the personal obligation undertaken by contract, it is tort, and it may be tort even though there may happen to be a contract between the parties, if the duty in fact arises independently of that contract. Breach of contract occurs where that which is complained of is a breach of duty arising out of the obligations undertaken by the contract.'

… [T]he third High Court case to which we were referred is *Somers* v. *Erskine* [[1943] IR 348]. There the question was whether an action commenced by a client against a solicitor for negligence, and sought to be continued against the solicitor's personal representative, had abated with the solicitor's death as an action in tort, or whether it survived his death as an action in contract. In an unreserved judgment Maguire P. applied the same test as was applied by O'Byrne J. in *Liston* v. *Munster and Leinster Bank* [[1940] IR 77], and held that the client's claim was essentially one in contract rather than in tort and that, therefore, the claim had survived the solicitor's death. In my opinion, the conclusion that an action by a client against a solicitor for damages for breach of his professional duty of care is necessarily and exclusively one in contract is incompatible with modern developments in the law of torts and should be overruled. In my view, the conclusion there reached does not follow from a correct application of the test laid down by Greer LJ in the *Jarvis Case* [[1936] 1 KB 194] …

The test adumbrated by Greer LJ, which commended itself to O'Byrne J in *Liston* v. *Munster and Leinster Bank* [[1940] IR 77] and to Maguire P in *Somers* v. *Erskine* [[1943] IR 348], correctly draws a distinction between a claim arising out of an obligation deriving from, and owing its existence to, a personal obligation undertaken pursuant to a contract (in which case it is an action in contract) and a claim arising out of a liability created independently of a contract and not deriving from any special obligation imposed by a contract (in which case an action lies in tort). The action in tort derives from an obligation which is imposed by the general law and is applicable to all persons in a certain relationship to each other. The action in contract is founded on the special law which was created by a contract and which was designed to fit the particular relationship of that contract ...

It has to be conceded that for over a hundred years there has been a divergence of judicial opinion as to whether a client who has engaged a solicitor to act for him, and who claims that the solicitor failed to show due professional care and skill, may sue in tort or whether he is confined to an action in contract. In *Somers* v. *Erskine* [[1943] IR 348], (and in some English cases) it was held that the sole cause of action was the solicitor's failure to observe the implied term in the contract of retainer that he would show due professional skill and care. It is undeniable that the client is entitled to sue in contract for breach of that implied term. But it does not follow that the client, because there is privity of contract between him and the solicitor and because he may sue the solicitor for breach of the contract, is debarred from suing also for the tort of negligence. Since the decision of the House of Lords in *Hedley Byrne & Co. Ltd.* v. *Heller & Partners Ltd* [[1964] AC 65] and the cases following in its wake, it is clear that, whether a contractual relationship exists or not, once the circumstances are such that a defendant undertakes to show professional care and skill towards a person who may be expected to rely on such care and skill and who does so rely, then if he has been damnified by such default that person may sue the defendant in the tort of negligence for failure to show such care and skill. For the purpose of such an action, the existence of a contract is merely an incident of the relationship. If, on the one side, there is a proximity of relationship creating a general duty and, on the other, a reliance on that duty, it matters not whether the parties are bound together in contract. For instance, if the defendant in the present case had not been retained for reward but had merely volunteered his services to the plaintiff, his liability in negligence would be the same as if he was to be paid for his services. The coincidence that the defendant's conduct amounts to a breach of contract cannot affect either the duty of care or the common-law liability for its breach, for it is the general relationship, and not any particular manifestation such as a contract, that gives rise to the tortious liability in such a case: see *per* Lord Devlin in the *Hedley Byrne Case* [[1964] AC 465] at p. 530 of the report.

A comprehensive survey of the law governing the liability of a solicitor to his client in negligence is to be found in the judgment of Oliver J in *Midland Bank* v. *Hett, Stubbs & Kemp* [1979] CH 384], in which it was held that the solicitor's liability in tort exists independently of any liability in contract. That conclusion, which was reached at first instance and with which I agree, may be said to be reinforced by dicta in the judgments of the Court of Appeal in *Batty* v.

Metropolitan Realisations Ltd. [[1978] QB 554 and *Photo Production Ltd.* v. *Securicor Ltd* [1978] 1 WLR 856.

On a consideration of those cases and of the authorities mentioned in them, I am satisfied that the general duty of care created by the relationship of solicitor and client entitles the client to sue in negligence if he has suffered damage because of the solicitor's failure to show due professional care and skill, notwithstanding that the client could sue alternatively in contract for breach of the implied term in the contract of retainer that the solicitor will deal with the matter in hand with due professional care and skill. The solicitor's liability in tort under the general duty of care extends not only to a client for reward, but to any person for whom the solicitor undertakes to act professionally without reward, and also to those (such as beneficiaries under a will, persons entitled under an intestacy, or those entitled to benefits in circumstances such as a claim in respect of a fatal injury) with whom he has made no arrangement to act but who, as he knows or ought to know, will be relying on his professional care and skill. For the same default there should be the same cause of action. If others are entitled to sue in tort for the solicitor's want of care, so also should the client; that is so unless the solicitor's default arises not from a breach of the general duty of care arising from the relationship but from a breach of a particular and special term of the contract in respect of which the solicitor would not be liable if the contract had not contained such a term. Thus, if the client's instructions were that the solicitor was to issue proceedings within a specified time, or to close a sale by a particular date or, generally, to do or not to do some act, and the solicitor defaulted in that respect, any resulting right of action which the client might have would be in contract only unless the act or default complained of falls within the general duty of care owed by the solicitor.

The modern law of tort shows that the existence of a contractual relationship which impliedly deals with a particular act or omission is not, in itself, sufficient to rule out an action in tort in respect of that act or omission. For instance, in *Northern Bank Finance Corporation Ltd.* v. *Charlton* [[1979] IR 149 it was unanimously held by this Court that a customer of a bank can sue the bank for the tort of deceit where the deceit arises from fraudulent misrepresentations made by the bank in the course of carrying out the contract between the bank and the customer. The existence of a contract, for the breach of which he could have sued, did not oust the customer's cause of action in tort.

Therefore, I conclude that where, as in the instant case, the client's complaint is that he has been damnified by the solicitor's default in his general duty of care, the client is entitled to sue in negligence as well as for breach of contract. In the plaintiff's statement of claim, after reciting his accident and his retainer of the defendant as the solicitor to prosecute his claim for damages in respect of it, the plaintiff pleads that the defendant 'negligently failed to issue proceedings on behalf of the plaintiff in respect of the accident aforesaid within the time limited by the Statute of Limitations, 1957.' That was intended to be, and is, a claim in negligence. Such being the case, by virtue of the provisions of s. 94 of the Courts of Justice Act, 1924, as amended, the plaintiff was entitled to serve notice of a trial by a judge and jury. Mr. Justice D'Arcy was correct in refusing to set aside the notice of trial so served. I would dismiss this appeal."

MEDICAL NEGLIGENCE

Duty of care

As is evident from the decision in *Finlay v Murtagh* [1979] I.R. 249, professionals may owe a duty of care in tort as well as in contract. To whom do they owe the duty of care? It is clear that a medical practitioner owes a duty of care to his/her patient, but this duty can also extend to people not party to that relationship. In *Dunne v National Maternity Hospital and Reginald Jackson* [1989] I.R. 91 a doctor was held to owe a duty of care to his patient's unborn twins. In *Allen v Ó Suilleabháin & Mid-Western Health Board,* unreported, High Court, July 28, 1995, one issue before the court was to whom the doctor owed a duty of care.

Allen v Ó Suilleabháin and Mid-Western Health Board
High Court unreported, July 28, 1995

Facts: The plaintiff to this action was a student seeking a qualification in midwifery. The second named defendant employed the plaintiff, and the first named defendant, Mr Ó Suilleabháin, was the senior obstetrician. The delivery ward was quite busy at the time of the accident. A patient was pregnant with twins; the first was delivered with no complications, but there were some difficulties with the second birth. Mr Ó Suilleabháin, in attempting to deliver the second twin, declined the use of the stirrups that were available. Instead, he required the plaintiff and a doctor to hold up the legs of the patient and to hold them in the same position as if stirrups were used. The patient was in a lot of pain and was pushing with her leg; there was also an imbalance as the doctor appeared to have no difficulty on his side. The plaintiff was in great pain and suffered a back injury.

Issue: Did the first named defendant owe the plaintiff a duty of care? It was held that he did owe the plaintiff a duty of care and that she was entitled to damages for the injuries sustained by her.

Kinlen J.:

"... There was evidence that this accident was entirely foreseeable. It should be anticipated that a patient would be moving and the use of stirrups would be more effective in controlling her. Standard practice ought not to put the midwife at risk. It is totally predictable that the patient will move and could cause injury. One matron went so far as to say that midwives should not be trained to cope with something which should not arise. Holding a leg of a woman in labour carries a very significant risk to anyone holding the leg. The patient may kick violently and suddenly and it is foreseeable that she may cause damage. It is mainly a question for management. Several features emerged from the evidence. Firstly, many midwives have been injured in the past by allowing a foot or leg to rest on the midwife's hip or from holding the leg. Midwives are now a strong profession. The use of stirrups is normal and usual. In some hospitals there have been rules (either written or unwritten) prohibiting holding, lifting or cradling a patient's leg or foot. However, one doctor states that he always delivers in the lateral position but this still requires a midwife to hold a leg.

It is a matter requiring urgent attention. It is for management in consultation with all parties to lay down the guidelines. Midwives should not be expected to support a bucking leg. However, it is significant that the rule of using stirrups exclusively, or at least normally, was not known to another senior midwife in Limerick Hospital.

It was not known at all by any of the obstetricians who gave evidence. There was great talk about team work. The obstetrician is the overall captain with overall responsibility. However, the senior midwife in the theatre or delivery ward is in charge of the midwifery services. The midwives are now treated, as indeed they should always have been, as a highly skilled and important group of professional people. However, there is a clear break down in communications. The midwives apparently decided they would not take any orders from consultants requiring them to endanger themselves. However, the Plaintiff here knew nothing of these rules nor did the obstetrician. Also, the senior midwives who gave evidence stated that if they were directed by the doctor to do so, they would—but 'under protest'. It is for the management to see that the various professions understand, not merely their own duties, but also their inter-relationship with other participants in the labour ward and in the operating theatre. It is not for the Court to lay down what these should be. It is purely a matter for management. The nurses and midwives are not there merely to facilitate the consultant.

The obstetrician owes a very real duty, not merely to the patient and unborn baby, but to the staff assisting. The arrogance of some consultants in the past has become legendary. It is regrettable that in the present case the obstetrician blamed the Plaintiff's accident on the patient! In the current case there was tension and time was moving fairly rapidly. It was not yet a full-blown emergency but it had the potential to become one. Professionals in conjunction with each other should have a management plan to cope not merely with what is normal but also foreseeable risks if there is tension or pressure or an emergency.

… Under the principles of 'the good neighbour' he certainly owed a duty to the Plaintiff."

Standard of care

The major distinction between a claim in general negligence and a claim for medical negligence is evident in the standard of care. In general negligence a person is expected to act in a manner in which a reasonable person with reasonable foresight and intelligence would. A medical practitioner is not necessarily negligent if his/her patient does not recover or dies. Perfection is not required; the essential test is whether the doctor behaved reasonably. The standard of care required by medical practitioners has been addressed in a number of decisions, for example, *Daniels v Heskin* [1954] I.R. 73.

Daniels v Heskin
Supreme Court [1954] I.R. 73

Facts: The plaintiff gave birth and after the birth, while she was being stitched by the doctor, the surgical needle broke, leaving about one-and-a-half inches of a needle buried deep in the plaintiff's perineum. The doctor searched for the needle but failed to retrieve it, and so left it in the patient advising the nurses to observe the patient, but no specific reference was made to the needle in his instructions. Neither the plaintiff nor her husband were informed of the needle. Every time the plaintiff bent down she claimed she felt as though a wire was inside her; some six weeks after birth she was X-rayed on the instructions of the nurse, and some two weeks later she was operated on and the needle was removed.

Issue: In this case the court reviewed the standard of care with which a medical practitioner should comply; they also reviewed the duty to disclose information to a patient. The following extract will address the issue of the standard of care; the issue of the duty to disclose is discussed later in this chapter. The patient failed to establish that the doctor was negligent in his actions and the case was accordingly dismissed.

Maguire C.J.:

"… A medical practitioner is liable for injury caused to another person to whom he owes a duty to take care if he fails to possess that amount of skill which is usual in his profession or if he neglects to use the skill which he possesses or the necessary degree of care demanded or professed. This statement is taken from Halsbury's Laws of England, vol. 21, at para 634, and appears to me correctly to summarise the law. It is conceded that the defendant did owe to the plaintiff, Mrs. Daniels, a duty to take care."

Lavery J. (Murnaghan and O'Byrne JJ. concurring):

"… The defendant undertook to treat the female plaintiff, to whom I shall hereafter refer as the plaintiff, as a medical man and he is responsible for damage caused by his treatment if he did not possess in a reasonable measure the skill necessary to perform what he undertook or if, possessing such skill, he failed to employ it with reasonable care …"

Kingsmill Moore J.:

"… A doctor owes certain well recognised duties to his patient. He must possess such knowledge and skill as conforms to the recognised contemporary standards of his profession and, if he is a specialist, such further and particularised skill and knowledge as he holds himself out to possess. He must use such skill and knowledge to form an honest and considered judgment as to what course, what action, what treatment, is in the best interests of his patient. He must display proper care and attention in treating, or in arranging suitable treatment for, his patient. Any attempt to substitute a rule of law, or even a rule of thumb practice, for the individual judgment of a qualified doctor, doing what he considers best for the particular patient, would be disastrous. There may be cases where the judgment of the physician is proved by subsequent events to have been wrong, but if it is honest and considered and if, in the circumstances known to him at the time, it can fairly be justified, he is not guilty of negligence. There may indeed be cases where the nature of the judgment formed or the advice given is such as to afford positive evidence that the physician has fallen short of the required standard of knowledge and skill, or that his judgment could not have been honest and considered, but it lies on the plaintiff to adduce evidence from which such a failure of duty can reasonably be inferred."

The Supreme Court in *Dunne v National Maternity Hospital* [1989] I.R. 91 established the authoritative statement as to the standard of care expected of medical practitioners in this jurisdiction and as to what constitutes a "general and approved practice". The Supreme Court attempted to achieve a balance between the necessity of medical practitioners to practice without constant fear of litigation and the rights of patients to an adequate standard of care in their treatment and diagnosis.

Dunne v National Maternity Hospital and Reginald Jackson
Supreme Court [1989] I.R. 91

Facts: The mother of the plaintiff was, at the time of the alleged negligence, pregnant with twins. During the labour the defendants only monitored one foetal heart, which was hospital policy. It was difficult to monitor both hearts, and it was felt that as they were in the same environment, monitoring one foetal heart was sufficient. In this case the plaintiff was severely brain-damaged and his twin was stillborn.

Issues: The court addressed the issue of the standard of care expected of a medical practitioner, reviewing the use of general and approved practices, inherent defects in such practices, and a divergence in schools of thought between practitioners. The court upheld the appeal by the defendants as regards the quantum of the award, and on one point of the trial judges' charge to the jury, and remitted the matter for a retrial. They also held, significantly, that the failure to monitor both foetal hearts amounted to a deviation from a general and approved practice.

Finlay C.J. (Griffin and Hederman JJ. concurring):

"… The courts have consistently recognised certain features in the general law of negligence which have particular reference to allegations of negligence made against professional persons in the carrying out of their professional duties. These particular features applicable to allegations of medical negligence have been fully set out by this Court in *O'Donovan v. Cork County Council* [1967] IR 173, which adopted and followed the decision of the former Supreme Court in *Daniels v. Heskin* [1954] IR 73. The reasoning of *O'Donovan v. Cork County Council* was expressly followed by this Court in *Reeves v. Carthy & O'Kelly* [1984] IR 348. It was again approved and applied to a case of professional negligence by a solicitor in *Roche v. Peilow* [1985] IR 232. There was no argument submitted to us on the hearing of this appeal which constituted any form of challenge to the correctness of the statements of principle thus laid down, although there was controversy concerning their application to the facts of this case. The principles thus laid down related to the issues raised in this case can in this manner be summarised.

1. The true test for establishing negligence in diagnosis or treatment on the part of a medical practitioner is whether he has been proved to be guilty of such failure as no medical practitioner of equal specialist or general status and skill would be guilty of if acting with ordinary care.
2. If the allegation of negligence against a medical practitioner is based on proof that he deviated from a general and approved practice, that will not establish negligence unless it is also proved that the course he did take was one which no medical practitioner of like specialisation and skill would have followed had he been taking the ordinary care required from a person of his qualifications.
3. If a medical practitioner charged with negligence defends his conduct by establishing that he followed a practice which was general, and which was

approved of by his colleagues of similar specialisation and skill, he cannot escape liability if in reply the plaintiff establishes that such practice has inherent defects which ought to be obvious to any person giving the matter due consideration.

4. An honest difference of opinion between doctors as to which is the better of two ways of treating a patient does not provide any ground for leaving a question to the jury as to whether a person who has followed one course rather than the other has been negligent.

5. It is not for a jury (or for a judge) to decide which of two alternative courses of treatment is in their (or his) opinion preferable, but their (or his) function is merely to decide whether the course of treatment followed, on the evidence, complied with the careful conduct of a medical practitioner of like specialisation and skill to that professed by the defendant.

6. If there is an issue of fact, the determination of which is necessary for the decision as to whether a particular medical practice is or is not general and approved within the meaning of these principles, that issue must in a trial held with a jury be left to the determination of the jury.

In order to make these general principles readily applicable to the facts of this case, with which I will later be dealing, it is necessary to state further conclusions not expressly referred to in the cases above mentioned. These are:

(a) 'General and approved practice' need not be universal but must be approved of and adhered to by a substantial number of reputable practitioners holding the relevant specialist or general qualifications.

(b) Though treatment only is referred to in some of these statements of principle, they must apply in identical fashion to questions of diagnosis.

(c) In an action against a hospital, where allegations are made of negligence against the medical administrators on the basis of a claim that practices and procedures laid down by them for the carrying out of treatment or diagnosis by medical or nursing staff were defective, their conduct is to be tested in accordance with the legal principles which would apply if they had personally carried out such treatment or diagnosis in accordance with such practice or procedure.

In order fully to understand these principles and their application to any particular set of facts, it is, I believe, helpful to set out certain broad parameters which would appear to underline their establishment. The development of medical science and the supreme importance of that development to humanity makes it particularly undesirable and inconsistent with the common good that doctors should be obliged to carry out their professional duties under frequent threat of unsustainable legal claims. The complete dependence of patients on the skill and care of their medical attendants and the gravity from their point of view of a failure in such care, makes it undesirable and unjustifiable to accept as a matter of law a lax or permissive standard of care for the purpose of assessing what is and is not medical negligence. In developing the legal principles outlined and in applying them to the facts of each individual case, the courts must constantly seek to give equal regard to both of these considerations."

Comments and Questions:
1. What are the elements necessary to show medical negligence?

2. The authoritative statement on medical negligence makes reference to questions to be left to the jury; what impact does the abolition of jury trials have on this authority?

3. How did the court define a "general and approved practice"?

General and approved practice

The English courts have held that where a medical practitioner follows a "general and approved practice" this may offer a defence. A "general and approved practice" is one which: is accepted as proper by a "responsible body of medical men" and a "standard of practice recognised as proper by a competent reasonable body of opinion": *Bolam v Friern Hospital Management Committee* [1957] 2 All E.R. 108; and refers to a "respectable body of professional opinion": *Maynard v West Midlands Regional Health Authority* [1984] 1 W.L.R. 634. As can be seen from the decision in *Dunne v National Maternity Hospital* [1989] I.R. 91, a medical practitioner will generally be afforded a defence where that practitioner follows a general and approved practice. The limitation with this defence is where such a practice contains an inherent defect. This issue was addressed in the case of *Collins v Mid-Western Health Board* [2000] 2 I. R. 154.

Collins v Mid-Western Health Board
Supreme Court [2000] 2 I.R. 154

Facts: The plaintiff's husband was taken ill and attended a general practitioner (second defendant), who was not his family doctor; the doctor was informed by the plaintiff that her husband was a reluctant patient. He was diagnosed with an upper respiratory tract infection and over the next few days his condition did not improve. A second examination elicited a history of "headaches". The family doctor on examining the patient arranged for his immediate admission to hospital. When the plaintiff's husband presented at the hospital (first named defendant), a junior doctor held that the plaintiff's husband needed further examination by a specialist, and sent him home. The plaintiff's husband suffered a severe brain haemorrhage the following day and died a short time later.

Issues: The plaintiff claimed negligence by the hospital in their refusal to admit her husband, and also against the first general practitioner in his failure to properly diagnose the patient's condition. The issues before the court related to the standard of care that a patient should expect from a general practitioner (see extract from this case below under Categories of Practitioner) and also whether the system of admissions operated by the hospital was a "medical practice". The court allowed the appeal and permitted the plaintiff to recover in negligence.

Barron J. (Hamilton C.J., Barrington and Lynch JJ. concurring):

"… [Dr Nur is the representative of the hospital, the first named defendant]. The case for the plaintiff is that Dr Nur should have admitted the deceased as an inpatient. At the time of his examination in the casualty department of the hospital Dr Nur was aware that Dr O'Brien had formed the opinion that the deceased should be referred for expert opinion. Accordingly, he started his examination with this knowledge …

He formed the opinion that the deceased required further examination. It did not seem to him that there was a matter of extreme urgency …

What is significant is the authority vested in Dr Nur a senior house officer in the accident and emergency ward. While he could refuse admission, he could not admit a patient without a second opinion. Again, Dr O'Brien's letter referred to the possibility of something sinister underlying the deceased's symptoms. But Dr Nur did not seek a further opinion, there was no evidence that if he had called in someone more senior that any different opinion would have been expressed by his senior. It might even be said that he took the same view as Dr O'Brien but differed from Dr O'Brien as to the circumstances in which the further examination of the deceased should take place.

It seems to me that any system which gives absolute authority to a junior doctor is inadvisable. By its very nature the position of a senior house officer is one where the holder is learning his profession. He must meet from time to time cases with which he is not familiar and in which he would welcome the opinion of a senior. If he is given absolute authority there is a danger that he may miss things which his seniors would not. I do not seek to impose greater liability on hospitals than is necessary. House officers should not be required to look over their shoulders on every occasion that a patient is brought to casualty. An absolute authority is inadvisable. It is a matter for the hospital authorities themselves to indicate a scheme to provide under what circumstances a house officer would be required to seek the advice of somebody more senior. In the present case, a member of the medical team might well have taken a different view.

It seems to me that the problem really arose from the system which gave Dr Nur such an absolute authority to refuse admission. All the indications were that he ought to have referred the deceased to the medical team having regard in particular to the letter from Dr O'Brien. In my view he was wrong not to do so. He was, in effect, ignoring Dr O'Brien's concerns and treating the case as calling solely for his own diagnosis. Perhaps he felt himself bound by the system in which case it is the authors of the system who must take the blame. In either case, there was breach of the duty of care for which the first defendant is liable …

The tort of negligence is not committed until there is both a breach of duty and loss flowing from it. Although I have used the word negligent to describe conduct in breach of a duty to take care, that was a colloquial use of the word. Whether loss flowed from the breaches of care which have been identified and, if so, to what extent was expressly left over by the parties to be determined only in the event of breach of duty being established. This has now been established. Accordingly, I would allow the appeal and remit the matter to the High Court to determine whether loss flowed from the breaches of duty …"

Keane J. (Hamilton C.J., Barrington J. and Lynch JJ. concurring):

"… In *Dunne v The National Maternity Hospital* [1989] IR 91, Finlay CJ, speaking for the court, set out the principles of law which are applicable to allegations of medical negligence. In particular, the learned Chief Justice said at p.109 that:—

> 'If a medical practitioner charged with negligence defends his conduct by establishing that he followed a practice which was general, and which was approved of by his colleagues of similar specialisation and skill, he cannot escape liability if in reply the plaintiff establishes that such practice has inherent defects which ought to be obvious to any person giving the matter due consideration.'

It can, I think, be safely said that, in general, a lay tribunal will be reluctant to condemn as unsafe a practice which has been universally approved in a particular profession. The defects in a practice universally followed by specialists in the field are unlikely to be as obvious as the test requires: if they were, it is a reasonable assumption that it would not be so followed. But the principle, which was first stated by the court in *O'Donovan v Cork County Council* [1967] IR 173, is an important reminder that, ultimately, the courts must reserve the power to find as unsafe practices which have been generally followed in a profession.

In the case of the first defendant, however, the court is not concerned with a medical practice as such. The allegation against the first defendant is that, under the admissions system operated in the hospital, Dr Nur, a senior house surgeon, was allowed to substitute his own judgment as to whether the plaintiff's husband required admission and investigation as a matter of urgency for the judgment already arrived at by an experienced general practitioner, Dr Maurice O'Brien, that he did. The claim that the first defendant was negligent and in breach of its duty to the deceased in operating such a system cannot be refuted, in my view, simply by demonstrating that it is a system in use in at least some other hospitals in these islands …

A system, which, according to the defendant's own evidence, allowed a junior hospital doctor, although admittedly one at a relatively senior level, effectively to disregard the opinion of an experienced general practitioner that his patient required further investigation as a matter of urgency without even obtaining an opinion from a doctor at a more senior level, clearly suffered from an inherent defect which should have been obvious to any person giving it due consideration. It cannot be equated to a medical practice followed by specialists in a particular field. The letter from Dr O'Brien should, in my view, have been sufficient to ensure that the plaintiff's husband was admitted for the investigation that his general practitioner correctly thought he urgently required and particular procedures applicable in the hospital for the admission of patients should not have prevented that happening …

I am satisfied that the appeal against the judgment dismissing the claim as against the first defendant must, for those reasons, be allowed …"

Categories of practitioners

There is not one general standard of care for all medical practitioners. A medical practitioner who holds himself or herself out as having a particular skill or expertise will be judged according to the same standards as others professing to have the same skill or expertise. This was addressed in *O'Donovan v Cork County Council* [1967] I.R. 173.

O'Donovan v Cork County Council
Supreme Court [1967] I.R. 173

Facts: The plaintiff's husband underwent surgery to have his appendix removed. There were complications during surgery and the patient suffered symptoms of ether convulsions, a very rare condition. The doctors present made efforts to stop the convulsions; the anaesthetist did not, however, administer a relaxant drug, which was part of the accepted procedure in such circumstances, because he did not think of doing so. The convulsions continued and the patient died. The anaesthetist was highly experienced, and no question arose in respect of the administration of the anaesthetic; the issue arose in his response to the very rare condition of ether convulsions.

Issues: The plaintiff brought an action claiming damages for the negligence of the defendants. This case is an appeal from the trial court's decision. The Supreme Court addressed a number of points, including the standard of care expected. The court held that this depends to a large extent on the degree of expertise that the professional holds themselves up as possessing. Therefore, a consultant would be compared with another consultant, a general practitioner with a general practitioner. The court also referred to the fact that reliance on a general and approved practice will not offer a defence where there are inherent defects in that practice.

Walsh J. (Ó Dálaigh C.J. concurring):

"... A medical practitioner who holds himself out as being a specialist in a particular field is required to attain to the ordinary level of skill amongst those who specialise in the same field. He is not required to attain to the highest degree of skill and competence in that particular field.

It was also alleged against Dr. O'Brien [anaesthetist] that he was lacking in care both in his preparations for the operation and in his conduct when the emergency arose. A medical practitioner's conduct so far as care is concerned is to be judged in the light of the particular circumstances prevailing at the time when he is called upon to act, and the degree of care required may vary in proportion to the magnitude of the risk involved ...

A medical practitioner cannot be held negligent if he follows general and approved practice in the situation with which he is faced: see *Daniels* v. *Heskin* [1954] IR 73 and the cases referred to therein.

That proposition is not, however, without qualification. If there is a common practice which has inherent defects, which ought to be obvious to any person giving the matter due consideration, the fact that it is shown to have been widely and generally adopted over a period of time does not make the practice any the less negligent. Neglect of duty does not cease by repetition to be neglect of duty. Furthermore, if there be a dispute of fact as to whether or not a particular practice is a general and approved practice, it is a matter for the jury to determine whether or not the impugned treatment is general and approved practice. In such circumstances a jury would be told that if they find that there is such a general and approved practice they must acquit the practitioner where there is not the qualification which I have referred to above.

If some witnesses say that a particular practice is a general and approved one and other medical witnesses deny that, then it is an issue of fact to be determined as any other issue of fact. This particular issue cannot be withdrawn from a jury merely because the practice finds support among some medical witnesses if there be others who deny the fact that it is general and approved practice ...

So far as the second period was concerned, the allegation against Mr. Hurley [surgeon] deals with his responsibility for the administration of the anaesthetics and the treatment of the convulsions which was really a matter within the field of anaesthetics ... A surgeon is entitled to rely on the careful administration of the anaesthetics by a skilled and competent anaesthetist and he is entitled to assume that the anaesthetist is skilled and competent until he has a reason to believe otherwise ...

The risk of ether convulsions developing is a risk inherent in the use of ether itself. In the use of ether it is a foreseeable though unavoidable risk. As in the case of all risks, a degree of care is required of the person undertaking the risk but the degree of care varies in proportion to the magnitude of the risk involved. On all available experience the risk of ether convulsions, while always present, is very slight because the condition is one of extreme rarity. Nevertheless a person undertaking to administer ether and holding himself out as having the necessary skill to do so must also be required to know how to deal with ether convulsions should that condition arise ...

I turn now to consider the allegations made in respect of Dr. O'Brien's conduct after the onset of the convulsions ... While it is a very rare condition, it is one which is referred to in the current standard text-books as one of the recognised risks in the administration of ether. When a patient develops ether convulsions it produces a shortage of oxygen because of the interference with the respiration caused by the convulsions and that condition of anoxia, if it is allowed to continue sufficiently long, would cause permanent brain damage and, unless he gets oxygen quickly enough and in sufficient quantities, the patient will inevitably die.

It was generally agreed by all the medical witnesses that the treatment must be very prompt and be as follows:— (*a*) to cut off the ether, (*b*) to get oxygen into the lungs and into the tissues and (*c*) to stop the convulsions if they have not passed off. It was also agreed that the general and accepted practice of achieving this result was, first to cut off or withdraw the ether; secondly, to administer a relaxant drug or, if the condition of the patient permitted it, an anticonvulsant drug so as to permit the entry of the oxygen into the lungs and the tissues if that was being rendered impossible by the convulsions or, if after initial entry, it was then being impeded by the convulsions; thirdly, the entry of the oxygen itself; and, fourthly, an anti-convulsant to stop the convulsions if they had not already stopped after the intake of the oxygen, after the relaxant had worn off ...

In my view on the evidence it was open to the jury to hold that there was a general and approved practice applicable to the condition of the patient in question in this case and it is not disputed that Dr. O'Brien did not follow that particular practice. That, of course, does not conclude the matter because before he could be found guilty of negligence it would have to be established that the course which he did take was one which no anaesthetist of ordinary skill would have taken had he been taking the ordinary care required from an anaesthetist ..."

Lavery J. (dissents on the issue of negligence of the anaesthetist):

"... The question of negligence on the part of a medical man has been examined in this Court in the case of *Daniels* v. *Heskin* [1954] IR 73. In the course of my judgment in that case I said at p. 79 of the report:—'The defendant was bound to possess and use reasonable skill, having regard to his position as a general practitioner and in the circumstances of the particular case. If I may quote Maugham L.J. in the case of *Marshall* v. *Lindsey County Council* [1935] I KB 516, 551:—"I refer to his evidence as an illustration of the fact that in this matter, as in so many others, the doctors differ, and in the presence of this undoubted honest difference of opinion it is not open in my opinion to a jury to hold that it is negligent to accept one view rather than the other."' I stated that this was my view of the law and with this judgment Murnaghan J. and O'Byrne J. agreed. Kingsmill Moore J., in a separate judgment, was of the same opinion; at p. 85 of the report he said:—'I should like to say with emphasis that an honest difference of opinion between eminent doctors, as to which is the better of two ways of treating a patient, does not provide any ground for leaving a question to the jury as to whether a person who has followed one course rather than the other has been guilty of negligence.' Maguire C.J., who differed in opinion on another issue, said at p. 76 of the report:—'As regards the first head of negligence [which was alleged negligence in the manner of operating] I am of opinion that there is no evidence upon which the jury could hold that the breaking of the needle was due to negligence on the part of the defendant. The second head of negligence is that the defendant failed to remove the broken needle promptly from the body of Mrs. Daniels. From the expert evidence which on this point was in agreement, two courses were open …' The Chief Justice described them and continued:—'The latter was the course adopted by the defendant and from the expert evidence given it is clear that to adopt either course is in accordance with accepted medical practice.'

There was therefore no difference of opinion in the Court on the standard to be applied in considering whether a medical man had been negligent in the treatment of a patient.

In the year 1955 the Court of Session in Scotland considered a similar question in *Hunter* v. *Hanley* [1955 SC 200]. *Daniels' Case* [[1954] IR 73] was not cited. It may be that notwithstanding the date of the report stated it had not in fact been published at the time.

I quote from the judgment of Lord President Clyde at p. 204 of the report:— 'To succeed in an action based on negligence, whether against a doctor or against anyone else, it is of course necessary to establish a breach of that duty to take care which the law requires, and the degree of want of care which constitutes negligence must vary with the circumstances—*Caswell* v. *Powell Duffryn Associated Collieries* [[1940] AC 152] per Lord Wright at pp. 175–6. But where the conduct of a doctor, or indeed of any professional man, is concerned, the circumstances are not so precise and clear cut as in the normal case. In the realm of diagnosis and treatment there is ample scope for genuine difference of opinion and one man clearly is not negligent merely because his conclusion differs from that of other professional men, nor because he has displayed less skill or knowledge than others would have shown. The true test for establishing negligence in diagnosis or treatment on the part of a doctor is whether he has been proved to be guilty of such failure as no doctor of ordinary skill would be guilty of if acting with ordinary care—Glegg, Reparation (3rd Ed.), p. 509. The standard seems to be the same in England—Salmond, Torts (11th Ed.), p. 511.' At p. 206 the Lord President continues:—'Even a substantial deviation from normal practice may be warranted by the particular circumstances. To establish liability by a doctor where deviation from normal practice is alleged, three facts require to be established. First of all it must be proved that there is a usual and normal practice; secondly it must be proved that the defender has not adopted that practice; and thirdly (and this is of crucial importance) it must be established that the course the doctor adopted is one which no professional man of ordinary skill would have taken if he had been acting with ordinary care.'

The principle is therefore well settled and is the same in the Courts of England, Scotland and Ireland. The course of events and the conduct and actions of the two defendants Surgeon Hurley and Dr. O'Brien, which appears in the evidence, is to be judged on this principle ...

[Lavery J. sets out the detail in relation to the conflicting evidence in respect of how the anaesthetist dealt with the crisis when it arose:]

Evidence was given by a number of medical men of the highest standing both on the surgical aspect of the case and in relation to the anaesthesia. On many points there was a definite conflict of opinion. There is no doubt about the qualifications of all the witnesses to express an opinion under the principles laid down in the cases to which I have referred. The issue is whether it was proper to submit to a jury the choice of which of two differing views they should accept. The defendants can only be held liable if there is evidence that they acted or failed to act otherwise than in a manner approved by a responsible body of opinion ...

This summary of the evidence ... in my opinion correctly states its effect. Mr. Justice Walsh takes a different view which he explains.

In my opinion the learned trial judge should have withdrawn the case from the jury and directed a verdict in favour of all the defendants. I consider, therefore, that the appeal should be allowed and that the action should be dismissed."

Comments and Questions:

1. Lavery J. dissented on the issue of liability of the anaesthetist; what were the reasons for his dissent? Compare the decisions of Walsh J. and Lavery J. on this point.

2. Where there is an honest difference of opinion between doctors, who determines which is the correct position to take?

As the court established in *O'Donovan v Cork County Council* [1976] I.R. 173, the standard of care required of a particular medical practitioner is that he possess and use reasonable skill having regard to the expertise he holds himself out as having. In *O'Doherty v Whelan*, Prof. Neg. L.R. 440, High Court, January 1993, a general practitioner was found to have failed in his duty to his patient by not responding to a call-out to a patient's house. The response was inadequate having regard to the particular circumstances of the case. The duty of general practitioners is more than a duty to hear what the patient has to say, but also to question the patient, and to take on board contact from family members as was seen in the case of *Collins v Mid-Western Health Board* [2000] 2 I.R. 154.

Collins v Mid-Western Health Board
Supreme Court [2000] 2 I.R. 154

Facts and issues: see above.

Barron J. (Hamilton C.J., Barrington, Keane and Lynch JJ. concurring):

"... The deceased had just suffered a serious traumatic experience and his first reaction as he felt well enough to go home was to want to consult a doctor. It was to be expected that when he saw the doctor he would have told him of the sudden and appalling headache and the manner of its onset and said 'What is wrong with me Doctor?' This did not happen. The nearest he got to telling the actual history was to tell the doctor that he had felt unwell at work.

While this is surprising, it is probably accounted for by several factors. The deceased was unaccustomed to visiting a doctor. By the time he did visit the second defendant he had recovered sufficiently to go to him on his own. The manner in which the second defendant conducted his surgery visits was in his own words:—

> 'when I see a new patient, when I have the drug history, allergies and that taken, I sit back in my chair and say "right, what is the problem. What can I do for you" and give the patient the opportunity to tell me what the problem his. His headache was one of a number of complaints on the first occasion. It was the main complaint on the second occasion.' ...

Having found that the second defendant was not told of the sudden onset of headache and that he had no reason as a result of his surgery consultation to go beyond his diagnosis of URTI, the learned trial judge found that in the course of that visit the second defendant had asked all the correct questions.

This finding was made in the light of the expert medical evidence that a general practitioner at a surgery visit had an obligation not only to listen to what the patient said but also to ask appropriate questions. This is in effect no more than a reiteration of the general principle that it is the duty of a professional person to satisfy himself or herself that he or she knows what is being asked of them and that it is proper in the interest of the patient or client to act on such instructions.

In the present case, the question arises as to whether the learned trial judge took too narrow a construction of the obligation of the general practitioner by confining it to what he was told by his patient at the surgery visit and not taking into account the circumstances under which he came to his surgery. These were the apparent urgency as expressed by the telephone call from the plaintiff inquiring whether he was still seeing patients as well as what was actually said by the plaintiff. Having asked the doctor to wait a few minutes she told him: 'Jim has a very bad headache. He does not usually go to doctors. He must be very bad.' ...

The effect of the evidence suggests that simple questions should be asked whenever pain is a significant presenting feature and that a doctor cannot rely only on what he has been told when it is reasonable to ask further questions. It also suggests that where there are inconsistencies between what the doctor is told and what he finds this is a further ground for making further inquiry ... [Barron J. sets out the position of the trial judge] ...

It is clear that the essence of the findings is that they were made having regard to the condition of the deceased at the time and that they were not made having regard to the contents or fact of the telephone call which preceded the first visit ...

The issue in this case is really a very simple one. It was accepted by the second defendant that he knew the significance of sudden onset of severe headache. If the questions had been asked, it is inconceivable that he would not have been told of the sudden onset. So the real issue is, should questions have been asked about headache ...

The second defendant was not expected to make the correct diagnosis. But he was expected to be in a position to know when his patient should be referred to a specialist. Undoubtedly, on both examinations there were negative findings which would have suggested that there was nothing seriously wrong. Nevertheless, history was said to be 80% of diagnosis. So that if no proper history in the sense of correct questions is taken the chance of an accurate diagnosis or decision to refer is seriously restricted.

The second defendant may well have failed to see the significance of the fact that the deceased was someone who did not go to doctors. There does not however seem to be any justification for his failure to follow up on the question of headaches having regard to the telephone call which he received from the plaintiff. Had he done so, he must have discovered that there was a sudden onset of headache from which on his own admission he would have known what the problem was.

In the present case, a question arises as to whether the second defendant was entitled to rely upon what he was told by the deceased. Obviously yes, but that did not absolve him from asking questions to establish that his patient had left nothing out that he as a doctor would have considered material to a proper diagnosis. Here, the information was given in reply to 'tell me all about it'. While that must be a good starting point, it should not be the finishing point also. He has to be satisfied that the patient has left out nothing which might be of significance to the doctor. Simple questions would probably be all that was necessary to satisfy the doctor that what he has been told does not mask anything else.

The visit was not just a simple surgery visit. It was preceded by a telephone call suggesting urgency and which at the same time gave him two further pieces of information, first, that his condition was likely to be serious because he didn't go to doctors, and secondly, that the principal symptom was severe headache. Even without the added element of urgency both these matters needed to be taken into account. Neither was the obvious element of urgency. In my view, to be satisfied with the diagnosis of URTI was negligence.

While the second defendant did ask specifically about headaches subsequently, he persisted with his diagnosis notwithstanding that the answers he was given tended to deny the diagnosis ...

The questions to be asked are, did the doctor do all that could reasonably be expected of a reasonably prudent general practitioner exercising ordinary care and, if not, would what he should have done have led to a correct diagnosis either by him or by a specialist to whom he would have been referred.

For the reasons which I have already indicated the second defendant failed the test on the first question. He did so on the 20th February and equally on the 23rd and the 25th. If he had not so failed the correct diagnosis would have been made probably by him but certainly following tests directed by a specialist to whom the deceased would have been referred ...

In the course of submissions, counsel for the plaintiff referred to a Canadian authority *Dale v Munthali* (1977) 78 D.L.R. (3d) 588. In that case, a general practitioner was found negligent in failing to realise that his patient's illness—subsequently diagnosed to be meningitis—was something more than flu. One of the grounds for such finding was that the doctor should have questioned both the patient and his wife more thoroughly concerning the high fever that had existed prior to his visit.

In *Langley v Campbell* (The Times, 5th November, 1975), a general practitioner was found negligent because he failed to consider the possibility that his patient, an Englishman who had recently returned from Uganda, could be suffering from a tropical disease—malaria. He had diagnosed flu, the symptoms being fever, headache and alternative sweating and shivering. The trial judge in reaching his decision accepted evidence from members of the patient's family that the doctor had been told that the patient had just returned from Uganda and that he had suffered from malaria previously.

This type of case depends upon its own facts. Nevertheless, both these cases show that the trial judge regarded as material what the patient said to the doctor, but also what he was or might have been told by his spouse or other family member.

I agree with that view. Where, as here, information is supplied by someone other than the patient whether in arranging the consultation or before or after a visit, it should be taken into account and, if necessary, further questions asked. This is particularly so when, as here, there is a discrepancy between what is said by the patient on the one hand and the family member on the other. The failure to heed what was said by the plaintiff in each of her three telephone calls and to follow it up was negligence.

The two cases to which I have referred both acknowledge the importance of what a doctor is told by relatives. I agree entirely. Such information is important. The weight to be given to it is a matter for the doctor, but it should not be completely ignored ..."

INFORMED CONSENT

Touching without consent is a battery; if that consent has been received as a result of incomplete information, then that consent is invalid. Most early actions in medical negligence were taken in battery; however, it is thought that negligence rather than battery is the more appropriate form of action: *Walsh v Family Planning Services* [1992] 1 I.R. 496 followed the Canadian decision of *Reibl v Hughes,* 114 D.L.R. (3d) 1, which stated that actions in battery should be confined to a complete absence of consent. The question this raises is whether a failure to inform a patient of potential risks, significant or otherwise, with regard to proposed treatment, amounts to negligence in the performance of a doctor's duty. If the duty to disclose risks is an issue of negligence, what is the test to determine whether the doctor has complied with that test? Three principle tests have been espoused.

The three tests

The first test is known as the *Bolam* test; this test determines that the decision of what to tell the patient is primarily a medical issue. Therefore, the decision of what information to give to a patient is an issue of medical judgment.

Bolam v Friern Hospital Management Committee
Queen's Bench Division [1957] 2 All E.R. 118,
[1957] 1 W.L.R. 582, 1 B.M.L.R. 1

Facts: The plaintiff to the action was suffering from mental illness and was advised to undergo electro-convulsive therapy. He signed a consent form to the treatment, but was not warned of the risk of fracture. There was evidence that the risk of fracture was small. The plaintiff did not receive a relaxant drug which would have excluded the risk of fracture. There were two bodies of medical opinion, one favouring the use of relaxants and the other confining its use to cases where there was a particular reason for their use; this was not such a case. The plaintiff, as a result of this treatment, sustained severe physical injuries consisting in the dislocation of both hip joints with fractures of the pelvis on each side which were caused by the head of the femur on each side being driven through the acetabulum or cup on the pelvis.

Issues: The court was faced with a number of issues. There were two schools of thought on the relevant treatment, both adhered to by bodies of competent opinion. A further consideration was whether a patient should be expressly warned about the risk of fracture before being treated. The issue for the purposes of this extract is the issue in respect of informing the patient—was there a duty to inform the patient of the risks relating to proposed treatment? Again, on this issue there were two different schools of thought. The court held that the doctor in this instance was not negligent in not informing the patient and the plaintiff did not succeed in his action.

McNair J.:

"... On the evidence it is clear, is it not, that the science of electro-convulsive therapy is a progressive science? Its development has been traced for you over the few years in which it has been used in this country. You may think on this evidence that, even today, there is no standard settled technique to which all competent doctors will agree. The doctors called before you have mentioned in turn different variants of the technique that they use. Some use restraining sheets, some use relaxant drugs, some use manual control ...

The plaintiff's case primarily depends on three points. First, it is said that the defendants were negligent in failing to give to the plaintiff a warning of the risks involved in electro-convulsive therapy, so that he might have had a chance to decide whether he was going to take those risks or not ...

Let us examine those three points. Bear in mind that your task is to see whether, in failing to take the action which it is said Dr. Allfrey should have taken, he has fallen below a standard of practice recognised as proper by a competent reasonable body of opinion? First let me deal with the question of warning. There are two questions that you have to consider. First—does good medical practice require that a warning should be given to a patient before he is submitted to electro-convulsive therapy? Secondly—if a warning had been given, what difference would it have made? Are you satisfied that the plaintiff would have said: 'You tell me what the risks are. I won't take those risks. I prefer not to have the treatment.' ...

[Evidence of different views to informing patients was presented.]

That is, in very summary form, the evidence on this point that you have to consider; and, having considered it, you have to make up your minds whether it has been proved to your satisfaction that when the defendants adopted the practice that they did (namely, the practice of saying very little and waiting for questions from the patient), they were falling below a proper standard of competent professional opinion on this question of whether or not it is right to warn. Members of the jury, though it is a matter entirely for you, you may well think that when a doctor is dealing with a mentally sick man and has a strong belief that his only hope of cure is submission to electro-convulsive therapy, the doctor cannot be criticised if he does not stress the dangers, which he believes to be minimal, which are involved in that treatment.

The second point on the question of giving a warning is this: Suppose you come to the conclusion that proper practice requires some warning to be given, if a warning had been given, would it have made any difference? Only the plaintiff can answer that question, and he was never asked it. The plaintiff dealt with the point quite shortly when he said:

> 'On Aug. 16 I was examined by Dr. de Bastarrechea. He told me he recommended convulsive treatment. I knew what it meant; but Dr. de Bastarrechea did not give me any warning of any risk.'

The question what the plaintiff would have done if he had been told that there was a one in ten thousand risk was never put. Surely, members of the jury, it is mere speculation on your part to decide what the answer would have been, and you might well take the view that unless the plaintiff has satisfied you that he would not have taken the treatment if he had been warned, there is really nothing in this point."

The Supreme Court of Canada set out the second approach, in the case of *Reibl v Hughes,* 114 D.L.R. (3d) 1 (*Reibl test*); in this decision the focus is on the rights of the patient. This approach to the issue of informed consent requires disclosure to the patient of all material risks of the proposed treatment to be carried out.

Reibl v Hughes
Supreme Court of Canada 114 D.L.R. (3d) 1; 1980 D.L.R. LEXIS 3486

Facts: The plaintiff suffered from headaches and consulted a physician whose examination revealed that the plaintiff had hypertension. Tests did not reveal the cause of the hypertension. The defendant, a neurosurgeon, was consulted and during the course of his examination discovered a build-up of plaque in the left carotid artery of the plaintiff's neck, significantly narrowing that artery. This was unrelated to the plaintiff's hypertension, and did not cause any disfunction at that moment, but the defendant's opinion was that it should be remedied surgically. This would reduce the risk of death or stroke caused by diminution of the blood supply to the brain. The risks of death or stroke were also risks attendant to the remedial surgery. The defendant recommended surgery to the plaintiff, who agreed. Either during or following the surgery, the plaintiff suffered a massive stroke, which paralysed the right side of his body.

Issues: Was the defendant negligent in failing to adequately disclose and advise the plaintiff of the specific risks attendant with the surgery? Does the relationship between surgeon and patient give rise to a duty of the surgeon to disclose to the patient all material risks attendant with the recommended surgery? The plaintiff was successful in proving negligence in this action.

Laskin C.J.C.:

"... It is now undoubted that the relationship between surgeon and patient gives rise to a duty of the surgeon to make disclosure to the patient of what I would call all material risks attending the surgery which is recommended. The scope of the duty of disclosure was considered in *Hopp v. Lepp*, a judgment of this Court, delivered on May 20, 1980, and as yet unreported [since reported 112 DLR (3d) 67, 22 AR 361, [1980] 4 WWR 645] where it was generalized as follows [at p. 81]:

> 'In summary, the decided cases appear to indicate that, in obtaining the consent of a patient for the performance upon him of a surgical operation, a surgeon, generally, should answer any specific questions posed by the patient as to the risks involved and should, without being questioned, disclose to him the nature of the proposed operation, its gravity, any material risks and any special or unusual risks attendant upon the performance of the operation. However, having said that, it should be added that the scope of the duty of disclosure and whether or not it has been breached are matters which must be decided in relation to the circumstances of each particular case.'

The Court in *Hopp v. Lepp* also pointed out that even if a certain risk is a mere possibility which ordinarily need not be disclosed, yet if its occurrence carries serious consequences, as for example, paralysis or even death, it should be regarded as a material risk requiring disclosure.

In the present case, the risk attending the surgery or its immediate aftermath was the risk of a stroke, of paralysis and, indeed, of death. This was, without question, a material risk. At the same time, the evidence made it clear that there was also a risk of a stroke and of resulting death if surgery for the removal of the occlusion was refused by the patient. The delicacy of the surgery is beyond question, and its execution is no longer in any way faulted ... How specific, therefore, must the information to the patient be, in a case such as this, to enable him to make an 'informed' choice between surgery and no surgery? One of the considerations weighing upon the plaintiff was the fact that he was about a year and a half away from earning a life-time retirement pension as a Ford Motor Company employee. The trial Judge noted (to use his words [at p. 45]) that 'Due to this tragedy befalling him at the time it did, he was not eligible for certain extended disability benefits available under the collective agreement between the Ford Motor Company of Canada Limited and its hourly employees of 10 years' standing.' At the time of the operation, the plaintiff had 8.4 years' service with his employer. He stated in his evidence that if he had been properly informed of the magnitude of the risk involved in the surgery he would have elected to forego it, at least until his pension had vested and, further, he would have opted for a shorter normal life than a longer one as a cripple because of the surgery. Although elective surgery was indicated for the condition from which the plaintiff suffered, there was (as the trial Judge found) no emergency in the sense that immediate surgical treatment was imperative ...

In respect of a claim in negligence, the issue of informed consent to treatment is a concomitant of the physician's duty of care. A surgeon's duty to exercise due skill and care in giving his patient reasonable information and advice with respect to the risks specifically attendant on a proposed operative procedure arises out of the special relationship between them. It is a particular case of the duty which is cast on professional persons in a fiduciary position called upon specifically or by implication to give information or advice to a client intending and entitled to rely on his statements to determine his course: *Nocton v. Lord Ashburton*, [1914] A.C. 932; *Kenny v. Lockwood*, [1932] O.R. 141. That duty does not require warning the patient of the dangers incident to or possible in any surgical procedure, such as the dangers of anaesthesia or the risk of infection, matters which men of ordinary knowledge are presumed to appreciate. It relates to the specific risks within the surgeon's knowledge peculiar to the contemplated treatment. The scope of this professional duty of care is defined by the evaluation of a variety of interrelated factors which bear uniquely on each case, factors such as the presence of an emergency requiring immediate treatment; the patient's emotional and intellectual make-up, and his ability to appreciate and cope with the relevant facts; the gravity of the known risks, both in terms of their likelihood and the severity of this realization. The difficulty evident for the independent evaluation of these factors by a lay tribunal has caused the law of this jurisdiction to leave the definition of the scope of this duty in any particular case a matter essentially of medical judgment, one to be determined by the court on the basis of expert medical evidence ...

Appeal allowed; judgment at trial restored."

The third test was set out in the House of Lords decision of *Sidaway v Governors of the Bethlem Royal Hospital* [1985] A.C. 871 (*Sidaway test*), which adopted a middle-of-the-road approach to the issue. This approach in effect adopts the *Bolam test* but adds a *caveat*, that is, where disclosure was "so obviously necessary to an informed choice on the part of the patient that no reasonably prudent medical man would fail to make it."

Sidaway v Governors of the Bethlem Royal Hospital
House of Lords [1985] A.C. 871

Facts: The plaintiff, who suffered recurrent pain in her neck, right shoulder and arms, underwent neuro-surgery at the first named defendant's hospital. The surgery carried with it an inherent material risk, which was put at between 1 and

2 per cent, of damage to the spinal column and the nerve roots. The risk of damage to the spinal column was substantially less than to a nerve root but the consequences were much more serious. In consequence of the operation the plaintiff was left severely disabled. There was a difficulty at the trial—the surgeon was deceased, and the judge was not prepared to accept Mrs Sidaway's evidence that he had given her no warning.

Issues: The plaintiff claimed damages for negligence against the hospital and the surgeon (at the time of the case the surgeon was deceased, so the action was continued against the executors of his estate). She relied solely on the alleged failure of the surgeon to disclose or explain to her the risks inherent in, or special to, the operation which he had advised. This surgery was elective rather than necessary, a fact that the surgeon did not, according to the trial judge, inform the plaintiff of. The trial judge held that the proper test to be applied was whether the surgeon was following a practice which would have been accepted as proper by a responsible body of skilled and experienced neuro-surgeons, as applied in *Bolam v Friern Hospital Management Committee* (above). The plaintiff did not succeed in the action as the court held that she did not establish that the surgeon had breached a duty to disclose to her. The plaintiff appealed.

Lord Bridge (Lord Keith concurred; Lord Diplock and Lord Templeman, in their judgments, were largely in agreement with Lord Bridge. Lord Scarman adopted a more patient-focused position, based on the US case of *Canterbury v Spence,* 464 F. 2d 772, but was clearly in the minority):

"… Broadly, a doctor's professional functions may be divided into three phases: diagnosis, advice and treatment. In performing his functions of diagnosis and treatment, the standard by which English law measures the doctor's duty of care to his patient is not open to doubt. 'The test is the standard of the ordinary skilled man exercising and professing to have that special skill.' These are the words of McNair J. in *Bolam v. Friern Hospital Management Committee* [1957] 1 W.L.R. 582, 586, approved by this House in *Whitehouse v. Jordan* [1981] 1 W.L.R. 246, 258, per Lord Edmund-Davies and in *Maynard v. West Midlands Regional Health Authority* [1984] 1 W.L.R. 634, 638 per Lord Scarman. The test is conveniently referred to as the *Bolam* test. In *Maynard's* case Lord Scarman, with whose speech the other four members of the Appellate Committee agreed, further cited with approval, at p. 638 the words of Lord President Clyde *in Hunter v. Hanley,* 1955 S.L.T. 213, 217:

> 'In the realm of diagnosis and treatment there is ample scope for genuine difference of opinion and one man clearly is not negligent merely because his conclusion differs from that of other professional men … The true test for establishing negligence in diagnosis or treatment on the part of a doctor is whether he has been proved to be guilty of such failure as no doctor of ordinary skill would be guilty of if acting with ordinary care …'

The language of the Bolam test clearly requires a different degree of skill from a specialist in his own special field than from a general practitioner. In the field of neuro-surgery it would be necessary to substitute for Lord President Clyde's phrase 'no doctor of ordinary skill,' the phrase 'no neuro-surgeon of ordinary skill.' All this is elementary and, in the light of the two recent decisions of this House referred to, firmly established law.

The important question which this appeal raises is whether the law imposes any, and if so what, different criterion as the measure of the medical man's duty of care to his patient when giving advice with respect to a proposed course of treatment. It is clearly right to recognise that a conscious adult patient of sound mind is entitled to decide for himself whether or not he will submit to a particular course of treatment proposed by the doctor, most significantly surgical treatment under general anaesthesia ...

There are, it appears to me, at least theoretically, two extreme positions which could be taken. It could be argued that, if the patient's consent is to be fully informed, the doctor must specifically warn him of all risks involved in the treatment offered, unless he has some sound clinical reason not to do so. Logically, this would seem to be the extreme to which a truly objective criterion of the doctor's duty would lead. Yet this position finds no support from any authority, to which we have been referred, in any jurisdiction. It seems to be generally accepted that there is no need to warn of the risks inherent in all surgery under general anaesthesia. This is variously explained on the ground that the patient may be expected to be aware of such risks or that they are relatively remote. If the law is to impose on the medical profession a duty to warn of risks to secure 'informed consent' independently of accepted medical opinion of what is appropriate, neither of these explanations for confining the duty to special as opposed to general surgical risks seems to me wholly convincing.

At the other extreme it could be argued that, once the doctor has decided what treatment is, on balance of advantages and disadvantages, in the patient's best interest, he should not alarm the patient by volunteering a warning of any risk involved, however grave and substantial, unless specifically asked by the patient. I cannot believe that contemporary medical opinion would support this view, which would effectively exclude the patient's right to decide in the very type of case where it is most important that he should be in a position to exercise that right and, perhaps even more significantly, to seek a second opinion as to whether he should submit himself to the significant risk which has been drawn to his attention. I should perhaps add at this point, although the issue does not strictly arise in this appeal, that, when questioned specifically by a patient of apparently sound mind about risks involved in a particular treatment proposed, the doctor's duty must, in my opinion be to answer both truthfully and as fully as the questioner requires.

The decision mainly relied on to establish a criterion of the doctor's duty to disclose the risks inherent in a proposed treatment which is prescribed by the law and can be applied independently of any medical opinion or practice is that of the District of Columbia Circuit Court of Appeals in *Canterbury v. Spence*, 464 F. 2d 772. The judgment of the Court (Wright, Leventhal and Robinson JJ.), delivered by Robinson J., expounds the view that an objective criterion of what is a sufficient disclosure of risk is necessary to ensure that the patient is enabled to make an intelligent decision and cannot be left to be determined by the doctors. He said, at p. 784:

> 'Respect for the patient's right of self-determination on particular therapy demands a standard set by law for physicians rather than one which physicians may or may not impose upon themselves.'

In an attempt to define the objective criterion it is said, at p. 787, that 'the issue on non-disclosure must be approached from the viewpoint of the reasonableness of the physician's divulgence in terms of what he knows or should know to be the patient's informational needs.' A risk is required to be disclosed 'when a reasonable person, in what the physician knows or should know to be the patient's position, would be likely to attach significance to the risk or cluster of risks in deciding whether or not to forego the proposed therapy': 464 F. 2d 772, 787. The judgment adds, at p. 788: 'Whenever non-disclosure of particular risk information is open to debate by reasonable-minded men, the issue is for the finder of facts.' ...

Expert medical evidence will be needed to indicate the nature and extent of the risks and benefits involved in the treatment (and presumably of any alternative course). But the court affirms, at p. 792: 'Experts are unnecessary to a showing of the materiality of a risk to a patient's decision on treatment, or to the reasonably, expectable effect of risk disclosure on the decision.' In English law, if this doctrine were adopted, expert medical opinion as to whether a particular risk should or should not have been disclosed would presumably be inadmissible in evidence.

I recognise the logical force of the Canterbury doctrine, proceeding from the premise that the patient's right to make his own decision must at all costs be safeguarded against the kind of medical paternalism which assumes that 'doctor knows best.' But, with all respect, I regard the doctrine as quite impractical in application for three principal reasons. First, it gives insufficient weight to the realities of the doctor/patient relationship ... Secondly, it would seem to me quite unrealistic in any medical negligence action to confine the expert medical evidence to an explanation of the primary medical factors involved and to deny the court the benefit of evidence of medical opinion and practice on the particular issue of disclosure which is under consideration. Thirdly, the objective test which Canterbury propounds seems to me to be so imprecise as to be almost meaningless. If it is to be left to individual judges to decide for themselves what 'a reasonable person in the patient's position' would consider a risk of sufficient significance that he should be told about it, the outcome of litigation in this field is likely to be quite unpredictable ...

I should also add that I find particularly cogent and convincing the reasons given for declining to follow Canterbury by the Supreme Court of *Virginia in Bly v. Rhoads* (1976) 222 S.E. 2d 783.

Having rejected the Canterbury doctrine as a solution to the problem of safeguarding the patient's right to decide whether he will undergo a particular treatment advised by his doctor, the question remains whether that right is sufficiently safeguarded by the application of the *Bolam* test without qualification to the determination of the question what risks inherent in a proposed treatment should be disclosed. The case against a simple application of the *Bolam* test is cogently stated by Laskin C.J.C., giving the judgment of the Supreme Court of Canada in *Reibl v. Hughes*, 114 D.L.R. (3d) 1, 13:

> 'To allow expert medical evidence to determine what risks are material and, hence, should be disclosed and, correlatively, what risks are not material is to hand over to the medical profession the entire question of the scope of the duty of disclosure, including the question whether there has been a breach of that duty. Expert medical evidence is, of course, relevant to findings as to the risks that reside in or are a result of recommended surgery or other treatment. It will also have a bearing on their materiality but this is not a question that is to be concluded on the basis of the expert medical evidence alone. The issue under consideration is a different issue from that involved where the question is whether the doctor carried out his professional activities by applicable professional standards. What is under consideration here is the patient's right to know what risks are involved in undergoing or foregoing certain surgery or other treatment.'

I fully appreciate the force of this reasoning, but can only accept it subject to the important qualification that a decision on what degree of disclosure of risks is best calculated to assist a particular patient to make a rational choice as to whether or not to undergo a particular treatment must primarily be a matter of clinical judgment. It would follow from this that the issue whether non-disclosure in a particular case should be condemned as a breach of the doctor's duty of care is an issue to be decided primarily on the basis of expert medical evidence, applying the *Bolam* test. But I do not see that this approach involves the necessity 'to hand over to the medical profession the entire question of the scope of the duty of disclosure, including the question whether there has been a breach of that duty.' Of course, if there is a conflict of evidence as to whether a responsible body of medical opinion approves of non-disclosure in a particular case, the judge will have to resolve that conflict. But even in a case where, as here, no expert witness in the relevant medical field condemns the non-disclosure as being in conflict with accepted and responsible medical practice, I am of opinion that the judge might in certain circumstances come to the conclusion that disclosure of a particular risk was so obviously necessary to an informed choice on the part of the patient that no reasonably prudent medical man would fail to make it ...

In the instant case I can see no reasonable ground on which the judge could properly reject the conclusion to which the unchallenged medical evidence led in the application of the *Bolam* test. The trial judge's assessment of the risk at one to two per cent covered both nerve root and spinal cord damage and covered a spectrum of possible ill effects 'ranging from the mild to the catastrophic.' In so far as it is possible and appropriate to measure such risks in percentage terms—some of the expert medical witnesses called expressed a marked and understandable reluctance to do so—the risk of damage to the spinal cord of such severity as the appellant in fact suffered was, it would appear, certainly less than one per cent. But there is no yardstick either in the judge's findings or in the evidence to measure what fraction of one per cent that risk represented. In these circumstances, the appellant's expert witness's agreement that the non-disclosure complained of accorded with a practice accepted as proper by a responsible body of neuro-surgical opinion afforded the respondents a complete defence to the appellant's claim.

I would dismiss the appeal."

Comments and Questions:
1. Three different approaches have been set out; which approach would you favour and why?

2. The approach adopted in *Bolam* contrasts most starkly with the approach adopted in *Reibl.* Do these approaches reflect the changing nature of the relationship between doctor and patient?

Irish approach

The confusion that is evident by virtue of the fact that there are three tests is also evident in Irish case law. In one of the first cases to address this issue it is apparent that there is little consensus on what a patient is entitled to know.

Daniels v Heskin
Supreme Court [1954] I.R. 73

Facts and issues: see above.

Maguire C.J.:

"The only case cited to the Court on this last question was *Gerber* v. *Pines* [79 Sol. Jo. 13]. There Mr. Justice du Parcq said that it seemed to him 'that a patient in whose body a doctor found that he had left some foreign substance was entitled to be told at once. That was a general rule, but there were exceptions.' Reference was also made to a note of an American case noted in Taylor's Medical Jurisprudence, 9th ed., vol. 1, at p. 83, *Eislein* v. *Palmer* [Amer. Law Dig., 1899, at p. 1870], in which it was apparently decided that there was no duty on a physician to tell a patient or her husband that a broken needle had been left in the patient's body as long as she remained a patient but that there was a duty to tell her when discharging her from his care.

To my mind Mr. Justice du Parcq has laid down the rule correctly. In this case no reason is given why the defendant should be excused what seems to me to be his obvious duty. There was no evidence that any serious consequence would be likely to follow telling the patient what had happened when it happened. Even if it were shown that to tell her might unduly shock Mrs. Daniels there is no reason why her husband should not have been informed. The fact that a choice lay between the two alternative courses of action mentioned above made it to my mind incumbent upon the defendant at least to inform the husband and to allow him to judge whether his wife should be told and in any case to allow the patient or her husband to make the choice. The defendant would clearly have advised that the stitching be completed and the operation of removing the broken needle deferred for some weeks. It was, however, the prerogative of the patient and her husband to decide whether they would accept or reject such advice if given.

In my view the jury should have been asked to consider the question whether or not the defendant was negligent in failing to inform the plaintiffs of the breaking of the needle.

The verdict and judgment should be set aside and a new trial should be ordered."

Lavery J. (Murnaghan and O'Byrne JJ. concurring):

"… The duty of a doctor to inform his patient of the treatment he is adopting and of incidents such as that under examination has been fully discussed in argument. It is clear that there are some matters which a doctor must disclose in order to afford his patient an opportunity of deciding whether she accepts his view or wishes to consult another doctor and an opportunity to make a choice between alternative courses. An example would be where a dangerous operation was contemplated.

On the other hand, there are matters which the doctor must decide for himself having accepted the responsibility of treating his patient and having regard to his professional skill and knowledge upon which she relies. A clear example would be where in the course of an operation an unexpected complication appears.

Into which category does the present case come?

The evidence establishes, in my opinion, that when the needle broke, the choice before the defendant was either to suspend operations, inform the husband and have the plaintiff removed immediately to hospital (assuming that were possible), and there X-rayed and operated on for the removal of the needle or to complete the stitching and defer the operation for removal.

I have already expressed the view that in deciding on the latter course the defendant acted reasonably and without negligence.

This decision having been taken the evidence establishes that the defendant and the nurse discussed the question whether the plaintiff should be told and agreed that it would be better not to tell her for fear it would damage her health.

A period of six weeks would have to elapse during which nothing could be done save to keep the patient under observation. In the words of the defendant in his letter of the 24th October, 1951, he did not inform the patient as he 'was of the opinion that if this fact were disclosed to her at that time it would only cause her unnecessary mental anxiety.'

This appears to me to be a reasonable decision and it involved non-disclosure to the husband as well. In the circumstances no purpose could have been served by informing either the patient or her husband.

It is not, however, necessary to hold that the decision was the right one. In order to establish negligence or breach of duty the plaintiff would have to show that it was a decision incompatible with the proper exercise of the defendant's functions as a doctor.

Moreover, in order to succeed in the action, even assuming the duty to tell, the plaintiff would have to prove that damage which is the gist of the action as pleaded was caused by the failure to tell. In fact, the needle was successfully removed by Dr. O'Keeffe at the appointed time and the event justified the course taken by the defendant. I cannot find any evidence that the non-disclosure caused any damage to the plaintiffs.

For these reasons I am of the opinion that the ruling of the learned trial Judge was correct in all respects and that this appeal should be dismissed."

Kingsmill Moore J.:

"… The third head of negligence alleged against the defendant was his failure to give immediate information to the patient or her husband that a portion of the needle was buried in the tissues.

Counsel for the plaintiffs suggested that there was a rule of law that such information should be given. He relied first on the words of Mr. Justice du Parcq in a case of *Gerber* v. *Pines*, very shortly reported in 79 Sol. Jo. 13. The learned Judge is there alleged to have said that 'it seemed to him that a patient in whose body a doctor found he had left some foreign substance was entitled to be told at once. That was a general rule, but there were exceptions.' Counsel next referred to an American case, noted in Taylor's Medical Jurisprudence, 9th ed., vol. 1, at p. 83, *Eislein* v. *Palmer*, [Amer. Law Dig. 1899, at p. 1870], in which it was apparently decided that there was no duty on a physician to tell a patient or her husband that a broken needle had been left in the patient's body so long as she remained a patient, but that there was a duty to tell her when discharging her from his care.

I doubt very much whether the judges in either of these cases intended to enunciate a rule of law. If they did I must respectfully disagree. A doctor owes certain well recognised duties to his patient. He must possess such knowledge and skill as conforms to the recognised contemporary standards of his profession and, if he is a specialist, such further and particularised skill and knowledge as he holds himself out to possess. He must use such skill and knowledge to form an honest and considered judgment as to what course, what action, what treatment, is in the best interests of his patient. He must display proper care and attention in treating, or in arranging suitable treatment for, his patient. Any attempt to substitute a rule of law, or even a rule of thumb practice, for the individual judgment of a qualified doctor, doing what he considers best for the particular patient, would be disastrous. There may be cases where the judgment of the physician is proved by subsequent events to have been wrong, but if it is honest and considered and if, in the circumstances known to him at the time, it can fairly be justified, he is not guilty of negligence. There may indeed be cases where the nature of the judgment formed or the advice given is such as to afford positive evidence that the physician has fallen short of the required standard of knowledge and skill, or that his judgment could not have been honest and considered, but it lies on the plaintiff to adduce evidence from which such a failure of duty can reasonably be inferred.

I cannot admit any abstract duty to tell patients what is the matter with them or, in particular, to say that a needle has been left in their tissues. All depends on the circumstances—the character of the patient, her health, her social position, her intelligence, the nature of the tissue in which the needle is embedded, the possibility of subsequent infection, the arrangements made for future observation and care, and innumerable other considerations. In the present case the patient was passing through a *post-partum* period in which the possibility of nervous or mental disturbance is notorious; the needle was not situate in a place where any immediate damage was to be anticipated; husband and wife were of a class and standard of education which would incline them to exaggerate the seriousness of the occurrence and to suffer needless alarm; and arrangements were made to keep the patient under observation during the period when sepsis might occur, and to have the patient X-rayed at a period when the bruising and injuries caused by the birth should have subsided. If it were open to me to speak as a juror I would say that the defendant's action was correct. That question is not directly before this Court. What we have to consider is whether it was so incorrect as to provide evidence on which a jury could reasonably conclude that the defendant had failed in any of the duties toward his patient which I have already enumerated. In my opinion there is no such evidence."

Comments and Questions:
1. There are a number of approaches adopted in this case; in your opinion, do any of them correlate with the three approaches outlined above?

2. In your opinion, should education and social class be factors a doctor considers when deciding whether to inform a patient of potential risks with a procedure?

The decision in *Dunne v National Maternity Hospital* [1989] I.R. 91 did not address the issue of consent to treatment, concerned as it was with the issues of diagnosis and treatment. A major case which addressed the issue of a duty to disclose was that of *Walsh v Family Planning Services, Orr and Kelly* [1992] 1 I.R. 496; a crucial point to note in relation to this case is that the surgery that was the subject of the litigation was elective as opposed to necessary surgery.

Walsh v Family Planning Services, Orr and Kelly
Supreme Court [1992] 1 I.R. 496

Facts: Mr Walsh underwent elective surgery, namely a vasectomy. The reason for the operation was for contraceptive, not medical, purposes. He was informed that the surgery would not affect his sex life in a negative way, that there might have been some discomfort after surgery, some swelling, and "very rarely, for no known reason, some patients experienced pain for some years after the operation." Mr Walsh, after surgery, developed orchialgia, which is a rare but known side-effect of vasectomies. The condition meant that Mr Walsh had severe pain in the groin, which was exacerbated during intercourse and his sex life stopped. He had various treatments to try to solve the problem including the removal of his left testicle.

At the High Court it was held that the plaintiff was successful in trespass; it was held that a technical assault and battery had been committed by the third defendant. The third defendant was undergoing training and actually carried out the operation; the plaintiff claimed not to have consented to him performing the procedure.

Issue: The case before the Supreme Court relates to an appeal against the finding of assault, and the plaintiff cross-appealed on the finding of no negligence. The issue of most significance to the negligence cross-appeal related to the court's attempt to address the duty, if any, owed by the doctor to inform a patient of the possible consequences of surgery, notwithstanding the rarity of those consequences. A crucial issue for the court related to the fact that the surgery complained of was elective rather than necessary. The court did not find for the plaintiff, holding that there was a duty to warn, but that the warning provided had been sufficient.

Finlay C.J.:

"... I am satisfied that there is, of course, where it is possible to do so, a clear obligation on a medical practitioner carrying out or arranging for the carrying out of an operation, to inform the patient of any possible harmful consequence arising from the operation, so as to permit the patient to give an informed consent to subjecting himself to the operation concerned. I am also satisfied that the extent of this obligation must, as a matter of common sense, vary with what might be described as the elective nature of the surgery concerned. Quite obviously, and apart even from cases of emergency surgery which has to be carried out to persons who are unconscious or incapable of giving or refusing consent, or to young children, there may be instances where as a matter of medical knowledge, notwithstanding substantial risks of harmful consequence, the carrying out of a particular surgical procedure is so necessary to maintain the life or health of the patient and the consequences of failing to carry it out are so clearly disadvantageous that limited discussion or warning concerning possible harmful side-effects may be appropriate and proper. On the other hand, the obligation to give warning of the possible harmful consequences of a surgical procedure which could be said to be at the other end of the scale to the extent to which it is elective, such as would undoubtedly be the operation of vasectomy, may be more stringent and more onerous. I am satisfied, however, that the standard of care to be exercised by a medical practitioner in the giving of the warning of the consequences of proposed surgical procedures is not in principle any different from the standard of care to be exercised by medical practitioners in the giving of treatment or advice, and that there are not good grounds for suggesting that the issue of negligence arising under this heading is outside the general principles which have been enunciated by this Court in previous cases concerning the standards of care and the methods of ascertaining them arising in medical negligence cases which were summarised in *Dunne (Infant) v. National Maternity Hospital* [1989] I.R. 91, which summary has been set out in the judgment about to be delivered by McCarthy J. It is, I am satisfied, true, however, that if a medical practitioner charged with negligence consisting of a failure to give sufficient warning of the possible consequences of an operation, defends his conduct by establishing that he followed a practice which was general, that it may be, certainly in relation to very clearly elective surgery, that the court might more readily reach a conclusion that the extent of warning given or omitted contained inherent defects which ought to have been obvious to any person giving the matter due consideration than it could do in a case of complicated medical or surgical procedures, and an allegation that, although generally adopted, they were inherently unsafe."

McCarthy J.:

"... All surgery, in a sense, is elective although the election may have to be implied from the circumstances rather than determined as express. The gravely wounded, the gravely ill may be unconscious but in urgent need of surgery. A patient's condition may be such as to demand surgical intervention as the only hope for survival. Such may be called non-elective surgery. The patient given the choice between enduring pain and having limb replacement surgery or fusion surgery may technically be electing as between the pain and the surgery but the election may be more apparent than real. An extreme of elective surgery would be what is purely cosmetic—simply to improve the natural appearance rather than to remedy the physical results of injury or disease. Even it may have an element of quasi-medical care because of the psychological reaction of the patient to personal appearance. A like argument may be advanced in respect of contraceptive surgery, male or female. Such surgery does not have a direct effect on the health or well being of the patient nor in prolongation of life; it may alleviate marital stress or other domestic pressure and in that sense be therapeutic. Essentially, however, it is for the improvement of the sex life of the couple concerned. At least since 1979 the danger of chronic orchialgia was known and documented; there had been one instance of it in the first defendant's clinic itself in 1983. It still remained a minor and elective surgical procedure ...

In McMahon & Binchy, *Irish Law of Torts* (2nd ed.) at p. 268 the authors deal with the duty of disclosure:—

> 'What is the proper test for deciding whether the doctor has given sufficient instruction to the patient? Three principal solutions have been proposed. The first resolves the question by reference to the generally accepted practice in the medical profession. This approach, which is an application of the *Bolam test* ([1957] 1 W.L.R. 582), stresses the fact that the decision of what to tell the patient has traditionally been regarded as primarily a matter of medical judgment and discretion. The second solution, at the other end of the spectrum, concentrates on the patient's right of self determination in regard to what is to be done to his body. It requires full disclosure of all material risks incident to the proposed treatment, so that the patient, rather than the doctor, makes the real choice as to whether treatment is to be carried out ... The third approach lies between these two extremes. While tilting somewhat towards the first, it applies the *Bolam* test save where disclosure of a particular risk "was so obviously necessary to an informed choice on the part of the patient that no reasonably prudent medical man would fail to make it ..." *Sidaway v. Governors of the Bethlehem Royal Hospital* [1985] A.C. 871 at 900.'

Despite the division identified by Messrs. McMahon & Binchy, in a case such as the present I believe that the second and third solutions propounded by them are essentially the same. In determining whether or not to have an operation in which sexual capacity is concerned, it seems to me that to supply the patient with the material facts is so obviously necessary to an informed choice on the part of the patient that no reasonably prudent medical doctor would fail to make it. What then is material? Apart from the success ratio of the operation, what could be more material than sexual capacity after the operation and its immediate sequelae? Whatever about temporary or protracted pain or discomfort, the only information given to the plaintiff and his wife on the score of sexual capacity, upon which they placed so much emphasis, was that contained in the brief paragraph headed 'Does it affect your sex-life? No'. This is not a question of merely determining that a particular outcome is so rare as not to warrant such disclosure that might upset a patient but, rather, that those concerned, and this includes the authors of the information sheet, if they knew of such a risk, however remote, had a duty to inform those so critically concerned with that risk. Remote percentages of risk lose their significance to those unfortunate enough to be 100% involved. In my view it is inescapable that the defendants, possessed as they were of this knowledge, were in breach of their duty to the plaintiff, and to his wife, for failing to identify the risk of impotence, whether it be functional due to pain and discomfort, or mechanical due to some other cause."

O'Flaherty J. (Hederman J. concurring):

"... In the alternative, it is submitted under this heading that because the possible risks of long term consequences and complications were not explained to the plaintiff his consent was not an 'informed consent' and, therefore, the operation as performed constituted an assault on him. Assuming for the sake of this argument that that was the factual position—though I will return to this topic later—I believe that if there had been such a failure to give a warning as to possible future risks that would not involve the artificial concept of an assault, but, rather, a possible breach of a duty of care giving rise to a claim in negligence.

... I do not accept that the question of whether a warning should be given in relation to a procedure such as this is to be determined in accordance with the criteria set out in *Dunne (Infant) v. National Maternity Hospital* [1989] I.R. 91 as regards general and approved practice. Rather I think it is a matter for the trial judge, in the first instance, to find whether there has been a breach of the duty of care owed by the defendants to a person such as the plaintiff. That is to be resolved on the established principles of negligence. This was the approach of the Supreme Court of Canada in the *Reibl v. Hughes* (1980) 114 D.L.R. (3d) 1.

I leave aside the requirements that may come into play in the case of emergency or essential surgery where questions of life and death arise as I do questions of possible emotional upset such as were considered by the Court in *Daniels and Another v. Heskin* [1954] I.R. 73 and I deal, exclusively, with the case in hand. I have no hesitation in saying that where there is a question of elective surgery which is not essential to health or bodily well-being, if there is a risk—however exceptional or remote—of grave consequences involving severe pain stretching for an appreciable time into the future and involving the possibility of further operative procedures, the exercise of the duty of care owed by the defendants requires that such possible consequences should be explained in the clearest language to the plaintiff ...

The plaintiff is bound by the primary finding of fact made by the trial judge in this regard, *viz.* that the warning was given to the plaintiff and, in those circumstances, it seems to me that I am precluded from engaging in any examination of whether if a more powerful warning was given the plaintiff would have acted on it in the light of his flat contradiction that any warning at all was given."

Egan J.:

"… In such a case both my learned colleagues are of opinion that if there is a risk, however exceptional or remote, of grave consequences involving severe pain stretching for an appreciable time into the future and involving further operative procedures, the exercise of the duty of care owed by the defendants requires that such possible consequences should be explained in the clearest language to the prospective patient …

The evidence given by Dr. Sheehy-Skeffington who dealt with this aspect of the case and whose evidence was accepted by the learned trial judge as being a true account of oral information given to the plaintiff fails to satisfy me that the plaintiff received adequate warning of the possible consequences of a vasectomy operation, however remote such consequences might be. Furthermore, literature with which he was supplied was equally defective in this regard. I instance the question in the document which is headed 'To start you thinking about vasectomy' and which reads 'Does it affect your sex life?' The stated answer is 'No' and there is not a word (even in the small print) to suggest that intercourse could become painful.

The plaintiff denied that he had received *any* warning from Dr. Sheehy-Skeffington but his evidence was rejected in this regard. I cannot accept the proposition, however, that his wrongful denial precludes the court from engaging in an examination of whether adequate warning was given to the plaintiff. Neither do I consider it necessary that there should be proof by the plaintiff that had a proper warning been given to him, he would not have submitted to the original operation. If he never in fact received a proper warning his answer to a question asking how it would have affected his attitude would necessarily be hypothetical and, unless it was by any unlikely chance in the negative, the court would be entitled to come to the conclusion that the failure to give the advice was negligent and actionable.

In the end result, therefore, I agree with the judgment of McCarthy J."

Comments and Questions:
1. How many tests were adopted by the Supreme Court to determine the issue of the duty to disclose?

2. What definitive statements can be made of the duty to disclose based on this decision?

3. For a full discussion on the different approaches adopted in this case see McMahon and Binchy, *The Law of Torts* (3rd ed., Butterworths, 2000).

The decision in *Walsh v Family Planning Services, Orr and Kelly* [1992] 1 I.R. 496, while not setting out a coherent approach on what the duty to disclose is in the context of necessary surgery, very clearly requires a duty to disclose for elective surgery. The next case to address the issue of a duty to disclose is that of *Farrell v Varian,* unreported, High Court, September 1994. This case was heard shortly after the decision in *Walsh v Family Planning Services,* but the High Court made no reference to that decision. O'Hanlon J. favoured the *Sidaway test* in his judgment.

Farrell v Varian
Unreported, High Court, September 1994

Facts: The plaintiff had been suffering from contractions of the fingers on his left hand. He underwent an operation to relieve this condition and the outcome was successful, although the complaint recurred again after the passage of a number of years. He noticed, around 1985, that the right hand was also becoming affected. He was referred to a consultant who specialised in hand surgery. He was diagnosed with bilateral Dupuytren's contractures; surgery was recommended and it was decided to operate on the right hand first and deal with the left hand at a later date. The condition of the hand operated on deteriorated, and was worse than when surgery was first mooted. On top of the original complaint a rare condition had also developed known as reflex sympathetic dystrophy syndrome, affecting not only his hand, but also his arm and shoulder. His whole hand was contracted, discoloured and covered with scaly skin, and he had constant severe pain. As a result he lost his employment, and was unemployable, as the pain and incapacity would continue, there being no known medical treatment which could offer relief.

Issues: There was a major conflict of fact between the plaintiff and the defendant. The plaintiff claimed that the defendant was negligent in failing to give the plaintiff due warning of the risks associated with the operation and that he therefore could not make an informed decision as to whether he wanted the surgery, or take the consequences of deciding against it. The plaintiff did not succeed in establishing his case.

O'Hanlon J.:

"… Did the Defendant, prior to operating on the Plaintiff, give such information to the Plaintiff as he was required by law to do as to risks involved in undergoing the operation so as to enable the Plaintiff to make an informed decision whether he wished to undergo the operation notwithstanding the existence of such risks? …

With regard to the nature and extent of the warning which should be given to a patient contemplating an operation, I am of opinion that the doctor's obligation does not extend to enumerating all the possible risks, however remote, which are involved. Such a procedure could only subject many patients to unnecessary fears and worries, and possibly have the effect of deterring many patients from submitting to treatment which it was obviously in their best interests to undergo.

If there is some significant danger involved of serious consequences the patient would have an entitlement to be warned about it. *In Sidaway v Board of Governors of Bethlem Royal Hospital,* (1985) AC 871, the House of Lords suggested, by way of example, that if there was an operation involving a substantial risk of grave adverse consequences such as a 10 per cent risk of a stroke, a judge would be entitled to conclude that in the absence of some cogent clinical reason why the patient should not be informed, a doctor, recognising and respecting his patient's right of decision, could hardly fail to appreciate the necessity for an appropriate warning.

All the expert medical evidence in the present case appears to concur in confirming that the onset of reflex sympathetic dystrophy in its severe form, as experienced by the Plaintiff, is a rare phenomenon. The Plaintiff's case was described by all the doctors as the worst case they had ever seen, and the general incidence of the condition in a severe form was put at lower than 1% of cases arising from operative treatment. In view of the extremely small number of actual cases seen by these medical gentlemen of great experience in their field, their evidence would suggest a much smaller incidence than 1%. There also appears to be an incidence of a much less serious character which clears up within a relatively short period even without remedial treatment, in a significantly larger number of cases.

I agree with the view expressed by the House of Lords in the *Sidaway* case that 'the decision what degree of disclosure of risks is best calculated to assist a particular patient to make a rational choice as to whether or not to undergo a particular treatment must primarily be a matter of clinical judgment', although, as also observed by their Lordships, a case might arise where a judge could conclude that disclosure of a particular risk was so obviously necessary to an informed choice on the part of the patient that no reasonably prudent medical man would fail to make it.

I am satisfied that the standard warning given by the Defendant to his patients who are considering undergoing the operation to correct Dupuytren's contracture, and which I believe he gave in the present case, was adequate in all the circumstances to meet his obligation in this respect."

In *Geoghegan v Harris* [2000] 3 I.R. 526 the courts were again faced with a case where they had to address the duty to disclose. The case in hand related to elective surgery, so there was more guidance available to the High Court in this instance. Kearns J. leans towards the *Reibl test,* and also defines what a material risk is.

Geoghegan v Harris
High Court [2000] 3 I.R. 526

Facts: The plaintiff decided to have dental implants in 1992. The operation necessitated that a bone graft be taken from the plaintiff's chin. The defendant carried out the operation. The graft damaged a nerve in the front of the plaintiff's chin and left him with severe mid-line chin pain which is a chronic neuropathic pain. The claim by the plaintiff was that his dentist did not disclose this risk to him. The dentist had given extensive information on the implant procedure but nothing on the graft. The procedure was elective, and the plaintiff claimed that even if there was the tiniest risk of constant pain he would not have continued. The defendant contended that the onset of chronic neuropathic pain was so remote a possibility that a warning as to this occurring was unnecessary.

Issues: Was the defendant obliged to give a warning to the plaintiff of any material risk which was a known or foreseeable complication of an operation? What test should the court adopt as to the risks that ought to be disclosed to a patient before an operation? It was held by the court that the defendant had a duty to disclose the risk of ongoing pain.

Kearns J.:

"… The obligation on a medical practitioner carrying out or arranging for the carrying out of an operation to inform the patient of any possible harmful consequence arising from the operation, was addressed by the Supreme Court in *Walsh v Family Planning Services Ltd.* [1992] 1 IR 496 …
    In Medical Negligence Actions by Dr John White, the author states at p. 190:—

> 'It is not unfair to observe that Walsh's case is bewildering both in the alternative criteria of decision adopted by its adjudicators and in the application of those criteria of decision to the facts of that case.'…

However, in relation to the issue which the court is called upon to address in this case, an analysis of the judgments in *Walsh v Family Planning Services Ltd.* [1992] 1 IR 496, yields the same answers, arrived at by the application of the different principles, in relation to two critical questions, that is to say:—

> (a) the requirement on a medical practitioner is to give a warning of any material risk which is a 'known complication' of an operative procedure properly carried out;
> (b) the test of materiality in elective surgery is to inquire only if there is any risk, however exceptional or remote, of grave consequences involving severe pain stretching for an appreciable time into the future.

All five judges of the Supreme Court clearly agreed in *Walsh v Family Planning Services Ltd.* [1992] 1 IR 496, that in elective surgery any risk which carries the possibility of grave consequences for the patient must be disclosed. The requirement is set out in the various judgments without qualification in respect of statistical frequency. In fact, this consideration is firmly ruled out ...

Bolton v Blackrock Clinic (Unreported, Supreme Court, 23rd January, 1997) did not purport to vary or alter the requirement for the type of warning necessary in elective surgery.

Hamilton CJ at p. 13 stated:—

> 'The surgery contemplated in this case on the 4th March, 1988, viz. the sleeve resection operation was undoubtedly elective surgery in the sense that it was a matter for the plaintiff to decide whether or not she would undergo such an operation and to give or withhold or consent thereto.'

Before obtaining such consent there was a clear obligation on Mr Wood to (i) satisfy himself as to the necessity for the operation; (ii) explain to the plaintiff the necessity for the operation and the consequences of failing to have the operation; (iii) explain to the plaintiff the nature of the operation, and (iv) inform the plaintiff ...

While the issue of quantum has been deferred to a later stage of this hearing, both the medical evidence I have heard in the context of liability and the plaintiff's own evidence satisfy me that the plaintiff does have an extremely painful and hitherto intractable version of this nerve damage ...

None of the medical practitioners have to this point queried the genuineness of the plaintiff's condition which, he says has destroyed his life ...

His condition merits the description of being severe, though clearly it is well short of the category which may include conditions such as paralysis, loss of a limb or reproductive function. The requirements of *Walsh v Family Planning Services Ltd.* [1992] 1 IR 496 are therefore met in the instant case.

Even though the views of the medical experts were all to the effect that no warning was necessary of the remote risk of neuropathic pain, the decision in *Walsh v Family Planning Services Ltd.* [1992] 1 IR 496 must nonetheless bind me. I accordingly, hold there was an obligation to warn ...

The application of the reasonable patient test seems more logical in respect of disclosure. This would establish the proposition that, as a general principle, the patient has the right to know and the practitioner a duty to advise of all material risks associated with a proposed form of treatment. The court must ultimately decide what is material. 'Materiality' includes consideration of both (a) the severity of the consequences and (b) the statistical frequency of the risk. That both are critical is obvious because a risk may have serious consequences and yet historically or predictably be so rare as not to be regarded as significant by many people. For example, a tourist might be deterred from visiting a country where there had been an earthquake causing loss of life, but if told the event happened fifty years ago without repetition since, he might well wonder why his travel agent caused him unnecessary worry by mentioning it at all.

The reasonable man, entitled as he must be to full information of material risks, does not have impossible expectations nor does he seek to impose impossible standards. He does not invoke only the wisdom of hindsight if things go wrong. He must be taken as needing medical practitioners to deliver on their medical expertise without excessive restraint or gross limitation on their ability to do so.

The decision in *Walsh v Family Planning Services Ltd.* [1992] 1 IR 496 effectively confines the test of materiality to severity of consequences only. This approach is best encapsulated in the memorable passage of McCarthy J when he stated at p. 521:—

> '... those concerned ... if they knew of such a risk, however remote, had a duty to inform those so critically concerned with that risk. Remote percentages of risk lose their significance to those unfortunate enough to be 100% involved.'

However, the attractiveness of the observation should not occlude the possibility that at times a risk may become so remote, in relation at any rate to the less than most serious consequences, that a reasonable man may not regard it as material or significant. While such cases may be few in number, they do suggest that an absolute requirement of disclosure in every case is unduly onerous, and perhaps in the end counter productive if it needlessly deters patients from undergoing operations which are in their best interest to have."

The Supreme Court was given the opportunity to clarify the law in this area in *Bolton v The Blackrock Clinic*, unreported, Supreme Court, January 1997. At High Court level Geoghegan J. favoured the approach taken by O'Flaherty in the *Walsh case,* which is most closely aligned with the *Reibl test.* While upholding the decision of Geoghegan J. in the Supreme Court, the Supreme Court judges appeared to take a different approach to the trial judge, but did not criticise the approach taken by the trial judge. This brought us no closer to a clarification of the position in Ireland.

Bolton v The Blackrock Clinic
Unreported, Supreme Court, January 1997

Facts: The first named defendant was the clinic, the second named defendant a cardio-thoracic surgeon, and the third named defendant a consultant thoracic physician. The first operation carried out on the plaintiff was a sleeve resection surgery. This operation led to restenosis which is the narrowing of her left bronchus and the consequent need for the pneumonectomy, which resulted in her personal injuries.

Issue: The issue at hand was that the operation was unnecessary and unwarranted; that the consent given by the plaintiff was not an informed consent because the doctor had not sufficiently informed himself with regard to the cause of the plaintiff's condition and therefore could not inform and advise the plaintiff. The plaintiff alleged that the pneumonectomy and its injurious consequences could have been avoided if the plaintiff had been treated conservatively in the first instance.

Hamilton C.J.:

"… It appears from the foregoing that there are two fundamental issues to be determined by this Court.
1. Whether the finding by the learned trial judge that the second and third named Defendants were not negligent in failing to fully investigate the cause of the Appellant's condition and the necessity for a sleeve resection operation was supported by the evidence before him?
2. Whether the finding of the learned trial judge that the Appellant had given a fully informed consent to the operation on the 4 day of March 1988 and the pneumonectomy which was carried out on the 8 day of August 1988, was supported by the evidence before him.

With regard to this latter issue, Finlay CJ in the course of his judgment *in Walsh v Family Planning Services Ltd and Others* [1992] 1 IR page 496 stated at page 510 of the Report that:—

> 'I am satisfied that there is, of course, where it is possible to do so, a clear obligation on a medical practitioner carrying out or arranging for the carrying out of an operation, to inform the patient of any possible harmful consequence arising from the operation, so as to permit the patient to give an informed consent to subjecting himself to the operation concerned. I am also satisfied that the extent of this obligation must, as a matter of common sense, vary with what might be described as the elective nature of the surgery concerned. Quite obviously, and apart even from cases of emergency surgery which has to be carried out to persons who are unconscious or incapable of giving or refusing consent, or to young children, there may be instances where as a matter of medical knowledge, notwithstanding substantial risks of harmful consequence, the carrying out of a particular surgical procedure is so necessary to maintain the life or health of the patient and the consequences of failing to carry it out are so clearly disadvantageous that limited discussion or warning concerning possible harmful side-effects may be appropriate and proper. On the other hand, the obligation to give warning of the possible harmful consequences of a surgical procedure which could be said to be at the other end of the scale to the extent to which it is elective, such as would undoubtedly be the operation of vasectomy, may be more stringent and more onerous. I am satisfied, however, that the standard of care to be exercised by a medical practitioner in the giving of the warning of the consequences of proposed surgical procedures is not in principle any different from the standard of care to be exercised by medical practitioners in the giving of treatment or advice, and

that there are not good grounds for suggesting that the issue of negligence arising under this heading is outside the general principles which have been enunciated by this Court in previous cases concerning the standards of care and the methods of ascertaining them arising in medical negligence cases which were summarised in *Dunne (Infant) v National Maternity Hospital* [1989] IR 91, which summary has been set out in the judgment about to be delivered by McCarthy J. It is, I am satisfied, true, however, that if a medical practitioner charged with negligence consisting of a failure to give sufficient warning of the possible consequences of an operation, defends his conduct by establishing that he followed a practice which was general, that it may be, certainly in relation to very clearly elective surgery, that the court might more readily reach a conclusion that the extent of warning given or omitted contained inherent defects which ought to have been obvious to any person giving the matter due consideration than it would have been in a case of complicated medical or surgical procedures, and an allegation that, although generally adopted, they were inherently unsafe.'

The summary referred to in the said judgments is set forth at Page 516 of the Report as follows and is relevant to the issue of whether the Respondents were negligent.

[He then set out the *Dunne* principles, see above] …

The statement of Finlay CJ clearly established that there was a clear obligation on Mr Wood who was arranging for the carrying out of the sleeve resection operation on the 4 day of March, 1988 to inform the Appellant of any possible harmful consequence arising from the operation so as to permit the patient to give an informed consent to subjecting herself to the operation and that the extent of this obligation must as a matter of common sense vary with what might be described as the elective nature of the surgery concerned.

Before obtaining such consent there was a clear obligation on Mr Wood to

(i)   satisfy himself as to the necessity for the operation;
(ii) explain to the Appellant the necessity for the operation and the consequences of failing to have the operation;
(iii) explain to the Appellant the nature of the operation, and
(iv) inform the Appellant of any possible harmful consequence arising from the operation …

The learned trial judge having accepted the evidence of Mr Wood was satisfied that the Appellant was informed of the risk of the occurrence of restenosis and that if such occurred a pneumonectomy would be inevitable and that the consent given to the said operation by the Appellant was an informed consent …"

Comments and Questions:

1. Craven suggests in relation to this case that: "Although *Bolton* presented the first opportunity at Supreme Court level since *Walsh* to resolve the issue of how the standard of care in disclosure in the obtaining of consent prior to diagnostic or therapeutic interventions should be assessed, the approach failed to address the central problem. In summary, therefore, the definitive determination of the standard of care in disclosure must await another day." (For further discussion and analysis of the duty to disclose and informed consent as a topic, see C. Craven, "Consent to Treatment by Patients— Disclosure revisited (Part I)", (2000) 6(1) *Bar Review* 56 at 58; and C. Craven, "Consent to Treatment by Patients—Disclosure revisited (Part II)", (2000) 6(2) *Bar Review* 111–114.)

A final case that is worthy of note is that of *Ewing v Northwestern Health Board,* unreported, High Court, December 1998. While no reference is made to any of the various tests espoused, Donovan J. makes an interesting observation on people's ability to consent when they suffer from chronic pain.

Ewing v Northwestern Health Board
Unreported, High Court, December 1998

Facts: The plaintiff in this case began to experience a severe pain in her abdomen which recurred about three times a week, lasting for a couple of hours on each occasion and accompanied by bouts of vomiting. She also began to experience a progressive weight loss and was required to absent herself from work. She went to her general practitioner who referred her to Sligo General Hospital, where she was admitted and subjected to several tests which disclosed no abnormality, but the symptoms persisted. She had to leave her employment as she was unable to guarantee that she would be present five days a week. Some time later she had a scan of her pelvis and discovered what appeared to be an ovarian cyst, but no firm diagnosis was confirmed. She underwent surgery for what she thought was the removal of the ovarian cyst and possibly one of her ovaries. The surgeon claimed to be operating for endemitriosis, although her medical records made no reference to such procedure. Most of the medical evidence presented agreed that there was no necessity for surgery for an ovarian cyst.

Issues: The plaintiff to this action claimed that the performing of the surgery was unnecessary, that the defendants failed to carry out a review of the ultrasound scan prior to the performing of the surgery, and that they did not have consent for the carrying out of the surgery, or for the carrying out of an unnecessary procedure of plication of the round ligaments. The court found for the plaintiff in this action.

O'Donovan J.:

"… As for Doctor Carroll, throughout his evidence, he emphasised that all his decisions with regard to his treatment of the Plaintiff were influenced by the fact that he accepted that she was experiencing very severe pain; indeed, he said that she presented to him on the 5 November 1992 as a young lady who had the appearance of being very unwell, and that he was very anxious to do everything within his power to diagnose the cause of her problems with a view to alleviating her symptoms. Accordingly, I have no doubt at all but that, when these two people met on the 5 November 1992, the Plaintiff was prepared to submit to any treatment which Doctor Carroll might have advised in the hope that it would alleviate her symptoms whereas Doctor Carroll, for his part, was concerned to do everything in his power to diagnose the cause of the Plaintiff's suffering with a view to ending it. That as it may be, however, I do not accept the evidence of Professor John Bonner, another Consultant Gynaecologist/ Obstetrician who gave evidence on behalf of the defence, that a patient can dictate the course of his or her treatment depending on the degree of pain which he/she is experiencing. In this connection Professor Bonner said that it is up to a patient, rather than to his/her medical specialist, to decide whether or not the degree of pain which he/she is experiencing is sufficient to warrant a particular form of treatment which has been suggested by the specialist as being an option. I cannot accept that that is so. While I can understand that a patient, who is in great distress, such as this Plaintiff was, might well be prepared to submit to any treatment which his/her specialist might suggest, it is my opinion that, ultimately, it is for the specialist and not for the patient to decide what form of treatment is in the best interests of the patient, particularly a patient who is only 18 years of age. Accordingly, whatever she may have said to Doctor Carroll, I do not think that Connie Ewing has any responsibility with regard to the treatment to which she was subjected by him. She herself said in evidence 'I left it to Doctor Carroll to decide what was best for me'. In my view, that is as it should be and as it was and it is in that light that I view what subsequently transpired between the Plaintiff and Doctor Carroll."

SOLICITORS' NEGLIGENCE

Duty of care

Solicitors, like doctors, can be liable in both tort and contract. In a contractual relationship solicitors will be responsible to the parties to the contract; the issue in tort is not so clear. To whom do solicitors owe a duty of care? This issue has been addressed in a number of cases, including *Wall v Hegarty* [1980] I.L.R.M. 124.

Wall v Hegarty
High Court [1980] I.L.R.M. 124

Facts: The plaintiff was a named beneficiary under a will, which was improperly attested and therefore ineffectual. The defendants were a firm of solicitors retained by the testator to draft his will. The signature of the testator had not been authenticated by two witnesses and one of the signatures was added subsequently in the solicitor's office. As a result the plaintiff was not entitled to a legacy of £15,000.

Issues: The plaintiff sought to establish that a solicitor owes a duty of care to the beneficiaries under a will he is responsible for drafting. The court agreed, allowing the plaintiff to recover.

Barrington J.:

"... The plaintiff, in his statement of claim, pleads that a solicitor retained by a testator to prepare a will owes a duty to an executor and beneficiary named in the will to ensure that the testator's benevolent intentions in respect of the executor and beneficiary are not frustrated through lack of reasonable care on the part of the solicitor. At paragraph 7 of the statement of claim he pleads:

> 'The defendants and each of them as solicitors for William Wall, deceased, were obliged at all material times to conduct the affairs of the deceased in such manner as would ensure and protect the best interests of the plaintiff as the person named as his executor by the deceased and as a beneficiary under his said will and of all persons entitled to benefit from, or concerned with, the will of the deceased, which said duty the defendants failed to discharge.'

Traditionally, English law did not regard a solicitor as owing any such duty to a legatee in a testator's will and, so far as I am aware, the law of Ireland was no different in this respect ...

However, since *Robertson v Fleming* was decided, there have been two major advances in the law, material to the consideration of the present question. First was the development of negligence as an independent tort and the line of authority running from *Donoghue v Stevenson* [1932] AC 562; to *Hedley Byrne & Co Ltd v Heller & Partners Ltd* [1964] 465. In particular, was the famous passage in Lord Aitkin's speech in *Donoghue v Stevenson* where he stressed the duty to take reasonable care to avoid injuring one's neighbour, and went on to inquire:

> 'Who, then, in law is my neighbour? The answer seems to be *"persons who are so closely and directly affected by my act that I ought reasonably to have them in contemplation as being so affected when I am directing my mind to the acts or omissions which are called into question".'*

Lord Atkin went on to stress that the concept of *'neighbour'* did not include merely persons in close physical proximity to the alleged tortfeasor; but also, all such persons as stood in such direct relationship with him, as to cause him to know that they would be directly affected by the careless act. (See [1932] AC 580.)

The second important legal development which has taken place since *Robertson v Fleming* is that it is now finally established, so far, at any rate, as the law of Ireland is concerned, that a solicitor owes two kinds of duties to his client. First, is his duty in contract to carry out the terms of his retainer. Second is a duty in tort to show reasonable professional skill in attending to his client's affairs. It is clear that this duty in tort arises simply because he is purporting to act as a solicitor for his client and is independent of whether he is providing his professional services voluntarily or for reward. (See the judgment of the Supreme Court in *Finlay v Murtagh* [1979] IR 249 and the judgment of Oliver J , in *Midland Bank Trust Co. Ltd v Hetts, Stubbs & Kemp* [1979] Ch 384.)

The Supreme Court in *Finlay v Murtagh* was merely dealing with a net point of law as to whether a solicitor owed a duty to a client in tort as well as in contract, but it is quite clear that the court, in holding that he did, derived the duty from the proximity principle outlined by Lord Atkin in *Donoghue v Stevenson*. For instance, the following passage appears at page 2 of the judgment of Kenny J:

> 'The professional person, however, owes the client a general duty and not one arising from contract from the *'proximity'* principle (*Donoghue v Stevenson, Hedley Byrne & Co., v Heller & Partners Ltd.*), to exercise reasonable care and skill in the performance of the work entrusted to him. This duty arises from the obligation which springs from the situation that he knew or ought to have known that his failure to exercise care and skill would probably cause loss and damage. This failure to have or to exercise reasonable skill and care is tortious or delictual in origin.'

Indeed, Henchy J, in a passage at page ten of his judgment, appears to anticipate the situation which has arisen in the present case. He says:

> 'The solicitor's liability in tort under the general duty of care extends not only to a client for reward, but to any person for whom he undertakes to act professionally without reward, and also to those (such as beneficiaries under a will, persons entitled under an intestacy, or those entitled to benefits in circumstances such as a claim in respect of a fatal injury) with whom he has made no arrangement to act, but who, as he knows or ought to know, will be relying on his professional care and skill. For the same default there should be the same cause of action. If others are entitled to sue in tort for the solicitor's want of care, so also should the client.'

Since the decision of the Supreme Court in *Finlay v Murtagh*, the specific question which arises in the present case arose for consideration in the English High Court in the case of *Ross v Caunters* [1980] Ch. 297.

In that case, the testator instructed solicitors to draw up his will to include gifts of chattels and a share of his residuary estate to the plaintiff, who was his sister-in-law. The solicitors drew up the will naming the plaintiff as legatee. The testator requested the solicitors to send the draft will to him at the plaintiff's home where he was staying, to be signed and attested. The solicitors sent the will to the testator with a covering letter giving instructions on executing it, but failed to warn him that under *s. 15 of the Wills Act, 1837*, attestation of the will by the beneficiary's spouse would invalidate the gift to the beneficiary. The plaintiff's husband attested the will which was then returned to the solicitors who failed to notice that he had attested it. In fact, prior to the execution of the will, the testator had, in correspondence, raised with his solicitor, the question *'Am I right in thinking that beneficiaries may not be witnesses?'* The solicitors unfortunately did not answer this question which clearly provided them with an opportunity to warn the testator that the spouse of a beneficiary should not be a witness either.

The testator died two years after the execution of the will. Some time later, the solicitors wrote to the plaintiff informing her that the gifts to her under the will were void because her husband had attested it. The plaintiff brought an action against the solicitors claiming damages for negligence for the loss of the gifts under the will. Sir Robert Megarry VC, after an exhaustive analysis of the authorities, held that she was entitled to succeed ...

I fully accept the reasoning of Sir Robert Megarry that, in a case such as the present, there is a close degree of proximity between the plaintiff and the defendant. If a solicitor is retained by a testator to draft a will, and one of the purposes of the will is to confer a benefit on a named legatee, the solicitor must know that if he fails in his professional duty properly to draft the will, there is considerable risk the legatee will suffer damage. To use Sir Robert's words, his contemplation of the plaintiff is *'actual nominate and direct.'*

Likewise, I accept Sir Robert's reasoning that there can be no conflict of public policy in holding that a solicitor has a duty to take care in drafting a will, not only to the testator but also to a named legatee in the will. There is no possible inconsistency between the duty to the testator and the duty to a legatee. Recognising a duty to a legatee tends to strengthen the chances that the testator's wishes will in fact be properly expressed in the will. The two duties march together.

The authorities are, as I said, analysed by Sir Robert Megarry with consummate ability in his judgment in *Ross v Caunters*, and it would be otiose for me to repeat here the exercise which he has carried out in his judgment. Suffice it to say that I am satisfied on the basis of the decision in *Finlay v Murtagh* that a solicitor does owe a duty to a legatee named in a draft will, to draft the will with such reasonable care and skill as to ensure that the wishes of the testator are not frustrated and the expectancy of the legatee defeated through lack of considerable care and skill on the part of the solicitor.

If a solicitor owes any duty to a named legatee, then it is quite clear that the solicitor in the present case has failed to show the appropriate care and skill. It is unnecessary to labour the point. The case has been frankly met. No effort has been made to defend what was done, except to say that the defendants owed no duty to the plaintiff."

The duty of care is therefore broader than a duty only to one's clients. In *Doran v Delaney* [1999] I.L.R.M. 225 it was held that a solicitor may owe a duty of care to the client of another solicitor. This case does rest largely on its unusual facts, but it is instructive on how the duty of care can be interpreted.

Doran v Delaney
Supreme Court [1998] 2 I.L.R.M. 1

Facts: This is quite a complex case. The plaintiffs purchased a site for a dwelling-house but were unable to build because of a defective title in the portion of the property sold. The vendors had previously started to build on the site but had to discontinue when they had disputes with their neighbours on the issue of encroachment. The vendors then reapplied for planning permission for a smaller house and decided to sell the land with the permission. The map, which was submitted for permission, showed an access route, which was actually in the possession of the neighbour. This route was vital for providing access to the builders. This dispute was not communicated to the plaintiffs who purchased the property. The plaintiffs were also shown the incorrect map and told that these were the correct boundaries. The property was in effect landlocked. The plaintiffs had made some efforts to have the exact extent of the property outlined, and their own solicitor suggested that a special condition be inserted into the contract to delineate the property. The vendors resisted this special condition and the purchaser's solicitors removed the special condition without reference to the purchasers. The parties entered into a contract. Furthermore, when questions were asked in relation to a requisition on title, the vendor replied that there were no boundary disputes with neighbours. The situation was that the neighbour did not resolve the dispute, and the purchaser ended up with a landlocked site, and significant debts.

Issues: The plaintiffs to the action successfully sued the vendors, and their own solicitors. They also took an action against the vendor's solicitors, who were initially absolved; this is the subject of this action. Do the vendor's solicitors owe a duty of care to the plaintiffs to this action? The Supreme Court found for the plaintiffs, holding that in certain circumstances a solicitor may owe the client of another solicitor a duty of care.

Keane J. (Barrington J. concurring; Barron J. did deliver a judgment but agreed in principle with Keane J.):

"... The applicable law
In the course of his speech in *Hedley Byrne & Co. v. Heller & Partners* , the case which, as applied in a number of decisions in this jurisdiction, is authority for the proposition that liability for negligent misstatements can arise in our law, even in the absence of a contractual relationship, Lord Devlin said ([1964] AC 465 at p. 528):

> 'I think, therefore, that there is ample authority to justify your lordships in saying now that the categories of special relationships which may give rise to a duty to take care in word as well as in deed are not limited to contractual relationships or to relationships of fiduciary duty, but include also relationships which in the words of Lord Shaw in *Nocton v. Lord Ashburton* [1914] AC 932 at p. 972 are '*equivalent to contract*' that is, where there is an assumption of responsibility in circumstances in which, but for the absence of consideration, there would be a contract. Where there is an express undertaking, an express warranty as distinct from mere representation, there can be little difficulty. The difficulty arises in discerning those cases in which the undertaking is to be implied. In this respect the absence of consideration is not relevant. Payment for information or advice is very good evidence that it has been relied on and that the informer or adviser knows that it is. Where there is no consideration, it will be necessary to exercise greater care in distinguishing social and professional relationships and between those which are of a contractual character and those which are not. It may often be material to consider whether the adviser is acting purely out of good nature or whether he is getting his reward in some indirect form.'

The latter part of that passage is of assistance in determining the nature of the duty of care, if any, which a vendor's solicitor owes to the purchaser in circumstances such as arose in the present case. While there was no contractual relationship between the vendors' solicitors and the purchasers, that would not of itself negate the existence of a duty of care. Moreover, in determining whether such a duty of care arose in the particular circumstances, it is a material factor that statements such as replies to requisitions are made by a solicitor acting as such and not in some casual social context. Again, while the primary duty of the solicitor acting for the vendor in circumstances such as arose here, is, under common law and by virtue of contract, to protect his own client, that obligation is perfectly consistent with the existence of a duty of care in certain circumstances to the purchaser.

It is also clear that the transmission by a solicitor to a third party of information which turns out to be inaccurate and upon which the third party relied to his detriment does not, of itself, afford a cause of action in negligence to the injured third party. The factors necessary to give rise to liability were set out by Lord Jauncey in the passage so frequently referred to in the present case in *Midland Bank plc v. Cameron, Tong, Peterkin and Duncans* as follows:

'In my opinion four factors are relevant to a determination of the question whether in a particular case a solicitor, while acting for a client, also owed a duty of care to a third party.

(1) The solicitor must assume responsibility for advice or information furnished to the third party;

(2) The solicitor must let it be known to the third party expressly or impliedly that he claims, by reason of his calling, to have the requisite skill or knowledge to give the advice or furnish the information;

(3) The third party must have relied on that information as a matter for which the solicitor has assumed personal responsibility;

(4) The solicitor must have been aware that the third party was likely so to rely.'

It is clear that, at least in cases where those four factors are present, a solicitor may be held liable in negligence to a third party under the more general principle laid down in *Hedley Byrne & Co. Ltd v. Heller & Partners Ltd.* An example of a case in which they were clearly met is the New Zealand decision of *Allied Finance and Investments Ltd v. Haddow & Co.* to which we were also referred.

In that case, the plaintiffs, a money lending company, lent a person money on the security of a yacht which the plaintiffs understood that he was buying. Before the loan was made, the plaintiffs' solicitors forwarded to the borrower's solicitors an instrument by way of security and asked them for a certain certificate. The borrower's solicitors returned the instrument signed by him and certified, *inter alia, 'that the instrument by way of security is fully binding on RKH.'* In fact, and to the knowledge of RKH's solicitors, the yacht was being purchased by a company of which he was a director and controlling shareholder. When the yacht was seized by the unpaid seller and H. became bankrupt, the plaintiffs sued its solicitors for the balance of their loan. The New Zealand Court of Appeal held that the solicitors were liable, Cooke J saying [1983] NZLR 22 at p. 24:

'... the relationship between two solicitors acting for their respective clients does not normally of itself impose a duty of care on one solicitor to the client of the other. Normally the relationship is not sufficiently proximate. Each solicitor is entitled to expect that the other party will look to his own solicitor for advice and protection ...

But surely the result of the established principle is different when on request a solicitor gives a certificate on which the other party must naturally be expected to act. That is a classic duty of care situation, now that it is accepted that the likelihood of economic loss only does not automatically rule out a duty. The proximity is almost as close as it could be short of contract ...'

The fact that the vendors in this case have been found to be liable to the plaintiffs for misrepresentations made directly by themselves to the plaintiffs or (as the learned trial judge found) in the form of statements transmitted in good faith by their solicitors is not a relevant consideration in determining whether the solicitors themselves were in breach of a duty of care which they owed to the plaintiffs. A different view was taken in England in *Gran Gelato v. Richcliff (Group) Ltd* [1992] Ch 560, but was not accepted in a subsequent English decision of *McCullagh v. Lane Fox & Partners Ltd*. I would adopt the view taken by Coleman J in the latter case that, in general, the fact that there will be a duplication of remedy should not negate the existence of liability.

Finally, it should always be borne in mind, in considering whether a particular statement amounts to a negligent misstatement, that the omission of significantly relevant facts may be sufficient to convert a literally accurate statement into a misstatement.

Conclusions
There are many occasions when, in furnishing replies to objections or requisitions in a contract for the sale of land, the solicitor for the vendor cannot be said to assume any responsibility for information being transmitted to the purchaser's solicitor. Typically in the course of such a contract the solicitor or counsel for the purchaser may raise an objection or requisition to the effect that, for example, a particular estate has not been got in or appropriate words of limitation have not been used in a deed forming part of the proffered title. The vendor's solicitor or counsel, in reply, may refer to some other document furnished or some legal principle as meeting the difficulty. In such cases, it cannot be said that the vendor's solicitor or counsel, in drafting the reply, is assuming responsibility for information being furnished in the sense in which that expression is used in *Midland Bank plc v. Cameron, Tong, Peterkin and Duncans*. The solicitors and counsel on either side are dealing with the same set of documents and doing no more than expressing their professional opinion on matters of title.

Similarly, there are many circumstances in which the vendor's solicitor in drafting a reply could be described as transmitting information but could not reasonably be regarded as assuming any particular responsibility for that information. Thus, in the present case, the standard requisition 11 asked whether any notice, certificate or order had been served on the vendor under a long series of listed statutes or *'under any other Act ...'* The answer was a terse *'no'*. The purchasers' solicitor from his own experience would be well aware that the most that could be inferred from such a reply was that the vendors' solicitor's clients had so instructed her. It would be wholly unreal to suppose that the vendors' solicitor was accepting any responsibility for the accuracy of the information being furnished.

But that is not to say that there are no circumstances in which the vendor's solicitor will not assume at least some degree of responsibility for the information being furnished to the purchaser's solicitors. Specifically, in a case such as the present, where the vendor's solicitor is asked whether there is any litigation pending or whether any adverse claim has been made to the property and is aware of his or her own knowledge of threats of litigation and adverse claims having been made, he or she assumes at least some responsibility for the information given in reply and cannot be exonerated from responsibility solely on the ground that he or she is simply transmitting the vendor's instructions. Whether he or she can be regarded as so relieved from responsibility must depend upon the circumstances of the particular case and whether it was reasonable, in those circumstances, for the vendor's solicitor simply to transmit what he or she was told without further enquiry.

It is also clear that, in such a situation, the vendor's solicitor in assessing the instructions he or she is given, determining whether further enquiries should be made and deciding on the information to which the vendors' solicitors are entitled, is acting in a professional capacity and must be assumed to be applying the skill and knowledge to be expected of a solicitor in such circumstances.

I would, accordingly, take the view, differing with respect from the learned trial judge, that the first two requirements indicated in *Midland Bank v. Cameron, Tong, Peterkin & Duncans* before a duty of care can arise as between a solicitor and a third party are met in this case.

As to the third and fourth requirements—that the plaintiffs were relying upon the reply and that the vendors' solicitors must have been aware that they were likely so to rely—the context in which the reply was given is crucial. The contract for sale had expressly provided that the site was being sold with the benefit of a specified planning permission. Not merely were the vendors' solicitors aware of this: they were also aware that there was no physical boundary between the site and Mrs McKimm's land and that she had threatened to institute proceedings if the vendors continued to gain access to the land from the main road, on the ground that they would be trespassing on the triangular area. They were also aware that she had claimed through her solicitors that the map on which the planning permission was based erroneously included the triangular area and that, accordingly, the planning permission was invalid. They were also aware of the first named plaintiff's concerns as to the boundary in question, since he had unsuccessfully sought to have the boundary staked out or an ordnance survey map incorporated in the contract. In these circumstances, they must have known that, whether or not their reply accurately reflected the vendors' instructions to them, it would unquestionably be relied on by the plaintiffs. In the event, of course, it was relied on, since the plaintiffs closed the sale wholly unaware of the fact that the vendors had been embroiled in a dispute concerning this very boundary which, as the learned trial judge found, had led to their selling on the property to the plaintiffs and the reply to the requisition, however else it may be viewed, certainly gave not the slightest hint of any trouble as to the boundary to the plaintiffs.

I conclude, accordingly, that the vendors' solicitors owed a duty of care to the plaintiffs when they replied to requisition 13.8. It remains to be considered whether they were in breach of that duty. In the circumstances of this case, I am satisfied that they were. There are many instances in which a solicitor acting in a transaction such as this would be perfectly entitled to convey without comment the information furnished to him by his client, but this was not one of them. It is not a question of the vendors' solicitors having to query the veracity of the instructions being furnished to them by their own client: even if those instructions were perfectly correct, it could have meant that the dispute had been settled on terms that the vendors acknowledged the title of Mrs McKimm to the triangular area. In failing to ascertain the terms on which the dispute had been settled and conveying that information to the plaintiffs, they were in breach of their duty of care to them. On one view—that urged on behalf of the plaintiffs—they had, in any event, not accurately transmitted the vendors' instructions, since those merely indicated that the dispute had been settled: they did not indicate, as the reply to the requisition on one reading did, that no claim to the triangular portion was at the date of the reply being made by Mrs McKimm. At the very least, however, the reply, because of the manner in which it was framed did not convey all the information to which the plaintiffs were entitled and, as I have already said, a partial statement in such circumstances may be equivalent to a misstatement or misrepresentation. It is right to say that no one in this case has suggested that the vendors' solicitors deliberately intended to mislead the plaintiffs or their solicitor: unfortunately, however, they had, in all the circumstances insufficient regard to the duty which they clearly owed to the plaintiffs. Had they got in touch with Cunningham & Co. it would have transpired that Mrs McKimm had not abandoned her claim to the 54 square metres and that her claim was well founded in law. The plaintiffs would then clearly have been in a position to rescind the contract and recover their deposit because of the vendors' misrepresentations."

Comments and Questions:
1. What factors or elements are necessary for a determination that a solicitor, while acting for a client, owes a duty of care to a third party?

Standard of care

Where it is established that a solicitor owes a duty of care, then the issue of the appropriate standard of care must be addressed. In *Hanafin v Gaynor,* High Court, May 1990, Egan J. held:

> "I should at this stage set out what I conceive to be the test when considering whether there has or has not been professional negligence by a solicitor. The Supreme Court held in *William Dunne (an infant) v The National Maternity Hospital and Jackson* [1989] ILRM 735, [1989] IR 91 that a medical practitioner was negligent in diagnosis or treatment only if guilty of such failure as no other practitioner of equal specialist or general status and skill would be guilty of if acting with ordinary care.

This was a claim in respect of medical negligence but it must surely follow in a claim for professional negligence against a solicitor that an analogous test should be applied. The question to be asked, therefore, would be whether the solicitor was guilty of such failure as no other solicitor of equal status and skill would be guilty of if acting with ordinary care. This would not mean that a solicitor following a practice which was general and which was approved of by his colleagues of similar skill would escape liability if it were established that such practice had inherent defects which ought to be obvious to any person giving the matter due consideration. *Roche v Peilow* [1985] IR 232; [1986] ILRM 177."

A solicitor should therefore exercise the degree of care that is to be expected in the circumstances from a solicitor of equal status. Solicitors in general should exercise this professionalism in their work, which can include: the advice they give—*Park Hall School Ltd v Overend* [1987] I.L.R.M. 345; the briefing of counsel—*Fallon v Gannon* [1988] I.L.R.M. 193; the choice of court—*Lopes v Walker,* unreported, Supreme Court, July 1997; and avoiding conflicts of interest—*Phelan Holdings v Hogan,* High Court, October 1996. Showing that a solicitor followed a practice that is common among solicitors can offer a defence in many instances. This issue and the exception to that rule were also addressed in *Roche v Peilow* [1986] I.L.R.M. 189.

Roche v Peilow
Supreme Court [1986] I.L.R.M. 189

Facts: The plaintiffs hired the defendants to act as solicitor for them in the purchase of a house by means of a building contract. This involved the plaintiffs making stage payments during the construction of the house; on completion, the purchaser would receive a 999-year lease on the site and the property. The solicitors for the construction company did, by letter, state that there were no dealings which would adversely affect the title to the property to be sold. The solicitors for the purchaser failed to discover that the property was the subject of a mortgage. The plaintiffs made a number of stage payments but, prior to the completion of the house, the company went into liquidation, resulting in significant financial loss to the purchasers.

Issues: The plaintiffs alleged that the respondents were negligent and in breach of their contract with them for not discovering the mortgage by making the appropriate searches in the Companies' Office and warning them of this risk. The court found for the plaintiffs.

Henchy J. (Hederman J. concurring; Walsh, Griffin and McCarthy JJ. delivered judgments largely in agreement with that of Henchy J.):

"... I have no doubt that the financial disaster that has befallen the plaintiffs may be said to result from the defendants' failure to discover and bring to their notice, before the contract, the existence of the bank's charge. The real question is whether that failure amounts to negligence by the defendants as solicitors.

The general duty owed by a solicitor to his client is to show him the degree of care to be expected in the circumstances from a reasonably careful and skilful solicitor. Usually the solicitor will be held to have discharged that duty if he follows a practice common among the members of his profession: see *Daniels v Heskin* [1954] IR 73 and the cases therein referred to. Conformity with the widely accepted practice of his colleagues will normally rebut an allegation of negligence against a professional man, for the degree of care which the law expects of him is no higher than that to be expected from an ordinary reasonable member of the profession or of the speciality in question. But there is an important exception to that rule of conduct. It was concisely put as follows by Walsh J in *O'Donovan v Cork County Council* [1967] IR 173, at p. 193:

'If there is a common practice which has inherent defects, which ought to be obvious to any person giving the matter due consideration, the fact that it is shown to have been widely and generally adopted over a period of time does not make the practice any the less negligent. Neglect of duty does not cease by repetition to be neglect of duty.'

The reason for that exception or qualification is that the duty imposed by the law rests on the standard to be expected from a reasonably careful member of the profession, and a person cannot be said to be acting reasonably if he automatically and mindlessly follows the practice of others when by taking thought he would have realised that the practice in question was fraught with peril for his client and was readily avoidable or remediable. The professional man is, of course, not to be judged with the benefit of hindsight, but if it can be said that if at the time, on giving the matter due consideration, he would have realised that the impugned practice was in the circumstances incompatible with his client's interests, and if an alternative and safe course of conduct was reasonably open to him, he will be held to have been negligent.

I consider it to be beyond doubt that it was inimical to the plaintiffs' interests for the defendants to allow them to enter into contractual relations with the building company, and in particular to bind themselves to make stage payments, without first making a search in the Companies' Office which would have shown that the beneficial owner of the site was the bank. Because of the defendants' default in that respect, the plaintiffs were left open to disappointment and financial disaster if, as happened, the building company proved to be unable to discharge their indebtedness to the bank. As the evidence in the High Court showed, in not making that search the defendants were following a conveyancing practice common at the time among solicitors. However, adherence to that practice can avail as a defence only if it be shown that a reasonable solicitor, giving consideration at the time to the interests of the client, would have justifiably concluded that a search in the Companies' Office was unnecessary or undesirable. Having regard to the fact that no undue delay, expense or difficulty was involved in making such a search, and bearing in mind that financial disaster of the kind actually sustained by the plaintiffs was reasonably foreseeable by the defendants as a risk for the plaintiffs, I consider that, notwithstanding that the defendants in not carrying out a search were conforming to a practice widespread at the time in the profession, they were nevertheless wanting in the duty of care owed by them to the plaintiffs. It is to avoid detectable pitfalls of the kind that beset the plaintiffs that prospective purchasers engage solicitors to act for them."

Where there is no general and approved practice it is still incumbent on a solicitor who holds himself or herself out to his or her clients as having adequate skill and knowledge to conduct his or her business in that manner. In *Kelly v Crowley* [1985] I.R. 212 the court had to review the duty of a solicitor in the purchase of licensed premises; while there was no general and approved practice, the court assessed what was expected of a reasonable practitioner in this regard.

Kelly v Crowley
High Court [1985] I.R. 212

Facts: The defendant solicitor was acting for the plaintiff in the purchase of a licensed premises, which the plaintiff wished to operate as a public house. The defendant negotiated the sale of the premises, and asked the vendor to specify the exact type of licence attaching to the premises. The vendor, by way of reply, furnished the licence to the defendant. The defendant made no inspection of the Register of Licences. The plaintiff took possession of the premises and operated them as a public house. When he sought to renew his licence it transpired that it was a hotel licence, and the renewal was refused as the premises were not operated as a hotel. As a result the plaintiff suffered a significant financial loss.

Issues: This action is a claim for damages for the negligence of the defendant in the performance of his contractual duty to render professional services as a solicitor.

Murphy J.:

"… Clearly the existence of a general practice—where such is established—can be of particular significance in a case of this nature. If a client can establish the existence of such a practice and show that his solicitor has failed to follow it with a consequent loss to the client this would ordinarily constitute compelling evidence of professional negligence. On the other hand, if a solicitor establishes for his part that there is a generally accepted practice in a particular aspect of his profession and that he has adhered to that practice and despite so doing that his client has suffered loss this would ordinarily provide a defence to a claim of negligence against him. Clearly stress must be placed on the word 'ordinarily' in both cases as it is obvious that many cases will turn upon their own particular facts and indeed there are cases in which professional practices and procedures themselves may be so deficient that reliance upon them would not provide a defence to a claim for negligence (see the observations of Mr. Justice Walsh in *O'Donovan* v. *Cork County Council* [1967] IR 173 at p.193). Indeed, it is unlikely that any professional man would contend that he discharged his duty to his client by a blind adherence to a procedure however sound. There must always be room for the application of the professional expertise of the individual lawyer to the particular circumstances of the individual case and the needs of his own client. However, in the absence of evidence as to the practice of the solicitors' profession the matter falls to be considered from first principles. This involves a consideration of the relevant provisions of the Licensing Acts and the nature of the functions carried out by a solicitor in investigating title on behalf of his client ...

Where a licence is granted on the basis that the premises constitute an hotel a certificate for the renewal of the licence will not be granted if the premises cease to be an hotel and furthermore where the licence was granted originally after the passing of the Act of 1960. Section 20, of that Act introduces a mandatory condition precedent to the renewal of the certificate: it must be shown to the satisfaction of the court hearing the application for the grant of the certificate that the hotel is registered in the Register of Hotels kept by Bord Fáilte Éireann ...

Undoubtedly a person familiar with the relevant legislation and the proper interpretation thereof would appreciate the importance of distinguishing between a licence granted to a public house and a licence granted to an hotel. It seems to me that the next question is, therefore, whether the defendant in the present case failed in his contractual obligation to the plaintiffs by neglecting to ensure that the licence attaching to the licensed premises in question was granted in respect of a public house rather than an hotel.

It is well settled law that a solicitor holds himself out to his clients as having adequate skill and knowledge properly to conduct all business that he undertakes. The solicitor has a duty in contract and tort to his client to possess and properly apply that degree of skill and knowledge in the conduct of his client's affairs. However, it is a duty to exercise care: not a guarantee that a particular result will be achieved. This aspect of the matter was adverted to in *Roche* v. *Peilow* [1985] I.R. 232 where Finlay P. Cashe then quoted with approval a passage in which Hodson L.J. in *Simmons* v. *Pennington & Son*[1955] 1 W.L.R. 183 (at p.189) had in turn cited from an earlier decision the following passage:—

'In *Cook* v. *Falconer's Representatives*, Lord Fullerton said "A professional man does not warrant that what he does will certainly have the effect which is expected from him. He warrants only that he should bestow on the matter committed to him the skill generally possessed by his brethren in the profession. It is not enough in order to recover damages from a professional man to show that something which was committed to him to do, has not had the effect which was expected from it; he must show an act of gross ignorance, such as could not have been committed by any other ordinarily informed member of the profession".'

Whilst it is clear that in *Roche* v. *Peilow* [1985] IR 232 the defendant solicitor did not achieve what was expected to be achieved from him, namely, securing to the plaintiff therein a good title to the premises on which he had spent his money the learned trial judge was satisfied first that the solicitor in that case 'throughout acted with general care and promptness and applied his mind to the various problems that arose in (that) transaction' and secondly 'that there were no members of the solicitors' profession in Ireland who in 1973 and 1974 had foreseen the particular series of events which in (that) case caused the plaintiff's loss.' ...

It seems to me that in every case in which a solicitor acts on behalf of a client in the purchase of premises in respect of which there has been granted a licence for the sale of intoxicating liquor, the solicitor is bound to concern himself with the nature of the licence attaching to the premises; the power of the vendor to procure such licence to be vested in the purchaser and the means by which such licence is transferred to or vested in the client. As the evidence in the present case demonstrates, a substantial part of the consideration for the sale may be attributable to the licence and certainly the nature of the licence and the means by which it is renewed and transferred is clearly a matter of law on which the lay client is necessarily dependent upon his professional adviser for guidance and assistance. As I understand it, in *Taylor's Case* (Unreported, High Court, Finlay P., 10th March, 1983) the learned President accepted that this was so and the substantive issue in the case was whether the enquiries made by the solicitor were sufficient having regard to the fact that his suspicions should have been aroused by his client on the one hand and his particular knowledge of the premises on the other hand. In the circumstances it seems to me that the conclusion is inescapable—even in the absence of evidence of any practice or custom in relation to the exercise of the solicitors' profession—that a solicitor acting on behalf of a lay client in the purchase of licensed premises is bound to make appropriate enquiries as to the nature of the licence attaching thereto."

CHAPTER 9

TRESPASS

INTRODUCTION

Trespass is one of the oldest established torts, and is an intentional tort concerned with the deliberate interference with the rights of another. There are three forms of trespass: trespass against the person; trespass onto land; and trespass to chattels.

CHARACTERISTICS OF TRESPASS

A number of characteristics must be present before the tort of trespass can be established. The trespass or injury must be the result of a direct impact, and the result of a voluntary act. Trespass is actionable *per se*. For an action in trespass to succeed the plaintiff must establish that the defendant either intended to bring the result about, or was negligent as to the harm that could result from his/her actions. *Scott v Shepherd* (1773) All E.R. Rep 295 describes an example of what can amount to a voluntary act; also of interest is the dissenting judgment where Blackstone J. discussed the issue of direct impact as opposed to consequential impact.

Scott v Shepherd
Court of Common Pleas [1558–1774] All E.R. Rep 295;
also reported 2 Wm. Bl. 892, 3 Wils 403, 96 E.R. 525

Facts: In this action, the defendant threw a firecracker made of gunpowder into a market where a large group of people were assembled. The firecracker fell on the stall of a third person, Willis, and, to prevent injury to himself and his goods, Willis threw it onwards. At this stage the firecracker landed on another stall and again it was thrown onwards, this time by Ryal, whereupon it exploded and injured the plaintiff.

Issues: In an action for trespass and assault, the defendant pleaded that as he had not directly hit the plaintiff, he was not liable. It was held for the plaintiff that, in order to maintain trespass, it was not necessary for the defendant personally to have touched the plaintiff. The question also arose as to whether an act of self-defence can render conduct involuntary.

Nares J.:

"... I am of opinion that trespass would well lie in the present case. The natural and probable consequence of the act done by the defendant was injury to somebody, and, therefore, the act was illegal at common law ... Being, therefore, unlawful, the defendant was liable to answer for the consequences, be the injury mediate or immediate. YEAR BOOK 21 Hen 7, 28, is express that *malus animus* is not necessary to constitute a trespass ... The principle I go on is what is laid down in *Reynolds v Clark* [(1725) Fortes Rep 212]; that if the act in the first instance be unlawful, trespass will lie. Wherever, therefore, an act is unlawful at first, trespass will lie for the consequences of it ... I do not think it necessary, to maintain trespass, that the defendant should personally touch the plaintiff; if he does it by a mean it is sufficient ... He is the person who, in the present case, gave the mischievous faculty to the squib. That mischievous faculty remained in it until the explosion. No new power of doing mischief was communicated to it by Willis or Ryal ... The person who turns him loose is answerable in trespass for whatever mischief he may do. The intermediate acts of Willis and Ryal will not purge the original tort in the defendant. But he who does the first wrong is answerable for all the consequential damages ..."

Blackstone J. (dissenting):

"... I am of opinion that an action of trespass does not lie for the plaintiff against the defendant on this Case. I take the settled distinction to be that, where the injury is immediate, an action of trespass will lie; where it is only consequential, it must be an action on the Case: *Reynolds v Clark* [(1725) Fortes Rep 212]; *Haward v Bankes* [(1760) 2 Burr 1114]; *Harker v Birkbeck* [(1764) 3 Burr 1556]. The lawfulness or unlawfulness of the original act is not the criterion, although something of that sort is put into LORD RAYMOND'S mouth in *Reynolds v Clark* [(1725) Fortes Rep 212] where it can only mean that if the act then in question, of erecting a spout, had been in itself unlawful, trespass might have lain; but as it was a lawful act (on the defendant's own ground) and the injury to the plaintiff only consequential, it must be an action on the case. But this cannot be the general rule, for it is held by the court in the same case that if I throw a log of timber into the highway (which is an unlawful act) and another man tumbles over it and is hurt, an action on the case only lies, it being a consequential damage; but if in throwing it I hit another man, he may bring trespass because it is an immediate wrong. Trespass may sometimes lie for the consequences of a lawful act. If in lopping my own trees a bough accidentally falls on my neighbour's ground and I go thereon to fetch it, trespass lies. This is the case cited from YB 6 Edw 4, fo 7, pl 18. But then the entry is of itself an immediate wrong. And case will sometimes lie for the consequence of an unlawful act ...

The solid distinction is between direct or immediate injuries on the one hand and mediate or consequential on the other, and trespass never lay for the latter.

If this be so, the only question will be whether the injury which the plaintiff suffered was immediate, or consequential only; and I hold it to be the latter."

Gould J.:

"... I agree with Nares, J, that, wherever a man does an unlawful act, he is answerable for all the consequences; and trespass will lie against him if the consequence be in nature of trespass. But, exclusive of this, I think that the defendant may be considered in the same view as if he himself had personally thrown the squib in the plaintiff's face. The terror impressed on Willis and Ryal excited self-defence and deprived them of the power of recollection. What they did was, therefore, the inevitable consequence of the defendant's unlawful act. Had the squib been thrown into a coach full of company, the person throwing it out again would not have been answerable for the consequences. What Willis and Ryal did was by necessity, and the defendant imposed that necessity on them."

De Grey C.J.:

"... The question here is whether the injury received by the plaintiff arises from the force of the original act of the defendant, or from a new force by a third person. I agree with Blackstone, J, as to the principles he has laid down but not in his application of those principles to the present case. The real question certainly does not turn on the lawfulness or unlawfulness of the original act; for actions of trespass will lie for legal acts when they become trespasses by accident, as in the cases cited of cutting thorns, lopping of a tree, shooting at a mark, defending oneself by a stick which strikes another behind, etc. They may also not lie for the consequences even of illegal acts, as that of casting a log in the highway, etc. But the true question is whether the injury is the direct and immediate act of the defendant; and I am of opinion that in this case it is. The throwing the squib was an act unlawful and tending to affright the bystanders. So far, mischief was originally intended; not any particular mischief, but mischief indiscriminate and wanton. Whatever mischief, therefore, follows he is the author of it ... It has been urged that the intervention of a free agent will make a difference; but I do not consider Willis and Ryal as free agents in the present case, but acting under a compulsive necessity for their own safety and self-preservation. On these reasons I concur with Gould and Nares, JJ, that the present action is maintainable."

Comments and Questions:

1. Compare and contrast the view taken of a voluntary act and direct impact by Nares J. and Blackstone J.

2. De Grey C.J. agrees with the principles laid down by Blackstone J., but comes to a different conclusion—how does he achieve this?

TRESPASS AGAINST THE PERSON

There are three torts contained within the general tort of trespass against the person. These are assault, battery and false imprisonment. McMahon and Binchy suggest a potential fourth trespass against the person, namely, the intentional infliction of emotional distress; see *The Law of Torts* (3rd edn., Butterworths, 2000), Chapter 22, for more information on this.

Assault

An assault is defined as "an act that places another person in reasonable apprehension of an immediate battery being committed upon him.": *Dullaghan v Hillen* [1957] Ir. Jur. Rep. Assault does not require touching, but for the victim of the assault to fear a battery.

Dullaghan v Hillen and King
Circuit Court [1957] Ir. Jur. Rep. 10

Facts: The plaintiff was stopped by customs officers while driving a motor van near the border. The four customs officers approached the motor van and commenced questioning the plaintiff. The plaintiff refused to answer questions, and was removed by one of the customs officers; blows were exchanged between them and the plaintiff was injured. The plaintiff was detained by the customs officers, brought to Dundalk police station and charged.

Issues: The plaintiff to the action took a case for assault and battery, false imprisonment and malicious prosecution against two of the customs officers. The court held that the plaintiff had been assaulted as the defendant had exceeded his powers. The plaintiff did not succeed on the other actions.

Fawsitt J.:

"The plaintiff claimed damages for assault and battery, false imprisonment, and malicious prosecution ...

Assault and battery: Security for the person is among the first conditions of civilized life. The law, therefore, protects us, not only against actual hurt and violence, but against every kind of bodily interference and restraint not justified or excused by allowed cause, and against the present (immediate) apprehension of any of these things. Blackstone said: 'The least touching of another's person wilfully, or in anger, is a battery; for the law cannot draw the line between different degrees of violence and, therefore, totally prohibits the first and lowest stage of it: every man's person being sacred and no other having a right to meddle with it in any the slightest manner.' Battery indicates assault, and the word 'assault' is to-day commonly made to include battery. Hostile or unlawful intention is necessary to constitute an indictable assault, and such touching, pushing or the little as belongs to the ordinary conduct of life and is free from the use of unnecessary force, is neither an offence nor a wrong. Words cannot of themselves amount to an assault, under any circumstances. When one is wrongfully assaulted, it is lawful to repel force by force, provided that no unnecessary violence is used. How much force and of what kind it is reasonable and proper to use, in the circumstances, is a question of fact. Resistance must 'not exceed the bounds of mere defence and prevention,' or that the force used in defence must be not more than commensurate with that which provoked it …

The first question which I have to determine is: did Hillen beat the plaintiff in self-defence? … [T]he plaintiff uttered a filthy and insulting remark towards Hillen, which still further inflamed Hillen's temper. But for his agitated state of mind Hillen would, no doubt, have recollected the commonplace but trite couplet which runs: 'Sticks and stones may break your bones but words will never hurt you,' and in which there is a definition of the law of assault, namely that mere words, no matter how harsh, lying, insulting and provocative they may be, can never amount in law to an assault. When the plaintiff refused to withdraw and apologise to Hillen for the insulting words which the plaintiff used towards and of Hillen, the assault on, and beating up of, the plaintiff, by Hillen, immediately followed. The plaintiff, his passion, too, now aroused, then made a kick at Hillen which, if it struck Hillen, did him no injury, and could, properly in the circumstances, be described as having been made by the plaintiff in his self defence. … This series of blows by Hillen on the plaintiff's nose was not delivered by him in his (Hillen's) self-defence … It was committed by Hillen in excess of the limits of the powers which he possessed as customs officer.

False imprisonment: The second ground of the plaintiff's claim is that he was held prisoner and arrested: that is, he was unlawfully detained and arrested: that is, he was unlawfully detained and arrested by the defendants. This is an allegation of false imprisonment. It has been judicially stated that 'interference with the liberty of the subject by a private person has ever been jealously guarded by the common law of the land. At common law a police constable may arrest a person if he has reasonable cause to suspect that a felony has been committed, although it afterwards appears that no felony had been committed, but that is not so when a private person makes or causes the arrest, for to justify his action, he must prove among other things that a felony has actually been committed.' (see per Lord Tenterden, CJ in *Beckwith v. Philby*) … Suspicion only, without a felony committed, is no cause for the arrest of another by a private person … Freedom of the person includes immunity, not only from the actual application of force, but from every kind of detention and restraint not authorised by law. The infliction of such restraint is the worry of false imprisonment, which though generally coupled with assault, is nevertheless a distinct wrong. False imprisonment is the unlawful and total restraint of the personal liberty of another whether by constraining him or compelling him to go to a particular place or confining him in a prison or police station or private place or by detaining him against his will in a public place. The essential element in the offence is the unlawful detention of the person, or the unlawful restraint on his liberty. The fact that a person is not actually aware that he is being imprisoned does not amount to evidence that he is not imprisoned, it being possible for a person to be imprisoned in law, without his being conscious of the fact and appreciating the position in which he is placed, laying hands upon the person of the party imprisoned not being essential. There may be an effectual imprisonment without walls of any kind. The detainer must be such as to limit the party's freedom of motion in all directions. In effect, imprisonment is a total restraint of the liberty of the person. The offence is committed by mere detention without violence.

When an action of false imprisonment is brought and defended, the real question in issue is: was the imprisonment justified? All the plaintiff has to prove is the detention: it is then for the defendant to show that he was justified in what he did, and that the imprisonment was lawful. The present defendants are persons with limited authority, under the customs statutes and regulations, to arrest person in certain circumstances. 'The general rule of law as to actions of trespass against persons having a limited authority is plain and clear. It they do any act beyond the limit of their authority ... they thereby subject themselves to an action of trespass; but if the act be within the limit of their authority, although it may be done through an erroneous or mistaken judgment, they are not liable to such action.' (*Doswell v. Impey*). Has the plaintiff in this action, proved that he was detained and imprisoned? [Evidence set out] ... On these facts I must find that there was a detaining and imprisonment of the person of the plaintiff by and at the instance of the defendant ... I must hold that the plaintiff's detention and imprisonment was within the limited powers of the defendant, King, as customs officer, and done in the discharge of his duty as such officer ..."

Comments and Questions:

1. Assault is defined as an act that places another person in reasonable apprehension of an immediate battery being committed upon him. Does this require the potential victim to fear such contact or is an awareness of the potential of such contact sufficient?

2. In this action Fawsitt J. defines assault, battery and trespass against the person. Assault is defined as the fear or anticipation of a battery and Fawsitt J. states that "words cannot of themselves amount to an assault, under any circumstances." In your opinion is this too broad an exception? Can you envisage situations where words alone may amount to an assault?

Fawsitt J. stated that words alone cannot amount to assault; this suggests that words would need to be accompanied by an act for an assault to arise. By the same rationale, where an action could amount to an assault, can words render that action innocent? This issue was addressed in *Turberville v Savage* [1669] 86 E.R. 684.

Turberville v Savage
[1669] 86 E.R. 684

Facts: The incident that gave rise to this case arose during assize time (assize time relates to a period where the court travelled from county to county in England and Wales at intervals). During a period of assize a man held his sword and stated: "If it were not assize time, I would not take such language from you."

Issue: Do words mitigate what could amount to an assault? The court held that words can mitigate an assault.

COURT

"The evidence to prove a provocation was, that the plaintiff put his hand upon his sword and said, '*If it were not assize-time, I would not take such language from you.*'—The question was, If that were an assault?—The Court agreed that it was not; for the declaration of the plaintiff was, that he would not assault him, the Judges being in town; and *the intention* as well *as the act* makes an assault. Therefore if one strike another upon the hand, or arm, or breast in discourse, it is no assault, there being no *intention* to assault; but if one, intending to assault, strike *at* another and miss him, this is an assault: so if he hold up his hand against another in a threatening in manner and say nothing, it is an assault. – In the principal case the plaintiff had judgment."

Comments and Questions:
1. The court held here that both action and intention was necessary. In the modern version of this tort it appears that negligence as to the outcome of your actions can replace intention in a given situation.

While words alone have been deemed not capable of amounting to an assault, and words can mitigate what would otherwise have been an assault, silence has been held capable of constituting an assault. The relevant case is *R. v Ireland* [1998] A.C. 147, a criminal case, where a person who made silent telephone calls was found guilty of assault. The court determined that a person receiving silent calls could apprehend physical contact as a result.

R. v Ireland; R. v Burstow
House of Lords [1998] A.C. 147

Facts: This case involved two appeals from criminal conviction; as they were addressing similar legal questions both cases were heard together. The appellant to the first case had been making a large number of telephone calls to three women and remaining silent when they answered. A psychiatrist who examined the women stated that, as a result of the repeated telephone calls, each of them had suffered psychological damage. The second appellant conducted a campaign of harassment of a woman with whom he had previously had a social relationship which she had terminated. For a period of about eight months in 1995 he made silent telephone calls, distributed offensive cards in the street where she lived, sent menacing notes to her, appeared at her home and place of work and took photographs of her and her family. A consultant psychiatrist stated that she was suffering from a severe depressive illness. For the purposes of this extract we will focus on the case of *R v Ireland.*

Issue: This chapter relates to the issue of assault. An assault may be committed by words and gestures depending on the circumstances. In this instance the court had to address whether the making of a silent telephone call which caused fear of immediate and unlawful violence amounted to an assault. The court held that it did amount to assault and so the convictions stood.

Lord Steyn (Lord Goff, Lord Slynn, Lord Craighead and Lord Hutton concurring):

"… My Lords, it is easy to understand the terrifying effect of a campaign of telephone calls at night by a silent caller to a woman living on her own. It would be natural for the victim to regard the calls as menacing. What may heighten her fear is that she will not know what the caller may do next. The spectre of the caller arriving at her doorstep bent on inflicting personal violence on her may come to dominate her thinking. After all, as a matter of common sense, what else would she be terrified about? The victim may suffer psychiatric illness such as anxiety neurosis or acute depression. Harassment of women by repeated silent telephone calls, accompanied on occasions by heavy breathing, is apparently a significant social problem. That the criminal law should be able to deal with this problem, and so far as is practicable, afford effective protection to victims is self-evident …

Before the Court of Appeal there were two principal issues … The second issue was whether Ireland's conduct was capable of amounting to an assault. In giving the judgment of the court in Ireland's case Swinton Thomas L.J. said, at p. 119:

'It has been recognised for many centuries that putting a person in fear may amount to an assault. The early cases predate the invention of the telephone. We must apply the law to conditions as they are in the 20th century.' …

It is now necessary to consider whether the making of silent telephone calls causing psychiatric injury is capable of constituting an assault under section 47. The Court of Appeal, as constituted in the Reg. v. Ireland case, answered that question in the affirmative. There has been substantial academic criticism of the conclusion and reasoning in *Reg. v. Ireland*: see Archbold News, Issue 6, 12 July 1996; Archbold's Criminal Pleading, Evidence & Practice, Supplement No. 4 (1996), pp. 345–347; Smith and Hogan, Criminal Law, 8th ed. (1996), 413; 'Assault by Telephone' by Jonathan Herring [1997] C.L.J. 11 and 'Assault' [1997] Crim. L.R. 434, 435–436. Counsel's arguments, broadly speaking, challenged the decision in *Reg. v. Ireland* on very similar lines. Having carefully considered the literature and counsel's arguments, I have come to the conclusion that the appeal ought to be dismissed ...

It is to assault in the form of an act causing the victim to fear an immediate application of force to her that I must turn. Counsel argued that as a matter of law an assault can never be committed by words alone and therefore it cannot be committed by silence. The premise depends on the slenderest authority, namely, an observation by Holroyd J. to a jury that 'no words or singing are equivalent to an assault:' *Rex v. Meade and Belt* (1823) 1 Lew. 184. The proposition that a gesture may amount to an assault, but that words can never suffice, is unrealistic and indefensible ...

That brings me to the critical question whether a silent caller may be guilty of an assault. The answer to this question seems to me to be 'Yes, depending on the facts.' It involves questions of fact within the province of the jury. After all, there is no reason why a telephone caller who says to a woman in a menacing way 'I will be at your door in a minute or two' may not be guilty of an assault if he causes his victim to apprehend immediate personal violence. Take now the case of the silent caller. He intends by his silence to cause fear and he is so understood. The victim is assailed by uncertainty about his intentions. Fear may dominate her emotions, and it may be the fear that the caller's arrival at her door may be imminent. She may fear the possibility of immediate personal violence. As a matter of law the caller may be guilty of an assault: whether he is or not will depend on the circumstance and in particular on the impact of the caller's potentially menacing call or calls on the victim. Such a prosecution case under section 47 may be fit to leave to the jury. And a trial judge may, depending on the circumstances, put a common sense consideration before the jury, namely what, if not the possibility of imminent personal violence, was the victim terrified about? I conclude that an assault may be committed in the particular factual circumstances which I have envisaged. For this reason I reject the submission that as a matter of law a silent telephone caller cannot ever be guilty of an offence under section 47. In these circumstances no useful purpose would be served by answering the vague certified question in *Reg. v. Ireland*."

Battery

For the tort of battery to be established a number of requirements must be fulfilled. There must be the direct application of physical contact with the person of another; this can be touching, kissing or spitting in a person's face (*R. v Cotesworth* (1704) 6 Mod. 172). Another element of this tort is that the touching, in whatever form it takes, must be touching without the consent, express or implied, of the person being touched. A battery may occur where a person initially touches another with their consent but then exceeds the consent given; this occurred in *Corcoran v W & R Jacob* [1954] I.R. 446 where a security guard was over-zealous in his search of an employee.

Corcoran v W & R Jacob
Supreme Court [1945] I.R. 446

Facts: The plaintiff was a storekeeper for the defendants. During the plaintiff's employment he left the defendant's premises on messages for them and, while so engaged, purchased a small shovel for himself. When returning to the defendant's premises he carried the shovel inserted in his dungarees so that very little of it was visible. He consented to be searched by a commissionaire employed by the defendants. The commissionaire attempted to assist the plaintiff in removing the shovel from his person and, in doing so, pulled the plaintiff's clothes about violently and slightly damaged them. The plaintiff then stopped the search, and alleged that an assault had taken place. The case at first instance held for the plaintiff on two counts, defamation and assault, and awarded £500 in damages but did not segregate the amounts between each claim. The defendants appealed.

Issues: The Supreme Court held that the defamation action would not succeed. The Supreme Court remitted the case to the High Court to assess damages on the claim for assault.

Murnaghan J. (Geoghegan, O'Byrne JJ. concurring; Black J. in his judgment agreed):

"... In his evidence the respondent said that on his return to the factory he purchased a copper shovel, and carried it on his bicycle until he reached the factory, where he removed it from the bicycle and put it inside his clothes in a way which was the subject of much discussion in this Court and at the trial. He said himself that it was inside his trousers and dungarees, over which he wore his coat and overcoat. The commissionaire asked him what he had inside his coat and Corcoran said he had a shovel. The commissionaire then asked him to come to the office to be searched. Having gone into the office the respondent says that he proceeded to remove the shovel to show it to Noonan. He also makes statements suggesting that both coats were open, but admits that he had difficulty in getting out the shovel. He says Noonan made a sudden rush—a 'power dive'—at him and pulled his clothes about. The respondent resented that, buttoned his coat, and refused to allow the search to proceed, and went away ...

As regards the respondent's claim in respect of an alleged assault, booklets have been produced here, and evidence was given at the trial of notices exhibited in the factory, showing the firm's regulations as to their employees' liability to be searched. As I understand it, the case proceeded on the basis that Corcoran agreed that he was liable to search, as that word is ordinarily understood. There was no limitation of the right of the searcher to put his hands upon the person searched.

The only question which arises, then, is whether there was any unnecessary violence used in Noonan's search of Corcoran. The respondent spoke of a 'power dive.' That is ambiguous, but might lead a jury to believe that excessive strength was used which might be unreasonable in the circumstances. The appellants' servant said he only used such force as was necessary, and desisted when objection was made, and it is agreed that he did at once desist. My view is that this is a question of fact, in one sense, for a jury. I do not think the mere pulling about of his clothes was such as in any way injuriously to affect the respondent. He was not injured, but merely lost a button. Counsel for the appellant practically admit that it was a question for the jury whether any unnecessary violence was used, and in these circumstances, I do not think that the Court should interfere with the jury's findings on this issue."

Comments and Questions:
1. Based on this definition batteries occur every day in many situations, for example, when queuing at a bar for a drink. It is not an attractive proposition that we permit litigation in all of those situations; one possible solution is to expand the concept of implied consent. Consent may be implied to cover a range of everyday events such as bumping into a person on a crowded street. This touching may otherwise be deemed unlawful.

2. McMahon and Binchy, in *The Law of Torts* (3rd ed., Butterworths, 2000), p.620, refer to three possible approaches to addressing the problem of everyday contact. One is implied consent, a second is the necessity for hostility in touching (see below), and a third is restricting actions in battery to offensive or harmful contact. This issue has not been resolved in the Irish context. Which approach would you favour?

The authorities lead one to the conclusion that for a battery to exist there must be an intentional touching or contact with the plaintiff by the defendant. This form of contact could arise in so many situations; sitting in a crowded lecture theatre could give rise to several technical batteries. It would not be desirable if all such contacts could lead to litigation, and in England they have attempted to deal with this by the introduction of the concept of "hostility"; that is, that the touching must be proved to be a hostile touching. This issue was addressed in *Wilson v Pringle* [1987] Q.B. 237 and it was held that hostility is not to be equated with ill-will or malevolence. It is to be determined by the facts of the case. In this case two school-children were involved in horseplay and one was injured; it was held that there was no hostility in the touching.

Wilson v Pringle
Court of Appeal [1987] Q.B. 237

Facts: The plaintiff and the defendant, both aged 13, were schoolboys in the same class. The plaintiff alleged that he suffered serious injury as a result of the defendant having intentionally jumped on him. The defendant denied liability, claiming that he had merely pulled the plaintiff's schoolbag off his shoulder in the course of ordinary horseplay and that as a result the plaintiff had fallen to the ground and sustained his injuries.

Issues: The plaintiff claimed damages from the defendant for trespass to the person, specifically battery. Battery was held to be an intentional and hostile touching of, or contact with, one person by another. The court focused on potential defences, and the Court of Appeal granted leave to appeal as the trial judge had not given enough consideration to all the elements of the tort of battery, particularly the defences.

Croom-Johnson L.J.:

"… The judgment of the Divisional Court was given by Robert Goff L.J. It is necessary to give a long quotation to do full justice to it. He said, at pp. 1177–1178:

'We are here concerned primarily with battery. The fundamental principle, plain and incontestable, is that every person's body is inviolate. It has long been established that any touching of another person, however slight, may amount to a battery. So Holt C.J. held in *Cole v. Turner* (1704) 6 Mod. 149 that "the least touching of another in anger is a battery." The breadth of the principle reflects the fundamental nature of the interest so protected. As Blackstone wrote in his Commentaries, 17th ed. (1830), vol. 3, p. 120: "the law cannot draw the line between different degrees of violence, and therefore totally prohibits the first and lowest stage of it; every man's person being sacred, and no other having a right to meddle with it, in any the slightest manner." The effect is that everybody is protected not only against physical injury but against any form of physical molestation.

But so widely drawn a principle must inevitably be subject to exceptions. For example, children may be subjected to reasonable punishment; people may be subjected to the lawful exercise of the power of arrest; and reasonable force may be used in self-defence or for the prevention of crime. But, apart from these special instances where the control or constraint is lawful, a broader exception has been created to allow for the exigencies of everyday life. Generally speaking, consent is a defence to battery; and most of the physical contacts of ordinary life are not actionable because they are impliedly consented to by all who move in society and so expose themselves to the risk of bodily contact. So nobody can complain of the jostling which is inevitable from his presence in, for example, a supermarket, an underground station or a busy street; nor can a person who attends a party complain if his hand is seized in friendship, or even if his back is, within reason, slapped: see *Turberville v. Savage* (1669) 1 Mod. 3. Although such cases are regarded as examples of implied consent, it is more common nowadays to treat them as falling within a general exception embracing all physical contact which is generally acceptable in the ordinary conduct of daily life. We observe that, although in the past it has sometimes been stated that a battery is only committed where the action is "angry, revengeful, rude, or insolent" (see Hawkins, Pleas of the Crown, 8th ed. (1824), vol. 1, c. 15, section 2), we think that nowadays it is more realistic, and indeed more accurate, to state the broad underlying principle, subject to the broad exception.

Among such forms of conduct, long held to be acceptable, is touching a person for the purpose of engaging his attention, though of course using no greater degree of physical contact than is reasonably necessary in the circumstances for that purpose. So, for example, it was held by the Court of Common Pleas in 1807 that a touch by a constable's staff on the shoulder of a man who had climbed on a gentleman's railing to gain a better view of a mad ox, the touch being only to engage the man's attention, did not amount to a battery: see *Wiffin v. Kincard* (1807) 2 Bos. & Pul. 471; for another example, see *Coward v. Baddeley* (1859) 4 H. & N. 478. But a distinction is drawn between a touch to draw a man's attention, which is generally acceptable, and a physical restraint, which is not. So we find Parke B. observing in *Rawlings v. Till* (1837) 3 M. & W. 28, 29, with reference to *Wiffin v. Kincard*, that "There the touch was merely to engage [a man's] attention, not to put a restraint upon his person." Furthermore, persistent touching to gain attention in the face of obvious disregard may transcend the norms of acceptable behaviour, and so be outside the exception. We do not say that more than one touch is never permitted; for example, the lost or distressed may surely be permitted a second touch, or possibly even more, on a reluctant or impervious sleeve or shoulder, as may a person who is acting reasonably in the exercise of a duty. In each case, the test must be whether the physical contact so persisted in has in the circumstances gone beyond generally acceptable standards of conduct; and the answer to that question will depend upon the facts of the particular case.'

This rationalisation by Robert Goff L.J. draws the so-called 'defences' to an action for trespass to the person (of which consent, self-defence, ejecting a trespasser, exercising parental authority, and statutory authority are some examples) under one umbrella of 'a general exception embracing all physical contact which is generally acceptable in the ordinary conduct of daily life.' ...

In our view, the authorities lead one to the conclusion that in a battery there must be an intentional touching or contact in one form or another of the plaintiff by the defendant. That touching must be proved to be a hostile touching. That still leaves unanswered the question 'when is a touching to be called hostile?' Hostility cannot be equated with ill-will or malevolence ... It may be imported from the circumstances ... Where the immediate act of touching does not itself demonstrate hostility, the plaintiff should plead the facts which are said to do so ...

Although we are all entitled to protection from physical molestation we live in a crowded world in which people must be considered as taking on themselves some risk of injury (where it occurs) from the acts of others which are not in themselves unlawful. If negligence cannot be proved, it may be that an injured plaintiff who is also unable to prove a battery, will be without redress.

Defences like self-defence, and exercising the right of arrest, are relevant here. Similarly, it may be that allowances must be made, where appropriate, for the idiosyncrasies of individuals or (as was demonstrated in *Walmsley v. Humenick* [1954] 2 D.L.R. 232) the irresponsibility of childhood and the degree of care and awareness which is to be expected of children ...

Accordingly we would allow this appeal, and give unconditional leave to defend. The court will invite submissions as to what directions are required for the further conduct of the action."

Comments and Questions:
1. Define "hostility". Are there, in your opinion, any difficulties with the approach adopted by the courts in this decision?

With regard to medical treatment, it is clear that a person is within their rights to refuse medical treatment even where it would be beneficial for them: *Re a Ward of Court* [1995] 2 I.L.R.M. 401. Forcing treatment on a person against their will constitutes a battery, except where a person is not in a position to consent, *i.e.* emergency cases, where the patient is unconscious or does not have the capacity to consent. In the case of a person who lacks the capacity to consent, consent may be given on their behalf, as in *F v West Berkshire Health Authority* [1990] 2 A.C. 1, where the court consented to the performance of a sterilisation procedure on an adult patient deemed incapable of consent.

F v West Berkshire Health Authority
(Mental Health Commission Intervening)
House of Lords [1990] 2 A.C. 1, [1989] 2 All E.R. 545, [1989] 2 W.L.R. 938,
[1989] 2 F.L.R. 476, [1989] Fam. Law. 390, 4 B.M.L.R. 1

Facts: A 36-year-old woman with a learning disability, F, who resided as a
voluntary in-patient in a mental hospital and who had the mental age of a small
child, had formed a sexual relationship with a male patient. The hospital staff
considered that she would be unable to cope with the effects of pregnancy and
giving birth, and that, since all other forms of contraception were unsuitable and it
was considered undesirable to further curtail F's limited freedom of movement in
order to prevent sexual activity, it would be in her best interests to be sterilised. F's
mother, who for the same reasons also wished her to be sterilised, issued an
originating summons seeking a declaration from the court under Ord.15, r.16 of
the Rules of the Superior Courts that such an operation would not amount to an
unlawful act by reason only of the absence of F's consent.

Issues: There were a number of issues facing the court, such as whether they
had jurisdiction to make this decision and, if so, what test should be employed
to determine that decision. The issue for the purposes of this chapter relates to
whether the common law permits an operation of sterilisation to be lawfully
performed on an adult who, by reason of learning disability, is unable to give
any meaningful consent. The court held that the sterilisation was permitted
under law.

Lord Brandon (Lord Jauncey and Lord Bridge concurring. Lord Goff gave a
full judgment and agreed in principle with Lord Brandon; Lord Griffiths agreed
in the main, but contended that the court should always give permission for such
a procedure):

"... At common law a doctor cannot lawfully operate on adult patients of sound
mind, or give them any other treatment involving the application of physical
force however small ('other treatment'), without their consent. If a doctor were
to operate on such patients, or give them other treatment, without their consent,
he would commit the actionable tort of trespass to the person. There are,
however, cases where adult patients cannot give or refuse their consent to an
operation or other treatment. One case is where, as a result of an accident or
otherwise, an adult patient is unconscious and an operation or other treatment
cannot be safely delayed until he or she recovers consciousness. Another case
is where a patient, though adult, cannot by reason of mental disability
understand the nature or purpose of an operation or other treatment. The
common law would be seriously defective if it failed to provide a solution to the
problem created by such inability to consent. In my opinion, however, the
common law does not so fail. In my opinion, the solution to the problem which

the common law provides is that a doctor can lawfully operate on, or give other treatment to, adult patients who are incapable, for one reason or another, of consenting to his doing so, provided that the operation or other treatment concerned is in the best interests of such patients. The operation or other treatment will be in their best interests if, but only if, it is carried out in order either to save their lives, or to ensure improvement or prevent deterioration in their physical or mental health ...

That is not the end of the matter, however, for there remains a further question to be considered. That question is whether, in the case of an operation for the sterilisation of an adult woman of child-bearing age, who is mentally disabled from giving or refusing her consent to it, although involvement of the court is not strictly necessary as a matter of law, it is nevertheless highly desirable as a matter of good practice. In considering that question, it is necessary to have regard to the special features of such an operation. These features are: first, the operation will in most cases be irreversible; secondly, by reason of the general irreversibility of the operation, the almost certain result of it will be to deprive the woman concerned of what is widely, and as I think rightly, regarded as one of the fundamental rights of a woman, namely, the right to bear children; thirdly, the deprivation of that right gives rise to moral and emotional considerations to which many people attach great importance; fourthly, if the question whether the operation is in the best interests of the woman is left to be decided without the involvement of the court, there may be a greater risk of it being decided wrongly, or at least of it being thought to have been decided wrongly; fifthly, if there is no involvement of the court, there is a risk of the operation being carried out for improper reasons or with improper motives; and, sixthly, involvement of the court in the decision to operate, if that is the decision reached, should serve to protect the doctor or doctors who perform the operation, and any others who may be concerned in it, from subsequent adverse criticisms or claims.

Having regard to all these matters, I am clearly of the opinion that, although in the case of an operation of the kind under discussion involvement of the court is not strictly necessary as a matter of law, it is nevertheless highly desirable as a matter of good practice."

False imprisonment

Fawsitt J. in *Dullaghan v Hillen* [1957] Ir. Jur. 10 defined false imprisonment thus:

> "False imprisonment is the unlawful and total restraint of the personal liberty of another whether by constraining him or compelling him to go to a particular place or confining him in a prison or police station or private place or by detaining him against his will in a public place. The essential element in the offence is the unlawful detention of the person, or the unlawful restraint

on his liberty. The fact that a person is not actually aware that he is being imprisoned does not amount to evidence that he is not imprisoned, it being possible for a person to be imprisoned in law, without his being conscious of the fact and appreciating the position in which he is placed, laying hands upon the person of the party imprisoned not being essential. There may be an effectual imprisonment without walls of any kind. The detainer must be such as to limit the party's freedom of motion in all directions. In effect, imprisonment is a total restraint of the liberty of the person. The offence is committed by mere detention without violence."

Thus, false imprisonment involves the denial of liberty. The victim does not need to be aware of this denial, the fact of imprisonment being sufficient to attract this tort. The denial of liberty does not require the victim to escape such confinement where this could cause humiliation or injury to the victim: *Sayers v Harlow Urban District Council* [1958] 1 W.L.R. 623. Imprisonment may be physical or psychological. The issue of psychological imprisonment was addressed in the case of *Phillips v GN Ry Co Ltd* (1903) 4 N.I.J.R. 154.

Phillips v Great Northern Railway Co. Ltd.
King's Bench Division 4 N.I.J.R. 154 (K.B.D. 1903)

Facts: The plaintiff travelled with her two daughters on the defendants' railway from Skerries to Dublin. The plaintiff and one of her daughters had second-class tickets, whilst one of the daughters had a third-class ticket on which the excess due had to be paid. Prior to their arrival in Dublin a guard examined their tickets; there was some confusion about their validity and she was required to go to the secretary's office, where some conversation took place. Both the ticket collector and the guard thought she was trying to defraud the company. The court later held that this was a mistaken belief. When the plaintiff arrived in Dublin her daughters were waiting for her and already had a cab hailed and the luggage on board. The cabman was ordered not to move, as was Mrs Phillips by the ticket collector. A scene ensued which was finally ended by the cabman driving away. A jury trial found that the plaintiff had been falsely imprisoned and awarded her £5. The defendants appealed.

Issues: The defendants argued that there was no evidence of false arrest. This case had to determine whether there was evidence of false imprisonment and assault. The court did not find for the plaintiff in this action, holding that there was not sufficient evidence of total restraint of the plaintiff; she had been subjected to a delay but was always in a position to leave the station.

Lord O'Brien L.C.J.:

"… When they arrived in Amiens Street Station the collector asserted that the plaintiff and her daughters had been travelling on a false ticket. While the altercation was going on, the daughter had the luggage placed in the cab. This is the critical period in the case, and I now turn to the plaintiff's evidence. She says, 'When I got round, one of my daughters said to me, "I have a cab, and the luggage is all right; come along." As I was stepping into the cab, and giving the cabman the address where to drive to, the ticket-collector told me not to move. I asked the cabman whom he was to obey—was it I or the ticket-collector? The cabman said "You; but we dare not move." The ticket-collector kept waving the wrong half of the ticket in my face. I was annoyed at this, and took it out of his fingers, and tore it up. The station-master said that I was a dishonest woman, that I was acting more dishonestly and that I was no lady, I gave him the bits of the torn ticket, and said I would report him. He laughed at that and said, "Oh, do, ma'am, and I will take the law on you." I got into the cab. The station-master shouted, "We have the number of that cab." We drove away.' Now, that is what the lady says. Turn now to what the cabman, John Keegan says:

> 'On the 1st of August I had a cab at Amiens Street. Was engaged by the young lady. The passengers were nearly all gone when the lady and her mother came to the cab. The ticket-collector told me to stay there till the station-master came. The station-master, after a few minutes, told me I might go. I did not mind what they were saying when I was driving away. There was some altercation.'

There were the facts as set out in evidence on the plaintiff's side. On the defendant's side there is a denial that there was any arrest or false imprisonment. It is plain from the evidence that the plaintiff experienced a certain delay. She would have left sooner but for the conduct of the station-master. On consideration, however, I think that there was no evidence of imprisonment within the meaning of the authorities. There is no evidence that the plaintiff was so dominated by the action of the ticket-collector that, succumbing to that domination, she lost her liberty. Her intended means of egress were interfered with, but she plainly could have left the station, and in the words of Mr Justice Patterson in *Bird v. Jones* 7 QB 742, there was not 'a total restraint of the liberty of the person.' In that case Mr Justice Coleridge said, 'And I am of opinion that there was no imprisonment; to call it so appears to me to confound partial obstruction and disturbance with total obstruction and detention.' In the same case, Mr Justice Williams, says, 'If a partial restraint of the will be sufficient to constitute an imprisonment, such undoubtedly took place.' But then he goes on to say that there was no total restraint by force—'I think that, in this case, there was no total restraint by force.' Mr Justice Patterson said:

> 'I have no doubt that in general if one man compels another to stay in any given place against his will, he imprisons that other just as much as if he

locked him up in a room, and I agree that it is not necessary, in order to constitute imprisonment, that a man's person should be touched; but I cannot bring my mind to accept that if one man merely obstructs the passage of another in a particular direction, whether by threat or personal violence or otherwise, leaving him at liberty to stay where he is, or to go in any other direction if he pleases, he can be said thereby to imprison him.'

Lord Denman, in that case dissented. He thought that there was evidence of false imprisonment, and said, 'The plaintiff, wishing to exercise his right of way, is stopped by force, and ordered to move in a direction which he wished not to take' but I do not think that there is anything in this case like that. I think there is no evidence of total restraint of the person, and the verdict therefore must be set aside, and judgment entered for the defendants with costs."

Comments and Questions:

1. Constraint of a person means to be confined within fixed bounds. That is generally taken to mean that there is an inability to go in any direction including returning from where you came. A victim is not required to injure themselves or property, or risk humiliation. The method of constraint required by this tort does not need to take any particular form; we have seen in this case that there can be constraint without walls, but equally constraints could be: prison—*Gildea v Hipwell* [1942] I.R. 489; barracks—*Dunne v Clinton*, unreported, Supreme Court, December 12, 1931; room—*Dillon v Dunnes' Stores Ltd.*, unreported, Supreme Court, December 20, 1968; polling booth—*Higgins v O'Reilly* [1940] Ir. Jur. Rep. 15; and a toilet— *Sayers v Harlow UDC* [1958] 1 W.L.R. 623.

In *Kane v Governor of Mountjoy Prison* [1988] I.R. 757 it was held that overt surveillance did not amount to detention as the person was at all times permitted to go where they wanted to go. A person who helps to continue a wrongful constraint of a person may be guilty of false imprisonment.

What is the position where a person fails to release a person who is falsely imprisoned? There are a number of older authorities which did not find employers guilty of false imprisonment where they refused to facilitate a worker leaving his or her place of work prematurely: *Herd v Weardale Steel & Coke Co. Ltd* [1915] A.C. 67, and *Burns v Johnston* [1916] 2 I.R. 455. The changes that have taken place in industrial relations and the recognition of workers' rights must call these authorities into question. In *Dullaghen v Hillen* [1957] Ir. Jur. Rep. 10, Fawsitt J. stated that a person need not be aware of their confinement. In *Murray v Minister for Defence* [1988] 1 W.L.R. 692, the House of Lords held that there was no requirement for consciousness of one's confinement. The "supreme importance" which the law attaches to a person's liberty makes it necessary to define the tort in a broad manner.

Murray v Ministry of Defence
House of Lords [1988] 1 W.L.R. 692

Facts: At an army briefing, Corporal D was told that the plaintiff was suspected of involvement with the IRA and of various other offences. She was instructed to go to the plaintiff's house with armed soldiers, arrest the plaintiff and bring her back to the army screening centre. Corporal D and the soldiers, when carrying out the arrest, entered the house, and every room in the house, assembled all the occupants in one room, then, when the plaintiff was ready, brought her to the screening centre. At the centre, the plaintiff was questioned and later released. The soldiers arrived at her house at 7 a.m., but did not arrest her until 7.30 a.m. and she alleged false imprisonment for that period.

Issues: The House of Lords dismissed the appeal, and held on the facts that the plaintiff had been under restraint from the moment she had been identified at 7 a.m. and must have realised that she was; that there was no valid distinction between detention to the knowledge of the detainee and arrest. For the purposes of this extract it is the discussion of the tort of false imprisonment that is relevant.

Lord Griffiths (Lord Keith of Kinkel, Lord Templeman, Lord Oliver, and Lord Jauncey concurring):

"My Lords, the plaintiff, Mrs. Margaret Murray, a resident of Andersonstown, Belfast, sued the Ministry of Defence for false imprisonment by the Army ...

The Court of Appeal rejected both these complaints of unlawful imprisonment. They gave the following reasons for rejecting the complaint of false imprisonment from 7 to 7.30 a.m.:

> 'Whether the plaintiff has any complaint in law on account of her treatment during the first half-hour before the formal words of arrest were spoken may depend upon whether in law she was already under arrest, or, if not, whether she was being falsely imprisoned. During that period the evidence was that had the plaintiff attempted to leave the house she would have been stopped. Had she been denied the right to leave, that refusal would have constituted an imprisonment in law. But it also appears from the terms of her inquiry that she did not appreciate that she would not have been free to leave the house. I am satisfied that because of this lack of any indication by any member of the Army that the plaintiff was being arrested or any appreciation on her part of what would have been the reaction had she attempted to leave, she was not during that period under arrest or falsely imprisoned. Knowledge of the fact of restraint by the suspect is an essential element of an arrest. There was some indication to the contrary in *Meering v. Grahame-White Aviation Co. Ltd.* (1919) 122 L.T. 44. In that case the Court of Appeal was divided on the question. Atkin L.J. expressly stated that awareness of the fact of detention was unnecessary. Warrington L.J. who concurred in the result does not appear

to have considered the question whether the knowledge was necessary and the report does not indicate whether this was a matter which was argued. The third member of the court, viz. Duke L.J., was of the opinion that a person could not claim to have been falsely imprisoned without knowledge of the fact of the denial of liberty. The opinion of Atkin L.J. has been subject to considerable criticism. In the first place it is plainly inconsistent with the decision of the Court of Exchequer in *Herring v. Boyle* (1834) 1 C. M. & R. 377, a decision of a court of equal authority which apparently was not cited to the court. Academic criticism of the opinion of Atkin L.J. may be found, for example, in *Smith and Hogan, Criminal Law*, 5th ed. (1983), pp. 385–386; *Street on Torts*, 7th ed. (1983), pp. 25–26; *Winfield and Jolowicz on Tort*, 12th ed. (1984), pp. 59–60 and *Goodhart, Restatement of the Law of Torts* (1935) 83 U. Pa. L. Rev. 411, 418. I consider that the conclusion in *Herring v. Boyle* is to be preferred to the dictum of Atkin L.J. which was not part of the ratio of the decision, and, therefore, that the plaintiff was not subject to imprisonment until formally arrested.'

Counsel for the plaintiff attacked the finding of the Court of Appeal that the plaintiff did not know that she was under restraint until she was told she was arrested ...

Although on the facts of this case I am sure that the plaintiff was aware of the restraint on her liberty from 7.00 a.m., I cannot agree with the Court of Appeal that it is an essential element of the tort of false imprisonment that the victim should be aware of the fact of denial of liberty. The Court of Appeal relied upon *Herring v. Boyle,* 1 C. M. & R. 377 for this proposition which they preferred to the view of Atkin L.J. to the opposite effect in *Meering v. Grahame-White Aviation Co. Ltd.,* 122 L.T. 44. *Herring v. Boyle* is an extraordinary decision of the Court of Exchequer: a mother went to fetch her 10-year-old son from school on 24 December 1833 to take him home for the Christmas holidays. The headmaster refused to allow her to take her son home because she had not paid the last term's fees, and he kept the boy at school over the holidays. An action for false imprisonment brought on behalf of the boy failed. In giving judgment Bolland B. said, at p. 381:

'as far as we know, the boy may have been willing to stay; he does not appear to have been cognisant of any restraint, and there was no evidence of any act whatsoever done by the defendant in his presence. I think that we cannot construe the refusal to the mother in the boy's absence, and without his being cognisant of any restraint, to be an imprisonment of him against his will; ... '

I suppose it is possible that there are schoolboys who prefer to stay at school rather than go home for the holidays but it is not an inference that I would draw, and I cannot believe that on the same facts the case would be similarly decided today. In *Meering v. Grahame-White Aviation Co. Ltd.,* the plaintiff's employers, who suspected him of theft, sent two of the works police to bring him in for questioning at the company's offices. He was taken to a waiting-room where he said that if he was not told why he was there he would leave. He was told he was wanted for the purpose of making inquiries about things that had been stolen and he was wanted to give evidence; he then agreed to stay. Unknown to the plaintiff, the works police had been instructed not to let him leave the waiting-room until the Metropolitan Police arrived. The works police therefore remained outside the waiting-room and would not have allowed the plaintiff to leave until he was handed over to the Metropolitan Police, who subsequently arrested him. The question for the Court of Appeal was whether on this evidence the plaintiff was falsely imprisoned during the hour he was in the waiting-room or whether there could be no 'imprisonment' sufficient to found a civil action unless the plaintiff was aware of the restraint on his liberty. Atkin L.J. said, at pp. 53–54:

> 'It appears to me that a person could be imprisoned without his knowing it. I think a person can be imprisoned while he is asleep, while he is in a state of drunkenness, while he is unconscious, and while he is a lunatic. Those are cases where it seems to me that the person might properly complain if he were imprisoned, though the imprisonment began and ceased while he was in that state. Of course, the damages might be diminished and would be affected by the question whether he was conscious of it or not. So a man might in fact, to my mind, be imprisoned by having the key of a door turned against him so that he is imprisoned in a room in fact although he does not know that the key has been turned. It may be that he is being detained in that room by persons who are anxious to make him believe that he is not in fact being imprisoned, and at the same time his captors outside that room may be boasting to persons that he is imprisoned, and it seems to me that if we were to take this case as an instance supposing it could be proved that Prudence had said while the plaintiff was waiting: "I have got him detained there waiting for the detective to come in and take him to prison"—it appears to me that that would be evidence of imprisonment. It is quite unnecessary to go on to show that in fact the man knew that he was imprisoned. If a man can be imprisoned by having the key turned upon him without his knowledge, so he can be imprisoned if, instead of a lock and key or bolts and bars, he is prevented from, in fact, exercising his liberty by guards and warders or policemen. They serve the same purpose. Therefore it appears to me to be a question of fact. It is true that in all cases of imprisonment so far as the law of civil liability is concerned that "stone walls do not a prison make," in the sense that they are not the only form of imprisonment, but any restraint within defined bounds which is a restraint in fact may be an imprisonment.'

I agree with this passage. In the first place it is not difficult to envisage cases in which harm may result from unlawful imprisonment even though the victim is unaware of it. Dean William L. Prosser gave two examples in his article in the Columbia Law Review, vol. 55 (June 1955), p. 847 ('False Imprisonment: Consciousness of Confinement'), in which he attacked section 42 of the *Restatement of Torts* which at that time stated the rule that 'there is no liability for intentionally confining another unless the person physically restrained knows of the confinement.' Dean Prosser wrote, at p. 849:

> 'Let us consider several illustrations. A locks B, a child two days old, in the vault of a bank. B. is, of course, unconscious of the confinement, but the bank vault cannot be opened for two days. In the meantime, B. suffers from hunger and thirst, and his health is seriously impaired; or it may be that he even dies. Is this no tort? Or suppose that A abducts B, a wealthy lunatic, and holds him for ransom for a week. B. is unaware of his confinement, but vaguely understands that he is in unfamiliar surroundings, and that something is wrong. He undergoes mental suffering affecting his health. At the end of the week, he is discovered by the police and released without ever having known that he has been imprisoned. Has he no action against B? ... If a child of two is kidnapped, confined, and deprived of the care of its mother for a month, is the kidnapping and the confinement in itself so minor a matter as to call for no redress in tort at all?'

... If a person is unaware that he has been falsely imprisoned and has suffered no harm, he can normally expect to recover no more than nominal damages, and it is tempting to redefine the tort in the terms of the present rule in the American *Restatement of Torts*. On reflection, however, I would not do so. The law attaches supreme importance to the liberty of the individual and if he suffers a wrongful interference with that liberty it should remain actionable even without proof of special damage."

TRESPASS TO LAND

Trespass to land occurs where a person either intentionally or negligently enters, remains on, or causes anything to be placed onto land in the possession of another, and this is done without lawful justification. Land includes whatever is affixed to the land or could be regarded as land, such as fences or trees. In *Hannabalson v Sessions* 116 Iowa 457 (1902) land was defined in the following terms: as "he who owns the soil owns upwards unto heaven and by analogy, downward to hell." There are exceptions to this statement such as: "republican" treasure trove—*Webb v Ireland* [1988] I.L.R.M. 565; state mineral rights—Minerals Development Act 1979; air travel—Air Navigation and Transport Act 1936, to name a few. The trespass occurs with the entry onto land. Entry onto land does not have to be extensive; in the case of *Whelan v Madigan* [1978] I.L.R.M. 136 the High Court held that the striking of a door with the intention of breaking it amounted to trespass.

Whelan v Madigan
High Court [1978] I.L.R.M. 136

Facts: The plaintiffs were tenants of the defendant and originally signed four different letting agreements which had long since expired. As a result they now held the flats as monthly tenants on the terms contained in the original letting agreements. The second and fourth named plaintiffs' original tenancy agreements contained covenants by the landlord that the tenant shall have quiet and peaceable enjoyment of the premises. Evidence was adduced that the defendant became indignant about the low rents he was receiving from the plaintiffs and decided to enforce each clause in their agreements. On January 5, 1978 he sent a letter to all the plaintiffs giving them notice that he would call and inspect the properties on January 7, 1978. On the said date the defendant arrived at the premises and, as he had no key to the main door, he forced open the hall door and, as the court stated, "by a strange coincidence, he had brought a screwdriver with him", with which he damaged the plaintiffs' letter-boxes, and caused further damage to the doors of some of the premises, including removing one door entirely. He rang one of the tenants and when she lifted the speaker he said nothing. The plaintiffs were frightened by his actions and instituted proceedings with a view to stopping his behaviour.

Issues: The plaintiffs instituted proceedings, claiming an injunction restraining the defendant from interfering with their peaceable enjoyment of the properties let to them and damages for breach of the obligation to give this and for trespass and intimidation. It was held that the first and second named plaintiffs were entitled to damages for trespass.

Kenny J.:

"… To assess the damages which should be awarded it is necessary to consider what legal wrongs Mr Madigan committed to each of the tenants. I think that he committed an act of trespass against Mr Thornhill when he damaged his door by striking it on a number of occasions with, I think, the intention of breaking it down and also when he made the hole in the partition wall. His removal of the chairs from the return landing was a trespass to chattels. The damage to the door and the partition was deliberate and not accidental. The right to use the letter boxes made the plaintiffs occupiers of them and their removal or damage to them was also an act of trespass. The removal of Miss Whelan's door was a trespass as was the interference with Miss Lynch's letter box. Miss Whelan has not the benefit of a covenant for quiet enjoyment because there is not one in her lease and it cannot be implied because she was in arrear with rent. Mr Thornhill and Miss Lynch have a covenant for quiet enjoyment and this extends to the letter boxes let to them. No damage was done to Miss Lynch's flat but she is, in my opinion, entitled to damages for breach of covenant for quiet enjoyment.

While there must be some physical interference with the enjoyment of the premises in order to sustain an action for breach of covenant for quiet enjoyment (see *Sanderson v The Mayor of Berwick Upon Tweed* (1884) 13 QBD 547; *Kenny v Preen* [1963] 1 QB 499), interference with the letter box is a sufficient act of interference to justify an award for the breach of the covenant for quiet enjoyment ...

I am convinced that awarding merely the cost of making good the damage done by Mr Madigan would not be the appropriate measure. His conduct, particularly as he is a solicitor, was disgraceful and caused considerable anxiety and nervous shock to the four plaintiffs."

As is evident from the decision in *Whelan v Madigan* [1978] I.L.R.M. 136, this tort protects the rights of those in possession of the land. In this case the tenants were in a position to take an action against the owner of the property.

This tort seeks to protect property rights, but the common law is not the only source of such protection. Bunreacht na hÉireann, the Constitution of Ireland, has two separate articles dealing with property rights; for the purposes of this tort Art.40.5 is most relevant and it states:

> "The dwelling of every citizen is inviolable and shall not be forcibly entered save in accordance with law."

The Supreme Court held that entry onto premises without a warrant could only be permitted where there were "extraordinary excusing circumstances": *People (Attorney-General) v O'Brien* [1965] I.R. 169.

People (Attorney-General) v O'Brien
Supreme Court [1965] I.R. 142, 1 Frewen 516

Facts: Gerald O'Brien was convicted of stealing and housebreaking, and Patrick O'Brien of housebreaking and receiving goods. These goods were identified by their owners at trial and were found during the course of a search of the defendants' premises by members of the Garda Síochána. This search was carried out pursuant to a search warrant, but the warrant was mistaken and described the premises as 118 Cashel Road, Crumlin, and not 118 Captain's Road, Crumlin, which was where the defendants lived and where the search took place. There was no question of a deliberate alteration of the warrant and it was not clear whether the gardaí noticed that they had a mistaken address prior to the search.

Issues: This is a criminal action, and the evidence for the conviction was mostly gathered during the course of the search. The challenge was to the search and the use of any evidence from the search on foot of an invalid search warrant and in violation of Art.40.5 of the Constitution of Ireland. The issue for the court to determine was whether the evidence should be excluded or not. For the purposes of this chapter, the reference by the court to the special protection afforded to private dwellings by virtue of Art.40.5 is crucial but, as is evidenced from this action, it is not absolute. The appeal was dismissed and the evidence was not excluded.

Walsh J. (Ó Dálaigh C.J. concurring; Kingsmill Moore J. in his judgment agreed in principle with the reasons set out by Walsh J.; Lavery and Budd JJ. concurred with Kingsmill Moore J.'s decision):

"… In my judgment the law in this country has been that the evidence in this particular case is not rendered inadmissible and that there is no discretion to rule it out by reason only of the fact that it was obtained by means of an illegal as distinct from an unconstitutional seizure. Members of the police make illegal searches and seizures at their peril and render themselves liable to the law of tort and in many instances also to the criminal law …

I come now to deal with the ground which was based upon the Constitutional issue. Article 40, para.5, of the Constitution provides as follows·—'The dwelling of every citizen is inviolable and shall not be forcibly entered save in accordance with law.' That does not mean that the guarantee is against forcible entry only. In my view, the reference to forcible entry is an intimation that forcible entry may be permitted by law but that in any event the dwelling of every citizen is inviolable save where entry is permitted by law and that, if necessary, such law may permit forcible entry. In a case where members of a family live together in the family house, the house as a whole is for the purpose of the Constitution the dwelling of each member of the family. If a member of a family occupies a clearly defined portion of the house apart from the other members of the family, then it may well be that the part not so occupied is no longer his dwelling and that the part he separately occupies is his dwelling as would be the case where a person not a member of the family occupied or was in possession of a clearly defined portion of the house. In this case the appellants are members of a family living in the family dwelling-house and also appear to have their own respective separate bedrooms. Each of the appellants would therefore have a constitutional right to the inviolability of No. 118 Captain's Road … When the illegality amounts to infringement of a constitutional right the matter assumes a far greater importance than is the case where the illegality does not amount to such infringement. The vindication and the protection of constitutional rights is a fundamental matter for all Courts established under the Constitution. That duty cannot yield place to any other competing interest. In Article 40 of the Constitution, the State has undertaken to defend and vindicate the inviolability of the dwelling of every citizen. The defence and vindication of the constitutional rights of the citizen is a duty superior to that of trying such citizen for a criminal offence. The Courts in exercising the judicial powers of government of the State must recognise the paramount position of constitutional rights and must uphold the objection of an accused person to the admissibility at his trial of evidence obtained or procured by the State or its servants or agents as a result of a deliberate and conscious violation of the constitutional rights of the accused person where no extraordinary excusing circumstances exist, such as the imminent destruction of vital evidence or the need to rescue a victim in peril. A suspect has no constitutional right to destroy or dispose of evidence or to imperil the victim. I would also place in the excusable category evidence obtained by a search incidental to and contemporaneous with a lawful arrest although made without a valid search warrant.

In my view evidence obtained in deliberate conscious breach of the constitutional rights of an accused person should, save in the excusable circumstances outlined above, be absolutely inadmissible. It follows therefore that evidence obtained without a deliberate and conscious violation of the accused's constitutional rights is not excludable by reason only of the violation of his constitutional right.

In the present case it is abundantly clear from the evidence that it was through an error that the wrong address appeared on the search warrant and that the searching officers were unaware of the error. There was no deliberate or conscious violation of the right of the appellants against arbitrary intrusion by the Garda officers. The evidence obtained by reason of this search is not inadmissible upon the constitutional ground.

For the reasons I have given as to both grounds, the appeal should be dismissed."

Clearly, where there are no "extraordinary circumstances", entries without lawful justification would be contrary to Art.40.5 of the Constitution. Trespass onto land occurs where there is an interference with land without lawful justification. Lawful justification can be granted by virtue of legislation or the common law. The common law, for example, provides for search warrants issued by a District Justice. There are a variety of legislative enactments that provide for the right of entry onto private property, such as: Factories Act 1955; Safety, Health and Welfare at Work Act 1989; Gaming and Lotteries Act 1956; Social Welfare (Consolidation) Act 1981; Fire Services Act 1981. Where entrants exceed their lawful authority to enter land, they then become trespassers. This position was addressed in *DPP v McMahon* [1987] I.L.R.M. 87.

Director of Public Prosecutions v McMahon
Supreme Court [1987] I.L.R.M. 87

Facts: Each of the defendants owned a licensed premises and were charged in the District Court and convicted with offences contrary to the Gaming and Lotteries Act 1956 (the 1956 Act). All three of the defendants appealed their convictions. Evidence was given at the rehearing by a ban garda that she and another garda entered the licensed premises of the defendants in their plain clothes in order to ascertain whether offences against the 1956 Act were being committed within.

Issues: The defendants sought a dismissal of the charges against them on the basis that the garda evidence was inadmissible as it had been obtained by illegal means in the absence of a search warrant. In the law of trespass this case determines that, where entrants exceed their lawful authority to enter, then they become trespassers in law. The gardaí in this case were trespassers and so the evidence was found as a result of an illegality, but it was permitted to use the evidence so found in this instance.

Finlay C.J. (Walsh, Henchy and Hederman JJ. concurring; McCarthy J. delivered a separate judgment in agreement with the Chief Justice):

"... Upon the hearing before the Circuit Court, evidence was given by a Ban Garda Berry that she and another member of the Garda, dressed in plain clothes, entered successively each of the licensed premises the property of the defendants, for the specific purpose of ascertaining whether offences against the *Gaming and Lotteries Act 1956* were being committed within them, and made certain observations while present in the premises, leading to evidence which *prima facie* established the commission of offences.

The witness further gave evidence that neither she nor her companion identified themselves as members of the Garda Síochána, stated what their purpose was, nor did they obtain any search warrant for the premises, pursuant to the provisions of *s. 39 of the Gaming and Lotteries Act 1956* (the Act of 1956).

At the conclusion of the evidence for the prosecution objection was made by counsel on behalf of each of the defendants (the cases being tried together) that the evidence with regard to the commission of the offences was inadmissible as it had been obtained by illegal means in the absence of a search warrant and that accordingly the defendants were entitled to a dismissal of the charges against them ...

Quite clearly a licensed premises does not come within the provisions of *s. 38.* ... a member of the Garda Siochana cannot, except with the agreement or by the invitation of the owner thereof, enter such premises for the purpose of ascertaining whether an offence against the Act of 1956 is being committed or not unless he be not below the rank of inspector and have already within 48 hours obtained a search warrant pursuant to *s. 39.*

It was correctly conceded on behalf of the Director of Public Prosecutions that on the findings of fact made by the learned Circuit Court judge in this case, namely, to the effect that the purpose of the Gardaí in entering each of the premises was solely to investigate the possibility of the commission of offences against the Act of 1956 that the general invitation implied by law in the case of a person running a licensed premises was not applicable to the Gardaí in this instance and in this case. It is clear that the owner of a licensed premises issues by implication an invitation to members of the public to have resort to his premises for the purpose of buying drink or consuming drink or food therein and for ancillary and consequential purposes. In the instant case, however, it is clear that the members of the Garda Síochána did not have that purpose and it is proper and commendable that they did not seek to colour their activity by pretending by the consumption of some food or drink that they had such a purpose ...

I am satisfied, therefore, that the Garda Síochána on entering each of the licensed premises involved in this case did not have any statutory authority so to do and were outside, by reason of their intention in so doing, the implied invitation of the owner of the licensed premises.

They were, therefore, in my view, in law trespassers, and the evidence which they obtained by inspecting the use of gaming machines within these premises was evidence obtained by unlawful means, though not, of course, by the commission of any offence against the criminal law.

The act of entering, as a trespasser, the public portion of a licensed premises which is open for trade does not, of course, constitute any invasion or infringement of any constitutional right of the owner of those premises ...

On the findings of fact contained in the case stated, unless altered by further evidence, it would appear that, in balancing the public interest that crime should be detected against the undesirability of using improper methods, particular importance may attach to the fact that the Gardaí in entering the public houses to view the machines were trespassers only, not involved in any criminal or opprobrious conduct and that the offence of permitting gaming on licensed premises may be considered as one with grave social consequences."

Where a person enters land with the authority of law, as opposed to a private invitation, and that person then abuses or exceeds their lawful authority, that person becomes a trespasser *ab initio,* that is, from the moment they enter the premises. A person can only become a trespasser *ab initio* by an act of positive misfeasance. This doctrine was applied in the case of *Webb v Ireland* [1988] I.L.R.M. 565.

Webb v Ireland and the Attorney-General
Supreme Court [1988] I.L.R.M. 565

Facts: In February 1980 the plaintiffs discovered an ancient chalice and other religious objects; this became known as the Derrynaflan Hoard. This discovery was effected by the use of a metal detector on land which was a national monument within the meaning of the National Monuments Act 1930. They delivered the hoard into the custody of the National Museum with a letter from their solicitor which stated that it had been delivered "to your care for the present and pending determination of the legal ownership" thereof. The landowners, a Mr O'Brien and Mr O'Leary, gave permission to the National Museum to carry out excavations on the site where the hoard was found and more items were recovered. The National Museum promised the plaintiffs that they were to be honourably treated, but were unable to negotiate a reward acceptable to both parties. The plaintiffs issued proceedings to recover the hoard. In the interim the landowners accepted an award of £25,000 each. In the High Court it was held by Blayney J., following *Byrne v Ireland* [1972] I.R. 241, that the royal prerogative of treasure trove had ceased to be part of Irish law on the enactment of the 1922 Constitution; that the transaction by which the plaintiffs handed over the hoard amounted to a bailment; that the State as bailee was estopped from denying the title of the plaintiffs as bailors; and that the plaintiffs were entitled to the return of the hoard or recovery of its value as assessed. The State appealed this decision.

Issues: The Supreme Court allowed the appeal, declaring the State to be the owner of the hoard subject to the rights of any person capable of proving ownership and paid the plaintiffs as finders an award of £25,000 each. As regards the issue of trespass, the court held that the fact that the plaintiffs were finders by act of trespass disentitled them to any rights in the hoard as between them and the landowners.

Finlay C.J. (Henchy and Griffin JJ. concurring; Walsh J., in a separate judgment, agreed with the outcome of the case, but by different means):

"… The decision of Chitty J. in *Elwes v The Brigg Gas Company* (1886) 33 Ch. D 562 , is a clear and unequivocal authority for the proposition that the owner of a fee simple interest in land is entitled to any chattel which may be in the land as against the finder of that chattel, even where the finder is excavating the land with the licence of the owner. I have carefully considered the judgment in that case and I find it a very persuasive precedent.

In the case of *South Staffordshire Water Co v Sharman* [1896] 2 QB 44, Lord Russell CJ quoted with approval the following passage in Pollock and Wright's *Possession in the Common Law*:

> 'The possession of land carries with it in general, by our law, possession of everything which is attached to or under that land, and, in the absence of a better title elsewhere, the right to possess it also. And it makes no difference that the possessor is not aware of the thing's existence … It is free to anyone who requires a specific intention as part of the *de facto* possession to treat this as a positive rule of law. But it seems preferable to say that the legal possession rests on a real *de facto* possession constituted by the occupier's general power and intent to exclude unauthorised interference.'

Later on in his judgment the Chief Justice stated this principle in somewhat different form and, in particular, appeared to apply it to things which may be upon or in the land, where the statement would appear to apply to everything which is attached to or under the land. This slight qualification, if it is such, of the earlier statement is dealt with in the judgment of McNair J. in *London City Corporation v Appleyard* [1963] 2 All ER 843. I am satisfied that the true legal position is that there must be distinguished, with regard to the question of control, things which are on land and things which are attached to or under it. This distinction makes consistent the decision in *Bridges v Hawkesworth* (1851) 21 LJ QB 75, and the decision in *Parker v The British Airways Board* [1982] 1 All ER 834 which dealt with objects on land and with an absence of control over them with the decisions in the cases to which I have referred, dealing with objects attached to or under the land. The extent to which, where objects are attached to or under the land, an absence of control may deprive the owner against a finder is probably limited to cases such as *Hanna v Peel* [1945] KB 509, where the owner of a house had never entered into possession of it though the title had developed upon him. There is no evidence in this case of anything approaching that type of absence of control on the part of the landowners. From a consideration of all these cases, although it is clearly *obiter* to the facts contained in it, I would find the general propositions set out by Dolandson LJ in *Parker v British Airways* to be a careful and, in my opinion, correct assertion of the relevant principles applicable. Two of the propositions he there states are relevant to the issues arising in this case, the first being that an occupier of land has rights superior to those of a finder over chattels in or attached to that land, and the second being that the finder of a chattel acquires very limited rights over it if he takes it into his care and control ... in the course of trespassing.

I, therefore, conclude that on the facts of this case the owners of the lands, Messrs O'Brien and O'Leary had a right to possession of these chattels, superior to the plaintiffs who were finders of them, and that by the agreements made between the State and those two landowners these rights have become vested in the State.

That conclusion would obviate the necessity to reach a conclusion as to whether the plaintiffs, by reason of the fact that their finding of these objects constituted a trespass by the digging in the soil would, in any event, lose any right to possession they might have. This matter was very fully argued, however, and I feel that although it is not necessary for the decision of this case that I should express a view upon it. I do not consider that having regard to the fact that the allegation that the plaintiffs acted contrary to *s. 14 of the National Monuments Act 1930* is an allegation of the commission of a criminal offence, that the evidence could support such a conclusion. The subsection involved is *s. 14(1)(6)* of the Act which makes it an offence to excavate, dig, plough or otherwise disturb the ground within, around, or in proximity to any such national monument without or otherwise than in accordance with the consent hereinafter mentioned. Such evidence as was given, and it does not appear to have been in any way emphasised or fully investigated with regard to the relationship between the area in which the hoard was found and the buildings constituting the national monument does not appear to me to form a safe base for even *prima facie* establishing a criminal offence.

With regard to the question of trespass, however, the position would appear to be as follows. The learned trial judge found that the act of digging was an act of trespass, and even though the plaintiffs may have entered with the implied licence of the owners, as was found by him, this would lead to the legal conclusion that they then became, upon commencing to dig, trespassers *ab initio*.

As such, the general principle of public policy seems clearly to be that they should not, because of that trespass, acquire any rights of ownership to the land or things found in it.

It was submitted on behalf of the plaintiffs that their trespass was minimal or certainly not very serious and that this altered what otherwise might have been the legal position.

There can be no doubt that the plaintiffs in this case behaved extremely responsibly once they found these objects and that their conduct subsequent to the finding of them, both in the discretion with which they approached the Museum and the expedition with which they did so, and in the very active co-operation which they subsequently gave to the officials of the Museum concerning the find, was exemplary.

The principle which I have shortly outlined, that the law leans against the acquisition by a person of property rights by trespass, save in cases of prescription, is based on the requirement of the common good that the ownership and right to possession of land shall be protected from an unlawful invasion of it. There does not appear to me to be any grounds in logic or justice for a rule of law that a person who by a trespass of little extent obtains possession of a very valuable chattel would be exempt from this provision of the law, whereas a person committing a larger or more extensive trespass, and possibly deriving a much smaller profit would be penalised by it.

I would, therefore, conclude that even if the right of ownership of the hoard as between the owners of the land and the finders were different from what I have stated it to be, that the fact that these plaintiffs are finders by an act of trespass would disentitle them to any rights in the objects found, certainly as between them and the owners of the land."

McCarthy J.:

"... Despite the authority cited by the Chief Justice, which, in this context, was not considered by the trial judge, who held against the State on estoppel No. 1, I am far from satisfied that ownership of land necessarily carries with it either ownership or a right to possession or other right in respect of chattels found in or over the land as against the claim of a finder. By definition, the owner, until the find, is unaware of the presence of the chattels; if the owner is a purchaser, he has bought and the vendor has sold for a price that takes no account of the chattels; these circumstances are quite apart from the problems that arise from the possible existence of a series of superior or inferior titles to the land, which term must, for this purpose, include real property of any kind. In this regard I find most persuasive the judgment of Whitehouse J, giving the judgment of the Supreme Judicial Court of Maine in *Weeks v Hackett* (1908) 71 Atl. Rep. 858 where English and American authorities up to that date (1908) were cited. In *Armory v Delamarie* 1 Strange 505, a chimney-sweeper's boy found a jewel (presumably in a chimney) and brought it to the defendant who was a goldsmith to know what it was; the goldsmith gave it to his apprentice who, under pretence of weighing it, took out the stones, and called to the goldsmith to let him know it came to three halfpence, where upon the goldsmith offered the boy the money; he refused to take it and insisted on having it back whereupon he got the socket without the stones. Pratt CJ ruled:

1. That the finder of a jewel, though he does not by such finding acquire an absolute property of ownership, yet he has such a property as will enable him to keep it against all but the rightful owner, and consequently may maintain trover.
2. That the action well lay against the master, who gives a credit to his apprentice, and is answerable for his neglect.
3. As to the value of the jewel several of the trade were examined to prove what a jewel of the finest water that would fit the socket would be worth; and the Chief Justice directed the jury that unless the defendant did produce the jewel and show it not to be of the finest water they should presume the strongest against him and make the value of the best jewels the measure of their damages; which they accordingly did.

In *Parker v British Airways Board* [1982] 1 All ER 834, Donaldson LJ cited *Armory's* case at 837 stating that the rule as stated by Pratt CJ must be right as a general proposition and proceeding to qualify it, particularly in the case of the trespassing finder. He said:

> 'The person *vis-a-vis* whom he is a trespasser has a better title. The fundamental basis of this is clearly public policy. Wrongdoers should not benefit from their wrong-doing. This requirement would be met if the trespassing finder acquired no rights. That would, however, produce the free-for-all situation to which I have already referred, in that anyone could take the article from the trespassing finder. Accordingly, the common law has been obliged to give rights to someone else, the owner *ex hypothesi* being unknown. The obvious candidate is the occupier of the property on which the finder was trespassing. Curiously enough, it is difficult to find any case in which the rule is stated in this simple form, but I have no doubt that this is the law.'

Public policy is an unruly horse; it is a form of judicial policy making, in this instance to be used to establish a right in someone who was unaware of the subject matter of that right until it was brought to his attention by the person who is to be denied that right. Because of the view I take on what I regard as the most fundamental issue in this appeal, I do not find it necessary to express any concluded view; I do not accept that the defendants have established a right consequent on the transaction of 7 July 1981."

Comments and Questions:
1. While visiting a friend's farm you find on the property a very valuable diamond necklace; this necklace does not form part of our antiquity. Based on the decision in *Webb v Ireland,* establish who is entitled to the necklace.

TRESPASS TO CHATTELS

This tort protects against the intentional, direct and unlawful interference or injury to chattels in the possession of another. The term chattels refers to items of property, generally moveable property, and does not include real estate.

Farrell v Minister for Agriculture and Food
Unreported, High Court, October 1995

Facts: The plaintiff is a farmer and cattle dealer. At the time of the incident complained of, his herd numbered 789 animals. His herd was tested for brucellosis and it was found that he had a number of reactors in his herd. These animals were slaughtered and Mr O'Neill, the departmental Regional Veterinary Superintendent of the South West Region, advised that the entire herd should be depopulated. On the back of each form there is an application by the owner to claim payment on slaughter of the reactors listed overleaf and accepting that payment will be subject to the conditions which are set out. The conditions provide that the Minister may at his discretion refuse payment where he is satisfied that the herd-owner has not complied with the provisions of the Diseases of Animals Act 1966 or with movement, identification or other controls under any official scheme for the eradication of animal diseases. Following the depopulation of the herd, the plaintiff, Mr Farrell, wrote to Mr O'Neill highlighting that he had yet to receive payment for the animals slaughtered. The reply stated that the department was experiencing difficulty in reconciling the identity cards for his herd received at the office with the animals shown in the test reports. It further stated that cards had been furnished for only about a third of the animals tested and that no further consideration could be given to grant payments until identity cards for all the animals tested were provided. At the time of the action payment was still pending.

Issues: The plaintiff denied any culpability and issued proceedings. He claimed he was entitled to payment in respect of the 380 cattle. He also claimed damages for trespass to his goods. The plaintiff succeeded in a number of elements of his claim.

Carroll J.:

"… But here one of the Plaintiff's alternative claims is that the tort of trespass has been committed. He claims that what the Minister did under the Regulations amounted to trespass because he used the Regulations to carry out a direct and immediate interference with the Plaintiff's chattels so that they had to be delivered for slaughter. The measure of damages therefore is *restitutio in integrum.*

Counsel for the Minister says there was no contact and because there was no contact there was no trespass. Trespass must be forcible and direct, not consequential. He cited the case of *McDonagh v The West of Ireland Fisheries Limited* (unreported 19 December, 1986 Blayney J) where it was held that the Defendant was not liable in trespass where a boat which the Defendant had temporarily removed from the moorings in harbour was later damaged in uncertain circumstances, on the basis that the injury was clearly not direct.

As Messrs McMahon and Binchy say in Irish Law on Torts (second edition) the law relating to wrongful interference with chattels lacks clarity and consistency. They also point out that where precisely the line is to be drawn between direct and indirect interference is not easy to say.

The tort consists of wrongfully and directly interfering with the possession of chattels. In my opinion there was a direct interference with the Plaintiff's right to possession of his cattle when the Minister, with the mantle of statutory Regulations assumed to be valid around him, constrained the Plaintiff to bring his herd to be slaughtered. The Minister did it knowingly and intended the consequences, though he did not act *mala fides* because he did not know the Regulations were *ultra vires.* To my mind that is a direct interference with the Plaintiff's right to possession of his animals and therefore the tort of trespass to chattels was committed and the Plaintiff is entitled to damages for the loss suffered.

One of the difficulties in this case is to establish exactly how many cattle were slaughtered, what type they were, how many of each type were or probably were reactors, what they were worth and what money was paid by the meat factories …

In my opinion the Plaintiff is not entitled to any general damages. He has succeeded in his claim that Article 8 of the 1980 Regulations (except for 8(1)(a)) is ultra vires. This carried with it the consequence that he was only entitled to compensation for healthy animals. He has got other consequential damage and in my view is not entitled to any general damages."

O'Carroll J. states that trespass to chattels "consists of wrongfully and directly interfering with the possession of chattels." As in the case of trespass to land, the law is concerned with protecting those in possession of property; ownership is not necessary. In *Keenan Bros Ltd v CIE* (1963) 97 I.L.T.R. 54 goods were delayed in train wagons due to an industrial dispute, and the owners were not permitted to remove the goods without the permission of CIE. An action can be maintained without the necessity of ownership, if no better claim can be shown; this issue was addressed in *Jennings v Quinn* [1968] I.R. 305.

Jennings v Quinn and Dooris
Supreme Court [1968] I.R. 305

Facts: The plaintiff had been arrested in Ireland and extradited to England pursuant to the provisions of Pt III of the Extradition Act 1965. The Irish police had seized, at the time of the arrest, certain goods which were then in the possession of the plaintiff. The plaintiff sued the defendants, who were gardaí, in the High Court for the return of the goods, and applied for an interlocutory injunction restraining the defendants from parting with their possession of the goods pending the trial of the action. The High Court did not grant the injunction; this decision was appealed to the Supreme Court.

Issues: The issue at stake was whether someone who could only highlight possession as opposed to ownership was entitled to lay a claim to the property.

O'Keeffe J. (Ó Dálaigh C.J. and Walsh J. concurring):

"… At the time of the arrest a search was made of the plaintiff's house, and possession was taken of a considerable amount of property …

The plaintiff originally claimed ownership of all the property and based his application for an interlocutory injunction upon the intention (declared to the solicitor then acting for the plaintiff) of the second defendant to hand the property over to the English police. In the High Court, the plaintiff subsequently applied for leave to base his claim on possession of the property and that claim has been repeated in this Court. An amendment to enable him to do so was not granted in the High Court … In this connection it is material to remark that some, at least, of the property was stated by Detective Sergeant Huddle of the London police to have been stolen.

An application of the kind which is now before the Court raises a number of important questions. The property in question is at present within the jurisdiction of the Court and proceedings have been instituted by the plaintiff claiming possession of it. If the property is handed over to the London police in accordance with the declared intention of the second defendant, it will be impossible for the Court to make an effective order for its return to the plaintiff.

It is said on behalf of the defendants that, even if the property is wrongfully handed over to parties outside the jurisdiction of the Court, a remedy by way of damages is available to the plaintiff, and it has been submitted that the Court ought not to interfere in aid of the plaintiff by restraining the defendants from parting with possession of the property ...

Before considering the question whether property taken at the time of the arrest of an accused person can properly be sent out of the State, it is desirable to consider what right, if any, the persons making the arrest have to seize the property at all. In the case of *Dillon* v. *O'Brien and Davis* [20 LR Ir 300] it was held by the Exchequer Division (Palles C.B., Dowse B. and Andrews J.) that, when a person is lawfully arrested to be brought before a court on a criminal charge, property seized at the time of the arrest and which is to be used as evidence on that charge may lawfully be retained for that purpose by the police. The Chief Baron, who delivered a judgment with which the other members of the court concurred, rested his decision on the principle that the State has an interest in having a person, who is guilty of a crime, brought to justice; and in ensuring that a prosecution, once commenced, is determined in accordance with law. In the course of his judgment, at p. 317 of the report, he said:—'But the interest of the State in the person charged being brought to trial in due course necessarily extends as well to the preservation of material evidence of his guilt or innocence as to his custody for the purpose of trial. His custody is of no value if the law is powerless to prevent the abstraction or destruction of this evidence, without which a trial would be no more than an empty form. But if there be a right to production or preservation of this evidence, I cannot see how it can be enforced otherwise than by capture.' ...

In so far as the property seized at the time of the arrest of the plaintiff might be required by the police officers as material evidence in any charge brought against the plaintiff in this jurisdiction, their taking and retention of that property, in my view, would clearly be excused.

The question as to the extent to which property, coming into the hands of the police at the time of a lawful arrest, may be sent out of the jurisdiction of this Court and into another jurisdiction appears not to have arisen for consideration either in this country or in England in any case to which reference was made, and accordingly it becomes necessary to determine the matter as one arising now for the first time. It appears to me that the public interest also requires that property, which the police might lawfully retain for use as material evidence in a charge against a person arrested if that charge were brought against him within the jurisdiction, may also be retained lawfully by them for the purpose of sending it, and that they may send it, into another jurisdiction where a charge on which that property is material evidence has been laid against the person arrested, at least in cases where the lawful arrest of the person within the jurisdiction was made in aid of the jurisdiction of the country in which the charge is laid. For this reason I would be prepared to hold that the defendants might lawfully retain in their possession any of the property which has come into their possession at the time of, or shortly after, the arrest of the plaintiff and which is required as material evidence on a charge laid against the plaintiff in the United Kingdom. At present, however, there is no satisfactory evidence before this Court that any of the property in the possession of the defendants is so required; and the defendants, when enquiry was made of them through their counsel, indicated that they did not wish to file at this stage any further evidence on this question. As matters stand, therefore, there is no evidence before the Court to show that the property ought to be sent out of the jurisdiction in aid of the jurisdiction of another State.

The case has been fought by the defendants in this Court, as in the High Court, principally on the ground that the plaintiff has not made out any real case of ownership or lawful possession of the property. It appears to me that the evidence of the second defendant establishes possession by the plaintiff of the property, or most of it, at the time of his arrest and that, in the circumstances, a claim to possession of the property was made for the plaintiff and that it is sufficient to enable him to maintain this application."

DEFENCES

There are a number of defences available: consent, necessity, discipline and defence of person or property.

Consent

As with all torts, consent can render contact lawful; this is based on the maxim of *volenti non fit injuria* (Chapter 14). Consent can be express or implied, assuming the person giving the consent has the capacity to do so. Where a party argues that a person does not have capacity, it is for them to prove such incapacity (*F v West Berkshire Health Authority* [1990] 2 A.C. 1 (HL)). The consent must be real, that is, it should not be the result of duress, illegality or fraud. In some cases the consent of a third party may be accepted—this arose in the case of *Holmes v Heatley* [1937] Ir. Jur. Rep. 74.

Holmes v Heatley
High Court [1937] Ir. Jur. Rep. 74

Facts: During the performance of a minor surgical operation upon a 16-year-old boy, to which the boy and his parents had consented on the understanding that only a local anaesthetic would be necessary, an emergency, the possibility of which had not been communicated to the boy or his parents, arose, and it became necessary to administer a general anaesthetic, as a result of which the boy died upon the operating table.

Issues: The parents took an action in assault against the surgeon for damages for the death of their son. They were unsuccessful in their action.

Witness action before a judge and jury

"The plaintiffs, the parents of a deceased minor, claimed damages under the Fatal Accidents Act 1846 (9 & 10 Vict c 93) (Lord Campbell's Act), from the defendant, a medical surgeon, for the death of the minor during a surgical operation which took place in a hospital in Dublin.

The statement of claim set out, *inter alia*:

> 'The plaintiffs have suffered damage from an assault and battery committed upon the 23rd day of November, 1934, by the defendant upon one Richard Holmes, a minor, at Mercer's Hospital, Dublin, by causing to be administered to the said Richard Holmes a drug or anaesthetic and by performing upon he said Richard Holmes a surgical incision or operation whereby the said Richard Holmes died upon the said day.'

The defence set out, *inter alia*: 'The defendant never assaulted or beat the said Richard Holmes as alleged or at all. The acts which are alleged to have constituted an assault and battery were done with the leave and by the consent of the said Richard Holmes and/or the plaintiffs.'

From the evidence at trial it appeared that advice had been obtained from a general medical practitioner to the effect that the minor, who was 16 years of age should undergo an operation for toxic exopthalmic goitre. The deceased and his parents (the plaintiffs) consented to the necessary operation, the plaintiff Annie Holmes having been informed that only a local anaesthetic would be required and that the proposed operation would not be serious. The minor spent several weeks in hospital during which, *inter alia*, a cardiograph and an X-ray photograph were prepared and revealed that the left auricle of the minor's heart was slightly enlarged.

The anaesthetist and members of the nursing staff attended under subpoena and gave evidence that at the actual operation the minor, who was of a nervous disposition, became restless and hysterical, was shouting and kicking, and had to be held down. He also put his hand to the incised part of his neck. In order to stitch up the wound it became necessary to administer a general anaesthetic, but on chloroform being administered the patient became weak and died upon the operation table.

An extract from the register of operations of the hospital which was put in evidence stated: 'Operation was started under local anaesthesia; patient became very restless and excitable. Chloroform about two drachms was administered in usual manner. Breathing became shallow and eventually ceased altogether. Usual stimulants were given and artificial respiration performed.'

At the close of evidence adduced on behalf of the plaintiffs, counsel for the defendant asked for a direction."

Kingsmill Moore S.C. (with him, Mr. Ernest Wood), for the defendant:

"In the case of an adult there is no relevant reported authority for the proposition that consent under such circumstances is necessary. 'A reasonable patient should be told what is about to be done to him that he may take courage and put himself in such a situation as to enable him to undergo the operation:' *Slater v. Baker and Stapleton.* Apparently a tacit consent may be implied even against the instructions of the patient where the operation is necessary: *Beatty v. Cullingsworth. Pollock on Torts* (at p. 160) expresses the view that consent is unnecessary. It appears that the necessity for preserving health and life justifies an assault even though the plaintiff has not consented, *e.g.* forcible feeding: *Leigh v. Gladstone.* It is not necessary formally to plead consent as a defence to trespass to the person since it is implied in the denial of assault: *Christopherson v. Bare: Pollock on Torts,* p.216, note (q).

In the case of an infant there is no reported authority as to the necessity for a parent's consent. By analogy the consent of the infant should be sufficient. An infant could take part in boxing or football without the consent of a parent being obtained in respect of anything that might happen to him, and the absence of the parent's consent would not give the infant a right of action against opponents who might injure him in the course of the sport. At common law the consent of an infant is a defence even in cases of indecent assault unless a breach of the peace is caused: *Reg. v. Banks; Reg. v. Meredith; Reg. v. Martin.*

Where a person is of such an age of discretion as to understand the nature of and necessity for an operation his consent is sufficient to prevent the operation being *wrongful,* and the Fatal Accidents Act, 1846, applies only where death is caused by a *wrongful* act, neglect, or default. As to the meaning of 'age of discretion' see of the *Oxford Dictionary,* vol. 3, p. 436. In the emergency which arose, if consent were necessary, the antecedent consent given in respect of a local anaesthetic tacitly implied consent to the general anaesthetic. A relevant test is whether the boy, had he recovered, could have maintained an action."

Mr Lennon, for the plaintiffs:

"It was impropore [*sic*] to perform such an operation without the consent of the parents: *Slater v. Baker and Stapleton; Mitchell v. (Magistrates of) Aberdeen; Sutherland v. (Magistrates of) Aberdeen; Halsbury; laws of England,* vol. 27, pp. 877–8 (including notes). The nature of the case and the possible dangers should have been previously communicated to the plaintiffs and their consent to the administration of the general anaesthetic obtained."

Maguire J.:

"I am of the opinion that the direction asked for should be granted. There is no evidence here which would entitle a jury to hold that there was an assault. I am not deciding the question as to whether there is any necessity for the consent of the parents for an operation or whether the consent of the boy of the age of the deceased is sufficient. In my view the surgeon was bound to act as he did in the emergency with which he was faced. On the uncontradicted evidence in this case the giving of the general anaesthetic was the only course open to him. I accordingly withdraw the case from the jury and direct a verdict for the defendant."

Consent can also be vitiated by fraud. In the criminal case of *R. v Williams* [1923] 1 K.B. 340 the court addressed the issue of fraud; a young girl consented to intercourse with her choir master after he told her it was a procedure to improve her voice.

R. v Williams
Court of Criminal Appeal [1923] 1 K.B. 340

Facts: The appellant, who was engaged to give lessons in singing and voice production to a girl of 16 years of age, had sexual intercourse with her under the pretence that her breathing was not quite right and that he had to perform an operation to enable her to produce her voice properly. The girl submitted to what was done under the belief that she was being medically and surgically treated by the appellant. The appellant was convicted of rape and appealed.

Issue: Was her consent valid? What are the necessary elements of a valid consent? It was held that the appellant had been properly convicted of rape.

Lord Hewart C.J. (Darling and Salter JJ. concurring):

"… Mr. Gorst has to-day taken one point and one point only on behalf of the appellant—namely, that in view of the evidence the appellant ought not to have been convicted of the crime of rape. In support of that argument the attention of the Court has been directed to *Reg. v. O'Shay* [19 Cox, C. C. 76] and to the provisions of the Criminal Law Amendment Act, 1885. There is no doubt that before the passing of the Act of 1885 a man who by fraudulent pretence succeeded in obtaining sexual intercourse with a woman might be guilty of rape. For example in *Reg. v. Case* [(1850) 4 Cox, C. C. 220; 19 L. J. (M. C.) 174] a medical practitioner had sexual connection with a girl of fourteen years of age upon the pretence that he was treating her medically and the girl made no resistance owing to a bona fide belief that she was being medically treated. It was held that he was properly convicted of an assault and might have been convicted of rape. In *Reg. v. Flattery* [2 Q.B.D. 410] the same principle was affirmed. But it has been argued that the position has been changed by the passing of the Criminal Law Amendment Act, 1885. Mr. Gorst, when the question was specifically put to him, did not contend that that Act would prevent the laying of an indictment for rape in such a case as *Reg. v. Flattery,* [2 Q. B. D. 410] but he said that that Act made an indictment for rape impossible in the present case. That argument is based upon the provisions of s. 3, sub-s. 2, of the Act of 1885, which provides that 'any person who … by false pretences or false representations procures any woman or girl, not being a common prostitute or of known immoral character, to have any unlawful carnal connexion, either within or without the Queen's dominions … shall be guilty of a misdemeanour.' It is obvious that those words go beyond a case of rape. It is easy to imagine a case which would come within the comprehensive scope of those words and yet fail to come within a charge of rape. No doubt in *Reg. v. O'Shay* [19 Cox, C. C. 76] Ridley J. did appear to say that after the passing of the Criminal Law Amendment Act *Reg. v. Flattery* [2 Q.B.D. 410] was no longer law. And the headnote of the case accordingly says that 'the effect of the Criminal Law Amendment Act, 1885, is to set aside *Reg. v. Flattery,* [2 Q.B.D. 410] and it is a good defence to an indictment for rape that the carnal knowledge alleged in the indictment was had with the consent of the woman, even though such consent had been obtained by fraud, but the prisoner may be convicted of an indecent assault.' It is however quite clear when one looks at the report of the case that the attention of the judge was not directed to s. 16 of the Act of 1885. That section makes it plain that the provisions of the statute were not in the least intended to interfere with the liability of a person for an offence punishable at common law, but were intended to supplement the offences punishable at common law. In the opinion of this Court the decision in *Reg. v. O'Shay* [19 Cox, C. C. 76] was given under a misapprehension.

Reference has been made in the course of the argument to *Reg. v. Dicken,* [14 Cox, C. C. 8.] which was tried at the Stafford Assizes in 1877. In that case a man was charged with rape upon a girl above the age of twelve and under the age of thirteen years. Mr. C. J. Darling (as he then was) argued that the prisoner could not be convicted of felony. He said that the prisoner 'was charged with rape. That offence consisted in his unlawfully and carnally knowing the girl against her will—i.e., without her consent. But such an offence was now defined in 38 & 39 Vict. c. 94, s.4, and thereby declared to be a misdemeanour. Consequently, with respect to girls between the age of twelve and thirteen the earlier statutes making that offence a felony were repealed.' That argument depended upon the words in the statute: 'whether with or without her consent.' Mellor J., who was the judge trying the case, said: 'The carnal abuse of children having excited the attention of the Legislature, they have been specially protected by Acts of Parliament. 24 & 25 Vict. c. 100, s. 51, enacted that "Whosoever shall unlawfully and carnally know and abuse any girl being above the age of ten years, and under the age of twelve years, shall be guilty of a misdemeanour." Under this provision an offender was punishable, whether the girl did or did not consent to his act. In 1875 it was thought desirable that further protection should be given to young girls, and the limit of ten years was extended, by 38 & 39 Vict. c. 94, s. 4, declaring that "Whosoever shall unlawfully and carnally know and abuse any girl being above the age of twelve years, and under the age of thirteen, whether with or without her consent, shall be guilty of a misdemeanour." Ex abundanti cautela the words "whether with or without her consent" were inserted in the later enactment; but, save in respect of the alteration in the age of the girl, the law remained exactly as it was previously—that is to say, if she consented, the prisoner might be convicted of the statutory misdemeanour; if she did not, a fortiori he might be so. But if she did not consent, his offence would amount also to the higher crime—the felony—of rape, and he might be indicted and tried for it quite irrespective of the modern statutes throwing special protection around children. The present indictment is for rape, and therefore if the girl consented to the carnal knowledge, the act was not done "against her will," and the crime is not made out. It would be preposterous to suppose that Parliament intended to repeal the law of rape as to girls of the very age during which extra statutory protection is cast over them, and I am clearly of opinion that no such repeal has been effected.' Those are the observations of a judge with regard to a statute which contained no such provision as is contained in s. 16 of the Act of 1885. There is a footnote to the report to the effect that Sir James F. Stephen in a note to 38 & 39 Vict. c. 94, s. 3, on p. 173 of his Digest of the Criminal Law, 3rd ed. writes of the phrase 'with or without her consent': 'These words are obviously a mistake. In the preceding section (where they do not appear) they would have been superfluous, but harmless. In this section they are mischievous; for if taken literally, they make it impossible to commit a rape upon a girl between twelve and thirteen, as they provide that carnally to know a girl between twelve and thirteen without her consent is a misdemeanour … it is impossible to suppose that Parliament can have intended the monstrous consequence pointed out above.'

In the present case the argument on behalf of the appellant must amount to this—if it be a sound argument at all—that after the passing of the Act of 1885 it is no longer possible to indict a man for rape in such cases as *Reg. v. Case* [4 Cox, C. C. 220] and *Reg. v. Flattery* [2 Q. B. D. 410]. That is to say that inasmuch as there is a statute which makes the obtaining of carnal connection with a woman by false pretences a misdemeanour that offence can no longer be a rape. That proposition cannot be the law for the same reason as that stated by Mellor J. in *Reg. v. Dicken* [14 Cox, C. C. 8.], even if s. 16 of the Act of 1885 be disregarded, but in view of that section the proposition is obviously untenable. Branson J. stated the law in the course of the summing up in the present case in accurate terms. He said: 'The law has laid it down that where a girl's consent is procured by the means which the girl says this prisoner adopted, that is to say, where she is persuaded that what is being done to her is not the ordinary act of sexual intercourse but is some medical or surgical operation in order to give her relief from some disability from which she is suffering, then that is rape although the actual thing that was done was done with her consent, because she never consented to the act of sexual intercourse. She was persuaded to consent to what he did because she thought it was not sexual intercourse and because she thought it was a surgical operation.'

As reference has been made to Stephen's Digest of the Criminal Law it may be pertinent to refer to a passage in Russell on Crimes, 7th ed., vol. i., p. 934, where reference is made to various cases on this point including *Reg. v. Young* [(1878) 14 Cox, C. C. 114]. The conclusion of the matter according to the editors is this: 'A consent or submission obtained by fraud is, it would seem, not a defence to a charge of rape or cognate offences.' In the opinion of this Court that is a true proposition and nothing contained in the Act of 1885 diminishes the offence of rape at common law in such cases as *Reg. v. Flattery* [2 Q. B. D. 410] and *Reg. v. Case* [4 Cox, C. C. 220]. The appeal must therefore be dismissed."

As the civil law is still very much in a state of development, the criminal cases provide guidance as to how the courts view the matter. A case of some significance is that of *Hegarty v Shine* (1878) L.R. (Ir.) 288, this case dealt with a man who infected his partner with a venereal disease and was not found guilty of a battery.

Hegarty v Shine
Appeal Court 1878 L.R. (Ir.) 288

Facts: The female plaintiff and the male defendant were engaged to be married, and were cohabiting; the marriage did not take place and the plaintiff was infected with a venereal disease. This action is brought by the female plaintiff against the male defendant for breach of promise of marriage, and for assault of the plaintiff, and infecting her with venereal disease.

Issues: Was the consent valid? The plaintiff in this action did not know that the defendant had a venereal disease, but he was aware of this fact. The court did not find for the plaintiff, but the fact that they were not married did appear to play a significant part in this judgment.

Lord Chancellor Ball C. (Palles C.B. and Deasy L.J. both delivered judgments concurring with the Lord Chancellor):

"I charged the jury, carefully reviewing the evidence. Without expressing any opinion on my own part, I adopted as law, and, as applicable to a civil action, the cases of *Reg. v. Bennett* [4 F. & F 1105] and *Reg. v. Sinclair* [13 Cox, C. C. 28], and I in substance directed the jury, as a matter of law, that an assault implied an act of violence committed upon a person against his or her will, and that, as a general rule, when the person consented to the act there was no assault; but that if the consent was obtained by fraud of the party committing the act, the fraud vitiated the consent, and the act became in view of the law an assault; and that therefore, if the Defendant, knowing that he had venereal disease, and that the probable and natural effect of his having connexion with the Plaintiff would be to communicate to her venereal disease, fraudulently concealed from her his condition, in order to induce, and did thereby induce, her to have connexion with him, and if but for that fraud she would not have consented to have had such connexion, and if he had with her the connexion so procured, and thereby communicated to her such venereal disease, he had committed an assault, and one for which they might on the evidence award substantial damages.

This charge and the objections to it were brought before the Queen's Bench Division, when a majority of the Judges held that the views presented by the learned Judge to the jury (not, indeed, according to his own opinion, but in deference to the authority of the two cases in the Criminal Courts cited by him) were a misdirection, and they consequently awarded a new trial upon this ground. The propriety of this ruling we have not to examine.

The charge of the learned Judge assumes that, in order to constitute an assault upon a person, the act done should be against his or her will, without his or her consent. With that proposition I entirely agree. To strike a person minaciously or in anger is a matter very different in character from a blow in sport or play. Sexual intercourse with the consent of the female (supposing no grounds for invalidating that consent) cannot be an assault on the part of the male. The charge then proceeds to assert, that although consent be given, yet if that consent was obtained by the fraud of the party committing the act, the fraud vitiated the consent, and the act became in view of the law an assault. From this proposition, when laid down in reference to the particular facts of the present case, I dissent. We are not dealing with deceit as to the nature of the act to be done, such as occurred in the instance cited in argument, of the innocent girl who was induced to believe that a surgical operation was being performed. There was here a lengthened cohabitation; deliberate consent to the act, out of which the cause of action has arisen. If deceit by one of the parties to such a cohabitation as to the condition of his health suffices to alter the whole relation between them, so as to transform their intercourse into an assault on his part, why should not any other deceit have the same effect? Suppose a woman to live with her paramour, under and with a distinct and reiterated promise of marriage, not fulfilled, nor, it may be, ever intended to be fulfilled—is every separate act of sexual intercourse an assault? Let the same happen in conjunction with a violated engagement to provide for her maintenance and protection against poverty does a similar consequence here also follow? No one, I think, would be prepared to answer these questions in the affirmative. In the present case, the fraud relied upon to annul the Plaintiff's consent is the concealment of a fact which if known would have induced her to withhold it; but before this effect is attributed to such concealment, it seems to me reasonable to demand—what is required in contract—that from the relation between the parties there should have arise a duty to disclose, capable of being legally enforced. And how can this be, when the relation is itself immoral and for the indulgence of immorality; the supposed duty with the object of aiding its continuance? To support obligation founded upon relation, it appears to me the relation must be one that we can recognise and sanction. I do not think these opinions conflict with the Criminal Courts referred to by the learned Judge in his charge. Considerations affect prosecutions not applicable to civil actions. In the former we are concerned with public interests and consequent public policy; in the latter, with the reciprocal rights and liabilities of individuals. Mutual consent to a prize-fight might prevent the pugilists having a remedy *inter se*; but would not make it less a breach of the peace, or exonerate those engaged from punishment.

These reasons, in my opinion, justify the order of the Queen's Bench Division directing a new trial upon the ground of misdirection by the learned Judge. I think it right to add that I also concur the majority of that Court in holding an action of this character cannot be maintained. The consequence of an immoral act—the direct consequence—is the subject of complaint. Courts of Justice no more exist to provide a remedy for the consequences of immoral or illegal acts and contracts, than to aid or enforce those acts or contracts themselves. Some striking illustrations of this are afforded by authorities cited in the argument of this appeal. Thus Judges have refused to partition the plunder obtained by robbery, to acknowledge or protect property in an indecent book or pictures, to compel payment of the wages of unchastity. Are the same tribunals to regulate the relative rights and duties of the parties to an illicit intercourse? No precedent has been cited, no authority suggested, for an action like the present; and I am not disposed to make, in the interest of immorality, either precedent or authority for it."

Comments and Questions:
1. Do you agree with the decision in this action?

2. Should the issue of morality form such a central part of this judgment?

3. What are the central elements of the Lord Chancellor's decision?

4. Consider a situation where a person is HIV positive. This person knows s/he is HIV positive, and has unprotected sexual intercourse with another and thereby infects that person. Based on this decision there is no cause of action. Is it time for a change of direction in the law? If you agree that a change is necessary, on what basis would you argue such a case?

Defence of persons or property

It is permissible to use reasonable force in the defence of another person or property. Self-defence is in response to a wrongful assault, and one is entitled to repel force with force. The force used must, however, be reasonable. What is reasonable depends on the circumstances of the case. In the case of *Gregan v Sullivan* [1937] Ir. Jur. 64, the defendant, a man in his thirties, had broken the arm of the 65-year-old plaintiff and also used a pitchfork to inflict a number of puncture wounds on his arms; this was in response to the plaintiff striking the defendant on the lip. Here the force used was deemed unreasonable and, in the course of the judgment, O'Byrne J. stated that he was "inclined to agree that we ought not to weigh a method of self-defence on too fine a scales, but steam hammers ought not to be used to crush flies." An example of defence of property occurred in *McKnight v Xtravision*, unreported, Circuit Court, July 1991.

McKnight v Xtravision
Unreported, Circuit Court, July 1991

Facts: The plaintiff was a security officer working in a shopping centre, where the defendants were the tenants of a lockup shop in a shopping centre in Dublin. At the time of the incident complained of there was a dispute between Xtravision and the owners of the shopping centre. As a result the defendants withheld payment of service charges. On the morning of the incident the staff arrived to find that they could not enter the shop because of a chain and lock placed there by the landlords. The Xtravision party, after some negotiations, turned up with bolt clippers; this party consisted of the manager of Xtravision, the head of security and a member of the security department who was a light-middleweight boxer. The Xtravision party, when they went to cut the locks, found their path blocked by the plaintiff who had anchored himself to the handles of the double doors of the shop facing the doors with an arm through each handle. There is conflicting evidence as to what happened next, but there was a struggle.

Issues: It seems clear that the actions of the landlord amounted to a trespass; this was further compounded by the actions of the plaintiff. The issue for the court was whether the force used by the defendants was reasonable.

Carroll J.:

"… The defence witnesses say that Mr Joyce gave the plaintiff a bear hug from the rear while Mr Murphy removed the plaintiff's left hand and arm from the door, the plaintiff at the time struggling violently, to allow Mr Conn to cut the chain with the bolt cutter, using no more force than was necessary: *molier manus imposuerunt*.

The plaintiff says that these witnesses were indeed in the positions so described but that both his arms were restrained and that Murphy and Joyce each punched him with their free arms. He succeeded in getting the bolt cutters nevertheless and giving them to Pomeroy who then ran off with them. Just about at this time Mr Moriarty came on the scene and opened the door, and the incident ended.

I prefer the plaintiff's account of what transpired, which I think is substantially true and which accords better with the findings of Dr McCarthy, who examined the plaintiff at around 4 pm. The doctor found the plaintiff very shocked, almost in tears, each arms bruised, with four fresh bruises on the upper chest. The plaintiff had a tender lower back was unable to bend over and had a generally tender lower abdomen.

When he saw the plaintiff a week later, the plaintiff, complained of severe pain in his back, as well as insomnia. The doctor prescribed pain-killers and advised the plaintiff not to work or drive in view of this marked restriction of back movement.

Again on 9 August, the doctor examined the plaintiff; he felt that the plaintiff should be fit for work in another week. The plaintiff himself claims that he was stiff and sore for several more weeks; but, on the basis merely of the doctor's evidence, I am satisfied that the plaintiff was given a 'roughing up' and beating which inflicted injuries which would certainly support a charge of assault causing actual bodily harm against each and every one of the employees of Xtravision who are defendants in this action. The question now is whether this can be justified upon the grounds that it was the consequence of using no more force than was reasonably necessary to remove from the shop doors a man who was undoubtedly a trespasser.

What is reasonable force? Is it merely the amount of energy which is required to move a man out of a room, a house, or, as here, to loosen his grip on a door and move him away from it, no matter what may be the other consequences? I think not. It is necessary to take into account the occasion upon which the force is used. It is here essential to point out that the present case bears only the remote resemblance to that of a householder who is disturbed by an intruder who invades his or her house or flat, the shopkeeper or tradesman who finds a person forcing his way into his shop or premises where business is being carried out so as to threaten or discommode his customers or staff or one who refuses to go when asked; even less does it resemble the case of any such person who has to deal with a criminal who forces or tries to force an entry with threat to life or limb or property.

The danger of causing confusion in the minds of such persons is one of the features of the case which has troubled me. The degree of force used here would be perfectly justifiable in such types of case and much more if necessary to defend a man's home. Nothing which I am about to say should in any way render such citizens hesitant or fearful about defending their person or property.

In this case, up to the arrival of Conn, Murphy and Joyce no one had been in any way threatened or put in fear: it was a simple case of the defendants being prevented from entering a lock-up shop and, no doubt, some threat to commercial interests.

The Xtravision party were undoubtedly entitled to lay hands lightly on the plaintiff to move him aside. But when that failed, in the circumstances of the case, they should have desisted. They were not upon such cause entitled to assault him so as to inflict the type of injuries described by Dr McCarthy.

On their way to Donnybrook to buy the bolt clippers and pick up the light-middleweight, Mr Joyce, they must have passed the open door of these courts where, their solicitors might have advised them, they could have had an injunction against Mr McKnight and his employers for the asking. It may be objected that this would have involved a delay which would have been damaging to their commercial interests. But it is of the essence of the civilised state regulated by law that its citizens in very many—indeed in all but a very small minority of—cases, forego the right to redress their grievances by private violence and instead look to the courts for their remedy. If parties were to resort to private violence in cases such as this, there would be an end to all law or order.

A particularly disturbing feature of the case is that the violence was employed by the defendants through the use of their own retainers, kept and maintained for such purpose. It will be recalled that Mr Murphy admitted under cross-examination that his party came to 'overawe and, if they failed in that, to do as they did.' I find in such a state of affairs an attitude that is quite intolerable.

As regards damages, the plaintiff's conduct in forcibly preventing the defendants' servants from entering the shop, trespasser as he was, was equally blameworthy."

Comments and Questions:
1. Carroll J. in her judgment tries to ensure that caution is employed before force is used. Do you think the situation in this case can be compared to the situation where a homeowner is seeking to protect his/her property?

Other defences

There is a defence of necessity; this is a relevant defence in cases of trespass to a person or to property in an emergency situation, or one of imminent peril. The actions of the person must be reasonable and proportionate. This defence permits a trespass to prevent a greater harm. For example, it may be acceptable to trespass in a person's house where that house is on fire, and the trespass is to rescue a child from that house.

A second defence is that of discipline. Reasonable discipline may be a defence. This defence generally applies in the context of children or others in appropriate situations, and the defence extends to parents and others *in loco parentis*. A school, for example, may have a policy banning the use of mobile phones. Confiscating or removing a person's phone would normally amount to a trespass to chattels, but the school may be in a position to avail of the defence, if this is reasonable.

Chapter 10

DEFAMATION

Introduction

The tort of defamation seeks to strike a balance between the right to free expression and a person's right to his/her good name and reputation. As an indication of the importance given to both rights, they are protected by the Constitution. The right to a good name is protected by Art.40.3.2, while freedom of expression is protected by Art.40.6.1. The right to free speech is a right which is protected by Art.10 of the European Convention on Human Rights. The area of defamation is also regulated in part by statute in the form of the Defamation Act 1961.

Given the sensitivity of the rights at issue in the tort of defamation, there have been numerous proposals which have called for reform and clarification of this area. In 1991 the Law Reform Commission published its *Report on the Civil Law of Defamation*. The most significant set of proposals was published in June 2003 by the Legal Advisory Group on Defamation (Advisory Group) established by the Department of Justice, Equality and Law Reform in September 2002. Its proposals are significant and far-reaching and touch on almost every aspect of the tort of defamation. The recently published Defamation Bill 2006 incorporates some of these proposals. The most significant aspects of the Bill are discussed, where relevant, throughout this chapter.

The tort of defamation is said to have been committed on (Walsh J., in *Quigley v Creation Ltd.* [1971] I.R. 269)

> "[t]he wrongful publication of a false statement about a person, which tends to lower that person in the eyes of right-thinking members of society or tends to hold that person up to hatred, ridicule or contempt, or causes that person to be shunned or avoided by right-thinking members of society."

Publication

To constitute a defamatory statement it must be published to a third party (*i.e.* somebody other than the plaintiff). Section 14(2) of the Defamation Act 1961 states that publication of words will include "a reference to visual images, gestures and other methods of signifying meaning."

A communication between a man and his wife or vice versa will not constitute publication as the married couple are seen as one unit. It is also a defence to show that publication was involuntary (as in the case, for instance, of employees acting on the instruction of employers).

Those who can be sued for publication include the initial communicator, distributors such as publishers, printers, retailers, printers and the media. A defence is available to distributors (other than the original publisher, media and printers) who can show that they had no knowledge of the defamatory content of the material; that nothing in the material or surrounding circumstances gave them grounds to suspect any defamatory content; and that they were not negligent in failing to discover the defamatory content.

Where publication is unintended or accidental, a person can still be liable if the publication was foreseen, as was demonstrated in the case of *Paul v Holt* (1935) 69 I.L.T.R. 157.

LIBEL OR SLANDER?

The publication of a defamatory statement can take the form of a slander or a libel. Libels are communication in a permanent or lasting form, such as the written word. Slanders on the other hand are communications in a transient form, such as spoken words.

Currently there are two important distinctions between the torts of libel and slander. First, a libel may be a crime as well as a tort and as such can be subject to criminal proceedings (see Pt III of the Defamation Act). Libel also is actionable *per se* (you do not have to show damage), whereas only some forms of slander are actionable without showing special damage.

The slanders which are actionable *per se* are as follows:

1. Words (including images, gestures or other methods of signifying meaning), which impute unchastity or adultery to any woman or girl (s.16 of Defamation Act 1961).
2. Slanders affecting a person's official, professional or business reputation (s.19 of the Defamation Act).
3. Slanders imputing a criminal offence punishable by death or imprisonment.
4. Slanders imputing a contagious disease which tends to exclude the sufferer from society.

If the slander communicated is not actionable *per se,* the plaintiff will have to show "special damage". Special damage in this context requires material damage of some sort, such as loss of business, loss or refusal of an office or employment, the dismissal from a situation or the loss of a client. In any event there must be some material loss. Loss of reputation or standing alone will not suffice (*Dinnegan and Dinnegan v Ryan and Ryan* [2002] 3 I.R. 178).

The Defamation Bill 2006 proposes to remove the distinction between libels and slanders, all such communications being described in the Bill as the "tort of defamation" (s.5).

Dinnegan and Dinnegan v Ryan and Ryan
High Court [2002] 3 I.R. 178

Facts: The plaintiffs arrived at the public house of the defendants on St Stephen's Day, 1998, following their wedding ceremony. On arrival, the plaintiffs and their wedding party were not served any drinks and were asked to leave. The plaintiffs contended that this was in breach of an agreement between the parties that the defendants would provide a small reception; in addition, they claimed that their characters had been defamed. The defendants, for their part, argued that no agreement existed, and that they had been asked to leave because the bar was too busy. The Circuit Court held in favour of the plaintiffs and awarded them damages for breach of contract and slander. The defendants appealed.

Issues: In the High Court, Murray J. was asked to consider whether, *inter alia*, the character of the defendants had been defamed. As the allegation was of slander, it fell on the court to consider whether "special damage" had been shown. Murray J. held that, as the plaintiffs could not show that they had suffered any "material loss", the action for slander must fail. Murray J. did, however, find that there had been a breach of contract and awarded damages on this basis.

Murray J.:

"Slander
    As regards the Plaintiffs' action for slander, it was accepted by Counsel for the Plaintiffs and properly so, that while at common law libel is always actionable per se, slander generally speaking, is not so actionable and therefore the general rule is that a person defamed by a slander can only succeed on proof of 'special damage' arising as the direct, natural and reasonable result of the publication of the words complained of (see M'Mullan v O'Mulhall and Farrell [1929] 1 IR 470) There are exceptions to this general rule where slander is actionable per se. However, there is no element in this case which would bring the slander within any of those particular exceptions and obviously this is why Counsel for the Plaintiffs (notwithstanding the pleadings) accepted that it was incumbent upon the Plaintiffs to prove special damage as well as the slander in order to succeed against the Defendants.
    While there is an arguable case that the words spoken by the Defendant to and concerning the Plaintiffs, in particular the first named Plaintiff, may have been slanderous given the circumstances and context in which they were spoken, the position in this case is that even if there was a slander it is not actionable in law unless there is proof of special damage. At this point the question to be considered is whether there is proof of any special damage. Counsel for the Plaintiff submitted that one background factor to take into account is the publicity given to the wedding in the local newspapers. This arose from the fact that some special publicity was given to the wedding in a local

newspaper due to the fact that it had to take place in the dark by candlelight only on account of the blackout. This meant the wedding was fairly widely known to have taken place. The ejection of Mr Dinnegan from the pub meant that people could well ask themselves is this the sort of fellow they would wish to do business with. Therefore, he might have difficulty cashing a cheque, looking for a job or seeking work as a PVC fitter which was work which he had subsequently undertaken. The special damage did not have to be for a specific amount.

Apart from the fact that Mr Dinnegan was unemployed at the time of the alleged slander it was not contended, and could not have been contended, that it was spoken of him concerning his trade or profession. Furthermore, there was no evidence that he had on any occasion been adversely affected in a particular way by the conduct of third parties arising from what was said and took place in the pub.

Gatley on Libel and Slander (9th edition, 1998, pg. 119) sums up what constitutes special damage by reference to a range of authorities and states 'special damage for this purpose is some "actual, temporal loss"—the loss of some "material" or "temporal advantage" which is "pecuniary" or "capable of being estimated in money". So, for example, the requirement is satisfied where there is the loss or refusal of an office or employment, or the dismissal from a situation, or the loss of a client, or of a dealing.' Gatley goes on to point out that mere social ostracism or disgrace is not enough even though its effect on the Plaintiff may be very painful. The special damage must have accrued before action is brought. Mere apprehension or possibility of temporal loss in the future is not sufficient. (Onslow -v- Horne (3 Wils. 177 at 188)) cited with approval in M'Mullan -v- Mulhall and Farrell (cited above). In Michael -v- Spiers and Pond Ltd (1909 101 L.T. 352), cited by Gatley, the Plaintiff was ejected from the Defendants' licensed premises by their servant who said that he was drunk. In that case it was held that a threat by the Plaintiff's father to remove him from the Directorate of a company of which he, the father, had control, unless the Plaintiff could clear his character, did not constitute special damage on the ground that a threat of temporal damage in the future was not sufficient to constitute such damage.

In any event in this case, there is no evidence of any actual, (or prospective) material or temporal loss on the part of the Plaintiff. In fact apart from the alleged defamatory nature of the words spoken, there was no evidence whatsoever of the effect of the alleged slander on third parties. Assuming, for present purposes, that the words were defamatory with the implication that the Plaintiff's reputation was damaged by reference to those who became aware of the slander, this would obviously not constitute special damage as defined by the authorities. In short, the Plaintiffs have not established that they suffered any special damage arising from the slander alleged in the Civil Bill. Therefore, even if there was a slander, it is not actionable and the Plaintiffs must fail on this ground alone. It is, therefore, not necessary to enter upon the question whether in fact the words spoken by the first named Defendant were, in the circumstances, slanderous."

Comments and Questions:
1. Slanders require "special damage" while libels do not. Is there any logical rationale in your view for such a distinction?

DEFAMATORY MEANING

The publication must be capable of lowering the person in the eyes of right-thinking members of society, or of holding them up to hatred, ridicule or contempt, or be capable of causing that person to be shunned or avoided by right-thinking members of society. In determining whether a statement is defamatory, the judge, or in the High Court, the judge and jury, seek to reflect the views of society. The standard is an objective one, concerned not with the plaintiff's intention but rather with the impact the publication will generate in the minds of others. A publication may be defamatory given the word's ordinary and natural meaning, or it may be defamatory as a result of innuendo (what the statements suggest).

In the case of *Reynolds v Malocco* [1999] 2 I.R. 203, [1999] 1 I.L.R.M. 289 the plaintiff was held to have been defamed in relation to his professional character and in his moral character by innuendo alleging criminal activity and by virtue of innuendo as to his sexual orientation.

Reynolds v Malocco
High Court [1999] 2 I.R. 203, [1999] 1 I.L.R.M. 289

Facts: The plaintiff, the director of a company that owned two well-known night-clubs in Dublin, learned that he was about to be the subject-matter of an article, edited by the first defendant, written by the second and third defendants, and due to be published by the fourth defendant, in a magazine owned by the fifth defendant.

In an application for an interlocutory injunction, the plaintiff alleged that the article was defamatory of him in a number of respects. First, it suggested that he had been charged with permitting the sale of drugs in his nightclubs and/or that he was turning a blind eye to their sale. Secondly, that he had benefited from the sale of drugs on his premises. Thirdly, that by reference to phrases such as 'gay bachelor' in the article, there was an implication that he was homosexual.

Issues: The court (Kelly J.) was called upon to decide, *inter alia*, whether the words in the article gave rise to the defamatory meanings alleged.

Kelly J. held that while the words relating to the drug dealing allegations did not in their "natural and ordinary meaning denote any criminal activity on the part of the plaintiff, looking at the article as a whole there was present a clear innuendo that the matter complained of was libellous." He further held that "use of the word 'gay' either in its natural and ordinary meaning or by innuendo, was an allegation of homosexuality."

Kelly J.:

"The article to which exception is taken by the plaintiff commences at p. 31 of the magazine and concludes at page 33. Apart from the heading which I have already reproduced in the first paragraph of this judgment, the other parts of the article in respect of which complaint is made read as follows:—'Pod and U2's Kitchen Nightclubs among 12 Dublin Nightclubs and late-night bars stung by undercover gardai buying illegal drugs.

So far, up to 30 people arrested in various clubs and pubs.

Gay bachelor John Reynolds is feeling far from gay these days. The face synonymous with what was once one of Dublin's top nightclubs, the Pod, is in big trouble. PATRICK magazine can exclusively reveal that the Pod nightclub has been visited by undercover gardai who have bought drugs there not once but on several occasions. Efforts were made by our journalists to contact Reynolds and give him an opportunity to speak about the drugs problem, but through his spokesperson he declined to comment. During the summer Reynolds approached two journalists from PATRICK in the Pod who were working on this story and told them to leave his club—that he did not want their "type" there.

This is not Reynolds' first brush with the law but the difficulties he faces now are far more serious. Should the gardai proceed with the prosecution and be successful Reynolds would be banned from holding a licence or operating a nightclub for five years. The gay bachelor, who is featured regularly in the tabloid gossip columns where the names of his latest model girlfriends are plugged, is seriously worried. The consequences of a successful prosecution by the National Drugs Unit for the Porsche-driving Reynolds could be devastating. Not only would he personally be banned but the Pod would lose its existing licence and would no longer be able to operate as a nightclub.

Furthermore, according to sources close to him, Reynolds is concerned that, if convicted, other business interests he has might also suffer, particularly if the banks were to call in their loans. But it would not be the first time that a nightclub owner was jailed if it came to that. In 1995, a Donegal nightclub owner was convicted and imprisoned for three years and fined £10,000 for allowing drugs to be sold on his premises where raves were a regular feature ...

However, it remains to be seen if any premises are to be closed down or any licensees jailed. Cynics believe that no club owners would ever be jailed and those club owners who are directly involved in drugs will continue for some time to make vast profits from allowing their venues to be used as drug havens. They claim that the people who will have the full force of the law brought down to bear on them will be the drug buyers.

Despite "Operation Nightcap" drugs continue to be widely available in several of Dublin's top nightspots. There are complaints that the gardai are dragging their feet on the matter and effectively allowing certain club owners to continue to profit from the sale of illegal drugs on their premises.

In October this year two undercover investigative journalists from PATRICK magazine had no difficulty in purchasing cocaine, ecstasy and cannabis in Lillies Bordello, the Kitchen Nightclub, the Pod, the Red Box and Bruxelles near the Westbury Hotel. It is unlikely that the owners of these clubs knew of these dealings as they have all adopted additional security measures to prevent these transactions. The journalists were able to ascertain the names of the drug dealers. When the journalists returned one week later drugs were still available in all five venues but there was a noticeable increase in club security. Maybe the message is finally getting across.'

On the first page of the article there is a photograph of the plaintiff in the company of a woman whose face has been excised from the picture. It bears the legend 'Reynolds continues to run the POD'. On the third page of the article there is a photograph of the plaintiff's Porsche motor car. This picture bears the legend 'Reynolds enjoys the high life'.

The plaintiff complains that the above extracts defame him in two respects. He says that the words, in their natural and ordinary meaning, or by innuendo, allege:—

(a) that he has been charged with permitting the sale of drugs in his nightclubs and/or that he permits the sale of drugs on the premises and is benefiting therefrom. Alternatively, he is turning a blind eye to the sale of drugs on his premises, and;
(b) that he is a homosexual.

The first defendant contends that insofar as the first of these complaints is concerned, the words do not bear the meanings ascribed to them. If they do, he says that he will plead justification at the trial of the action. Insofar as the second complaint is concerned, he says that the words do not bear the meaning contended for. He has stated in open court that the plaintiff is not a homosexual nor did he ever intend to allege such.

The plaintiff says that the libel is so serious that it is a case in which the court ought to intervene by the granting of an injunction. Without such injunction it is said the plaintiff will suffer loss which is incapable of being compensated for in damages.

The defendants say there should be no injunction because there is no libel and even if there is one concerning the drugs their intended plea of justification is fatal to the plaintiff's case.

I will shortly have to consider these contentions but before doing so it is necessary to deal with the principles applicable to the granting of interlocutory injunctions in cases of this type.

The legal principles applicable

[Before considering whether the article was defamatory, Kelly J. dealt with the question of whether an injunction should be granted. The court then went on to consider the allegations made in the article].

The drug dealing allegations

In looking at these allegations I note that the plaintiff accepts that he, together with 19 other nightclub operators in the greater Dublin area, has received notification from the police concerning drug activity and conduct relating to drugs on his club premises.

I have carefully read and re-read the parts of the article in respect of which complaint is made under this heading. The first defendant contends that in their natural and ordinary meaning the words in question do not allege any criminal activity on the part of the plaintiff. In that regard I believe him to be correct. Even if I am wrong on that and the words do, in their natural and ordinary meaning, make such allegations, they certainly do not do so with the degree of clarity required to enable me to say that the words are, without doubt, defamatory of and concerning the plaintiff.

I therefore must now turn to the contention of the plaintiff to the effect that by innuendo the words complained of amount to allegations of the wrong-doing alleged. The plaintiff's counsel says that that is the clear inference which is to be drawn from the article. Amongst other things he says that whilst the article purports to deal with drugs in clubs (as is apparent from the cover of the magazine) in fact it is directed almost exclusively at the plaintiff. A fair reading of the article supports this contention. The article speaks of the plaintiff being 'in big trouble'. It alleges that his premises have been visited by the police who bought drugs there on several occasions. It speaks about this not being the plaintiff's first brush with the law, but of him now facing difficulties which are 'far more serious'. It alleges that the plaintiff 'is seriously worried'. It speaks of the consequences for him of a successful prosecution. It then resorts to the device, frequently used by journalists, of citing anonymous 'sources close to' the plaintiff, and indicating that the plaintiff is concerned that 'if convicted' other business interests he has might also suffer. In the same paragraph it goes on to point out that it would not be the first time that a nightclub owner has been jailed. It then deals with a Donegal owner who was imprisoned for three years for allowing drugs to be sold on his premises.

Later in the article it speaks about it remaining to be seen if any premises are to be closed down or licensees jailed. In the same paragraph it mentions that cynics believe that no club owners will ever be jailed and that those club owners who are directly involved in drugs will continue for some time to make vast profits from allowing their venues to be used as drug havens. This paragraph is juxtaposed close to the photograph of the plaintiff's car where it speaks of him enjoying 'the high life'.

True it is, that the article then goes on to say that it is unlikely that the owners of these clubs knew of these particular drug dealings as they have all adopted additional security measures to prevent the transactions in question. That statement comes in the final paragraph of the article.

I have come to the conclusion that, looking at the parts of the article which are complained of as a whole, there is present an innuendo to the effect contended for by the plaintiff. Furthermore I am of the view that such an innuendo is clear and that in the absence of a successful plea of justification a jury would say that the matter complained of was libelous. If they did so I do not believe that the Supreme Court would set aside the verdict as unreasonable. If the jury did not do so its decision would be likely to be set aside. I do not think that the inclusion of a single sentence in the final paragraph of the article would have much prospect of neutralising the sting contained in the remainder of it.

It seems to me that the article is carefully written so as to avoid making the direct allegation of criminal wrong-doing whilst at the same time creating in the mind of the reader a clear impression that the plaintiff has connived at the use of his premises for drug dealing with considerable gain to himself.

If, of course, the defendants can satisfy me that they have a prospect of success in their plea of justification then there can be no question of an injunction being granted in favour of the plaintiff.

Apart from the stated intention to plead justification what admissible evidence is there to support that plea? I refer to 'admissible evidence' because earlier in the hearing I struck out portions of the defendants' principal replying affidavit together with the affidavit of the third defendant pursuant to O. 40, R 12 of the Rules of the Superior Courts because of the scandalous material contained in them.

Having examined the remaining portions of the affidavit evidence it seems to me that the only real evidence which could amount to justification is that contained in para. 15 of the first defendant's affidavit. He says:—

'I say and believe that between January and June, 1998, I have personally witnessed drugs being sold openly in both of these premises to young people. I say that I witnessed men and women who were dressed in the uniform of the club observing these drug dealings. I say that on the four occasions I was present myself I also witnessed the plaintiff, John Reynolds, moving around in the club and mixing with people.'

I do not think that that averment goes anywhere near demonstrating the existence of an arguable prospect of making out the defence of justification.

The allegation of homosexuality

Throughout the article the plaintiff is referred to on a number of occasions as a 'gay bachelor'. He says that in its natural and ordinary meaning, the word gay is nowadays taken as meaning homosexual. He says that that is clearly defamatory of and concerning him and on this aspect of the matter it is to be noted that the defendants disavow any intention to plead justification. On the contrary they accept that the plaintiff is not homosexual but say that they never alleged that he was. In support of this contention they make a number of arguments which I will deal with in turn.

First, they say that the term 'gay' is an adjective used to describe a person's demeanour as in 'lively, cheerful, vivacious, light-hearted, fond of pleasure and gaiety'.

Had this argument been made thirty years ago it would probably have succeeded. But it is an absurd proposition to put to the court in 1998.

Language is a living thing and words can change their meaning over the years. Sometimes the primary meaning of a word will undergo subtle or even profound changes. On other occasions the word may acquire a secondary meaning which it did not formerly have. The word 'gay' falls into the second category. Over the last 30 years or so it has come to be synonymous with homosexuals and homosexual activity. One would have to be resident on the moon not to be aware of this. Not merely has it acquired this secondary meaning but it has in fact eclipsed the primary meaning so that nowadays one rarely hears the term used other than as denoting homosexuals or homosexual activity. I reject the defendants' contention that the word is confined to the meanings asserted by them which I have reproduced in parenthesis above.

The next contention is that the use of the word 'gay', (as an adjective) qualifying the noun 'bachelor', is a term in common use to refer to men who are happily unmarried. The defendants contend that when the term 'gay bachelor' is used it never indicates that the person is a homosexual. Again it seems to me that this argument could be made with telling force had this case occurred in 1968 rather than 1998. It is true that the term 'gay bachelor' or 'bachelor gay' may still be used with slightly more frequency than the word 'gay' in its original meaning. Nonetheless it seems to me that nowadays the term has practically fallen out of use largely because of the secondary meaning of the word 'gay'. I therefore reject the contention made by the defendants that this term could not be defamatory.

The next contention made by the first defendant is to the effect that even if he is wrong in these contentions to allege of a person that he or she is 'gay' is not harmful to reputation. The first defendant says 'homosexuality is an accepted part of Irish life and the days are long gone when homosexuals were simply tolerated; they are now accepted and integrated into the fabric of Irish life like other minorities and this magazine fully endorses that reality'. Counsel for the plaintiff says that this argument holds no water. He says that an allegation of being gay is an allegation of deviant sexual practice which many people in Irish society find repellent. He therefore argues that it is clearly defamatory.

No cases were cited by either side in support of the conflicting positions which they argue for.

My own researches have however discovered a decision of the Court of Appeal in England which is of assistance. In Reg. v Bishop [1975] 1 Q.B. 274, that court had to consider a case where a defendant was tried at first instance on a charge involving theft from a bedroom. In evidence he explained the presence of his fingerprints in the room by saying that he had had a homosexual relationship with a prosecution witness, which that witness had denied. The prosecution sought leave to ask the defendant questions tending to show that he had been convicted of offences other than that charged because the nature and conduct of the defence was such as to involve imputations on the character of the witness for the prosecution within s.1(f)(ii) of the Criminal Evidence Act, 1898. The defendant objected on the grounds that, in view of s.1(1) of the Sexual Offences Act, 1967, an allegation that a man was a homosexual or practised homosexuality was not an imputation on his character within s.1(f)(ii) of the Act, 1898, and in any event the allegation had been made for the purpose of explaining the defendant's presence in the room and not for that of discrediting the testimony of the prosecution witness. The objection was rejected, questions about the defendant's previous convictions were asked, and he was convicted. He appealed to the Court of Appeal on the grounds that his objections to the evidence of his previous convictions had been wrongly rejected.

That Court (Stephenson LJ., MacKenna and O'Connor JJ.) dismissed the appeal. The Court held that the character of a witness was impugned by an allegation of homosexual conduct made against him and an imputation of homosexual immorality against a witness might reflect on his reliability, generally or in the witness box. The court also held that a defendant who made such an attack but disclaimed the intention to discredit the testimony of the witness nevertheless was still subject to the risk of cross-examination as to his own record. In the course of delivering the judgment of the court Stephenson LJ. said at p. 281:—

> 'Mr Bate submitted that in these progressive (or permissive) days it was no longer an imputation on a man's character to say of him that he was a homosexual or that he practised homosexuality. Since 1967, when section 1 of the Sexual Offences Act 1967 became law, it was no longer an offence to commit a homosexual act with another man of full age in private. No reasonable person would now think the worse of a man who committed such acts; he might not wish to associate with him but he would not condemn him. We think that this argument goes too far and that the gap between what is declared by Parliament to be illegal and punishable and what the common man or woman still regards as immoral or wrong is not wide enough to support it. We respectfully agree with the opinion of Lord Reid in Reg. v Knuller (Publishing, Printing and Promotions) Ltd. [1973] AC 435, 457 that "there is a material difference between merely exempting certain conduct from criminal penalties and making it lawful in the full sense", and with him we read the Act of 1967 as saying that even though homosexual acts between consenting adults in private may be corrupting, if people choose to corrupt themselves in this way, that is their affair and the law will not interfere. If Mr Price were to sue the defendant in respect of his allegation if repeated outside a court of law, we venture to think that a submission that the words were incapable of a defamatory meaning would be bound to fail and a jury would generally be likely to find them defamatory.'

Whilst this last statement is very much on point in respect of the issue that I have to deal with here it is of course a statement made obiter. Nonetheless it does appear to me to represent the legal position in England and in my view it also represents the legal position in Ireland.

Quite apart from the decision which I have just cited it does not appear to me to be sound to suggest that merely because an activity is no longer prohibited by the criminal law an allegation of engaging in such activity cannot be defamatory. The commission of adultery is not a criminal offence but nobody could seriously suggest that an allegation of adultery could not be defamatory. Similarly, to lie is not a criminal offence, but again can it be seriously suggested that to call a person a liar is not defamatory

I reject the defendants' contentions in this regard.

The defendants do however say that the photograph of the plaintiff with a woman (albeit with her face blocked out) on his arm, and the suggestion that the plaintiff is 'featured regularly in the tabloid gossip columns where the names of his latest model girlfriends are plugged' makes it plain that no allegation of homosexuality is being made. I do not agree. It seems to me that it would be perfectly open to a jury to hold that the use of the word 'gay' in relation to the plaintiff either in its natural or ordinary meaning or by innuendo was an allegation of homosexuality. A jury would be entitled to find in the plaintiff's favour in that regard and if they did it does not appear to me that their verdict could be regarded as perverse. I do not think that the sting is removed by the reference to the appearance of the plaintiff in the tabloid gossip columns or the photograph which accompanies the article.

As there is no plea of justification in respect of this complaint it follows that the plaintiff has made out a sufficiently strong case in my view to satisfy the test required for the granting of an interlocutory injunction."

The nature of what is defamatory will clearly change over time, as demonstrated in the case of *Berry v Irish Times Ltd* [1973] I.R. 368.

Berry v Irish Times Limited
Supreme Court [1973] I.R. 368

Facts: The plaintiff, Peter Berry, was a senior civil servant and the head of the Department of Justice. The defendants were newspaper publishers, who published a photograph which showed a man carrying a placard on which was written: "Peter Berry—20th Century Felon Setter—Helped Jail Republicans in England." The words on the placard were untrue. Beneath the photograph was printed a news item about two Irishmen who were stated to be serving sentences of imprisonment after convictions in England for having taken part in a raid for arms in that country. The plaintiff sued the defendants in the High Court for damages for libel. The High Court (with a jury) held that the words were not defamatory. The plaintiff appealed this finding to the Supreme Court.

Issues: The court (Ó Dálaigh C.J., Walsh and Budd JJ.; Fitzgerald and McLoughlin JJ. dissenting) held that as the statement involved the bringing of criminals to justice, the statement could not be seen to be defamatory. The dissenting judgments however, held that the statement was effectively branding the plaintiff as an "informer", an allegation which would be defamatory in this country.

Ó Dálaigh C.J. (Walsh and Budd JJ. concurring):

"The law in the matter is most recently set out in the judgment of this Court in *Quigley* v. *Creation Ltd.* [1971] I.R. 269 In the course of his judgment, Mr. Justice Walsh at p. 272 of the report stated the position in law to be as follows:—'Basically, the question of libel or no libel is a matter of opinion and opinions may vary reasonably within very wide limits. When a jury has found that there has been a libel, this Court would be more slow to set aside such a verdict than in other types of actions and it would only do so if it was of opinion that the conclusion reached by the jury was one to which reasonable men could not or ought not have come. It is true that if words only tend to lower a person in the minds of a particular class or section of society, particularly if the standard of that particular section of society is one which the Court cannot recognise or approve, the words will not be held to be defamatory. On the other hand, words are defamatory if they impute conduct which would tend to lower that person in the eyes of a considerable and respectable class of the community, though not in the eyes of the community as a whole. The test is whether it will lower him in the eyes of the average right-thinking man. If it will, then it is defamatory if untrue. It follows naturally that in an action in this country the standard would be that of the average right-thinking person in this community. The law recognises the right of the plaintiff to have the estimation in which he stands in the opinion of the right-minded people in this community unaffected by false statements to his discredit.' The judgment also goes on to state that in defamation, as in perhaps no other form of civil proceedings, the position of the jury is uniquely important. Mr. Justice Budd and Mr. Justice McLoughlin agreed.

There can be little doubt that the person who published on the placard, which appears in the photograph, the words complained of published a statement which, on the evidence, is indisputably false; it is a fair inference that the object of the author of the words (and of those displaying the poster) was to injure the plaintiff in his general reputation. The intent of the author or the publisher of a libel may be very relevant on the question of malice, but it does not determine the question whether the material complained of is or is not defamatory. In appropriate cases an action lies for willful injurious malicious falsehood, and such an action is not governed by the stringent rules of libel and slander: this matter is dealt with in s.20 of the Defamation Act, 1961. That is not the action before this Court, even though the material on the placard could be proved to be a malicious falsehood. In this case there is no allegation of express malice against the *Irish Times* in respect of their publication of the placard by its reproduction of the photograph in question …

… It is perhaps surprising that the Supreme Court should be asked to hold, as a matter of law, that it is necessarily defamatory to say of one of the citizens of this country that he assisted in the bringing to justice in another country of a fellow countryman who broke the laws of that country and who was tried and convicted for that offence in the ordinary course of the administration of criminal justice. This Court is bound to uphold the rule of law and its decisions must be conditioned by this duty. Is the matter to be considered differently because the person or persons so convicted were motivated by a desire to resolve, by force of arms, a dispute existing between their own country and the country in which the offence was committed when there is not a state of war between the two countries? To say, in those circumstances, that such an allegation must be defamatory would be to hold that ordinary right-thinking people in this country could not condemn such militant activities—to the extent that one could not but think that a person who assisted in curbing or putting down such militant activities was guilty of disgraceful conduct. That, in effect, is what was alleged against the plaintiff ...

... The learned trial judge asked the jury to consider the case on the basis of whether the allegation, if true, was such as would make the plaintiff's ordinary right-thinking neighbours think less of him. To that question the jury answered 'No.' It cannot be held as a matter of law that his right-thinking neighbours, or any other right-thinking people in the community in Ireland, must necessarily think less of him for taking such action if he had done so. The fact that the allegation is false does not make it defamatory. The plaintiff in his own evidence said he understood it to suggest that he was 'an informer.' If for historical reasons it is to be assumed that the word 'informer' has a special and defamatory meaning and is, because of such special meaning, to be distinguished from the word 'informant' which itself certainly is not defamatory in its ordinary meaning, the fact is that the word 'informer' was not used in the publication complained of and no innuendo was pleaded to suggest that the words actually published were so understood. This ground of appeal must fail."

McLoughlin J.:

"... To have one's name displayed on a placard in the public street is something which most people would regard as objectionable. It is almost axiomatic that if one's name is placarded one is blackguarded. Followed by the words '20th Century Felon Setter' makes it particularly obnoxious. What do the words mean? Literally, I suppose, designating some person a felon so that he may be proceeded against as such; but more, it means doing it in a malevolent way. As an expression it is clearly vituperative and reviling. The words which follow 'Helped jail Republicans in England' do not take away from the vituperative nature of the expression '20th Century Felon Setter.' They seem to convey only the reason why he is so vilified. He is called a felon setter because he has designated republicans, by giving information as to names and locations, addresses perhaps in England, and so assisted the British authorities to have such persons jailed. Put in other words, the suggestion is that this Irishman, the plaintiff, has acted as a spy and informer for the British police concerning republicans in England, thus putting the plaintiff into the same category as the spies and informers of earlier centuries who were regarded with loathing and abomination by all decent people.

It is the fact that there is no evidence of the effect of this publication in the minds of persons who saw it. There is evidence of its effect on the plaintiff. Asked why the publication appalled and distressed him, he said:—'I can think of nothing more ugly, more horrible in this life than to be called an informer. It has a peculiarly nauseating effect in Irish life. It was totally untrue.' Not only was he not cross-examined to suggest that this was not a reasonable reaction on his part to the publication but, on the contrary, it was suggested to him that placards with similar wording on an occasion prior to the publication by the defendants (one bearing the words 'Quisling Berry—helped Britain to gaol Irish political prisoners') were such that he would find them extremely offensive and hurtful.

Reading the charge of the learned trial judge, it is clear that he expected the jury to answer the second question in the affirmative. When charging on the question of damages he said:—'*Prima facie,* as a matter of reasonable inference, to suggest of a person of his standing, a reputable public servant, that he is an informer would lower his reputation.' He then goes on to tell the jury in so many words that there was no evidence to indicate that his reputation was in fact lowered. I think the jury may have been misled into thinking that, because there was no evidence that his reputation was in fact lowered by the publication, the publication was not defamatory *of him*; although nowhere in the charge or in the evidence is there any indication that a view could be taken of the publication which was not defamatory.

A publication is defamatory of a person if it injures or tends to injure his good reputation in the minds of right-thinking people. That is a simple definition but the difficulty is to discover what is meant by 'right-thinking people.' It does not mean all such people but only some such people, perhaps even only one, because if a plaintiff loses the respect for his reputation of some or even one right-thinking person he suffers some injury. I put the matter squarely to Mr. Micks and he said that some right-thinking people might regard a publication as defamatory and other right-thinking people might come to a diametrically opposite conclusion …

… It is my view that there must be many right-thinking persons who, although they do not approve of or positively disapprove of the acts of militant republicans in England, would regard the plaintiff with contempt if they believed that he had gone out of his way to supply information to the British police so as to have such persons jailed in England. It may be that one's views on matters of this sort are conditioned by one's up-bringing and education. The school sneak who, however justified, 'splits to the head' was regarded with contempt by all his fellows …

... A person's good name deserves the special protection of the law: see Article 40, s.3, of the Constitution (see p.361, *ante*) I do not think that the plaintiff's good name has received that protection."

Comments and Questions:

1. The dissenting judgment of McLoughlin J. above highlights the difficulty of determining whether a statement is defamatory. Given the political climate at the time, did you find the judgment of McLoughlin J. more convincing than that of Ó Dálaigh C.J.?

2. A case dealing with a similar political question but starkly demonstrating how the political climate was now far less ambiguous, was that of *McDonagh v News Group Newspapers Ltd.,* Supreme Court, November 23, 1993, which involved a barrister appointed to represent the Irish Government at the inquest into the killing of three people in Gibraltar. An article was written in the British *Sun* newspaper, stating that "Leftie Spies pack Gib Inquest". This was taken to mean that the plaintiff was a leftwing spy, and a sympathiser with terrorist causes. In finding for the plaintiff, Finlay C.J. stated that: "I am satisfied that there are not very many general classifications of defamatory accusation, which at present in Ireland would be considered significantly more serious."

IDENTIFICATION OF THE PLAINTIFF

In order for a defamation action to succeed the plaintiff must be identified. In some cases it will be clear that the person referred to is the plaintiff, in that s/he may be named specifically, and an address, or picture, or other description may be given. However, in other cases it may not be clear, in which case the question arises as to what will amount to sufficient identification of the plaintiff. Section 21 of the Defamation Act 1961 allows for a defence in respect of unintentional identification, based on the exercise of the defendant of reasonable care in ensuring that accidental identification had not taken place and the defendant making an offer of amends.

However, where the person named is part of a group it is more difficult for the plaintiff to establish that they have been identified (see *Knupffer v London Express Newspaper Ltd.* [1944] A.C. 116 below).

Knupffer v London Express Newspaper Ltd.
House of Lords [1944] A.C. 116

Facts: The plaintiff was a Russian migrant in England, who was head of the English branch of Young Russia. The defendants ran a newspaper which had published a disparaging article about the Young Russia movement, accusing them of being devotees of Hitler with a Fascist ideology. The newspaper wrote that one of their number would be recruited by Hitler, for the purpose of violently destroying existing structures within the Soviet Union. The plaintiff sued, presenting four of his friends who testified that they believed the article was about him. He succeeded in the trial court, but this was reversed in the Court of Appeal. He appealed this finding to the House of Lords.

Issues: The court had to consider whether the plaintiff, as a member of a group that the article published referred to, had been identified in the article.

The court held that, to be identified, the article must reasonably be capable of referring to the plaintiff and some people known to the plaintiff must have reasonably thought that the plaintiff had been referred to. On the basis of this test, they held that the article could not be held to have identified the plaintiff.

Viscount Simon L.C. (Atkin, Porter, Russell of Killowen L.JJ. delivered concurring judgments; Lord Thankerton concurring):

"My Lords, it is an essential element of the cause of action for defamation that the words complained of should be published 'of the plaintiff.' If the words are not so published, the plaintiff is not defamed and cannot have any right to ask that the defendant should be held responsible to him in respect of them.

In the words complained of in this case there is no specific mention of the appellant from beginning to end, and the only countries in which it is stated that this group of émigrés is established are France and the United States. Evidence was given at the trial that the appellant had joined the Young Russia Party in 1928, that in 1935 he became assistant representative of the Young Russia movement in Great Britain, and that in 1938 he was appointed representative of the movement in Great Britain and head of the British branch of the movement. The headquarters of the movement were in Paris until June, 1940, when they were removed to America.

These facts, standing alone, however, do not justify the conclusion that the words complained of are capable of being read as a defamation of the appellant. The words make allegations of a defamatory character about a body of persons—some thousands in number—who belong to a society whose members are to be found in many countries. In *O'Brien v. Eason & Son* [47 Ir. L. T. 266], Holmes and Cherry L.JJ. ruled that where comments of an alleged defamatory character were made on an association called the Ancient Order of Hibernians, an individual member of the order, who was not named nor in any way referred to, could not maintain an action of libel. They referred [Ibid. 266, 267, 268] to a well-known dictum of Willes J., uttered more than fifty years before, in *Eastwood v. Holmes* [1 F. & F. 347, 349], that 'if a man wrote that all lawyers were thieves, no particular lawyer could sue him unless there is something to point to the particular individual.' Where the plaintiff is not named, the test which decides whether the words used refer to him is the question whether the words are such as would reasonably lead persons acquainted with the plaintiff to believe that he was the person referred to. There are cases in which the language used in reference to a limited class may be reasonably understood to refer to every member of the class, in which case every member may have a cause of action. A good example is *Browne v. D. C. Thomson & Co.* [1912 S. C. 359], where a newspaper article stated in Queenstown 'instructions were issued by the Roman Catholic religious authorities that all Protestant shop assistants were to be discharged,' and where seven pursuers who averred that they were the sole persons who exercised religious authority in the name and on behalf of the Roman Catholic Church in Queenstown were held entitled to sue for libel as being individually defamed. Lord President Dunedin in that case said: 'I think it is quite evident that if a certain set of people are accused of having done something, and if such accusation is libellous, it is possible for the individuals in that set of people to show that they have been damnified, and it is right that they should have an opportunity of recovering damages as individuals.' In the present case, however, the appellant rejected the view that every member of the Young Russia Group could bring his own action on the words complained of, and relied on his own prominence or representative character in the movement as establishing that the words referred to himself. There is, however, nothing in the words which refers to one member of the group rather than another. *Le Fanu v. Malcolmson* [1 H. L. C. 637] was, it is true, a decision of this House in which Lord Cottenham L.C. and Lord Campbell held that the verdict of a jury awarding damages to the owners of a factory in the county of Waterford against the proprietor of a newspaper published in that county could be upheld notwithstanding that the letterpress, in the course of denouncing the alleged cruelty with which factory operatives were treated, did not specifically refer to the plaintiff's factory. It appears, however, in that case that there were circumstances, such as the location of the factory, which enabled the jurors to identify the plaintiff's factory as the factory pointed at, and the Lord Chancellor observed that 'if a party can publish a libel so framed as to describe individuals, though not naming them, and not specifically describing them by any express form of words, but still so describing them that it is known who they are, as the jurors have found it to be here, and if those who must be acquainted with the circumstances connected with the party described may also come to the same conclusion, and may have no doubt that the writer of the libel intended to mean those individuals, it would be opening a very wide door to defamation, if parties suffering all the inconvenience of being libelled were not permitted to have that protection which the law affords.' It will be observed that *Le Fanu v. Malcolmson* [1 H. L. C. 637] was a case where there were facts pointing to the particular factory which was meant to be referred to though the article spoke in more general terms of a factory in Waterford. In the present case the statement complained of is not made concerning a particular individual, whether named or unnamed, but concerning a group of people spread over several countries and including considerable numbers. No facts were proved in evidence which could identify the appellant as the person individually referred to. Witnesses called for the appellant were asked the carefully framed question: 'To whom did your mind go when you read that article?' and they not unnaturally replied by pointing to the appellant himself, but that is because they happened to know the appellant as the leading member of the society in this country and not because there is anything in the article itself which ought to suggest even to his friends that he is referred to as an individual.

There are two questions involved in the attempt to identify the appellant as the person defamed. The first question is a question of law—can the article, having regard to its language, be regarded as capable of referring to the appellant? The second question is a question of fact—Does the article, in fact, lead reasonable people, who know the appellant, to the conclusion that it does refer to him? Unless the first question can be answered in favour of the appellant, the second question does not arise, and where the trial judge went wrong was in treating evidence to support the identification in fact as governing the matter, when the first question is necessarily, as a matter of law, to be answered in the negative. I move that this appeal be dismissed."

Comments and Questions:
1. The test for identification on the basis of *Knupffer,* above, is therefore two-fold: first, that the publication could reasonably be held to have identified the plaintiff, and, secondly, that individuals who know the plaintiff believe that the publication refers to the plaintiff. As the first question was answered in the negative the plaintiff lost his action.

DEFENCES

In an effort to maintain the balance between free speech and the right to a good name, a number of defences have emerged. The primary defences are: justification, privilege, fair comment and consent. The offering of an apology and an offer of amends, while not complete defences, can go some way in mitigating liability.

The Defamation Bill 2006 proposes the introduction of a new defence of "fair and reasonable publication (s.24) on a matter of public importance".

Justification

Once a defamatory statement is made it is presumed to be false; it rests with the defendant to prove that the statement is true. If the defendant succeeds in proving the truth of the statement, the defence of justification provides a complete defence. The justification given has to be as wide as the defamation and encompass all the elements of the defamation. Section 22 of the Defamation Act 1961 states that that where two or more distinct charges are made against the plaintiff, the defence of justification will still apply even though the defendant cannot prove each one. This applies so long as the ones not proven do not cause any additional damage to the plaintiff's reputation given the damage done by the ones proven to be true. Where the statement made is substantially true, even if not true in all respects, the defence will succeed.

Bailey v Irish Mirror Group Ltd.
Unreported, Circuit Court, January 19, 2004

Facts: The plaintiff, Mr Bailey, was a suspect in the murder of a woman, Ms du Plantier, and was arrested but not charged with that crime. A number of newspapers reported the fact of his arrest and related matters, including statements as to his past. Mr Bailey argued that he had been defamed in these articles and sued in the Circuit Court. The defendants pleaded, *inter alia*, justification as a defence, including reliance on s.22 of the Defamation Act 1961.

Issues: The court (Moran J.) had to consider whether the contested statements in the articles complained of constituted defamatory statements. Furthermore, he had to consider whether justification could be pleaded as a defence to those statements. Moran J. ultimately held that a number of the statements were not capable of being defamatory. As regards statements as to his arrest on suspicion of murder and having beaten his ex-wife, he held that the plea of justification could apply to the statements as to Mr Bailey's arrest, but not as to his having beaten his ex-wife.

Moran J.:

"The Plaintiff in this case, Mr Bailey, is by occupation a journalist. Once this news broke about the discovery of the body of Madame du Plantier, he became involved in reporting the story of the murder. He made numerous reports and he furnished numerous reports to various newspapers … During that time of course one can only presume and assume that the area of West Cork was full of rumour and talk, reports and counter-reports as to what had happened to this unfortunate lady over the weekend of the 21/22 December. I am sure that fingers were pointed in various directions and there were various stories. I am not concerned with those.

In any event the Plaintiff was arrested on the morning of 10 February of 1997 and he was taken to Bandon Garda Station, and apparently when he got out of the Garda car he was photographed.

When the Garda make an arrest in any criminal offence, and particularly in a murder case, I suppose in any serious criminal offence, they do it for very strong reasons and they usually do it because they have a strong suspicion as to the involvement of the injured party, and I suspect that's what they did on this particular day.

The Plaintiff complains about his arrest and indeed of his treatment by the Garda, but that is not a matter for this court. If he has any complaints about his treatment by the Garda there are other authorities, and I think counsel referred to them, namely the Garda Complaints Board.

He was photographed and he was named, and following this arrest there was further publicity. That is natural and that is normal. He was arrested as a suspected person involved in the murder of Madame du Plantier. Various newspaper articles appeared and he complains of the treatment he has received from seven different publications, I think eight or nine articles in all.

I said at the outset of this case that this was not a murder trial. These are civil claims and they are actions in defamation. As the lawyers know, whatever about the general public, there is a difference in the standard of proof required in a criminal case as against a civil case. I was anxious that this trial should never take on the mantle of a criminal trial. I am afraid once or twice it may well have and I am sorry it did, but I want to emphasise this was not a criminal trial, not a criminal investigation, and it is not one.

I would have to say that evidence was given indeed during the course of these trials and these cases which would not be admitted for legal reasons in a criminal trial. Any findings of fact that I make in this case are made and based on the balance of probabilities, and nothing else.

The Plaintiff brings seven actions arising from the different articles. The first one is against the Mirror for a publication of 14 February of the year 1997; the second one against the Sunday Independent of 20 July of 1997; the third one is against the Independent on Sunday for an article of 26 April of 1998; the fourth is against the Times Newspapers: one against The Times itself in respect of a report of 11 February of 1997; and the other one against the Sunday Times in respect of an article on 16 February of 1997. The next one is against the Star and there are two incidents there: one of 22 February of 1997; and the other of 19 December of 1997. The next one is the Sun and the date is 14 February of 1997. The final one is the Daily Telegraph for 3 March of 1997. I do not propose going through these articles.

I have read them on several occasions myself. They have been read to me here, they have been dealt with in depth by counsel on behalf of the Plaintiff and in particular by counsel on behalf of the defence.

I just do not see any point in wasting time going through them again.

The first defence in these cases is one of justification, the second one is one of partial justification, and then the Defendants argue that if neither of those succeed they go on to rely on consent, on qualified privilege and contributory negligence.

The law in the case dealing with what is defamation was put very clearly to me by Mr Gallagher in his submission to me and in his closing address. He says that if one is defamed one must deal with the ordinary and natural meaning of the words. He quoted to me an extract from Duncan and Neill on Defamation which is as follows:

> 'In order to determine the natural and ordinary meaning of the words which the plaintiff complains of, it is necessary to take into account the context in which the words were used and the mode of publication. Thus, a plaintiff

cannot select an isolated passage in an article and complain of that alone if other parts of the article throw a different light on that passage.'

Mr Gallagher also told me that it was for me to determine the sense in which the words would reasonably have been understood by an ordinary man in the light of generally known facts and meaning of words.

The allegation of libel means that the person the libel is published about, his standing has been reduced in the eyes of an ordinary person. The defendants have assisted me by referring me to the Charleston case and the judgment of Lord Bridge, in which he said:

'At first blush this argument has considerable attractions, but I believe that it falls foul of two principles which are basic to the law of libel.

The first is that where no legal innuendo is alleged to arise from extrinsic circumstances known to some readers, the natural and ordinary meaning to be ascribed to the words of an allegedly defamatory publication is the meaning including inferential meaning which the words would convey to the mind of the ordinary, reasonable and fair-minded reader. This proposition is too well established to require citation of authority. The second principle which is perhaps a corollary of the first is that although a combination of words may in fact convey different meanings to the minds of different readers, the jury in a libel action applying the criterion in which the first principle dictates is required to determine the single meaning which the publication conveyed to the notional, reasonable reader and to place its verdict and any award of damages on the assumption that this was the one sense in which all readers would have understood it.'

That is very simply the law which must guide me in determining whether the Plaintiff has been defamed in these proceedings.

The evidence in this case consisted mainly of the evidence of the Plaintiff himself. I do not propose going through it, I just want to make some comments about it.

One thing that occurred to me, Mr Bailey having been in the witness box for, I think, three-and-a-half days, that he was what I would describe as a very cool witness. He never got annoyed during the very lengthy and protracted cross-examination by Mr Gallagher of him and that is quite exceptional and quite extraordinary, he just did not. The only time he showed any discomfort was in fact when he was making a complaint about something that had happened to him within the walls of this building.

He gave his version of events. He told me about his difficulties with Ms Thomas, not in any great detail or anything, and he told me the effects of these articles on him. He told me about the treatment he had from the Garda and he said he was being hounded by the media as a result of it all.

He was cross-examined at considerable length by Mr Gallagher. Mr Gallagher put to him that he was, first of all, a violent man, and then reminded him how, following his arrest, that he himself sought publicity and used publicity, how he allowed himself to be interviewed by the national television station RTE.

He allowed himself to be interviewed by the Pat Kenny programme, and he spoke to researchers first apparently, and then spoke to Mr Kenny himself. He certainly posed for photographs and he certainly had interviews on his own evidence, indeed, with some of the media.

This to me was quite unusual for somebody who had been arrested on suspicion of a serious charge of murder. Normally such people, I think, withdraw very much into the background following their release from custody and, I presume, wonder what is going to happen next, but Mr Bailey did not. He certainly gave the interviews to RTE on the news and to Mr Kenny and he also met members of the press. One can only presume from that that Mr Bailey is a man who likes a certain amount of notoriety, that he likes perhaps to be in the limelight, that he likes a bit of self-publicity.

The next witness was Ms Thomas. Ms Thomas was an equally cool witness. She was not cross-examined for very long, but there were some very unpleasant things put to her and she did not show any upset or anxiety. When it was put to her about the violence and the assaults of Mr Bailey on her she tended, if you like, to put them under the carpet and say [that] really these were all due to drink and they lasted for a very short time, and they were really nothing at all.

There was other evidence called on behalf of the Plaintiff as well. Mr Doyle of Paris Match and the gentlemen from Skibbereen and Schull, the two businessmen.

The Defendants then went into evidence and called a number of witnesses from the Toormore and Schull area. The purposes of their evidence was really to show inconsistencies, or flaws if you like, in the version that Mr Bailey and Ms Thomas had given me. The thrust of the Plaintiff's case is, as I see, that he is branded as a man who was violent towards women, and that he was branded as the murderer of Sophie du Plantier. There are other matters as well dealing with his ex-wife, that he had been violent towards her and the sale of property dealing with his previous marriage.

On the question of his being violent towards women, and this is a question of fact for me to decide, what came across, particularly as a result of Mr Gallagher's in-depth cross-examination, was that Ms Thomas had suffered three nasty assaults at the hands of Mr Bailey. In one of them he was brought before the District Court and he received a suspended sentence. The quotation from the newspaper was read or was put to him in which apparently the learned district justice said he battered her. He said that violence takes place, it's a domestic problem. What the newspapers have said about him in the various articles is that he is violent towards women. He says yes, he was violent against one woman and that is it.

In my experience dealing with family law here, and very few people would know anything about what goes on in family law cases [except] the parties or the practitioners, but one rarely comes across instances of beatings; occasionally one does. In this case we have three of them. I think to have violence once would be unusual, to have it twice would be very unusual, to have it three times exceptional. The learned district judge imposed a six-month suspended sentence when he was dealing with the matter that went to a criminal trial, and I suspect he did that because Ms Thomas came in and said that she had forgiven him. If I had such a case I would have the same attitude myself. If the partner did not come in and say I have forgiven him, I would impose a custodial sentence. I personally would have no hesitation in describing Mr Bailey as a violent man. I think the Defendants were perfectly justified in referring to him as being violent towards women in the plural, and I feel he has not been defamed by that.

The other matters of fact for me to decide on really are the inconsistencies which were dealt with during the course of the case. The first one is the question of whether or not the Plaintiff knew the late Madame Sophie du Plantier. He says he never met her. He said he had seen her from Mr Lyons' house when he was working there. Mr Lyons gave evidence to me and he said he was 80 or 90% sure that he had introduced the late Madame du Plantier to Mr Bailey.

On the balance of probability I accept this evidence of Mr Lyons. I accept that he did introduce them, but I look upon it as a very casual introduction. I otherwise accept Mr Bailey's evidence that he did not know her. By knowing her, to know her as somebody whose house he would visit, or somebody whom he would meet in the street and have conversations with, or go out for a drink with her, anything like that.

I am afraid I am not going through these witnesses by order as they were called. It is just that I made these notes as it occurred to me.

The next witness called by the defence in so far as inconsistencies are concerned that I am going to deal with is the evidence of Mrs Farrell, who said she did not know Mr Bailey, who described this man she had seen in Schull, who described the man she saw walking out of Schull early in the morning, who described the man she saw at Kealfadda Bridge in the early hours of the morning, and who described the man she later saw in Schull as all being the one man, and she said that was Mr Bailey and she was able to put a name on him.

Mrs Farrell said she came here reluctantly, and we also had certain discussion about the 'relationship', to use that word in inverted commas, between Mrs Farrell and Mr Bailey, which culminated in Mrs Farrell's solicitor writing a letter to Mr Bailey about his behaviour.

On the balance of probabilities I accept what Mrs Farrell told me, that the man she saw at Kealfadda Bridge was in her view Ian Bailey.

I would have to say of course that it is evidence of identification, and if it was very material to the issues I do not know to what extent it would stand.

The next aspect of the case is the evidence about the fires, the evidence that was given to me by Mrs Kennedy, I think, and Mr Jackson, who said that there were fires on the Ian Bailey/Jules Thomas property on St Stephen's day. I accept the fires were lit there on that day and I accept their evidence, but of course as to what was being burned is really anyone's guess. One of the witnesses said crackling sounds which would suggest timber of some nature or briars or something like that, and the other a mattress.

The other witnesses which I will refer to is the evidence of Mr and Mrs Shelley, who went with Mr Bailey and Ms Thomas to the Bailey/Thomas home on New Year's Eve of 1997 or 1998, I am not quite sure which. Mr and Mrs Shelley told me that Mr Bailey said to them at the end of the night: 'I did it, I did it.' Mr Bailey's evidence is no, I did not say that. What I said was they say I did it, I did it. I accept what Mr and Mrs Shelley told me that he did say that.

What is the effect of that admission? I think it goes back possibly to Mr Bailey being a man looking for notoriety, self-publicity seeking and was probably drink-induced as well.

Then there was the evidence of Malachi Reed, who was then a 14-year-old boy, who says that Mr Bailey said to him I did it. Again I accept his evidence as what he says that Mr Bailey told him. I think this was a form of bravado really on Mr Bailey's part, trying to impress this young 14-year-old for whatever reason, but the 14-year-old was quite concerned about it and told his mother, who became equally upset and concerned.

There was a lot of other evidence showing inconsistencies about time, about Ms Thomas' car being seen in the vicinity of the house on the day of the discovery of the body, the conversations with Mr Fuller and the conversations with Mr Belecki. I do not propose going into those. There certainly were inconsistencies.

That is really the evidence in the case.

The Plaintiffs say that what these articles say is that they portray Mr Bailey as being the murderer of the late Madame du Plantier. I have read the articles, as I say, not once, not twice, several times during the trial, over the vacation, and on Saturday and yesterday again. I put myself into the position that Lord Bridge says I should, as the ordinary reader. These articles do not convey to me that they say that he was the murderer. What they do convey is that he was the suspect and he was arrested on the suspicion of murder. The articles constantly go on to quote him and refer to what he says: 'I didn't do it.' They give it equal prominence.

I take the view that the plea of justification is established very strongly with the exception of three matters.

The first one is there has not been any evidence called about the Wellington boots and the washing of the Wellington boots in a stream. That has not been refuted and there is no evidence to suggest he was.

The other one is the burning of the clothes. There is no evidence to say that he burned clothes at all.

The third one is the one that he was violent towards his ex-wife and that's all.

In so far as the first two are concerned, namely the relevance to the Wellington boots and the burning of the clothes, the Defendants have urged upon me that the defence of partial justification is also there and they have referred me to s 22 of the Defamation Act 1961, and they have quoted it which reads as follows:

> 'In an action for libel or slander in respect of words containing two or more distinct charges against the plaintiff, defence of justification shall not fail by reason only that the truth of every charge proved to be true do not materially injure the plaintiff's reputation having regard to the truth of the charges which they have established.'

I do not think the reference to the Wellington boots, washing his Wellington boots, or the reference to burning the clothes in any way injure his reputation, having regard to the truth of the charges which have otherwise been established, namely that he was arrested on suspicion of murder. Therefore, that aspect of the claim fails.

The only other one remaining then is the claim that he was violent towards his ex-wife. There has been no evidence called to that. I have certainly found that he is a violent man, that is one thing; as to saying he was violent towards his ex-wife there has been absolutely no evidence and I find that he has been defamed in that regard, but of course that is outside the thrust of the main part of these cases.

In so far as the defamatory statement about his ex-wife is concerned, I take the view that he is entitled to damages, and I assess those in the sum of Euro 8,000.

In so far as all of the other allegations are concerned I dismiss them."

Comments and Questions:
1.   In relation to the reliance on the defence of s.22 of the Defamation Act 1961 for the unproven statements as to his washing his boots and burning his clothes, do you agree with Moran J. that reporting of these facts did not further harm the plaintiff's reputation, in a manner which was different to that of being arrested on suspicion of murder?

2.   As regards the claim that Mr Bailey beat his ex-wife, a number of cases have sounded a word of caution to publishers of statements ascribing to a person a general characteristic on the basis of a known incident. In the case of *Wakley v Cooke* (1849) 4 Exch. 511 for instance, the plaintiff called the defendant a "libellous journalist". Although the defendant could show that there had been one case of proven libel taken against the plaintiff, it was not enough to show the truth of the statement which imputed him to be generally libellous and the defence of justification failed.

Privilege

The defence of privilege can be pleaded in specific cases where the statement made, although untrue, is protected as it is in the public interest to allow uninhibited expression in certain cases.

There are two types of privilege: absolute privilege and qualified privilege.

Where absolute privilege applies the defendant is totally protected in respect of any statements which s/he may make, irrespective of motive or knowledge (these included parliamentary privilege, presidential privilege, reports of court proceedings, and state communications).

On the other hand, to rely on the defence of qualified privilege, the defendant must show that s/he had a duty to convey the information complained of, that the body or person to whom they communicated it had a legitimate interest in receiving it and that the communication was made free from malice. Qualified privilege can apply to statements ranging from mistaken suspicions of wrong-doings communicated to the police, to parental advice given to children, to complaints of misconduct by professionals. In the last scenario it is important for the defendant seeking to rely on the defence to show that s/he communicated the complaint to the correct body. As held in the case of *Hynes-O'Sullivan v O'Driscoll* [1989] I.L.R.M. 349, failure to do so will mean that the defence will not succeed.

Hynes-O'Sullivan v O'Driscoll
Supreme Court [1989] I.L.R.M. 349

Facts: The plaintiff was an acting consultant psychiatrist who was called to attend at a court hearing in Dublin by the defendant. She did not have to give evidence and sent a bill to the defendant requiring payment. He in turn required a breakdown of the charges, and from there ensued a series of communications to the Law Society and the Irish Medical Association (IMA) and the Irish Medical Council (IMC) on the matter. The plaintiff claims that she was defamed in a letter sent to the IMA, the IMC and the Law Society by the defendant. The defendant argued the defence of qualified privilege. The defendant succeeded in the High Court and the plaintiff appealed to the Supreme Court.

Issues: The court (Finlay C.J., Henchy, Griffin, Hederman and McCarthy JJ.) had to consider whether the defence of qualified privilege applied in this case, and in particular whether the communications were motivated by malice.

The court held that mere "honest belief" as to the appropriateness of the recipient was insufficient, "utmost care" had to be taken. As this was not done, the defence of qualified privilege failed. It was also open to the jury to consider the issue of malice, given the circumstances of the case, and the court held that the trial judge had erred in law, in not allowing the jury to consider the existence of malice.

Finlay C.J. (Griffin J. concurring):

"On 3 June 1982 the plaintiff wrote to the Incorporated Law Society enquiring as to whether the Society had laid down any guidelines with regard to the issuing of *subpoenas* to professional people to enforce their attendance at court at extremely short notice. In that letter she set out her version of her dealings with the defendant and complained that the defendant had acted in a reprehensible fashion to cause her such harassment. She also sought the help of the Society in obtaining her fees, stating that the seeking by the defendant of a breakdown of them was a further insult to her professional integrity.

The Law Society sent a copy of this letter to the defendant and asked him for his comments.

On 24 June 1982 the defendant wrote a lengthy letter to the Law Society commenting on the letter which the plaintiff had written and giving his version of the events leading to her attendance in court as a witness. In the course of that letter the defendant accused the plaintiff of duplicity and described her as a person *'who holds scant regard for professional ethics and even less for the solemnity of the law'*. He stated that when he informed the plaintiff that he would be obliged to serve a *subpoena* upon her to secure her attendance at court on behalf of his client, she replied that if he did she should send him a *'sick note'*. He also stated that she attempted to avoid service of the *subpoena* and that she was obsessed with the payment of her fees.

On 25 June 1982 the defendant sent a copy of this letter to the secretary of the Irish Medical Association (the IMA) with a covering letter making a formal complaint against the plaintiff:

(1) of a willingness alone or in conspiracy with other members of the medical profession to falsify a medical certificate on her behalf,
(2) of a lack of integrity demonstrated in the misleading complaint she made to the Law Society against the defendant, and
(3) of demanding exorbitant fees and expenses for a court appearance.

The secretary of the IMA acknowledged that letter and stated that his Association had no function in relation to such complaints which were a matter for the Medical Council.

The defendant on 13 July 1982 wrote to the secretary of the Medical Council in terms identical to those contained in his letter to the secretary of the IMA and enclosed a copy of his letter of 24 June 1982 to the Law Society.

The Medical Council sought the observations of the plaintiff upon the complaint made by the defendant and having considered them took no action on the complaints.

On 5 June 1985 the solicitors for the plaintiff wrote to the defendant claiming an apology, compensation and the payment of costs. In a portion of this letter the claim appeared to be for an apology and costs only. This request was repeated but no reply was made by the defendant to any of the letters. These proceedings were then instituted. The plaintiff claims damages for libel in respect of:

(1) The letter written to the Law Society,
(2) The letters written and sent to the IMA, and
(3) The letters written and sent to the Medical Council.

The defendant in his defence in addition to certain denials pleaded that the letters complained of were all written without malice on occasions of qualified privilege and furthermore pleaded justification of the allegations

(a) that the plaintiff threatened, if served with a *subpoena*, to send a sick note,
(b) that the plaintiff made a misleading complaint to the Law Society, and
(c) that the plaintiff demanded for appearance in the High Court fees that were exorbitant.

The action was tried in the High Court by a judge sitting with a jury. At the conclusion of the evidence for the plaintiff an application was made by the defendant to withdraw the case from the jury.

The learned trial judge then ruled that while he was satisfied that it had been established that the writing of the letter to the Law Society and to the Medical Council were each occasions of qualified privilege; since it had not been established that the plaintiff was a member of the IMA he (the judge) could not hold that the sending of the letters to that body was an occasion of qualified privilege unless the defendant in evidence established that he had an honest belief that the IMA was the appropriate body to which to make a complaint concerning the conduct of the plaintiff. Accordingly, he decided that the defendant had a case to meet.

Upon the conclusion of the evidence for the defendant the application for a dismissal was renewed. The learned trial judge then ruled that the defendant had an honest belief that the IMA was the appropriate body and that accordingly all the letters were published on occasions of qualified privilege.

He further ruled that there was no evidence in respect of any of the letters complained of which a jury could infer was more probably consistent with malice than otherwise and that accordingly the case must be dismissed ...

... **Plea of justification**

The plaintiff made the following admissions in evidence relevant to this issue:

(a) That when the defendant stated that he would be obliged to have a *subpoena* served upon her she said she would send him a sick certificate.
(b) That when a person came to serve a *subpoena* on her in her consulting rooms she heard the receptionist stating that she, the plaintiff, was not in, although she was standing in an adjoining corridor and was aware of the purpose of the visitor, namely, to seek to serve a *subpoena*, she did not correct her receptionist.
(c) That she did not pay a consultant any fees to carry out her duties on the occasion of her absence from Cork to attend the court in Dublin.

I am not satisfied that these admissions necessarily constitute conclusive evidence justifying all the charges made in the correspondence against the plaintiff. They are, in my view, capable of being accepted by a jury as such justification or capable of being accepted as failing to justify the charges made. I therefore conclude that there are no grounds upon which this Court could decide this appeal on the issue of justification.

Qualified privilege in respect of the letters to the IMA

There does not appear to be any direct Irish authority on the question as to whether an occasion of qualified privilege can arise where there is not actually an interest or duty in the person to whom a matter is published, although the person making the publication honestly believes that there is. In *Waring v McCaldin* (1873) IR 7 CL 282, FitzGerald B at p. 288 in the course of a ruling on a plea of demurrer stated as follows:

> 'If without express malice, I make a defamatory charge, which I bona fide believe to be true, against one whose conduct in the respect defamed has caused me injury, to one whose duty it is, or whose duty I reasonably believe it to be, to enquire into and redress such injury, the occasion is privileged, because I have an interest in the subject matter of my charge, and the person to whom I make the communication has, on hearing the communication, a duty to discharge in respect of it.'

A consideration of the report of the entire proceedings in that case clearly indicates that the statement which I have quoted from the judgment of Fitzgerald B, in so far as it dealt with reasonable belief, was *obiter* to the issues arising for decision.

In *Jenoure v Delmege* [1891] AC 73 which was an appeal to the Privy Council from the Supreme Court of Jamaica, Macnaghten LJ at p. 77 stated as follows:

> 'The Chief Justice went on to tell the jury that the proper authority to whom such a complaint should have been submitted was the superintending medical officer; but he also told them that if they thought that the appellant had addressed the letter to the inspector of constabulary by an honest unintentional mistake as to the proper authority to deal with the complaint, then the communication would not be deprived of any privilege to which it would have been entitled had it been addressed to the superintending medical officer. So far the summing-up seems to be open to no objection.'

The case in which this statement occurs was one in which the point on appeal before the Privy Council concerned an alleged misdirection by the Chief Justice of Jamaica to a jury on the question of privilege.

In *Hebditch v Macllwaine* [1894] 2 QB 54, the Court of Appeal in England decided that it was not sufficient that the maker of a statement honestly and reasonably believes that the person to whom it is made has an interest or duty to receive it in order to create an occasion of qualified privilege but that the actual existence of such duty or interest must be proved. This decision has since been followed in England and is quoted with approval in successive editions of *Gatley on Libel and Slander* being referred to at para. 507 of the 7th Edition. It was referred to by Black J in a judgment which was dissenting on other issues in *Kirkwood Hackett v Tierney* [1952] IR 185. The principle that in order to establish an occasion of qualified privilege it is necessary to prove the actual existence of a duty or interest in the person to whom the statement is communicated was clearly accepted by the former Supreme Court in *Reilly v Gill* (1951) 85 ILTR 165 as well as in *Kirkwood Hackett v Tierney* .

There does not appear to have been raised before this Court or before the former Supreme Court in any case the question as to whether an occasion of qualified privilege could also be established by proof of an honest belief in the person publishing the statement formed with reasonable care as to the interest or duty of the person to whom he communicates.

In the decision of the House of Lords in *London Association for Protection of Trade v Greenlands Ltd* [1916] 2 AC 15 it was decided that upon an enquiry being made to a person as to the financial circumstances and credit of a trader, that person is justified in giving such information and is deemed in law to do so on an occasion of qualified privilege provided that (1) he *bona fide* believes in the truth of the information which he gives and (2) *bona fide* believes that the person making the enquiry has an interest which justifies the enquiry. I am not aware of this decision having been considered by any Irish court.

If it were possible and desirable to extend the principle laid down in *London Association for Protection of Trade v Greenlands Ltd* to circumstances other than the credit of traders and even, as is urged in this case, to circumstances where an enquiry is not made, it would quite clearly be fundamental to any principle so developed that a person volunteering such a statement would take the utmost care in ascertaining as to whether the person to whom he was communicating it had an interest or duty to receive it.

In the instant case the defendant, a solicitor, before writing to the IMA took, on his own evidence, no step of any description to ascertain whether they were the appropriate body to which a complaint with regard to misconduct on the part of a doctor should be made. It is quite clear that either a reference by him to the *Medical Practitioners' Act 1978* or an enquiry made without involving the mentioning of any name to the IMA itself as to whether they were the appropriate body, would have yielded the immediate information that the appropriate body to whom such a communication should be made was the Medical Council.

In these circumstances, I am satisfied that even if a defence of qualified privilege can be established in the manner submitted on this appeal by the defendant that on the facts of this case it could not conceivably arise and I prefer not, in those circumstances, to express any view as to whether it is part of the law, or if it is the circumstances which would give rise to it.

Having regard to the consequences of the publication of such information I take the view that a mere honest belief in the appropriateness of the recipient is not sufficient under any circumstances to create privilege and since the decision of the learned trial judge that the publication to the IMA was privileged seems to have rested upon that principle, it was, in my view, in error.

With regard to the submission made on behalf of the defendant that the receipt by the IMA from the defendant's client of the fees due to the plaintiff which they transferred to her was proof of an actual duty or interest in the IMA to receive these letters, I am satisfied it must fail. The only evidence of the circumstances surrounding this payment was the production of a bank draft, apparently endorsed by the IMA and cashed by the plaintiff. Such evidence falls very far short indeed of the onus of proof which was upon the defendant of proving a relevant duty or interest in the IMA to receive the communication concerned.

I am, therefore, satisfied that the publication of these letters to the IMA should have been left to the jury without concerning any issue on the question of malice.

Rulings on malice

I am satisfied that although there are some difficulties in accurately understanding from the transcript in this case what precisely was said by the learned trial judge in his ruling that there are no grounds for the submission made on behalf of the plaintiff to the effect that his ruling on malice should be interpreted as a consideration of each separate item of evidence alleged by the plaintiff to constitute evidence of malice and a ruling that the matter should not be left to the jury because in more instances the plaintiff had failed to establish a probability of malice than in the instances in which she succeeded. The first submission made with regard to the issue of malice on behalf of the plaintiff must therefore fail.

With regard to the more general submission, the position would appear to me to be as follows. It was agreed by counsel both for the plaintiff and the defendant in this case that the appropriate test for malice was that laid down in the judgment of O'Byrne J in the former Supreme Court in the case of *Kirkwood Hackett v Tierney* [1952] IR 185. This firstly was that a trial judge should leave an issue of malice to the jury only if he was satisfied that the evidence given was more consistent with the existence of malice than with its absence, or to put the matter in another but identical way, that the existence of malice as a matter of probability, was an inference which the jury would be entitled to draw from the evidence given. Secondly, that judgment appears to establish that, as was stated at p. 204 having recited the principle laid down by Porter LJ in *Turner v Metro-Goldwyn-Mayer Pictures Ltd* [1950] WN 83:

> 'Applying the foregoing principle, which I consider to be sound in law, it is clear that you cannot get evidence of malice from a number of items of evidence, no one of which is, in itself, evidence of malice.'

I do not construe this second proposition as prohibiting a trial judge from having regard to different pieces of evidence which appear to him to be interrelated so as to reach a conclusion as to whether the evidence supports the probability of malice in the manner which I have indicated above. Rather do I construe it as simply laying down a principle which may indeed be of more general application than merely to the question of a judge's ruling concerning malice, that a number of separate items of evidence establishing a mere possibility of the existence of malice cannot by reason of their multiplicity alone convert that mere possibility into a probability.

In the instant case the plaintiff relied in the court below and relies on this appeal on a number of separate portions of the evidence as constituting evidence of the probability of malice. Some of those may well be capable of being considered interrelated. The main matters upon which reliance was placed may be summarised as follows.

1. Delay on the defendant's part in making any complaint concerning the plaintiff's conduct until such time as the plaintiff had herself made a complaint with regard to the defendant to the Law Society.
2. The length and scope of the defendant's letter to the Law Society which it is alleged was so far outside necessary or relevant comment on the matters contained in the plaintiff's letter to the Law Society as to constitute evidence of a motive of revenge or retaliation rather than a motive of a duty to make the complaint concerned.
3. The violence of some of the language used in the letter, particular complaint being made of the allegation that the plaintiff was a person who held scant regard for professional ethics and even less for the solemnity of the law; that she was obsessed with her fees and that she was guilty of duplicity and a lack of integrity in the contents of her letter written to the Law Society.
4. It was asserted that the reference in the letter to the Law Society setting out the history of the family law case giving rise to the request to the plaintiff to give evidence could be construed as a slur on the plaintiff's professional competence in that it could be construed as indicating that the unfortunate history of the wife in the family law case was due to inappropriate advice or treatment.
5. The failure of the defendant upon request to comply with the demand made on behalf of the plaintiff prior to action for an apology and the payment of costs or even for an apology, compensation and the payment of costs.
6. The plaintiff also relied on the fact that copies of the correspondence sent to the Law Society, to the IMA and to the Medical Council were sent by the defendant to the plaintiff as indicating some element of spite or hostility towards her from him.

With regard to these various allegations of malice I have come to the conclusion that the learned trial judge erred in law in holding that it would not have been open to a jury to reach a conclusion that the probability of the existence of malice in the communications made by the defendant was established by the length and scope of the letter written by him to the Law Society, having regard to the matters which that Society asked for his comments on and by the violence of some of the language used in that letter. In reaching this view I am, of course, expressing no opinion as to whether I would accept from all the facts of this case that malice was proved, but rather expressing a view on the legal question which fell to be determined by the learned trial judge as to whether the probability of malice was an inference open to the jury on the evidence which was given.

It is quite clear that the failure or refusal of the defendant to apologise and pay costs, with or without compensation, could not be evidence of malice, having regard to the defence of justification which he subsequently filed in the proceedings. I do not construe the portion of the letter dealing with the history of the treatment by the plaintiff of the wife in the family law case as containing an implication that that treatment was incompetent or negligent, and I do not consider that this was an item of malice which should have been left to a jury. The sending by the defendant of copies of the letters to the plaintiff could not be evidence of malice.

Quite clearly the fact that the defendant made no complaint concerning the conduct of the plaintiff until such time as she made a complaint to the Law Society is inter-related with the alleged violence of language contained in his letter to that society and can be considered with it. Having regard to the above conclusions I am satisfied that this appeal should be allowed and that a new trial of this action should be ordered in accordance with the principles which I have set out in this judgment."

Comments and Questions:
1. In addition to illustrating the need to take the "utmost care" in identifying the correct recipient for a privileged communication, this case is also useful for its discussion regarding malice. How easy is it, in your view, to show malice?

Fair comment on matters of public interest

Publications made in good faith on a matter of public interest are protected by the defence of fair comment.

To benefit from the defence a defendant must show that the comment, as well as being in the public interest, was also clearly comment as opposed to a statement of fact, and that the comment was fair in the sense of being honestly made. The comment must be based on the facts and these facts must be accurately reported (except in cases where the facts are readily available or accessible to the public).

Section 23 of the Defamation Act 1961 qualifies the defence in a similar manner to that of justification by stating that in the case of:

> "words consisting partly of allegations of fact and partly of expression of opinion, a defence of fair comment shall not fail by reason only that the truth of every allegation of fact is not proved, if the expression of opinion is fair comment having regard to such of the facts alleged or referred to in the words complained of as are proved."

Foley v Independent Newspapers (Ireland) Limited, McCormack, Collins, Ross and Tunney
Unreported, High Court, December 21, 1993

Facts: The plaintiff was a barrister appointed by the State to investigate a company called Greencore. The defendants published an article outlining the fees paid to the plaintiff. The article was written in such a manner as to suggest that the fees were imposed on the State and were exorbitant given the work carried out. The fees had in fact been negotiated in advance. The plaintiff successfully sued in the Circuit Court, the defendants having failed to make out their defence of fair comment. The defendants appealed to the High Court.

Issues: The court (Geoghegan J.) was asked to consider whether the defence of fair comment had been established. He held that it had not, in that, first, the facts of the case had not been clearly stated, and that, secondly, the attack on the plaintiff's professional character was not fair in the sense of being honest and based on fact.

Geoghegan J.:

"This is an appeal by the first and fourth named Defendants from a decree of the Circuit Court for £30,000 damages awarded against them for libel. It is also an appeal by the same Defendants against an Order for costs over in respect of the costs of the fifth named Defendant who had been successful in the Circuit Court and who had obtained an Order for costs against the Plaintiff.

For obvious reasons it is necessary to determine the libel appeal first. The complaint of libel arises out of an article or column by Senator Shane Ross, the fourth named Defendant in the Sunday Independent of the 8 March 1992. The first named Defendant is the publisher and printer of that newspaper. The alleged libelous passage in the article reads as follows:—

> 'The inspectors were ripping off the State. They were sent into Greencore to unveil skullduggery. They appear to have done an efficient job, but in the process they have decided to charge fees of an immoral not illegal magnitude.
>
> £250,000 per inspector for six months work is a public scandal in itself. Certainly, a Minister could be forgiven for seven or eight impulsive telephone calls when he saw the bill reaching the million mark. Mr O'Malley has a notoriously short fuse.
>
> The Minister has exposed a piece of institutionalised hypocrisy. The inspectors were appointed to counter the culture of greed; they have turned out to be part of it. Their brief was to protect the tax-payer; they're milking him.
>
> The inspector's fees are indefensible. They undermine the whole basis of the investigation. Excesses of capitalism always tread a fine line between legality and illegality. The comparative merits of tax avoidance and tax

evasion have no moral difference but simply a legal distinction. These fees come into the tax avoidance category.

The Government turns out to be a good mark, an easy target for predators. Public money can be thrown away like confetti, if it is in the name of protecting the tax-payer!

No fees were agreed in advance. The Minister rightly saw the danger. His instincts were correct. It is a pity he offered so many hostages to fortune in his cavalier approach to the solution.'

There is no plea of justification but there is a plea of fair comment in the form of a rolled up plea.

As Gatley and all the other textbook writers point out the authorities establish that for a comment to escape being defamatory solely on the grounds of it being a fair comment on some matter of public interest the following requirements must be complied with.

(1) It must be based on facts truly stated subject to the qualification contained in Section 23 of the Defamation Act 1961 which is similar to Section 6 of the English Defamation Act 1952.
(2) It must not contain imputations of corrupt or dishonourable motives on the person whose conduct or work is criticised save insofar as such imputations are warranted by the facts.
(3) It must be the honest expression of the writer's real opinion.

I am satisfied that neither the first nor the second of these requirements has been complied with in this case and that accordingly the defence of fair comment fails on two quite separate grounds

In the first place the relevant facts have not been truly stated. A true statement of grounding facts is not necessarily constituted by a series of sentences which are literally accurate. In the seventh edition of Gatley on Libel at paragraph 722 the following passage appears.

'Again, the defence of fair comment will fail if the Defendant omits from the statement of facts on which the comment purports to be based, some important fact which had it been mentioned would falsify or alter the complexion of the facts that are stated.'

Two cases the reports of which I have been unable to obtain are cited in support of this proposition Harris v White Limited (1926) OPD 104 and Seligman Limited v Investors Review Limited The Times, 4 July 1929. But I have no doubt that the passage represents good law and good sense.

In this case a fact of fundamental importance has been omitted from the article. The £250,000 was a cumulative figure based on a particular mode and particular rates of remuneration negotiated and agreed with the State within a relatively short period of the appointment. Any ordinary reader of the article unaware of the facts would have understood the author to be saying that the Plaintiff and his colleague sent in their respective bills totalling £250,000 each without any prior agreement with the State as to the manner of remuneration. If the article had explained that the fees were agreed, as was the case, following negotiations at a meeting involving officers of the Department of Finance, Department of Justice, Department of Industry and Commerce and the Attorney General's Office or had even referred to these negotiations and subsequent agreement in a general way the facts would have been truly stated, but that was not done. The omission in my view is fatal to the plea of fair comment in this case.

But even if I am wrong about that, I am satisfied that the offending passage in the article imputed dishonourable and immoral conduct on the part of the Plaintiff as an appointed inspector especially having regard to his professional position as a Senior Counsel. In a long line of authorities it has been established that this is not permissible under a plea of fair comment. The principle was first articulated in Campbell v Spottiswoode (1863) 3 B & S 769. In his judgment in that case Cockburn CJ observed.

> 'A line must be drawn between criticism upon public conduct and the imputation of motives by which that conduct may be supposed to be actuated; one man has no right to impute to another, whose conduct may be fairly open to ridicule or disapprobation, base, sordid and wicked motives unless there is so much ground for the imputation that a jury shall find, not only that he had an honest belief in the truth of his statements, but that his belief was not without foundation.'

... I now turn to consider more fully the application of that principle to this case. In my view, the words complained of in their natural and ordinary meaning do not just constitute an allegation that the Plaintiff's fees were exorbitant. The author is clearly suggesting by way of paradox that the Plaintiff who was appointed to investigate immoral conduct himself acted immorally. The clear allegation is that the Plaintiff deliberately took advantage of the State and the tax-payer perceiving the State as a kind of easy target or 'soft touch' in order to obtain what he knew was excessive remuneration. I do not accept that 'ripping off' should be interpreted as meaning merely 'charging too much'. It is quite true that a patron of a restaurant or a customer of a shop may well complain that the prices are a 'rip off' without necessarily suggesting immoral conduct on the part of the restaurateur or the shopkeeper but the sentence 'the inspectors were ripping off the State' introduces a direct personal accusation. It implies that the inspectors were stealing in the moral sense though not of course in the sense that a prosecution could be brought under the Larceny Act. In the context of the article I also believe that an ordinary reader would interpret the word 'predators' as meaning something like moral equivalents of robbers or plunderers and not as suggested by Senator Ross, an equivalent merely to a projected takeover bidder in the financial world, though I do of course accept that the expression can have that meaning in a business context. Even if Senator Ross's readers in the Sunday Independent were confined to those with a specialist interest in business and finance, which I do not accept, I believe that they would have read the article in the sense which I have suggested. The offending article went well beyond strident criticism of the magnitude of the fees. It quite clearly imputed immoral conduct on the part of the two inspectors."

Consent

A person cannot bring an action in defamation if s/he has consented to the publication of the offending statement under contract. Likewise, a person cannot complain if s/he has agreed to waive his/her legal rights in respect of it, whether or not for value.

Apology

An apology is not a defence in a traditional sense but, if made before the commencement of an action or as soon as practicable afterwards, it will be admissible in mitigation of damages.

CHAPTER 11

NUISANCE

INTRODUCTION

Nuisance as a tort is difficult to define; generally speaking it covers all wrongs arising from the unreasonable interference with another person's rights, and those rights are usually connected to land. This tort can be divided into both public and private nuisance. Private nuisances involve the unreasonable interference with the rights that relate to the ownership of, or other rights in connection with, land; a public nuisance relates to the unreasonable interference with a right belonging to a person as a member of the public. Generally speaking it is not a defence to show reasonable care, but see *Daly & Daly v McMullan* below, as an exception to the general rule.

PUBLIC NUISANCE

Public nuisances, in general, impact on the public at large. It is usually, therefore, the preserve of the Attorney General to take civil actions for public nuisance. Members of the public may only take an action in public nuisance where they can establish a particular or special damage. Special or particular damage is damage to the plaintiff to the action that is greater or more serious than that suffered by the general public.

Boyd v The Great Northern Railway Co.
Exchequer Division [1895] 2 I.R. 555 (Ex. Div.)

Facts: The plaintiff was a doctor who was detained at a level crossing for 20 minutes by reason of the defendant's negligence. The plaintiff had a large practice and his time had a pecuniary value. The doctor's contention was that this unnecessary delay had a more detrimental impact on him than on others. At the initial trial the defendants were successful; the case was appealed.

Issues: The issue was whether the doctor could show that the damage he suffered was special or particular. At appeal the court found for the doctor.

Andrews J. (Murphy J. concurring):

"The Railway Company are not entitled either under the 47th sect of Railways Clauses Consolidation Act 1845, or any other enactment to obstruct the public highway, which they obtained power to cross on a level, for a longer period than is reasonably necessary for their own authorised purposes, and the protection of the public using the highway; and even without any such expression of judicial opinion as is to be found in the case of *Wyatt v. The Great Western Railway Co* 6 B & S 709, 34 LJ, QB 204, I should have been quite prepared to hold the defendants liable in the present case. By the findings the only two material questions of fact are affirmatively determined, viz whether the defendants on the occasion in question unreasonably and unnecessarily obstructed the highway, and if so, whether the plaintiff suffered thereby some appreciable damage peculiar to himself beyond that suffered by other members of the public ordinarily using the highway? The learned judge has found that an actual delay of twenty minutes was occasioned by the defendants, not by any necessity arising from their traffic or otherwise, and that the delay was unreasonable, and the result of negligence on the part of the defendants. He also found that the plaintiff is a medical man, in very large practice whose time was of pecuniary value, and that he has sustained personal pecuniary damage for the delay of twenty minutes, which the learned judge estimated at ten shillings. Everything, therefore, which is necessary in point of law to entitle the plaintiff to recover damages in this action, has been established in point of fact, and our answer to the question reserved for our opinion must be that on the facts proved the defendants are liable to the plaintiff.

The learned judge will, upon our decision being communicated to him, reverse the dismiss, and give the plaintiff a decree for ten shillings, with such costs he shall think it proper to award, and we shall order the defendants to pay the plaintiff £10 for the costs of the argument before us."

A public nuisance can take a variety of forms, including obstructions, damage and dangers on the public highway. There is case law to support the proposition that making the highway dangerous or unsafe to persons lawfully using it may amount to a nuisance: *Hasset v O'Loughlin* (1943) 78 I.L.T.R. 47. In *Connolly v South of Ireland Asphalt Co.* [1977] I.R. 99 the public nuisance consisted of a danger created on the road; in *Cunningham v MacGrath Bros* [1964] I.R. 209 an obstruction of the footpath amounted to a public nuisance.

Connolly v South of Ireland Asphalt Co.
Supreme Court [1977] I.R. 99

Facts: A motorcyclist, Mr Wade, was travelling on a damaged public road when he lost his balance and fell off his bike. While he was picking up his bike he was struck and killed by the plaintiff's motorcar. The damage to the road consisted of potholes at the entrance to the defendant's premises. The defendant's heavy lorries travelled to and from the public road, and it was held that this use of the road had resulted in several unconnected potholes in a line along the margin of the road, and that these potholes extended onto the public road. It was also established that on the night of the accident there was a heavy rain followed by a sharp drop in temperature and that patches of ice had formed in the vicinity of the potholes.

Issues: Mr Wade's widow had succeeded in an action for negligence against Mr Connolly who is the plaintiff to this action. The purpose of this action was to see whether the defendant to this action could be held liable in law for the death of Mr Wade. The court held that the defendant had caused a public nuisance and was therefore partly responsible for the death of Mr Wade.

O'Higgins C.J. (Kenny and Parke JJ. both agreed in principle with the Chief Justice's position):

"... It has been said that actionable nuisance is incapable of exact definition. The term nuisance contemplates an act or omission which amounts to an unreasonable interference with, disturbance of, or annoyance to another person in the exercise of his rights. If the rights so interfered with belong to the person as a member of the public, the act or omission is a public nuisance. If these rights relate to the ownership or occupation of land, or of some easement, profit, or other right enjoyed in connection with land, then the acts or omissions amount to a private nuisance. In this case we are concerned with the allegation that the third party were guilty of causing a public nuisance.

The third party used heavy lorries for the purpose of their business and the lorries travelled, laden and unladen, to and from the premises of the third party over the junction of the entrance with the roadway. This, in itself, was a lawful exercise of the third party's right to carry on their business and to use for that purpose lorries of their own choosing. However, what the third party did resulted in damage to the roadway upon which these lorries travelled; the damage was caused at the point where the entrance joined the public road on the Dublin side of the third party's premises. It was clear that at this point the lorries used could not be supported by the road surface, either because of their weight or their number. The result was that breaks and holes appeared, not rarely, but on numerous occasions. Were the third party entitled to carry on regardless of the damage so caused merely because of their proprietary rights? *Sic utere tuo ut alienum non laedas* is a maxim which expresses the view that people should have regard to the rights and conveniences of others in the way they use what is theirs. While it may lack preciseness, it has here a sufficient application to prescribe a limit to what it was permissible for the third party to do in pursuance of their legitimate business interests. In my view the third party were not entitled to exercise their rights without regard to whether damage was being or would be caused to the public road.

Damage was caused not only to the third party's own entrance but also to the roadway, and this consisted of the seven holes already described. In my view the question is whether this damage, so caused, constituted a danger to members of the public using the roadway. That the breaks or holes initiated on the third party's own property appears to me to be immaterial. It is well established that an excavation or interference with one's own land can be regarded as actionable where the land is so adjacent to the roadway as to constitute a danger to a person who, while using that roadway, turns into or travels thereon and thereby suffers damage: *Barnes* v. *Ward* [(1850) 9 CB 392]; *Hardcastle* v. *South Yorkshire Railway* [(1859) 4 H & N 67]; *Carshalton U.D.C.* v. *Burrage* [[1911] 2 Ch 133].

Here the damage to the road surface extended from the third party's premises out on to the roadway itself. That this damage could constitute a danger to a person using a motor-cycle on that roadway at night is, in my view, not open to question. Once the holes appeared it was to be expected that in wet weather they would retain water which in turn would be splashed by passing traffic. In winter time this led inevitably to the added hazard of an icy patch being formed contiguous to the line of pot-holes. The learned trial judge was satisfied on the evidence that either the pot-holes or one or more of them or this ice caused the deceased to get into difficulties on his cycle and to fall. This in my view is a finding that the deceased's fall was caused by the danger on the roadway created by the acts and omissions of the third party.

The deceased, having been caused to fall on the public road, was struck and killed by the defendant's passing car. Not only was he killed because he had fallen in the path of an approaching car but, in my view, the likelihood of such a misfortune happening to him was present from the very moment he was caused to fall.

In my view, the result is that the third party, having so damaged the surface of their own entrance and the adjoining roadway as to create a danger on the roadway, were guilty of committing a public nuisance thereon. The plaintiff, being the widow of the deceased, suffered particular damage because of this nuisance in that it was a factor contributing to his death. On this account she could have maintained an action against the third party in respect of the damage she suffered."

In *Cunningham v MacGrath Bros* [1964] I.R. 209 an obstruction amounted to a public nuisance. The court suggested that the creation of the obstruction was not in itself sufficient to allow for an action in public nuisance, and intimated the necessity for foreseeability.

Cunningham v MacGrath Bros
Supreme Court [1964] I.R. 209

Facts: The plaintiff was employed by Brown Thomas and left the premises to go for lunch. The MacGrath Brothers had been working on a blind outside of Brown Thomas's premises and needed to use double ladders. The work had commenced in the morning; the workers had left to complete the repairs on the blinds and left the ladders in position and unattended, causing a partial obstruction on the footpath. The ladder was moved by someone unknown onto a small side street; as the plaintiff was passing the ladder fell and she suffered personal injuries.

Issues: The Supreme Court had to determine whether the ladders amounted to a public nuisance. The court also addressed whether a person responsible for creating a nuisance should anticipate as a reasonable and probable consequence of the public nuisance that some person would attempt to abate the nuisance and in so doing create a danger. The court applied this test to the actions of the defendant in this action. The court held that the plaintiff was entitled to succeed in nuisance.

Kingsmill Moore J. (Ó Dálaigh C.J. and Lavery, Haugh and Walsh JJ. concurring):

"… Now, speaking generally, any obstruction of the public highway is a public nuisance, prosecutable on indictment and a tort sounding in damages if any member of the public should suffer particular injury thereby. But the owner of property abutting on the highway may, for proper purposes connected with his property, cause such an obstruction, provided that neither in quantum nor duration does it extend beyond what is necessary; and this exception would extend to cover those doing the necessary work. Thus, although the ladders when in position obstructed the footpath, so long as their presence was necessary for chipping the plaster or fixing the blind they did not constitute a public nuisance: but as soon as the chipping was done and there was no need for the ladders to remain in position they did become a public nuisance and if anyone had been injured by them in the position in which they had been left by the defendants' workmen the defendants would clearly have been liable. But it is contended for the defendants that there was no direct causal connection between the leaving of the ladders in a safe position and the injury to the plaintiff. The accident was due to the intervention of an unknown person who removed at least one of the ladders from a position of relative safety to a position of danger. There was a '*novus actus interveniens.*'

It is not every '*novus actus*' which breaks the chain of causation. If what is relied upon as *novus actus interveniens* is the very kind of thing which is likely to happen if the want of care which is alleged takes place, the principle embodied in the maxim is no defence. The whole question is whether or not, to use the words of the leading case, *Hadley* v. *Baxendale* [(1854) 9 Ex 341)] the accident can be said to be 'the natural and probable result' of the breach of duty. If it is the very thing which ought to be anticipated … or one of the things likely to arise as a consequence of his wrongful act, it is no defence; it is only a step in the way of proving that the damage is the result of the wrongful act …

'It is not necessary to show that this particular accident and this particular damage were probable; it is sufficient if the accident is of a class that might well be anticipated as one of the reasonable and probable results of the wrongful act:' *Hayes* v. *Harwood* [[1935] 1 KB 146], per Greer L.J., at p. 156

A case which bears some resemblance to the present was *Clark* v. *Chambers* [3 QBD 327]. The defendant had unlawfully placed a spiked barrier so as partially to obstruct a private road. Someone removed the barrier and put it on the neighbouring footpath. A lawful user of the road, coming along it in the dark, felt his way to that portion of the road which he knew to be unobstructed and then, going on to the footpath, ran into the spikes on the portion of the barrier which had been removed. Cockburn C.J., giving the judgment of the Divisional Court, held the plaintiff entitled to recover. After a detailed review of authorities dealing with the defence of *novus actus interveniens*, he said, at p. 338:—'... a man who unlawfully places an obstruction across either a public or private way may anticipate the removal of the obstruction, by some one entitled to use the way, as a thing likely to happen; and if this should be done, the probability is that the obstruction so removed will, instead of being carried away altogether, be placed somewhere near; thus, if the obstruction be to the carriageway, it will very likely be placed, as was the case here, on the footpath. If the obstruction be a dangerous one, wheresoever placed, it may, as was the case here, become a source of damage, from which, should injury to an innocent party occur, the original author of the mischief should be held responsible.'

I am of opinion that the test to be applied is whether the person responsible for creating the nuisance should anticipate as a reasonable and probable consequence that some person in pursuance of his rights would attempt to abate the nuisance and in so doing would create a danger. Applying this test it seems to me that Mr. MacGrath should have anticipated as reasonable and probable that someone—a passer-by, a frontager, or an employee of Brown Thomas Ltd.—would remove the ladder and put it somewhere near in a position where it would be less of an obstruction but might constitute more of a danger. This is what happened. The ladder was moved round the corner to Duke Lane, a relatively unimportant side street which is not a thoroughfare. It was probably folded up and put leaning against the wall. In this position, though more dangerous, it would be less of an obstruction to pedestrians and would not obscure the window display of Brown Thomas Ltd. That an unattended ladder, even if spread out, involves some element of danger is recognised by the admitted practice of the men to take down the ladders during the luncheon interval and put them on a hand cart, and by Mr. MacGrath's acquiescence in the suggestions that 'it would be unsafe to leave a ladder unattended in a public place' and that 'it was a thing you would not do.' Indeed, the whole tenor of his evidence was that he only left the ladders because he thought they would be taken care of by Mr. Murphy. A jury were entitled to consider that he should have made an express stipulation to that effect and that, as he did not do so, the accident was a reasonable and probable result of his action in leaving the ladders without making some provision for their removal to a safe place when no longer needed. I would dismiss the appeal."

Comments and Questions:
1. In this action the courts introduce a test that is to be applied to determine whether a person is responsible for creating the nuisance or not. The test requires an obstruction and the necessity for the person who created the obstruction to anticipate "as a reasonable and probable consequence that some person in pursuance of his rights would attempt to abate the nuisance and in so doing would create a danger."

2. In your opinion is there a necessity for a person to attempt to abate the nuisance, if the obstruction caused could reasonably be thought to be a danger?

In *Wall v Morrissey* [1969] I.R. 10 the court held that damage to the highway without foreseeability could not give rise to a public nuisance. The creation of a public nuisance was also held to attract the principle of a non-delegable duty.

Wall v Morrissey
Supreme Court [1969] I.R. 10

Facts: The defendant sought and obtained permission from the local authority to make a trench in the public highway with a view to laying water pipes across the highway, in order to provide a water supply for his cattle. The contractor employed by the defendant opened a trench across the highway, laid the pipes and refilled the trench to the level of the surrounding roadway; the next day the defendant added more filling material, in order to compensate for subsidence. That evening the plaintiff was injured when he fell from his bicycle as he was crossing the refilled trench.

Issues: The plaintiff claimed damages alleging both negligence and that the defendant had created a public nuisance. The issue in nuisance was that of foreseeability of the damage; also look for references to the principle of non-delegable duty. The plaintiff did not succeed in this action, as the nuisance was not deemed foreseeable, and negligence was not established.

Walsh J. (Budd J. concurring):

"For the purpose of this appeal I am assuming that the condition of the road which brought about the plaintiff's accident did amount to a public nuisance.
    I do not think that the agreement with the County Council, which was in effect an indemnity to the County Council on the question of the resurfacing of

the portion of the highway involved, affects the matter at all. The County Council cannot give a licence to the defendant to commit a public nuisance, nor can it in any way absolve him from the consequences of one. Furthermore, I do not consider that the defendant's position is in any way altered on the question of nuisance by the fact that he employed an independent contractor. A person who makes an excavation on the highway has imposed upon him a duty of care which cannot be discharged by the employment of an independent contractor, nor can such person delegate to a contractor the work of taking the precautions necessary to prevent the mischievous consequences of the excavation on the highway. The person who procures the excavation is primarily liable for the actionable consequences which may flow therefrom; he is not simply liable vicariously for the acts of the independent contractor.

The temporary excavation of the highway is not itself a public nuisance so long as it does not offend by exceeding, in either degree or duration, the temporary requirements of a person whose premises adjoin the highway. A public nuisance is constituted by exceeding this temporary requirement, or by failing to restore the position to the point where it does not operate as a withdrawal of part of the highway from the public, or by leaving the highway dangerous for members of the public using it.

It is true that the facts giving rise to a public nuisance often ground a cause of action in negligence also, and in many cases it may matter nothing which of these causes of action is relied upon. It is true, however, as has been submitted by counsel for the plaintiff, that negligence is not an essential element in nuisance: see the examples given by Lord Reid in *Overseas Tankship (U.K.) Ltd.* v. *The Miller Steamship Co. Pty. [The Wagon Mound (No. 2)]* [1967] A.C. 617, 639]. However, I am also content to adopt the reasoning of Lord Reid in the same case and to accept the conclusion which he arrives at, namely, that, while negligence is not an essential ingredient of nuisance in an action on public nuisance, foreseeability is an essential ingredient. In the present case the defendant created a danger on the highway which did amount to a public nuisance, but before the plaintiff can establish his right to damages he must satisfy the jury that the injury which he suffered was a reasonably foreseeable event on the part of the defendant.

From such information as the Court has been able to learn from the course of the trial in the High Court, it would appear that the point taken by counsel for the plaintiff in requesting the trial judge to leave the question of nuisance to the jury was the point that foreseeability was not an essential ingredient of that cause of action. That was the course of the trial and in the circumstances, therefore, I am satisfied that it is not necessary or relevant to consider any other matters which might have arisen when the only point which did arise was, in my view, unfounded in law ...

The view that foreseeability is an essential ingredient is supported by the decision of Lavery J. in *Gillen* v. *Fair* [(1956) 90 I.L.T.R. 119]. That was an action, laid both in nuisance and in negligence, resulting from the branch of a tree growing beside the public highway falling on a passing motor car and killing the driver. The learned judge dismissed the action in negligence on the grounds that the damage was not foreseeable (on the particular facts of that case) and he appears also to have taken the same view on the question of the claim in nuisance which he also dismissed. Finally I turn to the decision of this Court in *Cunningham v. McGrath Brothers* [[1964] I.R. 209]. While in that case the question whether foreseeability was an essential ingredient or not in actionable public nuisance was not in issue, the decision clearly accepted and proceeded on the basis that it was an essential ingredient. The contest was whether, on the evidence, it could be held that the mischief was foreseeable and the answer was in the affirmative.

As this appeal has turned upon the question of whether the trial judge was correct or not in applying the test of foreseeability, I would dismiss the appeal for the reasons I have already given."

Comments and Questions:

1. This case adopts the position taken by Lord Reid in *Overseas Tankship (UK) Ltd. v The Miller Steamship Co. Pty [The Wagon Mound (No. 2)]* [1967] A.C. 617, who stated that "while negligence is not an essential ingredient of nuisance in an action on public nuisance, foreseeability is an essential ingredient."

For a public nuisance to be created a causal connection must be shown between the actions of the defendant and the actual nuisance created.

Convery v Dublin County Council
Supreme Court [1996] 3 I.R. 153

Facts: The facts of this case were not in dispute. The plaintiff to the action represented people living in three residential roads in Tallaght. These roads had, by the time of the action, been carrying volumes of traffic which were far greater than the volumes for which they were designed. This congestion had increased significantly because of developments such as The Square Tallaght (shopping complex), and were expected to increase further with a proposed hospital and the new headquarters of Dublin Bus. These particular roads were used as a shortcut, or what is commonly known as a "rat run". The plaintiffs sought a number of orders including injunctions to abate the public nuisance. The plaintiffs sought an interlocutory injunction trying to prevent the traffic; this case came to be heard in the High Court before Carroll J. Carroll J. accepted that the traffic conditions amounted to a public nuisance; she went on to say that the County Council, as planning authority, had permitted extensive development in the area without ensuring that the infrastructure was adequate. She added that, in her opinion, the failure of the County Council to take tangible steps to address the problem amounted to negligence. She required the County Council to abate the nuisance within a reasonable time, and allowed the Council to choose the most appropriate measure. The County Council attempted to comply with the judgment, but its efforts were both physically and legally frustrated by residents in other parts of the estate. The County Council then decided to abandon the attempts to close off the access and the High Court was so informed. Carroll J. then made an order requiring the County Council to close Alderwood Park at its junction with Old Blessington Road within seven days. The County Council appealed this order to the Supreme Court.

Issues: Did the County Council cause in a legal sense the public nuisance complained of? The court held that the County Council could not be held responsible for the public nuisance, as the traffic did not originate in any premises owned or occupied by the County Council; they had, in fact, little control over the excess traffic.

Keane J. (O'Flaherty and Barrington JJ. concurring):

"... The County Council is a body which has duties, powers and functions which it must exercise for the benefit of the public. The High Court is invested with a supervisory jurisdiction designed to ensure that such bodies act in accordance with the law and, in particular, do not act in a way which is arbitrary, unreasonable or oppressive or offends against any constitutional norms. That jurisdiction is invoked in our modern law by the judicial review procedure.

Various acts and omissions of the County Council which have come under scrutiny in the present proceedings arose from its statutory role as a planning authority and roads authority. The judicial review procedure has not been invoked by the plaintiff in the present case and it is agreed by the parties that, in the result, no questions of public law, which would have been relevant in such proceedings, arise in the present case. This, it is accepted, is a case in which the plaintiff could only succeed if she established that the County Council had been guilty of an actionable tort. The claim on her behalf is that the actions or omissions of the County Council amounted to a public nuisance or to negligence.

A public nuisance consists of an act or omission which causes injury to, or materially affects the reasonable comfort and convenience of, the public, or a section of the public. It is, however, only actionable at the suit of an individual, if he has suffered particular damage over and above that suffered by other members of the public.

While the authorities demonstrate that the use of land in such a way as to alter the character of an area by bringing greater volumes of people and traffic to it may give rise to an action in private nuisance (see *Dewar v City and Suburban Racecourse Company* [1899] 1 IR 345; *O'Kane v Campbell* [1985] IR 115), they have no relevance to the present case, where the acts or omissions complained of do not arise from operations on land of the County Council and the action is framed as one in public nuisance. The same can be said of the decision of *Kelly v Dublin County Council* (Unreported, High Court, O'Hanlon J, 21st February, 1986) which arose out of the operations by the defendant local authority on a particular plot of land in their ownership and occupation.

It has been held in England—in *Gillingham Borough Council v Medway (Chatham) Dock Co Ltd.* [1993] Q.B. 343—that even a lawful use of the public highway may, in extreme circumstances, amount to a public nuisance. In that case, the defendants were operating a commercial port on the site of a former naval dockyard and the plaintiffs, the relevant local authority, alleged that the use of the roads leading to the port by heavy goods vehicles amounted to a public nuisance for which the defendants were responsible. The court rejected that claim, noting that the plaintiffs themselves had given permission under the relevant legislation for the activities by the defendants which had led to the increased traffic and that the control of the traffic was a matter for it in its capacity as planning authority and not for the courts. Buckley J observed at p. 358 that:—

> 'It is not necessary for me to hold that otherwise lawful use of a highway can never amount to a public nuisance, whatever the circumstances and however excessive the use. Extreme circumstances may arise when it could be right so to hold (*see Halsey v Esso Petroleum Company Ltd.* [1961] 1 DPP 683).'

No authority was cited to us for the proposition that a local authority, in its capacity as a planning or road authority or in any other capacity, can be held liable in public nuisance because of volumes of traffic on the highway resulting, not from any operations carried on by it, but indirectly from decisions taken by it as a local authority ...

There can be no doubt that the plaintiff and the other residents of these roads have had to endure a serious interference with the normal amenities of life in a residential area as a result of a volume of traffic which is greatly in excess of the design capacity of the roads. At the same time, the difficulties encountered by the County Council in attempting to cope with the problem should not be underestimated. While the weight to be given to them is a matter on which different views could doubtless be taken, it could hardly be expected wholly to disregard the claims by other residents in this area that closing off the access to these roads would simply create problems for them.

As to the claim founded on nuisance, the traffic did not originate in any premises owned or occupied by the County Council and was not generated as a result of any activities carried on by it on land in the area. The fact that the traffic reached a volume which caused significant inconvenience and discomfort for the residents was the result of a combination of factors: the development of large scale residential and commercial projects by private interests, the decisions of thousands of individual drivers to use this particular route, and the failure of central government to allocate funds for the provision of the necessary roads infrastructure, to mention the most obvious. The decisions of the County

il to which objection is taken is only one of a number of factors which has
:d in the present position. To treat the County Council, in these
circumstances, as being the legal author of a public nuisance would be entirely
contrary to principle and wholly unsupported by authority."

Comments and Questions:
1. Public nuisance requires an obstruction on the public highway, or public
    footpath, and damage must be foreseeable. Does this case add a third
    element necessary to establish public nuisance?

PRIVATE NUISANCE

Private nuisance relates primarily to the unreasonable interference with rights
related to the ownership or occupation of land. The tort of private nuisance
essentially endorses the principle that what an occupier of land is "entitled as
against his neighbour is the comfortable and healthy enjoyment of the land to
the degree that would be expected by an ordinary person whose requirements
are objectively reasonable in all the particular circumstances" (*Hanrahan v
Merck Sharpe and Dohme* [1988] I.L.R.M. 629). This is in effect a balancing
operation between competing land rights.

Hanrahan v Merck Sharpe and Dohme
Supreme Court [1988] I.L.R.M. 629

Facts: The plaintiffs to this action, the Hanrahan family, farmed land situated
about a mile from the defendants' factory. The factory engaged in the processing
of pharmaceutical products, which involved the storage and use of large quantities
of toxic substances as well as the disposal in the factory of toxic and dangerous
chemical residues. The plaintiffs claimed that as a result of the manner in which
the defendants conducted their operation the plaintiffs, their farm animals, and the
plant life on the farm suffered severe injury and damage.

Issues: The court addressed constitutional arguments, and arguments based in
negligence and nuisance. For the purposes of this chapter we are going to focus
on the arguments based on the tort of nuisance. The court had to assess the onus
of proof necessary to establish a case in private nuisance; it was held that in this
instance the plaintiffs had reached the necessary standard of proof in
establishing their claim in private nuisance.

Henchy J. (Finlay C.J. and Hederman J. concurring):

"... To provide a basis for the award of damages for the private nuisance relied
on, the plaintiffs have to show that they have been interfered with, over a

substantial period of time, in the use and enjoyment of their farm, as a result of the way the defendants conducted their operations in the factory. The plaintiffs do not have to prove want of reasonable care on the part of the defendants. It is sufficient if it is shown as a matter of probability that what they complain of was suffered by them as occupiers of their farm in consequence of the way the defendants ran their factory …

It is common case that the probative aspect of a claim in nuisance has been correctly expressed by Gannon J in the following passage from his judgment in *Halpin and Ors v Tara Mines Ltd* High Court 1973, No. 1516P, 16 February 1976.

'A party asserting that he has sustained material damage to his property by reason of an alleged nuisance must establish the fact of such damage and that it was caused by the nuisance as alleged. It is no defence to such a claim, if established, that the activities complained of were carried out with the highest standards of care, skill and supervision and equipment or that such activities are of great public importance and cannot conveniently be carried out in any other way. In so far as the nuisance alleged consists of interference with the ordinary comfort and enjoyment of the property of the plaintiff, his evidence must show sensible personal discomfort, including injurious affection of the nerves or senses of such a nature as would materially diminish the comfort and enjoyment of, or cause annoyance to, a reasonable man accustomed to living in the same locality. To my mind the reasonable man connotes a person whose notions and standards of behaviour and responsibility correspond with those generally pertaining among ordinary people in our society at the present time, who seldom allows his emotions to overbear his reason, whose habits are moderate and whose disposition is equable.'

It is clear from the authorities on the law of nuisance that what an occupier of land is entitled to as against his neighbour is the comfortable and healthy enjoyment of the land to the degree that would be expected by an ordinary person whose requirements are objectively reasonable in all the particular circumstances. It is difficult to state the law more precisely than that.

In this case the plaintiffs' main complaints, namely that the emissions from the factory damaged their health and that of the livestock on the farm, are of so pronounced and serious a nature that no question of nicety of reaction arises. Either those complaints were caused by the emissions from the factory or they were not. If on the balance of probabilities they can be said to derive from factory emissions, then the case for nuisance has been made out. Anything short of that degree of proof would not support a finding of nuisance.

The ordinary rule is that a person who alleges a particular tort must, in order to succeed, prove (save where there are admissions) all the necessary ingredients of that tort and it is not for the defendant to disprove anything. Such exceptions as have been allowed to that general rule seem to be confined to cases where a particular element of the tort lies or is deemed to lie, pre-eminently within the defendants' knowledge, in which case the onus of proof as to that matter passes to the defendant. Thus, in the tort of negligence, where damage has been caused to the plaintiff in circumstances in which such damage would not usually be caused without negligence on the part of the defendant, the rule of *res ipsa loquitur* will allow the act relied on to be evidence of negligence in the absence of proof by the defendant that it occurred without want of due care on his part. The rationale behind the shifting of the onus of proof to the defendant in such cases would appear to lie in the fact that it would be palpably unfair to require a plaintiff to prove something which is beyond his reach and which is peculiarly within the range of the defendant's capacity of proof.

That is not the case here. What the plaintiffs have to prove in support of their claim in nuisance is that they suffered some or all of the mischief complained of and that it was caused by emissions from the defendants' factory. To hold that it is for the defendants to disprove either or both of those matters would be contrary to authority and not be demanded by the requirements of justice. There are of course difficulties facing the plaintiffs in regard to proof of those matters, particularly as to the question of causation, but mere difficulty of proof does not call for a shifting of the onus of proof. Many claims in tort fail because the plaintiff has not access to full information as to the true nature of the defendant's conduct. The onus of disproof rests on the defendant only when the act or default complained of is such that it would be fundamentally unjust to require the plaintiff to prove a positive averment when the particular circumstances show that fairness and justice call for disproof by the defendant. The argument put forward in this case for putting a duty of disproof on the defendants would be more sustainable if the plaintiffs had to prove that the emissions complained of were caused by the defendants' negligence. Such is not the case. In my view, having regard to the replies given by the defendants to interrogatories and notices for particulars and to the full discovery of documents made by them, it is not open to the plaintiffs to complain that for want of knowledge on their part it would be unjust or unfair to require them to bear the ordinary onus of proof.

The plaintiffs have also invoked the Constitution in support of their argument as to the onus of proof. They contend that the tort relied on by them in support of their claim is but a reflection of the duty imposed on the State by *Article 40.3* of the Constitution in regard to their personal rights and property rights. The relevant constitutional provisions are:

1° The State guarantees in its laws to respect, and as far as practicable, by its laws to defend and vindicate the personal rights of the citizen.
2° The State shall, in particular, by its laws protect as best it may from unjust attack and in the case of injustice done, vindicate the life, person, good name, and property rights of every citizen.

I agree that the tort of nuisance relied on in this case may be said to be an implementation of the State's duties under those provisions as to the personal rights and property rights of the plaintiffs as citizens. The particular duty pointed to by the plaintiffs is the duty to vindicate the personal right to bodily integrity and the property right to their land and livestock. They say that vindication of those rights under the constitutional guarantee is not properly effective by leaving them to their rights as plaintiffs in an action for nuisance and that the vindication they are guaranteed requires that once they show that they have been damnified in their person or property as alleged, it should be for the defendants to show that emissions from their factory were not the cause.

So far as I am aware, the constitutional provisions relied on have never been used in the courts to shape the form of any existing tort or to change the normal onus of proof. The implementation of those constitutional rights is primarily a matter for the State and the courts are entitled to intervene only when there has been a failure to implement or, where the implementation relied on is plainly inadequate, to effectuate the constitutional guarantee in question. In many torts—for example, negligence, defamation, trespass to person or property—a plaintiff may give evidence of what he claims to be a breach of a constitutional right, but he may fail in the action because of what is usually a matter of onus of proof or because of some other legal or technical defence. A person may of course in the absence of a common law or statutory cause of action, sue directly for breach of a constitutional right (see *Meskell v C.I.E.* [1973] IR 121); but when he founds his action on an existing tort he is normally confined to the limitations of that tort. It might be different if it could be shown that the tort in question is basically ineffective to protect his constitutional right. But that is not alleged here. What is said is that he may not succeed in having his constitutional rights vindicated if he is required to carry the normal onus of proof. However, the same may be said about many other causes of action. Lack of knowledge as to the true nature of the defendants' conduct or course of conduct may cause the plaintiff difficulty, but it does not change the onus of proof.

It is also to be noted that the guarantee to respect and defend personal rights given in *Article 40.3.1°* applies only *'as far as practicable'* and the guarantee to vindicate property rights given in *Article 40.3.2°* refers only to cases of *'injustice done.'* The guarantees, therefore, are not unqualified or absolute. I find it impossible to hold that *Article 40.3.1°* means that a plaintiff in an action in nuisance is to be relieved of the onus of proving the necessary ingredients of that tort. Neither, in my view, does *Article 40.3.2°* warrant such a dispensation, for the guarantee of vindication there given arises only *'in the case of injustice done,'* so it is for the plaintiff to prove that the injustice relied on was actually suffered by him and that it was caused by the defendant.

I would hold that the trial judge correctly rejected the submission of the plaintiffs that an onus of disproving the allegation as to causation should rest on the defendants …

I would allow this appeal by the plaintiffs to the extent of holding that the three plaintiffs have established that the defendants are liable to them in damages for the offensive smells emitted from the factory, that John Hanrahan is entitled to damages for the injurious effect on his health of the factory emissions, and that the defendants are also liable in damages for the cattle ailments to the extent that they were caused by factory emissions. Since it is desirable that all the damages should, at least at first instance, be assessed by the same tribunal, I would remit the case to the High Court for both the assessment of the damages and the making of the findings necessary for such assessment."

Comments and Questions:
1. What is the standard of proof for an action in nuisance? Is this a realistic standard for a private individual when faced, as the Hanrahans were, with a large multi-national company?

Private nuisance is not actionable *per se*; there is a necessity to show damage. Damage may consist of injury to the land, or to the occupiers of the land or interference with the enjoyment of land. Injury to land can take many forms including: the encroachment of roots onto another person's property causing damage (*Middleton v Humphries* (1912) 47 I.L.T.R. 160); overhanging branches (*Lemmon v Webb* [1894] 3 Ch. 1), emission of toxic substances (*Hanrahan v Merck Sharpe and Dohme (Ireland) Ltd.* [1988] I.L.R.M. 629); vibrations and dust (*Patterson v Murphy* [1978] I.L.R.M. 85).

Halpin v Tara Mines Ltd.
High Court [1976–1977] I.L.R.M. 28

Facts: The plaintiffs sought damages for nuisance. The nuisance alleged related to excessive and intolerable noise as a result of the blasting involved in the mining work of the defendants. The plaintiffs also alleged that this work involved vibrations which damaged the structure of their houses and they sought compensation for this damage.

Issues: The court had to consider whether the defendants' activities amounted to an unreasonable interference with the ordinary human comfort of human existence for the plaintiffs. The court also had to consider whether the defendants' activities caused material damage to the plaintiff's property. The court held for the plaintiffs and awarded damages for the damage caused.

Gannon J.:

"As a general proposition I take it to be the law that an occupier of land, or of premises thereon, who embarks on operations or activities out of the ordinary must not cause or permit, *inter alia*, noises or vibrations to pass into his neighbour's property in such a way as materially to interfere with the ordinary comfort of the occupier of such property or in such a way as to cause physical damage to the property of his neighbour. Where such interference or such damage is shown to be a matter of some continuity, repetition, or persistence it founds an action for nuisance for which the appropriate remedy would be an order of the court restraining the harmful activities or operations whether accompanied or not by an award of damages by way of recompense. A party asserting that he has sustained material damage to his property by reason of an alleged nuisance must establish the fact of such damage and that it was caused by the nuisance as alleged. It is no defence to such a claim, if established, that the activities complained of were carried out with the highest standards of care, skill and supervision and equipment or that such activities are of great public importance and cannot conveniently be carried out in any other way. Insofar as the nuisance alleged consists of interference with the ordinary comfort of existence and enjoyment of the property of the plaintiff his evidence must show sensible personal discomfort, including injurious affection of the nerves or senses of such a nature as would materially diminish the comfort and enjoyment of, or cause annoyance to a reasonable man accustomed to living in the same locality. To my mind the reasonable man connotes a person whose notions and standards of behaviour and responsibility correspond with those generally pertaining among ordinary people in our society at the present time who seldom allows his emotions to overbear his reason and whose habits are moderate and whose disposition is equable ...

The order of enquiry therefore would seem to be first to ascertain what are the standards of peace, comfort and enjoyment normal to homes in this locality by the standards of ordinary reasonable people. Having ascertained what normal activities were carried on in general in the neighbourhood of each plaintiff's home and what noises and disturbances are the normal regular feature of the neighbourhood then, to determine whether the activities of the defendants have introduced new and additional noises and disturbances materially increasing the burden of tolerance so as to diminish sensibly the reasonable peace and comfort of living in the locality. Insofar as the disturbances complained of are alleged to consist of vibrations to which structural and decorative damage to property is attributed, the enquiry involves consideration of the nature and causes of such damage. If the plaintiffs establish their claims there remains the question of whether a restraining order must be made and whether damages should be awarded ... [Each plaintiff set out their complaint].

The evidence in relation to all these complaints was carefully tested by the defendants and related to background noises including the noises from the joinery works and the volume of road traffic. The sensitivity of the witnesses was tested and related to the results of scientific research. The defendants adduced evidence of the nature of the work undertaken by them and the necessary pattern of their operations and showed by their records and the oral evidence of their staff the skill and care taken by them to reduce to the minimum the degree of interference with their neighbours which might be caused by their activities. It transpired in the course of the hearing of the evidence, which went over from July to October 1973, that the defendants' standards of care in these respects improved to a considerable degree. With helpful technical detail they related their efforts to the standards recommended by researchers based on statistical records and showed by their evidence the manner in which they had successfully adjusted their standards because of local experience well within the limits recommended from statistical research.

But standards based on statistics are necessarily founded upon averages, not only of the sensibilities of persons, but also averages for localities. As they are arrived at by counterbalancing or offsetting variations above or below the mean arrived at, they do not give a true or fair assessment for persons or localities which, although reasonable, fall above or below such mean. The evidence of the records of tests of the amplitude of sounds made by the defendants showed that a truck or motor bicycle passing near a transducer might make a noise which would obscure the sound of an explosion at blasting made some distance further away. I do not accept that it must follow from this that the noise of the explosion is not disturbing to the domestic peace of a reasonable person living in a place where the passing of trucks or motor bicycles is normal, whether frequent or occasional. Indeed such normally accepted noises such as that of a motor bicycle could be a nuisance if sustained for what might seem to be an excessive period or if repeated at what might appear excessively frequent intervals. Intermittent noises of their nature unusual to a locality which come at irregular or unpredictable intervals are likely to be more disagreeable than such noises which form part of the norm for the locality, such as passing traffic. When these unusual noises are of such nature that they instil apprehension and anxiety into the mind of the listener the sensitivity of the ear is likely to be more acutely perceptive of such noises, despite the amplitude of other more familiar and more acceptable noises simultaneously heard but instinctively disregarded ...

The evidence of the defendants confirmed the fact that their activities necessarily introduced into the neighbourhood of the plaintiffs' homes noises and vibrations which were totally alien to the normality of that locality as it was, prior to the commencement of their undertakings. The evidence of the defendants also convinced me that these noises and vibrations were of such a nature that they were known to be, were likely to be, and were expected to be a cause of disturbance of the peace and comfort of the homes of ordinary reasonable people ...

Having ascertained the standards of peace and comfort normal to the enjoyment by the plaintiffs of their homes in this locality by the standards of ordinary reasonable people, I find as fact that the activities of the defendants have introduced new and additional noises and disturbances of continuous, of intermittent, and of repetitious natures which materially increased the burden of tolerance for the plaintiffs and for each of the plaintiffs have sensibly diminished the reasonable comfort and peace of living in the locality. I am not satisfied that any of the physical damage to property of which the several plaintiffs complained is attributable to the activities of the defendants, but I accept that the apprehensions of the plaintiffs in these respects are reasonable and are a significant constituent in the disturbance of the enjoyment of the comfort of their homes.

As to the relief to which the plaintiffs are entitled on these findings, it seems to me that if the situation had remained as shown by the evidence up to the end of July 1973, I would have felt compelled to make an order restraining the defendants by injunction from continuing further the activities to which the nuisances alleged are attributable. But thereafter the defendants, with the co-operation of a degree of forbearance on the part of the plaintiffs, achieved a formula and improved working standards which made it unnecessary to continue the interim injunction granted on 7 June 1973 or to make a further order of injunction so long as the matter remained pending before the court ... [Damages awarded.]"

Comments and Questions:

1. Gannon J. in this action defines the reasonable man as "a person whose notions and standards of behaviour and responsibility correspond with those generally pertaining among ordinary people in our society at the present time who seldom allows his emotions to overbear his reason and whose habits are moderate and whose disposition is equable." Is this the modern day equivalent of the "man on the Clapham Omnibus" as defined by Greer L.J. in *Hall v Brooklands Auto Racing Club* [1933] 1 K.B. 205?

2. How do the courts assess what is the "ordinary comfort of existence and enjoyment of the property"?

3. The court distinguished in this action between noises of different types but similar levels. In your opinion, is this the correct approach to take?

Private nuisances may occur by omission as well as by action. The failure to act, may give rise to a cause of action. Unusually in this case, the court considered, in deciding liability the question of whether the defendant had taken reasonable care. This appears to arise where the defendant does not cause the nuisance by a positive act, but rather inherits the nuisance and fails to remedy it.

Daly & Daly v McMullan
Circuit Court, April 11, 1997

Facts: The defendant's property included an embankment which ran down behind the plaintiff's house; a further portion of the embankment was owned by another party and previously belonged to the defendant. The plaintiffs purchased their house in 1964. Over the years there were a number of falls of soil from the embankment, some quite significant. In August 1996 a considerable quantity of soil came into the plaintiffs' garden from the embankment. The defendants arranged for the removal of the soil and the hiring of tree surgeons to clear the foliage.

Issues: What is a person's liability where they continue a nuisance, or do not remedy the nuisance, on the purchase of property containing a nuisance? In this action there had been several soil spills and the court held that, as a result, the defendant was on notice of the nuisance from the date of the first spill and that that notice certainly gave rise to the existence of a duty to ameliorate the nuisance.

Buckley J.:

"Of the cases opened to me the one in which the facts are most similar to the facts in this case, though with two significant differences, is *Leakey v National Trust* [1980] 1 QB 485. Unlike most of the other cases opened to me, or referred to in the cases opened to me, the *Leakey case* was one of slippage from a large mound onto houses at the foot of the large mound. The first difference between the *Leakey case* and the present case is that, while there was some evidence in that case of cutting into the mound, it was accepted by the parties that the legal rights and liabilities were to be ascertained on the assumption that the contours of the Defendant's property were as nature made or developed them.

The second difference between the *Leakey case* and this case is that both the Plaintiffs and the Defendant derive their title to their properties from the Howth Estate. It is clear that the Howth Estate must have at the very least consented to any cutting into the Hill of Howth so as to enable a site for the house to be made available. Even if the Plaintiffs' engineers view that the site of the house could have existed naturally were to be accepted, the Howth Estate granted a lease of the site to the Plaintiff's predecessors in title with the unstable bank already in existence ...

Accordingly, it seems to me that, whatever might have been the position of the Plaintiffs' predecessors in title vis-a-vis the Howth Estate in relation to the creation of the unstable bank, the unstable bank was in existence when the Defendant took the lease of his property and the Defendant must have had notice of the existence of the bank, if not precise knowledge that it was unstable. The fact that both the Plaintiffs and the Defendant derive title from the Howth Estate seems to me to leave the position that no claim of third party alteration of the natural contour is relevant since any such alteration was either carried out by or with the consent of the Howth Estate to which the Plaintiffs and the Defendant are successors in title in the Plaintiffs' case and lessee in the Defendant's case ...

The authorities are reviewed with great care by Megaw LJ in the *Leakey case* commencing with an extract from Salmond, The Law of Torts (5th ed, 1920) at p 260 which was subsequently expressly approved by two of the judges in *Sedleigh-Denfield v O'Callaghan* [1940] AC 880:

> 'When a nuisance has been created by the act of a trespasser or otherwise without the act, authority or permission of the occupier, the occupier is not responsible for that nuisance unless, with knowledge or means of knowledge

of its existence, he suffers it to continue without taking reasonably prompt and efficient means for its abatement.'

Megaw LJ also refers to the judgement of Rowlatt J in *Noble v Harrison* [1926] 2 KB 332 in which he said at p 338:

'A person is liable for a nuisance constituted by the state of his property (1) if he causes it; (2) if by the neglect of some duty he allowed it to arise; and (3) if when it has arisen without his own act or default, he omits to remedy it within a reasonable time after he did become aware of it.'

The position at (3) appears to be of as much relevance in the present case as Megaw LJ considered it to be in the *Leakey case*. While *Sedleigh-Denfield v O'Callaghan* is a case in which third party intervention was significant, a passage in Lord Wright's speech at pp 904–905 is of relevance:

'The liability for a nuisance is not, at least in modern law, a strict or absolute liability. If the Defendant by himself or those for whom he is responsible has created what constitutes a nuisance and if it causes damage, the difficulty now being considered does not arise. But he may have taken over the nuisance, ready made it as it were, when he acquired the property, or the nuisance may be due to a latent defect or to the act of a trespasser, or stranger. Then he is not liable unless he continued or adopted the nuisance or, more accurately, did not without undue delay remedy it when he became aware of it or with ordinary and reasonable care should have become aware of it.'

The Court of Appeal in the *Leakey case* was concerned with the question of whether the law of England and Wales was the same as the law of Australia as found by the Privy Council in *Goldman v Hargrave* [1967] AC 645. In *Goldman v Hargrave* at p 661 the Privy Council found support in the opinions of the House of Lords in *Sedleigh-Denfield v O'Callaghan* and the dissenting judgment of Scrutton LJ in *Job Edwards Ltd v Birmingham Navigation* [1924] 1 KB 341 and the extract from the 5th edition of Salmond for the existence of a general duty upon occupiers in relation to hazards occurring on their land whether natural or man-made. Accepting that the law as stated by the Privy Council in *Goldman v Hargrave* did represent the law of England and Wales Megaw LJ at p 524 said:

'The duty is a duty to do that which is reasonable in all the circumstances, and no more than what, if anything, is reasonable, to prevent or minimise the known risk of damage or injury to one's neighbour or his property.'

What are the relevant sources of law in this jurisdiction?

In the 2nd edition of McMahon & Binchy, Irish Law of Torts it is stated at p 470:

'Thus, where the nuisance is created by a trespasser or stranger or results from natural causes, the occupier will be liable if, within a reasonable time after acquiring knowledge or presumed knowledge of its existence, he fails to take reasonable steps to bring it to an end. The same applies to cases where the occupier acquires property with a nuisance already existing on it. So also where the nuisance results from the escape of things naturally on the land: the occupier will be made liable where he has failed to take reasonable care, due allowances being made for the fact that the hazard has been 'thrust upon him through no seeking or fault of his own'. The courts will have regard to the fact that his resources may be of a very modest character either in relation to the magnitude of the hazard or as compared to those of his threatened neighbour. The standard required of him is thus no more than what is reasonable to expect of him in his individual circumstances' ...

In coming to the conclusion that the law in this jurisdiction is as set out in the case of *Goldman v Hargrave* and as adopted by the Court of Appeal in the *Leakey case*, I am comforted to find that a similar view has been taken on the law in Northern Ireland by McDermott LJ in *Neill v Department of the Environment for Northern Ireland* [1990] NI 84 in which he accepted that the principle of *Goldman v Hargrave* applied in Northern Ireland law.

It is clear that in the present case the Defendant was on notice of the nuisance from the date of the first spill and that notice certainly gave rise to the existence of a duty to ameliorate the nuisance."

A person can also be liable for private nuisance where they unreasonably interfere with another's right to the quiet enjoyment of their land. The central requirement is that the defendant's conduct is unreasonable.

Patterson v Murphy
High Court [1978] I.L.R.M. 85

Facts: The plaintiffs, a married couple, purchased a house from the first-named defendant in 1973. Prior to the purchase, the first-named plaintiff noticed work being carried out on a field owned by the defendant. He inspected the planning register and ascertained that no permission had been granted to use the field as a quarry. In May 1977, an oral agreement was entered into by the son of the first named defendant, acting on her behalf, and the managing director of the second named defendant. The written memorandum records the fact that the second named defendant would take a lease of the field for three years. It was expressly agreed that permission was given for the installation in the field of "crusher screeners and conveyors and necessary equipment for the manufacture of stone." Pursuant to this agreement blasting operations commenced on a regular and extensive basis; on one occasion causing cracks to appear in the walls of the plaintiffs' house, breaking a window and causing shock and alarm to the second named plaintiff who was pregnant at the time. Evidence was given that dust from the operations was extensive and that the plaintiffs were unable to sit in their garden. There were also complaints in relation to the noise from the lorries, and the condition of the roads as a result of their user.

Issues: The issue relates to what can be deemed unreasonable. To determine this issue the courts have traditionally sought to strike a balance between the utility of the defendant's conduct and the gravity of the harm likely to result from the conduct at issue. In this action the plaintiff succeeded in getting an injunction to prevent the defendant's activities. Costello J., in granting the injunction, referred specifically to the fact that the defendants in their actions did little to alleviate the nuisance suffered by the plaintiffs.

Costello J.:

"… I should begin my examination of the nuisance claim by considering a submission of the second-named defendant. It is this. In ascertaining whether the noise, vibration and dust complained of in these proceedings amounts in law to a nuisance it is submitted that the standard of comfort to be applied is that of the ordinary and reasonable man in the locality in which the plaintiffs reside (see *Salmond on the Law of Torts* 17 edition p. 56); that as the plaintiffs came to reside in what was termed a *'mining area'* the standard of comfort to which they are entitled is less than would apply in an ordinary rural area; that by applying the proper standards no nuisance has been established. In connection with this submission evidence was adduced both as to the nature of the locality in which Shillelagh Lodge was situated, and, also, the user of the quarry field adjoining the plaintiffs' home. From the evidence I find the following facts:

1. Shillelagh Lodge is in fact situated on a hillside. It is surrounded by fields which are used for coarse grazing. The quarry field itself was covered to a considerable extent by heather …
2. Later I will examine the use of the quarry field prior to October 1964. For the purposes of this part of the case I find that from 1964 to 1969 the quarry field was used very intermittently by Mr Murphy to obtain shale. For this purpose a mechanical shovel was used to scrape the top of the soil and to put the shale into lorries.
3. The quarry field was more intensively worked by a Mr Mansfield in the year 1969 (not the year 1970 as he thought) …
4. After Mr Mansfield vacated the field it was, again, only used very intermittently for the purpose of obtaining shale. It was, in fact, let from time to time by Mr Murphy for sheep grazing …

I conclude, therefore, that the existence of the gravel pits and the quarry some distance away from Shillelagh Lodge and the use actually made by the defendant of the quarry field do not reduce the standard of comfort to which the plaintiff was entitled when he purchased his new home. The standard to which he was entitled and which I should apply in considering the nuisance claim is that which an ordinary reasonable person would expect whose home was on a country lane in an area used for normal and common agricultural purposes.

The new developments which occurred from about the middle of 1977 were these ... From time to time large quantities of rock were blasted by means of explosives. The blasted rock was loaded by the excavator into a dumper. The dumper transferred the rock into a hopper at the rear of the crusher. The material travelled by conveyor belt (having been crushed in the crushing machine) to the screening plant. The crushed stones fell from the screening plant into a hopper, and the four inch stones were loaded into lorries and taken away ... Large 30 ton lorries were used to take away the stone, and these, naturally, were driven up and down the laneway close to the plaintiffs' house. The intensity of the traffic varied. Sometimes lorries came in convoys of four and five and on some days more than 80 lorries would pass by the plaintiffs' entrance ... To obtain the raw material for the manufacture of stone blasting occurred on 26 July, 8 August, 15 September, 28 September, 11 October, 20 October, 8 December. By arrangement made in the course of these proceedings a further blast occurred on 30 March of the present year. The total amount of explosives used in each blast varied. On 30 March last a total charge was 30 pounds; whilst on 8 August 1977 well over 2000 pounds were used. Blasting took place at distances from 500 feet from the plaintiffs' house to about 675 feet or thereabouts. The rock face of the quarry is now 10 to 12 metres high at its highest point. The crusher is about 175 yards from the house.

I have heard evidence from Mr and Mrs Patterson and Mr and Mrs O'Sullivan as to the effect of the operations which I have described. I have no hesitation in accepting their evidence. Each gave their testimony without exaggeration, with care for accuracy, and conscientiously. None could be regarded as being in any way abnormally sensitive. Turning, firstly to the allegation relating to noise and dust, I accept that the noise from the operations in the quarry field was continuous and loud and calculated to fray the nerves of any normal person. The noise came from the plant, including the crushing plant which was used continuously; it came from the movement of the rocks and stones as they were shifted in the different parts of the operation which I have described. I accept that the noise became so intolerable that Mrs Patterson was forced to leave her home and live elsewhere and that, similarly, Mrs O'Sullivan was driven from her home by it. Equally, I accept that serious nuisance from dust was created by the operations in the quarry field. The level of dust, naturally, varied according to the climatic conditions but I accept the evidence that on some occasions the dust could actually be felt on the face; that it created a film over the house and gardens; that it was such as to require windows to be kept closed, and prohibited Mr and Mrs Patterson from sitting in their garden.

Apart from the noise and dust emanating from the quarry field the evidence establishes to my satisfaction that further acts of nuisance were occasioned by the lorries travelling to and from the quarry field. The laneway was unmetalled and in fine weather very considerable dust came into the plaintiffs' house and garden both from the loads being carried on the lorries but principally from the surface of the laneway. In addition the size of the lorries and the frequency of the journeys created an excessive amount of noise. In wet conditions the laneway became a morass and almost impassable on occasions, and the laying of stones from the quarry on the laneway proved an ineffective remedy.

I find, accordingly, that the plaintiffs have established acts of nuisance to a serious degree arising from the emanation of noise and dust from the quarry field and from the emanation of noise and dust from the laneway. I will now turn to deal with the allegations relating to the blasting operations ...

[Scientific evidence in relation to measuring the impact of blasts was explained by Costello J.] The evidence establishes that there are two recognised methods for fragmenting an explosion, and for ease of reference I will refer to the process as the use of *'delayed detonators.'* The records show that when the blasts were supervised by Irish Industrial Explosives delayed detonators were used. As a result the *'maximum instantaneous charge'* was kept between 155 pounds and 80 pounds, the difference in the figures in the main being attributable to the extent of the *'burden'* and the depth of the charge. If, as happened in this case, blasts took place and delayed detonators were not used then the *'maximum instantaneous charge'* would have equalled the amount of the explosives used, thus setting up vibrations greatly in excess of those set up on the occasions when delayed detonators were used ...

The evidence satisfies me that if delayed detonators had been used in the blasting operations no physical damage to the plaintiffs' house would have occurred. Unfortunately, on 29 September when Mr Daragh personally supervised the blasting operation delayed detonators were not used. A very considerable amount of explosives were used on that occasion and physical damage was, I am quite satisfied, caused to the plaintiffs' house by the blast set off on that day. I will now examine the claim arising out of this damage.

The blast of 29 September was a very severe one. The window of the living-room was shattered, and part of an old boundary wall was knocked down. Mr Patterson gave evidence of cracking appearing on the interior walls of the house which was not there before the blast and Mr Purcell, the well known architect, described these cracks as he saw them on his visit on 3 October ... Mr Purcell again examined the house after 30 March explosions. Some of the cracks had increased in width and length and for the first time he noticed external cracks ... These external cracks (which he described in detail) were not present when he examined the premises in October ... I am satisfied that the plaintiffs have discharged the onus which is on them of establishing that, on the balance of probabilities, all the cracks described by Mr Purcell were attributable to vibration from explosion and not otherwise. I am, however, not satisfied that the explosions caused any damage to the plaintiffs' chimney as has been alleged. It had been imperfectly constructed and had, in fact, given trouble long before the plaintiffs purchased the premises ...

I will now consider the other aspects of the claim arising from the blasting operations. The blast on 29 September occurred in the afternoon. Mrs Patterson was lying down (she was then expecting a baby) and had actually gone to sleep. She was awoken by a very loud explosion which actually threw her up into the air, causing her to hit her head on the head-rest of the bed. She thought a bomb had gone off. She found the living-room in chaos and the couch (on which normally she would have been resting) was covered in glass from the blown-in window. Her first reaction was anger at what had been done and she immediately went down to the quarry to see someone in charge. Later she got a severe pain in her chest and she then started to worry that she might have a miscarriage. The experience was, I am quite satisfied, a very frightening one. She was present on subsequent occasions when blasting took place. She found them very frightening and she is now of the view that she could not stay in the house if she thought any future explosions would take place.

The evidence establishes to my satisfaction that if delayed detonators had been used, no physical damage would have been caused to the premises. But the blasting constituted an actionable interference with the enjoyment by the plaintiffs of their home. The evidence further satisfies me that if blasting operations were continued with the volume of charges employed by Trading Services as heretofore that their effect would be in the future to cause material discomfort to the plaintiffs' enjoyment of their premises both by the noise involved and the nervous strain associated with the explosives ...

I should add that even if a lower standard of comfort, as urged on behalf of the defendants, was to be applied that the conditions produced by the operations I have described fell far short of the standards which an ordinary reasonable person would expect to enjoy in the sort of *'mining area'* envisaged by the defendant's counsel.

... In the present case there are no circumstances which can deprive the plaintiffs of the relief to which they are *prima facie* entitled. The infringement of their rights is a most serious one; the injury which they have suffered and will suffer if the nuisance is permitted to continue has been and will be a considerable one; damages would not adequately compensate them. I should add that whilst I am conscious of the financial consequences for the defendants of the granting of an injunction I do not think bearing in mind that the sale to the plaintiffs took place at a time when Mr Murphy was aware of the possibility that quarrying operations in the adjoining field might take place, and bearing in mind that both defendants must have fully appreciated the great inconvenience to the plaintiffs which the quarrying operations would cause, that relief by way of an injunction could be termed oppressive."

The greater the utility of the defendant's conduct, the less likely the courts are to prohibit it. However, the rights of those living in proximity to such activities must also be respected. In the case of *Clifford v Drug Treatment Centre Board* [1997] I.E.H.C. 171, the court succeeded in balancing competing interests. The plaintiffs in this case objected to the operation and expansion of a treatment centre for drug addicts as they argued that it interfered with the running of their business. In declining to grant an injunction reducing the number of drug addicts, McCracken J. stated that to do so would go "clearly against the public interest, besides depriving possibly hundreds of individuals of badly needed treatment." As a compromise, however, he did award an injunction to prevent further expansion of the centre.

Clifford v The Drug Treatment Centre Board
High Court [1997] I.E.H.C. 171

Facts: The plaintiffs were owners or occupiers of business premises on Pearse Street in Dublin or in its immediate vicinity. The defendant was a body established by the Minister for Health pursuant to the provisions of the Health (Corporate Bodies) Act 1961, and was set up under the Drug Treatment Centre Board (Establishment) Order 1988 as amended in 1992. The defendants provided a treatment centre for drug addicts, and the plaintiffs objected to any expansion of this system, alleging that it interfered with their business.

Issues: The court had to consider the public utility of the defendant's actions and balance the competing interests of the property-owners. The response of the court was not to grant an injunction to reduce the numbers but to grant the injunction to prevent further expansion.

McCracken J:

"... A number of Affidavits have been filed on behalf of the Plaintiffs giving accounts of the difficulties, and in some cases the dangers, which have arisen by reason of the presence of a large number of drug addicts attending the Defendant's premises in connection with one or more of their functions. There are complaints of harassment, of theft, of threats of violence and of actual violence involving the use of syringes, which it is not necessary to set out in detail in this judgment. It is particularly alleged that such incidents have increased substantially in the last five years, and are having a serious effect on the businesses carried on by the Plaintiffs. It is also alleged by the Plaintiffs, and to some degree confirmed by the Defendant, that it intends to increase the services being provided by it in the near future. The Defendant, on the other hand, says that the problems facing the Plaintiffs are no different from problems encountered by business people anywhere in the inner city, and in fact that the incidence of crime in the Pearse Street area is less than in many other inner city areas.

The case made by the Plaintiffs is that their difficulties arise from the numbers which are attending the Defendant's Centre, and the inability of the Centre to cope with such numbers. They say that the problem has now got to such an extent that it constitutes a public nuisance which affects them personally, or alternatively constitutes a private nuisance against them in relation to their use of their premises. The Plaintiffs also make the case that the Defendant conducts its business negligently, and that it is an act of negligence on the part of the Defendant to accept more patients than the Centre can treat without causing a nuisance.

I have no doubt that the Plaintiffs have a good arguable case, that the actions of the persons visiting the Defendant's Centre are such as to seriously affect the Plaintiffs in the conduct of their businesses and in their use of their premises, and also have made out a good arguable case that this is a nuisance caused by the numbers attending the Centre. There remains, however, a legal question as to whether this nuisance is actionable.

It is argued on behalf of the Defendant that there is considerable authority that where a statutory body is carrying out its statutory functions, no action will lie against that body for nuisance unless the body is carrying out its functions negligently. This principle was set out by Lord Wilberforce in *Alan v. Gulf Oil Refining Limited* (1981) All E.R. 353 at page 356 where he said:—

> 'We are here in the well chartered field of statutory authority. It is now well settled that where Parliament by express direction or by necessary implication has authorised the construction and use of an undertaking or works, that carries with it an authority to do what is authorised with immunity from any action based on nuisance. The right of action is taken away (see *Hammersmith and City Railway Co. v. Brand* (1869) LR 4 HL 171...)
>
> To this there is made the qualification, or condition, that the statutory powers are exercised without "negligence", that word here being used in a special sense so as to require the undertaker, as a condition of obtaining immunity from action, to carry out the work and conduct the operation with all reasonable regard and care for the interests of other persons.'

The matter was put slightly differently by Viscount Duneden in *Manchester Corporation v. Farnworth* (1930) A.C. 171 at page 183 where he said:—

> 'When Parliament has authorised a certain thing to be made or done in a certain place, there can be no action for nuisance caused by the making or doing of that thing if the nuisance is the inevitable result of the making or doing so authorised. The onus of proving that the result is inevitable is on those who wish to escape liability for nuisance, but the criterion of inevitability is not what is theoretically possible but what is possible according to the state of scientific knowledge at the time, having also in view a certain common sense appreciation, which cannot be rigidly defined, of practical feasibility in view of situation and of expense.'

It does not seem to me that these authorities preclude the Plaintiffs from bringing or succeeding in an action for nuisance. I accept that it may well be at the trial of the action that the Defendant would prove that any nuisance caused to the Plaintiffs was the inevitable consequence of the performance of a statutory duty or power by the Defendant, but I do not think that such a case has been made on Affidavit by the Defendant in the present circumstances. This is a matter which will have to be determined on oral evidence ...

Finally, I turn to consider the balance of convenience. It is urged on me on behalf of the Defendant, and I think rightly urged, that I must take into account, not only the convenience of the Defendant, but also the convenience or damage to the persons attending the Centre, and indeed the public at large. The Plaintiffs are seeking to reduce the numbers at present attending the Centre to the 1992 level. The immediate result of this would be that less drug addicts would be treated, which is clearly against the public interest, besides depriving possibly hundreds of individuals of badly needed treatment. I certainly do not think that I would be justified in taking such a step at interlocutory stage and on possibly a temporary basis.

On the other hand, I accept that the Defendant intends to expand the use of the Centre. An injunction restraining such expansion will not affect existing patients. Furthermore, if the Plaintiffs were to succeed at the trial, it might well be that a Judge would order treatment to cease in respect of any additional patients since the issue of proceedings. I do think, therefore, that the status quo should be maintained, and I would propose to grant an Interlocutory Injunction restraining the Defendant by itself, its servants or agents or otherwise howsoever, from using its premises at Trinity Court, 31/32 Pearse Street, Dublin 2, as a Centre for referral of drug addicted patients for numbers in excess of the number for which the premises was so used on 21st July, 1997, the date of issue of these proceedings."

In deciding whether the behaviour is "unreasonable" the courts will also look to the nature of the area in which the nuisance takes place. In *Molumby v Kearns* [1999] I.E.H.C. 86 the location in which the nuisance arose was central in the decision of the court. The plaintiffs sought an injunction restraining the activities of a nearby industrial estate that operated on a 24-hour basis. As the industrial estate was located near a residential area the court ordered that the industrial estate operate only within normal working hours from Monday to Friday and on Saturday mornings as a way of reconciling both interests.

Molumby v Kearns
High Court [1999] I.E.H.C. 86

Facts: The plaintiffs to this action resided in the residential street of Foster Avenue in Dublin. The defendants operated an industrial estate which was accessed by a lane off Foster Avenue. The industrial estate had been operating for some period but the complaint related to what was described as a "dramatic increase in the number and size of vehicles together with the hours at which they come and go". The nuisance alleged related to noise, fumes, the obstruction of gates, damage to the property of some of the plaintiffs and traffic congestion. The plaintiffs also complained about the increased opening hours of the industrial estate, which they claimed operated on a 24-hour basis. There was considerable disagreement between the parties as to the facts of the alleged nuisance.

Issues: The issue in this action relates to the balancing of competing property rights, but the court also dealt with the issue of who could sue in nuisance. The court found that a person does not have to be the owner of the property to base an action in nuisance; occupation of the property will suffice. The court found for the plaintiffs in this action.

O'Sullivan J.:

"… The Defendants submit that Mrs Kirrane has no *locus standi* to bring the nuisance claim nor have the Careys. They accept that Dr. Kirrane has *locus standi* but the title shows that he and he alone has a legal interest. In the case of the Careys it is submitted that there is not sufficient evidence to show that they have an interest in their property. The Defendants accept that the Molumbys have established such an interest. This latter is because Ronan Molumby's Affidavit, sworn on the 14th February, 1997, states that their dwelling house was *'purchased in our joint names in or about the month of July 1994.'*

With regard to the Careys, the position is that Dominique Carey in her Affidavit of the same date at paragraph 8 says that *'the house is the only asset that we have and I say that it is likely that we will suffer a major financial loss.'* This is stated in the context of her having sworn immediately beforehand that she would have no option *'but to sell my house'* if the nuisance continued. Her husband, Colm Carey, swore an Affidavit on the 19th March, 1997 and makes no reference to ownership or interest in the house. His wife swore a further supplemental Affidavit of the 19th March, 1997 where she alludes to *'my house.'* Mr. Herbert S.C. submits that this leaves the Court in a position of having to speculate as to whether Dominique Carey owns their house or whether they both own the house or whether either of them have any legal interest in it.

This submission relies on a distinction which appears to have developed on the law of nuisance in the United Kingdom and which is particularly articulated in *Hunter and Others v. Canary Wharf Limited* [1997] 2 All ER 426. A majority of the House of Lords held that in order to sue in nuisance a plaintiff had to have an interest in the land. For example, Lord Goff of Chievley (at page 436) said:-

> 'Subject to this exception, however, it has for many years been regarded as settled law that a person who has no right in the land cannot sue in private nuisance.'

On the other hand Irish law on nuisance has been authoritatively re-stated in *Hanrahan and Others v. Merck Sharp and Dohme (Ireland) Ltd.* [1988] ILRM 629. In the Supreme Court decision delivered by Henchy J. (and in particular at page 634) it is stated:—

'It is clear from the authorities on the law of nuisance that what an occupier of land is entitled to as against his neighbour is the comfortable and healthy enjoyment of the land to the degree that would be expected by an ordinary person whose requirements are objectively reasonable in all the particular circumstances. It is difficult to state the law more precisely than that.'

Later on at pages 635/6 he said:—

'I agree that the tort of nuisance relied on in this case may be said to be an implementation of the State's duties under those provisions [of the Constitution] as to the personal rights and property rights of the Plaintiffs as citizens'.

On this particular point I accept that *locus standi* is established by a plaintiff who sues in nuisance if he or she is the occupier of the land. I do not think it is necessary that the plaintiff establish a legal interest over and above this.

In passing from this topic it is interesting to note that Lord Hoffmann who was in the majority in *Hunter* observed (at page 453):—

'The Courts today will readily assume that a wife has acquired a beneficial interest in the matrimonial home. If so, she will be entitled to sue for damage to that interest.'

I would also hold on the basis of the averments in the Affidavits to which I have referred above that even if it was necessary for the Careys to establish, as a matter of probability, that they had a legal interest in their home, that such an onus had been discharged. I take the observation of Lord Hoffmann, for example, to indicate that the Court will readily infer such an interest from relatively slight evidence. Accordingly, in my view, both the Careys and Maire Kirrane would have established that they had a legal interest in their respective homes if that were a necessary precondition to asserting a claim in nuisance.

Accordingly, all Plaintiffs have *locus standi* to bring the action in nuisance.

I have been referred to a large number of cases, and I have considered these. However, I think that in the last analysis the statement of law which I have already cited from the judgment of Henchy J. in *Hanrahan* not only captures the essence of the tort in Irish law but indicates that it is difficult to state the law more precisely. This in turn shows, I think, as was submitted by Mr. Collins S.C. on behalf of the Plaintiffs, that ultimately the question of nuisance is one of impression.

In forming an impression on the evidence I have had regard, to all of the evidence, but in particular I note that the acoustic experts were in reasonably close agreement as between themselves, and concluded that the impact of the noise in the back garden of the Molumbys' house was such as would give rise to a serious consideration of prosecution … I consider that the recurring movements of the larger vehicles which occur in the lane adjoining the Plaintiffs' residences and in particular immediately adjoining the Molumbys' residence, breaches what the Plaintiffs and in particular the Molumbys as occupiers of their land are entitled to as against the occupiers of the industrial estate, to use the phraseology employed by Henchy J. in *Hanrahan*.

I do not think the Plaintiffs and in particular the Molumbys have been afforded *'the comfortable and healthy enjoyment'* of their property on the basis set out by Henchy J. in *Hanrahan*. In reaching this conclusion, I have had regard to all the evidence and not just the evidence of the acoustic experts. I have had regard to the evidence of Mr. McGill. I think the locality in which these events have occurred is one which, on the one hand, is zoned residential in the most recent development plan so that the policy of the planning authority is to protect the amenities of residences. On the other hand, the Plaintiffs' houses front onto a busy national route taking traffic to the West from Dun Laoghaire Harbour. Furthermore, I accept that the probability is that the industrial estate is authorised by a permission granted under the previous planning code but this is also true of the houses occupied by the Plaintiffs.

I treat the locality not as an exclusively residential area but as a residential area, so zoned, adjoining a busy road in front and with an industrial estate authorised by appropriate planning permission, in its midst.

I do not think that the fact that the residences immediately adjoin the industrial estate means that the estate must close down. I do not think this would be reasonable. Equally, I do not think that the noise, fumes and general activity and traffic movements on the estate should be such as to cause an undue impact on the amenities of the nearby residences.

The Plaintiffs have indicated that they would accept Hiace type vans or possibly slightly larger vans (which would include the van owned by Chervil Limited) servicing the estate. They would object, however, to large rigid trucks or any kind of articulated truck.

They are seeking an Order limiting the hours of access to the historic hours, namely, 8.30 a.m. to 5.30 p.m.

The parties are agreed that I should deal with the case upon the basis that a lodgment which was accepted means that the Molumbys are free, if they wish, to re-instate the wall between their property and the lane servicing the estate to its condition prior to any damage done by passing vehicles.

I have had the benefit of a site visit and on that occasion an articulated truck and others accessed the lane and I had the opportunity of standing in the Molumbys' rear garden while the engine was left running. It is clear that, even with their wall restored to its original substantial condition, the noise carries to the rear garden and in the case of a number of trucks the exhaust fumes would emit from a high point behind the driver's cab. I do not think it is reasonable to require residents to have to accept such impact on the amenity of their gardens on any kind of regular basis. Of course domestic occupiers will, from time to time, permit exceptional vehicles to visit their premises. Again, occasionally, construction work will be carried out on houses in residential areas. The Glenville Industrial Estate has been in place for a great number of years and will continue there. In my view, it can only so continue in compliance with the Irish law of nuisance if the working hours are strictly regulated by the closing of the access gates, if relatively quiet and relatively small commercial vehicles service the estate, if there is no commercial overnight parking, if the distribution activity servicing Dell Computers is removed and if the use of noisy pallets or fork-lift vehicles is excluded (both on the ground and in vehicles themselves).

In order to give effect to these criteria, I consider that the gates should remain closed except between 8.15 a.m. and 6.15 p.m. Mondays to Fridays and 9 a.m. and 1 p.m. on Saturdays. No commercial vehicles should be permitted access to the estate when the gates are closed. I consider, however, that the Defendants should be entitled to park up to three private vehicles in the estate outside opening hours to facilitate senior employees working late.

There should be a large clear notice at the entrance of the estate limiting speed to 8 miles an hour and prohibiting the running of engines during loading and unloading. No fork-lift or pallet trucks should be used on the estate other than electric or battery operated units with rubber wheels. There should be no obstruction of the entrances to any one of the Plaintiffs' houses by vehicles servicing the estate or of the entrance and access to the garage usually used by Dr. Kirrane. A notice to this effect should be erected near the entrance to the laneway servicing the estate."

Sensitivity of the defendant

Not only must the activity of the defendant be reasonable but the demands of the plaintiff must also be that of a reasonable person before they can seek a remedy in nuisance. Unreasonable sensitivities or unusual demands will rarely be entertained: *Robinson v Kilvert* (1889) 41 Ch. D. 88.

Robinson v Kilvert
Court of Appeal (1889) 41 Ch. D. 88.

Facts: The plaintiff to this action hired premises in a warehouse for his business, which was paper and twine. At a later date the premises below the plaintiffs were rented out. The lessors commenced business as paper-box makers for which they required warm and dry air. For this they used a boiler and set up some steam piping in connection with it, the effect of which was that heat escaped into the plaintiff's premises. The plaintiff's complaint was that this heat caused injury to some of his paper stock by making it too dry, and lessened its value and impacted on his profits. The plaintiff sought to restrain the defendants from heating and drying the air in his warehouse so as to cause damage to him in his business.

Issue: The sensitivity of the plaintiff's business meant that the interference which did impact on him was not necessarily unreasonable. The court did not find for the defendant in this instance.

Cotton L.J.:

"… It was first argued as a case of nuisance. Now the heat is not excessive, it does not rise above 80° at the floor, and in the room itself it is not nearly so great. If a person does what in itself is noxious, or which interferes with the ordinary use and enjoyment of a neighbour's property, it is a nuisance. But no case has been cited where the doing something not in itself noxious has been held a nuisance, unless it interferes with the ordinary enjoyment of life, or the ordinary use of property for the purposes of residence or business. It would, in my opinion, be wrong to say that the doing something not in itself noxious is a nuisance because it does harm to some particular trade in the adjoining property, although it would not prejudicially affect any ordinary trade carried on there, and does not interfere with the ordinary enjoyment of life. Here it is shewn that ordinary paper would not be damaged by what the Defendants are doing, but only a particular kind of paper, and it is not shewn that there is heat such as to incommode the workpeople on the Plaintiff's premises. I am of opinion, therefore, that the Plaintiff is not entitled to relief on the ground that what the Defendants are doing is a nuisance."

Lindley L.J.:

"I have come to the same conclusion as the Vice-Chancellor though I do not quite agree with him as to the way of arriving at it …

As regards the question of nuisance, the lessors heat the air of their cellar so as to raise the temperature of the Plaintiff's room. There is no evidence to shew that the heat is such as to interfere with the comfort of the Plaintiff's workpeople, but there is evidence to shew that it damages one sort of paper sold by the Plaintiff, and so to some extent interferes with his use of the demised property. The Plaintiff contends that this establishes a case of nuisance, and he relies upon *Cooke v. Forbes* [Law Rep. 5 Eq. 166], in the head-note to which it is laid down that 'It is no answer to a complaint by a manufacturer of a nuisance to his trade, to say that the injury is felt only by reason of the delicate nature of the manufacture.' But that head-note goes too far, further than is warranted by the case. The defendants there were pouring into the air sulphuretted hydrogen, a gas of an offensive and noxious character. Now, if a man pours gas of that description into the atmosphere he does it at his own risk, and it may well be that he is liable for any damage done by it to a neighbour, although such damage would not accrue if the neighbour's manufacture were not of a delicate description. But there is a very broad difference between poisoning the atmosphere with sulphuretted hydrogen and doing something not in itself noxious, and which makes the neighbouring property no worse for any of the ordinary purposes of trade …"

Lopes L.J.:

"I am of the same opinion. I think the Plaintiff cannot complain of what is being done as a nuisance. A man who carries on an exceptionally delicate trade cannot complain because it is injured by his neighbour doing something lawful on his property, if it is something which would not injure anything but an exceptionally delicate trade. *Cooke v. Forbes* [Law Rep. 5 Eq. 166] has been disposed of by Lord Justice Lindley. In the present case the Defendants are not shewn to have done anything which would injure an ordinary trade, and cannot, in my opinion, be held liable on the ground of nuisance ...

I agree, therefore, that the appeal must be dismissed."

Comments and Questions:
1. This judgment highlights the importance the courts attach to the issue of reasonableness in nuisance actions. Not only do they look to the reasonableness or otherwise of the defendant's actions, but also that of the plaintiff's claims.

The courts stress that some allowances should be made for the ordinary incidents of neighbourly relations and that injury should be of a substantial character, not fleeting or passing. The nature of the plaintiff is relevant in an action in nuisance.

O'Kane v Campbell
High Court [1985] I.R. 115

Facts: The plaintiff resided in Glengarriff Parade, the second house from the corner of that road where it meets North Circular Road. The defendant owned the corner premises on the opposite side of the road from the plaintiff. The defendant operated a "24-hour" shop from his premises. The plaintiff claimed that the use of the premises for all-night trading constituted a nuisance to her enjoyment of her premises; this activity created noise late into the night.

Issues: Was the plaintiff to the action overly sensitive? The characteristics of plaintiffs can be considered. In this case Lynch J. held that elderly people may sleep more lightly than others, but that does not mean they are overly sensitive, as the elderly as well as the young are entitled to their night's sleep. The court found for the plaintiff in this action.

Lynch J.:

"... These are the normal and inevitable noises of ordinary law abiding people going to and from the shop from and to cars, motor-bikes, vans, trucks and on foot. Such noises are the revving of engines, the banging of doors (and they have to be banged to some extent to close them at all), the playing of radios in the vehicles and cordial 'hellos' and 'goodbyes' between people meeting each other, as well also as the clacking of hard heeled shoes on the footpaths and roads ...

The noise is not such as to call for garda intervention. There was no breach of the peace nor disorderly behaviour on these occasions. But Inspector Finn who investigated the complaints on a couple of occasions said that in his opinion the noise was sufficient to disturb sleep in the plaintiff's house. Elderly residents of Glengarriff Parade gave similar evidence of disturbance.

On the other hand, younger people gave contrary evidence. Most of these witnesses, however, lived on the North Circular Road itself, where different conditions apply from those obtaining in Glengarriff Parade. Nurse Horan gave evidence that when she lived in No. 6 Glengarriff Parade which is next door to the plaintiff's house she was not disturbed. Perhaps this contradiction between the evidence of the various witnesses is simply an example of the perennial generation gap. Young people can sleep in spartan conditions such as youth hostels, camping, sleeping bags or mattresses on floors. Nurses have necessarily to acquire the ability to sleep in difficult circumstances. Elderly people perhaps sleep more lightly but they are not abnormal for that and they are entitled to their night's sleep ...

As Henchy J. said in *Mullin* v. *Hynes* (unrep. Supreme Court, 13th November, 1972) which is reported in McMahon and Binchy's Casebook on the Irish Law of Torts at page 524 and 529 and in particular at page 526:—

> 'In a claim for a private nuisance of this kind the judge has to act as an arbiter between the competing interests of the respective property users. He has to decide which is to prevail, the defendant's claim to use his property in the impugned manner or the plaintiff's claim to use his property free from the damage caused by the defendant.'

Leaving aside altogether the evidence of the plaintiff herself and the other witnesses called on behalf of the plaintiff, I accept the evidence of Miss Hilda Hunt, Mr. Edward Brown, and Miss Pauline McKinney that the advent of the 24 hour shop trading 7 days per week has drastically altered the amenity of Glengarriff Parade as a residential street. I am satisfied that this night trading constitutes a nuisance to the plaintiff in the enjoyment of her house and subject to the issue of delay she is entitled to relief ...

The plaintiff in this case is therefore entitled to relief but the defendant is to be disturbed in the use and enjoyment of his property to the minimum extent consistent with giving reasonable relief to the plaintiff. I considered whether I should limit the injunction so as to prohibit only night trading in such a way as to cause a nuisance but I have come to the conclusion that this would be unworkable because any night trading at all will cause an actionable nuisance by the noise made by ordinary law abiding citizens in resorting to the premises.

I therefore affirm the order of the learned Circuit Court Judge but I vary it as follows:—

'The defendant is hereby prohibited and injuncted from opening or keeping open to the public or trading or carrying on business with the public in or from the premises known as Campbell's corner No. 409 North Circular Road in the City of Dublin between the hours of midnight and 6 a.m., during all seasons of the year.' ...

I award costs to the plaintiff in both the High Court and the Circuit Court and each party shall have liberty to apply to the Circuit Court."

Who may sue for private nuisance?

This issue was addressed in *Molumby v Kearns* [1999] I.E.H.C. 86 and the court took the view that occupation of the property was sufficient to maintain an action in nuisance. In *Hanrahan v Merck Sharpe and Dohme* [1988] I.L.R.M. 629 the owner, the spouse of the owner, and their children, were entitled to take an action in nuisance. In England the position was clarified in *Hunter v Canary Wharf Ltd.* [1997] 2 W.L.R. 685; it was held that only a person with an interest in the land or premises may sue for private nuisance. The House of Lords contend that such a limitation was necessary for the tort. In Ireland the issue was addressed in *Royal Dublin Society v Yates*, unreported, High Court, July 1997.

Royal Dublin Society v Yates
High Court, July 31, 1997

Facts: The plaintiff, a body corporate, alleged that Mr Yates, the defendant, had been guilty of acts of both trespass and nuisance. The Royal Dublin Society alleged private nuisance in the form of trespass and intimidation by the defendant.

Issues: Who is entitled to take an action in private nuisance? The court in this action held that a body corporate, as owner and occupier of the premises, could maintain an action in nuisance.

Shanley J.:

"Private nuisance consists of any interference without lawful justification with a person's use and enjoyment of his property ...

In *Hunter & Others v Canary Wharf Limited, Hunters & Others v London Dockland Development Corporation* [1997] All ER 426, the House of Lords was considering the extent to which a nuisance had been committed by defendant developers in relation to television reception by the plaintiffs in their homes. In considering the issue of the right to sue for damages for nuisance, Lord Hoffman stated at page 448 that:—

'Up to about 20 years ago no-one would have had the slightest doubt about who could sue. Nuisance is a tort against land including interests in land such as easements and profits. A plaintiff must therefore have an interest in the land affected by the nuisance.'

He went on to refer to the fact that the leading case or the need for exclusive possession to found an action in nuisance is the case of *Malone v Laskey*, [1907] 2 KB 141. Mrs Malone in that case lived in a house belonging to her husband's employer; he (her husband) was a service occupier. She was injured by the falling of a bracket supporting a water-tank which had been dislodged by vibration caused by an engine worked by the defendants on the adjoining premises. She sued in negligence and nuisance and lost on both counts. On the nuisance issue, however, her claim was rejected because she had no interest in the property. She was the licensee of her husband or his employer. In other words she was a mere occupier of the premises and had no entitlement to possession of the premises.

In the Irish case of *Mary Hanrahan & Others v Merck Sharp and Dohme (Ireland)* [1988] ILRM 629, a different and more flexible approach appears to have been taken on the issue of who has the right to sue. In that case, Mr Justice Henchy, delivering the judgment of the Court said at page 634:—

'It is clear from the authorities on the law of nuisance that what an occupier of land is entitled to as against his neighbour is the comfortable and healthy enjoyment of the land to the degree that would be expected by an ordinary person whose requirements are objectively reasonable in all the particular circumstances. It is difficult to state it more precisely than that'.

In that case the plaintiff Mary Hanrahan was the registered owner of the farm of about 264 acres at Ballycurkeen, Carrick-on-Suir, County Tipperary. The second and third named plaintiff was a husband and wife. John Hanrahan, the second named Plaintiff, was the son of the registered owner of the farm but neither he nor his wife had any right to the exclusive possession of the farm.

The Court of Appeal in England recently considered the question of the entitlement of an occupier of premises to sue in respect of the tort of nuisance. In the case of *Khorasand Jian v Bush*, [1993], 3 All ER 669, the plaintiff was a young woman aged 18 living with her mother, the defendant was a former friend who pestered her with telephone calls. In the ordinary sense of the word as the Court noted he was 'making a nuisance of himself'; the problem was to find a cause of action which could justify the grant of an injunction to stop him. A majority of the Court of Appeal (Peter Gibson LJ dissenting) held that she was entitled to sue in respect of nuisance. Dillon, Lord Justice, brushed Malone's case aside. He said at page 675:—

'To my mind it is ridiculous if in this present age the law is that the making of deliberately harassing and pestering telephone calls to a person is only actionable in the Civil Courts if the recipient of the calls happens to have the freehold or a leasehold proprietary interest in the premises in which he or she has received the calls.'

Lord Hoffman, in *Hunter v Canary Wharf Limited* (supra), was of the view that Lord Justice Dillon was mistaken in his statement of his reasons for allowing an action for nuisance to be brought at the suit of the daughter who had no interest in the premises in question. He said as follows:—

'In the case of nuisances 'productive of sensible personal discomfort', the action is not for causing discomfort to the person but, as in the case of the first category for causing injury to the land. True it is that the land has not suffered "sensible" injury, but its utility has been diminished by the existence of the nuisance. It is for an unlawful threat to the utility of his land the possessor or occupier is entitled to an injunction and it is for the diminution and such utility that he is entitled to compensation' (at page 451).

In the present case, the Royal Dublin Society is not just the occupier of the lands at Ballsbridge in the City of Dublin but also the owner of those lands and entitled to the exclusive possession of them. Accordingly, in asking the question as to whether the Society is entitled to sue in respect of any private nuisance committed by Mr Yates, it is unnecessary to consider the difference of approach which appears to have emerged between the Irish Supreme Court as exemplified by the judgment of Mr Justice Henchy in *Hanrahan v Merck Sharp and Dohme*, supra, and in the House of Lords in the speeches of a majority of their Lordships in the case of *Hunter and Canary Wharf Limited*, supra. It is, however, worthwhile referring to a statement of principle that Mr Justice Henchy quoted with approval in the case *of Hanrahan v Merck Sharp and Dohme* Supra at page 634: he was referring to a decision (unreported) of Gannon J in the case of *Halpin and Others v Tara Mines Limited*, High Court 1973 No 1516p the 16 February 1976 in which Mr Justice Gannon stated as follows:—

'A party asserting that he has sustained material damage to his property by reason of an alleged nuisance must establish the fact of such damage and that it was caused by the nuisance as alleged. It is no defence to such a claim if established that the activities complained of were carried out with the highest standards of care, skill and supervision and equipment or that the activities are of such great public importance and cannot conveniently be carried out in any other way. Insofar as the nuisance alleged consists of interference with the ordinary comfort and enjoyment of the property of the plaintiff his evidence must show sensible personal discomfort including injurious affection of the nerves or senses of such a nature as would materially diminish the comfort and enjoyment of or cause annoyance to, a reasonable man accustomed to living in the same locality. To my mind the reasonable man connotes a person whose notions and standards of behaviour and responsibility correspond with those generally pertaining among ordinary people in our society at the present time who seldom allow his emotions to over-bear his reason, whose habits are moderate and whose disposition is equitable.'

The test propounded by Mr Justice Gannon *in Halpin and Others v Tara Mines Limited*, 16 February 1976 seems to me the appropriate test to be applied to the position as between the Society and Mr Yates …

While I have found that Mr Yates has been guilty of private nuisance, I do not propose to award to the Society any damages in respect of that nuisance."

Comments and Questions:
1.   Shanley J. highlights the distinction between the position adopted in *Hunter v Canary Wharf Ltd.* [1997] 2 W.L.R. 685 and *Hanrahan v Merck Sharpe and Dohme* [1988] I.L.R.M. 629; what are those distinctions? How significant might these distinctions prove to be in practice?

Who may be sued in private nuisance?

With regard to public nuisance it was established in *Convery v Dublin County Council* [1996] I.R. 153 that the County Council could not be held responsible for a public nuisance that did not originate in any premises owned or occupied by the Council. The position for private nuisance is somewhat similar in that it is the creator of the nuisance or anyone who authorises the nuisance that can be sued.

Goldfarb v Williams & Co.
High Court [1945] I.R. 433

Facts: The plaintiff to the action was in occupation of the first and third floor of the premises in Henry Street in Dublin. The plaintiff used the third floor as a residence and operated a hairdressers from the first floor. The defendant was the landlord of the premises, and in 1944 let the second floor to the co-defendants, who ran a social and athletic club. The premises were used for holding dances, which were held twice weekly. On account of the construction of the premises the sounds "were transmitted with exceptional clearness and loudness to the floors above and below".

Issue: Is there the potential to take an action against someone who is not causing the nuisance, but permits the creation of a nuisance? The court held that the landlord was capable of being sued for failing to take reasonable steps to abate the nuisance.

Overand J.:

"These premises were designed and erected about 1917/18. The ground floor and basement for Messrs. Williams' shop premises; the upper floors for offices and show rooms. These floors are in the main carried on rolled steel H joists, 10" x 5", on the lower flanges of which are stout wooden plates on which rest the ends of the wooden joists which run from one steel joist to the next. The wooden joists are 7" x 2", to the underside of which are nailed the plasterboards which form the ceiling of the room below, and to the upper side is nailed the flooring of the room itself. It is obvious that the entire thickness of floor and ceiling is 9" or less, and that the steel joists must project some inches below the ceilings of the under rooms. It occurred to me that such a floor would act as a sounding-board, especially in the case of an instrument in direct physical contact with it, such as a piano, and would conduct sound unless there was provision for deadening noise. I put a question on the point to Mr. Donnelly, who told me that such a floor would definitely transmit sound more than an ordinary floor laid on joists built into brick walls ...

Now, in addition to these opinions I have direct evidence from Mr. Munden, who went to the premises on two dance evenings. On the first floor in the cubicles he could hear the dance music and the sound of dancing feet overhead and he observed vibration in the lamp-shades during the dancing. On the third floor he could hear the music plainly and also hear singing. Mr. Caffrey also deposed that he could hear the music of a band and a lady's voice singing. I think this was from the wireless set. I have also conclusive evidence that Mr. Grant offered, and Mr. Goldfarb refused to accept, a reduction in rent of £50 per annum, as adequate compensation for the inconvenience caused to him ...

I now pass to the third floor. Mr. Goldfarb, who had enjoyed the premises from 1939, as sole occupant, lost no time in making complaints, and lost no opportunity either. He started early in September to complain of the noise of moving in, a purely temporary inconvenience, and he made every conceivable complaint, reasonable and unreasonable, to such an extent as to lend credence to the view that he was determined to root out Arnott's club, and to make me regard his evidence as unreliable save so far as it is corroborated. I am of opinion that this is due in no small measure to the club's somewhat enthusiastic start, which got on his nerves, till every sound became to him a source of violent and undue irritation. This seems to me to be established by his own evidence as to vibration, which he said was not noticeable when standing up and occupied, but extremely annoying when sitting down ...

The evidence satisfies me that the club used the premises demised to their trustees for dancing, in a reasonable and normal manner for such a purpose, that the members of the club were orderly in their behaviour and that anything unduly noisy or objectionable in a dance room was at once checked by the steward of the evening. At the same time I am convinced that the sounds which are ordinarily associated with dancing were transmitted with exceptional clearness and loudness to the floors above and below, and that such sounds, occurring twice weekly from 7.30 to 11 p.m., did amount to a nuisance and were a serious interference with the comfort and health of the plaintiff, Mr. Goldfarb, and other inhabitants of the third floor. Few things could be more exasperating than the knowledge that for three and a half hours every Wednesday and Saturday evening one must listen to jazz or rhythm dances, or leave one's home as the only means of escape. It is a matter of legitimate comment that no one on behalf of the defendant company accepted the plaintiff's invitation to come to his premises and hear for themselves. As regards the first floor, I am satisfied that the second floor has been so used as to cause annoyance and inconvenience to Ono Ltd, though not to so great an extent, since the overlap with business hours is relatively small. No customer of Ono Ltd., has been called to prove that she suffered any actual annoyance. In *Jenkins* v. *Jackson* 40 [Ch. D. 71.] Kekewich J. held that dancing overhead in business premises, though outside normal business hours, was a nuisance, but he did not grant an injunction for a reason not applicable in the present case, since I must grant an injunction to Mr. Goldfarb.

In *Ball* v. *Ray* [LR 8 Ch App 467], Lord Selborne and Sir George Mellish point out that an unusual use of premises which materially disturbs the comfort of adjoining occupiers, may be a nuisance, though a similar amount of noise arising from the ordinary use of such premises would not be a nuisance. In my opinion the use of these premises for dancing is an unusual one, for which the premises were never designed, and for which, though sufficiently strong and safe, they are otherwise unsuitable ...

The fact that such annoyance is caused to the plaintiffs by the use of the premises in a manner, reasonable for the purpose for which they were demised to the club's trustees, proves their unsuitability.

As between the club and their lessors I am of opinion that, inasmuch as dancing was one of the purposes specifically mentioned during the negotiations, the club was entitled to use the premises for that purpose in a reasonable manner, notwithstanding the restrictive provision against causing nuisance or annoyance. I therefore think the lessors are responsible as having authorised such nuisance, which was inevitable if the premises were used as intended: *Harris* v. *James* [45 LJ QB 545]. The lessors must be deemed to know the construction and properties of their own building.

In my opinion the plaintiffs have completely failed to prove the major part of the exaggerated averments in their statement of claim, but have proved sufficient to warrant an injunction. I shall not restrain the defendants in the form asked for; nuisance is often a question of degree, and in my opinion the holding of an isolated dance now and then is a very different matter from bi-weekly dancing; again, an occasional concert during reasonable hours might be permissible and unobjectionable.

I shall merely restrain the defendants from permitting the premises to be used in such manner as to be a nuisance to the other occupiers of the building, 45/47 Henry Street.

I think that from first to last the plaintiffs have been unreasonable. Much of the time occupied by the hearing was due to the plaintiffs' attempts to prove the extravagant averments which they failed to substantiate and to the defendants' evidence to counter these attempts.

I think I shall be treating the plaintiffs at least fairly if I award them one-half of one set of costs of the action.

As between the defendants, I am of opinion that, upon the whole, the defendant trustees, as lessees of the second floor, used the demised premises reasonably for purposes authorised by the lease, and that therefore the defendant company should bear the costs awarded to the plaintiffs."

DEFENCES

All torts are capable of relying on the general defences; some torts, including nuisance, have some specific remedies. If a defendant can raise the defence of statutory authority or prescription, s/he may be able to avoid an action in nuisance.

Statutory authority

Where a person carries out an activity pursuant to legislation, these actions may not amount to a private nuisance.

Superquinn Ltd. v Bray Urban District Council
High Court [1998] 3 I.R. 542

Facts: The plaintiff owned a premises situated on the banks of a river. The action was initially lodged against five potential defendants, but continued only as against the first, third and fourth. The first defendant was a sanitary authority; the third a drainage construction company (working for the first defendant); and the fourth the owner of an artificial lake located upstream from the plaintiff's premises. The incident occurred on the night of August 26, 1986 during a storm known as "Hurricane Charlie", when the river burst its banks and caused extensive flooding to the plaintiff's premises. It was alleged that the first defendant contributed to the flooding because of the manner in which the drainage construction works had obstructed the flow of the river. It was alleged that the third defendant was liable for the manner in which the works were carried out. It was alleged that the fourth defendant was liable for failing to properly use and maintain the dam and to provide and maintain an effective arrangement for releasing waters from the reservoir when the level of the reservoir rose.

Issue: Here the court had to determine whether an action in nuisance lay against Bray Urban District Council. The court held that the actions of Bray Urban District Council were carried out pursuant to legislation and therefore they had successfully raised the defence of statutory authority.

Laffoy J.:

"It was submitted by counsel, on behalf of the first defendant, that, as the sanitary authority for the Bray area, it was under a statutory duty, by virtue of s.17 of the Public Health (Ireland) Act, 1878, to cause to be made such sewers as might be necessary for effectually draining the Bray area and that on the 25th

August, 1986, the drainage construction works being carried out in the Dargle at Bray were being executed in pursuance of that duty and in the only manner in which they could reasonably be executed. That being the case, it was submitted, as a matter of law, the first defendant was immune from an action based on nuisance and was free from liability unless it was negligent in the exercise of its statutory duty and power. I am satisfied that this proposition is correct and that, in the absence of proof of negligence, no liability attaches to the first defendant or to the third defendant, which executed the works under contract with the first defendant."

Prescription

Prescription is the acquiring of rights as a result of continuous use without objection. In effect, where a potential plaintiff acquiesces in allowing a private nuisance to continue without objection for a considerable period of time, this acquiescence may grant the creator of the nuisance a defence. A person who comes to an area where a nuisance exists, comes with all their rights attached: *Bliss v Hall* (1838) 4 Bing NC 183, 132 E.R. 758.

Sturges v Bridgman
Court of Appeal 11 Ch. D.

Facts: A confectioner had for more than 20 years used a pestle and mortar in the back of his premises, which were alongside the garden of a doctor. The noise and vibration of this work were not felt or complained of. In 1873 the doctor erected a consulting room at the end of his garden and then the noise and vibration became a nuisance to him. He sought an injunction.

Issues: The main issue was whether the confectioner had acquired a right to make noise. In other words, could he establish a claim founded on the basis of a long period of uninterrupted use, or long-standing custom; *i.e.* that if there was a nuisance it had been legalised by prescription? The plaintiff in this action succeeded in showing that prescription had not in fact occurred.

Jessel M.R.:

"I think this is a clear case for the Plaintiff. There is really no dispute as to this being a nuisance; in fact, the evidence is all one way, and, as has been often said in these cases, the Plaintiff is not bound to go on bringing actions for damages every day, when he is entitled to an injunction.

The only serious point which has been argued for the Defendant is that by virtue of the statute, or by prescription, he was entitled as against the Plaintiff to make this noise and commit a nuisance. Now the facts seem to be that until a very recent period it was not a nuisance at all. There was an open garden at the back of and attached to the Plaintiff's house, and the noise, it seems, if it went anywhere, went over the garden, and, of course, was rapidly dispersed; as far as I can see upon the evidence before me, there was until a recent period no nuisance to anybody—no actionable nuisance at all. The actionable nuisance began when the Plaintiff did what he had a right to do, namely, built a consulting-room in his garden, and when, on attempting to use the consulting-room for a proper purpose, he found this noise too great for anything like comfort. That was the time to bring an action for nuisance.

Now, under those circumstances, it appears to me that neither the defence of the statute, nor the defence of the right by prescription, can possibly avail ...

I will state the authorities as shortly and in as few words as I can. There are a great many authorities on the subject, but there is one authority which I have been looking at for another purpose, to which I shall refer. That is the case of *Webb v. Bird* [13 CB (NS) 841], which states the law as explicitly as it possibly can be stated. There Justice *Wightman*, who delivered the judgment of the Court, says, 'We think, in accordance with the Court of Common Pleas, and the judgment of the House of Lords in *Chasemore v. Richards* [7 HLC 349], that the presumption of a grant from long-continued enjoyment only arises where the person against whom the right is claimed might have interrupted or prevented the exercise of the subject of the supposed grant.'

Now in the case before me that was simply impossible. The noise was made on the Defendant's own premises—in his kitchen. Of course you could not go into his kitchen without being a trespasser. You could not interrupt it there, nor could you interrupt it on your own land, because you had no control over the waves of sound; nor could you even have interrupted it by an action, because there was originally no actionable nuisance. It did not hurt anybody as long as the Plaintiff's premises remained as a garden. It did not hurt anybody until the room was built. Therefore it is quite plain that independent of the technical ground, namely the fact of there having been two leases, there would have been no ground for presuming a grant. That puts an end to any notion of prescription ..."

From this decision the defendant appealed. The appeal court held:

Thesiger L.J. (James, Baggalay JJ. concurring):

"The Defendant in this case is the occupier, for the purpose of his business as a confectioner, of a house in *Wigmore Street*. In the rear of the house is a kitchen, and in that kitchen there are now, and have been for over twenty years, two large mortars in which the meat and other materials of the confectionery are pounded. The Plaintiff, who is a physician, is the occupier of a house in *Wimpole Street*, which until recently had a garden at the rear, the wall of which garden was a party-wall between the Plaintiff's and the Defendant's premises, and formed the back wall of the Defendant's kitchen. The Plaintiff has, however, recently built upon the site of the garden a consulting-room, one of the side walls of which is the wall just described. It has been proved that in the case of the mortars, before and at the time of action brought, a noise was caused which seriously inconvenienced the Plaintiff in the use of his consulting-room, and which, unless the Defendant had acquired a right to impose the inconvenience, would constitute an actionable nuisance ...

Here then arises the objection to the acquisition by the Defendant of any easement. That which was done by him was in its nature such that it could not be physically interrupted; it could not at the same time be put a stop to by action. Can user which is neither preventible nor actionable found an easement? We think not ... [T]he laws governing the acquisition of easements by user stands thus: Consent or acquiescence of the owner of the servient tenement lies at the root of prescription, and of the fiction of a lost grant, and hence the acts or user, which go to the proof of either the one or the other, must be, in the language of the civil law, *nec vi nec clam nec precario;* for a man cannot, as a general rule, be said to consent to or acquiesce in the acquisition by his neighbour of an easement through an enjoyment of which he has no knowledge, actual or constructive, or which he contests and endeavours to interrupt, or which he temporarily licenses. It is a mere extension of the same notion, or rather it is a principle into which by strict analysis it may be resolved, to hold, that an enjoyment which a man cannot prevent raises no presumption of consent or acquiescence.

Upon this principle it was decided in *Webb v. Bird* [13 CBA (NS) 841] that currents of air blowing from a particular quarter of the compass, and in *Chasemore v. Richards* [7 HLC 349] that subterranean water percolating through the strata in no known channels, could not be acquired as an easement by user; and in *Angus v. Dalton* [4 QBD 162] a case of lateral support of buildings by adjacent soil, which came on appeal to this Court, the principle was in no way impugned, although it was held by the majority of the Court not to be applicable so as to prevent the acquisition of that particular easement. It is a principle which must be equally appropriate to the case of affirmative as of negative easements; in other words, it is equally unreasonable to imply your consent to your neighbour enjoying something which passes from your tenement to his, as to his subjecting your tenement to something which comes from his, when in both cases you have no power of prevention. But the affirmative easement differs from the negative easement in this, that the latter can under no circumstances be interrupted except by acts done upon the servient tenement, but the former, constituting, as it does, a direct interference with the enjoyment by the servient owner of his tenement, may be the subject of legal proceedings as well as of physical interruption. To put concrete cases—the passage of light and air to your neighbour's windows may be physically interrupted by you, but gives you no legal grounds of complaint against him. The passage of water from his land on to yours may be physically interrupted, or may be treated as a trespass and made the ground of action for damages, or for an injunction, or both. Noise is similar to currents of air and the flow of subterranean and uncertain streams in its practical incapability of physical interruption, but it differs from them in its capability of grounding an action. *Webb v. Bird* and *Chase-more v. Richards* are not, therefore, direct authorities governing the present case. They are, however, illustrations of the principle which ought to govern it; for until the noise, to take this case, became an actionable nuisance, which it did not at any time before the consulting-room was built, the basis of the presumption of the consent, viz., the power of prevention physically or by action, was never present.

It is said that if this principle is applied in cases like the present, and were carried out to its logical consequences, it would result in the most serious practical inconveniences, for a man might go—say into the midst of the tanneries of *Bermondsey*, or into any other locality devoted to a particular trade or manufacture of a noisy or unsavoury character, and, by building a private residence upon a vacant piece of land, put a stop to such trade or manufacture altogether. The case also is put of a blacksmith's forge built away from all habitations, but to which, in course of time, habitations approach. We do not think that either of these hypothetical cases presents any real difficulty. As regards the first, it may be answered that whether anything is a nuisance or not is a question to be determined, not merely by an abstract consideration of the thing itself, but in reference to its circumstances; what would be a nuisance in *Belgrave Square* would not necessarily be so in *Bermondsey*; and where a locality is devoted to a particular trade or manufacture carried on by the traders or manufacturers in a particular and established manner not constituting a public nuisance, Judges and juries would be justified in finding, and may be trusted to find, that the trade or manufacture so carried on in that locality is not a private or actionable wrong. As regards the blacksmith's forge, that is really an idem per idem case with the present. It would be on the one hand in a very high degree unreasonable and undesirable that there should be a right of action for acts which are not in the present condition of the adjoining land, and possibly never will be any annoyance or inconvenience to either its owner or occupier; and it would be on the other hand in an equally degree unjust, and, from a public point of view, inexpedient that the use and value of the adjoining land should, for all time and under all circumstances, be restricted and diminished by reason of the continuance of acts incapable of physical interruption, and which the law gives no power to prevent. The smith in the case supposed might protect himself by taking a sufficient curtilage to ensure what he does from being at any time an annoyance to his neighbour, but the neighbour himself would be powerless in the matter. Individual cases of hardship may occur in the strict carrying out of the principle upon which we found our judgment, but the negation of the principle would lead even more to individual hardship, and would at the same time produce a prejudicial effect upon the development of land for residential purposes. The Master of the Rolls in the Court below took substantially the same view of the matter as ourselves and granted the relief which the Plaintiff prayed for, and we are of opinion that his order is right and should be affirmed, and that this appeal should be dismissed with costs."

CHAPTER 12

RYLANDS v FLETCHER

INTRODUCTION

This tort arose out of a particular case, that of *Rylands v Fletcher* (1868) L.R. 3 H.L. 330. The court granted a remedy for the plaintiffs in this action and in so doing developed a new rule, and what today is recognised as a tort in itself. The rule in *Rylands v Fletcher* imposes liability where the defendant brings onto his or her land a non-natural thing that causes injury by virtue of its escape.

RYLANDS V FLETCHER

Initially this case was considered to be a form of nuisance; today the tort of nuisance and the rule in *Rylands v Fletcher* are considered separate torts.

Rylands v Fletcher
House of Lords (1868) L.R. 3 H.L. 330

Facts: The defendants were mill-owners who had engaged independent contractors to build a reservoir. The independent contractors, unknown to the defendants, built a reservoir over a disused mine shaft which collapsed and flooded the plaintiff's mine. The mine became unworkable as a result.

Issue: The plaintiffs sued in negligence, nuisance and trespass for the damage to the mine. The plaintiff did not succeed under any of these headings, as the case did not fulfill all the elements of the respective torts. Despite the fact that the case did not succeed under these torts, liability was imposed on the defendant, on the basis of a new principle, which is now known as the rule in *Rylands v Fletcher.*

Blackburn J.:

"The plaintiff, though free from all blame on his part, must bear the loss, unless he can establish that it was the consequence of some default for which the defendants are reponsible. The question of law therefore arises, what is the obligation which the law casts on a person who, like the defendants, lawfully brings on his land something which, though harmless whilst it remains there, will naturally do mischief if it escape out of his land. It is agreed on all hands that he must take care to keep in that which he has brought on the land and keeps there, in order that it may not escape and damage his neighbours, but the question arises whether the duty which the law casts upon him, under such circumstances, is an absolute duty to keep it in at his peril, or is, as the majority of the Court of Exchequer have thought, merely a duty to take all reasonable and prudent precautions, in order to keep it in, but no more. If the first be the law, the person who has brought on his land and kept there something dangerous, and failed to keep it in, is responsible for all the natural consequences of its escape. If the second be the limit of his duty, he would not be answerable except on proof of negligence, and consequently would not be answerable for escape arising from any latent defect which ordinary prudence and skill could not detect.

Supposing the second to be the correct view of the law, a further question arises subsidiary to the first, viz., whether the defendants are not so far identified with the contractors whom they employed, as to be responsible for the consequences of their want of care and skill in making the reservoir in fact insufficient with reference to the old shafts, of the existence of which they were aware, though they had not ascertained where the shafts went to.

We think that the true rule of law is, that the person who for his own purposes brings on his lands and collects and keeps there anything likely to do mischief if it escapes, must keep it in at his peril, and, if he does not do so, is *prima facie* answerable for all the damage which is the natural consequence of its escape. He can excuse himself by shewing that the escape was owing to the plaintiff's default; or perhaps that the escape was the consequence of vis major, or the act of God; but as nothing of this sort exists here, it is unnecessary to inquire what excuse would be sufficient. The general rule, as above stated, seems on principle just. The person whose grass or corn is eaten down by the escaping cattle of his neighbour, or whose mine is flooded by the water from his neighbour's reservoir, or whose cellar is invaded by the filth of his neighbour's privy, or whose habitation is made unhealthy by the fumes and noisome vapours of his neighbour's alkali works, is damnified without any fault of his own; and it seems but reasonable and just that the neighbour, who has brought something on his own property which was not naturally there, harmless to others so long as it is confined to his own property, but which he knows to be mischievous if it gets on his neighbour's, should be obliged to make good the damage which ensues if he does not succeed in confining it to his own property. But for his act in bringing it there no mischief could have accrued, and it seems but just that he should at his peril keep it there so that no mischief may accrue, or answer for the natural and anticipated consequences. And upon authority, this we think is established to be the law whether the things so brought be beasts, or water, or filth, or stenches."

Comments and Questions:

1. What are the necessary elements to establish the rule in *Rylands v Fletcher?*

2.   Blackburn J. in his judgment refers to "the person whose grass or corn is eaten down by the escaping cattle", suggesting that cattle can fulfill the rule in *Rylands v Fletcher.* In your opinion would the bringing of cattle onto land be a non-natural use?

3.   The reference to cattle may be misleading; compare Blackburn J.'s judgment on this point to the issue of cattle trespass in Chapter 13.

Non-natural use

Blackburn J. states that a number of elements are necessary to ensure that the rule in *Rylands v Fletcher* is met, including the necessity for the item brought onto the land to be a non-natural use.

Miller v Addie & Sons (Collieries) Ltd.
2D Division [1934] S.C. 150.

Facts: Due to an escape of gas from a service pipe which led to a number of houses, gas made its way into the plaintiff's house while she and her family were asleep. Her husband died and she and her daughter were seriously injured through gas poisoning. The defendants were responsible for the pipes, their upkeep, maintenance and renewal. The pipes were in poor condition, and not protected from corrosion in any way.

Issue: The plaintiff raised a number of arguments, including nuisance, negligence and the rule in *Rylands v Fletcher.* The issue for the court was whether a gas pipe for commercial use was a non-natural use of property. The court held that the laying of gas pipes by a landlord for the supply of gas to dwelling-houses owned by him was a natural and not a non-natural use of his property and, accordingly, that ownership of an ordinary service pipe for the conveyance of gas to a tenant's house was insufficient *per se* and without proof of negligence, to render the landlord liable for injury resulting to the occupants of the house through an escape of gas from the pipe.

Lord Justice-Clerk Aitchison (Lords Hunter and Murray agree in principle):

"It was maintained by the pursuer that, in any event and apart from *culpa*, the defenders were answerable to the pursuer upon the familiar doctrine of *Rylands v. Fletcher* [LR 3 HL 330] and *Kerr v. Earl of Orkney* [20 D. 298]. Coal gas, it was said, is a thing dangerous in itself, and the person who brings it either on to his own land or through land through which he has an access or way leave does so at his own peril so as to make him liable, independently of negligence, for any injury or mischief done to persons or property by its escape. The duty to control and to prevent escape is absolute; the liability where escape occurs is the liability of an insurer, so that the mere happening of the mischief makes the person in possession and control answerable without proof of negligence.

I am unable to agree that these propositions are supported by the authorities referred to. The foundation of the rule in *Rylands v. Fletcher* and *Kerr v. Earl of Orkney* was that the land was put to what was termed a non-natural use what Lord Buckmaster in *Rainham Chemical Works* [[1921] 2 A. C. 465, at p. 471] termed 'the use of land in an exceptional manner' and that thereby there was entailed a special and exceptional obligation to prevent mischief arising through the absence of effective control.

I do not think that that principle can reasonably be applied to the provision of coal gas in an ordinary service pipe. Although such a provision entails risk where care is not exercised, it is not reasonably to be regarded as the introduction of a danger, but rather as the provision of an amenity for domestic use. It is not a non-natural use of land; on the contrary, it is a familiar everyday use both in urban and in rural areas. It cannot, in my view, be classified as an *opus manufactum* such as a dam or reservoir, or fall within the category of nuisance, or something that can only be kept or used at the peril of those who provide it. That does not mean that no liability can arise from its escape, but it does mean that the liability when it arises is a liability based upon negligence, positive or negative, and not upon the mere occurrence of the event. In *Rickards v. Lothian*, [[1913] A. C. 263] which was a case of damage done through an overflow of water from a top floor due to the malicious act of a third party, Lord Moulton, in delivering the judgment of the Privy Council, said this (at p. 274): 'The only duty incumbent upon the defendant in such a case would have been to take reasonable precautions to prevent such an act causing damage.' He further said (at p. 275): 'The legal principle that underlies the decision in *Rylands v. Fletcher* was well known in English law from a very early period, but it was explained and formulated in a strikingly clear and authoritative manner in that case, and therefore is usually referred to by that name. It is nothing more than an application of the old maxim *sic utere tuo ut alienum non laedas*.' Again (at p. 279 *et seq.*) Lord Moulton says: 'There is another ground upon which their Lordships are of opinion that the present case does not come within the principle laid down in *Rylands v. Fletcher*. It is not every use to which land is put that brings into play that principle. It must be some special use bringing with it increased danger to others, and must not merely be the ordinary use of the land or such a use as is proper for the general benefit of the community. To use the language of Lord Robertson in *Eastern and South African Telegraph Co. v. Cape Town Tramways Companies*, [[1902] AC 381 AT 393] the principle of *Rylands v. Fletcher* subjects to a high liability the owner who uses his property for purposes other than those which are natural. In such matters as the domestic supply of water or gas it is essential that the mode of supply should be such as to permit ready access for the purpose of use, and hence it is impossible to guard against wilful mischief. In having on his premises (*i.e.* the premises of the landlord or occupier) such means of supply he is only using those premises in an ordinary and proper manner, and, although he is bound to exercise all reasonable care, he is not responsible for damage not due to his own default, whether that damage be caused by inevitable accident or the wrongful acts of third persons.'

These passages appear to me to make it clear beyond all doubt that the owner of an ordinary service pipe, whether conveying water or gas, from which an escape occurs and does damage, does not *ipso facto* become answerable for the mischief done, but is liable to the person suffering hurt only where the escape is due to negligence on his part. Although the doctrine of *Rylands v. Fletcher* has been recognised in the law of Scotland, I think it is open to doubt whether it has ever been treated as a doctrine of absolute liability."

Lord Anderson:

"The pursuer has also tabled three issues which are based, not on negligence, but on the principle of absolute obligation recognised in the case of *Rylands v. Fletcher*. The main question raised in the appeal was whether these issues fall to be allowed or disallowed ...

The circumstances in which the principle becomes applicable are where property is put to a use which has been variously described as non-natural, exceptional, or extraordinary. Such use is at the peril of the proprietor. If damage results therefrom he is under absolute obligation to make it good; it is not essential that negligence should be charged and proved against him. This doctrine of absolute obligation was authoritatively declared to be part of the common law of England in *Rylands v. Fletcher*, and in later cases in that country the rule has been applied to a variety of differing circumstances. The pursuer contended that this rule of absolute obligation was also part of the common law of Scotland. In my opinion this contention is fully documented by the authorities which were founded on, viz., *Kerr*, [20 D. 298] *Chalmers*, [3 R. 461] and *Caledonian Railway Co.* [1917 SC (H. L.) 56, [1917] A. C. 556].

Do, then, the averments of the pursuer disclose a case of extraordinary or of ordinary user of property? I am of opinion that it is the latter mode of user and not the former which is disclosed. To lead gas or water into a dwelling-house is an ordinary act of necessary administration for the purpose of making the house habitable according to modern standards. This topic is dealt with by Lord Moulton in delivering the judgment of the Privy Council in the case of *Rickards* [[1913] AC 263]. Referring to the principle of *Rylands v. Fletcher*, Lord Moulton (at p. 280) says: 'It is not every use to which land is put that brings into play that principle. It must be some special use bringing with it increased danger to others, and must not merely be the ordinary use of the land or such a use as is proper for the general benefit of the community.' And again (at p. 281) he observes: 'The provision of a proper supply of water to the various parts of a house is not only reasonable, but has become, in accordance with modern sanitary views, an almost necessary feature of town life. It is recognised as being so desirable in the interests of the community that in some form or other it is usually made obligatory in civilised countries. Such a supply cannot be installed without causing some concurrent danger of leakage or overflow. It would be unreasonable for the law to regard those who install or maintain such a system of supply as doing so at their own peril, with an absolute liability for any damage resulting from its presence even when there has been no negligence.' These observations are equally applicable to the taking into a dwelling-house of a supply of gas.

I am therefore of opinion that the pursuer has no relevant averments to support the three issues which rest on the principle of absolute obligation, and that these issues ought therefore to be disallowed."

Comments and Questions:
1. This court here held that the collection of gas for residential property did not amount to a non-natural use. Compare this to the statements made by Blackburn J. in *Rylands v Fletcher* about what amounted to a non-natural user. Based on Blackburn J.'s statements, is the decision in this case too restrictive an interpretation of the rule?

2. Based on this decision the court was of the view that the collection or gathering of gas for the provision of services to a residential property was not a non-natural use. In your opinion, would the court have had a different attitude to the collection of gas for commercial purposes?

Defendant must accumulate or collect the non-natural item

A second element of the rule in *Rylands v Fletcher* is the necessity for the defendant to accumulate or collect the non-natural item onto the property.

Healy v Bray Urban District Council
Supreme Court [1963–1964] Ir. Jur. Rep. 9

Facts: The plaintiff was walking on a public footpath which runs around Bray Head about 100 feet above sea level. She was struck, and seriously injured, by a loose rock which had rolled down the hill.

Issues: The plaintiff sued and relied on the rule laid down in *Rylands v Fletcher*, claiming that the rock which hit her was something of a dangerous nature brought and kept by the council on their land, and that they were responsible for the escape and subsequent damage. The issue the court focused on was the issue of bringing the item onto the property. The court did not find for the plaintiff on the basis that they did not bring the rock onto the property. The rock was on the property as a result of geology and natural forces.

Kingsmill Moore J.:

"Bray Head is a solid bluff of Cambrian rock rising to about 700 feet above sea level, sloping seawards at varying angles. At its base, some 50 feet above sea, runs the railway line, in steep sided cuttings and tunnels cut through the live rock and on rocky ledges and shelves. About fifty feet higher on the landward side and closely parallel with the railway line runs the path. It is separated from the steep slope of the railway cutting by a carefully built masonry wall 2'6" high and on the other side of the path a mass concrete wall 2' high supports the earth and prevents it from shingling down on to the path. The surface of the path appears to be compacted stones and gravel and from the photographs it is clear that the path, at all events where the accident occurred, was at some time cut out of the hillside and, with its side walls, artificially constructed at a considerable expenditure of time and labour. Above the path the side of the head stretches up to a height of over 600 feet. The gradient is at an angle of 30° to 38° and the surface is covered with a natural growth of bracken, furze, brambles and coarse grass. In this vegetation, buried or partially buried, lie some stones and boulders, the result of past erosion, and in places the rock outcrops in small knolls of bare stone, the lower sides of which lie at a somewhat steeper angle than the main slope. Except for the walls to which I am about to refer the slope appears never to have been interfered with by the hand of man and to have reached its present state as a result of natural agencies—water, wind, ice, sun and frost—operating throughout the many millions of years since the formation was laid down.

There are on the hillside two stone walls substantially built and apparently of considerable age, which are admittedly boundary walls of the property conveyed by the deed of 1923, though in age antedating that conveyance. One stretches straight up the slope and forms the boundary between that property and the Meath estate. The other runs parallel with the path and about 25 feet above it and constitutes the boundary between the property and the land formerly owned by the railway. It was claimed by the plaintiff that this wall was built as a protection for persons using the path against any stones that might roll down the slope, and undoubtedly, so long as it was intact, it would have served to intercept anything but a large boulder: but the trial judge, on a comparison of this wall with the other wall and on admitted fact that it ran along the boundary of the two properties, told the jury, rightly in my opinion, that it should be regarded as a boundary wall and that there was nothing to warrant the conclusion that it was built to protect the path. This wall, though clearly very old, is generally in good repair but over one stretch of about 30 yards someone has removed the coping stones and immediately above the spot where the accident happened there is a gap about 15 feet wide at the top and 9 feet wide at ground level. It is not a new gap, for the grass has grown over it and there is no sign of the stones which must have come from it; and no evidence was given to fix even its approximate age.

The circumstances which led to the fall of the stone are established in broad outline. Six boys were descending the Head in a straggling group and the stone was dislodged from where it was lying by one of them, either accidentally or wantonly. It rolled down the hill, found its way through the gap in the wall and came to rest in the middle of the path, striking the plaintiff just as it came to rest. In weight it was between two and three hundred-weight …

The rule in *Rylands v Fletcher* has no application. In that case the rule was stated by Blackburn J in the Exchequer Chamber as follows—'The true rule of the law is that the person who for his own purpose brings on his lands and collects and keeps there anything likely to do mischief if it escapes, must keep it at his peril.' The defendant did not bring the rocks or outcrop on to [their] land for their own purpose (or at all). They are there as a result of natural forces operation in geological time, as indeed is the land. They are, in short, the land itself and not things brought on to it. See also *Pondardawe RDC v. Moore-Gwyn* [1929 1 Ch 656, a decision of Eve J which appears to me to be clearly correct."

Escape

A third element of the rule in *Rylands v Fletcher* is the necessity for there to be an escape of the dangerous or non-natural substance. This means that the non-natural substance or item must leave the boundaries of the defendant's property.

Read v J Lyons & Co. Ltd.
House of Lords [1947] A.C. 156

Facts: The appellant was employed as an inspector of munitions by the Ministry of Supply, and in the course of her duties she was injured by an explosion in a munitions factory. In the same explosion a man was killed and the inspector and others were injured. The explosion occurred during the manufacturing process and no negligence was alleged.

Issue: The plaintiff sought to rely on the rule in *Rylands v Fletcher*. The issue before the court was whether all elements of the rule had been met; the focus was the issue of escape, and there was also an important discussion of the issue of unnatural use of the land. The court held that the plaintiff could not succeed in damages as there had been no escape of any dangerous thing from the premises of the defendant and accordingly an essential condition for the application of the rule in *Rylands v Fletcher* was not present.

Viscount Simon (Lord Macmillan, Lord Simonds and Lord Uthwatt agreed in principle with both Viscount Simon and Lord Porter):

"Blackburn J., in delivering the judgment of the Court of Exchequer Chamber in *Fletcher v. Rylands* laid down the proposition that 'the person who for his own purposes brings on his lands and collects and keeps there anything likely to do mischief if it escapes, must keep it in at his peril, and, if he does not do so, is prima facie answerable for all the damage which is the natural consequence of its escape.' ...

Now, the strict liability recognized by this House to exist in *Rylands v. Fletcher* is conditioned by two elements which I may call the condition of 'escape' from the land of something likely to do mischief if it escapes, and the condition of 'non-natural use' of the land. This second condition has in some later cases, which did not reach this House, been otherwise expressed, e.g., as 'exceptional' user, when such user is not regarded as 'natural' and at the same time is likely to produce mischief if there is an 'escape.' Dr. Stallybrass, in a learned article on Dangerous Things and Non-Natural User of Land in 3 Cambridge Law Journal, p. 376, has collected the large variety of epithets that have been judicially employed in this connexion. The American Restatement of the Law of Torts, vol. 3, s. 519, speaks of 'ultra-hazardous activity,' but attaches qualifications which would appear in the present instance to exonerate the respondents. It is not necessary to analyse this second condition on the present occasion, for in the case now before us the first essential condition of 'escape' does not seem to me to be present at all. 'Escape,' for the purpose of applying the proposition in *Rylands v. Fletcher*, means escape from a place where the defendant has occupation of or control over land to a place which is outside his occupation or control. Blackburn J. several times refers to the defendant's duty as being the duty of 'keeping a thing in' at the defendant's peril and by 'keeping in' he does not mean preventing an explosive substance from exploding but preventing a thing which may inflict mischief from escaping from the area which the defendant occupies or controls. In two well-known cases the same principle of strict liability for escape was applied to defendants who held a franchise to lay pipes under a highway and to conduct water (or gas) under pressure through them *(Charing Cross Electricity Supply Co. v. Hydraulic Power Co.* [[1914] 3 K. B. 772]; *Northwestern Utilities, Ld. v. London Guarantee & Accident Co.* [1936] A. C. 108). In *Howard v. Furness Houlder Argentine Lines, Ld.* [41 Com. Cas. 290], Lewis J. had before him a case of injury caused by an escape of steam on board a ship where the plaintiff was working. The learned judge was, I think, right in refusing to apply the doctrine of *Rylands v. Fletcher*, on the ground that the injuries were caused on the premises of the defendants. Apart altogether from the judge's doubt (which I share) whether the owners of the steamship by generating steam therein are making a non-natural use of their steamship, the other condition upon which the proposition in *Rylands v. Fletcher* depends was not present, any more than it is in the case with which we have now to deal. Here there is no escape of the relevant kind at all and the appellant's action fails on that ground ...

On the much litigated question of what amounts to 'non-natural' use of land, the discussion of which is also unnecessary in the present appeal, I content myself with two further observations. The first is that when it becomes essential for the House to examine this question it will, I think, be found that Lord

Moulton's analysis in delivering the judgment of the Privy Council in *Rickards v. Lothian* [1913] AC 263 is of the first importance. The other observation is as to the decision of this House in *Rainham Chemical Works, Ld. v. Belvedere Fish Guano Co., Ld.* [[1921] 2 AC 465], to which the appellant's counsel in the present case made considerable reference in support of the proposition that manufacturing explosives was a 'non-natural' use of land ... I think it not improper to put on record, with all due regard to the admission and dicta in that case, that if the question had hereafter to be decided whether the making of munitions in a factory at the Government's request in time of war for the purpose of helping to defeat the enemy is a 'non-natural' use of land, adopted by the occupier 'for his own purposes,' it would not seem to me that the House would be bound by this authority to say that it was. In this appeal the question is immaterial, as I hold that the appellant fails for the reason that there was no 'escape' from the respondents' factory. I move that the appeal be dismissed with costs."

Lord Porter:

"[A]re the occupiers of a munitions factory liable to one of those working in that factory who is injured in the factory itself by an explosion occurring there without any negligence on the part of the occupiers or their servants? Normally at the present time in an action of tort for personal injuries if there is no negligence there is no liability. To this rule however the appellant contends that there are certain exceptions, one of the best known of which is to be found under the principle laid down in *Rylands v. Fletcher*. The appellant relied upon that case and naturally put it in the forefront of his argument. To make the rule applicable, it is at least necessary for the person whom it is sought to hold liable to have brought on to his premises or at any rate to some place over which he has a measure of control, something which is dangerous in the sense that, if it escapes, it will do damage. Possibly a further requisite is that to bring the thing to the position in which it is found is to make a non-natural use of that place. Such at any rate appears to have been the opinion of Lord Cairns L.C. and this limitation has more than once been repeated and approved—see *Rickards v. Lothian* [[1913] A. C. 263, 280], per Lord Moulton. Manifestly these require-ments must give rise to difficulty in applying the rule in individual cases and necessitate at least a decision as to what can be dangerous and what is a non-natural use ... I do not, however, think that it is necessary for your Lordships to decide these matters now, in as much as the defence admits that high-explosive shells are dangerous things and, whatever view may be formed as to whether the filling of them is or is not a non-natural use of land, the present case can, in my opinion, be determined upon a narrower ground. In all cases which have been decided, it has been held necessary, in order to establish liability, that there should have been some form of escape from the place in which the dangerous object has been retained by the defendant to some other place not subject to his control. In *Rylands v. Fletcher* it was water, in *Rainham Chemical Works, Ld. v. Belvedere Fish Guano Co., Ld.* [[1921] 2 A. C. 465], it was explosive matter, in *National Telephone Co. v. Baker* [[1933] 2 Ch. 186], it was electricity, in *Northwestern Utilities, Ld. v. London Guarantee & Accident Co., Ld.* [(1936) A. C. 108], it was gas which escaped from the defendant's mains into property belonging to the plaintiff, and so on, in the other instances. In every case, even in *Charing Cross Electricity Supply Co. v. Hydraulic Power Co.* [[1914] 3 K. B. 772], there was escape from the container in which the defendants had a right to carry the dangerous substance, and which they had at least a licence to use, and also an escape into property over which they had no control. Such escape is, I think, necessary if the principle of *Rylands v. Fletcher* is to apply. The often quoted words of Blackburn J. in that case in the Court of Exchequer Chamber are 'it seems but reasonable and just that the neighbour, who has brought something on his own property which was not naturally there, harmless to others so long as it is confined to his own property, but which he knows to be mischievous if it gets to his neighbour's, should be obliged to make good the damage which ensues if he does not succeed in confining it to his own property,' and in *Howard v. Furness Houlder Argentine Lines, Ld.* [41 Com. Cas. 290], Lewis J. so decided in a judgment with the result of which I agree. The limitations within which the judgment of Blackburn J. confines the doctrine have all been the subject of discussion, more particularly as to who is a neighbour, whether knowledge of the danger is a condition of liability and how far personal injuries are covered, but I know of no case where liability was imposed for injury occurring on the property in which the dangerous thing was confined.

It was urged upon your Lordships that it would be a strange result to hold the respondents liable if the injured person was just outside their premises but not liable if she was just within them. There is force in the objection, but the liability is itself an extension of the general rule and, in my view, it is undesirable to extend it further. As Lindley L. J. said in *Green v. Chelsea Waterworks Co.* [70 L. T. 547]: 'That case, *(Rylands v. Fletcher)* is not to be extended beyond the legitimate principle on which the House of Lords decided it. If it were extended as far as strict logic might require, it would be a very oppressive decision.' Much of the width of principle which has been ascribed to it is derived not from the decision itself but from the illustrations by which Blackburn J. supported it. Too much stress must not in my opinion be laid upon these illustrations. They are but instances of the application of the rule of strict liability, having for the most part separate historical origins and though they support the view that liability may exist in cases where neither negligence, nuisance nor trespass are to be found, yet it need not as I think necessarily be said that they form a separate coherent class, in which liability is created by the same elements throughout."

Comments and Questions:
1. Assume there were two munitions inspectors. Both were in the process of leaving; one was outside the premises and the other was a few steps behind, but still on the premises. The explosion occurred and both were injured. How would you advise the munitions inspectors?

Damage

An essential element of *Rylands v Fletcher* is the necessity for damage to occur as a result of the escape. In the case of *Healy v Bray UDC* above it seems clear that the Irish courts were willing to consider the right of a non-occupier of land to sue for personal injuries under the rule in *Rylands v Fletcher.* In *Hanrahan v Merck Sharpe & Dohme* [1988] I.L.R.M. 629 the plaintiff claimed for personal injuries under the rule in *Rylands v Fletcher,* and while the case was ultimately determined as a case of nuisance (see Chapter 11), the court raised no objection to the plaintiff's claim. The position in the United Kingdom is different on this issue as can be seen in the case of *Transco v Stockport MBC* [2003] 3 W.L.R. 1467.

Transco v Stockport Metropolitan Borough Council
House of Lords [2003] U.K.H.L. 61, [2004] 1 All E.R. 589, 91 Con. L.R. 28

Facts: The defendant, a local authority, owned a block of flats. The flats were supplied with water for the domestic use of the residents. The water was carried to the flats by means of a pipe which led to a storage tank in the basement. The pipe failed and due to the fact that the leak was not detected for some time a considerable amount of water escaped. The water percolated an embankment which supported the plaintiff's high pressure gas main, and caused the embankment to collapse leaving the gas main exposed and unsupported. The plaintiff repaired the damage and sought to recover the cost of the repairs relying on the rule in *Rylands v Fletcher.*

Issue: This case gave the House of Lords a chance to review the scope and application, in modern conditions, of the rule of law laid down in *Rylands v Fletcher.* A number of issues arose in this case; one such issue was the request that the House of Lords follow Australian authority and treat the rule in *Rylands v Fletcher* as having been absorbed by the principles of ordinary negligence. The House of Lords decided not to follow the Australian example. The issue that is highlighted below relates to their Lordships' views on the type of damage actionable under the rule in *Rylands v Fletcher.*

Lord Bingham (Lord Hobhouse, Lord Scott and Lord Walker were in general agreement on this issue):

"… The rule in *Rylands v Fletcher* is a sub-species of nuisance, which is itself a tort based on the interference by one occupier of land with the right in or enjoyment of land by another occupier of land as such. From this simple proposition two consequences at once flow. First, as very clearly decided by the House in *Read v J Lyons & Co Ltd* [1946] 2 All ER 471, [1947] AC 156, no claim in nuisance or under the rule can arise if the events complained of take place wholly on the land of a single occupier. There must, in other words, be an escape from one tenement to another. Second, the claim cannot include a claim for death or personal injury, since such a claim does not relate to any right in or enjoyment of land. This proposition has not been authoritatively affirmed by any decision at the highest level. It was left open by Parker LJ in *Perry v Kendricks Transport Ltd* [1956] 1 All ER 154 at 160–161, [1956] 1 WLR 85 at 92, and is inconsistent with decisions such as *Shiffman v Venerable Order of the Hospital of St John of Jerusalem* [1936] 1 All ER 557 and *Miles v Forest Rock Granite Co (Leicestershire) Ltd* (1918) 34 TLR 500. It is however clear from Lord Macmillan's opinion in *Read's* case [1946] 2 All ER 471 at 476, [1947] AC 156 at 170–171 that he regarded a personal injury claim as outside the scope of the rule, and his approach is in my opinion strongly fortified by the decisions of the House in the *Cambridge Water case* [1994] 1 All ER 53, [1994] 2 AC 264 *and Hunter v Canary Wharf Ltd, Hunter v London Docklands Development Corp* [1997] 2 All ER 426, [1997] AC 655, in each of which nuisance was identified as a tort directed, and directed only, to the protection of interests in land …"

Lord Hoffmann:

"… In some cases in the first half of the twentieth century plaintiffs recovered damages under the rule for personal injury: *Shiffman v Venerable Order of the Hospital of St John of Jerusalem* [1936] 1 All ER 557 and *Hale v Jennings Bros* [1938] 1 All ER 579 are examples. But dicta in *Read's* case cast doubt upon whether the rule protected anything beyond interests in land. Lord Macmillan ([1946] 2 All ER 471 at 476, [1947] AC 156 at 170–171) was clear that it had no application to personal injury and Lord Simonds ([1946] 2 All ER 471 at 481, [1947] AC 156 at 180) was doubtful. But I think that the point is now settled by two recent decisions of the House of Lords: *Cambridge Water Co Ltd v Eastern Counties Leather plc* [1994] 1 All ER 53, [1994] 2 AC 264, which decided that *Rylands v Fletcher* is a special form of nuisance and *Hunter v Canary Wharf Ltd, Hunter v London Docklands Development Corp* [1997] 2 All ER 426, [1997] AC 655, which decided that nuisance is a tort against land. It must, I think, follow that damages for personal injuries are not recoverable under the rule …

I pause at this point to summarise the very limited circumstances to which the rule has been confined. First, it is a remedy for damage to land or interests in land. As there can be few properties in the country, commercial or domestic, which are not insured against damage by flood and the like, this means that disputes over the application of the rule will tend to be between property insurers and liability insurers. Secondly, it does not apply to works or enterprises authorised by statute. That means that it will usually have no application to really high-risk activities. As Professor Simpson points out ([1984] 13 JLS 225) the Bradfield Reservoir was built under statutory powers. In the absence of negligence, the occupiers whose lands had been inundated would have had no remedy. Thirdly, it is not particularly strict because it excludes liability when the escape is for the most common reasons, namely vandalism or unusual natural events. Fourthly, the cases in which there is an escape which is not attributable to an unusual natural event or the act of a third party will, by the same token, usually give rise to an inference of negligence. Fifthly, there is a broad and ill-defined exception for 'natural' uses of land. It is perhaps not surprising that counsel could not find a reported case since the 1939–45 war in which anyone had succeeded in a claim under the rule. It is hard to escape the conclusion that the intellectual effort devoted to the rule by judges and writers over many years has brought forth a mouse."

Comments and Questions:
1. The distinction between the Irish position and the English position is significant. The refusal of a remedy under the rule in *Rylands v Fletcher* for personal injury narrows the scope of the rule considerably in the English courts.

Defences

The final element of the rule in *Rylands v Fletcher* concerns defences. There are a number of defences available: act of a stranger, act of God, or statutory authority, as well as the general defences which are reviewed in Chapter 14.

Act of a stranger

Perry v Kendricks Transport Ltd.
Court of Appeal [1956] 1 W.L.R. 85

Facts: The plaintiff, a boy of 10, was injured by the explosion of petrol fumes from the tank of a disused coach on the defendant's parking grounds. The petrol had been drained out and a cap screwed onto the tank. As the plaintiff approached the parking ground he saw two other boys standing on the edge of the grounds and when he was level with the coach the boys jumped away and immediately the explosion occurred. The trial judge found that the screw cap had been removed by someone unknown and that one of the two boys had thrown a lighted match into the tank.

Issue: The plaintiff claimed that the rule in *Rylands v Fletcher* applied and that the defendants had kept on their land a dangerous object likely to do mischief if it escaped. The court focused on the issue of the escape of the dangerous fumes and the explosion caused by the acts of a stranger, and had to determine whether the defendant could be held responsible for those acts. In this case the court did not address whether the rule applied to personal injuries or not, as it was shown that the escape of the dangerous fumes and the explosion were caused by the act of a stranger. Therefore, the defendant came within the exception to the rule in *Rylands v Fletcher*, unless the plaintiff could show that the act which caused the escape was of a kind that the defendant could reasonably foresee and protect against. The plaintiff was unable to do this, and so failed in his action.

Singleton L.J.:

"... The second way in which the case is put by the plaintiff is that the motor-coach placed upon the defendants' land was something of a kind likely to do mischief if it escaped, or if something from it escaped, and that the defendants, having it upon their land, must keep it and fumes or flames from it upon their land at their peril ... I suppose that an ordinary person would have thought that the tank or the coach and the tank would be safer if the petrol was removed from the tank than if the petrol was left in the tank, but upon the evidence given by the inspector of the Dudley Fire Brigade it may be said that an empty tank is more dangerous than a full tank, that is, if there has been petrol in it. Upon the evidence of the inspector, Mr. King-Hamilton submitted that here was a dangerous coach, for there might well be an accident through fumes from the tank escaping if the cap was taken off. It appears clear upon the facts, and upon the case put forward by the plaintiff, that there was interference by someone with the coach and with the cap on the top of the tank.

The principle laid down in *Fletcher v. Rylands* may be avoided or may cease to be applicable if the harm done was due to the act of a stranger. If the mischievous, deliberate and conscious act of a stranger causes the damage, the occupier can escape liability; he is absolved. That is clear from a number of authorities. The one referred to by the judge is *Box v. Jubb* [(1879) 4 Ex. D. 76]. I do not cite it directly. It is sufficient if I take a passage from the speech of Lord Moulton in *Rickards v. Lothian* [[1913] AC 263, 279; 29 TLR 281]. Lord Moulton, having referred to *Rylands v. Fletcher,* said:

> 'Following the language of this judgment their Lordships are of opinion that no better example could be given of an agent that the defendant cannot control than that of a third party surreptitiously and by a malicious act causing the overflow. The same principle is affirmed in the case of *Box v. Jubb*. In that case the defendants had a reservoir on their land which was connected both for supply and discharge with a watercourse or main drain. Through the sudden emptying of another reservoir into the drain at a higher level than their reservoir and by the blocking of the main drain below, the defendants' reservoir was made to overflow, and damage was done to the lands of the plaintiff. The defendants were guilty of no negligence either in the construction or maintenance of the reservoir, and the acts which led to its overflow were done by

persons over whom they had no control. In giving judgment Kelly C.B. says: "The question is, what was the cause of this overflow? Was it anything for which the defendants are responsible? Did it proceed from their act or default, or from that of a stranger over which they had no control? The case is abundantly clear on this, proving beyond a doubt that the defendants had no control over the causes of the overflow and no knowledge of the existence of the obstruction. The matters complained of took place through no default or breach of duty of the defendants, but were caused by a stranger over whom and at a spot where they had no control. It seems to me to be immaterial whether this is called vis major or the unlawful act of a stranger; it is sufficient to say that the defendants had no means of preventing the occurrence. I think the defendants could not possibly have been expected to anticipate that which happened here, and the law does not require them to construct their reservoir and the sluices and gates leading to it to meet any amount of pressure which the wrongful act of a third person may impose." Their Lordships agree with the law as laid down in the judgments above cited, and are of opinion that a defendant is not liable on the principle of *Fletcher v. Rylands* for damage caused by the wrongful acts of third persons.'

In the present case there were two acts which had to happen before the damage could be done. The first was the removal of the cap. By whom that was done there is nothing to show. The second is the throwing into the tank of a lighted match which immediately brought about flames and which caused injury to this young boy. The two boys who were near the plaintiff, and who were up against the coach as he approached, were about the same age as the plaintiff, about 10 years old ...

I am prepared to accept this position. If the person who interferes with something of the defendants is a person whom they might expect to be upon their ground, and if the character of the interference is something which they ought to anticipate, then they do owe some duty. The measure of that duty depends upon the circumstances, the nature of the object, and the age of the children. I do not think that it can extend to that which happened in this case. Someone removed the cap. Someone threw the lighted match into the tank. There is no evidence to show that either of those things ought to be anticipated. If it is said that because boys pass through a parking ground there is a duty on the owner of the vehicle or the occupier of the parking ground who has a vehicle there to see that the cap is not removed from the petrol tank, in other words, to lock by a padlock or otherwise the cap, that is something new, in my view. I do not know the basis on which it can be said that the occupier must anticipate that kind of thing: still less do I think that the occupier ought to anticipate that a boy of 10 would throw a lighted match into the tank. There is nothing to show that it has ever been done before and I hope it will never be done again. A boy of 10 years of age knows that it is wrong. He knows that he is asking for trouble if he does it. That, I think, is shown by the fact that both boys jumped back. The match was thrown into the tank mischievously and deliberately. It cannot be said that it was something which the defendants ought to have anticipated, and it was the act of one who was not under their control in any sense. He was a stranger."

Jenkins L.J.:

"… I am prepared to accept the view that this motor-coach, in the condition in which it was on the defendants' land, was an object of the class to which the rule in *Rylands v. Fletcher* applies, that is to say, that it was for this purpose a dangerous thing, so that the defendants were under an obligation under the rule to prevent it, or the dangerous element in it, escaping on to a neighbour's land and doing damage there. It was a dangerous thing for this purpose in that its tank contained inflammable petrol vapour. But the fact that it was a thing to which the rule in *Rylands v. Fletcher* applied, and the fact that the vapour escaped and was ignited and did damage, cannot conclude the matter against the defendants, because, as is well settled, an occupant of land cannot be held liable under the rule if the act bringing about the escape was the act of a stranger, and not any act or omission of the occupier himself or his servant or agent, or any defect, latent or patent, in the arrangements made for keeping the dangerous thing under control. In this case, it seems to me plain that the escape was caused by the act of a stranger or strangers in the shape of one or both of the two small boys Whittaker and Rawlinson.

Mr. King-Hamilton submitted that a child cannot for this purpose be a stranger because ability should not be imputed to a child of doing a conscious and deliberate act when he does such a thing as setting fire to petrol vapour in the tank of a vehicle. Speaking for myself, I see no necessity to confine the exception from the rule in *Rylands v. Fletcher* of acts of strangers to acts which proceed from the conscious volition or the deliberate act of the stranger. It seems to me that the relevance of the exception is that the stranger is regarded as a person over whose acts the occupier of the land has no control. Then the real cause of the escape is not the occupier's action in having the dangerous thing on his land: nor is it any failure on his part, or on the part of his agents, in keeping the dangerous thing on the land: nor is it due to any latent or patent defect in his protective measures. The real cause is none of these things. The real cause is the act of the stranger, for whose acts the occupier of the land is in no sense responsible, because he cannot control them."

Parker L.J.:

"… It has for a long time been an exception to the rule if the defendants can show that the act which brought about the escape was the act of a stranger, meaning thereby, someone over whom they had no control. The acts in question here, firstly, of removing the petrol cap, and, secondly, of inserting a lighted match, are, as it seems to me, prima facie undoubtedly the acts of strangers in that sense. Mr. King-Hamilton, however, contends that, nevertheless, since at any rate the last of those acts, the insertion of the lighted match, was almost certainly the act of a young child, the exception does not apply, and for this reason, so he says, that in law the act of a young child is not a novus actus interveniens. Speaking for myself, I do not think the matter can be approached in quite that way. In a *Rylands v. Fletcher* case the plaintiff need only prove the escape. The onus is then on the defendants to bring themselves within one of the exceptions. Once they prove that the escape was caused by the act of a stranger, whether an adult or a child, they escape liability, unless the plaintiff can go on to show that the act which caused the escape was an act of the kind which the occupier could reasonably have anticipated and guarded against. In that connexion it seems to me that it is not sufficient for the plaintiff to show that the defendants knew that children played in the vehicle park, played on the roof of a motor or inside a coach. They must show that the defendants reasonably should have anticipated an act of a kind which would cause the escape."

Comments and Questions:

1. The involvement of the act of a stranger does not in itself raise this defence. If a plaintiff can establish that the act which caused the escape was of a kind that a defendant could reasonably foresee and protect against then the defendant may still be liable.

Act of God

Superquinn Ltd. v Bray Urban District Council
High Court [1998] 3 I.R. 542

Facts: The plaintiff owned a premises on the banks of a river. The action was initially lodged against five potential defendants, but continued only as against the first, third and fourth. The first defendant was a sanitary authority; the third a drainage construction company (working for the first defendant); and the fourth was the owner of an artificial lake located upstream from the plaintiff's premises. The incident occurred on the night of August 26, 1986 during a storm known as "Hurricane Charlie"; the river burst its banks and caused extensive flooding to the plaintiff's premises. It was alleged that the first defendant contributed to the flooding because of the manner in which the drainage construction works had obstructed the flow of the river. It was alleged that the third defendant was liable in the manner the works were carried out. It was alleged that the fourth defendant was liable for failing to properly use and maintain the dam and to provide and maintain an effective arrangement for releasing waters from the reservoir when the level of the reservoir rose.

Issues: An action under the rule in *Rylands v Fletcher* was only raised against the fourth defendant. The question for the court was to determine whether the fourth defendant was absolved from liability for the consequence of the dam failure by reliance on the defence of Act of God or *vis major.* The court had to address what test was to be applied; and whether the defendant could reasonably have anticipated or guarded against this occurrence. The court held that the first named defendant (and the third defendant who worked for them) was immune from an action based on nuisance and free from liability unless it was negligent in the exercise of its statutory duty (see Chapter 11). The court determined that there was an Act of God or *vis major* and that the test to be applied was whether the storm could reasonably have been anticipated or guarded against by the fourth named defendants.

Laffoy J.:

"The Storm

The Little Bray area had experienced flooding prior to 1986. There had been flooding within living memory in November, 1965, and there were records of severe flooding in 1905, coincidentally on the 25th August in that year. However, the storm, which was caused by an offshoot depression from 'Hurricane Charlie', which hit the Wicklow and Dublin areas on the 25th August, 1986, was exceptional. It occasioned publication by the meteorological service of a supplement to the Monthly Weather Bulletin for August, 1986 ...

That gloomy picture is reflected in the rainfall records maintained by the meteorological service. Over the twenty-four hour duration of the storm from 8.00 a.m. (0900 GMT) on the 25th August to 8.00 a.m. (0900 GMT) on the 26th August, the recorded rainfall in the Dargle and Upper Dodder catchments ranged from 80 mm in low lying areas to at least 250 mm in the highest areas with a considerable amount of the catchment which was located at middle levels recording 150 mm to 200 mm rainfall. At Bray garda station 86 mm was recorded during that twenty-four hour period. Rainfall of that magnitude at a low lying station has a return period of one hundred years ...

The overall picture which the data recorded by the meteorological service paints of the storm on the 25th and 26th August, 1986, is of heavy persistent rain which produced exceptional one day rainfall totals which, applying the methodology of the Flood Studies Report, to which I will refer later, produced a return period from one in fifty years to one in one hundred years. The rainfall was accompanied by strong to gale force winds. The storm followed a number of other active weather systems which affected Ireland and gave high rainfalls earlier in the month. There was very little soil moisture deficit even in low lying areas ...

Is the fourth defendant liable under the rule—in Rylands v. Fletcher?

... The decision in *Rylands v. Fletcher* itself is authority for the proposition that the creation of an artificial lake or reservoir is a non-natural use. The nature of the liability of a defendant for the escape of dangerous things has been clarified recently by the House of Lords in *Cambridge Water Co. v. Eastern Counties Plc.*

[1994] 2 A.C. 264, in which it was held that forseeability of harm of the relevant type by the defendant is a prerequisite of the recovery of damages both in nuisance and under the rule in *Rylands v. Fletcher*. In the light of that decision the nature of the liability of a defendant under the rule in *Rylands v. Fletcher* is summarised as follows in *Charlesworth and Percy on Negligence*, 9th ed., at p. 893:—

> 'The escape of a dangerous thing does not found an action unless the defendant knew of, or could reasonably have foreseen, the type of damage that would arise if it escaped and upon which the claim is based. Liability is strict only in the sense that if the defendant did know of the risk, or at least could reasonably have foreseen it, he is liable for the damage caused, notwithstanding the exercise of reasonable care to prevent an escape.'

In my view, the fourth defendant could reasonably have foreseen that, if the dam at Paddock pond failed and the impounded water escaped, it would flow *via* the gorge and the watercourse into the Dargle and that damage in the nature of flooding of the riparian properties downstream would ensue. In my view, the circumstances of the escape of water from the Paddock pond on the night of the 25th August, 1986, came fairly and squarely within the ambit of the rule in *Rylands v Fletcher* and, unless the fourth defendant has established one of the excusing factors recognised as constituting a defence to liability under that rule, the fourth defendant is liable to the plaintiff provided the plaintiff has established that the flooding of its premises was caused or contributed to by the water from the Paddock pond.

The defence which the fourth defendant claims absolves it from liability is Act of God. Counsel, on behalf of the fourth defendant, relied on *Nichols v. Marsland* (1876) 2 Ex. D. 1, which is described in McMahon and Binchy on *Irish Law of Torts,* 2nd ed., at p. 491 as the only reported decision in which the defence of Act of God has been successful, in support of his contention that the dam failure was caused by Act of God. The facts in that case, as set out in the judgment of Mellish L.J., were that the defendant was the owner of a series of artificial ornamental lakes, which had existed for a great number of years, and had never previous to the 18th June, 1872, caused any damage. On that day, however, after a most unusual fall of rain, the lakes overflowed, the dams at their end gave way, and the water out of the lakes carried away the county bridges lower downstream. The jury found that there was no negligence either in the construction or the maintenance of the reservoirs, but that, if the flood could have been anticipated, the effect might have been prevented. Mellish, L.J. distinguished the case before him on the facts from *Rylands v. Fletcher* stating:—

> 'But the present case is distinguished from that of *Rylands v. Fletcher* in this, that it is not the act of the defendant in keeping this reservoir, an act in itself lawful, which alone leads to the escape of the water, and so renders wrongful that which but for such escape would have been lawful. It is the supervening *vis major* of the water caused by the flood, which, superadded to the water in the reservoir (which of itself would have been innocuous), causes the disaster.'

Having stated that the opinion of the Court of Appeal was that the defendant was entitled to excuse herself by proving that the water escaped through the Act of God, Mellish L.J. went on to say:—

> 'The remaining question is, did the defendant make out that the escape of the water was owing to the Act of God? Now the jury have distinctly found, not only that there was no negligence in the construction or the maintenance of the reservoirs, but that the flood was so great that it could not reasonably have been anticipated, although, if it had been anticipated the effect might have been prevented; and this seems to us in substance a finding that the escape of the water was owing to the act of God. However great the flood had been, if it had not been greater than floods that had happened before and might be expected to occur again, the defendant might not have made out that she was free from fault; but we think she ought not to be held liable because she did not prevent the effect of an extraordinary act of nature, which she could not anticipate ...'

It was indeed ingeniously argued for the appellant that at any rate the escape of the water was not owing solely to the Act of God, because the weight of the water originally in the reservoirs must have contributed to break down the dams, as well as the extraordinary water brought in by the flood. We think, however, that the extraordinary quantity of water brought in by the flood is in point of law the sole proximate cause of the escape of the water. It is the last drop which makes the cup overflow.

Counsel for the fourth defendant emphasised the similarity on the facts of *Nichols v. Marsland* (1876) 2 Ex.D. 1 and the instant case and urged that *Nichols v. Marsland* should be followed. He submitted that the decision in *Dockeray v. Manor Park Homebuilders Ltd.* (Unreported, High Court, O'Hanlon J., the 10th April, 1995), the only recent Irish authority in which the defence of Act of God in a similar context to this case was considered, is distinguishable on the facts. Having recognised that Act of God or *vis major* could, in appropriate circumstances, afford a defence to a claim under the rule in *Rylands v. Fletcher*, and having quoted a passage from McMahon and Binchy at p. 492 to the effect that it would appear that 'only the most extreme of natural phenomena' will afford a good defence, O'Hanlon J. went on to says:—

> 'In the present case, while the rainfall on the 26th May, 1993, and again on the 11th June, 1993, was of extraordinarily high proportions, I do not consider that it was of such a phenomenal nature as to justify the description of Act of God. It will be recalled that some of the witnesses giving expert evidence on the topic indicated that such events might be expected to recur on a 20 year cycle, and other expert evidence indicated clearly that it was a wise precaution when developing a building site not to leave the entire sewerage and drainage system wide open to the ingress of storm-waters at any time.'

The plaintiff's response to the fourth defendant's submission was that in *Greenock Corporation v. Caledonian Railway* [1917] A.C. 556, the finding of fact by the jury in *Nichols v. Marsland* (1876) 2 Ex.D. 1 was thought to be wrong by the House of Lords, which approved of the decision in *Kerr v. Earl of Orkney* (1857) 20 D. Sess. Cas. 298 on which the plaintiff relied. In the latter case Clerk Hope L.J. said at p. 302:—

> '… if a person chooses upon a stream to make a great operation for collecting and damming up the water for whatever purpose, he is bound, as the necessary condition of such an operation, to accomplish his object in such a way as to protect all persons lower down the stream from all danger. He must secure them against danger. It is not sufficient that he took all the pains which were thought at the time necessary and sufficient. They were exposed to no danger before the operation. He creates the danger, and he must secure them against danger, so as to make them as safe notwithstanding his dam as they were before. It is no defence in such a case to allege the dam would have stood against all ordinary rains—it gave way in an extraordinary and unprecedented fall of rain, which could not be expected. The dam must be made perfect against all extraordinary falls of rain—else the protection is not afforded against the operation which the party must accomplish.'

It is stated in *Charlesworth and Percy* at p. 902 that to be an Act of God an occurrence must be:—

(i) the consequence of natural causes, exclusively;
(ii) of an extraordinary nature; and
(iii) such that it could not be anticipated or provided against by the defendant.

The third requirement was adopted by the House of Lords in *Greenock Corporation v. Caledonian Railway*, and, while supported by a line of authority, that decision departed from another line of authority represented by cases such as *Nichols v. Marsland* and *Nitro-Phosphate and Odam's Chemical Manure Co. v. London and St. Katherine Docks Co.*[1878] 9 Ch. D. 503, to which I will refer later in another context, cases in which it was held that to constitute an Act of God it was sufficient to show that the occurrence could not reasonably be anticipated or guarded against. The authors of *Charlesworth and Percy* state that, in order for the defence to succeed now, it must be proved by the defendant that it was impossible to anticipate the occurrence or to guard effectively against it and they point out that the defence was not established where there had been an exceptional storm; a rainfall of extraordinary violence (*Greenock Corporation v. Caledonian Railway* [1917] A.C. 556); an exceptionally heavy snow storm; a very high wind; or an extraordinarily high tide. They go on to suggest that the only circumstances in which the defence would be likely to succeed in the United Kingdom would be if some catastrophe happened as a result of an earthquake, a volcanic eruption or a tidal wave of vast proportions. The views expressed by the authors of Charlesworth and Percy are obviously informed by the supremacy of the decision in *Greenock Corporation v. Caledonian Railway* [1917] A.C. 556, over the decision in *Nichols v. Marsland* (1876) 2 Ex. D. 1. Apart from the distinguishing feature which I have already referred to, that the finding of fact in *Nichols v. Marsland* was made by a jury, *Nichols v. Marsland* was also distinguished in *Greenock Corporation v. Caledonian Railway* on the basis that, having reference merely to the storage of water as in *Rylands v. Fletcher*, it did not affect the question of liability for interference with the course of a natural stream as laid down in other authorities, such as, *Kerr v. Earl of Orkney* (1857) 20 D. Sess. Cas. 298, to which I have already referred (see the speech of Finlay, L.C. at p. 573 and the judgment of Wrenbury L.J. at p. 584). Another distinguishing feature was that *Greenock Corporation v. Caledonian Railway* was an appeal from the Court of Session in Scotland and the issue was whether the extraordinary rainfall which caused the stream to overflow in that case was a *damnum fatale* under Scottish Law. In his speech Finlay L.C. stated at p. 571 that the authorities justified the view of the law propounded by Professor *Rankine* in his work on the Law of Land Ownership in Scotland in the following passage:—

> 'The sound view seems to be that even in the case of an unprecedented disaster the person who constructs an opus manufactum on the course of a stream or diverts its flow will be liable in damages provided the injured proprietor can show (1) that the opus has not been fortified by prescription, and (2) that but for it the phenomena would have passed him scathless.'

I have quoted this passage because it discloses that even under the law of Scotland the strictures of the concept of *damnum fatale* gave way to the existence of a state of things for a period of long prescription. Immediately before the 25th August, 1986, the dam at Paddock pond was of sufficient antiquity to be 'fortified by prescription'.

In my view, the principle to be derived from the line of authorities which includes *Nichols v. Marsland* (1876) 2 Ex.D.1 and *Nitro-Phosphate v. London and St. Katherine Dock Co.*(1878) 9 Ch. D. 503, is more in line with the current concept of tortious liability under the rule in *Rylands v. Fletcher*, as exemplified by the decision of the House of Lords in *Cambridge Water Co. v. Eastern Counties Plc.* [1994] 2 A.C. 264, than the decision in *Greenock Corporation v. Caledonian Railway*. Moreover, on the facts, the instant case is closer to *Nicholas v. Marsland* than to *Greenock Corporation v. Caledonian Railway*. Accordingly, in determining whether the fourth defendant is absolved from liability for the consequences of the dam failure by reliance on the defence of Act of God, I consider that the test to be applied is whether the storm on the 25th August, 1986, could reasonably have been anticipated or guarded against by the fourth defendant. I am satisfied that the evidence shows that the storm did fall within the category of the most extreme natural phenomena and could not reasonably have been anticipated or guarded against, so that the defence of Act of God succeeds.

Accordingly, the plaintiff's claim against the fourth defendant under the rule in *Rylands v. Fletcher* fails."

CHAPTER 13

ANIMAL LIABILITY

INTRODUCTION

Any person in control of animals may be liable under both the general rules of tort (negligence, nuisance, trespass or *Rylands v Fletcher*) or the special rules in respect of animals (*scienter* and cattle trespass). The special rules provide for strict liability. The legislature has also introduced a number of relevant provisions including the Control of Dogs Act 1986–1992 and the Animals Act 1985.

GENERAL RULES OF LIABILITY

Negligence

An owner or person in control of an animal which causes damage may be liable in negligence.

Kavanagh v Stokes
High Court [1942] I.R. 596

Facts: The plaintiff was a paying guest at the defendant's house. The plaintiff went to a dance and had informed the defendant of her intention to do so, and had arranged with her that the hall door would be left on the latch. She returned to the house that night and, on her arrival, a watch-dog had been left loose in the grounds of the house and barked loudly. The plaintiff closed the gate and went to pat the dog; the dog then jumped up on her and bit her on the lip. The defendant, on hearing the scream, got up and dressed the wound. There was evidence to suggest that the dog had bitten a child a few years previously.

Issues: This case is an appeal from the decision in the Circuit Court which had dismissed the action. The plaintiff to this action sued in negligence; this case highlights that, while there are special rules in respect of animal liability, the general rules are also applicable. The court held that the defendant was liable to the plaintiff in damages as it was her duty to provide a reasonably safe access from the road to the hall-door of her house for people staying in the house and she had failed to do so.

Gavan Duffy J.:

"The plaintiff was an invitee and paying guest staying in the defendant's house, and in my opinion it was the duty of the defendant in this case to provide reasonably safe access from the road to the hall-door of her house for people staying in the house, and in my opinion she failed to do so.

I think that negligence has been proved and that, in the special circumstances, there is no need to examine the doctrine of *scienter*, though there was evidence of a previous bite by the dog in question.

The dog was a largish sheep dog, kept as a watch-dog, and its principal duty as such would be to guard the house during the night. The dog hardly knew the girls, of whom the plaintiff was one. They were guests in the house, and had only arrived there the day before. They went to the neighbouring town of Gorey for a dance and told the defendant that they would be back about 11 or 11.30 p.m., and arranged that she should leave the hall-door on the latch for them. They came in about 11.30 p.m. It was the watch-dog's duty and nature to give warning of intruders at night, and of course it might go further than give warning when a number of strange people came to the house late at night.

It is not unusual for young people returning from a dance to be somewhat noisy, though these girls seem to have come in quietly enough, and I think that the defendant, in leaving the dog at large when she knew that the girls, new visitors, would be returning home at a late hour, was careless for the safety of her guests on a dark night, and failed to act reasonably in leaving the dog at large, where he might well be a danger to the girls.

There was evidence that the dog was a dog that rather distrusted strangers. The girls all came in together; four of them ran in, because the dog barked excitedly, but the plaintiff stayed behind to close the gate and the dog bit the plaintiff. There was no evidence before me that the plaintiff had irritated the dog; the suggestion was that she patted him; and I think that the evidence of the plaintiff generally was correct.

Mr. Crivon referred to the observations of Greer L.J. in *Sycamore* v. *Ley* [147 LTR 342, at p. 345], which are in point.

I hold that, in leaving this watch-dog out under the circumstances that I have outlined, the defendant failed in her duty to take reasonable precautions to ensure the safety of, or prevent danger to, the plaintiff and those accompanying her, and that there was no negligence on the part of the plaintiff."

Comments and Questions:
1. In this action Gavan Duffy J. allowed the plaintiff to recover in negligence; in your opinion is there any benefit to taking an action in negligence for animal liability over *scienter?*

Nuisance

A nuisance can arise where there is an unreasonable interference with the rights of another; the rights are usually those associated with property or land. This position applies equally when the nuisance is caused by animals.

Gillick v O'Reilly
High Court [1984] I.L.R.M. 402

Facts: The plaintiff was injured when he was driving at night and his car collided with a bullock owned by the defendant. The animal was one of a herd that had strayed onto the road through an open gate. It was not established who had left the gate open. Neighbours of the defendant found the cattle and were herding them back when the accident occurred.

Issues: The plaintiff sued in nuisance and negligence. The question for the court was whether animals on the road could constitute a public nuisance. The court agreed that animals could constitute a nuisance, but held that in this instant case the plaintiff had failed to establish that there was any breach of duty by the defendant.

McWilliam J.:

"Under these circumstances, the plaintiff claims that the cattle on the road constituted a nuisance for which the defendant is liable, that Mr Yore and his cousin [the neighbour who discovered the cattle on the road and who were herding them back to the field] were negligent in their management of the cattle and that the defendant is liable for this negligence either because Mr York [*sic*] was in his employment or because Mr York and his cousin were acting on his behalf in such a manner as to make the defendant responsible.

Apart from contesting that there was either negligence or nuisance, the defendant has contended that there can be no liability for cattle escaping on to the road and that there can be no liability for any negligence on the part of the two men who were volunteers and servants or agents of his ...

In the case of *Cunningham v McGrath Brothers* [1964] IR 209, Kingsmill-Moore J said, at page 213, *'Now, speaking generally, an obstruction of the public highway is a public nuisance, prosecutable on indictment and a tort sounding in damages if any member of the public should suffer any particular damage thereby.'* Whether the number of cattle was six or twelve I am satisfied that such can constitute a nuisance on a busy main road constructed for fast traffic and, under the circumstances of this case, I am satisfied that they did constitute a nuisance. See *Hall v Wightman* (1926) NI 72 and *Cunningham v Whelan* (1918) 52 ILTR 67.

In *Cunningham v McGrath* the cause of the obstruction was a ladder which had been left on the footpath by the defendants and was subsequently moved by a third party and the only real question at issue was the effect of the intervention of the third party and I think that there should be added to the short statement I have quoted from the judgment of Kingsmill-Moore J, a statement to the effect that a person is only liable in nuisance if he does something or permits something or authorises something of which the natural and probable consequence is that it will give rise to the nuisance. The ground of action is, therefore, very similar to that in negligence. There must be some act or omission constituting a breach of duty to someone else. Accordingly it does not seem to be very material whether an action such as this is framed in negligence or nuisance ...

In the present case the plaintiff has failed to establish that there was any breach of duty on the part of the defendant. There is no evidence to show how the gate came to be open, one of the cattle was a bullock and I think I may assume from the field being in the nature of an out-farm that all the cattle were dry cattle so that there would have been no question of evening milking, and it is improbable that the defendant would have left the gate open so that his cattle could escape into danger on a road such as this."

Rylands v Fletcher

In the decision of *Rylands v Fletcher* (1868) L.R. 1 Ex. 265 the court developed a new tort (see Chapter 12). This tort requires the accumulation or collection of an item or substance onto the property that would amount to a non-natural use of land. There is a necessity for the non-natural substance or the dangerous thing to escape and to cause damage. It is accepted in law that the non-natural substance or the dangerous thing may in certain circumstances be an animal.

Robson v Marquis of Londonderry
Circuit Cases (1900) 34 I.L.T.R. 88

Facts: The plaintiff claimed damages for injuries done to his crops of wheat and oats by pheasants from the defendant's demesne. The damage was caused by the pheasants trampling down and pecking at the growing crops. The defendant had brought pheasant eggs and hatched them under hens in coops on his land. There were an estimated 2000 pheasants hatched in that season. The evidence produced in court held that the pheasants causing the damage must be older than the batch of 2000, as they would not have been on the wing at the time of the damage.

Issue: The plaintiff took an action in *Rylands v Fletcher*, claiming that the defendant had brought animals onto his property in sufficient numbers to amount to a non-natural use. The collecting of the animals was for the benefit of the defendant and the escape caused the damage. The plaintiff did not succeed in his action.

Barton J.:

"Mr. Robb [for the plaintiff] relied on the case of *Farrer v. Nelson*. In that case Baron Pollock held that where a man collected 450 pheasants in coops in an acre of land within five yards of a neighbour's lands, he was liable for damage caused by such unnatural, extraordinary, and unreasonable user of his lands. In that case the defendant had practically turned his land into a game farm, and the birds were brought by him on to his lands and kept in these excessive numbers in coops. The present case is very different. Lord Londonderry, as it appears from the evidence, breeds pheasants in the proportion of about two pheasants per acre of his demesne, and breeds them at a distance from his neighbours where they cannot and do not escape to their lands. The birds in this case are some older birds remaining unshot from former years, which, in comparatively small quantities, breed in the woods along the demesne wall. I cannot hold this to be an unreasonable user of a demesne, and I do not think that wild birds are in the same category with birds practically tame and cooped."

SCIENTER

This rule refers to the nature of the animal. There are two separate rules depending on whether the animal is wild or tame. Wild animals (*ferae naturae*) are presumed to be dangerous and, where any damage occurs, the person in control of that animal will be strictly liable (*Behrens v Bertram Mills Circus Ltd.* [1957] 1 All E.R. 583). With regard to tame animals (*mansuetae naturae*), knowledge of a vicious or mischievous propensity in the particular animal must be shown (*Duggan v Armstrong* [1992] I.R. 161) before strict liability is imposed (*Forster v Donovan, Ireland and the Attorney-General* (1980) 114 I.L.T.R. 104).

Wild animals

To determine whether an animal is wild or tame the courts will review the traits of the species as a whole, taking on board issues such as the danger the animal poses to humans and whether the animal is indigenous to the country in question. Once it is determined that an animal is a wild animal then the liability for that animal is strict.

Behrens v Bertram Mills Circus Ltd.
Queens Bench Division [1957] 2 Q.B. 1, [1957] 1 All E.R. 583,
[1957] 2 W.L.R. 404.

Facts: In this case a circus elephant was held to be a wild animal. The plaintiffs
to this action were injured when the elephant knocked down a booth in which
they were working. The plaintiffs' barking dog had scared the elephants, but the
defendants were held strictly liable for the injuries.

Issue: The court held that the "defendants were under an absolute duty so to
confine and control elephants kept by them that the elephants did no injury." The
passage relating to the distinction between a wild and tame animal is of interest.
The personal characteristics of the animal are not relevant. In this action the
court found for the plaintiff to the action.

Devlin J.:

"A person who keeps an animal with knowledge (*scienter retinuit*) of its
tendency to do harm is strictly liable for damage that it does if it escapes; he is
under an absolute duty to confine or control it so that it shall not do injury to
others. All animals *ferae naturae*, that is, all animals which are not by nature
harmless, such as a rabbit, or have not been tamed by man and domesticated,
such as a horse, are conclusively presumed to have such a tendency, so that the
scienter need not in their case be proved. All animals in the second class,
mansuetae naturae, are conclusively presumed to be harmless until they have
manifested a savage or vicious propensity; proof of such a manifestation is
proof of *scienter* and serves to transfer the animal, so to speak, out of its natural
class into the class *ferae naturae* ...

The particular rigidity in the *scienter* action which is involved in this case—
there are many others which are not—is the rule which requires the harmfulness
of the offending animal to be judged, not by reference to its particular training
and habits, but by reference to the general habits of the species to which it
belongs. The law ignores the world of difference between the wild elephant in
the jungle and the trained elephant in the circus. The elephant Bullu is, in fact,
no more dangerous than a cow; she reacted in the same way as a cow would do
to the irritation of a small dog; if perhaps her bulk made her capable of doing
more damage, her higher training enabled her to be more swiftly checked. I am,
however, compelled to assess the defendants' liability in this case in just the
same way as I would assess it if they had loosed a wild elephant into the fun
fair. This is a branch of the law which, as Lord Goddard CJ (quoting Blackburn
J) said recently in *Wormald v. Cole* [[1954] 1 All ER 683 at p. 686], has been
settled by authority rather than by reason. But once the fundamental irrationality

is accepted of treating circus elephants as if they were wild, I think it is possible to determine sensibly in the light of the scienter rule the other points on liability which arise in this case ...

If a person wakes up in the middle of the night and finds an escaping tiger on top of his bed and suffers a heart attack, it would be nothing to the point that the intentions of the tiger were quite amiable. If a tiger is let loose in a fun fair, it seems to me to be irrelevant whether a person is injured as the result of a direct attack, or because, on seeing it, he runs away and falls over. The feature of this present case which is constantly arising to blur the reasoning is the fact that this particular elephant, Bullu, was tame; but that, as I have said, is a fact which must be ignored. She is to be treated as if she were a wild elephant, and, if a wild elephant were let loose in the fun fair and were stampeding around, I do not think that there would be much difficulty in holding that a person who was injured by falling timber had a right of redress. It is not, in my judgment, practicable to introduce conceptions of *mens rea* and malevolence in the case of animals ...

The distinction between those animals which are *ferae naturae* by virtue of their genus and those which become so by the exhibition of a particular habit seems to me to be this: that in the case of the former it is assumed (and the assumption is true of a really dangerous animal such as a tiger) that whenever they get out of control they are practically bound to do injury, while in the case of the latter the assumption is that they will do injury only to the extent of the propensity which they have peculiarly manifested. It would not be at all irrational if the law were to recognise a limited distinction of this sort while holding that both classes of animals are governed by the same *scienter* rule. In the case of dangerous chattels, for example, the law has recognised, although it is not perhaps now of much importance, the distinction between chattels that are dangerous in themselves and chattels that are dangerous when used for certain purposes; and animals *ferae nature* have frequently been compared with chattels in the former class; see, for example, per Hilbery J, in *Parker v. Oloxo Ltd. & Senior* [[1937] 3 All ER 524 at p. 528], and per Lord Wright in *Glasgow Corpn. v. Muir* [[1943] 2 All ER 44 at p. 52] ..."

Tame animals

Where an animal is deemed to fall into the category of tame animals, then the principle of *scienter* does not apply unless it can be shown that the animal has a dangerous propensity. Once it is established that an animal has a dangerous propensity then liability for damage caused by that animal is strict.

Forster v Donovan, Ireland and the Attorney-General
High Court (1980) 114 I.L.T.R. 104

Facts: The plaintiff was a postman who worked for the second named defendant; the first named defendant owned the dog in question, which he kept on his premises. The plaintiff was a share postman, who delivered post to the first named defendant's house; it was only his second day on this route when the incident occurred. When he delivered the post to the hall-door of the first named defendant, he was attacked and bitten by the defendant's dog. The defendant had in fact placed a letter box near the entrance to the driveway of his house, which would not necessitate the postman coming to the front door. The defendant had also placed a notice on the entrance which read "Beware of Alsation". On the first occasion that the plaintiff had delivered post to the hall-door the guard dog was in the house. The first named defendant's wife telephoned the local post office and informed them that the postman was not to come to the door again and that the post was to be delivered by placing it in the box provided near the entrance. The post office failed to pass on this message to the plaintiff. In the Circuit Court the plaintiff succeeded against the owner of the dog, and the other defendants. There was evidence to suggest that the first named defendant had done all that he could to prevent the injury of the plaintiff.

The defendant appealed.

Issue: The appeal on the matter also decided in favour of the plaintiff. When one keeps an animal with a vicious propensity one does so at one's peril.

Costello J.:

"In my opinion the plaintiff must succeed in his claim ... I have sympathy for the first-named defendant but when he keeps a dog, like the one referred to in the evidence, he runs the risk of some person being injured. This defendant had knowledge of the propensity of the dog and, accordingly, the plaintiff must succeed against him and there must be a decree against him.

A question then arises as to whether the Post Office are liable due to their failure to warn the plaintiff of the presence of the dog on the first-named defendant's premises. I am satisfied that Mrs. Donovan did telephone the day before to the local post office but there was a break in communications there due to this being the vacation period. The warning in the sorting office by means of the pink card system was not suitable in the circumstances as the plaintiff was a share postman. There was, accordingly, a breach of duty on the part of the Post Office in not warning the plaintiff. Thus the plaintiff must also succeed against the second and third-named defendants and there must be a decree against them.

Then the question of contributory negligence on the part of the plaintiff arises. Had he been informed of the existence of the dog on the premises he would not have proceeded up to the hall door. I accept his evidence that he did not see the post box or the warning notice. Accordingly there was no contributory negligence on his part.

A question now arises as to whether there should be an order for indemnity or contribution as between the defendants. I have to consider how the degrees of fault should be apportioned seeing that the plaintiff is a postman. The first-named defendant was required to keep a dog to protect his home, and in the circumstances, I hold that the full responsibility rests with the second and third-named defendants. Accordingly, I give a decree for the agreed sum of £1,259 damages and costs with benefit of an order for contribution amount to full indemnity to the first-named defendant."

Comments and Questions:
1. In your opinion would the result in this case have been different had the plaintiff only sued the first named defendant?

2. Do you think the imposition of strict liability for having an animal with a dangerous propensity is unduly harsh?

Vicious propensity

In *Forster v Donovan, Ireland and the Attorney-General* (1980) 114 I.L.T.R. 104 the propensity of the animal was not in question. The owner had the dog because of its vicious propensity to act as a guard dog. The concept of vicious propensity is a broad concept as McCarthy J. points out in *Duggan v Armstrong and Tighe* [1992] 2 I.R. 161.

Duggan v Armstrong and Tighe
Supreme Court [1992] 2 I.R. 161

Facts: The plaintiff, a young girl, was on holiday with her family at a hotel in Donegal. When in the foyer of the hotel with other children she was attacked by a dog. The hotel was owned by the first named defendant and managed by the second defendant. She took an action in both negligence and *scienter* against the owner and manager of the hotel (the defendants). In the High Court, evidence was given that the dog had displayed a mischievous or vicious propensity, particularly towards young girls. It was also shown that the second defendant's son had known of this; and that the dog was allowed to roam freely about the hotel. The claim was dismissed by the trial judge. The plaintiff appealed.

Issue: The issue before the Supreme Court was whether the dog in this action had displayed a mischievous or vicious propensity, a fact which the defendants knew or ought to know. The Supreme Court allowed the plaintiff's case and stated that the requirement of *scienter* was that, having displayed a mischievous or vicious propensity, a dog might bite, as it did in this case.

McCarthy J. (Hederman and Costello JJ. concurring):

"The defendants contested both the alleged vicious nature of the dog and their knowledge, in particular, the knowledge of Mr. Tighe. Jalisco Shortt had testified that 'it appeared a vicious dog because it was always growling and anytime I went up there it would run at me and I usually got on my bike and got out of there or Daragh [Mr. Tighe's son] would come out and call it away.' Daragh Tighe was about 9 years old at the time. Evidence was also given by other witnesses as to seeing the dog trying to mount young girls, apparently a known habit of what are called male dominant dogs. This was analysed in evidence by an expert in pet animal behaviour.

In my view there was evidence to support the conclusion that the dog had a mischievous or vicious propensity. One does not have to wait for the growling and frightening dog to bite somebody in order to know that it may do so; the requirement of *scienter* is not that the dog *will* bite somebody, but that, having displayed a vicious propensity, it *may* do so. Whatever about the direct knowledge of Mr. Tighe, certainly there was evidence that his 9 year old son had knowledge of complaints being made about the dog; such knowledge must be imputed to the father. In this regard I would express approval of the views of Judge Davitt as he then was, in the Circuit Court, in *Bennett & anor. v. Walsh* (1936) 70 ILTR 252. No submission was made to this Court as to whether or not the doctrine called *scienter* survived into modern times and, in particular, survived the guarantees contained in the constitutional framework, but, in my judgment, it goes against common sense that the family of the owner can have an intimate knowledge of a dog's vicious propensities but the owner himself can escape liability unless one can prove direct communication to him.

Common law liability
This is the liability of the occupier of the hotel premises to a guest on the premises. No niceties of distinction between licensee and invitee arise here, if they could arise at all anywhere. It is not in issue that the plaintiff was on the premises as a hotel guest. In an area where a large number of people, including children, tended to congregate, a fairly large dog with a known propensity to jump on children, if not to growl and chase them, was permitted to run free. What some might think inevitable happened—a child got bitten. The knowledge of the manager, Mr. Tighe, is the knowledge of the owner. There was clear evidence of a breach of the duty owed to the plaintiff as a guest."

Comments and Questions:
1. What principle does McCarthy J. establish in this case, to show when an animal has a vicious propensity?

Knowledge of an animal's vicious or dangerous propensity is an essential element of the tort of *scienter.*

Quinn v Quinn
Circuit Court (1905) 39 I.L.T.R. 163

Facts: The plaintiff and the defendant occupied the same yard, and had the joint use of a stall, with a timber partition dividing the plaintiff's portion from the defendant's. The plaintiff had requested that the defendant put up a substantial partition which the defendant did not do. As there was not a sufficient partition the defendant's sows got into the portion of the stall occupied by the plaintiff's cow, attacked it and tore its paps, as a result of which the cow died. Evidence was given by the plaintiff that on a previous occasion the same sow, in the presence of the defendant, had attacked and killed some cocks and hens.

Issues: The action was taken in *scienter*, claiming that the animal had a vicious propensity. The question the court had to address was whether the defendant had knowledge of the vicious propensity of the sow. The court found for the plaintiff in this action.

Lord O'Brien L.C.J.:

"This case, as presented before me, has a perfectly different aspect from that which it presented before the County Court Judge, for a new volume of evidence has been adduced here. I believe that the sow eat the cocks and hens in the presence of the defendant, as deposed to by the plaintiff. The question then is whether this particular sow was a sow of mischievous propensities with a taste for blood. A cock or hen is an animal, and a cow is an animal, and they both have blood. Therefore the sow had a mischievous disposition to take blood, and I am certain the defendant saw the birds being attacked, the mischievous disposition was evidenced before the defendant. It pre-eminently stands out in the case that the sow bit the cow, blood poisoning ensued, the plaintiff lost her cow. It was killed by a sow with mischievous propensities known to the defendant, and consequently I give a decree for £10."

Comments and Questions:
1. In this case it seems clear that the defendant had direct knowledge of the vicious propensity of the sow; compare this to the approach to knowledge taken by the Supreme Court in *Duggan v Armstrong and Tighe* [1992] 2 I.R. 161.

CATTLE TRESPASS

This is a very ancient tort which imposes strict liability where cattle, of their own volition, stray onto neighbouring land and cause damage. The tort requires that the cattle stray directly onto the neighbouring land, or via the highway (*Kennedy v McCabe* 103 I.L.T.R. 110). This tort does not apply where the cattle are driven onto someone else's property.

Defining cattle

The term cattle is broadly defined for the purposes of this rule and includes horses, sheep, goats, pigs and domestic deer as well as cows. Wild animals are not covered by this rule (*Brady v Warren* [1900] 2 I.R. 632).

Brady v Warren
Queens Bench Division [1900] 2 I.R. 632

Facts: The farms of Mr Brady and Mr Warren were beside one another. Mr Warren only recently became possessed of the property. There were rabbits and deer on the property which trespassed onto Mr Brady's property. Mr Warren's predecessor had on two occasions let loose foreign rabbits with a view to improving the breed. Since Mr Warren had come into possession of the property he trapped the rabbits for profit and had done nothing to improve them or increase their numbers, but they bred in considerable numbers. The deer, which had at one time been confined within a walled deer park, broke lose in 1893 (some five years prior to this action) through a temporary breach in the wall, and only a portion were recaptured. The remainder had since been loose on Mr Warren's property and trespassed onto Mr Brady's property.

Issues: For the purposes of cattle trespass do rabbits and deer qualify as cattle? The court held that rabbits are not cattle, but that deer are.

Palles C.B. (Boyd, and Johnson JJ. delivered judgments which agreed in principle with Palles C.B.):

"... The question then is, was there evidence from which the jury might reasonably arrive at the conclusion that these deer in the demesne were tame; for it is admitted that if they were, there is abundant evidence that they were kept by the defendant.

Is there, then, evidence that they were tame? The reason of the distinction between the right of property in animals which are of a tame and domestic nature, as distinct from *ferae naturae,* is elementary. Blackstone states it to be (vol. ii., book ii., chap. I), because the former 'continue to perpetually in his occupation, and will not stray from his house or person, unless by accident or fraudulent enticement, in either of which cases the owner does not lose his property.' This distinction is kept in view in determining whether animals *ferae naturae* have been tamed, and they by habit go and return, fly away and fly back, such as *deer,* swans, and sea-fowl, doves and such like; another rule has been approved, that they 'are so long considered as ours, as long as they have the disposition to return,' *quamdiu habuerint animum revertendi.* 'For if they have no disposition to return, they cease to be ours; but they seem to cease to have the disposition to return when they have abandoned the habit of returning:' *revertendi autem animum videntur disinere habere cum consuetudinem revertendi desinuerint.* This view, which is taken from the civil law (Gaius, ii. 68; Inst. 2, i. 15), is to be found in all our law books which treat of this subject. It is to be observed of the civil law, that in the passage from Gaius, from which Bracton probably took the words I have read, deer are, as they are in Bracton, specially mentioned as being among the class of animals which may have this habit of going and returning, and by reason of this habit may be subjects of property ...

Further, the fact that deer are more usually domesticated now than they were in feudal times has, for more than a century and a half, been recognised as matter of law. In *Davies v. Powell* [Willes' Rep., 46, 48] the question was whether deer in an enclosed place were distrainable. Willes, C.J., in contrasting the view which the law took of deer, in the time of Lord Coke, with that then held, says: "Besides, the nature of things is now very much altered, and the reason which is given for the rule fails. Deer were formerly kept only in forests or chases, or such parks as were parks either by grant or prescription, and were considered rather as things of pleasure than of profit; but now they are frequently kept in enclosed grounds which are not properly parks, and are kept principally for the sake of profit, and, therefore, must be considered as other cattle.' Again he adds: 'When the nature of things changes, the rules of law must change too. When it was holden that deer were not distrainable, it was because they were kept principally for pleasure, and not for profit, and were not sold and turned into money as they are now. But they are become as much a sort of husbandry as horses, cows, sheep or other cattle. Whenever they are so, and it is universally known, it would be ridiculous to say that, when they are kept merely for profit, they are not distrainable as other cattle, though it has been holden that they were not so when they were kept for pleasure.' ...

Therefore, the present case can be well determined on one or other, or both of two separate considerations, viz.:

(1.) That it is a reasonable inference from the evidence that these deer had the habit of remaining in the demesne, a place of *quasi* captivity, although they had the opportunity of escaping from it, and the habit of returning to it when they occasionally left it for the plaintiff's farm.

(2.) That it is also a reasonable inference from the evidence that they were managed in the same way as other domestic cattle, oxen sheep &c., making allowance for their difference of their nature.

Having regard to these considerations, taken in connection with the nature of the animals in question, fallow deer, always easily tameable, and in the present day usually tamed and kept for profit, I entertain no doubt that there was evidence to go to the jury that the deer in the demesne were tame, were under the defendant's control, in his possession, were *his,* and were kept by him, and that the findings in the affirmative of these questions were in accordance with the weight of the evidence.

The verdict, therefore, on this head of the plaintiff's claim must stand.

The second claim was for trespass by rabbits. As to this there is more difficulty. It is laid down in *Boulston's Case* [Rep., Part V., 104b; more fully Cro. Eliz. 547 (21)], that 'if a man makes cony burrows in his own land, which increase in so great numbers that they destroy his neighbour's land next adjoining, his neighbour cannot have an action on the case against him who makes the said cony burrows;' and the reason is given, 'for as soon as the conies go on his neighbour's land he may kill them, for they are *ferae naturae,* and he who makes the cony burrows has no property in them.'... Accordingly, the Lord Justice directed the jury that the defendant was not answerable for any amount of damage caused by the natural and reasonably to be expected trespass of rabbits, having regard to the existence of rabbits in the locality. To this direction no objection was taken."

For an action to lie in cattle trespass the cattle must stray of their own volition and should not be driven onto the property of another.

Kennedy v McCabe
Circuit Court 103 I.L.T.R. 110

Facts: The defendant's cattle were found on the plaintiff's land up a private laneway leading from a public road adjoining the defendant's land.

Issue: The defendant claimed that no liability could attach to her without proof of negligence. The court determined that the plaintiff was entitled to succeed unless the defendant established that the cattle trespassed from the highway while lawfully using it for the purpose of passing or re-passing, in effect being driven. The court found for the plaintiff.

Ryan J.:

"The plaintiff must succeed in this case. I reserved my judgment to enable me to refer to Glanville Williams on 'Liability for Animals.' The following passage from that work at page 373 appears to cover this case: 'The animals that escaped must have been lawfully on the highway – i.e., they must have been there in pursuance of the right of passage, and not merely straying upon it. This was laid down in *Dovaston v. Payne* (1795); the rule is analogous to that which exists in the case of prescriptive and statutory duties to fence. Its justification at the present day is that damage done by straying cattle is not one of the risks that those who have property adjacent to a highway may be expected to assume. Where cattle stray in this way the landowner may lawfully replace them on the highway or distrain them damage feasant; in the former case he may also bring an action of cattle-trespass.'

Decree for the plaintiff."

Possession and control

Ownership of the animals is not a pre-requisite for an action in cattle trespass. Actions in cattle trespass should be taken against the person who has control or possession over the animals that strayed.

Dalton v O'Sullivan
Circuit Court [1947] Ir. Jur. 25

Facts: Cattle who were in the possession of an agister escaped and caused damage to the property of a neighbour. The agister had placed them on his lands in pursuance of an agistment agreement. There was no evidence of the fences being in poor condition but some of the cattle succeeded in jumping over a portion of the fences and then causing damage in the plaintiff's property.

Issue: The plaintiff took an action against the owner of the cattle. The question for the court was whether the basis of liability for cattle trespass depends upon occupancy of the land from which the cattle have strayed or if it is based upon possession of the cattle at the material time. It was held that since the defendant was neither in occupation of the lands from which the cattle escaped nor in possession of the cattle at the material time, no liability attached to him for the damage caused.

O'Briain J.:

"The question in this case is whether or not the owner of cattle is liable for damage caused by his cattle escaping from lands of a third party who had them there under a contract of agistment with the owner, and trespassing upon lands of the plaintiff. In the present case the owner alone is sued ...

I have been referred to and I have read with interest and advantage to myself the decision of Judge Davies in *Hammond v. Mallinson and Bowie*. In that case the second defendant had on his land under a contract of agistment, sheep belonging to the first defendant. The sheep escaped from the field in which they were, crossed the land belonging to a third party, and damaged a crop on the plaintiff's property. There was no definite evidence as to how the sheep came to escape on to the plaintiff's lands. It was held that (1) the second defendant was liable for the damage, and (2) the first defendant as owner of the sheep was not liable, and the claim against him failed. After observing upon the lack of authority on this point in England, the learned judge goes on to say (at p. 360): 'The foundation of the action in modern times is that there is a duty to prevent the animals from straying, and the fact that the defendant was not guilty of negligence does not exempt him from liability if they stray and do damage. See the judgement of Blackburn J. in *Rylands v. Fletcher,* where the case of damage by straying cattle is mentioned by him as an instance of the duty to prevent damage which was expounded in that case. I agree with Mr. Southall that Bowie was a bailee of the sheep and an independent contractor. It is clear that a defendant cannot escape liability for a breach of the duty laid down in *Rylands v. Fletcher* by entrusting its fulfilment to an independent contractor whether under a contract of bailment or otherwise: see *Black v. Christchurch Finance Co.* ([1984] AC 480). But the question remains whether the duty is imposed upon the owner of the animals or upon the person who has allowed the animals to be brought upon the land of which he is the occupier. It is true that in some cases, e.g., *Cox v. Burbridge* (13 CB, NS 430) it is said that the owner of straying animals is responsible for the damage they do, but as already stated there appears to be no case in which the owner of agisted cattle has been held responsible for damage done by them when straying from the agister's lands. And the rule in *Rylands v. Fletcher* is based upon ownership or occupation of the land from which the water or cattle or other source of mischief escapes, not upon ownership of the source of mischief itself. To hold that the owner of sheep which are being agisted upon another's land is responsible if they escape and do damage would, in my opinion, be an extension of the rule in *Rylands v. Fletcher* for which there is no warrant in authority. In my opinion therefore, Mallinson is not liable for this damage.'

I find that in *Hunt on Fences and Boundaries* the view is expressed that liability for trespass of animals is based upon the rule in *Rylands v. Fletcher.* In *Underhill on Torts* (8th edn.) it is stated, at p.180, that this rule (with some modification) is the foundation of the liability for damage done by animals. Mr. Williams points out, at page 197, certain differences between liability under the rule in *Rylands v. Fletcher,* and in cases of cattle trespass, and observes in Note 5 at page 199: 'Liability under *Rylands v. Fletcher* in some sense presupposes the use of "dangerous things" and the "non-natural user of land"—expressions that can hardly apply to the age-old practice of keeping cattle. Hence in *Manton v. Brocklebank* ([1923] 2 KB 212) it was held that an injury by the defendant's mare to the plaintiff's horse did not come within *Rylands v. Fletcher,* although had there been a trespass to land damages could undoubtedly have been recovered in cattle-trespass.'

It is to be observed that the liability for cattle-trespass may be attributed, on the one hand to occupancy of land from which the cattle stray, as appears to be the ground for the decision in *Hammond v. Mallinson and Bowie,* or, on the other hand, to possession of the offending cattle. I refrain from going further than expressing the view that the strict liability for cattle trespass is attributable to one or the other, if in law they be distinct. I do not think that for the purpose of this case it is necessary to go further, because the defendant living at Killarney—nearly 100 miles away from the lands of Mr. Lloyd where the cattle were agisted, cannot be liable on either view.

Accordingly I affirm the order of the learned District Justice. The appeal is dismissed with costs."

Defences

While liability is strict, there is a defence where the defendant can show that the reason for the trespass was the fault of the plaintiff, an act of God or the act of a third party (*Moloney v Stephens* [1945] Ir. Jur. Rep. 37).

Moloney v Stephens
Circuit Court [1945] Ir. Jur. Rep. 37

Facts: The plaintiff and the defendant were the owners of adjoining farms, and a third party had a right of way over both farms. There was a gate at the boundary fence between the farms, which the third party was meant to close. There were several trespasses by the defendant's horses onto the land of the plaintiff. These trespasses were the result of the third party forgetting to close the gate after him.

Issues: The initial action was taken in the District Court, where the court found for the plaintiff. This decision was appealed to the Circuit Court, where they had to decide whether the actions of a third party were a defence to cattle trespass. The Circuit Court also found for the defendant.

O'Briain J.:

"This case involves an interesting question of law, and one which, as appears from the reports, has not received much consideration. My personal reaction to the case apart from authority was that the defendant should not be held liable. As I read *M'Gibbon v. M'Curry* it is an authority binding on me and in favour of the defendant. The report is not free from ambiguity, but the several references in it to trespass, and the fact that *Salmond on Torts* in repeated editions, has taken it as an authority on cattle trespass, determine my attitude.

I am faced with a decision of the Courts prior to 1922 but incorporated into the law of this State by the Constitution. I hold that the defendant has established a good defence in law to this action by showing that the trespass complained of was caused by the wrongful acts of a third party. Accordingly I affirm the order of the learned District Justice, and dismiss the appeal."

LEGISLATION

In recent years a number of provisions have been introduced which change the old common law provisions. The Animals Act of 1985 replaces an old common law immunity that provided that the owner of an animal was not liable for the damage caused by that animal if it strayed onto the highway (*Searle v Wallbank* [1947] A.C. 341 which was applied in Ireland in *Dunphy v Bryan* (1963) I.L.T.R.). The rule was finally reformed by s.2 of the Animals Act. Section 2 of the Animals Act provides that the principle of negligence must be applied to determine cases where animals escape onto the public road and cause damage. Defective fencing may assist in showing that there was a lack of reasonable care, unless the area is one where fencing is not customary.

Animals Act 1985

ANIMALS ACT, 1985

Section 2
Duty to take care to prevent damage by animals straying on to public road.
  2.—(1) So much of the rules of the common law relating to liability for negligence as excludes or restricts the duty which a person might owe to others to take such care as is reasonable to see that damage is not caused by an animal straying on to a public road is hereby abolished.
  (2) (*a*) Where damage is caused by an animal straying from unfenced land on to a public road, a person who placed the animal on the land shall not be regarded as having committed a breach of the duty to take care by reason only of placing it there if—
    (i) the land is situated in an area where fencing is not customary, and
    (ii) he had a right to place the animal on that land.
  (*b*) In this subsection 'fencing' includes the construction of any obstacle designed to prevent animals from straying, and 'unfenced' shall be construed accordingly—there was an old common law immunity, which provided that the owner of an animal, which strayed onto the highway, was not liable for damage caused by that animal— ..."

Comments and Questions:
1. Section 1 defines relevant terms such as "animal", which means "a bovine animal, horse, ass or other equine animal, sheep or goat." The term "damage" is also defined and it includes "the death of, or injury to, any person (including any disease and any impairment of a person's physical or mental condition) and injury to or total or partial destruction of property."

The Supreme Court decision of *O'Shea v Anhold and Horse Holiday Farm Ltd.*, unreported, Supreme Court, 1996 gives an interpretation of the impact of s.2 of the Animals Act 1985.

O'Shea v Anhold and Horse Holiday Farm Ltd.
Unreported, Supreme Court, October 1996

Facts: The plaintiff was driving his motor car on the public road when he collided with a horse that was owned by the second named defendant. Evidence produced at trial suggested that the fencing was adequate and that it was unlikely that the horse would have escaped on its own. The plaintiff sustained quite serious injuries. In the High Court Costello J. found in favour of the plaintiff; he found that the second named defendants were negligent. The defendants appealed this decision to the Supreme Court.

Issues: The appeal was allowed, on the basis that the evidence did not support a finding of negligence.

O'Flaherty J. (Hamilton J. concurring):

"Dr Joe Hart, an agricultural consultant, gave evidence that he was satisfied that the fencing was adequate for ordinary commercial horse purposes. He said that the horse would not itself have got out. It would not jump over the wall onto the road. On the public road, the horse would have been in a panic and would behave differently. He believed that someone must have let it out onto the road. In a similar vein, Mr Ray Gallagher, an equestrian expert, testified that the only way that the horse would get out was for somebody to have opened the gate. While he agreed that a horse could jump from three to seven feet, he said he would be surprised if a horse would do so without being urged or forced. Section 2(1) of the Animals Act, 1985, provides:—

> So much of the rules of the common law relating to liability for negligence as excludes or restricts the duty which a person might owe to others to take such care as is reasonable to see that damage is not caused by an animal straying on to a public road is hereby abolished.

The 'rules of the common law' are well summarised for our present purposes in the decision of the House of Lords in *Searle v Wallbank* [1947] AC 341. For example, Lord du Parcq, in the course of his speech in that case said, at p 361:—

> 'Counsel disclaimed any suggestion that the respondent was bound to maintain a fence, and he recognised that for centuries both the law and the general sense of the community have sanctioned the depasturing of cattle on unfenced land. He contended, however, that one who keeps his cattle on land adjoining the highway behind an apparently secure fence must see to it that it is in fact secure, for otherwise (he said) a deceptive feeling of safety will be induced in the passing cyclist or motorist. My Lords, I should have thought that, on principle, where there is no duty to maintain a fence at all, it cannot be a breach of duty to maintain one which is imperfect. But, however that may be, the argument takes little account of rural conditions. A stray horse, even if it has come from the nearest field and not from one a mile or more away, may have escaped, not through a gap in the fence, but through a gate left open by a trespasser. Moreover, the suggested duty could only be to take reasonable care to maintain a reasonably secure fence, and it must be a very high fence which a horse cannot jump; indeed, we have it on the authority of Byles J that, in or about the year 1858, it was proved that a bull had leaped over an iron fence six feet high (Bessant v Great Western Ry Co [(1860) 8CB NS 368,372]. The truth is that, at least on country roads and in market towns, users of the highway, including cyclists and motorists, must be prepared to meet from time to time a stray horse or cow, just as they must expect to encounter a herd of cattle in the care of a drover. An underlying principle of the law of the highway is that all those lawfully using the highway, or land adjacent to it, must show mutual respect and forbearance. The motorist must put up with the farmer's cattle: the farmer must endure the motorist.'

The position as recounted in *Searle v Wallbank* also represented the law in Ireland: see McMahon and Binchy, The Irish Law of Torts (2nd ed) pp 518–521 and the cases cited therein. But then the legislature stepped in to change the law. This was a recognition, no doubt, that public roads had got much busier with the increase in motor traffic and so, from everyone's point of view, it was best to impose a duty on landowners to provide proper fencing adjacent to the highway to prevent animals from straying thereon except where 'the land is situated in an area where fencing is not customary' (see s 2(2) of the Animals Act, 1985). The trial judge was faced with the question: in the circumstances, were the owners of the horse liable to the plaintiff? He concluded:—

> 'The situation was that either the fencing on the laneway or field was inadequate or someone had opened the gate, let out one horse and closed the gate again. On balance the first possibility was much more likely than the second. The problem of fencing is a difficult one and the defendant was unable to discharge the onus of proof on it. The plaintiff has shown a breach of duty. There was no contributory negligence on the part of the plaintiff.'

There is no doubt that having regard to the statutory provision an onus rested on the defendants to show that they had taken reasonable care; nonetheless, that is the extent of the burden that rested on them. They disproved any negligence on their part through the evidence of their expert witnesses that the fencing was adequate, which testimony was not contradicted by the plaintiff's engineer. They were not required to take the further step of proving how the animal came to be on the highway: whether through the act of a trespasser or however. The most that is required of a defendant in this situation where the onus of proof rests on him is to disprove any negligence on his part: cf *Lindsay Mid-Western Health Board* [1993] 2 IR 147. It is not as if this was a case of strict or absolute liability. The learned trial judge approached the matter on the basis that one possibility was more likely than another; however, that was not the proper frame in which to resolve the problem that was presented to him. The trial judge's essential task was to decide whether reasonable care had been taken by the owners of the horse in the circumstances of the case, as required by the Act. The judge, in effect, went close to imposing strict liability on the defendants. This is to go too far. Legislation enacted in the future may provide for strict liability dispensing with the necessity to prove negligence, but that is not now the law.

In any event, as between the two possibilities, I would regard the possibility that someone opened the gate and let the horse out as less unlikely than that the horse cleared the fencing.

In the circumstances, I would allow the appeal."

Keane J. (Hamilton J. concurring):

"Section 2 of the Animals Act 1985 has abolished the somewhat anomalous immunity from the ordinary law of negligence which the owners of land from which animals strayed on to the highway previously enjoyed. It has not, however, imposed any form of absolute liability on such persons. To hold the Defendants liable for negligence in the circumstances of this case where the admitted evidence was that they had taken all the precautions which a reasonable person would take to prevent the particular animals, a herd of horses, from straying on to the road, would be to impose a higher duty than the duty 'to take such care as is reasonable' recognised by the Oireachtas as applying to such persons."

Control of Dogs Act 1986 and 1992

The Control of Dogs Act 1986 and 1992 deals with the liability of dog-owners for damage caused by that animal. The Act imposes strict liability for injuries to the person where there is an attack, or for any injury to livestock. Strict liability is not imposed in the case of a dog injuring livestock that have strayed onto the defendant's land, unless the dog was caused to attack the livestock. The ordinary rules of negligence apply where a trespasser is injured by a dog.

CONTROL OF DOGS ACT, 1986 and 1992

Section 21
Liability of owner for damage by dog.

21.—(1) The owner of a dog shall be liable in damages for damage caused in an attack on any person by the dog and for injury done by it to any livestock; and it shall not be necessary for the person seeking such damages to show a previous mischievous propensity in the dog, or the owner's knowledge of such previous propensity, or to show that such injury or damage was attributable to neglect on the part of the owner.

(2) Where livestock are injured by a dog on land on to which they had strayed, and either the dog belonged to the occupier of the land or its presence on the land was authorised by the occupier, a person shall not be liable under this section in respect of injury done to the livestock, unless the person caused the dog to attack the livestock.

(3) A person is liable in damages for any damage caused by a dog kept on any premises or structure to a person trespassing thereon only in accordance with the rules of law relating to liability for negligence.

(4) (*a*)   Any damage or injury for which a person is made liable under this section shall be deemed to be attributable to a wrong within the meaning of the Civil Liability Act, 1961, and the provisions of that Act shall apply accordingly.

   (*b*)   Sections 11 (2) (*a*) and 11 (2) (*b*) of the Statute of Limitations, 1957, shall apply to such damage.

Comments and Questions:
1.   Section 1 of the 1986 Act defines a number of terms. "Damage" is held to include "death or injury to any person (including any disease caused to a person or any impairment of his physical or mental condition) and includes injury to, or total or partial destruction of, property." "Livestock" includes cattle, sheep, swine, horses and all other equine animals, poultry, goats and deer not in the wild state. "Poultry" are further defined as "domestic fowls, turkeys, geese, ducks, guinea-fowls, pigeons and peafowl and includes, whilst in captivity, pheasants, partridges, grouse and quail."

2.   This provision does not abolish *scienter* actions, or the general torts available to a plaintiff. The major impact of this provision is that as regards dogs, in the case of an attack or injury to livestock, there is no necessity to prove that the dog had a mischievous propensity. Where the damage caused does not amount to an attack or injury to livestock, then the plaintiff may still rely on both *scienter* or the general principles of tort.

CHAPTER 14

DEFENCES

INTRODUCTION

For a tort action to succeed the claimant must ensure that his/her case does not come within one of the general defences available for all torts. Certain torts have specific defences, such as trespass, defamation, the rule in *Rylands v Fletcher* and nuisance, which are discussed in the individual chapters. This chapter focuses on the general defences applicable to all torts. The Civil Liability Act 1961 regulates these defences to a large degree. The defences are contributory negligence, *volenti non fit injuria,* and illegality.

CONTRIBUTORY NEGLIGENCE

The Civil Liability Act 1961 introduced the concept of contributory negligence, which operates as a partial defence to an action in tort. Prior to this legislative provision, if a defendant could show the existence of contributory negligence it acted as a complete defence. This rule was particularly harsh on plaintiffs and the courts attempted to avoid it where possible. Section 34 of the Civil Liability Act 1961 ensures that where a plaintiff has contributed to his/her injury then damages will be reduced in proportion to his/her fault. A failure to mitigate his/her damage will also be deemed to amount to contributory negligence and result in damages being reduced accordingly.

All sections highlighted below are referred to in the case law to follow. The most important section for the purposes of this chapter is s.34, which provides the statutory definition of contributory negligence.

Civil Liability Act 1961

CIVIL LIABILITY ACT 1961

AN ACT TO REFORM THE LAW RELATING TO CIVIL LIABILITY, PROVIDING IN PARTICULAR FOR THE SURVIVAL OF CAUSES OF ACTION ON DEATH, FOR PROCEEDINGS AGAINST AND CONTRIBUTION BETWEEN CONCURRENT WRONGDOERS AND FOR LIABILITY IN CASES OF CONTRIBUTORY NEGLIGENCE, TO PROVIDE FOR DAMAGES FOR THE BENEFIT OF THE DEPENDANTS OF ANY PERSON FATALLY INJURED BY THE WRONGFUL ACT,

NEGLECT OR DEFAULT OF ANOTHER, AND TO PROVIDE FOR OTHER MATTERS CONNECTED WITH THE FOREGOING.

...

PART III CONCURRENT FAULT
CHAPTER I *Liability of concurrent wrongdoers*

Persons who are concurrent wrongdoers.

11.—(1) For the purpose of this Part, two or more persons are concurrent wrongdoers when both or all are wrongdoers and are responsible to a third person (in this Part called the injured person or the plaintiff) for the same damage, whether or not judgment has been recovered against some or all of them.

(2) Without prejudice to the generality of subsection (1) of this section—

(*a*) persons may become concurrent wrongdoers as a result of vicarious liability of one for another, breach of joint duty, conspiracy, concerted action to a common end or independent acts causing the same damage;

(*b*) the wrong on the part of one or both may be a tort, breach of contract or breach of trust, or any combination of them;

(*c*) it is immaterial whether the acts constituting concurrent wrongs are contemporaneous or successive.

(3) Where two or more persons are at fault and one or more of them is or are responsible for damage while the other or others is or are free from causal responsibility, but it is not possible to establish which is the case, such two or more persons shall be deemed to be concurrent wrongdoers in respect of the damage.

(4) Where there is a joint libel in circumstances normally protected by the defences of qualified privilege or fair comment upon a matter of public interest, the malice of one person shall not defeat the defence for the other, unless that other is vicariously liable for the malice of the first.

(5) Where the same or substantially the same libel or slander or injurious falsehood is published by different persons, the court shall take into consideration the extent to which it is probable that the statement in question was published directly or indirectly to the same persons, and to that extent may find the wrongdoers to be concurrent wrongdoers.

(6) For the purpose of any enactment referring to a specific tort, an action for a conspiracy to commit that tort shall be deemed to be an action for that tort.

...

CHAPTER III *Contributory negligence*

Apportionment of liability in case of contributory negligence.

34.—(1) Where, in any action brought by one person in respect of a wrong committed by any other person, it is proved that the damage suffered by the plaintiff was caused partly by the negligence or want of care of the plaintiff or of one for whose acts he is responsible (in this Part called contributory negligence) and partly by the wrong of the defendant, the damages recoverable in respect of the said wrong shall be reduced by such amount as the court thinks just and equitable having regard to the degrees of fault of the plaintiff and defendant: provided that—

(*a*) if, having regard to all the circumstances of the case, it is not possible to establish different degrees of fault, the liability shall be apportioned equally;

(*b*) this subsection shall not operate to defeat any defence arising under a contract or the defence that the plaintiff before the act complained of agreed to waive his legal rights in respect of it, whether or not for value; but, subject as aforesaid, the provisions of this subsection shall apply notwithstanding that the defendant might, apart from this subsection, have the defence of voluntary assumption of risk;

(*c*) where any contract or enactment providing for the limitation of liability is applicable to the claim, the amount of damages awarded to the plaintiff by virtue of this subsection shall not exceed the maximum limit so applicable.

(2) For the purpose of subsection (1) of this section—

(*a*) damage suffered by the plaintiff may include damages paid by the plaintiff to a third person who has suffered damage owing to the concurrent wrongs of the plaintiff and the defendant, and the period of limitation for claiming such damages shall be the same as is provided by section 31 for actions for contribution;

(*b*) a negligent or careless failure to mitigate damage shall be deemed to be contributory negligence in respect of the amount by which such damage exceeds the damage that would otherwise have occurred;

(*c*) the plaintiff's failure to exercise reasonable care for his own protection shall not amount to contributory negligence in respect of damage unless that damage results from the particular risk to which his conduct has exposed him, and the plaintiff's breach of statutory duty shall not amount to contributory negligence unless the damage of which he complains is damage that the statute was designed to prevent;

(*d*) the plaintiff's failure to exercise reasonable care in the protection of his own property shall, except to the extent that the defendant has been unjustly enriched, be deemed to be contributory negligence in an action for conversion of the property;

(*e*) damage may be held to be caused by the wrong of the defendant notwithstanding any rule of law by which the scope of the defendant's duty is limited to cases where the plaintiff has not been guilty of contributory negligence: but this paragraph shall not render the defendant liable for any damage in respect of which he or a person for whose acts he is responsible has not been careless in fact;

(*f*) where an action is brought for negligence in respect of a thing that has caused damage, fact that there was a reasonable possibility or probability of examination after the thing had left the hands of the defendant shall not, by itself, exclude the defendant's duty, but may be taken as evidence that he was not in the circumstances negligent in parting with the thing in its dangerous state.

(3) Article 21 of the Warsaw Convention (which empowers a court to exonerate wholly or partly a carrier who proves that the damage was caused by or contributed to by the negligence of the injured person) shall have effect subject to the provisions of this Part.

...

Special Findings

40. —(1) Where damages are awarded to any person by virtue of subsection (1) of section 34, the jury or if there is no jury then the judge or arbitrator shall find and record—

(*a*) the total damages that would have been awarded if there had not been contributory negligence;

(*b*) where the plaintiff's damages are reduced under the said subsection, the proportion of such damages that shall not be awarded to the plaintiff and the proportion that shall be payable by the defendant, or the respective proportions that shall be payable by each of the defendants if more than one, expressed in each case in percentage of the total fault of the plaintiff and defendant or defendants;

(*c*) whose negligence, want of care or caution, or wrong contributed to whose or what damage, and in what respects.

(2) It shall be the duty of the judge or arbitrator to make the requisite calculations following upon such findings.

...

CHAPTER IV *General*

Application to breaches of strict duty.

43. —In determining the amount of contribution or of reduction of damages under subsection (1) of section 34 for contributory negligence the court may take account of the fact that the negligence or wrong of one person consisted only in a breach of strict statutory or common-law duty without fault, and may accordingly hold that it is not just and equitable to cast any part of the damage upon such person.

...

PART VII MISCELLANEOUS

...

Abolition of defences.

57. —(1) It shall not be a defence in an action of tort merely to show that the plaintiff is in breach of the civil or criminal law.

(2) It shall not be a defence in an action for breach of statutory duty merely to show that the defendant delegated the performance of the duty to the plaintiff.

To establish a case for contributory negligence the defendant must establish that the plaintiff behaved unreasonably given the circumstances. The court must determine what is reasonable; in *Stewart v Killeen Paper Mills Ltd.* [1959] I.R. 436 it was held that continuing a poor work practice where the practice is a common practice that has gone uncorrected at the place of work does not necessarily amount to contributory negligence on the part of the employee.

Sheehy v The Devil's Glen Tours Equestrian Centre Ltd.
High Court [2001] I.E.H.C. 176

Facts: The plaintiff to the action, when entering the reception area of the equestrian centre, fell on a strip of wood in the doorway which had a metal strip projecting upwards. The evidence presented in the case noted that the top of the metal strip was approximately two inches above ground level, and that a normal door saddle is usually around a half to three quarters of an inch off the ground. This door saddle was at the entrance to the premises and as a result of her fall she suffered severe personal injury, loss and damage. The defendants gave evidence that thousands of people used the centre and that there had never been a problem with the door.

Issue: In this action the defendants alleged that the plaintiff should have looked where she was going, and in failing to do so her actions were unreasonable and she was therefore partially to blame for her injuries. The court held that the plaintiff to this action was not guilty of contributory negligence.

Lavan J.:

"... Essentially the Defendants submit that the threshold was not a hazard or danger to the visitor. That in so far as there is a conflict between the engineers this is academic as the Plaintiff accepts that she did not see the threshold at all and the Plaintiff's engineer accepts that one inch is sufficient to cause a trip of the kind that occurred. That I should take account of the fact that thousands of visitors have stepped over this saddle without injury or complaint ...

Turning to the issue of contributory negligence in the particular circumstances of this case I am guided by the following view of the law. There is an essential difference between contributory negligence arising out of a breach of statutory duty and contributory negligence arising out of a breach of a common law duty of care. In the latter case

> 'An act of inadvertence if it is an act which a reasonably careful workman (person) would not do will constitute contributory negligence'

See *Higgins v SIAC* 101 ILTR at 168. In that same case I also noticed the opinion of O'Dálaigh CJ at page 171 to the following effect

> 'There may be act of momentary inadvertence which a jury will properly excuse as being the acts which a reasonably careful (person) will do'

These principals have been implemented in practice by Barron J in *Dunne v Honeywell Control Systems Limited and Virginia Milk Products Limited* [1991] ILRM at 595; by Budd J in *Kelly v McNamara* (unreported, The High Court 5th June, 1996) and by myself in a number of cases including *Connell v McGing* (unreported, The High Court 8th December, 2000).

I also note that the Supreme Court have pointed out in a number of cases the view that a Plaintiff, whilst walking is not required to look down at the ground.

In the case before me I'm satisfied that the Plaintiff and her family were visiting what, on any view of the case, was an interesting equestrian centre all of which was new to the Plaintiff on her first visit thereto.

I have seriously considered whether the actions of the Plaintiff constituted an act of inadvertence which a reasonably careful person would not do and likewise have considered the matter from the point of view as to whether I should deem the Plaintiff's actions in talking to her family and walking through the door as such an act of momentary inadvertence which a jury (and in this care which I) would properly excuse of being an act which a reasonably careful person will do. Taking all these matters into account I have concluded that it would be unreasonable to find the Plaintiff guilty of contributory negligence in the particular circumstances as pleaded in this case.

In the circumstances I find the Defendant liable in negligence. I find the Plaintiff not guilty of contributory negligence.

The Parties very sensibly had agreed the medical reports at outset of this case. Upon my invitation they agreed the general damages and the special damages."

Comments and Questions:
1. The court has taken a very pragmatic view about what is deemed to be reasonable behaviour on the part of the plaintiff. The plaintiff is not required to be perfect in her actions and behaviour. Momentary inadvertence will not give rise to an action in contributory negligence.

Contributory negligence effectively focuses the court on the actions of the plaintiff, to assess whether his/her actions added to the damage suffered. The issue of intoxication of a plaintiff was addressed in *Boyne v Bus Átha Cliath* [2003] 4 I.R. 47.

Boyne v Bus Átha Cliath
High Court [2003] 4 I.R. 47

Facts: The plaintiff to the action was on a bus belonging to the defendant, and had consumed six pints of beer. When the plaintiff was getting off, he somehow came in contact with the bus and, according to one witness, was spun by its motion and run over by its rear wheel. The bus continued on its journey. The plaintiff suffered personal injuries.

Issues: Does intoxication attract the defence of contributory negligence? Does a court assess the actions of an intoxicated person by reference to the actions of other intoxicated persons or by reference to persons not intoxicated? The court determined that, when assessing the issue of contributory negligence, the person's intoxicated state is to be disregarded. In this case the court held that the plaintiff to the action was guilty of contributory negligence.

Finnegan P.:

"… Contributory negligence
   The defendants plead contributory negligence and give the following particulars:—
   (a) failing to have any or adequate regard for his own safety;
   (b) failing to look where he was going;
   (c) exposing himself to a risk of danger or injury of which he knew or ought to have known;
   (d) needlessly endangering himself;
   (e) failing to pay attention or sufficient attention to what he was about;
   (f) failing to have any regard for his own safety in exposing himself to a risk of injury by reason of the excessive consumption of alcohol;
   (g) if [he] did fall, by causing himself to fall;
   (h) that the plaintiff was the author of his own misfortune.

The onus of establishing contributory negligence is on the defendants. Where there is no direct evidence, reliance must be placed on inference as a matter of probability as to what occurred: *Clancy v. Commissioners of Public Works in Ireland* [1992] 2 I.R. 449 at p. 467. Upon this basis I find that the plaintiff, due to his intoxicated state, while on the roadway and before attaining the footpath, stumbled and fell against the bus and then under the wheels of the bus. Counsel were unable to assist me with authorities as to how the court should approach the issue of contributory negligence having regard to the plaintiff's state of intoxication.

The matter is dealt with in Charlesworth on Negligence (8th ed.) at para. 3.48 as follows:—

> 'The excuse of drunkenness has to be disregarded, when considering contributory negligence. It is no excuse for failing to take reasonable care to prove that the person in question was unable to take proper care, owing to the influence of drink or drugs, which he had taken voluntarily. A drunken man cannot demand from his neighbour a higher standard of care than a sober man or plead drunkenness as an excuse for not taking the same care of himself when drunk, as he would have taken when sober. (*M'Cormick v. Caledonian Railway* (1903) 5 F. 362).'

In *Kilminster v. Rule* (1983) 32 S.A.S.R. 39, where a person under the influence of drink stepped into the roadway in front of a car at night and was killed, he was held to have contributed to the accident to the extent of 35%. I cannot see that this differs in any way from the outcome which would be expected if the plaintiff had been sober.

In a number of cases this issue arose in circumstances where the plaintiff was so intoxicated that he did not realise that the driver of the car in which he had taken a lift was himself unfit to drive through drink. The first of these, *Dann v. Hamilton* [1939] 1 K.B. 509, was argued and determined on the basis of *volenti non fit injuria*, the plaintiff's counsel having declined the trial judge's invitation to amend his pleadings to include a plea of contributory negligence: see letter from Lord Asquith discussing his decision in this case in (1953) 69 L.Q.R. 317. I find the discussion in other such cases, e.g., *Nettleship v. Weston* [1971] 2 Q.B. 691 unhelpful. However, in an Australian case, *Insurance Commissioner v. Joyce* (1948) 77 C.L.R. 39 at p. 47, Latham L. J. said:—

> 'If ... the plaintiff was sober enough to know and understand the danger of driving with (the defendant) in a drunken condition, he was guilty of contributory negligence ... but if he was not sober enough to know and understand such a danger ... if he drank himself into a condition of stupidity or worse, he thereby disabled himself from avoiding the consequences of negligent driving by (the defendant), and his action fails on the ground of contributory negligence.'

As I understand this, whether the defendant was under the influence of drink only to the extent that he knew or ought to have known and understood the risk he was running, or whether he was so under the influence that he was incapable of so knowing, he is, nonetheless, guilty of contributory negligence.

In *McKevitt v. Ireland* [1987] I.L.R.M. 541 at p. 546, Finlay C.J. said:—

> 'The finding by the jury that the plaintiff was guilty of contributory negligence implies a finding that he had by the time of the commencement of the fire sufficiently recovered from his drunken condition to owe a duty to take reasonable care for his own safety, which he failed to discharge.'

At first sight this might be seen as authority for the proposition that a plaintiff so under the influence of drink that he did not know or ought not to have known of the risk to his own safety would not be guilty of contributory negligence. The statement must be read in conjunction with the facts of the case. The plaintiff was in police custody while drunk and injured himself by setting fire to his cell with matches which a search had not uncovered. The Supreme Court held that a finding of 15% proportion of fault against the plaintiff was unreasonable to the extent that it should be set aside. I think it likely that Finlay C.J. was having regard to the duty which rested upon the defendant in the circumstances of that case: in short, the greater the degree of intoxication of the plaintiff to the knowledge of the defendant, the more onerous the duty of care on the defendant. The statement merely acknowledges the effect of *Donoghue v. Stevenson* [1932] A.C. 562 on the principle enunciated in *M'Cormick v. Caledonian Railway* (1903) 5 F. 362.

In *McEleney v. McCarron* [1993] 2 I.R. 132, an accident occurred when the plaintiff, who was drunk, was being assisted to his home by two girls and he fell onto the road. The girls had succeeded in moving his body such that his legs were on the footpath and his torso on the road when the second defendant's car approached. The girls moved onto the footpath and attempted to attract the attention of the defendant. The defendant believed the girls wished to thumb a lift and did not stop his car and ran over the plaintiff's head, causing him severe personal injuries. In the High Court the plaintiff was found guilty of contributory negligence and fault was apportioned 30% to him. The defendant appealed to the Supreme Court where it was held that the defendant in the circumstances of that case was not negligent. The court expressed no opinion on the questions of contributory negligence and the apportionment of fault.

In *Judge v. Reape* [1968] IR 226 the facts were that the plaintiff had consumed a considerable amount of alcohol before accepting a lift in the defendant's motor car when he knew or ought to have known that the defendant was drunk. The defendant did not deny negligence but pleaded that the plaintiff well knew that the defendant was drunk and so was guilty of contributory negligence. The jury found that the plaintiff had not been negligent. The Supreme Court on appeal found that there was plain evidence of contributory negligence and ordered a retrial. Counsel for the respondent on the appeal relied on passages from *Insurance Commissioner v. Joyce* (1948) 77 CLR 39 but not on the passage which I have quoted above. The passage quoted from Charlesworth on Negligence (4th ed.) para. 1139 at p. 229 in the judgment, and, it appears to me, accepted as correct by the Supreme Court, is as follows:—

> 'If a passenger in a motor car is himself drunk so that he does not realise that the driver of the car is also drunk and allows himself to be driven, he is guilty of contributory negligence in the event of a collision.'

From the foregoing it seems to me that the following principles can be gathered:—

(1) if the plaintiff is under the influence of drink to an extent that affects his ability to take care of himself, and whether he knows or ought to know of the risk he is running, this is a factor relevant to the existence and the extent of the defendant's duty of care;

(2) in assessing the plaintiff's conduct for the purposes of contributory negligence, his intoxicated state is to be disregarded and this is so whether, notwithstanding his intoxicated state, he knew or ought to have known of the risk which he was running or was incapable of so knowing.

In the circumstances of this case, in apportioning liability I take into account the circumstance that the second defendant was aware of the intoxicated condition of the plaintiff and the extent of his intoxication and to evaluate his conduct accordingly. In so far as the plaintiff is concerned, I evaluate his conduct as if he were sober. I am satisfied that the plaintiff on that basis did not take reasonable care for his own safety. If sober, he would have moved himself promptly to a position of safety some little way from the bus and would not have stumbled against and under the bus as he did. I apportion liability 75% to the defendant and 25% to the plaintiff."

Comments and Questions:

1. Do you think that the apportionment of 25 per cent was reasonable given the facts of the case?

The court determines how to apportion the damage between the plaintiff and the defendant. Section 34(1) of the Civil Liability Act provides that this is done "as the court thinks just and equitable" and it is based on the degree of fault of each party. Where it is not possible to establish different degrees of fault between the parties, s.34(1)(a) provides that "liability shall be apportioned equally."

O'Sullivan v Dwyer
Supreme Court [1971] I.R. 275

Facts: The plaintiff was a carpenter who had agreed with the defendant to work on the roofing of a number of houses for a fixed sum of money. While working on the roof the plaintiff fell about 10 feet to the ground and suffered serious injuries which resulted in paralysis of the lower body. To apportion damage in a case is an attempt to assess the level of "fault" or "blame" that can attach to each party to the incident. At the trial of the action in the High Court, the jury found for the plaintiff, but then found the plaintiff guilty of contributory negligence. The jury apportioned to the plaintiff 40 per cent of the fault and 60 per cent of the fault to the defendant. The defendant appealed to the Supreme Court, disagreeing with the apportionment, and asking for a retrial on the amount awarded for general damages.

Issues: The issue for the court was how to determine the correct apportionment of fault.

Walsh J. (Ó Dálaigh C.J. and Fitzgerald J. concurring):

"… It was also submitted on behalf of the defendant that the apportionment of fault in this case was such that no reasonable jury could have attributed 60% of the fault to the defendant and only 40% to the plaintiff and that, therefore, the apportionment ought to be set aside. In support of this it was submitted, as set out in the notice of appeal, that the learned trial judge should have directed the jury that the apportionment of degrees of fault should be on the basis of culpability and that he did not fully or correctly direct the jury on this topic in accordance with the provisions of the Civil Liability Act, 1961…

It is quite clear that no question of the apportionment of fault arises at all unless both the plaintiff and the defendant have contributed causatively. If the defendant has not contributed causatively there can be no verdict against him, and if the defendant has contributed causatively but the plaintiff has not then there is no question of apportionment of fault …

Under the provisions of s.34 of the Act of 1961 the question of apportionment of fault only arises when the plaintiff has been found guilty of contributory negligence and not in the case of any other wrong on the part of the plaintiff, although the defendant's wrong may not necessarily be negligence at all. The provisions of the Act of 1961 indicate clearly that fault is not equated to causation but that it does flow from causation in the sense that if there is no causation there can be no fault …

Under our statutory provision one party may be guilty of several wrongs and the other be guilty of one only, or vice versa, but it appears to me that fault, in the sense in which it is used in the Act of 1961, is not apportioned by comparing the sum of the wrongs on one side with the sum of the wrongs on the other side. A single wrong on one side may have done far more to bring about the damage than the sum of the wrongs on the other side. This seems to me to indicate that blameworthiness is involved in the sense of a party being more to blame or less to blame, as the case may be, in the normal sense—as if one were to say, in respect of somebody's action, that he ought to have known better or that he could hardly have been expected to know that. That this is so appears to be recognised by the provisions of s.43 of the Act of 1961 which provide that where the defendant's wrong is the breach of strict statutory or common-law duty without fault there shall be no apportionment of fault as against him.

However, it appears to me that in the apportionment of fault this indicates that, where a defendant's causative contribution to damage has been his breach of such strict duty, there must also be negligence on his part before any apportionment of the fault can be attributed to him. In my view, this indicates that under our law an action for breach of strict duty is not an action for negligence although some breaches of statutory duty may give rise to an action for negligence: see the definition of 'negligence' in s. 2 of the Act of 1961. Breach of strict duty is in itself actionable and appears to me to be a cause of action in which foreseeability is not a necessary ingredient. On the other hand the torts of negligence and of public nuisance, as distinct from the tort of breach of strict duty, are based upon personal culpability arising from the failure to avoid the foreseeable. It appears to me that this conclusion necessarily follows from the statutory distinction which the Act of 1961 makes between the wrong of breach of strict duty and the wrongs importing fault. Of course, it is possible to show that in many (if not most) cases of breach of strict duty there has also been culpable wrong or fault on the part of the defendant, but that is a different situation.

The result, however, appears to be somewhat anomalous. Under the terms of the Act of 1961 a person who has caused damage by the commission of a wrong which amounts to a breach of strict duty is liable in damages to the person injured thereby, even though the wrongdoer was not guilty of any fault, provided that the person injured was not guilty of contributory negligence. The position appears to be that, once he has been found guilty of contributory negligence, the person injured will fail to recover anything if the defendant wrongdoer cannot be shown to have been at fault. For example, the occupier of a factory may be under a strict duty not to use a certain piece of equipment unless it is of adequate strength, which is a continuing obligation; if the equipment proves not to be of adequate strength because of a defect which was not patent and which could not have been discovered by reasonable care or inspection (as in *Doherty* v. *Bowaters Irish Wallboard Mills Ltd.* [[1968] IR 277]) and this causes injury, the defendant would be liable in full to the injured party if the latter is not shown to have been guilty of any contributory negligence. On the other hand, if the injured party is shown in such case to have been guilty of any degree of contributory negligence amounting to causation, no part of the fault would be attributed to the defendant unless it could be shown that he was at fault in addition to being guilty of breach of strict duty. In such a case, therefore, it would be necessary to prove that the defendant was guilty not merely of breach of strict duty but also of some other causative factor from which fault could be deduced. It is right, however, to add that in a case of breach of strict duty only, a plaintiff could scarcely be found guilty of contributory negligence unless he had knowledge of the breach of strict duty found against the defendant.

It appears to me then that ... a judge, in directing a jury, must direct their minds to the distinction between causation and fault and that they should be instructed that degrees of fault between the parties are not to be apportioned on the basis of the relative causative potency of their respective causative contributions to the damage, but rather on the basis of the moral blameworthiness of their respective causative contributions. However, there are limits to this since fault is not to be measured by purely subjective standards but by objective standards. The degree of incapacity or ignorance peculiar to a particular person is not to be the basis of measuring the blameworthiness of that person. Blameworthiness is to be measured against the degree of capacity or knowledge which such a person ought to have had if he were an ordinary reasonable person: see the judgment of this Court in *Kingston* v. *Kingston* [(9168) 102 ILTR 65]. To that extent the act can be divorced from the actor. In many cases greater knowledge may attract a greater share of the blame or fault, but so also may greater ignorance. Fault or blame is to be measured against the standard of conduct required of the ordinary reasonable man in the class or category to which the party whose fault is to be measured belongs; but both common sense and public policy require that ignorance of the law is not a factor to be taken into account in the diminution of fault …

So far as the amount of fault attributed to the plaintiff is concerned, the jury might very well in this case have divided the fault equally but, in my view, the evidence is not coercive to the point where a reasonable jury could not attribute more of the fault to the defendant than to the plaintiff. There was ample evidence upon which the jury could have held that the plaintiff was, or ought to have been, as fully alive to the necessity for safeguards as the defendant but, in apportioning blame between the parties, the jury would be quite entitled to take into account that the plaintiff, by reason of his preoccupation with the particular work he was doing, might well overlook the immediate danger when it arose and that the defendant ought to have foreseen such an event. Therefore, in apportioning blame between the parties, a jury might reasonably come to the conclusion that the defendant was really more to blame than the plaintiff; on such a view the apportionment of 60% of the fault to the defendant and 40% to the plaintiff would be quite sustainable. In my view, therefore, the apportionment is not one which no reasonable jury could arrive at and there are no grounds for disturbing it."

Comments and Questions:
1. What is meant by blameworthiness, and is this different from moral blameworthiness?

2. How do the courts treat the rule in contributory negligence for a breach of a strict duty as opposed to a breach of a tort such as negligence or nuisance?

The issue of "fault" is further defined in the case of *Carroll v Clare County Council* [1975] I.R. 221. Here the court reviewed the use of the term "moral blameworthiness", as used by Walsh J. in *O'Sullivan v Dwyer* (above). The court in this instance linked the term "blameworthiness" with the causative contributions to the accident, which is measured by what is to be expected from a reasonable person in the circumstances.

Carroll v Clare County Council
Supreme Court [1975] I.R. 221

Facts: The plaintiff to this action, while driving at night, collided with a traffic island at the junction of a minor and a major road. The plaintiff approached the junction from the minor road and, while he had passed a warning sign and road markings, the traffic island was not illuminated. Evidence suggested it was possible that the plaintiff could have been misled by old traffic markings on the road. The plaintiff had consumed a number of beers before driving. As a result of the action he suffered severe personal injuries. The jury in the action apportioned 70 per cent of the blame to the defendant and 30 per cent to the plaintiff.

Issues: At the trial of the plaintiff's action in the High Court, the jury found that the plaintiff had been negligent in driving too fast and failing to keep a proper look out. The jury held that the plaintiff was 30 per cent at fault and the defendants 70 per cent. In determining the appeal the Supreme Court reviewed how the apportionment of fault pursuant to s.34(1) of the Civil Liability Act 1961 should be effected. The court reviewed the issue of blameworthiness, and linked it to the causative contributions to the damage done. Therefore, the percentage by which each party caused the damage is the correct apportionment in an action, and the actions of each party are measured by the standard of care to be expected from a reasonable person in the circumstances. The test imposed in this action is an objective test. The court upheld the appeal; they held that the apportionment was grossly disproportionate, so reversed the findings, holding the plaintiff to be 70 per cent at fault and the defendant 30 per cent.

Kenny J. (Henchy and Griffin JJ. concurring):

"The principal grounds of appeal in this case are (1) that the trial judge erred in the way in which he advised the jury to apportion the fault for the accident if they held that both parties were negligent; (2) that the apportionment which the jury made was grossly disproportionate to the admitted facts; and (3) that the general damages were excessive. The case raises important questions about the construction of s.34 of the Civil Liability Act, 1961, and as to the form of questions to be submitted to the jury in regard to general damages, when these are claimed for disability and pain suffered before the trial and to be suffered after it ...

Section 34, sub-s. 1, of the Civil Liability Act, 1961 in so far as it is relevant to this action, reads:—

'(1) Where, in any action brought by one person in respect of a wrong committed by any other person, it is proved that the damage suffered by the plaintiff was caused partly by the negligence or want of care of the plaintiff or of one for whose acts he is responsible (in this Part called contributory negligence) and partly by the wrong of the defendant, the damages recoverable in respect of the said wrong shall be reduced by such amount as the court thinks just and equitable having regard to the degrees of fault of the plaintiff and defendant...'

The section does not say that the damages are to be reduced by such amount as the court thinks just and equitable having regard to the degrees of negligence, but the section refers to fault of the plaintiff and the defendant.

In *O'Sullivan* v. *Dwyer* [[1971] IR 275] Mr. Justice Walsh (with whose judgment Ó Dálaigh CJ and FitzGerald J agreed) said at p. 286 of the report:

'It appears to me then that Mr. Liston is correct in his general submission that a judge, in directing a jury, must direct their minds to the distinction between causation and fault and that they should be instructed that degrees of fault between the parties are not to be apportioned on the basis of the relative causative potency of their respective causative contributions to the damage but rather on the basis of the moral blameworthiness of their respective causative contributions. However, there are limits to this since fault is not to be measured by purely subjective standards but by objective standards. The degree of incapacity or ignorance peculiar to a particular person is not to be the basis of measuring the blameworthiness of that person. Blameworthiness is to be measured against the degree of capacity or knowledge which such a person ought to have had if he were an ordinary reasonable person: see the judgment of this Court in *Kingston v. Kingston* [(1968) 102 ILTR 65].'

I think that 'fault' in s.34 of the Act of 1961 means a departure from a norm by a person who, as a result of such departure, has been found to have been negligent and that 'degrees of fault' expresses the extent of his departure from the standard of behaviour to be expected from a reasonable man or woman in the circumstances. The extent of that departure is not to be measured by moral considerations, for to do so would introduce a subjective element while the true view is that the test is objective only. It is the blameworthiness, by reference to what a reasonable man or woman would have done in the circumstances, of the contributions of the plaintiff and defendant to the happening of the accident which is to be the basis of the apportionment. I think that the use of the word 'moral', when addressing a jury in connection with blameworthiness, is likely to mislead them. Two examples may illustrate this: if an elderly lady is driving a motor car towards a traffic light which is showing red to her and if she, intending to put her foot on the brake, puts her foot on the accelerator and causes a serious accident, she is morally blameless but seriously blameworthy. If the plaintiff admits that some hours before the accident he had a glass of beer and if a member of the jury is of opinion that one should not drive when one has any alcoholic drink taken, the juryman may apply his particular standard of morality to apportioning blameworthiness and may decide to attribute blameworthiness to the plaintiff on moral grounds although no suggestion is made by either party that the plaintiff was unfit to drive or that his driving was affected by the alcoholic drink which he had consumed. Therefore I think that judges, when addressing juries, should not under any circumstances use the word 'moral' when speaking of blameworthiness, but that they should emphasise that the jury are to apportion the fault according to their view of the blameworthiness of the causative contributions to the accident and that it is to be measured and judged by the standards of conduct and care to be expected from a reasonable person in the circumstances.

I wish to emphasise that I agree with the principle in the passage which I have quoted from the judgment of Mr. Justice Walsh and I make these remarks only because 'moral blameworthiness' (which he was so careful to define in exact language) when used to a jury introduces a subjective element which is not consistent with the objective standard laid down in the passage and which will probably be misunderstood by juries and so will produce verdicts of apportionment on a wrong legal basis.

The trial judge put before the jury for their consideration the view that somebody who maintains a danger must be the more blameworthy when compared with a driver who is guilty of one act of negligence. When the jury had retired, Mr. Liston (for the defendants) objected to this passage in the charge and the judge said that the view that a person who maintains a danger is more blameworthy than a person guilty of a casual act of negligence approaching that danger was supported by the decision of this Court in *Walsh* v. *The Galway Harbour Commissioners* (18th December, 1972). The trial judge in this case said that his statement of this had been approved by Ó Dálaigh CJ in his judgment in the Supreme Court in *Walsh's Case, supra*. That case was heard at first instance by Mr. Justice Butler sitting without a jury; in the course of his judgment in that case he said that in normal circumstances he would be inclined to apply the principle that when there has been an accident, a person who maintains or permits an unusual danger must be more at fault than one who is guilty of what might be described as a casual act of negligence which contributes to the accident. In his judgment in the Supreme Court, Ó Dálaigh CJ did not either approve or disapprove of this statement—though he did say that the trial judge's apportionment of 50% to the defendants was the least which he could have allocated.

However, it is not a principle of law that a person who maintains or permits an unusual danger must bear a higher share of fault than that attributed to a person guilty of a casual act of negligence. Pressed to its logical conclusion, this leads to the result that a motorist is entitled to recover more than half the damages resulting from a collision at night between his vehicle and a traffic island which was insufficiently lighted, even though he had passed warning signs and had consumed far too much alcoholic drink and had been driving at an excessive speed. This is not the law.

In each case it is a question of fact whether a person who creates or maintains a danger is more blameworthy than a person who collides with it. As Lord Wright said in *Tidy* v. *Battman* [[1934] 1 KB 319] it is unfortunate that questions which are questions of fact alone should be confused by importing into them, as principles of law, a course of reasoning which has properly been applied in deciding other cases on other sets of facts. The dangers of stating general principles in relation to what are essentially questions of fact is well illustrated in our law reports. In *O'Beirne* v. *Hannigan*, [[1937] IR 237] FitzGibbon J. said that a motorist who plunged into a 'black shadow' without being able to see in front of him, and who collided with a stationary vehicle, must be held to have been guilty of contributory negligence. This statement was made at a time when contributory negligence was a complete defence to an action. Mr. Justice FitzGibbon's remarks were frequently distinguished and explained (though much of the explaining was explained away) until they were finally overruled in *Hayes* v. *Finnegan* [[1952] IR 98].

As it is not a principle of law that a driver who drives on when he cannot see ahead of him and collides with an unlighted object is necessarily guilty of contributory negligence (because this is essentially a question of fact which should not be judged by general principles), so in the same way someone who erects or maintains what is a danger in a public place need not, in the particular circumstances, necessarily have attributed to him the greater share of fault for an accident.

This Court will not generally interfere with the apportionment of fault made by a jury if it is not substantially different from the way in which the Court would have apportioned it. However, if there is gross disproportion between the apportionment by the jury and that which this Court would have made having regard to the undisputed facts, or if there has been a gross error on the part of the jury on the undisputed facts, this Court will reverse or review the verdict of the jury on this issue: *Donoghue* v. *Burke,* [[1960] IR 314]; *Murphy* v. *Cronin* [[1966] IR 699]; and *O'Leary* v. *O'Connell* [[1968] IR 149].

In this case the jury found that the defendants were negligent in failing to light the traffic islands and in failing to ensure that the old traffic lines did not become visible in any way: for this the jury held that the defendants were 70% at fault. They also found that the plaintiff was negligent in failing to take reasonable care because he did not keep a proper look out and because he drove too fast: for that they attributed 30% of the fault to him. In my opinion this apportionment bore no relation to the undisputed facts and to a proper and rational assessment of the degrees of fault of the plaintiff and the defendants for this unfortunate accident.

The plaintiff must have known that he was tired and should have known that his reaction was bound to be slow because his day had started at 8 a.m. in Dublin. He saw the 'major road ahead' sign and continued to drive at 40/50 m.p.h. He failed to see the vivid cross-hatched marks on the road, which he drove over, and the double line on the road. These together measured 158 feet and the plaintiff could have stopped his car so that there would have been no accident if he had slowed down when he had seen the 'major road ahead' sign, and if he had seen the stop sign which he could not have failed to see for a considerable distance if he had kept any reasonable look out. Drinking four or six beers at his friends' house certainly did not help his concentration. If he had been paying any attention to the road in front of him, the plaintiff would have seen the vivid crosshatched part of the road and the stop sign and he would have realised that he had to keep to the left of the cross-hatched part and of the white double line which led to the island. The defendants were negligent in failing to light the islands and in failing to ensure that the marks of the old line did not become visible again. In my opinion the proper apportionment of fault in this case is 30% to the defendants and 70% to the plaintiff."

Comments and Questions:
1.   What test is used to determine the correct apportionment in a case? Does the issue of morality play any role in that decision?

Duty to mitigate damage

Section 34(2)(b) of the Civil Liability Act of 1961 states that "a negligent or careless failure to mitigate damage shall be deemed to be contributory negligence in respect of the amount by which such damage exceeds the damage that would otherwise have occurred." In *Bohan v Finn DPIJ: Trinity and Michaelmas Terms 1994*, the court held that the failure of the plaintiff to undergo treatment for a psychosomatic illness, which was likely to be cured, could amount to contributory negligence. A more common occurrence relates to the use of seat-belts in cars which was addressed in *Hamill v Oliver* [1977] I.R. 73.

Hamill v Oliver
Supreme Court [1977] I.R. 73

Facts: The plaintiff was a passenger in the front seat of a car which was in a collision with the defendant's car. The car in which the plaintiff was travelling was equipped with a safety belt but she was not wearing the belt at the time of the accident. The defendant to the action did not deny liability, but requested the trial judge to leave a question to the jury asking them whether or not the plaintiff had been guilty of contributory negligence in failing to wear the safety belt. The trial judge refused to leave the question to the jury, on the basis that the wearing of a safety belt would not have prevented the accident. This point was appealed to the Supreme Court.

Issues: The court had to determine whether the use or non-use of a seat belt was relevant in determining the issue of contributory negligence. The court held that the failure to wear the safety belt did amount to contributory negligence as the injuries received by the plaintiff would have been prevented or reduced by wearing the safety belt.

Griffin J. (O'Higgins C.J. and Henchy J. concurring):

"... The two questions which arise for consideration in this appeal are (1) whether the judge was correct in deciding that the question of contributory negligence did not arise, and (2) whether the jury's award of £6,000 for general damages was excessive.

The first question is whether the trial judge should have ruled out contributory negligence although the plaintiff was not wearing the seat belt provided in her husband's car. Neither the plaintiff nor her husband was wearing a seat belt at the time. This was a new car, being only a few months old, but she said in evidence that they had never worn the seat belts provided.

The Road Traffic (Construction, Equipment and Use of Vehicles) (Amendment) Regulations, 1971—S.I. No. 96 of 1971—made it obligatory to fit safety belts and anchorage points in motor cars for use by the driver and the front-seat passenger farthest from him. The regulations apply to all cars first registered on or after the 1st June, 1971, and the car in which the plaintiff was travelling was so fitted. Since March, 1973, all main roads in the country display large road-safety posters with the slogan 'Live with a safety belt' painted in very large letters thereon. Advertisements appear regularly on television advocating the wearing of seat belts and drawing attention to the risks involved to those who travel in the front seats of a motor car without wearing such belts. When the Oireachtas made it compulsory to fit seat belts to a motor car, it must have been intended that they should be worn although the *wearing* of seat belts was not made compulsory. The plaintiff cannot but have been aware of the advisability of wearing a seat belt and of the risks incurred if she failed to do so.

In the accident, the plaintiff, as she herself described it, was 'thrown on to the gear handle' of the car, and received injuries to her chest and ribs. She fractured the fifth, sixth and seventh ribs on the right side, and she suffered a right pneumothorax with collapse of the lung on that side. The nature of the accident, coupled with these injuries, shows that the primary cause of her injuries was an impact with the gear lever, which would have been situated to her right. She was obviously thrown forward and to the right. This was a type of accident which could not have happened if she had been wearing a seat belt.

Prima facie, therefore, there was contributory negligence on her part. As was held in *Froom* v. *Butcher*, [1976] QB 286 any person who travels in the front seat of a motor car, be he passenger or driver, without wearing an available seat belt must normally be held guilty of contributory negligence if the injuries in respect of which he sues were caused wholly or in part as a result of his failure to wear a seat belt. There may be excusing circumstances for not wearing the seat belt, such as obesity, pregnancy, post-operative convalescence, and the like, where the wearing of a seat belt may be thought to do more harm than good; but it is for the plaintiff who has not worn it to raise and prove such excusing circumstances.

In this case, the trial judge ruled out contributory negligence on the ground that there was no evidence that the wearing of a seat belt would have prevented the accident. However, as was decided in *Froom* v. *Butcher*, [[1976] QB 286] that is not the correct test. The question is whether the wearing of a safety belt would have prevented or reduced the injuries. Here, as in most cases, no special evidence was required on the point. The jury could not but have come to the conclusion that the impact injuries the plaintiff received when her right chest and ribs struck the gear lever would not have happened if she had been wearing a seat belt. Therefore, the issue of contributory negligence was incorrectly ruled out."

Comments and Questions:
1. What, in your opinion, is the position with regard to seat-belts in the back seat of a motor car? Or the use of baby seats in a motor car?

VOLENTI NON FIT INJURIA

In its early form any form of voluntary assumption of risk was fatal to the plaintiff's case. Section 34(1)(b) of the Civil Liability Act 1961 removed this defence except in two specific situations: where a contract exists which amounts to a clear undertaking of the risk; or where the complainant has agreed to waive his or her legal rights to an action. Where either of those situations arise, the partial defence afforded by contributory negligence will apply.

Contract

Where the plaintiff and the defendant have entered into a contract which states that the parties are prepared to adopt the risk associated with the activity, then the plaintiff will be held to have assumed the risk, and will not be permitted to take a case. This issue was addressed in *O'Hanlon v ESB* [1969] I.R. 75.

O'Hanlon v Electricity Supply Board
Supreme Court [1969] I.R. 75

Facts: The plaintiff to the action was an experienced electrician who worked for the defendant. The nature of the work being carried out meant that he needed a particular fuse extractor to carry out the work without danger to himself. He failed to obtain the fuse extractor and continued to carry out the work, knowing that he would work in close proximity to an un-insulated power line. This was not a practice approved of by the employer. The plaintiff received a shock and suffered personal injuries. The defendant denied negligence and successfully pleaded *volenti non fit injuria* in the High Court. The plaintiff appealed.

Issues: Did the Civil Liability Act 1961 remove the defence of *volenti non fit injuria*? Once it is determined that the defence is now governed by the Civil

Liability Act 1961, did the evidence in the action establish an absolute statutory defence within the terms of that Act? Could an uncommunicated decision to undergo a risk constitute a prior agreement as set out by s.34(1)(b) in the Act? The court found for the plaintiff in this action, and held that the defence did not arise.

Walsh J. (Ó Dálaigh C.J., Budd and Fitzgerald JJ. concurring; Haugh J. dissenting):

"… It appears to me that the whole gist of the defendants' cross-appeal, and of their application to have the plaintiff's claim withdrawn from the jury, is the question of causation and what used to be called the defence of *volenti non fit injuria* but which can now only properly be described in the words of the Civil Liability Act, 1961, as 'the defence that the plaintiff before the act complained of agreed to waive his legal rights in respect of it.' The defendants' submissions in respect of the causation factor also covered many of the points relied upon in support of the statutory defence, in as much as it was submitted that the effective cause of the accident was solely the plaintiff's action in unforeseeably undertaking what he admittedly knew to be the dangerous task of working upon, or in close proximity to, the live electric wire. I might observe, in passing, that my use of the phrase 'statutory defence' is advisedly made as, in my view, the defence set out in the terms of the statute is now to be properly regarded as a statutory defence and should be so pleaded. For the purposes of this appeal the defence may be treated as if it had been raised in the terms of the statute.

This is an appropriate point at which to deal with this defence. It is stated in the 14th edition of Salmond on Torts at p. 47 that the maxim *volenti non fit injuria* had its origin in the process by which Roman Law validated the act of a free citizen in selling himself into slavery. It may be fairly stated that the true nature of the defence reflects this historical origin. In the nineteenth century it found its way into the law of torts in which it had a double application in intentional and accidental harms. The present case has reference only to the latter. It is unnecessary to recite in any detail the history of this defence and its treatment by the courts since it entered into the law of torts. In recent years this defence has virtually disappeared in master and servant cases which turn on common-law negligence. It is not allowable at all where a breach of statutory duty is proved against an employer. In England, however, there is some authority for its continued survival in cases of breach of statutory duty imposed on a fellow workman where it is sought to make the master, who has not been guilty of any breach of statutory duty, vicariously liable: see *Imperial Chemical Industries Ltd. v. Shatwell* [[1965] AC 656]. The burden of establishing this defence falls on the defendant in all cases. In *Bowater v. Rowley Regis Corporation* [[1944] KB 476] Lord Goddard said:—'The maxim *"volenti non fit injuria"* is one which in the case of master and servant is to be applied with extreme caution. Indeed, I would say that it can hardly ever be applicable where the act to which the servant is said to be *"volens"* arises out of his ordinary duty, unless the work for which he is engaged is one in which danger is necessarily involved.' For example, there are some occupations which cannot be carried on in perfect safety and where the presence of the danger is mutually recognised in that the servant undertakes the risk for the sake of higher pay. It was well settled, however, that knowledge of the danger and acquiescence in it did not establish the defence, although knowledge and acquiescence were necessary links in the chain of proof which a defendant undertook when he set out to prove that the plaintiff had voluntarily agreed that, if an injury should befall him, the loss should be on him and not on the defendant. Unless a defendant could obtain a finding to that effect he could not have succeeded in his defence. If there was no negligence on the part of the defendant, the point of the defence never arose. Likewise it did not arise if the negligence on the part of the defendant was not a causative factor in the accident.

It now becomes necessary to consider the wording of the relevant provision in the Civil Liability Act, 1961. Section 34 of that Act, which provides for the apportionment of fault in cases of contributory negligence, enacts at sub-s. 1(*b*) that 'this subsection shall not operate to defeat any defence arising under a contract or the defence that the plaintiff before the act complained of agreed to waive his legal rights in respect of it, whether or not for value; but, subject as aforesaid, the provisions of this subsection shall apply notwithstanding that the defendant might, apart from this subsection, have the defence of voluntary assumption of risk.' In s. 2, sub-s. 1, of the Act the word 'contract' is defined as meaning a contract under seal or by parol. This clearly refers to a contract supported by consideration or one under seal. There is no such contract alleged in this case and it is not necessary to consider this point further. It is already settled that such contracts are construed strictly against the party claiming the benefit of the exemption and there are instances where such contracts are actually prohibited by statute.

Under the terms of the Act of 1961 the defendants must establish that the plaintiff agreed to waive his legal rights in respect of the act complained of and that such agreement was made before that act. As no question of statutory duty arises in this appeal it is unnecessary to consider whether any such agreement, if it did exist, would be contrary to statute or to public policy. In my opinion, the use of the word 'agreed' in the Act of 1961 necessarily contemplates some sort of intercourse or communication between the plaintiff and the defendants from which it could be reasonably inferred that the plaintiff had assured the defendants that he waived any right of action that he might have in respect of the negligence of the defendants. A one-sided secret determination on the part of the plaintiff to give up his right of action for negligence would not amount to an agreement to do so. Such a determination or consent may be regarded as 'voluntary assumption of risk' in the terms of the Act but, by virtue of the provisions of the Act and for the purposes of the Act, this would be contributory negligence and not the absolute defence mentioned in the first part of sub-s. 1(*b*)

507

of section 34. According to the text-books the position of the defence of *volenti non fit injuria* prevailing in the first half of the last century was that it was in practice indistinguishable from the then defence of contributory negligence, being generally based upon the finding that a plaintiff was himself the cause of the injury or that the injury resulted from his own act alone. A careful perusal of the arguments advanced by the defendants in the present case shows that they were really submissions to the learned trial judge and to this Court that the plaintiff's injury resulted solely from his own act which, being based upon his knowledge of the risk and his willingness to undergo it in the light of that knowledge, amounted to clear evidence of negligence on the plaintiff's part ...

The defendants' case left open for the jury the consideration of whether the plaintiff's negligence was the sole cause of the accident or whether the negligence on the part of the defendants was also a cause of the accident. In the latter case it would be the duty of the jury to apportion the degrees of fault and the damages would be apportioned accordingly. The statutory absolute defence would not arise for consideration unless the jury were satisfied that the negligence of the defendants was a causative factor. The defendants' submissions as to knowledge of the risk and the willingness to undergo it, or even the choice to undergo it in the light of the knowledge, simply highlights what has been well established since *Smith* v. *Baker & Sons* [[1891] AC 325], namely, that *sciens* is not *volens*. It is difficult to discover any negligence action in modern times where the defence of *volenti non fit injuria* has succeeded. This is understandable when it is remembered that the defence was restrictively construed and that cases in which a person truly consented (not only to run the risk of physical injury from another person's wrongdoing but also to waive his legal rights in respect of it) must be extremely rare in the realm of negligence, apart from those cases where there is in existence a contract within the meaning of the Act of 1961 such as the excursion ticket on the railway or the terms of entry to certain premises.

In the present case there is evidence, which the jury accepted, which discloses that the plaintiff was instructed by the defendants, or their employees who were in authority, to do a certain job which required particular equipment and that the defendants permitted the plaintiff to depart and to carry out the job without the necessary equipment. Assuming for the moment that this negligence of the defendants was a causative factor in the injury suffered by the plaintiff, the question then arises whether it constitutes (with the plaintiff undertaking the job) evidence of a communication between the parties from which it can be inferred that it was agreed that the danger, created by the defendants' negligence, was accepted by the plaintiff to the point of waiving his legal rights if he should be injured by that danger. In my view the answer must be 'No.' It does no more than evidence knowledge of the risk of injury on the plaintiff's part. Knowledge is an essential link in the chain of proof but, if it is the only link in the chain, it is insufficient proof. The evidence did not warrant leaving the question of the statutory defence to the jury. The plaintiff's appeal on that ground should be allowed ...

The real question, and it was not put to the jury, was whether the plaintiff undertook the operation in question in circumstances from which it could be inferred, if it was not actually expressed, that he had agreed with the defendants before the dangerous operation was undertaken that he was exonerating them from liability for their negligence in not furnishing him with the means of disconnecting the current. The judge's charge erroneously permitted the jury to infer agreement from knowledge only and erroneously permitted them to equate a unilateral private determination with an agreement between two parties. In my view this is not permitted by the words of the statute which are 'agreed to waive his legal rights ... whether or not for value.'"

Comments and Questions:
1.   Does the defence of *volenti non fit injuria* exist in Irish law any more?

2.   What replaces the defence of *volenti non fit injuria?*

The defence may arise where there is a clear agreement between the parties or a contract agreeing to waive one's right of action for negligence. The subject of *Regan v Irish Automobile Club*, unreported, High Court, November, 1989 was whether such a contract existed.

Regan v Irish Automobile Club
Unreported, High Court, November 1989

Facts: A motor race was being held in Phoenix Park in Dublin. The plaintiff was officiating at the race as a flag marshal and was injured when a competing motor racing car went out of control, left the track and knocked the plaintiff down causing her serious injuries. The plaintiff alleged that there was a lack of protection for flag marshals at certain posts including the post to which she was assigned.

Issues: The plaintiff took an action in negligence. The defendants counter-claimed that the plaintiff had signed an agreement which gave her the benefit of a personal accident policy, and which agreed to absolve all persons having any connection with the promotion or organisation of RIAC from liability arising out of accidents. The issue was whether this contract was an agreement within the terms of the Civil Liability Act 1961.

Lynch J.:

"... The evidence established to my satisfaction that the Plaintiff and other officials camped in the Phoenix Park on the night of the 13–14 September 1985 and reported for duty to an administration caravan between 6 am and 7 am on the morning of Saturday the 14 September 1985. There the Plaintiff and the other intending officials signed a form proffered to them by the Clerical Officer in charge of the administration caravan. The form contained the following passage:

> 'I agree to act in an official capacity at this meeting and in consideration of the organising club(s) having effected for my benefit a personal accident policy for death or benefits as prescribed more specifically by RIAC requirements, I agree to absolve all persons having any connection with the promotion and/or organisation and/or conduct of the meeting including the (RIAC) the promoting club(s) the owner of the land, entrants and drivers and owners of vehicles from liability arising out of accidents however caused, resulting in damage and/or personal injury to my person and/or property.'

The evidence further established that an insurance policy such as is referred to in the form had been obtained and was in existence at the time when the Plaintiff signed the form although the precise amounts payable thereunder were not clearly established. This imprecision does not seem to me to be material however.

The Plaintiff did not know the details of the insurance policy taken out by the defendants for the benefit of officials at races but she did know that some such provision had been made and she also knew what was in the documents she signed to the extent at least that it contained an exemption clause which purported to restrict her rights to compensation in the event of an accident causing injury to her …

Paragraph 9 of the defence as impliedly denied raises the question of the construction of the terms of the form signed by the Plaintiff before officiating at the motor race meeting and the really relevant portion of that form that falls for construction is the second half of the paragraph already quoted that is to say:

> 'I agree to absolve all persons having any connection with the promotion and/or organisation and/or conduct of the meeting including the (RIAC) the promoting club(s) the owner of the land entrants and drivers and owners of vehicles from liability arising out of accidents howsoever caused, resulting in damage and/or personal injury to my person and/or property.'

Counsel for the Defendants (the moving party in the issue) conceded that the form did not expressly refer to negligence but submitted that it necessarily extended to and included negligence. He cited the following authorities:

O'Hanlon v ESB [1969] IR 75:
Chitty on Contract (24th Edition) paragraph 818 and *Smith v South Wales Switchgear Limited* [1978] 1 All ER 18, [1978] 1 WLR 165

Counsel for the Plaintiff submitted that in the absence of an express reference to negligence and in the light of the rule of law that the contract should be construed strictly against the person who drafted and proffered it, the document should be construed as referring only to accidents without negligence. He submitted that such accidents could readily happen at such an event as a motor race and he cited the following authorities:

Charlesworth on Negligence
Wilks and anor v Cheltenham Homeguard Motor Cycle and Light Car Club and Another [1971] 1 WLR 668, [1971] 2 All ER 369 and *Clayton Love and Sons (Dublin) Limited v British and Irish Steam Packet Company Limited* (1970) 104 ILTR 157.

I am satisfied that it is not fanciful or unreal to envisage accidents happening without negligence on the part of anyone at an event such as that at which the Plaintiff was officiating. Therefore while accidents usually occur due to some carelessness or other on the part of someone and a reference to 'accidents' would usually imply and include negligent accidents the mere reference to accidents in this case would not necessarily imply negligent accidents. However I have to give effect to the words used and the word 'accidents' is not left unqualified. It is qualified by the words 'howsoever caused' and these words are obviously wide enough to embrace negligent accidents for which someone is responsible in law as well as pure accidents for which no one is responsible in law. In addition the use of the word 'liability' presupposes some form of wrong. A pure accident for which no one is responsible would create no liability in anyone and therefore the reference to liability necessarily brings within the ambit of the clause accidents resulting from the wrongful or negligent conduct of others.

It follows that my decision on the preliminary issue actually referred to me by the Order of the 27 February 1989 is that the Plaintiff agreed for valuable consideration to absolve the Defendants from liability in respect of the accident which in fact happened to her and further that the Plaintiff before the accident complained of agreed to waive her legal rights as against the Defendants in respect of it.

Accordingly I rule that, subject to the issue as to whether there was a fundamental breach of contract by the Defendants and if so the effect thereof, the Plaintiff is barred from maintaining these proceedings against the Defendants."

Agreement to waive rights

Walsh J. in *O'Hanlon v ESB* [1969] I.R. 75 said as regards agreements that "a one-sided secret determination on the part of the plaintiff to give up his right of action for negligence would not amount to an agreement to do so." This suggests the necessity for some communication between the parties to such an agreement so that it could reasonably be inferred that the plaintiff has waived his or her legal rights. Failing such a clear agreement it will not be possible to raise this defence. In *McComiskey v McDermott* [1974] I.R. 75 this issue was addressed.

McComiskey v McDermott
Supreme Court [1974] I.R. 75

Facts: The plaintiff and the defendant were travelling at night as passenger and driver in the defendant's motor car. They were taking part as a team in a motor rally; the defendant was the driver and the plaintiff the navigator, when having driven around a corner on a muddy laneway the defendant was faced with an obstruction. Believing he could not stop before reaching the obstruction, he drove his car into a ditch where it overturned and the plaintiff was injured. The dashboard of the defendant's car carried a notice stating that passengers travelled in the car at their own risk. This notice was on the car when the defendant purchased it, and he had not removed it.

Issues: The plaintiff claimed damages in the High Court for the negligence of the defendant. At the trial the jury held that the plaintiff had implicitly agreed to waive his legal rights in respect of injury caused by the negligence of the defendant. While the Supreme Court did not find for the plaintiff, they did agree that the question in respect of the waiver of rights should not have gone to the jury.

Henchy J.:

"… The plaintiff instituted proceedings in the High Court in which he claimed damages for negligence against the defendant, but judgment was given against him for the jury held (*a*) that his claim was defeated because he had impliedly agreed to waive his legal right in respect of any negligence of the defendant causing injury to him, and (*b*) that the defendant was not negligent. From those findings the plaintiff now appeals to this Court.

The question whether the plaintiff had agreed to waive his legal rights in respect of the defendant's negligence so as to enable the defendant to rely on the statutory defence given by s.34, sub-s.1, of the Civil Liability Act, 1961, arose in this way. When the defendant purchased this car in England it had attached to the instrument fascia a notice to the effect that passengers travelled in the car at their own risk. The defendant had not bothered to remove the notice. The plaintiff was present when the car was bought by the defendant and consequently knew of the notice. The only reference made to it before the accident was on one occasion when the plaintiff jokingly said to the defendant that unless he removed the notice no one would sit in the car. The plaintiff denied in evidence that he took the notice seriously when he travelled as a passenger in the car; and the defendant, although his defence formally pleaded that the plaintiff had waived his right to sue, failed to state in evidence that he was relying on the notice when he carried the plaintiff as a passenger. Because the plaintiff was present when the defendant bought this car, he knew that it was the former owner who put the warning notice in the car, so the mere continuance of the notice in the car would not be sufficient to absolve the defendant unless it was proved, or could be inferred, that the defendant adopted the notice as one coming from him and intended to bind the plaintiff and that the plaintiff so accepted it: see *O'Hanlon* v. *Electricity Supply Board* [[1969] IR 75]. The evidence fell short of that. In fact, the plaintiff said in evidence that he disregarded the notice, and the defendant failed to assert that he intended or expected the plaintiff to treat the notice as a binding or effective one. In these circumstances, I consider the jury's verdict that the plaintiff had waived his right to sue to be unsupported by evidence and to be therefore invalid."

Griffin J.:

"... Affixed to the dash-board of the car on the passenger side was a notice to the effect that any person travelling as a passenger in the car did so at his own risk. Neither the plaintiff nor the defendant was able to recollect the exact wording or terms of this notice but they agreed that the effect was as stated. This car had been purchased in England some months previously when the plaintiff and the defendant were working together in England; at the time of the purchase the notice was already affixed to the dash-board and the defendant did not remove it. The plaintiff was with the defendant when the purchase of the car took place. The plaintiff stated that sometime prior to the accident the defendant made some flippant or jocose remark about the notice but the defendant stated that there was no discussion whatever between him and the plaintiff in connection with this notice at any time subsequent to the purchase of the motor car ...

The plaintiff has appealed to this Court on the ground that the trial judge was wrong in law in leaving the first question to the jury; he submits that there was no evidence to justify leaving this particular question to the jury and that they were wrong in answering it in the affirmative ...

The first question is based on what used to be called the defence of *volenti non fit injuria* which, since the Civil Liability Act, 1961, is 'the defence that the plaintiff before the act complained of agreed to waive his legal rights in respect of it.' The law on this topic was settled by this Court in *O'Hanlon* v. *Electricity Supply Board* [1969] IR 75. The majority decision of the Court was delivered by Mr. Justice Walsh and, having set out the terms of s. 34 of the Act of 1961, he stated at pp.91–2 of the report:—'Under the terms of the Act of 1961 the defendants must establish that the plaintiff agreed to waive his legal rights in respect of the act complained of and that such agreement was made before that act. As no question of statutory duty arises in this appeal it is unnecessary to consider whether any such agreement, if it did exist, would be contrary to statute or to public policy. In my opinion, the use of the word "agreed" in the Act of 1961 necessarily contemplates some sort of intercourse or commu-nication between the plaintiff and the defendants from which it could be reasonably inferred that the plaintiff had assured the defendants that he waived any right of action that he might have in respect of the negligence of the defendants. A one-sided secret determination on the part of the plaintiff to give up his right of action for negligence would not amount to an agreement to do so. Such a determination or consent may be regarded as "voluntary assumption of risk" in terms of the Act but, by virtue of the provisions of the Act and for the purposes of the Act, this would be contributory negligence and not the absolute defence mentioned in the first part of sub-s. 1(*b*) of section 34.' Later, at p. 95, Mr. Justice Walsh stated:—'The real question, and it was not put to the jury, was whether the plaintiff undertook the operation in question in circumstances from which it could be inferred, if it was not actually expressed, that he had agreed with the defendants before the dangerous operation was undertaken that he was exonerating them from liability for their negligence in not furnishing him with the means of disconnecting the current. The judge's charge erroneously permitted the jury to infer agreement from knowledge only and erroneously permitted them to equate a unilateral private determination with an agreement between two parties.'

Counsel for the plaintiff submitted that there was no evidence of any 'communication' between the plaintiff and the defendant from which the inference could be drawn that the plaintiff waived his right of action against the defendant, and that the existence of the notice on the dash-board of the car did not convey a message from the defendant to the plaintiff nor did it represent the state of mind of the defendant. Counsel for the defendant cited *Bennett* v. *Tugwell* [[1971] 2 QB 267] in which the defendant successfully relied on the defence of *volenti non fit injuria* where the plaintiff was injured whilst travelling in the defendant's car to which had been affixed a notice stating:—'Passengers travelling in this vehicle do so at their own risk.' On the facts of that case Ackner J. held that the consent of the plaintiff was clearly to be inferred from the facts. The trial judge in that case did not, of course, have to consider the provisions of s. 34 of the Act of 1961. In an appropriate case the affixing of a notice to the dashboard might lead to the inference that there was agreement between the passenger and the owner sufficient to set up the statutory defence under the Act of 1961, but such an inference could not, in my view, be drawn from the facts in the present case. In view of the fact that the defendant himself in evidence at no time relied on the notice, Mr. Ellis was driven to concede that there was no evidence to indicate that the notice in the car on this occasion did in fact represent a communication to the plaintiff by the defendant or the state of mind of the defendant and, in my opinion, there was no evidence which warranted leaving the first question to the jury and, accordingly, the question should not have been left for their consideration."

(Walsh J. concurred on this issue but not on the second issue under dispute.)

Comments and Questions:
1. As stated in *O'Hanlon v ESB* [1969] I.R. 75 there are only two ways to rely on the defence that there is a contract or an agreement to waive your legal remedy. Based on these cases, in your opinion, is this defence unnecessarily difficult to raise?

Employments that carry inherent risks

Certain forms of employment, such as the police, army, or the emergency services, by their very nature carry inherent risks. Are such employees entitled to recover for negligently inflicted injury in the course of such employment? The issue of whether a serving soldier in operations involving armed conflict was entitled to recover was addressed in the case of *Ryan v Ireland, Attorney-General and Minister for Defence* [1989] I.R. 177. The defendant contended that there was no negligence, and that the plaintiff had voluntarily assumed the risk of injury through the action of hostile forces and had waived his legal rights in respect of such injury. The excerpt below will address the issue of the voluntary assumption of risk, in this context.

Ryan v Ireland, Attorney-General and Minister for Defence
Supreme Court [1989] I.R. 177

Facts: The plaintiff was a soldier serving in the United Nations Interim Force in Lebanon under the control of the defendants. In the course of lengthy hostile engagement the plaintiff was ordered by his commanding officer to take a rest from sentry duty in an exposed and unprotected billet near his guard post and was injured in the legs by shrapnel from a mortar attack which hit the billet. In the High Court the defendants denied negligence and pleaded that the plaintiff had voluntarily assumed the risk of his injuries; the trial judge refused to withdraw the case. The plaintiff appealed; the defendants cross-appealed and argued that, at common law, the plaintiff was precluded from suing the State for injury or damage occasioned by any negligence of his superior officers.

Issues: The court found for the plaintiff, holding that there was no rule at common law that those responsible for a serving soldier, even in operations involving armed conflict or hostilities, did not owe him a duty of care or that they were immune from any action for negligence causing him injury.

Finlay C.J. (Hamilton P., Walsh J., Griffin J., and Hederman J. concur):

"... Reliance was placed on the decision of this Court in *Attorney General v. Ryan's Car Hire Ltd.* [1965] IR 642 ... the judgment of Kingsmill Moore J. identifies a similarity between the position of a member of the defence forces and soldiers of other common law countries, it is submitted that decisions of those countries on the liability of the State to serving soldiers injured by the torts of persons for whose acts the State might be vicariously liable are relevant.

The Court was referred to the following decisions: *Dawkins v. Lord Paulet* (1869) LR 5 QB 94; *Wilson v. First Edinburgh City Royal Garrison Artillery Volunteers* (1904) 7 F 168; *Shaw, Savill & Albion Co. Ltd. v. The Commonwealth* (1940) 66 CLR 344; *Parker v. The Commonwealth* (1965) 112 CLR 295 and *Feres v. United States* (1950) 340 US 135. The decision in *Dawkins v. Lord Paulet* which was a majority decision was to the effect that communications made by an officer of the army in the course of his duty concerning the military capacity, competence and character of an inferior officer were absolutely privileged and could not be sued upon. The underlying reason for the decision would appear to have been the necessity for giving to the officer reporting a complete freedom in the nature of his report, having regard to the importance of an accurate and honest appraisal of the military capacity of a serving officer.

The decision in *Wilson v. First Edinburgh City Royal Garrison Artillery Volunteers* (1904) 7 F. 168 as dealt with in Robertson: Civil Proceedings by and against the Crown (1908) would appear to have turned on the immunity of the funds of a regiment from suit because they were funds the property of the sovereign, though it would appear that the individual officer alleged to have been guilty of negligence in the carrying out of a military parade might well have been personally liable to the injured party. In *Shaw, Savill & Albion Co. Ltd. v. The Commonwealth* (1940) 66 CLR 344 the High Court of Australia decided that an action for negligence against the Crown for damage caused by a naval ship whilst it was being navigated in the course of a naval operation against the enemy must fail since the forces of the Crown while in the course of such operations are under no duty of care to avoid loss or damage to private individuals. The underlying principle involved in support of this decision would appear to be the prime and dominant importance of the defence of the realm. In *Parker v. The Commonwealth* (1965) 112 CLR 295 it was held that a civilian employee of the naval service could sue the Commonwealth for injuries caused by the negligent control of a naval ship on peacetime manoeuvres. It is tentatively, though not finally, stated in the judgment of Windeyer J. that a serving member of the navy could not have sued in like circumstances. The reason stated for that view was that it would be prejudicial to the discipline and morale of the armed forces to permit of such an action.

In *Feres v. United States* (1950) 340 US 135 the major issue which arose was the interpretation of the Federal Tort Claims Act, but in the course of the opinion of the US Supreme Court at p. 141 the following statement occurs:—'We know of no American law which ever has permitted a soldier to recover for negligence against either his superior officers or the Government he is serving.' The absolute nature of this proposition for which no principle was advanced is witnessed by the fact that one of the cases, which as a result of the opinion of the Court failed, was one in which a serving soldier who had undergone a stomach operation carried out by an army surgeon, who had removed from his stomach in a subsequent operation a piece of towelling 30 inches by 18 inches marked 'Medical Department of the U.S. Army', was held not entitled to sue.

Counsel on behalf of the State does not contend for such a widespread immunity as is laid down in *Feres' case* but confines his submission to negligence alleged during armed conflict or in a theatre of war. The reason for this distinction and the boundary line between maintainable and prohibited suits arising from the submissions of the State in this case is not very clear to me, and would appear to be based more on pragmatism than principle.

Having regard to these decisions and the submissions made, two questions of law, in my view, arise. 1. Does the common law applicable in Ireland appear to create an immunity for the State in the circumstances of the instant case? 2. If it appears so to do, could such immunity be consistent with the provisions of the Constitution? In my view, the answer to both these questions must be in the negative.

By virtue of the provisions of s.4 of the Defence (Amendment) Act, 1960, a soldier serving with the United Nations Emergency Forces is deemed, for the purpose of the Defence Act, 1954, to be 'on active service.' The consequence of this provision is largely related to discipline and the punishment for military offences. The provision does not, however, in any way, equate service with the United Nations with war, nor do considerations of the defence of the State arise in such service. No question of a dominant priority for the effectiveness of armed action against an enemy occurs.

Article 28 of the Constitution provides the most ample and unrestricted powers to the Oireachtas to legislate to secure public safety and the preservation of the State in time of war, as there defined, or in time of armed rebellion. Nothing in the Constitution shall be invoked to invalidate such legislation expressed to be for such purposes.

It is impossible, having regard to these provisions, to accept the application of a common law doctrine arising from the necessity to ensure the safety of the State during a period of war or armed rebellion, which has the effect of abrogating constitutional rights. In so far, therefore, as the principle apparently supporting some of the decisions to which we have been referred is the question of the dominant priority in regard to the defence of the State, such decisions would not appear to be applicable and cannot be applied to the question of service with the United Nations peacekeeping force.

Section 111 of the Defence Act, 1954, provides certain conditions applicable, *inter alia*, to actions or other proceedings in respect of any alleged neglect or default in the execution of the Act. No argument was presented to the Court with regard to any possible relevance of this section, and these proceedings clearly do not come within it. It would appear, however, to me to be inconsistent with the existence of any common law principle giving immunity from suit for the purpose of preserving the discipline and morale of the Defence Forces.

I, therefore, conclude that an immunity from suit by, or the negation of any duty of care to, a serving soldier in respect of operations consisting of armed conflict or hostilities has not been established as part of our common law. Even if it had, I conclude that in the blanket form which has been contended for it would be inconsistent with the guarantees by the State to respect, defend and vindicate the rights of the citizens contained in Article 40, s. 3, sub-ss. 1 and 2 of the Constitution. This ground of appeal must therefore fail.

Voluntary assumption of risk

Having regard to the decision of this Court in *O'Hanlon v. Electricity Supply Board* [1969] IR 75, for the defendants to succeed in this defence it would be necessary for them to establish that the plaintiff by enlisting and by volunteering for United Nations service, had entered into a contract waiving his right to sue if injured by the negligence of his superior officers. No express contract to that effect is suggested and, while it is correct to say that by enlisting and subsequently volunteering the plaintiff accepted the risks inherent in the possibility of being involved in armed conflict, it cannot be implied that he accepted the risk of being unnecessarily exposed to injury by negligence. This ground of appeal also fails."

Rescuers

It was originally assumed that rescuers had voluntarily assumed the risk of negligently inflicted injury; this is no longer the position. Common law courts have begun to recognise the rights of rescuers to recover in law. This issue was addressed in *Phillips v Durgan* [1991] I.L.R.M. 321.

Phillips v Durgan
Supreme Court [1991] I.L.R.M. 321

Facts: The plaintiffs, who were husband and wife, claimed damages against the defendant in respect of personal injuries suffered by them in a fire in the defendant's house. The plaintiffs were hired to clean the kitchen of the house prior to painting and decorating it. The defendant did not warn the plaintiffs of the state of the kitchen, which was in a condition of extreme dirt and filth consisting of many years' accumulation of grease. The first named plaintiff was cleaning around the cooker area, and fell due to the greasy conditions of the floor; a cloth she was holding came in contact with a flame on the cooker and resulted in a fire in which she received extensive burn injuries. The second named plaintiff was injured in his attempt to rescue her. The High Court held that the fire was not started by the "immediate negligence" of the defendant, but went on to impose liability on him in respect of the injuries sustained by applying a principle akin to the "*rescue*" principle. The learned trial judge refused to make any finding of contributory negligence. The defendant appealed against the finding of liability and against the failure of the trial judge to make a finding of contributory negligence in the case of both plaintiffs.

Issue: The Supreme Court dismissed the defendant's appeal but held that the principle of rescue is essentially a doctrine of foreseeability and cannot come into operation without an initial negligent act or omission.

Finlay C.J. (Hederman J. concurring):

"… I have come to the conclusion, with regard to the legal issues arising in this case, that the following is the position. I am satisfied that what is described as the principle of rescue, and what is dealt with in the case of *Ogwo v Taylor* [1987] 3 All ER 961, truly consists only of a situation in which the court will rule as a foreseeable consequence of the negligent commencement of a fire that persons seeking to put out that fire, either by reason of their duty as officers of a fire brigade or by reason of their desire to prevent damage, whether to persons or property, may be injured by the existence of the fire. It is essentially, therefore, a doctrine of foreseeability and cannot, in my view, come into operation without an initial negligence causing the fire. [Finding negligence to have occurred, Finlay C.J. considered the position of the second named plaintiff in the following manner:]

I do not consider that the plaintiff Liam Phillips [second named plaintiff] could be found guilty of any negligence contributing to this accident. What he did after the fire had started was the natural and obvious thing to do, and could not be an act of contributory negligence, namely, an attempt to put out the fire and to save his wife."

Griffin J.:

"I agree with the judgment delivered by the Chief Justice. I would like to add a few comments.

Whilst holding that the fire started without the negligence of either party, the learned trial judge nevertheless held by applying a principle akin to the *'rescue'* principle, that because the dirty condition of the house owned by the defendant in some way contributed to the occurrence of the fire, the plaintiffs were entitled to succeed in these actions. On the hearing of the appeal it was accepted by counsel that the *'rescue'* principle was neither raised nor argued in the High Court. That principle cannot apply unless there has been negligence on the part of the tortfeasor. The principle is succinctly stated by Lord Denning MR in *Videan v British Transport Commission* [1963] 3 WLR 374 at p. 385, where he says:

'… if a person by his fault creates a situation of peril, he must answer for it to any person who attempts to rescue the person who is in danger. He owes a duty to such a person above all others. The rescuer may act instinctively out of humanity or deliberately out of courage. But whichever it is, so long as it is not wanton interference, if the rescuer is killed or injured in the attempt, he can recover damages from the one whose fault has been the cause of it.'

Likewise, in a number of cases of which *Ogwo v Taylor* [1987] 3 All ER 961 (to which the Chief Justice has referred) is one, it has been held that where a person who by his negligent act had started a fire, and injuries were suffered by another person as a result of fighting the fire, and the person starting the fire should have foreseen that there was a real risk of injury inherent in the situation, there was a clear duty of care on the part of such person, and with no break in the chain of causation, he would be liable for such injuries as were suffered by the person fighting the fire.

It is clear therefore that in both rescue and fire-fighting cases there can be no liability unless there was negligence on the part of the person creating the situation of peril in the former case and on the part of the person starting the fire in the latter case.

On the uncontested facts in this case, the defendant could not, in my opinion, escape a finding of negligence on his part. The walls of the kitchen and the top and sides of the cooker and the floor of the kitchen were all covered with grease. As the plaintiff said in evidence, *'the grease was so thick on the cooker it was like candle grease.'* Three of the four rings on the gas cooker were not working as the jets were all stuffed with grease; on the remaining ring only some of the jets were in working order and the flame from those was unsatisfactory. All these facts were known to the defendant. He should clearly have foreseen that it would be necessary for his sister to have boiling water available to her for the purpose of cleaning the walls before painting. In its then condition, the gas cooker was an extremely high fire hazard. He should therefore have had the geyser and the gas cooker put into efficient working order before she commenced the work she was to do for him. He should also have informed her in advance of the condition of the kitchen so that she could bring with her the necessary materials and tools for carrying out the task she was to perform. The defendant did none of these things, and was clearly in breach of the duty he owed to her.

With regard to the finding of the learned trial judge that, when the plaintiffs arrived on the premises they could see quite clearly that the floor was greasy, and that the failure of the defendant to warn them of the greasiness was therefore irrelevant, that is a finding which in my view is not sustainable. The cases decided by this Court to which the Chief Justice has referred in his judgment establish that knowledge on the part of the plaintiff, whether imparted to her by the defendant or independently possessed by her, would not excuse the defendant unless she could, by virtue of such knowledge, efficiently carry out the work for which she was engaged without exposing herself to the risk of injury. Having regard to the condition of the floor and of the cooker in this case, in my view the plaintiff could not efficiently carry out the work she was doing for the defendant without exposing herself to the risk of injury."

Comments and Questions:
1. Should there be a specific rule protecting the actions of rescuers from the doctrine of contributory negligence? Without such a rule are we at risk of preventing people from going to the aid of others?

ILLEGALITY

The old common law principle of *ex turpi causa non oritur actio* is replaced by
the defence of illegality. Illegality means that a person cannot seek a remedy
under an illegal transaction in which they have participated. Section 57(1) of the
Civil Liability Act 1961 establishes the principle that showing that a plaintiff is
in breach of the civil or criminal law will not in itself be a bar to an action. This
issue was addressed in *Anderson v Cooke* [2005] I.E.H.C. 221.

Anderson v Cooke
High Court [2005] I.E.H.C. 221

Facts: The plaintiff was a passenger in the defendant's car. It was alleged that
the purpose of the journey was to obtain photographic evidence of it performing
at maximum speed for submission to an internet website, MAXED.ie.net. There
was photographic evidence to suggest that on one occasion the car reached the
speed of 126 mph. The car was involved in an accident and the plaintiff
sustained personal injuries. The defendant claimed that the plaintiff had
consented to the risks involved in travelling at such speed, and alleged that as
they were at all material times engaged in a common or joint criminal
enterprise, that the plaintiff was precluded from pursuing the claim on the basis
of the doctrine of *ex turpi causa non oritur actio.*

Issues: Section 57(1) of the Civil Liability Act 1961 provides that: "It shall not be
a defence in an action of tort merely to show that the plaintiff is in breach of the
civil or criminal law." The defence argued that as the plaintiff and the defendants
were engaged in a joint criminal enterprise the doctrine of *ex turpi causa non oritur
actio* applied. The court agreed, finding against the plaintiff in this action.

Finnegan P.:

"… In relation to the defence of ex turpi causa the Civil Liability Act section 57
is relevant. This provides as follows—

> '57(1) It shall not be a defence in an action of tort merely to show that the
> plaintiff is in breach of the civil or criminal law.'

The effect of section 57(1) is to modify but not to abolish the defence of *ex turpi
causa*. While for some time there appears to have been doubt as to whether the
maxim applied to actions based on contract only it is now well settled that it
applies equally to actions grounded in tort: *Hegarty v Shine* 2 LRI 273, and 4
LRI 288 Palles CB at 299, *O'Connor v McDonnell* The High Court Unreported
30th June 1970 Murnaghan J., *National Coal Board v England* 1954 1 All ER
546. In *O'Connor v McDonnell* Murnaghan J. cited with approval the statement
of the law by Lord Mansfield in *Holman v Johnston* 1 Cooper 341—

'No court will lend its aid to a man who founds his cause of action upon an immoral or an illegal act if from the Plaintiff's own stating or otherwise the cause of action appears to arise *ex turpi causa* or the transgression of a positive law of this country then the court says he has no right to be assisted. It is upon that ground the court goes: not for the sake of the defendant.'

The principle however was refined and it was not every crime committed by the Plaintiff which would cause his claim to be non suited. Thus in *National Coal Board v England* the Plaintiff was in breach of the Explosives in Coalmines Order 1934 the contravention of which was an offence. This was held not to bar him succeeding in his action. Lord Porter cited with approval from the judgment of Cohen L.J. in *Cakebread v Hopping Brothers (Whetstone) Limited* 1947 1 All E.R. 389

'The maxim ex turpi causa is based on public policy, and it seems to me plain that on the facts of this case public policy, far from requiring that the action shall be dismissed, requires that it shall be entertained and decided on its merits. The policy of the (Factories Act 1937) makes it plain that such a defence as was put forward by Counsel for the employers in this case would be inconsistent with the intention of Parliament when it passed the Act.'

He held that the policy of the Act was to ensure a safe method of working.

This policy based approach was also adopted in Canada in *Henwood v Municipal Tramways Trust (S.A)* (1938) 60 CLR 438. The Plaintiff was a passenger in a tram and becoming affected by nausea put his head outside the window and was struck by two standards while the tram was in motion. His conduct was in breach of a byelaw which exposed him to a penalty. The Defendant was found liable and it was held that the Plaintiff's breach of the byelaw was not a defence to his action. It was there held that there is no general rule denying to a person who is doing an unlawful act the protection of the general law imposing upon others duties of care for his safety. Thus at common law an occupier could incur liability to a trespasser. See also *Revill v Newbery* 1996 1 All ER 291 an occupiers liability case in which the occupier shot the Plaintiff who was attempting to break into his premises and in which the Defendant was found liable.

The maxim is more likely to have application in circumstances of joint illegal activity. This was the case in *O'Connor v McDonnell* where the Plaintiff and the Defendant with others were engaged in the poaching of deer when the Defendant accidentally shot the Plaintiff. Murnaghan J. held that the maxim applied and that the Plaintiff must fail. The applicability of the maxim to joint unlawful activities has been considered in a number of Australian cases—*Smith v Jenkins* 1970 119 CLR 397, *Jackson v Harrison* 1978 138 CLR 438 and *Gala & Ors v Preston* 100 ALR 29. In *Gala* the Plaintiff together with the three Defendants drank all afternoon and then stole a motor vehicle. They drove for some four hours drinking beer and sharing the driving after which the vehicle crashed while being driven by the first Defendant. On appeal it was held that the

Plaintiff and the first Defendant were engaged in a joint illegal enterprise. It was held that the driver of the vehicle owed no duty of care to the Plaintiff as the parties were not in a relationship of proximity such as to give rise to a relevant duty of care since it was not possible or feasible for a court to determine what was an appropriate standard of care to be expected in the circumstances. In the course of a Judgment delivered by Mason CJ Deane, Gaudron & McHugh JJ the Court said—

> 'Commencing with *Jaensch v Coffey* (1984) 155 CLR 549 this Court, in a series of decisions, has accepted that a relevant duty of care will arise under the common law of negligence only in a case where the requirement of a relationship of proximity between the Plaintiff and the Defendant has been satisfied. The requirement of proximity constitutes the general determinant of the categories of case in which the common law of negligence recognises the existence of a duty to take reasonable care to avoid reasonably foreseeable and real risk of injury. In determining whether the requirement is satisfied in a particular category of case in a developing area of the law of negligence, the relevant factors will include policy considerations. Where, as in the present case, the parties are involved in a joint criminal activity, those factors will include the appropriateness and feasibility of seeking to define the content of a relevant duty of care. Thus, it would border on the grotesque for the Court to seek to find the content of a duty of care owed by one bank robber to another in blowing up a safe which they were seeking to rob. On the other hand to take an extreme example the other way, it would be unjust and wrong for the Court to deny the existence of the ordinary relationship of proximity which exists between the driver of a motor vehicle and a passenger merely because the driver was, with the encouragement of the only passenger, momentarily driving in a traffic lane reserved for the use of cars with three or more occupants.'

The Court went on to find that the onus lies on the party who asserts that by reason of special and exceptional facts, the ordinary relationship of a driver towards a passenger is transformed into one which lacks the requisite relationship of proximity to give rise to a relevant duty of care. The same view as to onus was taken in the Canadian *case Hall v Hebert* 1993 101 DLR (Fourth) 129. Insofar as this conflicts with the statement of the Law by Lord Mansfield cited by Murnaghan J. in *Holman v Johnston* I prefer the latter view. As the issue historically was policy based I consider it appropriate that the Court may itself raise the issue even if the Defendant does not: there are cases in which the Court has regarded it as contrary to policy to lend assistance to a Plaintiff involved in joint illegal activity even though the defence of *ex turpi causa* is not raised by the Defendant by way of defence—I recall an action for an account of a joint venture between two highwaymen. The Defendant in this case has in fact pleaded *ex turpi causa* and has discharged the onus which rests upon a Defendant.

   The approach adopted in *Gala* save in relation to onus, it seems to me, reflects the common law—it is not in every case in which the parties had acted together in a manner which was illegal that the illegality would be a bar to the action.

This being the case what is then the effect of section 57(1)? Firstly, it seems to envisage the approach adopted by the Court in *National Coal Board v England* [1954] A.C. 403 and *Henwood v Municipal Tramways Trust* (J.A.) (1938) 60 C.L.R. 438, that is, to examine the policy of the statute or common law under which the Plaintiff's illegality arises and then determine if a duty of care exists. Secondly, it seems to me that the Civil Liability Act 1961, even in cases of a criminal act in which both the plaintiff and defendant are jointly engaged, the court is required to enquire upon the basis of proximity whether a duty of care and if so, what duty arose on the part of the defendant to the plaintiff in the circumstances of the particular case. If the court is unable to determine if, and if so what duty of care arose the Plaintiff's claim will fail.

This being the view which I have formed as to the law I am satisfied that in the circumstances of this case it is not possible to determine the duty of care which the Defendant owed to the Plaintiff having regard to the illegal enterprise upon which they were both engaged. If the joint enterprise was that the car should be driven at 70 mph where speed was limited by regulation to 60 mph the Court might well be in a position to establish the standard of care owed by the driver to the passenger: each case must turn upon its own circumstances. In the present case I cannot establish the duty of care if any which was owned by the Defendant to the Plaintiff in order to determine if there was a breach of the same. Insofar as there is authority for the proposition that the Court in a case in which the Plaintiff and Defendant were joint participants in illegal conduct will not hear evidence to enable it to establish whether and if so what duty of care is owed by the Defendant to the Plaintiff by reason of section 57(1) of the Civil Liability Act 1961 that is no longer the law. The denial of relief is related not to the illegal character of the activity but rather to the character and incidents of the enterprise upon which the Plaintiff and the Defendant are engaged and to the hazards which are necessarily inherent in its execution. In the circumstances of this case as I am unable to determine the duty if any which was owed by the defendant to the plaintiff and accordingly to determine whether or not there was a breach of the same the plaintiff fails."

CHAPTER 15

DAMAGES

INTRODUCTION

There are principally three types of remedies available to a claimant in a tort action. One is the legal remedy of damages. Legal remedies are available, as of right, once the tort is proven. The second is the equitable remedy of an injunction. Equitable remedies are by their nature discretionary, *i.e.* it is up to the court to decide in any particular case if it is reasonable to provide an equitable remedy. The third remedy is that of "self-help" *i.e.* where the plaintiff takes action to remedy the wrong. This can arise in cases of trespass, for instance where the plaintiff can take reasonable steps to prevent injury to person or to land. Similarly, with nuisance cases, the plaintiff can take reasonable steps to abate the nuisance.

While damages are often the most appropriate remedy, in some cases, such as that of nuisance, an injunction may also be awarded. Both of these remedies are available through the courts.

Damages are also available by way of application to the Personal Injuries Assessment Board (PIAB).

This chapter will deal with the issue of damages as a remedy only.

DAMAGES

The principle underlying all awards of damages is that of *restitutio in integrum,* which is to restore the person to the position they would have been in had the tort not arisen. Damages are awarded as a lump sum.

It is unusual for an appellate court to interfere with the *quantum* of damages awarded but this will be done if the award is grossly disproportionate to the injury suffered, particularly if the figure has been arrived at with the assistance of a jury.

Where the action is dealt with by the PIAB (as may occur with employers' liability, motor liability and public liability cases) the Board will assess the amount of general damages available by reference to their Book of Quantum (see www.piab.ie). Special damages reflecting actual financial loss are also available. Under s.22 of the Civil Liability and Courts Act 2004 courts must have regard to the *Book of Quantum* of the PIAB.

CATEGORIES OF DAMAGES

Damages can take various forms depending on the finding of the court. A successful plaintiff can be awarded either: contemptuous damages, nominal damages, compensatory damages or exemplary damages.

Contemptuous damages are awarded where a party wins his/her case but the court feels that, morally, s/he does not have a right to damages.

Nominal damages are awarded where no actual damage has occurred but a right has been infringed. This might occur for instance with the tort of trespass which is actionable *per se*. As described by O'Sullivan J., in *O'Keeffe v Kilcullen,* High Court, June 24, 1998: "Nominal damages means a sum of money that may be spoken of but has no existence in point of quantity, the purposes of such damages being twofold, namely, either to assert a right or as a 'peg' on which to hang an order for costs."

Exemplary damages

Exemplary damages are damages awarded not to compensate the victim for harm suffered but rather to punish the defendant for the manner in which the tort was committed and to deter future wrongful conduct by teaching the "wrongdoer that tort does not pay". The decision in *Rookes v Barnard* [1964] A.C. 1129 demonstrates the position as regards the awarding of exemplary damages in England. In that case Lord Devlin laid down three categories where an award of exemplary damages could be made, namely, arbitrary, oppressive or unconstitutional action by the servants of government; wrongdoing calculated to make a profit; or statutory cases. The decision has been greeted with some disapproval in other common law jurisdictions but in Ireland the courts have not categorically rejected Lord Devlin's categorisations (for a contrary view see McCarthy J. in the case of *McIntyre* which follows.) In the following decision in *McIntyre v Lewis* [1991] 1 I.R. 121 the punitive aspect of exemplary damages were highlighted, as was the use of exemplary damages as a means by which the court could mark its strong disapproval for the behaviour of the defendant.

McIntyre v Lewis, Dolan, Ireland and the Attorney-General
Supreme Court [1991] 1 I.R. 121

Facts: The plaintiff had been arrested by the first two defendants, members of the Garda Síochána, in Birr, County Offaly, and held on charges of assaulting the first named defendant, for which he was acquitted when the case came to trial. The plaintiff subsequently sued the defendants for assault, false imprisonment and malicious prosecution. He succeeded in the High Court where the jury awarded him damages. The defendants appealed to the Supreme Court on the basis of, *inter alia*, the award of damages.

Issues: The court (Hederman, McCarthy and O'Flaherty JJ.) was required to consider, *inter alia,* whether exemplary damages had to be expressly pleaded by the plaintiff in order to be awarded and secondly, whether an award of exemplary damages was appropriate in this case.

The court held that "while a claim for exemplary damages need not be expressly pleaded, it was desirable that a plaintiff gave some indication to his opponent that such would constitute part of his claim at the trial". In addition, the court held that "the jury in all the circumstances was clearly entitled to make an award of exemplary damages where there was an abuse of power by employees of the State in breach of the plaintiff's constitutional rights."

McCarthy J. further held that it was "inconsistent with the dynamism of the common law to delimit in any restrictive way the nature of the development of awards of aggravated or exemplary damages."

Hederman J.:

"... Exemplary damages

It is true that exemplary damages were not claimed in the pleadings but they do not have to be expressly claimed in the pleadings under the rules of court. I believe it might be desirable if the plaintiff did indicate in advance (even if it does not form part of the formal pleadings) that he does intend to claim exemplary damages. This is to afford a defendant an opportunity to meet such a case. We were assured by counsel for the plaintiff that they did ask for damages over and above the ordinary general damages but whether what they were seeking were aggravated damages or exemplary damages may not have been altogether clear and, certainly, was not dealt with in any great detail by the learned trial judge beyond what I have already quoted from his charge.

When the jury first returned to court with their verdict they had entered an award of £30,000 for 'special damages' and £30,000 for 'general damages' in respect of the malicious prosecution. The judge pointed out that the agreed special damages were only £1,787.50 and the jury after a very short retrial returned to court and the appropriate sum had been entered for special damages but the sum for general damages had been increased to £60,000.

The question for resolution, now, is whether the total award for damages for malicious prosecution consisting as it must of compensatory damages and an element of exemplary damages is excessive.

I believe that in the circumstances of this case the jury were entitled to award exemplary damages both for the assault and false imprisonment on the one hand and for the malicious prosecution on the other. Equally they were entitled to award exemplary damages in respect of one or other or both. They choose to award what were obviously exemplary damages in relation to the malicious prosecution.

In cases, like this, where there is an abuse of power by employees of the State the jury are entitled to award exemplary damages. One of the ways in which the rights of the citizen are vindicated, when subjected to oppressive conduct by the employees of the State, is by an award of exemplary damages.

I come now to the actual quantum of damages awarded. There was no appeal in respect of the damages awarded for the assault. Counsel for the plaintiff agreed that while, as he contended, it was on the low side it was not such as would call for the intervention of this Court. I believe that the damages awarded for the assault and for the malicious prosecution have to bear some relation to each other.

The medical evidence called on his behalf suggested that he had a mild reactive depression. I have already mentioned that he was worried about what he thought was a certain fear as a result of having brought the present proceedings, as I understand his evidence. On the evidence before the jury, in my view, the maximum award that could be given for general damages for malicious prosecution would be in the region of £5,000. However, in assessing the exemplary damages the jury were entitled to have regard to the conduct of the members of gardaí concerned who, acting in their capacity as gardaí—

(a) brought a false charge against the plaintiff;
(b) gave evidence at the criminal trial to support this false charge; and
(c) in repeating in the civil action what the jury had found to be false evidence given by the same gardaí against the plaintiff in the criminal trial.

However, as I have said, the amount awarded for exemplary damages should bear some relation to the amount that would be proper for general damages. I would substitute an award of £20,000 exemplary damages in the circumstances of this case."

McCarthy J.:

"… Damages

Counsel for the Plaintiff has informed us that reference was made both in the opening and closing speeches for the Plaintiff to the right of the jury to award exemplary damages; it is difficult to believe that such a point was not taken; there is a reflection of such a proposition in observations made by the trial Judge in the course of his direction to the jury both initially and after requisition on damages where he referred to the special elements in the case apart from the compensatory factor. Indeed, the initial verdict of the jury in which sums of £30,000 were written into the issue paper in respect of both special and general damages suggested that the jury, itself, was contemplating a separate award in that regard. In my view, the award did contain a significant element in respect of exemplary damages because of the abuse of power in the breach of the Plaintiff's constitutional rights by the first and second Defendants.

The Plaintiff, from the time of the original incident, until his trial, had to undergo a period of some 15 months of significant anxiety and concern not knowing what the outcome might be and knowing that the Gardaí were conspiring against him. How was he to know that he would be acquitted? He might well have believed that he had little chance of acquittal and would inevitably have to serve a sentence of imprisonment. If one assumes that approximately half of the damages were compensatory in nature, in my view they are in no way excessive. Compared to the anguish caused by defamatory material published of any citizen, the plight of the Plaintiff in this case seems to me to have been considerably worse. Yet awards of damages for defamation well in excess of £30,000 have become a feature of our Courts. As exemplary damages for the shocking abuse of police power by the first and second Defendants I consider a further sum of £30,000 as a perfectly acceptable level of award.

Exemplary or punitive damages are intended to reflect disapproval—they are peculiarly appropriate for assessment by a jury. The damages reflect the standing of both the abused and the abuser but one should look, in particular, to the standing of those responsible for the malicious prosecution. Such an action may be brought against an ordinary member of the public, but here it is against two individuals charged with the guarding of the peace and the protection of the public. It seems clear that from the very beginning they conspired together to concoct a malicious prosecution and conceal their own assault; they conspired to pervert the course of justice. In my opinion, the damages appropriate to a case of this kind must reflect the proper indignation of the public at this conduct, whatever windfall it may prove for the Plaintiff in the result. Some reference was made in the course of the hearing to the decision in Rookes v Barnard [1964] AC 1129; [1964] 2 WLR 269, [1964] 1 All ER 367; [1964] 1 Lloyd's Rep 28 where three categories of cases were stated where exemplary damages might be awarded. The decision has been the subject of significant adverse comment in other common law jurisdictions. In my view, it is inconsistent with the dynamism that characterizes the common law to delimit in any restrictive way the nature of its development. It is beyond question that the present is a case of oppressive, arbitrary and unconstitutional action by the servants of government; I reserve for another and more appropriate occasion the further consideration of cases where exemplary damages may be awarded. I see no real difference of meaning between punitive and exemplary in relation to damages. As stated in McMahon and Binchy (page 777) 'the inconsistency in terminology in the 1961 Act may thus be traced, not to nuances of meaning between the concepts of "punitive" and "exemplary" damages, but to the promiscuity of our borrowings from British legislation.'

O'Flaherty J.:

"The proper categorisation of damages has presented difficulties in this as in other cases. In this case the learned trial judge, through an oversight, initially did not address the jury on the question of damages at all. He was asked to do so though he was not specifically asked to say anything about the question of exemplary damages and it is clear that neither the word 'punitive' nor 'exemplary' was used by him when he did address the jury on damages though the words used by him might be regarded as appropriate in suggesting to the jury that they were entitled to award this latter type of damages. Counsel for the plaintiff have assured us that in the course of their addresses to the jury they asked for damages over and above basic compensatory damages but that could have included what are known as aggravated damages. I took them to accept that the distinction between aggravated damages and exemplary damages may not have been elucidated by them in the course of their speeches.

I believe that while 'exemplary' damages are referred to in s 7(2) of the Civil Liability Act, 1961 and 'punitive' damages in s 14(4) of the Act the terms are synonymous. I believe this to be so because it is impossible to articulate separate concepts of 'exemplary' and 'punitive' damages.

Some of the old cases interchange the words punitive, exemplary and, indeed, vindictive to describe these type of damages. They are all used in a passage of Molony CJ's judgment in Worthington v Tipperary Co Council [1920] 2 IR 233 at p 245 where he said:—

> 'punitive or vindictive damages stand upon an entirely different footing, and are given not merely to repay the plaintiff for temporal loss, but to punish the defendant in an exemplary manner.'

In this judgment I shall prefer the description exemplary damages. That these damages can properly be awarded for the torts committed in the circumstances of this case cannot be in doubt. (See the decision of this Court in Dillon v Dunnes Stores; [1966] IR 397 noted in MacMahon and Binchy: A Case Book on the Irish Law of Torts at p 126).

After the division of general and special damages one is down to compensatory, aggravated and exemplary damages and the distinction between them is well put in Salmond and Heuston: Law of Torts (Nineteenth Ed) at p 594:— Compensatory damages are awarded as compensation for, and are measured by, the material loss suffered by the plaintiff. A distinct category is that of aggravated damages, which may be awarded when the motives and conduct of the defendant aggravate the injury to the plaintiff. Insult and injured feelings are a proper subject for compensation. So a substantial sum was awarded for an 'insolent and high-handed trespass' by an inquiry agent. In such a case damages are at large precisely because the 'real' damage cannot be ascertained: it is not a matter of determining the 'real' damage and adding to that a sum by way of aggravated damages. Yet another distinct category is that of exemplary damages, which reflect the jury's view of the defendant's outrageous conduct. Aggravated damages are given for conduct which shocks the plaintiff: exemplary damages for conduct which shocks the jury.

I would add this important point, however. While aggravated damages are distinct they are still meant to compensate the plaintiff. So, more accurately, they should be regarded—when they are awarded—as a sub-head of the compensatory damages awarded to the plaintiff. On the other hand, exemplary damages are a separate category. They are not compensatory at all.

This is obviously not the case to decide whether or not exemplary damages can only be awarded along the lines of the three categories referred to by Lord Devlin in the course of his speech in the case of Rookes v Barnard [1964] AC 1129, [1964] 2 WLR 269, [1964] 1 All ER 367, [1964] 1 Lloyd's Rep 28. However, I think I can safely say that the majority of cases of injured feelings will be met by an award of aggravated damages rather than exemplary damages. As Lord Devlin said: 'Aggravated damages in this type of case can do most, if not all, of the work that could be done by exemplary damages' (at p 1230).

Further, I would respectfully adopt the three considerations which Lord Devlin said should always be borne in mind when awards of exemplary damages are being considered. They are, in summary:

1. The plaintiff cannot recover exemplary damages unless he is the victim of the punishable behaviour. The anomaly inherent in exemplary damages would become an absurdity if a plaintiff totally unaffected by some oppressive conduct which the jury wished to punish obtained a windfall in consequence.
2. The power to award exemplary damages constitutes a weapon that, while it can be used in defence of liberty, can also be used against liberty. The judge was pointing to the need for restraint in the amount of damages that should be awarded.
3. The means of the parties, irrelevant in the assessment of compensation, are material in the assessment of exemplary damages. Everything which aggravates or mitigates the defendant's conduct is relevant.

Taking all these considerations into account, when I look at the actual amounts awarded in this case there is no dispute that the award of £5,000 for assault and false imprisonment was appropriate. I would accept that that award cannot have any exemplary component in it. It represented rather modest damages. Accepting that the award of £60,000 damages for malicious prosecution has an exemplary component, nevertheless, in my judgment a reasonable proportion must be kept between the two awards. In fact one exceeds the other by a multiple of twelve. This is too great a disparity.

The award of exemplary damages is anomalous and where such damages are awarded—which should be very rarely in my judgment—the judge or jury must keep them on a tight rein. If the compensatory amount awarded includes aggravated damages then I believe if any award is made by way of exemplary damages it should properly be a fraction rather than a multiple of the amount awarded by way of compensatory damages (including aggravated damages).

In the particular circumstances of this case where the damages awarded were modest I am prepared to agree with the amount proposed to be substituted by Hederman J in respect of the award for malicious damages. It follows, therefore, that I believe that the amount awarded by the jury under this heading was so excessive as to call for the intervention of this Court."

Comments and Questions:

1. Given that the purpose of tort law is to place the defendant in the position s/he would have been in had the tort not arisen, is there any basis for awarding exemplary damages to a claimant?

2. The *McIntyre* case appears to disapprove of the restrictive nature of the categories of claim where exemplary damages would be appropriate; see also *Conway v Irish National Teachers Organisation* [1991] 2 I.R. 305, where Finlay C.J. similarly disapproved of strict categories when he said:

   "Punitive or exemplary damages arising from the nature of the wrong which was committed and/or the manner of its commission which are intended to mark the court's particular disapproval of the defendant's conduct in all the circumstances of the case and its decision that it should publicly be seen to have punished the defendant for such conduct ..."

3. In considering whether the categorisation of Lord Devlin in *Rookes v Barnard* should be adopted, do you favour the view of McCarthy J. or O'Flaherty J. above?

Compensatory damages

Compensatory damages are awarded to compensate the victim for the harm done. This category of damage is made up of an award for special damages, general damages and aggravated damages, where appropriate.

Aggravated damages will be awarded to compensate the plaintiff for additional harm suffered as a result of the manner in which the defendant has behaved but unlike exemplary damages they are still compensatory in nature (see O'Flaherty J. in *McIntyre v Lewis* above).

Connellan v St Joseph's Kilkenny
High Court [2006] I.E.H.C. 119

Facts: The plaintiff was a victim of sexual and physical abuse while a resident in the first defendant's orphanage. He sued for damages for the abuse suffered.

Issues: As liability for the abuse was accepted, the issue that had to be determined by the court (O'Donovan J.) was whether aggravated damages ought to be awarded in addition to compensatory damages.

O'Donovan J.:

"[O'Donovan J. considered at length the evidence submitted by both parties before considering the question of what damages were appropriate:]

... Conclusions

In the light of the evidence which I have heard, I have no doubt whatsoever, that, over a five year period, while he was a resident at St. Joseph's, Kilkenny i.e. when he was in St. Joseph's, itself, and when he was in Summerhill, he was subjected to physical, sexual, emotional and racial abuse at the hands of Theresa Connolly, David Murray and Breffney O'Rourke; abuse which was vicious and demeaning over a long period of time and was calculated to kill his spirit, as it did. I am equally satisfied that, as a result of that abuse, the plaintiff lost his self esteem, confidence and his ability to trust people; that he lacks stability and that he is riddled with indecision and is very much a loner. I am also persuaded that this abuse affected his ability to concentrate when he was at school with the result that, educationally, he never achieved his potential and is now less capable as an administrator than he might have been were it not for that abuse. In this regard, in the light of the evidence of Dr. McInerney coupled with that of Mr. Paul Glennon and Mr. Dermot Curran I am not persuaded, despite the suggestion of Mr. Stephen Kealey, the Consultant Psychologist, that the plaintiff had learning difficulties when he was at Saint Josephs. While I accept that he has had emotional problems as a result of that abuse which necessitated appropriate medication and counselling which is ongoing, I am not persuaded that he had, or has a significant problem with alcohol on account of it, as he asserted, for the reason that he does not appear to have required any medical help in that regard and was never institutionalised on account of over indulgence of alcohol. While I do not doubt that the fact that he was abandoned by his parents, that he was institutionalised for the first sixteen years of his life and that he was a coloured person in a predominantly white environment significantly inhibited his emotional and educational development, nevertheless, having regard to the severity of the abuse to which he was subjected and the fact that it was ongoing for a long period of time, I am satisfied that it was the abuse, rather than the other matters, which predominantly affected his development and which is primarily responsible for his current educational and emotional problems. In fact, notwithstanding the appalling ill treatment to which he was subjected in the course of his upbringing and the problems which that brought in its wake, it seems to me that David Connellan has done remarkably well in life, in that, since he left school, he has rarely been unemployed; albeit that some of the jobs which he got were well below his capabilities, that he sustained a marriage for twenty two years and that, so far, two of his children have been very successful in their careers. To that extent, it seems to me that he has had the fortitude to be able to overcome some of the unhappy events which he experienced in the course of his upbringing.

I also feel that the tragic death of his son, David, contributed to some of his past and present emotional problems. Nevertheless, his period at Saint Josephs was, in my view, a very hard cross to bear and if he is to be properly compensated for all the wrongs to which he was subjected during that period and the knock on effect which those wrongs have had on him since that time and are likely to have on him for some time into the future, I believe that only a substantial sum of money would be appropriate. In that regard, as laid down by the President of the High Court, Mr. Justice Finnegan, in the case of Noctor v Ireland & Others [2005] 1 I.R. at p.433 where, as in this case, damages are claimed under the headings of negligence, breach of duty, assault and breach of and failure to vindicate constitutional rights, the award has to comprehend each of those headings and, in assessing the amount to which I think that the plaintiff is entitled, I propose to do just that. I also propose to have regard to the regulations made under the Residential Institutions Redress Act, 2002, (Assessment of Redress) Regulations, 2002, because I think that the provisions of those regulations have a relevance in this case although I do not consider myself in anyway bound by them. Although no out of pocket expenses have been proved by the plaintiff nor, indeed, has he sought to quantify any future expenditure attributable to ongoing psychological problems, his psychiatrist, Dr. McInerney, gave evidence that it was appropriate that he should continue to take anti-depressant medication and that he would benefit from attending a private counsellor. In my view, that is a reasonable suggestion and, accordingly, when assessing the plaintiff's compensation for the future, I propose to build into it a figure to cover the costs of future medication and counselling. In addition, counsel for the plaintiff has submitted that this is a case in which it would be appropriate to award aggravated damages. In the case of Conway v Irish National Teachers Organisation [1991] 2 I.R. at p.305, Chief Justice Finlay stated:

> 'Aggravated damages being exemplary damages increased by reason of;
> (a) The manner in which the wrong was committed, involving such elements of oppressiveness, arrogance and outrage or
> (b) The conduct of the wrongdoer after the commission of the wrong, such as a refusal to apologise or to ameliorate the harm done or the making of threats to repeat the wrong or
> (c) Conduct of the wrongdoer and/or his representatives in the defence of the claim of the wronged plaintiff, up to and including the trial of the action.

Such a list of circumstances which may aggravate compensatory damages until they can properly be classified as aggravated damages is not intended to be in any way finite or complete. Furthermore, circumstances which may properly form an aggravating feature in the measurement of compensatory damages must in many instances be in part a recognition of the added hurt or insult to the plaintiff who has been wronged. It is in part also a recognition of the cavalier or outrageous conduct of the defendant.'

While doubts have been expressed as to whether aggravated damages should be awarded in negligence claims (see the Judgment of Keane C.J. in Swaine v Commissioners of Public Works [2003] 1 I.R. at p.521) McCracken J. in the course of a judgment which he delivered in a case of Philip v Ryan [2004] 4 I.R. at p.257 stated that he had no doubt but that, in an appropriate case, such damages can and should be awarded. While Finnegan P. in the course of his judgment in Noctor v Ireland, hereinbefore referred to, seems to suggest that it would not have been appropriate for him to award aggravated damages in that case, he, nevertheless, said that the award of general damages which he made was intended to take into account all the circumstances which surrounded the sexual and physical abuse to which the plaintiff in that case had been subjected. That seems to me to suggest that, in fact, he included an allowance for aggravated damages in the award of general damages which he made. However, whether or not he did so, it seems to me that, in this case, whatever about the abuse to which the plaintiff was subjected at the hands of David Murray and Breffney O'Rourke, that to which he was subjected at the hands of Theresa Connolly had elements of oppressiveness, arrogance and outrage of the type contemplated by Finlay C.J. in the course of his judgment in Conway v Irish National Teachers Organisation, hereinbefore referred to, and accordingly, is deserving of aggravated damages. In that regard, I would refer to the fact that, in addition to the physical and sexual abuse to which the plaintiff was subjected at the hands of Theresa Connolly, she taunted him making him sing a song 'I'm nobody's child', she abused him racially, she instilled in him that he was totally under her control, that she could do with him whatever she wanted and that all the abuse to which she subjected him was done in the presence of other boys. If that is not arrogance and outrage deserving of aggravated damages, I do not know what is.

In all the foregoing circumstances, for the five years during which he was subjected to abuse at the hands of Theresa Connolly, David Murray and Breffney O'Rourke and for the consequential loss of self esteem, loss of confidence and failure to achieve educational potential, I will award the plaintiff the sum of €200,000 for general damages. For the future, allowing that he is going to continue to experience emotional problems attributable to his experience at Saint Josephs, for the next two years or so and that, during that period, is going to have to purchase anti-depressant medication and to pay for private counselling I will allow a sum of €50,000 for general damages. On top of all that, I will allow a sum of €50,000 for aggravated damages. Accordingly, there will be judgment for the plaintiff for €300,000."

COMPUTATION OF DAMAGES

Damages are awarded to make good any loss arising by virtue of physical damage to property and personal injuries. The damages awarded represent the loss suffered by the plaintiff from the time of injury to when the case came to trial and future losses.

In terms of personal injury, damages have traditionally been divided into two categories, special damages (to compensate pecuniary loss) and general damages (to cover non-pecuniary loss).

Special damages (pecuniary loss)

Special damages include those damages capable of measurement in monetary terms such as loss of earnings, hospital expenses and other medical expenses. Actuarial evidence is relied on to aid in the assessment of pecuniary loss and awards of damages are tax-free. Any collateral benefits the plaintiff might also recover by virtue of the injury (such as benefits from private insurance, pensions, or any benefit payable under statute or otherwise), will not be deducted from the award of damages made by the court (s.2 Civil Liability (Amendment) Act 1964). By virtue of s.75 of the Social Welfare (Consolidation) Act 1993, all statutory disability benefit or injury benefit must be deducted from the amounts calculated. Section 2 of the Health (Amendment) Act 1986 provides that defendants will also have to pay for any hospital or health board costs arising from road accidents. This applies even where the treatment ought otherwise to have been free.

Loss of earnings in particular have given rise to difficulties as their computation requires a consideration of a wide range of factors, from the skills and employability of the employee to considerations as to the labour market, risk of unemployment, retirement age and so on. In the following case of *Reddy v Bates* [1983] I.R. 141, [1984] I.L.R.M. 197, the court overturned the High Court award of a jury and judge for loss of earnings on the basis that it failed to take into account any of these considerations.

Reddy v Bates
Supreme Court [1983] I.R. 141, [1984] I.L.R.M. 197

Facts: The plaintiff, who was severely injured in a motor car accident, sued the defendant who caused the accident for damages. She was left barely able to walk. The defendant admitted his negligence and damages were awarded by a judge and jury in the High Court. The defendant appealed, arguing that the damages awarded were excessive.

Issues: The court (Griffin, Hederman and McCarthy JJ.) was asked to consider whether the damages awarded for loss of earnings, the cost of a housekeeper and general damages were excessive. The court did not consider it necessary to disturb the award for the cost of a housekeeper but held that both the figure for loss of earnings and the award for general damages was excessive. The loss of earnings figure had not taken into account the possibility of unemployment, marriage, illness, redundancy and other breaks in employment and was therefore flawed.

Griffin J. (Hederman J. concurring):

"[The headings of damage contested were future loss of earnings, future cost of a housekeeper and future general damages. After concluding that in his view the award of damages was excessive, Griffin J. then went on to consider what an appropriate award under these headings would be, in light of the facts presented].

It is well settled that this Court cannot set aside the verdict of a jury on the grounds that the damages are excessive unless, adopting a view of the facts which is most favourable to the plaintiff, no reasonable proportion exists between the amount awarded and the circumstances of the case: see McGrath v Bourne [(1876) IR 10 CL 160] and Foley v Thermocement Ltd. [(1954) 90 ILT.R. 92.]. Applying that standard, it is my opinion that the amount of the damages awarded in this case is excessive; but this is not to minimise the gravity of the injuries sustained by the plaintiff. In assessing the damages, the jury were required to consider the evidence not only with sympathy and understanding for the plaintiff but also with fairness to both the plaintiff and the defendant, as the administration of justice is not a one-way operation. Counsel on behalf of the plaintiff submitted that the plaintiff's condition was as bad as is that of a paraplegic; I cannot agree. But, even if it was, the amount awarded for general damages (£250,000) is considerably in excess of any sum awarded in any case that has come to this Court, even for a paraplegic or a quadriplegic.

We have been invited by both the plaintiff and the defendant to assess the damages rather than send the case back for a retrial. Therefore, it is necessary to consider each of the four items of damage in dispute.

Loss of earnings
Under this heading the jury were required to assess the prospective value of the earnings which the plaintiff, if uninjured, would have been likely to earn. It has been decided by this Court in many cases over the past 20 years that where future loss of earnings, or a likelihood of regular necessary payments for medical, hospital or other expenses, form a substantial element of a plaintiff's claim, an actuary should give evidence. That was done in this case and Mr Reddin, who is a well-known actuary practising in Dublin, gave evidence on behalf of the plaintiff. His evidence establishes that the present value of £100 p.a. to the age of sixty is £1,606; to the age of sixty-five is £1,684; and for life is £1,812. In calculating the present value of £100 p.a., the actuary allowed for the possibility of death, using standard mortality tables, having regard to the sex of the plaintiff, and allowing for changing interest rates. Using the figure given for an age of sixty-five as a multiplier, the loss suffered by the plaintiff on that basis would be about £123,000. However, this figure does not take into account the marriage prospects of the plaintiff; nor does it take into account any risk of unemployment, redundancy, illness, accident or the like. It assumes that the plaintiff, if uninjured, would have continued to work, week in and week out, until retirement. In effect, it is based on the assumption that there would have been guaranteed employment, at a constantly increasing annual rate of wages, until retirement or prior death.

When actuarial evidence first came into regular use in our courts in cases such as this, employment was reasonably stable and so continued for many years thereafter. During that period of comparative stability, actuarial figures could be applied by juries with reasonable confidence, even though they have always been directed by trial judges that such figures are intended only as a guideline for the assistance of juries and that they are not bound to accept the figures. Whilst the mathematical calculations made by an actuary may be constant and correct, they should be applied in the particular circumstances of every case with due regard to reality and common sense. There is now a high rate of unemployment not only in this country but in Great Britain and in most of the member States of the European Economic Community. The great increase in recent years in the number of employees becoming redundant and in the number of firms being closed—firms which would have been regarded hitherto as of unshakeable financial soundness—must inevitably lead to the conclusion that there is no longer any safe, much less guaranteed, employment. In my view, this is a factor which juries should be required to take into account in assessing future loss of earnings in any given case, but the matter should be canvassed in evidence and in argument. In the case of a seriously injured plaintiff, experience shows that there is a tendency for the jury to take the highest multiplier and the highest possible multiplicand to arrive at the prospective loss of earnings; this is understandable when they have a seriously injured plaintiff before them.

The jury awarded £144,000 for loss of earnings even though it was accepted by the plaintiff's counsel that the highest sum, using the actuary's figure, should have been £123,000. Even that figure took no account of the matters to which I have referred but, as they were not canvassed in this case, I would only reduce the sum awarded under this heading to £123,000.

Cost of housekeeper
Under this heading the jury awarded a sum of £115,000. At the actuarial calculation of £1,812, this works out at a sum of £123 per week, 'constantly increasing annually throughout life'. The plaintiff was contending for £170 per week, but the jury clearly did not accept that figure. The learned trial judge invited the jury 'to keep their feet on the ground' in considering the damages under this heading and he invited the jury to be reasonable about this particular heading of damage. It is unlikely that the plaintiff will require any more assistance than would an elderly feeble person. Although the sum awarded was higher than the figure I would award in the particular circumstances, and was clearly higher than the sum the learned trial judge would have awarded had he been assessing the damages, it is nevertheless within the range of damages which, on the evidence, could be found by the jury and I would not interfere with it.

General damages

The jury awarded general damages of £100,000 for the period ending at the date of the award, and the sum of £150,000 for the future. In my judgment, each of these figures is excessive. In respect of the three years to the date of the trial, I would award the sum of £50,000. In respect of the future, I would award the sum of £70,000. The plaintiff's injury is unusual; indeed, in so far as the cases which have come before the Courts are concerned, it is almost unique. Notwithstanding, or even in spite of, her disabilities, the plaintiff is able to pay regular visits to the members of her close-knit and loving family. Without their support, it is unlikely that she would have reached her present state of rehabilitation. She has travelled with members of her family on holidays to the United States, to Spain, to England, and to Waterford with some regularity, and she seems to enjoy these holidays. She will now have a substantial capital sum to enable her to enjoy life even more.

In relation to general damages and in particular to general damages for the future, in my view the fact that a plaintiff has been awarded what is considered to be sufficient damages to cover all her prospective losses, to provide for all her bodily needs, and to enable her to live in comparative comfort (having due regard to her disabilities), should be reflected in the amount of general damages to be awarded. In my view, it would be desirable in a case such as this that the jury should be directed along those lines.

I should like to add one further general comment. In a case of this nature where damages are to be assessed under several headings, the jury, having added the various amounts awarded and having arrived at a total figure for damages, should consider the total sum (as should this Court on any appeal) for the purpose of ascertaining whether the total sum is, in the circumstances of the case, fair compensation for the plaintiff for the injury suffered or whether it is out of all proportion to such circumstances. In my view, the income which that capital sum would generate with reasonably careful and prudent investment is a factor which the jury (and this Court on appeal) should take into consideration in arriving at a conclusion in this behalf. Notwithstanding the ravages of inflation, a very substantial income can be obtained from a large capital sum, whilst preserving the capital intact. This is a factor which has been taken into consideration by this Court in very many cases within the past ten years.

The total of the sums of which I approve is £400,354. I would allow the appeal, reduce the damages to that sum, and give judgment accordingly.

On this appeal the damages have been assessed by the Court at the request, and with the consent, of both parties. Therefore, the question of the 'right' of the Court to assess the damages notwithstanding objection on the part of one or both parties does not arise. However, I should point out that the Court has on many occasions in the past ten years, of which I can speak with some knowledge, exercised this right in many cases in which the Court considered it was appropriate to do so, and I am aware that prior to that time the Court also exercised this right in appropriate cases. I mention this matter only lest my silence on the question might indicate acquiescence in a possible contrary view."

McCarthy J.:

"... The conventional approach to the assessment of damages to be awarded for personal injuries sustained through the tortious act of another is to ask the jury to award such sum as will, so far as money can do so, put the plaintiff in the same position as he or she would have been in if the tortious act had not occurred. In any case where the damages include any element other than direct compensation for objective monetary loss, it is self-evident that this method of compensation is imperfect. Such imperfection, however, whilst offending against the principle of justice, is not confined to the circumstances of this action. Imprisonment of a criminal provides no true remedy for an individual who has been damaged by the crime; damages for defamation cannot recall the defamatory matter. The law is, indeed, always an imperfect and inadequate human division of the divine concept of justice into compartments. It is, to say the least, unlikely that an individual would willingly submit to a given injury on being offered a sum of money which might be thought commensurate with such an injury when damages came to be assessed by a jury. Equally, it would be poor consolation to the injured individual to be given the opportunity of inflicting the self-same injury on the person who had injured him.

In the result, the formula already outlined, albeit unsatisfactory, is the established method and must be used both at the trial and as the template to be applied by this Court when called upon to review any such award. There are, however, certain principles that appear to me to be of general application when such an award comes for review.

1. The plaintiff must provide a concrete evidential basis for the calculation of his direct monetary loss, both as to past and future loss.
2. In the calculation of future loss, that evidence must include a satisfactory basis of assessment by way of an appropriate multiplier being applied to a reasonably accurate continuing item of loss.
3. The application of such a multiplier is to be regarded only as a guide. It is a pathway and not a tram-line and it may be coloured, as the jury may consider proper, by such factors (if relevant) as marriage, taxation, and prospects of permanent employment. This is not to exclude other factors which may prove relevant.
4. The total of the amount so calculated—as to loss, past and future—is not, of itself, an argument for interference with the award. In other words, the fact that such total may appear to be a high figure is no ground for interference where each individual figure, making up the total, is reasonably supportable on the evidence.

5. In contrast with the approach to a review of an award under the headings of past and future actual loss, the Court's approach in reviewing an award of general damages may, essentially, be one of first impression. Such damages are frequently stated to be for pain and suffering; they would be better described as compensation in money terms for the damage, past and future, sustained to the plaintiff's amenity of life in all its aspects, including actual pain and suffering, both physical and mental, both private to the plaintiff and in the plaintiff's relationships with family, with friends, in working and social life and in lost opportunity.

6. It is only in respect of general damages that it is appropriate to adopt the method of approach set out by the former Supreme Court in Foley v Thermocement Ltd. [(1954) 90 I.LT.R. 92.]

7. In order to warrant interference with an award of general damages, the disparity between the views of the individual members of this Court and each item of the award, however large it may be expressed in isolation, must be a significant percentage of that item of the award and, as a general rule, should not be less than 25 per cent. Despite pressures from time to time for legislation removing from the province of a jury the assessment of such damages, the legislature has consistently refused to do so. This factor emphasises that this Court should be reluctant so to interfere and, in particular, that it should avoid relatively petty paring from, or adding to, awards.

8. The annual or other income which may, on its face, be obtainable from the whole or any part of a total award is irrelevant to any such review. I profess no competence to determine the relative effects of varying interest rates, the falling value of money, the hazards of even the most apparently solvent companies in which money may be invested for capital growth, and the many other factors which exercise the minds of merchant bankers and the like—not always with success.

The instant appeal

The damages were awarded under six headings. (a) £41,404 being special damages to date, including loss of earnings, but excluding dental treatment. This was an agreed figure and does not require comment. (b) £950 for dental treatment. This item was the subject of the notice of appeal, but has not been pursued. (c) £100,000 as general damages to date. (d) £144,000 as loss of earnings in the future. (e) £115,000 as the cost of a housekeeper in the future. (f) £150,000 for general damages in the future.

Future loss of earnings

The plaintiff sought to make a case that such damages should be assessed on the basis of her prospects of her earning, while working in England, a salary significantly greater than that which she enjoyed with the P.M.P.A. Insurance Co Ltd. It is clear that the jury rejected that claim as being wholly unsustainable. It is equally clear that the jury did not limit the plaintiff to the level of earnings, subject to average increases, that she would have earned with the insurance company for, on that basis, this item would have been limited to not more than about £123,000. At the hearing, no attempt was made to determine the impact, if any, of marriage statistics or taxation on this item of assessment. I do not apportion responsibility for this absence of evidence on either side; it seems to me to be the responsibility of both sides to explore such questions. Were it not for the expressed request on behalf of both parties that in this, as in all other items of the jury's award, this Court, if interfering with any such item, should reassess the same, I would be disposed to direct a new trial on this issue. It may well be, however, that the impact of these two factors would have been negligible and that, on the one hand, those employed by the insurance company do not give up their employment on marriage and that, on the other hand, the amount of the multiplier would be so increased as to compensate for the reduction in the multiplicand.

Future cost of housekeeper
The learned trial judge clearly and succinctly directed the jury that they were entitled to award the plaintiff a sum significantly greater than the figure of £115,000 under this heading, albeit that he made a miscalculation in the multiplier which he applied by way of example. However, the jury had heard the evidence (the relevant evidence being that of the last witness) and I am not prepared to hold that the jury were misled by the judge's calculation. At the end of the judge's charge, no objection was taken to his suggestion that the jury might, as it were, water down the total under this heading, and I would not entertain any such objection now. For that matter, I would wish to express in the strongest terms my reluctance to entertain any criticism of the rulings of, or charge by, a trial judge when no such objections were made at the trial. I would uphold this item of the award.

General damages
Despite the observations I have made in respect of criticism of the total amount of the award, it does seem to me appropriate that this Court, in reviewing awards under the heading of general damages, should look to the items both separately and as a whole. Mr Maguire has painted a moving picture of the plaintiff's plight. The members of this Court have seen the plaintiff in private; she was attended by her solicitor and the solicitor for the defendant. She is, obviously, a rather pathetic young woman who has been grievously injured; she has to face some 40 or 50 years of life suffering from a severe impairment of that enjoyment of life to which she was entitled. She is, however, far from being as disabled as a paraplegic or a tetraplegic; there are many things she can do which are quite outside their compass. It may well be that awards of the size that she obtained can be justified in the case of those who sustain such dreadful paralysing injuries, but such is not the case here. Applying, as I do, the tests

outlined in Foley's Case [(1954) 90 ILT.R. 92] I am of opinion that both separately and jointly the awards under this heading bear no reasonable relationship to the injuries sustained and must be set aside. In re-assessing these amounts, however, I believe this Court should seek to adopt a generous approach. I would assess the general damages for the past at £60,000, which is the figure suggested by counsel for the defendant; and I would assess general damages for the future at £100,000, which sum is £10,000 more than that suggested by such counsel.

In the result, I would reduce the total award by the sum of £90,000. The plaintiff has cross-appealed the award in respect of the cost of a housekeeper, but that appeal was not pursued.

I have not heard argument and I reserve for future consideration, if necessary, the question as to whether or not, without the consent of both parties, this Court has power to substitute its own assessment of damages in place of that of a jury."

Comments and Questions:
1. Note that in the above case the court highlighted the reluctance of any appeal court to overturn the finding of a jury on damages. This, they considered, could only be done where "no reasonable proportion exists between the amount awarded and the circumstances of the case".

General damages (non-pecuniary loss)

General damages reflect the award for non-pecuniary loss, and includes pain and suffering and, for generally lesser amounts, loss of expectation of life (also described as loss of amenity, *i.e.* the degree to which the victim's capacity to enjoy life has been impaired). Given the subjective nature of these losses they are notoriously difficult to quantify in monetary terms. In terms of pain and suffering the courts have attempted to develop guidelines for what should be the highest award possible for the most serious injuries by which other awards can then be measured.

In the case of *Synott* [*sic*] *v Quinnsworth Ltd.* [1984] I.L.R.M. 523 a young man involved in a motor accident was rendered a quadriplegic and left with other physical difficulties which left him entirely dependent on others. He was awarded what was considered the maximum award for such injuries of £150,000. This figure has since increased in line with inflation with an award of £250,000 made in the case of *Kealy v Minister for Health*, High Court, April 19, 1999 to a woman who had been infected with contaminated Anti-D in 1977. More recently an award of £300,000 was made in the case of *McEneaney v Monaghan County Council*, unreported, High Court, July 26, 2001.

As the damages are to compensate for pain and suffering and loss of expectation in life, a person who responds with optimism to an otherwise debilitating injury might well recover less than a more pessimistic person.

In the case of *McFadden v Weir* which follows, Budd J. in the High Court had to consider the degree of damages to be awarded to an optimistic victim with very serious injuries.

McFadden v Weir
High Court [2005] I.E.H.C. 473

Facts: The plaintiff, a man aged 50, was injured when a car drove at speed into the rear of his car while he was stopped at a set of traffic lights. He suffered damage to his spine and teeth which resulted in severe pain and significantly impaired mobility. He sued the driver of the second car for the injuries suffered.

Issues: As liability was not contested it fell to the court (Budd J.) to consider the amount of damages to be awarded, including the amount to be awarded in general damages. Budd J. held that, in relation to general damages, the issue was highly dependent on the facts of the case, and any award had to be reasonable and in line with judicially agreed maximum awards. He considered reference to the *Book of Quantum* of the PIAB to be of limited use.

Budd J.:

"... I take cognisance of the Supreme Court's view that the general damages should represent fair and reasonable compensation for the loss and injury sustained by the Plaintiff, taking account of the total sum awarded in respect of past and future loss or expense, ordinary living standards prevailing in the country, the general level of incomes and the things on which the Plaintiff might reasonably be expected to spend money. Synott v. Quinnsworth Ltd (S.C.) [1984] ILRM 523 was decided at a time when the return on funds invested would have been much greater than at present. It was also stated that in addition, on the facts of a particular case, other matters may arise for consideration in assessing what, in the circumstances, should be considered as reasonable.

In McEneaney v. County Council of the County of Monaghan and Coillte Teo (Unreported, High Court, O'Sullivan J., 26th July, 2001) in his considered judgment, O'Sullivan J. dealt with the question of the appropriate rate to be applied in actuarial calculations in respect of the cost of medical aids and appliances as these rates were running at more than the prevalent rate of inflation. Happily this issue was not in conflict in the present case but it is helpful that O'Sullivan J. held that a reasonable equivalent to the €150,000 for general damages in Synnott would back in 1991 be a sum of £300,000. I note that Denham J. in M.N. v. S.M. on 18th March, 2005, remarked that she was satisfied that the equivalent figure then to the £150,000 of Synnott, is in excess of €300,000.

This remark seems unsurprising since O'Sullivan J. in his judgment in McEneaney on 26th July, 2001, after careful consideration of the change in value of money found that the equivalent would be £300,000 and that there is the further aspect that more than four years of some inflation have passed since July 2001, and there has also been the currency conversion into euro. Accordingly the equivalent of £300,000 back in July 2001, must be well in excess of €300,000 by now. Even back six years ago in 1999, Morris P. in Kealy v. Minister for Health [1999] 2 IR 456 at p 459 stated:

> 'My own day to day experience in the courts ruling in infant settlements is the clearest possible test for me that the cap of €150,000 is no longer regarded as applicable by practitioners ... In my view the correct measure of damages for the appellant for general damages for a lady whose life has been effectively ruined is £250,000.'

I note that in Gough v. Neary [2003] 3 IR 92 at p 130 Geoghegan J said that the test to be applied by the Supreme Court as to whether it will alter an award of damages either upwards or downwards is a test of proportionality as explained by the judgment of Fennelly J. in the Supreme Court in Rossiter v. Dun Laoghaire Rathdown Borough Council [2001] 3 IR 578. At p 583 of the report Fennelly J said the following:

> 'The more or less unvarying test has been, therefore, whether there is any "reasonable proportion" between the actual award of damages and what the Court, sitting on appeal, "would be inclined to give".'

The words of the inner quotations were taken from Pallen CB in McGrath v. Bourne [1876] IR 10 CL160, one of the great seminal Irish cases on damages. Another is Foley v. Thermocement Products Ltd (1954) 90 ILTR 92 at 94 (S.C.) in which Lavery J. reflected on the difficulty in assessing damages in a personal injury case and said:

> 'It is especially difficult in a case where personal injuries are the subject of the claim. There is no standard by which pain and suffering, facial disfigurement or indeed any continuing disability can be measured in terms of money. All that can be said is that the estimate must be reasonable and different minds will inevitably arrive at widely differing conclusions as to what is reasonable. The task must, however be undertaken.'

Acting on this, I have carefully and unobtrusively studied and scrutinised the Plaintiff, his demeanour, appearance and bearing throughout this trial and, having started from a sceptical position, having heard the witnesses about the Plaintiff and his injuries, I too have been convinced of the genuineness of his evidence and of his seriously painful and vulnerable condition. Incidentally, I note that Dr. Valerie Pollard did say that the Plaintiff's 'pain varied in intensity from 3-8/10 in severity on the visual analogue pain scale. Usually it was rated 6/10 in severity.' Furthermore, the evidence from Professor Bolger, Dr. Clarke, Dr. Hayes and Dr. Pollard is all strongly and reasonably expressed to the effect that it is highly unlikely that the Plaintiff will ever be able to do remunerative work in future, however determined he himself may be in persevering in the hope of returning to some type of employability.

Finally I turn to the matter of figures in respect of quantum of damage.

To date pain and suffering for the trauma of the collisions on 7th August, 2000, in which accident the Plaintiff suffered tetra-paresis, so that he was trapped with the fear of the peril of fire for one-and-a-half hours before being extracted from his car by the fire brigade ambulance men. The Plaintiff had the terror of having to sit, unable to move in the car and of still being paralysed after being put in the ambulance. For over a period of five-and-a-half hours he gradually regained partial power. He then had the experience over days of having to undergo x-rays, MRI scans and examinations which led to the dire warning that his neck was in such a condition that an impact or fall could cause the traumatic result of his becoming a quadriplegic. The Plaintiff had to undergo his first neck operation on 6th December, 2000, when the osteophyte damaging the spinal cord was reduced and the compression of the spinal cord at C3/4 was decreased. The injuries suffered to his spinal cord afflicted left him with left sided weakness and had a devastating impact on his lifestyle and his enjoyment of the amenities of life and affected his working, social, domestic and sporting life in a devastating manner. While I propose to allocate sums to particular aspects of the pain and suffering to date, I have also reflected on the global figures for each aspect of the case and for the total global figure having listed provisional figures against each heading. I have considered the individual figures which I have placed provisionally against each aspect and I have then considered the total figures in respect of pain and suffering to date and pain and suffering in the future together with the figures for special damages. Then I have also considered and reflected upon the total figure in the light of experience in other similar cases.

I note that s.22(1) of the Civil Liability and Courts Act 2004 provides that the court shall, in assessing damages in a personal injuries action, have regard to the book of quantum under the Personal Injuries Assessment Board Act 2003. I note that s.22(2) provides that s.22(1) shall not operate to prohibit a court from having regard to matters other than the book of quantum when assessing damages in a personal injuries action. The book of quantum states that it contains a guideline of injuries and related values. It lists injuries and the levels of compensation. The guidelines relate to head injuries, arm injuries, neck, back and trunk injuries, and leg injuries. The highest level type of awards are spinal cord injuries, in relation to which it states:

'The courts set the maximum compensation with the exact value being based on a number of considerations:

(a) level of movement,
(b) level of pain and suffering,
(c) depression—level of achievable rehabilitation,
(d) age and life expectancy, paraplegia up to €300,000 and quadriplegia up to €300,000.'

The Plaintiff has restricted level of movement with the need to take care of his fragile neck but a fall or jerk may paralyse him completely. He has a chronic and persistent high level of pain estimated as high on the pain scale by Dr. Pollard, the pain specialist, and by Dr. Clarke, his GP, who has high regard for the patient's valiant fight to carry on and to try to rehabilitate himself and keep fit despite being in much pain. The Plaintiff has been on medication both for pain and to stave off depression. He is now 55 and will be afflicted with pain and problems of weakness and lack of mobility for the rest of his life. This chronic pain is a special feature of this case with its capacity to wear the patient's reserves down and to make life miserable as was stressed by Professor Bolger. The Plaintiff has done very well to keep his fitness by walking and playing golf as prescribed by Professor Bolger, both for physical health and for preserving his morale and socialising.

The Supreme Court (Denham, Geoghegan and McCracken JJ.) in M.N. v. S.M. on 18th March, 2005, said this Book of Quantum was informative, but added in the context of that sexual abuse case:

'Its usefulness is limited, however, by the fact that it does not relate to purely psychological damage, and it does not relate to injuries for sexual abuse. However, it does indicate that in the most serious injuries, paraplegia and quadriplegia, the general damages are the highest awarded and that in general such an award may be up to €300,000.'

I have considerable reservations about the usefulness of the P.I.A.B. Book of Quantum as so much depends on one's assessment of the personality of the individual Plaintiff and how devastating the effect of the particular injuries have been on such a person with the relevant particular circumstances and character. Furthermore in this specific case there is a very special element being the constant and debilitating aspect of incessant pain. I have had an opportunity over ten days at intervals to assess the Plaintiff and I accept the medical evidence that he is in very chronic continual pain. The debilitating effect of such pain can be very serious. Professor Bolger commented on how such pain can sap away reserves of morale. It is not surprising that in this case Dr. Power and Dr. Clarke have had to treat the Plaintiff for depression and certainly it is not unexpected that the Plaintiff should be suffering from lowering of spirits and frustration at his inability to perform so as to be able to work in practice, with no hope of ever aspiring to the high levels of which he was previously capable. For the frightening impact in the collision, the transient paresis and the terror which this paralysis must have caused the Plaintiff while he was trapped in peril and pain for one-and-a-half hours in fear of fire in his car, I assess a figure of €15,000. The fear of a fall or the peril of a traumatic impact to his neck during the period between the road traffic accident and the first operation on 6th December, 2000, while the Plaintiff had to be wary of any physical contact which could cause a jerk of his neck or any fall, either of which could cause paralysis and then the first operation, the discectomy with also the reducing of the osteophyte impinging on the spinal cord, €10,000. The period of increasing pain and instability of his neck up to 17th November, 2003, when he had the nine-and-a-half hour second operation on his neck near the spinal cord in which stenosis was reduced and fusions were achieved in order to give more stability in the neck together with the insertion of metal to achieve this, €20,000.

The Plaintiff also suffered chest infections since 6th December, 2000, his first operation, and clearly this new tribulation can be ascribed to his injury. The scars caused during and by the two operations, the first on the front of the neck and the other at the back are significant although the Plaintiff clearly has not let these unsightly scars get him down, unlike the irksome nature of his other injuries. He has also suffered from tinnitus, which is a frequent and distressing result of such a neck injury. A sum of €10,044 would be appropriate, although arguably minimalist or conservative, as recognition for these after-effects of his injury and I allocate this under injuries to date for simplicity, while acknowledging that the scars, and probably the chest infections triggered by the first operation and the tinnitus all may persist.

Pain and suffering and loss of amenities of life in respect of teeth €7,500 to date.

In addition to this for all the pain, suffering, the psychological effects, depression and the loss of power on his left side together with the impairment of his capacity for previous strong healthy activities, including pain frustrating him in very private and intimate matters, and a loss of the amenities of life and the enjoyment thereof, a sum of €90,000, is appropriate, giving a total of €152,544 for general damages for pain and suffering to date …

… Future General Damages:
As for pain and suffering in the future re dental injuries, including anticipation of further work and the anaesthetics, implants and anguish involved, a sum of €7,500 is appropriate. There is the prospect of a further serious operation near the spinal cord. I do not think that the P.I.A.B. Book figures are much help as they appear to be comparatively generous for some minor injuries but not really helpful except in the general indication that spinal cord injuries tend to attract highest figures. Here one is dealing with an injury to the spinal cord where the Plaintiff is likely to continue to suffer from left sided weakness and constant pain and concern about the worrying vulnerability of his failed neck, with all the frustrations and the lowering of spirits which this can cause in a person who

was, previous to injury, very fit and energetic, both at work and in recreation and in a wide range of activities. There is likely to be a drastic reduction in his capacity in performance of tasks in the house and garden, and in his enjoyment of the amenities of life. I think that the appropriate figure, bearing in mind the constant nasty pain and impaired capacity, for future pain and suffering, including the dental aspect, is €157,500."

Comments and Questions:
1. As noted by Budd J. above in deciding on the award of general damages, s.22(1) of the Civil Liability and Courts Act 2004 requires courts to make reference to the *Book of Quantum* of the PIAB. However, Budd J. feels that such an exercise is of limited value given the subjective nature of the assessment and the characteristics and interests of the individual concerned. Do you agree?

2. As in all cases courts not only make an assessment for individual losses but then consider whether the cumulative damages figure represents a fair award. Do you agree with this method of calculating damages? Does it make the final figure arbitrary as opposed to an accurate representation of the individual heads of loss?

INDEX